TITANIC
VOICES

To Jonathan, Jack & Oscar

TITANIC VOICES

63 Survivors Tell Their
Extraordinary Stories

HANNAH HOLMAN

AMBERLEY

Cover illustrations: Front: Four survivors from *Titanic*. From left to right, first class passenger Margaret 'Molly' Brown lifeboat 6. © Jonathan Reeve JR2093f83 1912. Frederick Fleet, lifeboat 6, the Lookout on *Titanic* who spotted the iceberg. © Jonathan Reeve JR2099f89 1912. Stuart Collett, second class passenger, lifeboat 9. © Jonathan Reeve JR2081f71 1912. First class passenger, Madeleine Astor, lifeboat 4. © Jonathan Reeve JR2130f120 1912. *Spine*: Eva Hart who survived in lifeboat 14. Eva was one of the longest surviving survivors and died in 1996. © Ron Denney. *Back*: *Titanic* survivors in collapsible lifeboat D, one of the last to be launched at 2.05 a.m. © Jonathan Reeve JR2016f44 1912.

First published 2011

Amberley Publishing
The Hill, Stroud
Gloucestershire, GL5 4EP

www.amberley-books.com

Copyright © Hannah Holman 2011

The right of Hannah Holman to be identified as the Author
of this work has been asserted in accordance with the
Copyrights, Designs and Patents Act 1988.

British Library Cataloguing in Publication Data.
A catalogue record for this book is available from the British Library.

ISBN 978 1 4456 0222 6

Typesetting and origination by Amberley Publishing
Printed in Great Britain

Contents

Introduction

The Survivor Accounts

'The wreckage and bodies seemed to be all hanging in one cluster. When we got up to it we got one man, a passenger it was, and he died shortly after we got him into the boat. We got two others then as we pushed our way towards the wreckage, and as we got towards the centre we saw one man there, he was on top of a staircase; it seemed to be a large piece of wreckage anyhow. He was kneeling there as if he was praying, and at the same time he was calling for help. I am sorry to say there were more bodies than there was wreckage. It took us a good half-hour to get that distance to that man to get through the bodies. We could not row the boat, we had to push them out of the way and force our boat up to this man.' *Able Seaman Joseph Scarrott describing returning in lifeboat 14 to the spot where* Titanic *had sunk*

The survivor testimony from the wreck of the *Titanic* is extraordinary. Over 700 people survived, and a significant number of these fortunates were courted and cajoled into reliving the horrific event by beaurocrats (at the two major inquiries into the sinking) or journalists (almost every English county, US state and European country had a representative in the survivor list). Many others clearly wanted their experiences that night recorded as a tribute to those that died. This book includes over 60 of the best accounts – including the canonical Archibald Gracie and Lawrence Beesley in their entirety – assembled in the order in which they escaped from the sinking ship by lifeboat.

The tone of the testimony changes wildly during the two and a half hours from when the *Titanic* hit the iceberg at 11.40 p.m. to when the last few survivors were swept off the last square of *Titanic's* decks. Constance Willard left at about 1.00 a.m. on lifeboat 8:

Two men took hold of me and almost pushed me into a boat. I did not appreciate the danger and I struggled until they released me. 'Do not waste time; let her go if she will not get in,' an officer said.

For wireless operator Harold Bride, who was washed into the freezing Atlantic still holding onto the lifeboat he was trying to launch, the experience was very different:

> I had seen the collapsible boat on the boat deck… and was just lending a hand when a
> large wave came awash of the deck. The big wave carried the boat off. I had hold of an
> oarlock and I went off with it. I was in the boat and the boat was upside down and I was
> under it… I knew I had to fight for it and I did. How I got out from under the boat I do
> not know, but I felt a breath of air at last. There were men all around me – hundreds of
> them. The sea was dotted with them, all depending on their lifebelts.

The aim of this book is to capture this diverse experience using the words of those who were there. It is not another reinvention of the *Titanic* story but a rediscovery of the wealth of first-hand material already written. Some are classic accounts, others were reported at the time and then largely forgotten. Accounts by all the surviving officers, Second Officer Charles Lightoller, Third Officer Herbert Pitman, Fourth Officer Joseph Boxhall and Fifth Officer Harold Lowe are included. I focus on what it was like to be on board; what it was like to hear the cries of people drowning in the water and not to know whether your husband was amongst them; to be deep in the boiler rooms when water came gushing in through the side of the ship; to be one of the officers responsible for loading lifeboats or a steward leading your third class passengers through the warren of companionways, decks stairways and ladders. James Cameron's 1997 film reawakened interest in the *Titanic* from this human angle, and although his two central characters were fictional, many of the minor characters such as Molly Brown were based on real people.

Contemporary media reports often highlighted the stories of the rich. I have tried to redress this balance by including the stories of under-represented groups such as immigrants and passengers travelling third class, often known as 'steerage'. This was still a peak period of mass immigration to America. In the first decade of the twentieth century, 11 million Europeans crossed the Atlantic to settle in the USA, 3.2 million of them from the UK and Ireland.

Some of the most fascinating accounts come from those who had failed in the struggle to find a place in a lifeboat or in many cases had never even tried. They were swept off the ship, pulled down below and in a few lucky cases lived to tell the tale.

With such loss of life it didn't take long until survivors, the media and the public were looking for explanations for the collision. Official public inquiries and a very modern-style 'trial by media' followed. Candidates for blame included ignored ice warnings, excessive speed and lack of binoculars. Further questions were raised about the resulting huge loss of life, where blame for this should lie and whether there was class discrimination in the loading of lifeboats.

Some testimonies given to the two official inquiries held in the aftermath of the sinking are included. The first, given that many of the lives lost were American, was the US Senate Inquiry, chaired by Senator William Alden Smith between 19 April and 25 May 1912. The British Board of Trade Wreck Inquiry began on 2 May 1912 in London and was chaired by John Bigham, Lord Mersey. Those who testify were often nervous, under pressure to present their own actions in the best possible light and, in the case of current employees of the White Star Line, not to incriminate their employer. These testimonies and cross-examinations must be seen in this context.

Eyewitness accounts are arranged in approximate lifeboat departure order. Whilst the British inquiry attempted to establish lifeboat departure times, these have subsequently been revised by numerous *Titanic* historians and are still subject to much debate. I have used the timings suggested by *Titanic* experts Bill Wormstedt, Tad Fitch and George Behe in *Titanic: The Lifeboat Launching Sequence Re-Examined.* Trying to piece the sequence together is difficult: survivors often don't agree on the departure times for their lifeboat, and an extraordinary number believe themselves to have got away in 'the last boat'. This can be explained by the fact that lifeboats were launched from four locations, port, forward and rear, and starboard, forward and rear. It is conceivable, especially at night, that passengers would only really have a clear understanding of what was going on in their immediate vicinity. In addition some would claim to be in the last boat as this was the 'chivalric' place to be.

The lifeboat survivor grouping allows the reader to see how survivors recollect the same events differently and in some cases what they thought of the other occupants of their lifeboat. Common themes reappear throughout. Men often 'blamed' their survival on others — it was simply not seen as heroic to survive the sinking of the *Titanic*. 'Foreigners' and the 'lower orders' get a bad press and are regularly accused of trying to jump the lifeboat queue or behaving badly once they had secured a place. Any 'bad behaviour' not explainable by casual racism could be explained by language problems. Instructions and assurances given in English may simply not have been understood. Many women claim to have had babies entrusted into their care and an unfeasibly large number of people claim to owe their life to either the personal intervention of Captain Edward Smith or the richest man on the ship, John Jacob Astor.

Panic levels and emotions increase as the night goes on. Filling the early lifeboats was a challenge. Messages about the amount of damage caused by the iceberg were mixed. Some knew the truth, but concealed it to prevent panic, others still believed the *Titanic* was unsinkable and preferred to stay on board rather than be lowered in a small boat onto the Atlantic Ocean. Women were often coaxed into the early boats, but tended to be thrown into later ones. As the night wore on lifeboats became increasingly easy to fill and average passenger numbers rose. By the time the last few lifeboats were leaving the boat deck, shots were fired to maintain order and Second Officer Charles Lightoller ordered crew to lock arms in a wide ring around lifeboat D to keep people back.

Nobody can be sure of the exact numbers of either passengers on board or eventual survivors but the *Titanic* carried approximately 322 first class passengers, 277 second class passengers, 709 third class passengers and 898 crew members. The picture is confused by the presence of stowaways, by passengers travelling under a pseudonym and others whose names were incorrectly transcribed. All figures should therefore be treated with caution.

Approximately 703 to 711 people survived, including nearly all first class women, most second class women and less than half of the third class female passengers. This pattern is broadly repeated for children with nearly all first and second class children surviving but tragically only about a third of third class children surviving.

For men survival rates were lowest amongst the second class passengers (8 per cent) and highest amongst the first class where a third of male passengers survived. Of the 885 male crew members 22 per cent survived, which, compared with some other groups' survival rates, is very high.

Lifeboats were filled to an average of 60 per cent capacity. The figure for individual lifeboats varies widely from lifeboat 1, which left with just 12 passengers, to lifeboat 11, which was at maximum capacity; but the pattern that broadly emerges is this: the first half dozen or so lifeboats were loaded with almost exclusively first class passengers, then second class women start to be loaded in, followed by third class passengers, who make up a larger portion of later lifeboats. Lifeboats got steadily fuller throughout the night.

There were several reasons why lifeboats were not fully filled. Some officers mistakenly thought that there was a difference between the lowering capacity and the actual capacity of a lifeboat. Many passengers could see a light and thought they would be rescued before the ship sank and didn't want to get in a lifeboat. This false hope was also held by some officers – 'I didn't realise it was urgent then' was the explanation given by Second Officer Lightoller for the underfilling of lifeboats. Lack of strong leadership from Captain Smith was doubtless an issue. Smith was one of the few people in full possession of all the facts; he knew that *Titanic* was going to sink, that there weren't enough lifeboats and that the nearest ship to respond to their distress calls was four hours away. Had all lifeboats been filled perhaps 450 more lives could have been saved and Smith should have made sure this happened.

Lifeboats on the port side contained only women, children and crew with Second Officer Lightoller adhering to a policy of 'women and children only'. When there were no more women or children waiting for a place the lifeboat was launched even if there were still places left. On the starboard side men stood more chance with First Officer William Murdoch operating a policy of women and children first but allowing men to board when there were no more women coming forward.

Despite this preferential treatment 52 of the 79 children travelling third class tragically died that night. Setting aside any debate about the justice of male passengers being at the back of the queue, the question has to be asked why were third class women and children not up on the boat deck ready to take a lifeboat place? Some of the accounts within this book begin to answer this question. We hear of locked gates, passengers struggling to navigate their way up to the boat deck, and a general alarm not being raised so passengers were not necessarily aware of the danger. Survivor Olaus Abelseth describes fellow passengers climbing along cranes to get to the boat deck where the lifeboats were stowed.

The British inquiry concluded there was no class discrimination in the loading of lifeboats. Whilst there may not have been 'active' discrimination against third class passengers it is evident that the barriers that they had to overcome to get a place in a lifeboat were high. Firstly they needed to be aware of the gravity of the situation and with crew to passenger ratios as much as ten times higher in third class there was a certain amount of luck involved here. Then they needed to negotiate their way up to the boat deck either on their own initiative or by being lucky enough to be under the care of one of the stewards (e.g. John Hart, see chapter 37) who diligently carried out this duty. Those still on deck in the final minutes report a wave of steerage passengers suddenly appearing. This was a good two hours after the order went out for all passengers to get lifebelts on – why did it take so long before they reached the only place that could provide a hope of survival?

The last two collapsible lifeboats drifted off the deck when the *Titanic* finally sank and were a refuge for a lucky few. Lifeboat A drifted off right side up, but with her canvas sides unraised and taking on a lot of water. Lifeboat B was upturned – survivors had to cling onto the wooden slats at the bottom. Their position on board was precarious and men had to refuse to help others climb on board for fear that they might capsize the lifeboat.

The Ship

Titanic was the largest and most opulent ship of its day. The transatlantic passenger market was competitive and the White Star Line had commissioned a ship which would give a stable crossing in luxurious surroundings. On board was a swimming pool, gym, barbers, a squash court and a Turkish bath. The communal areas for those travelling first class included the Café Parisien, smoking room and the grand staircase. *The Shipbuilder* commented that the fittings were 'more than equal to that provided in the finest hotels on shore'. Passengers report feeling in awe of her immense size and luxurious interior:

> Like everyone else I was entranced with the beauty of the liner. I had never dreamt of travelling in such luxury. I remember being childishly pleased on finding strawberries on my breakfast table. Fancy, strawberries in April and in mid-ocean. The whole thing is positively uncanny. I kept saying to my husband, 'Why, you would think you were at the Ritz.' *Lady Lucy Duff-Gordon, Lifeboat 1*

Third class accommodation was also of an improved standard over previous ships. Cabins were less like the dormitory styles available elsewhere and had fewer berths. They had electricity and running water and a dedicated, although basic, social area.

In 1912 ocean liner was the only way of getting across the Atlantic and ports were the airports of their day. Newspapers employed ship reporters to report on the comings and goings at port, the airport paparazzi of their day, reporting on the rich and famous arriving at port. One such ship reporter, Jack Lawrence, said of the *Titanic*: 'I never saw a passenger list that contained so many well-known names. It seems highly probable now that no ship ever began an Atlantic crossing with so much wealth represented in her first cabin.'

She was built in Belfast by Harland & Wolff. Sold as 'unsinkable', *Titanic* was designed with 15 bulkheads (partition walls) which provided 16 separate watertight compartments. Four of these compartments could be flooded and *Titanic* would stay afloat. The collision with the iceberg caused the ship's hull to buckle along its starboard side and water to flood the first five compartments. As *Titanic* went gradually down by the bow, water began to flow over the top of each successive bulkhead, pulling her bow further down.

The *Titanic* was equipped with 14 full-sized lifeboats designed to carry 65 people each. There were two further 'emergency' lifeboats with a capacity of 40, and four 'collapsible' or 'Engelhardt' lifeboats with capacities of 47. Lifeboats 1, 3, 5, 7, 9, 11, 13, C and A were on the starboard side, and 2, 4, 6, 8, 10, 12, 14, 16, D and B were on the port side. Lifeboats 1 and 2 were the emergency boats – kept ready for immediate use. The collapsible lifeboats were named A, B, C and D. The boat deck plan (see illustration 66) shows the position of the lifeboats relative to other parts of the deck such as the first class stairway. Total lifeboat capacity was 1,178 and there were approximately 2,240 people on board.

The Maiden Voyage

Titanic left Southampton on Wednesday 10 April 1912 and made two stops before beginning to cross the Atlantic. Firstly in Cherbourg, France, to pick up mostly first and second class passengers, and secondly on 11 April in Queenstown (now renamed Cobh), Ireland, picking up over 100 third class passengers, who were mostly emigrating to America. *Titanic* was expected to arrive in New York on the morning of Wednesday 17 April. Although ice warnings had been received from ships nearby this first voyage was largely uneventful with few clues as to what was about to happen.

It was 11.39 p.m. on the evening of Sunday 14 April when Lookout Frederick Fleet spotted the iceberg. He called down to the bridge where Sixth Officer James Moody receives the warning 'Iceberg, right ahead!' First Officer Murdoch and Quartermaster Robert Hichens immediately tried to steer away from the iceberg but at 11.40 p.m. *Titanic* struck, her starboard side buckled and her fate was sealed.

The watertight doors were closed and Captain Smith soon arrived on the bridge. The ship's designer Thomas Andrews went to inspect the damage caused and soon returned to report that it was fatal. By midnight Captain Smith knew that *Titanic* was going to sink. Orders were sent out to uncover the lifeboats and get passengers into lifebelts.

Wireless Operators Harold Bride and Jack Phillips began sending out distress calls at about 12.15 a.m. asking for assistance from neighbouring vessels. The *Carpathia* picked up their call at 12.35 a.m. and Captain Rostron quickly ordered his ship to make for the *Titanic*. There was another ship much closer to *Titanic*, the *Californian*. Many passengers and crew report seeing a ship only a few miles away and the false hope that this ship would come to their aid was one of the reasons for passengers' subsequent reluctance to board the lifeboats. Why the *Californian* failed to come to *Titanic's* aid has been much debated but the failure undoubtedly cost lives.

In addition to the wireless distress messages, Fourth Officer Joseph Boxhall started sending up distress flares at 12.50 a.m. and continued doing so for another hour. Boxhall also tried to contact the mystery ship seen in the distance by using a Morse code lamp.

As the first lifeboats were being loaded and launched at around 12.40 a.m. the ship's band started to play. They would play until the very end and none would survive the night. The *Titanic's* engineering crew also worked to ensure that the ship's generators provided electricity until the very end.

For the next hour and a quarter lifeboats were launched with increased haste until by 2.00 a.m. only the canvas-sided collapsible lifeboats (A, B, C and D) were yet to leave the ship. By 2.05 a.m. the bow was under water and Captain Smith told wireless operators Bride and Phillips that it was time to leave their posts stating 'now it's every man for themselves'.

Survivors watching the last few minutes from the lifeboats reported different things, but it is generally agreed that *Titanic* continued to sink at the bow until by 2.10 a.m. the keel at the stern was above water exposing her propellers. By approximately 2.15 a.m. waves began to wash over the boat deck and collapsible lifeboats B and A floated off. The stern continued to rise out of the water and the angle of the deck became so steep that the forward funnel broke off and fell into the bridge, crushing many. Those 1,500 or so people still on board and not already trapped below, frantically climbed higher towards the stern or jumped overboard. Some reported that the ship broke in two before its final descent at 2.20 a.m., whilst others were sure that she remained intact. This was resolved in 1985 with the discovery of the wreck site; *Titanic* was found lying in two parts on the seabed.

Captain Smith went down with the ship. Whilst four of the ship's seven officers survived, eyewitnesses report that an officer (possibly First Officer William Murdoch) committed suicide just before the final descent.

It was after 4 a.m. on the morning of Monday 15 April when the *Carpathia* arrived at the scene and the last lifeboat was picking up at 8.30 a.m. The *Carpathia* arrived in New York on Thursday 18 April carrying less than a third of *Titanic's* original passengers to meet the assembled crowds.

Notable Crew & Passengers

THOMAS ANDREWS, Ship Designer employed by Harland & Wolff, died. Sometimes referred to as the ship's carpenter or builder.

COLONEL JOHN JACOB ASTOR IV, died. Very rich 'celebrity' American travelling with his 18-year-old wife Madeleine. His wife survived.

LAWRENCE BEESLEY, survived. An English second class survivor. Beesley was a schoolteacher who published a noted account of the disaster in 1912.

JOSEPH G. BOXHALL, Fourth Officer, survived. Tried to summon help with flares and a Morse lamp.

MARGARET 'MOLLY' BROWN, survived. The famous 'unsinkable' Molly Brown.

MAJOR ARCHIBALD BUTT, died. Famous for being an important aide to the then current American President William Howard Taft.

LORD & LADY DUFF-GORDON, both survived. Members of the English aristocracy. Lady Duff-Gordon was a famous fashion designer and her husband a renowned sportsman. Their actions on the night of the sinking were heavily criticised.

ARCHIBALD GRACIE, survived. An American first class survivor. Important because he wrote a very detailed memoir in 1912 of his experiences and researched the fates of many other passengers.

BENJAMIN GUGGENHEIM, died. Another immensely rich American 'celebrity' passenger, the fate of whom fascinated journalists.

ROBERT HICHENS, Quartermaster (*Titanic* had eight quartermasters in total), survived. Hichens was at the wheel when *Titanic* struck the iceberg.

BRUCE ISMAY, Managing Director of the White Star Line, survived. Ismay's conduct was closely scrutinised in the aftermath. In particular he was much pilloried for taking a lifeboat place.

CHARLES H. LIGHTOLLER, Second Officer, survived. In charge of lowering lifeboats on the port side.

HAROLD G. LOWE, Fifth Officer, survived. In charge of the only lifeboat to return to the scene of the sinking to save passengers in the water.

JAMES P. MOODY, Sixth Officer, died. The youngest of the officers who stayed with the ship until the very end helping to load lifeboats.

WILLIAM M. MURDOCH, First Officer, died. In charge of lowering lifeboats on the starboard side of the ship.

HERBERT J. PITMAN, Third Officer, survived. In charge of lifeboat 5, the second lifeboat to be launched.

COUNTESS OF ROTHES, survived. English aristocrat who received a lot of coverage in the aftermath of the sinking.

EDWARD J. SMITH, Captain, died. Went down with his ship. References to Smith in the survivor testimony (including amongst the crew) are relatively few considering he was the captain of a sinking ship.

ISIDOR & IDA STRAUS, both died. Famous for Ida's refusal to leave her husband when offered a lifeboat place.

HENRY T. WILDE, Chief Officer, died. Assisted lowering lifeboats mostly on the port side.

Note to the Reader

Editorial commentary is in the same font style as this notice. Material in square brackets is the editor's. The source of each extract is given in italics immediately preceding the extract.

LIFEBOAT 7
Starboard Side, Launched 12.40 a.m.

First Officer Murdoch supervised the loading of this first lifeboat in which 26 passengers got away. All passengers were first class, although there was a mixture of genders. There were two honeymooning couples in this lifeboat and I have included accounts from one of these: Helen and Dickinson Bishop.

The launching of lifeboat 7 was relatively calm, with Lookout George Hogg put in charge of the boat. All *Titanic*'s lookouts managed to survive the disaster.

By now *Titanic* would be noticeably down at the bow, as each successive compartment was flooded and water poured over the bulkheads, but it still proved difficult to fill the lifeboat quickly and Murdoch presumably decided it was better to send the lifeboat away promptly rather than wait for more passengers. Male crew: three; male passengers: four; women and children: 20; total for lifeboat: 27 (British Board of Inquiry).

I

Helen & Dickinson Bishop, First Class Passengers

Originally from Dowagiac in Michigan, the Bishops were newly married and returning from honeymoon. In the *Dowagiac Daily News* article Helen recounts an order to 'put in the brides and grooms' first, but this is not repeated in her later testimony and may be an attempt by Helen to 'blame' others for their escape and hence alleviate the guilt many passengers felt about their survival. Both Helen and Dickinson survived.

Helen's dog Freu Freu was one of a number of dogs on the *Titanic*. There was a kennel on board, most likely on the boat deck. The ship's butcher was responsible for the kennels, hence Helen's claim that 'the steward wouldn't let me take her to the butcher… she was too pretty'. It was claimed that as the ship began its final descent the kennel doors were opened to allow the dogs on board a chance of survival.

The *New York Times* article contains a vivid description of the sinking as witnessed from a lifeboat.

Dowagiac Daily News, 20 April 1912 We had been in Europe since January, and had visited Egypt, Italy, France and Algiers. We sailed on the *Titanic* on the 10th and had had a most enjoyable voyage until the night of the disaster. I had retired when our ship struck the iceberg, but Mr Bishop was sitting in our stateroom, reading. I didn't hear the shock, and it was several minutes before someone came to our door and told us to come on deck. I got up and dressed; then we went above. Officers told us we might as well go below and retire; that there was no danger. We did not do so for some time, however. Finally we did, and soon afterward we were again summoned. We dressed quietly and had plenty of time.

The girl who occupied a stateroom across from us refused to get up and the stewards pulled her out of bed; she got back in and sank with the ship.

When we got on deck there were few people there, but were tons of ice on the fore part of the ship. We were in the first lifeboat to be lowered over the side. Someone said, 'Put in the brides and grooms first.'

There were two newly married couples who went in that boat. Altogether, there were 28 in our boat. There might as well have been 40 or so, but the half hundred men on deck refused to leave, even though there was room for them.

John Jacob Astor was standing at the foot of the stairway as I started to go back the second time. He told us to get on our lifebelts and we did. Before our boat was lowered into the water, Mr and Mrs Astor were on the deck. She didn't want to go, saying that she thought we were all silly, that the *Titanic* couldn't sink. Because the Astors' stateroom was close to ours, we had had considerable to do with them on the voyage and I disliked to leave them on deck. As a matter of fact I believed much as they did that there was little chance of being picked up in the lifeboats.

The water was like glass. There wasn't even the ripple usually found on a small lake. By the time we had pulled 100 yards [*c.* 91 metres] the lower row of portholes had disappeared. When we were a mile away the second row had gone, but there was still no confusion. Indeed everything seemed to be quiet on the ship until her stern was raised out of the water by the list forward. Then a veritable wave of humanity surged up out of the steerage and shut the lights from our view. We were too far away to see the passengers individually, but we could see the black masses of human forms and hear their death cries and groans.

For a moment the ship seemed to be pointing straight down, looking like a gigantic whale submerging itself, head first.

One dining room steward, who was in our boat, was thoughtful enough to bring green lights – the kind you burn on the 4th of July. They cast a ghastly light over the boat, but you know we had no light of any kind. I think all lifeboats ought to be equipped with lights, crackers and water and compasses. Whenever we would light one of these diminutive torches we would hear cries from the people perishing aboard. They thought it was help coming.

We were afloat in the lifeboat from about 12.30 a.m. Sunday night until five o'clock Monday morning. Although we were the first boat to leave the *Titanic*, we were about the fourth picked up by the *Carpathia*. The scenes on that little craft adrift in mid-ocean with little hope of rescue were most heart-rending. Still the characteristics of the individuals appealed to me.

For instance, there was a German baron aboard who smoked an obnoxious pipe incessantly and refused to pull an oar. The men were worn out with the work, and I rowed for a considerable time myself. There was a little French aviator in our boat, Pierre Maréchal, a partner of Paulhan, who never took his monocle from his eye all the time we were on the water, but he did assist in the rowing.

It broke my heart to leave my little dog Freu Freu in my stateroom. I had purchased her in Florence, Italy, and she was the pet of the ship. The steward wouldn't let me take her to the butcher. He said she was too pretty, and she was the only one allowed to stay in the cabin. I made a little den for her in our room behind two of my suitcases, but when I started to leave her she tore my dress to bits, tugging at it. I realised, however, that there would be little sympathy for a woman carrying a dog in her arms when there were lives of women and children to be saved.

Whenever a light, however small, was flashed in a lifeboat those in the other drifting crafts were given false hopes of rescue. After we had been afloat for several hours without food or water and everyone suffering from the cold, I felt certain we should all perish. I took off my stockings and gave them to a little girl who hadn't as much time to dress as I had.

When the day broke and the *Carpathia* was sighted, there were indescribable scenes of joy. After we had pulled alongside of the rescue ship, many of the women were lifted aboard in chairs, tied to a rope. I was sufficiently composed to climb the ladder alongside to the deck. When the last of the survivors were taken on, the recounting of the experience began.

I think the story told us by Colonel Archibald Gracie, of Washington, DC, was the most remarkable of any we heard. He remained on deck and clung to the rail until he struck the water. He must have been sucked under 50 or 60 feet [*c.* 15–18 metres], Colonel Gracie told us. When he came to the surface he said he found himself among a mass of wreckage, but he is an excellent swimmer and finally succeeded in reaching a small collapsible which had a few passengers aboard. Imagine a man as old as Colonel Gracie scrambling with 1,700 people in water two miles deep. It is remarkable that he succeeded.

Colonel Gracie was peevish, though. He did not want to tell of his experiences.

Those on board the *Carpathia* did everything in their power for our comfort. They shared everything with us and the captain of that boat was not like Captain Smith of the *Titanic*. You didn't see him at fashionable dinners. He was always on duty.

Mrs Lucien Smith of Huntington, West Virginia, a dear little woman, who lost her husband in the disaster, said that before they parted on the deck he told her he had seen Captain Smith at a dinner at 11 p.m. that night. When he left the dining room, the captain was still there; although he may have gone to the bridge before the collision, it doesn't seem likely. For some reason, which we will probably never know, the bulkhead doors refused to work. I watched the men for several minutes endeavouring to turn the screws that would lower them and make the compartments watertight, but they were unsuccessful. It may be that the impact so wrenched them as to throw them out of line.

Helen Bishop, New York Times, 19 April 1912 We did not understand the situation till we were perhaps a mile away form the *Titanic*. Then we could see the rows of lights along the decks begin to slant gradually upwards from the bow. Very slowly the lines of light began to point downward at a greater and greater angle. The sinking was so slow that you could not perceive the lights of the deck changing their position. The slant seemed to be greater every quarter of an hour.

In a couple of hours, though, she began to go down more rapidly. Then the fearful sight began. The people in the ship were just beginning to realise how great the danger was. When the forward part of the ship dropped suddenly at a faster rate so that the upward slope became marked, there was a sudden rush of passengers on all decks toward the stern. It was like a wave. We could see the great black mass of people in the steerage sweeping to the rear part of the boat and breaking through into the upper decks. At the distance of about a mile we could distinguish everything through the night, which was perfectly clear. We could make out the increasing excitement on board the boat, as the people, rushing to and fro, caused the deck lights to disappear and reappear as they passed in front of them.

The panic went on, it seemed, for an hour. Then suddenly the ship seemed to shoot up out of the water and stand there perpendicularly. It seemed to us that it stood upright in the water for four full minutes.

Then it began to slide gently downwards. Its speed increased as it went down head first, so that the stern shot down with a rush.

The lights continued to burn till it sank. We could see the people packed densely in the stern till it was gone.

There were three sailors in our boat. There were six oars to be manned, and I took my turn with the men.

As the ship sank we could hear the screaming a mile away. Gradually it became fainter and fainter and died away. Some of the lifeboats that had room for more might have gone to their rescue, but it would have meant that those who were in the water would have swarmed aboard and sunk her.

We rowed for five or six hours I think. The Northern Lights were fading away when the *Carpathia* came.

I don't think the sinking of the boat caused much suction. The disturbance of the water was not great enough to reach our boat. Perhaps the explosion of the boilers counteracted the suction. A second after the boat sunk there was a noise like the roll of thunder.

Dickinson Bishop, Dowagiac Daily News, 10 May 1912 We waited over to take passage on this particular ship. We could have sailed earlier, but waited at Cherbourg to come across on this monster new passenger boat, which was the largest and most sumptuous of the transatlantic boats.

Up to the time of the wreck we had a beautified passage. The sea was delightful.

It was delightful that Sunday night, as calm and as quiet as a mill pond. I will never forget the sunset that night; everybody had enjoyed it.

We had spent the evening in the lounge, and at 11 o'clock retired to our stateroom on B deck. I sat up in bed and read until 11.40 when the ship struck the iceberg.

I hurriedly dressed and told Mrs Bishop to do the same. I then went to the A deck, and finally to the boat deck. There seemed to be no commotion. The stewards laughed at the suggestion of danger.

I felt assured all was safe and returned to our stateroom. We both undressed and retired. I once more began to read and so occupied myself for 10 minutes. Presently Mr Stewart, a friend we had made on board ship, who had been across the ocean many times, rapped at the door and called me outside. He informed me we had best get up and dress. He then called my attention to the listing of the boat which began soon after the iceberg was struck.

We then dressed completely and prepared for comfort in an emergency. We went up to the boat deck but no preparation had been made for lowering any of the boats. We returned to A deck and there met Mr and Mrs Astor, who seemed to feel little alarm. Mrs Bishop wanted a muff and I went for it, and while in the stateroom she came in and said we had been ordered to put on lifebelts. This we did and again went to the boat deck.

The lowering of the lifeboats was done deliberately, and it was not even commenced until we had been on deck for several minutes. It was then almost impossible to get people to venture into them. We entered the first boat lowered, and I am sure there were six or seven single men in the boat with us. The officers implored people to get aboard, but they seemed to fear hanging out over the water at a height of 75 feet [*c.* 23 metres], and the officers ordered the boat lowered away with only a small portion of what it could carry.

It was exceedingly difficult to be understood on the deck, such was the noise from the escaping steam which began to blow off as soon as the engines stopped.

US Senate Inquiry (inquiry question is followed immediately by Helen Bishop's answer)
You were on board the *Titanic* on this ill-fated voyage? Yes.

Did anything in particular occur to attract your attention to the ship or any special feature of the ship while you were en route from Southampton to the place of this accident? We thought of nothing at all except the luxury of the ship; how wonderful it was.

I wish you would tell the committee what you did after learning of this accident. *Witness answers:* My husband awakened me at about a quarter of 12 and told me that the boat had struck something. We both dressed and went up on the deck, looked around, and could find nothing. We noticed the intense cold; in fact, we had noticed that about 11 o'clock that night. It was uncomfortably cold in the lounge. We looked all over the deck; walked up and down a couple of times, and one of the stewards met us and laughed at us. He said, 'You go back downstairs. There is nothing to be afraid of. We have only struck a little piece of ice and passed it.' So we returned to our stateroom and retired. About 15 minutes later we were awakened by a man who had a stateroom near us. We were on B deck, number 47. He told us to come upstairs. So we dressed again thoroughly and looked over all our belongings in our room and went upstairs. After being there about five or 10 minutes one of the men we were with ran up and spoke to the captain, who was just then coming down the stairs.

Who was the man? Mr Astor.

Colonel Astor? Yes. The captain told him something in an undertone. He came back and told six of us, who were standing with his wife, that we had better put on our lifebelts. I had gotten down two flights of stairs to tell my husband, who had returned to the stateroom for a moment, before I heard the captain announce that the lifebelts should be put on. That was about three or four minutes later that the captain announced the lifebelts should be put on. We came back upstairs and found very few people up.

When you say upstairs, which deck do you mean? We were on B deck, and we came back up to A deck. There was very little confusion; only the older women were a little frightened. They were up, partially dressed. So I sent a number of them back and saw that they were thoroughly dressed before they came up again. Then we went up on to the boat deck on the starboard side. We looked around, and there were so very few people up there that my husband and I went to the port side to see if there was anyone there. There were only two people, a young French bride and groom, on that side of the boat, and they followed us immediately to the starboard side. By that time an old man had come upstairs and found Mr and Mrs Harder, of New York. He brought us all together and told us to be sure and stay together; that he would be back in a moment. We never saw him again. About five minutes later the boats were lowered, and we were pushed in. At the time our lifeboat was lowered I had no idea that it was time to get off.

Tell me which lifeboat you refer to? The first lifeboat that was taken off the *Titanic* on the starboard side. I think it was No. 7. Officer Lowe told us that.

All right. Proceed. *Witness answers:* We had no idea that it was time to get off, but the officer took my arm and told me to be very quiet and get in immediately. They put the families in the first two boats. My husband was pushed in with me, and we were lowered away with 28 people in the boat.

Was that a large lifeboat? Yes. It was a wooden lifeboat.

And there were 28 people in it? Yes. We counted off after we reached the water.

How many women were there? There were only about 12 women.

And the rest were – *Witness answers:* Were men.

Yes; but I want to divide the rest into two classes, the crew and the passengers. *Witness answers:* There were three of the crew. The rest of them were passengers. We had no officer in our boat.

Three of the crew? Three of the crew.

And 13 passengers? 13 passengers; yes. Among those there were several unmarried men in our boat, I noticed, and three or four foreigners in our boat. After we had been out in the water about 15 minutes – the *Titanic* had not yet sunk – five boats were gathered together, and five people were put into our boat from another one, making 33 people in our boat.

Do you know from what boat these persons were transferred to your boat? No; I cannot say. The man in charge was an officer with a moustache. I have never seen him since.

Did the boat from which these people were transferred seem to have more people than yours? Yes, sir; they had 30, I believe, or 37, or something like that.

Do you remember the number of the boat? No; I do not.

Go ahead. *Witness answers:* We had been rowing for some time when the other people were transferred into our boat. Then we rowed still farther away, as the women were nervous about the suction. We waited out in the water perhaps three quarters of an hour after we had rowed this distance when we saw the *Titanic* sink. For some time after that we were separated from all of the boats except one; that tied to us and stayed with us. We found we had no compass, no light, and I do not know about the crackers or water; but we had no compass and no light. We were out there until just before daylight, I think it was, when we saw the lights of the *Carpathia* and rowed as hard as we could and arrived at the *Carpathia* five or 10 minutes after five o'clock in the morning.

I suppose your experience was the same as that of the others as to the presence of ice and your proximity to icebergs? Yes; we saw a number of icebergs.

Is there anything else you care to say which will throw any light upon our inquiry as to the causes of this catastrophe or the conduct of the officers and crew of the *Titanic*? The conduct of the crew, as far as I could see, was absolutely beyond criticism. It was perfect. The men in our boat were wonderful. One man lost his brother. When the *Titanic* was going down I remember he just put his hand over his face; and immediately after she sank he did the best he could to keep the women feeling cheerful all the rest of the time. We all thought a great deal of that man.

What was his name? I do not know. He was on the lookout immediately after the boat had struck.

Was it Fleet? No; it was not.

Was it Lee? I do not think I ever heard his name. I know the name of one man in the boat was Jack Edmunds; I think it was.

That was this lookout? No; the man at the other end. They were great friends, I remember.

Is there anything else you care to say? No; that is all.

Very well; you may be excused.

2

Archie Jewell, Lookout

The loading of lifeboat 7 was marked by the lack of any sense of urgency. As part of the crew responsible for loading, lowering and manning the lifeboat, Archie Jewell gives a clear description of the difficulty in persuading passengers to leave the apparent security of the 'unsinkable' *Titanic*, to enter what amounted to a large rowing boat, be lowered 75 feet (c. 23 metres), and cast adrift into the middle of the Atlantic Ocean. This probably explains why several men were allowed to get in. The following is an edited version of the testimony he gave at the British Board of Trade Inquiry into the sinking.

British Board of Trade Inquiry (inquiry question is followed immediately by witness's answer) When you went off duty at 10 o'clock and went below, did you go to bed – turn in? Yes, I went to bed.

And what was the next thing you knew? The boatswain came below and called all hands on deck. I heard the crash first; that woke me up.

You were woken up were you by the crash? Yes.

What did you do then? Ran on deck to see what it was.

What did you see? I saw some ice on the well deck on the starboard side.

What did you do then? Went down and put on some clothes. We all went below. They did not think there was any harm.

Then you spoke about the boatswain coming. How long after was that? Not long. I cannot say exactly the time. He came and called all hands on deck. I could not tell you exactly the time; it was not long.

Then, when the boatswain came and called all hands on deck, did you go on deck with the others? Yes, all hands went on the deck.

Had you got a station? Yes, at my own boat.

Which was your boat? Lifeboat 7.

You say that when you were ordered up on deck and there was the muster, you went to No. 7? Yes.

Just tell us what was done with boat No. 7? We all cleared away the boats. The orders were for all hands to clear the boats, and we all went and cleared the boats. I helped to clear away No. 7, cleared away the falls, and got them all ready and the first officer, Murdoch, told us to lower away the boats to the level of the rail.

That was Mr Murdoch you say? Yes, he was in charge of us.

And he gave the order to lower the boat to the level of the rail? Yes.

And, of course, up to that time the boat would be empty? Yes.

Then, when she was lowered down level with the rail, what were the orders then? 'Women and children in the boat.'

Had any seamen been put into the boat? Not then. We were all standing by that belonged to the boat.

How many men man one of these boats? There are two sailors to each boat, so many firemen, and so many stewards. I do not know how many firemen; I have never seen their list.

Two seamen and a certain number of the firemen, and a certain number of the stewards? Yes.

Did you count as one of the two seamen for this boat? Yes.

Who was the other? Weller.

You say Mr Murdoch said, 'Women and children first,' and what was done? Well, we put all the women in that was there, and children. Up to that time there was not many people; we could not get them up; they were rather afraid to go into the boat; they did not think there was anything wrong.

Were there men passengers there too? Yes, we had some men passengers.

Did any of them get into your boat? Yes. I do not know how many. There was three or four there. Three or four Frenchmen there – I do not know whether they got into the boat.

I only just want to know; did any men passengers get into No. 7? Yes.

Three or four? Yes.

Was there excitement? No, Sir, none at all; very quiet.

And how many people got into No. 7 before she was lowered? I could not say; it looked pretty full; there was not much room to work in her.

But you do not know the number? No, I could not say the number at all.

Did you get into her? Yes, there were three seamen into that boat.

Where was the third? I never see no fireman or no stewards up there at that time; it was about the first boat to be lowered.

And how is it done on a big liner like this: when you lower the boat from the rail down to the water, is it done from the boat or from the deck? From the deck.

So that the people in the boat would not do the lowering away? No, just keep the boat off the ship's side.

Did she get down to the water safely? Yes.

Were there oars in the boat? Yes.

Was she provisioned? I never saw any biscuits or nothing; I do not know whether there was any; I do not know that there was anybody looking for any.

Had she got any light? No.

And where is the light kept? In the after-locker; the locker in the after end of the boat.

Did anyone take it out and light it? No; there was none there. We had a look to see if we could find a light, and there was none there.

Who was in charge of the boat? Hogg [another *Titanic* lookout].

There was Hogg and yourself and Weller? Yes.

Were those the only three members of the crew in the boat? That is all.

When you got down to the water, had you got any of these men passengers in them? Yes.

You say you thought about four? Well, I should say about that; I could not say the exact number.

Then the rest of them would be women and children? Yes.

Were there any children? We had one I think, that was all; the rest were women.

You say Mr Murdoch was giving orders about lowering the boat; did he give orders to launch her down to the water? To lower her right down to the water.

And what were the orders about, what was she to do? He told us to stand by the gangway.

I do not quite know what you mean by that. What is the gangway you are referring to? The doors that open in the ship's side.

Where the gangway would be if she were in port, I suppose? Yes, that is right.

And you were told to remain in the water below that gangway? Yes.

Those were your orders. How far off from the ship did you keep? We kept right alongside.

Was the sea smooth? Yes, very smooth.

Just tell us what happened after that? Well, we see all the other boats lowered away and pull away from the ship. Then we saw the ship settling away, and we had to pull away clear.

Let us just see if we can get clear about these other boats, if we can. Did you keep on the starboard side? Yes.

And you pulled away from her side because you saw these other boats were pulling away? Yes.

And how far off did you go? We only just went a little way at first, just kept so that we could speak to them on board the ship in case we were wanted.

Did anybody speak to you from the deck? No.

That would be some little distance off. Give me an idea how far off it would be? About 20 yards [c. 18 metres] or something like that, and we stopped there.

And when you were in that position, some 20 yards from the ship, so that you could be hailed from the deck, did you see any signs of her settling down then? Yes, you could notice her going away by the head.

Was that gradual or sudden? No, very slow.

Were the other boats on the starboard side about the same distance off, or further off? Further off.

Then when was it that you made a move again? The forecastle head was getting close down to the water then.

And what did you do then with your boat? Pulled away clear.

Now can you give me any idea about how long that was before she disappeared? I could not say that; not more than about half an hour I should say.

And how far from the ship did you pull away then? Oh, a long way. We met with the Third Officer, and he moored his boat alongside of ours all night.

What is the Third Officer's name? Mr Pitman.

And you met Pitman in his boat? Yes.

And he moored his boat alongside of yours? Yes, alongside of ours all night.

Lashed together, I think? Yes.

3

James McGough, First Class Passenger

The following is the affidavit James McGough supplied to the US Senate Inquiry. The 36-year-old American also added to his statement that some of the women in lifeboat 7 had objected to the suggestion of going back to pick up passengers who were in the water.

I was awakened at 11.40 p.m., ship time; my stateroom was on the starboard side – deck E – and was shared with me by John Flynn, a buyer for Gimbel Bros., New York, at 33rd and Broadway. Soon after leaving our stateroom we came in contact with the second dining room steward, George Dodd, in the companionway, of whom we asked the question, 'Is there any danger?' and he answered, 'Not in the least,' and suggested that we go back to bed, which we did not, however, do.

It was our intention to go up on the promenade deck, but before doing so I rapped on the door of the stateroom opposite mine, which was occupied by a lady, and suggested to her that she had better get up at once and dress as there was apparently something wrong.

Mr Flynn and I then ascended to promenade deck A, and after being up there about 10 minutes were notified to put on life preservers as a matter of precaution. We then had to go all the way from promenade deck back to our stateroom, which was on E deck. After procuring our life preservers we went back again to the top deck, and after reaching there discovered that orders had been given to launch the lifeboats, and that they were already being launched at that time.

They called for the women and children to board the boats first. Both women and men, however, hesitated, and did not feel inclined to get into the small boats, thinking the larger boat was the safer. I had my back turned looking in the opposite direction at that time and was caught by the shoulder by one of the officers, who gave me a push, saying, 'Here, you are a big fellow; get into the boat.'

Our boat was launched with 28 people; we, however, transferred five from one of the other boats after we were out in the ocean, which was some time after the ship went down.

When our lifeboats left the vessel, we were directed to row away a short distance from the large boat, feeling it would be but a short time until we would be taken back on the *Titanic*. We then rested on our oars; but after realising that the *Titanic* was really sinking, we rowed away for about half a mile, being afraid that the suction would draw us down.

Although there were several of us wanted drinking water, it was unknown to us that there was a tank of water and also some crackers in our boat, having no light on our boat; and we did not discover this fact – that is, as to the tank of water – until after reaching the *Carpathia*.

LIFEBOAT 5
Starboard Side, Launched 12.45 a.m.

First Officer Murdoch ordered Third Officer Herbert Pitman to load lifeboat 5. Approximately 37 people were in this lifeboat, all first class passengers and a small number of crew. Pitman states to the British inquiry that although the lifeboat was not full 'it took as many as it would take off the davits'. There was a misconception on the part of a number of officers that the lifeboats would buckle if *lowered* at maximum capacity.

This lifeboat was tied-up in the night to lifeboat 7 to make the flotilla easier for rescuers to spot. A small number of passengers were also transferred across to lifeboat 7 during the night.

Male crew: five; male passengers: six; women and children: 30; total for lifeboat: 41 (British Board of Inquiry).

4
Eleanor Genevieve Cassebeer,
First Class Passenger

Cassebeer thought her boat was the sixth to leave the ship. She describes that Pitman tried to go back but was prevented from doing so by the other passengers. This was first published in the *Binghamton Press*, 29 April 1912.

My being aboard the *Titanic* was merely a matter of chance. I was visiting in Paris and being desirous of coming to America, I took the first available steamer, which, as luck would have it, happened to be the *Titanic*.

I have travelled considerably and this was the tenth time that I have crossed the Atlantic ocean. My cabin was situated on D deck on the starboard side of the boat, and I felt the full impact of the iceberg when we struck it.

I was reclining on a couch in my room at the time and I had summoned a stewardess to inquire if it would be safe for me to allow the electric grate to burn throughout the night. She assured me that it would and immediately after she had left my cabin the shock of the cabin came. It sounded as if something were grinding and tearing away the very entrails of the monster liner. I knew immediately that there was something radically wrong and, slipping on a kimono and slippers, I hurried on deck where I met Harry Anderson, a fellow passenger, and together we made our way to the bow of the boat where we found a litter of small particles of ice which was torn from the iceberg by force of the impact. We could see the berg towering some 75 to 100 feet [*c.* 23–30 metres] out of the sea, and, as I afterwards learned only one fifth of the iceberg shows above the water, you can imagine the enormous size of that mountain of ice. Here we also met Thomas Andrews, who, I understand, was the designer of the *Titanic*. In answer to many questions he assured everybody that we were absolutely safe and that the *Titanic* was absolutely unsinkable. He said that she could break in three separate and distinct parts and that each part would stay afloat indefinitely.

It was not long after this, however, that the pursers started to go among the passengers ordering them to go below and put on warm clothing and be prepared to embark in the lifeboats. I hurried below and dressed and when I came on deck again I found that the deck had started to list in a very alarming manner. I had already donned a life preserver, which I found with some difficulty, and when I reached the deck I met Mr Andrews again and he took me by the arm and led me to the lifeboat.

I could not hear just what he said to me at the time on account of the din, but I saw him motion to me to get into the boat, which was about to be swung over the rail 90 feet [*c.* 27 metres] above the water. I asked him why he did not get in also, and he said, 'No, women and children first.'

Right here I wish to say that Bruce Ismay was there also, helping to load the women and children into the boat. He was dressed in pyjamas and slippers with a coat thrown over his shoulders, and as the boat I was in was the sixth to leave the ship you can see that reports that he was in one of the first boats are absolutely false.

There was absolutely no panic. The discipline was excellent. I was in the boat commanded by Third Officer H. J. Pitman. There were 37 people in the boat, five of them being seamen. The boat could not hold any more at the time, as it would have been foolhardy to attempt to overload it, inasmuch as it would have buckled and broken in two from the extra weight the moment it was swung from the davits.

We saw the *Titanic* when it made its final plunge. The lights were burning until the very last moment and it was a spectacular as well as awesome sight. After the *Titanic* had sunk there were thousands of people struggling in the water crying piteously for help. Three times Officer Pitman ordered his men to turn about so that he could pick up some of them, but each time they were prevented from doing so by some of the passengers in the lifeboat who called upon the seamen frantically to go ahead and when they grasped the oars and interfered with the proper handling of the boat so that the seamen were finally forced to give up their efforts of turning back to rescue any of the unfortunates.

We were all wrapped warmly in rugs which the stewards and pursers had pinned about our waists before we got into the boat. When we were picked up by the

Carpathia we were treated beautifully by both officers and the passengers. Many of whom gave up their quarters for our accommodation.

Aboard the *Titanic* I sat at the same table with Dr O'Loughlin, the ship's surgeon, and Thomas Andrews of the Harland & Wolff Building Company, I believe the name of the firm is. Mr Andrews is said to have designed the *Titanic*. Harry Anderson was also a member of our party.

When the boat first started to list so alarmingly I immediately started to make my way to where the men were assembled because I knew that there I would assuredly be safe. I am a staunch admirer in American and British manhood.

A fact that is not generally known is that it was very hard for the men to coax the women into the lifeboats and it became necessary for some of the men to get into the lifeboats first before the women would venture into them, so confident were they that the big steamship was absolutely unsinkable. Then again some of the women absolutely refused to leave their husbands' sides and it almost became necessary for Mr Ismay and Mr Andrews to use force in making some of the men get into the boats with the womenfolk so that they might be saved.

Another thing that is not generally known is that the *Titanic* was not ready to sail at the time she did. Mr Andrews told me himself and said that the only reason they allowed her to go when they did was that the sailing date had already been fixed and they just simply had to start. While the ship was fitted up most sumptuously one could not help but notice that she was not prepared to sail.

There were none of the usual printed notices in the cabins. The frames for them were on the walls, but the notices themselves were not there and when I tried to find a life preserver I did not know where to look for it and was compelled to inquire of some stewards who showed me where to find it.

While I knew matters were very serious I did not realise just how badly we were off until I came up on deck the last time and stumbled over the ropes with which they were preparing to lower the lifeboats. My boat was the third to leave the starboard side and the sixth to leave the ship.

5

Herbert Pitman, Third Officer

Third Officer Pitman was from Somerset. Pitman later said it was only when Murdoch gravely wished him 'good luck' as he stepped into the boat that he knew the situation was serious. When questioned about why the lifeboat did not go back to help those struggling in the sea, Pitman replies that he doesn't think it would have been safe to do so. Other witnesses in the boat suggest that Pitman had in fact suggested picking up survivors but was dissuaded from doing so by the other passengers.

British Board of Trade Inquiry (inquiry question is followed immediately by witness's answer) As you have said, you were turned in at the time the vessel struck the iceberg, and, I believe, asleep? Yes.

You were aroused and at first did you think much had happened? No, I did not.

What was it aroused you; was it a noise, or a jar, or what? A noise; I thought the ship was coming to anchor.

Did you lie on in your bunk for some few minutes? I did.

At the end of those few minutes did you do anything? Yes. I went on deck.

Was that curiosity; or what took you there? Yes, I suppose it was.

Getting on deck, what did you see or hear? I saw nothing and heard nothing.

Did you go to the forward part of the navigation bridge? No, I only just went outside the quarters.

The officers' quarters? That is all.

As it were, put your head out and saw nothing? No, I went on deck.

Seeing and hearing nothing, what did you do then? I went back inside again.

And turned in again? No, I met Mr Lightoller first of all, and I asked him what had happened, if we had hit something, and he said, 'Yes, evidently.'

He said, 'Evidently'? Yes, evidently something had happened.

After you had received that information what did you do? I went to bed.

How long did you remain in bed? It may have been five minutes.

And at the end of five minutes what did you do? I thought I might as well get up, as it was no use trying to go to sleep again, as I was due on watch in a few minutes.

Your watch was the middle watch, from 12 to 4? That night, yes.

Did you get up and proceed to dress? Yes.

While you were dressing did you receive any information? Mr Boxhall came to my room and said the mail room was afloat.

How long do you think had elapsed between the time you were aroused and Mr Boxhall coming and telling you this? I should think it must be 20 minutes.

Did he give you any information as to what had caused the mail room to be afloat? Yes; I asked him what we had struck, and he said an iceberg.

After that did you quickly proceed with your dressing? Yes, I put my coat on and went on deck.

When you got on deck, did you see anything being done? The men were uncovering the boats.

On which side was that? That was on the port side.

Did you meet the Sixth Officer when you went on deck, Mr Moody? Yes; I met him on the after part of the deck.

Did he give you any information? No, I asked him if he had seen the iceberg; he answered no, but there was ice on the forward well deck.

I believe you at that time did not think anything serious had happened, did you? I did not.

Then, I think, you went and looked at some ice, and, after having looked at the ice, did you then go under the forecastle head to see if any structural damage had been done to the bow of the ship? Exactly.

I believe you saw none. As you were coming from the forecastle, did you see any firemen? Yes, I saw a whole crowd of them coming up from below.

Did you ask them what was causing them to come up? Yes.

What was their answer? That the water was coming into their quarters.

Which side were the firemen coming, the port or starboard side? The starboard side.

In consequence of what they told you, did you go and do anything? No, I simply looked down No. 1 hatch and saw water rushing up No. 1 hatch, or at least round it.

Is that the hatch which has the coamings which I think we were told was on G deck? Yes.

Was the water coming in fast or slow, or how? Quite a little stream, both sides of the hatch.

Did you notice what direction it was flowing from; was it flowing from forward to aft, or how, or did not you notice? Well, I think it was running mostly from the starboard side.

Running from the starboard side? Yes.

Seeing that, did you then go back to the boat deck? Yes.

Were the boats still being uncovered, or had they finished the uncovering of the boats then? I could not say what had happened on the port side. I then returned to the starboard side and they were still uncovering the boats.

You are now on the starboard side, and I think you remained on the starboard side, did you not? Yes.

Did you see the First Officer taking part in getting the boats ready? No, I did not see him.

Did you hear any orders being given? No more than getting the boats filled with women and children; that is all I heard.

Did you go to any one of these boats? Yes, I went to No. 5.

Did you go to No. 7 first? No, Mr Murdoch was there. I did not see him.

Which was your boat? No. 1 is my boat usually in case of emergency.

If there was an emergency you would take charge of No. 1, is that so? Yes, that is in case of a man overboard and things like that.

Was your name on the boat list, as being the officer to look after that boat? Yes, as an emergency.

We have been told that there are boat lists put up about the ship; that is so, is it not? That is so.

Did you ever read your name on any list? I did not, as it is an understood thing the Third Officer looks after No. 1 boat.

You did not see your name on any list? No.

Would it be your duty to inform yourself as to what your boat was according to the list? No, it is quite an understood thing in the company for the third and fourth officers to have No. 1 and No. 2 boat.

Apart from understandings, would it be your duty at the beginning of the voyage to go and ascertain what boat was your boat? No.

Now you went in fact to No. 5. Why was that? Mr Murdoch ordered me there.

Was there any other officer there? I did not see anyone.

Of course, you know all the officers? Oh, yes.

If there had been one there you would have known? Mr Murdoch was there before the boat was lowered.

Had you seen Murdoch there at No. 5, or merely heard his voice? Oh, no, I saw him.

At No. 5? At No. 5, after the boat was out and practically filled with passengers.

When you got to No. 5, in what state was No. 5? Well, the cover was still on.

How long do you think had elapsed from the time of striking the berg up to the time you got to No. 5? It is difficult, I know, to be certain about time. Was it half an hour or 45 minutes? Let me help you. You gave me one space of time – about 20 minutes? Yes, I remember that.

Will that help you to approximate what you think was the time between the striking of the iceberg and your getting to boat No. 5? Was it an hour, do you think? No, I should think it would be about 12.20.

You say the cover was still on. Was the cover being stripped at the time you got there? It was being uncovered then – yes.

Did you see Mr Ismay close to this boat? I did.

Was he taking any part, saying anything, or doing anything? He remarked to me as we were uncovering the boat, 'There is no time to lose.' Of course, I did not know who he was then, and therefore did not take any notice.

You have since learned that that gentleman was Mr Ismay, have you? Yes.

How many men had you helping at this boat? I think four.

Were they sailor men, or could you tell in the darkness of the night? Well, I knew that two were.

And was the boat uncovered and swung out? Yes.

What was done with it? Was it then lowered to the level of the boat deck? It was lowered level.

And after you had got out to the level of the boat deck, what did you do with regard to passengers? Mr Ismay remarked to me to get it filled with women and children, to which I replied, 'I will await the commander's orders.' I then went to the bridge, and I saw Captain Smith, and I told him what Mr Ismay had said. He said, 'Carry on.'

What does that mean? Go ahead.

At this time, did you realise that this gentleman was Mr Ismay, or did you still think he was one of the passengers? Oh, I knew then that it was Mr Ismay – yes, judging by the descriptions I had had given me of him.

The captain told you to 'carry on'. Did you then return to the boat deck? I was already there; I returned to No. 5.

Yes, you were on it. You returned to your boat No. 5? Yes.

When you got back, were any people being put into it? None at all.

What happened then? I simply stood in the boat and said, 'Come along, ladies,' and helped them in – Mr Ismay helped to get them there.

How many ladies did you get in? I do not know; between 30 and 40, I should imagine.

Were there any children? Yes, we had two.

Could you tell whether these women were first, second or third class passengers that were getting into the boat? Most, I should say, would be first class.

In addition to those women that you got into the boat, did you take any male passengers in? Yes, I should say about half a dozen or more.

Why did you let the male passengers in? Simply because there were no more women around – at least, there were two there, but they would not come.

Did they give you any reason for refusing to come? No.

You say there were no other women around? Could you see whether there were other women in other parts of the boat deck? Did you notice at that time? There were none in sight at that time – at least, not on the starboard deck.

In view of the number that you had got into the boat at this time, did you think that that was as many as this boat would safely carry before she was lowered to the water? No, I did not decide how many she should take.

Who decided that? Mr Murdoch; he came along just then.

What did he say? Well, I jumped out of the boat then, ready to lower away, and he said, 'You go in charge of this boat, and also look after the others, and stand by to come along the after gangway when hailed.'

Did you go in charge of this boat? I did.

There were 30 to 40 women you have told us, two children, about half a dozen male passengers, yourself, and how many of the crew? Four.

Did the four include yourself? No, my Lord.

Did you say something about Mr Murdoch saying he would hail you when he wanted you alongside the gangway? Yes. He said, 'Keep handy to come to the after gangway.' Therefore, I understood he would hail us.

You understood it? Yes.

Was the boat properly lowered away? It was.

And you got put down to the water's edge? Yes.

On reaching the water what was done with that boat? We pulled away about 100 yards [*c.* 91 metres] from the side of the ship.

And then? Lay on our oars.

Did you take her in the direction of the gangway, in case Mr Murdoch might hail you and order you back? Well, we dropped astern a little.

That would be somewhere in the direction towards the gangway? Yes.

That is right aft? Yes, he said the after gangway.

Before you left the ship had you heard any order given about lowering the gangway or opening the gangway door? No, that was the first I knew of it.

After you were in the boat and had rowed out this 100 yards [*c.* 91 metres] somewhat astern did you notice whether the gangway door was open or not? I do not think it was.

You probably were looking in that direction? Well, I was watching the ship the whole time.

And you do not think it was opened? I do not.

Two on D deck amidships – one on E deck forward and aft; that would make four on the one side and four on the other. If I might go back for one moment – I do not know whether it is important or not, but it might become important – did Mr Murdoch, in addition to telling you to keep handy to come back to the gangway, say anything more to you? No; he only shook hands and said, 'Goodbye, good luck.' That was all.

When he said 'Goodbye' to you in that way, did you think the situation was serious; did you think the ship was doomed then? I did not, but I thought he must have thought so.

Again, with regard to the time, how long do you think it was between the time of striking the berg and your boat reaching the water? You have given me two estimates of time, 20 minutes, and 12.20. Could you help me on this matter? Well, I should think it would be about 12.30 when No. 5 boat reached the water.

I do not know whether this will help you to see whether that is right. Was your boat in the water about an hour before the *Titanic* went down? I think it was longer than that.

Much longer or a little longer? It is hard to say.

Now, I have got you in the boat somewhere about 100 yards [*c.* 91 metres] from the ship, you watching the ship. Whilst you were watching the ship, did you then begin to think she was in a condition in which it was probable she might be lost? No, I did not give up hope until I saw the last line of lights on the forecastle head disappear.

When you reached the water and were in the boat, did you see then that her head was getting deeper and deeper in the water? Oh, yes, I watched the different lines of lights disappear.

Did you see any other boat on the water anywhere near you after your boat had reached the water? *Witness answers:* Are you alluding to one of our boats?

Yes, I mean one of the *Titanic* boats? Yes, No. 7 was quite close to me.

Was No. 7, as far as you know, in the water before yours or after? No. 7 was before; it was the first boat launched on the starboard side.

No. 7? No. 7.

And the second boat was? No. 5, and No. 3 next.

How do you know No. 3 came next? Did you see it? I saw it coming down; I saw it being lowered.

Did you notice any other boats on that side being lowered? I did not.

You speak of 7, 5, and 3? 7, 5 and 3, yes.

In that order? [The Solicitor-General points out that Jewell refers to this saying that No. 7 was the first boat on the starboard side. Jewell says he was in the boat, and it was the first to go on the starboard side.] *Witness answers:* That is right.

Tell me with regard to the equipment of the boat you were in, do you know whether it had a lamp or not? Mine had not.

Did you look for it? I did.

And would you, as an officer, know what was the right place to look for the lamp? Exactly.

Was there any compass in your boat? No.

Did you look for it? Well, I did not at the time, because it would be absolutely useless to me.

But how do you know there was no compass? You say you did not look at the time. Did you look at some later time? Yes, after the boats were on the *Carpathia*.

Was there any water in your boat? Yes.

In what? Breakers? In two breakers.

Two breakers? Yes.

Were there any biscuits? Yes.

In what? A tank in the stern of the boat.

Whilst you were in the boat and before the ship sank, did you see any light or lights which you took to be the light or lights of another steamer? I saw a white light which I took to be the stern light of a sailing ship.

How far away did you judge it to be? I thought it was about five miles.

That would be a good distance to see a stern light, would it not? Yes, it may have been less.

Was it a good night for seeing a light; for seeing a good stern light? An excellent night.

They would be visible at a long distance? Yes.

Whilst you were in the boat did you notice the *Titanic* sending up rockets? Yes, she did.

We have heard this in detail. Was there good discipline and order maintained in your boat? Well, that is not for me to say; it is for other people to say that.

No, but you are asked your opinion? As regards the passengers, yes, and the crew.

I am not suggesting you did not behave well; I am only asking the question for the information of the court. It is a general question asked with regard to all the boats. I am not suggesting for one moment that there was anything wrong. You behaved well, I have no doubt. *Witness answers*: I do not know about myself; it is not for me to say that.

You say the passengers and the crew behaved well? They did.

Well, that exhausts it. Now you saw the vessel go down? Yes.

What did she do when she went down; you were an officer, perhaps you can tell us. Inquiries have been made of others. How did she sink? She sank by the head, we know that? Yes.

Did her after part ever right itself? I should not think so; I did not see it.

Before she finally disappeared? No.

Could you have seen it if it had happened? I think so; I was only barely 100 yards [*c.* 91 metres] away.

Were you keeping your eyes upon her? I was.

You know this is suggested – supposing that is the head of the ship and going down in this way with the after part coming up in that way; a number of witnesses have said that before she finally foundered, plunged into the sea, the after part righted itself like that and then she went down. The question is whether you think that is true that she broke in two in that way bringing her after part level with the water again and then went down in that way. Did she crack in the middle? *Witness answers:* I do not think so. If the after part had broken off it would have remained afloat.

Not broken off, but cracked in that way? No.

At all events, the point is this: did you see the after end of the ship – you saw it up in the air – right itself and come flush with the water again? It did not.

And you say you looked, and if it had happened you would have seen it? Certainly.

While you were in the water, before the *Titanic* sank, did you hear any hail either from Mr Murdoch or the captain or from anybody else to come back near the gangway? No.

Did you hear anybody on the *Titanic* using a megaphone? I did not.

Did you transfer any of your passengers to any other boat? Yes, I transferred four, I think it was.

Into what boat? I am not quite certain of the number, but I think it was No. 7.

Why did you transfer those passengers? Because they had a lesser number of passengers in that boat than I had.

As the *Titanic* sank and immediately after did you hear any screams? *Witness answers:* Immediately after she sank?

Yes? Yes.

Were you able to go in the direction of the screams and render any assistance? I did not go.

But do you think you could have gone? I am not suggesting anything; I only want to get the facts from you. Do you think it would have been safe or reasonable to go? I do not.

What is your reason? Well, there was such a mass of people in the water we should have been swamped.

In your view you had a sufficient number of people on your boat. Is that so? No, but I had too many in the boat to go back to the wreck.

And I think you remained on, the men more or less lying on their oars till daylight, and then you were picked up by the *Carpathia*? Yes; we lay at rest the remainder of the night.

Whereabouts were you when the *Titanic* sank? About 200 yards [*c.* 182 metres] away.

On what side? On the starboard quarter.

Would that be about abreast of the mainmast? About that, my Lord.

Do you consider that the system of launching boats from davits so high above the water, as the davits necessarily must have been on a vessel of the size of the *Titanic*, is a safe operation? Apparently so; it was that night.

But supposing the weather conditions had not been so favourable, would your answer be that it would not be? I do not know; I would not make any suggestion.

You will not make any suggestions? No, I am not making any suggestions.

Do you not think the system of lowering the boats to one of the lower decks and filling them either through the gangway doors or from the third deck would be less hazardous? It is too long a job.

And less calculated to inspire passengers with terror? Oh, no, it is too long a job to lower them from there.

To lower the boats empty and fill them from one of the lower decks? Yes, provided they had to get on a ladder it is too long.

Apart from the rope ladders, were there companion ladders for this boat, the *Titanic*? Yes, one.

Would it not have been possible to have lowered the boats half filled and then filled them down the companion ladders? No, not if there had been the slightest bit of swell.

But under the conditions that actually took place it would have been possible? Yes, but we did not know it was so calm until we got into the water.

I suppose you knew that there was not a heavy swell on, did you not? We did not; you could not tell from that ship.

Can you tell us whether the *Titanic's* head was going round at all under her helm when you left the ship, or after the collision? She remained stationary from the time I left the ship till she disappeared.

No altering her heading? No.

At the time your boat was lowered was she very much down by the head? It was noticeable.

Would it make very much difference in the amount of drop that you had to the water? Slightly, yes.

Not very much? No.

And you lowered your boat without any difficulty? Oh, yes.

Can you, therefore, say whether at the time the ship had much of a list on? None whatever.

None at all when you were launched? No.

Did you watch the list change after you were in the water? She had no list when I left the ship.

But afterwards, before she went down, did the list increase? I could not see that she had a list at all at any time.

Did you see a list to starboard, ever? I saw no list at all, my Lord.

Do you mean to say that before the ship went down you did not notice a list? No.

You only noticed her down by the head? That is all.

Did you hear anything in the nature of explosions before she went down? Yes, I heard four reports.

What do you estimate they were? Boilers leaving the bedplates and crashing through the bulkheads.

When the ship actually went down, did you experience any suction in your boat? Oh, none at all.

Although you had no lamp in your boat, did you see other of the ship's boats in the water with lamps in them? Several.

Was the boat into which you transferred some of your passengers one that had a lamp in it? I cannot recollect.

Did you tie up your boat eventually to that boat in order to keep together during the night? Yes, we did for some time.

And did you arrive at the *Carpathia* in that way? No.

You cast loose again before that? Yes, they cast off some time before the *Carpathia* came in sight.

Have you been in any other White Star boat? Yes, I have been in five of them.

Were you on the *Olympic*? No.

Have you been in a White Star ship with these iron gangway doors? I really forget – the *Oceanic* may have them. I forget.

Yes, she has them. Is it not part of the duty of an officer to take charge of these gangway doors on the arrival of a ship in port? Yes, we go and attend to them.

Have you ever carried out that duty? Yes, I have been there.

Can you give us any idea of the size and weight of the forward iron doors on the *Titanic*? No, I cannot give you any size or weight. Probably the builders can.

Will you tell us how many men it would take to open one of those doors? Four.

Four men? Yes.

And are not they very awkward to close again once they are opened – once when they are pushed back against the ship's side? No.

What is the method of closing them again? Simply attach a rope to them and pull and they come up themselves.

I suggest to you if you put a rope against an iron door flush against the ship's side, it would be very awkward to pull round unless you had some leverage to fetch it away from the ship's side. Is not that the fact? Of course if the thing had not been opened for years, yes.

Did you hear Mr Lightoller's evidence [see Lightoller chapter 60 later in this book] yesterday? Yes. I heard part of it.

He states he sent the boatswain down to open these doors. Now I am suggesting if those doors were opened and he found out he had made a mistake, he would have a hard job to get them closed again; is not that a fact? No, they could be closed easily enough.

Did you ever see them opened? Yes, the carpenter usually does that with about two hands.

And he could close them with two hands? Yes.

How many people do you say you took away in your boat? Between 40 and 50.

How many would the boat hold? I do not know – 60, I think, according to the Board of Trade Regulations, or something like that.

Were there people on the deck when you left the ship? Oh, yes, there were a few there.

Why did not you take in 60 then? Simply because the people did not want to go – they thought they were safer on the ship.

We have heard it stated by Mr Lightoller that he lowered the boats because he thought there were enough people in them to lower with safety. Will you tell us what you consider is the weakest part of the tackle for lowering a boat? Is it the block or the falls or the shackles or what? We want to find out, because Mr Lightoller said he was afraid of something giving way. *Witness answers:* I do not know.

Is that your idea, that the boat might buckle or the shackles might give way? I do not know whether they would or not.

Do you think it would be safe to lower 60 people in one of those boats from a height of 70 feet [*c.* 21 metres]? I do not know what I might do if I was placed in that position.

I say now, supposing you had to go through the operation again, do you think it would be safe to put 70 people in or 68 people? I would do now, yes, because I have found out since you could lower 80 in them.

When you were on the *Oceanic* did you ever see bulkhead door drill take place? I did not witness it, no.

Is it not the duty of the officer, either the chief officer or first officer, to go round at 11 o'clock each day and see the bulkhead doors closed? The commander does, yes.

Was it done on the *Titanic*? That I cannot say.

You do not know. Do you know where the hand bulkhead doors are situated there? Yes, I know where some of them are.

Did you see any closed that night? I did not go below that night.

You said you took two men off in the boat. Do you know who they were? *Witness answers:* I took two men?

Six men passengers you took. Who was in the boat with you? Do you know any of the crew that were in the boat with you? Yes, a steward by the name of Guy was one.

Were the rest seamen or firemen? One seaman, one fireman and two stewards.

6

Catherine Crosby, First Class Passenger

Catherine and her grown-up daughter Harriete were originally loaded into lifeboat 5. When lifeboats 5 and 7 were tied together in the night, the couple were transferred over to lifeboat 7 to even up the numbers.

US Senate Inquiry Extract from Affidavit Deponent further says that, on the 10th day of April, 1912, at Southampton, England, she embarked as a passenger on the steamer *Titanic* for the port of New York; that her husband, Edward G. Crosby, and her daughter, Harriete H. Crosby, were with her on said steamer; that she and her husband occupied stateroom No. 22 and her daughter occupied stateroom No. 26, they being first class passengers on said steamer. Deponent noticed nothing unusual or out of the ordinary, either in the equipment of the vessel or in the handling of her, and nothing unusual occurred until Sunday, the 14th day of April, 1912, when deponent noticed that the seamen on board the *Titanic* were taking the temperature of the water on the afternoon of that day, and it was stated by those engaged in doing this that the temperature of the water was colder and indicated that the boat was in the vicinity of icefields; this was about the middle of the afternoon, as I recollect it.

At that time my husband and I were walking up and down the promenade deck, which, as I recollect it, was the deck below the hurricane deck, and it was while we were walking up and down this deck that I first noticed these seamen taking the temperature of the water. My husband was a sailor all his lifetime, and he told me all about it, and it was from that that I knew what they were doing. I could see what they were doing. My husband retired at about nine o'clock that evening, and I retired about 10.30. Elmer Taylor, one of the passengers who went over with us on the steamer, told me afterwards, when we were on the *Carpathia*, that at the time I retired that night he noticed the boat was going full speed. I had not retired long when I was suddenly awakened by the thumping of the boat. The engines stopped suddenly. This was about 11.30. Captain Crosby got up, dressed, and went out, and came back again and said to me, 'You will lie there and drown,' and went out again. He said to my daughter, 'The boat is badly damaged; but I think the watertight compartments will hold her up.' I then got up and dressed, and my daughter dressed, and followed my husband on deck, and she got up on deck, and the officer told her to go back and get on her life preserver and come back on deck as soon as possible. She reported that to me, and we both went out on deck where the officer told us to come. I think it was the first or second boat that we got into. I do not recollect other boats being lowered at that time. I did not see them. This was on the left-hand side where the officer told us to come, and it was the deck above the one on which our staterooms were located; our staterooms were located on the B deck, and we went to the A deck where the officer and lifeboat were. We got into the lifeboat that was hanging over the rail alongside the deck; we got in and men and women, with their families, got in the boat with us; there was no discrimination between men and women. About 36 persons got in the boat with us. There were only two officers in the boat, and the rest were all first class passengers. My husband did not come back again after he left me, and I don't know what became of him, except that his body was found and brought to Milwaukee and buried.

There were absolutely no lights in the lifeboats, and they did not even know whether the plug was in the bottom of the boat to prevent the boat from sinking; there were no lanterns, no provisions, no lights, nothing at all in these boats but the oars. One of the officers asked one of the passengers for a watch with which to light up the bottom of the boat to see if the plug was in place; the officers rowed the boat a short distance from the *Titanic*, and I was unable to see the lowering of any other boats, and we must have rowed quite a distance, but could see the steamer very plainly; saw them firing rockets, and heard a gun fired as distress signals to indicate that the steamer was in danger; we continued a safe distance away from the steamer, probably a quarter of a mile at least, and finally saw the steamer go down very distinctly; we did not see nor hear about any trouble on the steamer that is reported to have taken place afterwards; we got away first, and got away a safe distance, so that we could not see nor hear what took place, until the steamer went down, which was about 2.20 a.m. on the morning of the 15th; I heard the terrible cries of the people that were on board when the boat went down, and heard repeated explosions, as though the boilers had exploded, and we then knew that the steamer had gone down, as her lights were out, and the cries of the people and the explosions were terrible; our boat drifted around in that vicinity until about daybreak, when the *Carpathia* was sighted and we were taken on board; we had to row quite a long time and quite a distance before we were taken on board the *Carpathia*; I was suffering from the cold while I was drifting around, and one of the officers put a sail around me and over my head to keep me warm, and I was hindered from seeing any of the other lifeboats drifting in the vicinity or observing anything that took place while we were drifting around until the *Carpathia* took us on board: we received very good treatment on the *Carpathia*, and finally arrived to New York; it was reported on the *Carpathia* by passengers, whose names I do not recollect, that the lookout who was on duty at the time the *Titanic* struck the iceberg had said, 'I know they will blame me for it, because I was on duty, but it was not my fault; I had warned the officers three or four times before striking the iceberg that we were in the vicinity of icebergs, but the officer on the bridge paid no attention to my signals.' I cannot give the name of any passenger who made that statement, but it was common talk on the *Carpathia* that that is what the lookout said.

I don't know anything about workmen being on the boat, and that the boat was not finished, and that the watertight compartments refused to work: I have read it in the papers, but I personally know nothing about it; I also heard that there were no glasses on board the vessel; they were loaned from a vessel to be used on the voyage from Liverpool to Southampton and then returned to the vessel, and the *Titanic* proceeded without any glasses; Mr Elmer Taylor informed me after we got on the *Carpathia* that a dinner was in progress at the time the boat struck; this banquet was given for the captain, and the wine flowed freely. Personally I know nothing or did not recollect anything of importance that occurred any more than I have stated.

7

Norman Chambers, First Class Passenger

Travelling with his wife Bertha, Chambers was an engineer from New York. Chambers' testimony highlights a key problem with the loading of the early lifeboats; passengers simply didn't take the threat seriously. Chambers thought the *Titanic*'s bulkheads made her unsinkable and he consequently felt 'no sense of danger' even when he saw the mail room underwater. He draws our attention to the 'terrific loud noise' on deck caused by steam escaping from the funnels. This impediment to communication must be considered when reflecting on the actions of those on board that fateful night. Not only were officers dealing with an unfamiliar ship and crew, but the noise levels on the boat deck must have made communication very difficult.

US Senate Inquiry Extract from Affidavit Our stateroom was E-8, on the starboard side; that is the lowest berth deck, and as far as I know, we were as far forward as any of the first cabin passengers on that deck.

At the time of the collision I was in bed, and I noticed no very great shock, the loudest noise by far being that of jangling chains whipping along the side of the ship. This passed so quickly that I assumed something had gone wrong with the engines on the starboard side.

At the request of my wife I prepared to investigate what had happened, leaving her dressing. I threw on sufficient clothes, including my overcoat. I went up, in a leisurely manner, as far as the A deck on the starboard side. There I noted only an unusual coldness of the air. Looking over the side I was unable to see anything in any direction.

I returned below, where I was joined by my wife, and we came up again to investigate, still finding nothing. However, there was then a noticeable list to starboard, with probably a few degrees of pitch; and as the ship had a list to port nearly all afternoon, I decided to remain up, in spite of a feeling of perfect safety.

Upon returning to the stateroom for the purpose of completing dressing, I looked at the starboard end of our passage, where there was the companion leading to the quarters of the mail clerks and farther on to the baggage room and, I believe, the mail-sorting room; at the top of these stairs I found a couple of mail clerks wet to their knees, who had just come up from below, bringing their registered mail bags. As the door in the bulkhead in the next deck was open, I was able to look directly into the trunk room, which was then filled with water, and was within 18 inches [*c.* 46 cm] or 2 feet [*c.* 60 cm] of the deck above.

We were standing there joking about our baggage being completely soaked and about the correspondence which was seen floating about on the top of the water. I personally felt no sense of danger, as this water was forward of the bulkhead.

While we were standing there three of the ship's officers – I did not notice their rank or department – descended the first companion and looked into the baggage room, coming back up immediately, saying that we were not making any more water. This was not an announcement, but merely a remark passed from one to the other. Then my wife and myself returned in the direction of our stateroom, a matter of a few yards away only, and as we were going down our own alleyway to the stateroom door our steward came by and told us that we could go back to bed again; that there was no danger. In this I agreed with him, personally.

However, I finished dressing, my wife being already fully and warmly clothed, and she, in the meanwhile having gone out into the passage to note any later developments, came rushing back to me, saying that she had seen another passenger who informed her that the call had been given out for lifebelts and on the boat deck. I went out, myself, and found my room steward passing down the alleyway and had the order verified.

As I was at the time fully dressed and wore my heavy overcoat, in the pockets of which I had already placed certain necessities, we started up. My wife had presence of mind enough to take a lifebelt. I opened my steamer trunk and took out a small pocket compass, and, sending my wife on ahead, opened my bag and removed my automatic pistol.

We then proceeded immediately upward, my wife being rather alarmed, as she had also been at the time of the collision. But for her I should have remained in bed, reading.

We kept on upward, passing, at the various landings, people who did not appear to be particularly frightened, until we arrived on the A deck, going out on the port side, where I shortly found the deck steward; joked with him about opening his little office room, and obtained our two steamer rugs.

We then proceeded up the port outside companion on to the boat deck. There did not at any time seem to be any particular group of passengers around the boats on the port side, although there were seamen there unlimbering the gear.

Owing to the list being to the starboard, I assumed that the boats which were lowered on the starboard side would be sure to clear the ship, while those on the port side might have some difficulty. This was only an assumption, as I have not heard of any such difficulty since.

We then proceeded over the raised deck caused by the unusual height of the ceiling in the lounge, and came down again on to the boat deck proper on the starboard side. Then I gave my wife a drink from my flask, filled my pipe, put on my lifebelt at her urgent request, she having hers already on, and we stood at the rail for a few moments.

I would like to call particular attention to the fact that from the moment the engines were stopped steam was of course blown out from the boilers. This, coming through one single steam pipe on the starboard side of the forward funnel, made a terrific loud noise; so loud, indeed, that persons on the boat deck could only communicate by getting as close as possible and speaking loudly. As a matter of fact, I shouted in my wife's ear.

All this time I considered that the lifeboats were merely a precaution and, upon my wife's suggestion, we moved up forward of the entry from the deck house.

There were still quite a number of passengers coming out, the stewards standing there directing them to the boats aft.

Instead of going aft, we stepped behind the projection of this entry, which was of the vestibule type, and waited until people had apparently ceased coming and the steward was no longer there. Then we started forward again, and, as nearly as I can remember, stopped at the last one of the forward starboard group of lifeboats. This was already swung out level with the deck, and to my eyes, appeared sufficiently loaded.

However, my wife said that she was going in that boat, and proceeded to jump in, calling me to come. As I knew she would get out again had I not come, I finally jumped into the boat, although I did not consider it, from the looks of things, safe to put very many more people in that boat.

As I remember it, there were two more men, both called by their wives, who jumped in after I did. One of them – a German, I believe – told me, as I recollect it, later on the *Carpathia* that he had looked around and had seen no one else and no one to ask whether he should go in or not, and he jumped in.

... By the time we were settled and I began to take note of the things on the ship I noticed a tall young officer clad in a long overcoat, which may help identify him, giving orders to another officer to go into our boat and take charge of the boats on our side. As a parting injunction he gave our officer (whom I later found to be a Mr Pitman) instructions to hold on to his painter and pull up alongside the gangway after the boat had reached the water.

Preliminary to this, and before lowering, all of which was done with absolute calm, I heard someone in authority say, 'That is enough before lowering. We can get more in after she is in the water.'

I remember these conversations particularly, as at the time I was wondering at the source of the order, being morally certain, myself, that no doors in the ship's side had been opened.

We were then lowered away in a manner which I would consider very satisfactory, taking into account the apparent absolute lack of training of the rank and file of the crew.

Shortly before we reached the water our officer called and finally blew his whistle for them to stop lowering, that he might find out if the plug was in or not. The inquiry was called in a loud tone of voice, to which one of the crew in our boat replied that it was, that he himself had put it in. Meanwhile a voice from above called down, as nearly as I can recollect it, 'It is your own blooming business to see that the plug is in, anyhow.'

When we reached the water, we then had difficulty in casting off the falls. The little quartermaster had to crawl between our legs to the amidship portion of the boat in order to reach what was apparently called the 'trigger', which is, I believe, a mechanism used to release both falls simultaneously.

We then put out our oars and crawled away slowly from the ship until we lay some three or four hundred yards off [*c.* 274–365 metres].

In connection with my statement that a large percentage of the steward part of the crew were new, I may say that my own room steward complained to me on the second day out that he did not know where anything was on the ship, and that no one would tell him.

LIFEBOAT 3
Starboard Side, Launched 12.55 a.m.

The third in the series of lifeboats overseen by First Officer Murdoch and launched on the starboard side, this lifeboat was again filled with first class passengers and some crew. Fifth Officer Lowe assisted Murdoch in loading this boat. In Lowe's US inquiry testimony he stated that the filling of lifeboats 5 and 3 was 'quiet and orderly', and when quizzed about the order that people were put into boats he replied, 'There was no such thing as selecting. It was simply the first woman, whether first class, second class, third class, or sixty-seventh class. It was all the same; women and children were first.' Male crew: 15; male passengers: 10; women and children: 25; total for lifeboat: 50 (British Board of Inquiry).

By this time distress rockets were being fired every few minutes by Fourth Officer Boxhall. Approximately eight rockets were fired with stocks exhausted by about 1.45 a.m.

8
Elizabeth Shutes, First Class Passenger

Elizabeth was a governess travelling with her charge, Margaret Graham, and Margaret's mother, Edith. An account from Edith is also included in this book. Shutes recollections were first published in Gracie's book *The Truth About the Titanic* and are elegiac in style.

Such a biting cold air poured into my stateroom that I could not sleep, and the air had so strange an odour, as if it came from a clammy cave. I had noticed that same odour in the ice cave on the Eiger glacier. It all came back to me so vividly that I could not sleep, but lay in my berth until the cabin grew so very cold that I got up and turned on my electric stove. It threw a cheerful red glow around, and the room was soon comfortable; but I lay waiting. I have always loved both day and night on board ship, and am never fearful of anything, but now I was nervous about the icy air.

Suddenly a queer quivering ran under me, apparently the whole length of the ship. Startled by the very strangeness of the shivering motion, I sprang to the floor. With too perfect a trust in that mighty vessel I again lay down. Someone knocked at my door, and the voice of a friend said, 'Come quickly to my cabin; an iceberg has just passed our window; I know we have just struck one.'

No confusion, no noise of any kind, one could believe no danger imminent. Our stewardess came and said she could learn nothing. Looking out into the companionway, I saw heads appearing asking questions from half-closed doors. All sepulchrally still, no excitement. I sat down again. My friend was by this time dressed; still her daughter and I talked on, Margaret pretending to eat a sandwich. Her hand shook so that the bread kept parting company from the chicken. Then I saw she was frightened, and for the first time I was too, but why get dressed, as no one had given the slightest hint of any possible danger? An officer's cap passed the door. I asked, 'Is there an accident or danger of any kind?' 'None, so far as I know,' was his courteous answer, spoken quietly and most kindly. This same officer then entered a cabin a little distance down the companionway and, by this time distrustful of everything, I listened intently, and distinctly heard, 'We can keep the water out for a while.' Then, and not until then, did I realise the horror of an accident at sea. Now it was too late to dress; no time for a waist, but a coat and skirt were soon on; slippers were quicker than shoes; the stewardess put on our life preservers, and we were just ready when Mr Roebling came to tell us he would take us to our friend's mother, who was waiting above.

We passed by the palm room, where two short hours before we had listened to a beautiful concert, just as one might sit in one's own home. With never a realising sense of being on the ocean, why should not one forget? No motion, no noise of machinery, nothing suggestive of a ship. Happy, laughing men and women constantly passing up and down those broad, strong staircases, and the music went on and the ship went on – nearer and nearer to its end. So short a life, so horrible a death for that great, great ship. What is a more stupendous work than a ship! The almost human pieces of machinery, yet a helpless child, powerless in its struggle with an almighty sea, and the great boat sank, fragile as a rowboat.

How different are these staircases now! No laughing throng, but on either side stand quietly, bravely, the stewards, all equipped with the white, ghostly life preservers. Always the thing one tries not to see even crossing a ferry. Now only pale faces, each form strapped about with those white bars. So gruesome a scene. We passed on. The awful goodbyes. The quiet look of hope in the brave men's eyes as the wives were put into the lifeboats. Nothing escaped one at this fearful moment. We left from the Sun Deck, 75 feet [*c.* 23 metres] above the water. Mr Case and Mr Roebling, brave American men, saw us to the lifeboat, made no effort to save themselves, but stepped back on deck. Later they went to an honoured grave.

Our lifeboat, with 36 in it, began lowering to the sea. This was done amid the greatest confusion. Rough seamen all giving different orders. No officer aboard. As only one side of the ropes worked, the lifeboat at one time was in such a position that it seemed we must capsize in mid-air. At last the ropes worked together, and we drew nearer and nearer the black, oily water. The first touch of our lifeboat on that black sea came to me as a last goodbye to life, and so we put off – a tiny boat on a great sea rowed away from what had been a safe home for five days. The first wish on the part of all was to stay near the *Titanic*. We all felt so much safer near the ship. Surely such a vessel could not sink. I thought the danger must be exaggerated, and we could all be taken aboard again. But surely the outline of that great, good ship was growing less. The bow of the boat was getting black. Light after light was disappearing, and now those rough seamen put to their oars and we were told to hunt under seats, any place, anywhere, for a lantern, a light of any kind. Every place was empty. There was no water – no stimulant – of any kind. Not a biscuit – nothing to keep us alive had we drifted long. Had no good *Carpathia*, with its splendid Captain Rostron, its orderly crew, come to our rescue we must have all perished. Our men knew nothing about the position of the stars, hardly how to pull together. Two oars were soon overboard. The men's hands were too cold to hold on. We stopped while they beat their hands and arms, then started on again. A sea, calm as a pond, kept our boat steady, and now that mammoth ship is fast, fast disappearing. Only one tiny light is left – a powerless little spark, a lantern fastened to the mast. Fascinated, I watched that black outline until the end. Then across the water swept that awful wail, the cry of those drowning people. In my ears I heard, 'She's gone, lads; row like hell or we'll get the devil of a swell.' And the horror, the helpless horror, the worst of all – need it have been?

Today the question is being asked, 'Would the *Titanic* disaster be so discussed had it not been for the great wealth gathered there?' It surely would be, for at a time like this wealth counts for nothing, but man's philanthropy, man's brains, man's heroism, count forever. So many men that stood for the making of a great nation, morally and politically, were swept away by the sinking of that big ship. That is why, day after day, the world goes on asking the why of it all. Had a kind Providence a guiding hand in this? Did our nation need so mighty a stroke to prove that man had grown too self-reliant, too sure of his own power over God's sea? God's part was the saving of the few souls on that calmest of oceans on that fearful night. Man's part was the pushing of the good ship, pushing against all reason, to save what? A few hours and lose a thousand souls – to have the largest of ships arrive in port even a few hours sooner than anticipated. Risk all, but push, push on, on. The icebergs could be avoided. Surely man's experience ought to have lent aid, but just so surely it did not.

In years past a tendency to live more simply away from pomp and display led to the founding of our American nation. Now what are we demanding today? Those same needless luxuries. If they were not demanded they would not be supplied. Gymnasiums, swimming pools, tea rooms had better give way to make space for the necessary number of lifeboats; lifeboats for the crew, also, who help pilot the good ship across the sea.

Sitting by me in the lifeboat were a mother and daughter (Mrs Hays and Mrs Davidson). The mother had left a husband on the *Titanic*, and the daughter a father and husband, and while we were near the other boats those two stricken women would call out a name and ask, 'Are you there?' 'No,' would come back the awful answer, but these brave women never lost courage, forgot their own sorrow, telling me to sit close to them to keep warm. Now I began to wish for the warm velvet suit I left hanging in my cabin. I had thought of it for a minute, and then had quickly thrown on a lighter-weight skirt. I knew the heavier one would make the life preserver less useful. Had I only known how calm the ocean was that night, I would have felt that death was not so sure, and would have dressed for life rather than for the end. The life preservers helped to keep us warm, but the night was bitter cold, and it grew colder and colder, and just before dawn, the coldest, darkest hour of all, no help seemed possible. As we put off from the *Titanic* never was a sky more brilliant, never have I seen so many falling stars. All tended to make those distress rockets that were sent up from the sinking ship look so small, so dull and futile. The brilliancy of the sky only intensified the blackness of the water, our utter loneliness on the sea. The other boats had drifted away from us; we must wait now for dawn and what the day was to bring us we dare not even hope. To see if I could not make the night seem shorter, I tried to imagine myself again in Japan. We had made two strange night departures there, and I was unafraid, and this Atlantic now was calmer than the inland sea had been at that time. This helped a while, but my hands were freezing cold, and I had to give up pretending and think of the dawn that must soon come.

Two rough-looking men had jumped into our boat as we were about to lower, and they kept striking matches, lighting cigars, until I feared we would have no matches left and might need them, so I asked them not to use any more, but they kept on. I do not know what they looked like. It was too dark to really distinguish features clearly, and when the dawn brought the light it brought something so wonderful with it no one looked at anything else or anyone else. Someone asked, 'What time is it?' Matches were still left; one was struck. Four o'clock! Where had the hours of the night gone? Yes, dawn would soon be here; and it came, so surely, so strong with cheer. The stars slowly disappeared, and in their place came the faint pink glow of another day. Then I heard, 'A light, a ship.' I could not, would not, look while there was a bit of doubt, but kept my eyes away. All night long I had heard, 'A light!' Each time it proved to be one of our other lifeboats, someone lighting a piece of paper, anything they could find to burn, and now I could not believe. Someone found a newspaper; it was lighted and held up. Then I looked and saw a ship. A ship bright with lights; strong and steady she waited, and we were to be saved. A straw hat was offered (Mrs Davidson's); it would burn longer. That same ship that had come to save us might run us down. But no; she is still. The two, the ship and the dawn, came together, a living painting. White was the vessel, but whiter still were those horribly beautiful icebergs, and as we drew nearer and nearer that good ship, we drew nearer to those mountains of ice. As far as the eye could reach they rose. Each one more fantastically chiselled than its neighbour. The floe glistened like an ever-ending meadow covered with new-fallen snow. Those same white mountains, marvellous in their purity, had made of the just-ended night one of the blackest the sea has ever known. And near them stood the ship which had come in such quick response to the *Titanic*'s call for help. The man who works over hours is always the worthwhile kind, and the Marconi operator awaiting a belated message had heard the poor ship's call for help, and we few out of so many were saved.

From the *Carpathia* a rope forming a tiny swing was lowered into our lifeboat, and one by one we were drawn into safety. The lady pulled up just ahead of me was very large, and I felt myself being jerked fearfully, when I heard someone say:

'Careful, fellers; she's a lightweight.' I bumped and bumped against the side of the ship until I felt like a bag of meal. My hands were so cold I could hardly hold on to the rope, and I was fearful of letting go. Again I heard, 'Steady, fellers; not so fast!' I felt I should let go and bounce out of the ropes; I hardly think that would have been possible, but I felt so at the time. At last I found myself at an opening of some kind and there a kind doctor wrapped me in a warm rug and led me to the dining room, where warm stimulants were given us immediately and everything possible was done for us all. Lifeboats kept coming in, and heart-rending was the sight as widow after widow was brought aboard. Each hoped some lifeboat ahead of hers might have brought her husband safely to this waiting vessel. But always no.

I was still so cold that I had to get a towel and tie it around my waist. Then I went back to the dining room and found dear little Louis, the French baby, lying alone; his cold, bare feet had become unwrapped. I put a hot water bottle against this very beautiful boy. He smiled his thanks.

Knowing how much better I felt after taking the hot stimulant, I tried to get others to take something; but often they just shook their heads and said, 'Oh, I can't.'

Towards night we remembered we had nothing – no comb, brush, nothing of any kind – so we went to the barber shop. The barber always has everything, but now he had only a few toothbrushes left. I bought a cloth cap of doubtful style, and felt like a walking orphan asylum, but very glad to have anything to cover my head. There were also a few showy silk handkerchiefs left. On the corner of each was embroidered in scarlet 'From a friend'. These we bought and we were now fitted out for our three remaining days at sea.

Patiently through the dismal, foggy days we lived, waiting for land and possible news of the lost. For the brave American man, a heart full of gratitude, too deep for words, sends out a thanksgiving. That such men are born, live and die for others is a cause for deep gratitude. What country could have shown such men as belong to our American manhood? Thank God for them and for their noble death.

9

Edith & Margaret Graham, First Class Passengers

Edith Graham was an American travelling with her 19-year-old daughter Margaret and her governess Elizabeth Shutes. Neither Washington Roebling or Howard Case survived.

New York Times, 20 April 1912 My daughter and I had a stateroom on the port side near the stern, and we were awake, although in bed, when the iceberg was struck. It was a grinding, tearing sound. We didn't regard it as serious. I dressed lightly, but my daughter tried to go to sleep.

With us, in an adjoining stateroom, was my daughter's companion, Miss E. W. Shutes, a teacher. She was the only other member in our party and was later saved with us. She got up, too, but my daughter insisted that the danger was imaginary and told us to go to sleep.

Shortly after, there was a rap at the door. It was a passenger we had met shortly after the ship left Liverpool, Washington A. Roebling. He told us that it would be best to be prepared for an emergency. I looked out of my window and saw a big iceberg. We lost no time getting into the saloon. In one of the passages I met an officer of the ship.

'What is the matter?' I asked him.

'We've only burst two pipes,' he said. 'Everything is all right; don't worry.'

'But what makes the ship list so?' I asked.

'Oh, that's nothing,' he replied, and walked away.

On the deck we met Howard Case. We had been introduced to him. We had had many pleasant talks with Mr Case and I asked his advice, because I had already seen one boatload of passengers lowered and I wanted to know if it would be safer to stay on board. Mr Case advised us to get into a boat.

'And what are you going to do?' we asked him.

'Oh,' he replied, 'I'll take a chance and stay here.'

Just at that time they were filling up the third lifeboat on the port side. I thought at the time that it was the third boat which had been lowered, but I found out later that they had lowered other boats on the other side, where the people were more excited because they were sinking on that side.

Just then Mr Roebling came up, too. He told us to hurry and get into the boat. Mr Roebling and Mr Case bustled our party of three into that boat in less time than it takes to tell it. They were both working hard to help the women and children. The boat was fairly crowded when we three were pushed into it. A few men jumped in at the last moment, but Mr Roebling and Mr Case stood at the rail and made no attempt to get into the boat.

They shouted goodbye to us, and – what do you think Mr Case did then? He just calmly lighted a cigarette and waved us goodbye with his hand. Mr Roebling stood there, too – I can see him now. I am sure that he knew that the ship would go to the bottom. But both just stood there.

I counted our fellow passengers. We were 34, including two sailors, two ship's boys, and half a dozen or more other men. The men didn't say a word. The women quarrelled a little because some of them didn't have room to sit down. Then there was a lot of argument as to how far we should go out. Some seemed to think that we ought to stay very near, because, they said, the ship wouldn't sink anyway. Others were in favour of going away out.

The trouble was that there was no one in command, and the two sailors couldn't do much. The men were silent, and that is why the women did most of the talking. There were 16 oar locks in our boat, but we lost three oars right off because those who handled them didn't know anything about rowing. Then I took an oar myself. I don't think I helped very much. It was snappy cold and I was dressed very lightly. Everybody seemed rather dazed, but not so very excited. That came later.

We went out about three quarters of a mile, I think, following another boat which carried some green lanterns. That was the only thing we had to go by. Behind us the lights on the *Titanic* went out, and in an hour and a half the big ship went down. It was in that hour and a half that the passengers got their fright. We couldn't tell what was going on on the ship – but those shrieks and cries! I'll never forget them. And there were many shots, I don't know how many.

I saw many dead. That was frightful. I saw Mrs Harris on the *Carpathia*. She appeared dazed and didn't say anything. I saw Mrs Astor, too. She didn't appear ill when I saw her. Throughout the journey to New York I didn't see Mr Ismay. You see, he remained in his cabin.

10

Robert Daniel, First Class Passenger

This article was published in the *New York Times* a few days after the sinking and is reflective of the sensationalist, headline-grabbing style of many contemporary newspaper accounts. Much of this article is fantasy. There is no evidence that 'men and women fought, bit and scratched to be in line for the lifeboats'; indeed at this stage of the night it was still a struggle to persuade people to leave the 'unsinkable' ship. It is also clearly untrue that 'five minutes after the crash everybody seemed to have gone insane'. Whether these and numerous other fabrications are courtesy of Daniel himself or a sensation-hungry journalist is unclear, but the piece remains gripping nonetheless. There are no reports that lifeboat 3 picked up survivors from the water. Did he invent this to explain why he came to be in a lifeboat reserved for women and children?

A banker from Philadelphia, Robert Daniel was 27 at the time of the sinking. In 1914 Robert Daniel married another *Titanic* survivor, Mary Smith.

New York Times, 19 April 1912 'I had just left the music room and disrobed and was in my bunk, when there was a terrific crash. The boat quivered and the lights went out. In the darkness I rushed out on the deck almost naked.

'There seemed to be thousands fighting and shouting in the dark. Then they got the storage batteries going, and that gave us a little light.

'Captain Smith was the biggest hero I ever saw. He stood on the bridge and shouted himself heard. The crew obeyed his orders as well as could be expected.

'Five minutes after the crash everybody seemed to have gone insane. Men and women fought, bit and scratched to be in line for the lifeboats. Look at my black eye and cut chin. I got these in the fight.

'Then Captain Smith seemed to get some order, and the passengers were sent to the fore and aft of the boat.

Continuing, Mr Daniel said there was a frightful grinding noise throughout.

'I saw men praying as I struggled to get to the rail. Curses and prayers filled the air. Women, who had been in the music room, where a concert had been in progress, were still dressed in evening attire and wearing diamonds. Other women had just got to their bunks and were dressed in flimsy night attire. All rushed with one object – to get to the lifeboats.

'Captain Smith remained on the bridge, trying to make himself heard. He was still shouting when I last saw him.

'As the passengers got into the lifeboats – women were thrown in if they did not move fast enough – an officer jumped into command, the boats were swung from their davits, and down into the water.

'Hundreds, it seemed, did not wait for the lifeboats. They could see there was no chance for them and they jumped overboard.

'What happened to you?' Mr Daniel was asked.

'Oh, I can't tell you what happened. I hardly know myself,' he returned. 'I was naked. I grabbed something and uttered one prayer. Then I went over the side of the boat – over the side of the boat.

At this point Daniel was so overcome that he had to be led to a rail, where he rested for a few moments.

'Let me smoke a cigarette before I go on,' he said. 'After waiting for an interminable time with the collapsible boat in my hands I felt the *Titanic* sinking under my feet. I could feel her going under at the bows. The storage batteries furnishing the light again gave out, and there was darkness. I tried to wait, but suddenly found myself leaping from the rail, away up in the air, and I fell an eternity before I hit the water. When I came to I felt myself drawn into the suction, and when I felt a cake of ice near I clung to it. I was naked. For five hours I battled with icecakes, and when I saw other boats near I almost gave up.

Describing his trip in the *Carpathia* Daniel said, 'I did not see Bruce Ismay on board the *Carpathia*. If my understanding of Captain Smith is a correct one, I know Smith never would have permitted a man to enter one of those lifeboats.

'I recall that when I got aboard the *Carpathia* Mrs John Jacob Astor was assigned to a cabin, given her by one of the passengers in the *Carpathia*. I did not see Mrs Astor since Monday morning. But I know she was in the care of a ship's surgeon.

Mr Daniel thought the horrible grinding and knocking he heard in the last hours of the *Titanic*'s struggle to keep afloat was due to some part of the monster vessel's machinery having given out. He did not think the boat remained close enough to the iceberg to have been pounding against the ice.

Mr Daniel was asked what was the condition of the survivors when picked up on the lifeboats.

'Horrible, horrible' was his reply. He added, 'Every one of the persons rescued was on the open sea for hours. We had not a bite to eat. The wind, coming over the sea of ice and the great bergs, chilled us to the marrow of our bones. One or two of the persons in the boats were frozen, I think, to death.

'The *Titanic* struck the berg at 10.20 o'clock. We could tell from the first that she was sinking. The whole front part of the steamer, it seemed, was torn away.'

Continuing, Mr Daniel said, 'We knew from the first there was no hope. We were doomed. We were confident of that. The vessel gradually went down. The bow entered the water first. When I got into the boat, I saw a throng of insane, struggling persons at the rail of the doomed ship.

'I know two of three lifeboats were drawn under the wrecked steamer and were lost. Each was filled with passengers.

'A number of passengers, I am confident, were in the bow of the vessel when that part sank. Why they did not go or were not allowed to go to another part of the steamer I don't know.

'It was not possible for us to save personal property. I had a number of things in my stateroom that I would have very much liked to have saved. When the crash came – it seemed as if the whole thing was over in a minute – the passengers were apparently insane. Many of the women, fearing death in many cases, collapsed. Perhaps they died where they were.

Removing a tattered deity that had been given to him by a passenger on the *Carpathia*, he said, 'I did the best I could.'

Then he reeled and was caught by a crowd of men, who had gathered about him.

LIFEBOAT 8
Port Side, Launched 1.00 a.m.

Probably the first lifeboat to be launched from the port side. Second Officer Charles Lightoller enforced a strict women and children only policy. Indeed, Ida Straus had tried to board lifeboat 8 with her husband Isidor, but turned back when Isidor was refused. This lifeboat was placed under the command of Able Seaman Thomas Jones.

Male crew: four; male passengers: 0; women and children: 35; total for lifeboat: 39 (British Board of Inquiry). This lifeboat had capacity for another 20 or so passengers.

11

Ella White, First Class Passenger

Ella White was travelling to New York accompanied by her maid, Amelia Bessetti. Ella White's manservant, Sante Ringhini, who was just 22, went down with the ship. His body was recovered a month later and identified by a ring he was wearing with the initials 'R.S.'.

US Senate Inquiry (inquiry question is followed immediately by witness's answer) Were you aroused especially by the impact? No; not at all. I was just sitting on the bed, just ready to turn the lights out. It did not seem to me that there was any very great impact at all. It was just as though we went over about a thousand marbles. There was nothing terrifying about it at all.

Were you aroused by any one of the ship's officers or crew? No.

Do you know whether there was any alarm turned on for the passengers? We heard no alarm whatever. We went immediately on deck ourselves.

You went on deck? We went right up on deck ourselves.

On the upper deck? Yes, sir.

And Miss Young and your maid were with you? Yes; and my manservant.

What were they doing then? Simply all standing around.

Was anything being done about the lifeboats? No; we were all standing around inside, waiting to know what the result was.

The lifeboats had not been cleared? Nothing had been said about the lifeboats in any way, when suddenly Captain Smith came down the stairway and ordered us all to put on our life preservers, which we did. We stood around for another 20 minutes, then, I should think.

Still on that deck? No, on deck B.

You went down to deck B? Yes, he said we must go back again, then, to deck A, which we did, to get into the boats.

Where did you enter the lifeboat? I entered the lifeboat from the top deck, where the boats were. We had to enter the boat there. There was no other deck to the steamer except the top deck. It was a perfect rat trap. There was no other deck that was open, at all.

Do you recollect what boat you entered? Boat 8, the second boat off.

On which side of the ship? I could not tell you. It was the side going this way – the left side, as we were going.

That would be the port side? Yes. I got in the second boat that was lowered.

What officer stood there? I could not tell you that; I have no idea.

What officer supervised this work? I have no idea. I could not even tell whether it was an officer or the captain. I know we were told to get into the boat.

Did you have any difficulty in getting into the boat? None whatever. They handled me very carefully, because I could hardly step. They lifted me in very carefully and very nicely.

How far out from the side of the ship did the lifeboat hang? Were you able to step into it? Oh, yes.

Or were you passed into it? No we stepped into it. It did not hang far out.

Did you see how far out it was? No, sir; I have no idea. We got into it very easily. We got into the lifeboat without any inconvenience whatever. As I said, my condition was such that I had to be handled rather carefully, and there was no inconvenience at all.

Did you see anything after the accident bearing upon the discipline of the officers or crew, or their conduct, which you desire to speak of? Yes; lots about them.

Tell me about that. *Witness answers:* For instance, before we cut loose from the ship two of the seamen with us – the men, I should say; I do not call them seamen; I think they were dining room stewards – before we were cut loose from the ship they took out cigarettes and lighted them on an occasion like that! That is one thing that we saw. All of those men escaped under the pretence of being oarsmen. The man who rowed me took his oar and rowed all over the boat, in every direction. I said to him, 'Why don't you put the oar in the oarlock?' He said, 'Do you put it in that hole?' I said, 'Certainly.' He said, 'I never had an oar in my hand before.' I spoke to the other man and he said, 'I have never had an oar in my hand before, but I think I can row.' Those were the men that we were put to sea with at night – with all these magnificent fellows left on board, who would have been such a protection to us. Those were the kind of men with whom we were put out to sea that night.

How many were there in your boat? There were 22 women and four men.

None of the men seemed to understand the management of a boat? Yes; there was one there, one who was supposed to be a seaman, up at the end of our boat, who gave the orders.

Do you know who he was? No; I do not know. I do not know the names of any of those men. But he seemed to know something about it.

I wish you would describe, as nearly as you can, just what took place after your lifeboat got away from the *Titanic. Witness answers:* We simply rowed away. We had the order, on leaving the ship, to do that. The officer who put us in the boat – I do not know who he was – gave strict orders to the seamen, or the men, to make for the light opposite and land the passengers and get back just as soon as possible. That was the light that everybody saw in the distance.

Did you see it? Yes; I saw it distinctly.

What was it? It was a boat of some kind.

How far away was it? Oh, it was 10 miles away, but we could see it distinctly. There was no doubt but that it was a boat. But we rowed and rowed and rowed, and then we all suggested that it was simply impossible for us to get to it; that we never could get to it, and the thing to do was to go back and see what we could do for the others. We only had 22 in our boat.

Then we turned and went back, and lingered around there for a long time, trying to locate the other boats, but we could not locate them except by hearing them. The only way they could locate us was by my electric lamp. The lamp on the boat was absolutely worth nothing. They tinkered with it all along, but they could not get it in shape. I had an electric cane – a cane with an electric light in it – and that was the only light we had. We sat there for a long time, and we saw the ship go down, distinctly.

What was your impression of it as it went down? It was something dreadful. Nobody ever thought the ship was going down. I do not think there was a person that night, I do not think there was a man on the boat who thought the ship was going down. They speak of the bravery of the men. I do not think there was any particular bravery, because none of the men thought it was going down. If they had thought the ship was going down, they would not have frivoled as they did about it. Some of them said, 'When you come back you will need a pass,' and, 'You can not get on tomorrow morning without a pass.' They never would have said these things if anybody had had any idea that the ship was going to sink. In my opinion the ship when it went down was broken in two. I think very probably it broke in two. I heard four distinct explosions, which we supposed were the boilers. Of course, we did not know anything about it.

How loud were those explosions? They were tremendous. We did what we were ordered to do. We went toward the light. That seemed to be the verdict of everybody in the boat. We had strict orders to do that from the officer or whoever started us off – land the passengers and come right back for the others. We all supposed that boat was coming toward us, on account of all the rockets that we had sent up.

Did you urge the man in charge of your lifeboat to go back? One of us did.

Did you urge him to go back to seek to pick up more people? Not until we had gone out for half an hour and found it perfectly useless to attempt to reach that boat or that light. Then everybody suggested going back and we did, too, but we could not.

You went back? Yes. The sailor changed our course and tried to go back. That was after trying to reach that light for three quarters of an hour. It was evidently impossible to reach it. It seemed to be going in the same direction in which we were going, and we made no headway toward it at all. Then we turned and tried to go back.

Did anybody try to get in or get out of your boat? No.

Did you land alongside the *Carpathia* with the same party with which you started from the boat deck of the *Titanic*? Exactly.

You all landed safely? We all landed safely. We had a great deal of trouble, but we all landed safely.

How many were there in your party? Three; Miss Young, myself, and my maid. My valet was lost.

Did you make any attempt to communicate with your friends after you got aboard the *Carpathia*, by wireless or otherwise? That was the first thing we did.

Did you succeed? No; we did not succeed. They never received the telegram until last Monday night in this hotel. They took our telegram first thing when we got on board the *Carpathia*, Monday morning. They took our Marconigram. I think the people on land had a much more serious time than we had, so far as real suffering was concerned.

Will you describe what you saw after daybreak, with regard to ice or icebergs? We saw one iceberg in front of us. Of course, we could not see it, because I was standing this way (indicating). I did not even see the *Carpathia* until my attention was called to her. I stood up all night long because I could not get up on to the seats, which were very high, on account of my foot being bound up. I had no strength in my foot, and I stood all night long.

After we got aboard the *Carpathia*, we could see 13 icebergs and 45 miles of floating ice, distinctly, right around us in every direction.

Everybody knew we were in the vicinity of icebergs. Even in our staterooms it was so cold that we could not leave the porthole open. It was terribly cold. I made the remark to Miss Young, on Sunday morning: 'We must be very near icebergs to have such cold weather as this.' It was unusually cold.

It was a careless, reckless thing. It seems almost useless to speak of it.

No one was frightened on the ship. There was no panic. I insisted on Miss Young getting into something warm, and I got into something warm, and we locked our trunks and bags and went on deck.

There was no excitement whatever. Nobody seemed frightened. Nobody was panic-stricken. There was a lot of pathos when husbands and wives kissed each other goodbye, of course.

We were the second boat pushed away from the ship, and we saw nothing that happened after that. We were not near enough. We heard the yells of the steerage passengers as they went down, but we saw none of the harrowing part of it at all.

As I have said before, the men in our boat were anything but seamen, with the exception of one man. The women all rowed, every one of them. Miss Young rowed every mile. The men could not row. They did not know the first thing about it. Miss

Swift, from Brooklyn, rowed every mile, from the steamer to the *Carpathia*. Miss Young rowed every minute also, except when she was throwing up, which she did six or seven times. Countess Rothes stood at the tiller. Where would we have been if it had not been for our women, with such men as that put in charge of the boat? Our head seaman would give an order and those men who knew nothing about the handling of a boat would say, 'If you don't stop talking through that hole in your face there will be one less in the boat.' We were in the hands of men of that kind. I settled two or three fights between them, and quieted them down. Imagine getting right out there and taking out a pipe and filling it and standing there smoking, with the women rowing, which was most dangerous; we had woollen rugs all around us.

Another thing which I think is a disgraceful point. The men were asked, when they got into our boat, if they could row. Imagine asking men who are supposed to be at the head of lifeboats – imagine asking them if they can row.

There is another point that has never been brought out in regard to this accident and that is that that steamer had no open decks except the top deck. How could they fill the lifeboats properly? They could not lower a lifeboat 70 feet [*c.* 21 metres] with any degree of safety with more than 20 people in it. Where were they going to get any more in them on the way down? There were no other open decks.

Just to think that on a beautiful starlit night – you could see the stars reflected in the water – with all those Marconi warnings, that they would allow such an accident to happen, with such a terrible loss of life and property. It is simply unbearable, I think.

There were no male passengers in your boat? Not one.

Do you know who any of the other women were in your boat? Mrs Kenyon, Mrs Dr Leder [sic. Leader], of Brooklyn; Mrs Swift, and the Countess Rothes, who was at the tiller, and her maid, and Miss Young, my maid, and myself. I did not know any other ladies. Those were the ladies right around me.

I never saw a finer body of men in my life than the men passengers on this trip – athletes and men of sense – and if they had been permitted to enter these lifeboats with their families the boats would have been appropriately manned and many more lives saved, instead of allowing the stewards to get in the boats and save their lives, under the pretence that they could row, when they knew nothing whatever about it.

12

Alice Leader & Countess Rothes, First Class Passengers

Alice Leader, a doctor from New York, describes the Countess Rothes taking charge of the boat once the women on board decided the seamen in their lifeboat were incompetent. The countess was a well-known aristocrat. Describing her as attractive and full of energy, Thomas Jones spoke highly of the Countess's conduct in lifeboat 8 and they maintained a correspondence for many years afterwards. Extract is from Everett, *Wreck & Sinking of the Titanic*.

Alice Leader: The countess is an expert oarswoman and thoroughly at home on the water. She practically took command of our boat when it was found that the seamen who had been placed at the oars could not row skilfully. Several of the women took their place with the countess at the oars, and rowed in turns, while the weak and unskilled stewards sat quietly in one end of the boat.

Countess Rothes: It was pitiful, our rowing towards the lights of a ship that disappeared. We in boat No. 8 saw some tramp steamer's mast headlights and then saw the glow of red as it swung towards us for a few minutes, then darkness and despair.

There were two stewards in boat No. 8 with us and 31 women. The name of one of the stewards was Crawford. We were lowered quietly to the water and when we had pushed off from the *Titanic*'s side I asked the seaman if he would care to have me take the tiller as I knew something about boats. He said, 'Certainly, lady.' I climbed aft into the stern and asked my cousin [Gladys Cherry] to help me.

The first impression I had as we left the ship was that, above all things, we mustn't lose our self-possession; we had no officer to take command of our boat and the little seaman had to assume all responsibility. He did it nobly, alternately cheering us with works of encouragement, then rowing doggedly. Then Signora de Satode Penasco began to scream for her husband. It was too horrible. I left the tiller to my cousin and slipped down beside her, to be of what comfort I could. Poor woman, her sobs tore our hearts and her moans were unspeakable in their sadness. Miss Cherry stayed at the tiller of our boat until the *Carpathia* picked us up.

The most terrible part of the whole thing was seeing the rows of portholes vanishing one by one. Several of us wanted to row back and see if there was not some chance of rescuing anyone that had possibly survived, but the majority in the boat argued that we had no right to risk their lives on the bare chance of finding anyone alive after the final plunge.

Indeed I saw – we all saw – a ship's lights not more than three miles away. For three hours we pulled steadily for the two masthead lights that showed brilliantly in the darkness. For a few minutes we saw the ship's port light, then it vanished, and the masthead lights got dimmer on the horizon until they too disappeared.

13

Constance Willard, First Class Passenger

Constance was from Minnesota and 21 years old at the time of travelling. The story surrounding a father begging Willard to take his child may or may not be true. There are a large number of reports of this happening; it seems to have been a favoured story amongst journalists reporting on the *Titanic*.

Chicago Tribune, 21 April 1912 One subject talked of after we were on board the *Carpathia* was the fact the *Titanic* had no searchlight. The crew said that it had been the intention of the owners to equip the vessel with a searchlight after its arrival in New York.

When I reached the deck after the collision the crew were getting the boats ready to lower, and many of the women were running about looking for their husbands and children. The women were being placed in the boats, and two men took hold of me and almost pushed me into a boat. I did not appreciate the danger and I struggled until they released me.

'Do not waste time; let her go if she will not get in,' an officer said. I hurried back to my cabin again and went from cabin to cabin looking for my friends, but could not find them. A little English girl about 15 years old ran up to me and threw her arms about me.

'O, I am all alone,' she sobbed, 'won't you let me go with you?' I then began to realise the real danger and saw that all but two of the boats had been lowered. Some men called to us and we hurried to where they were loading a boat. All the women had been provided with lifebelts. As the men lifted us into the boat they smiled at us and told us to be brave. The night was cold and the men who were standing about, especially the steerage passengers, looked chilled, but the men who were helping the women into the boats seemed different. Even while they smiled at us, great beads of perspiration stood out on their foreheads.

I never will forget an incident that occurred just as we were about to be lowered into the water. I had just been lifted into the boat and was still standing, when a foreigner rushed up to the side of the vessel and, holding out a bundle in his arms, cried with tears running down his face: 'O, please, kind lady, won't you save my little girl, my baby. For myself it is no difference, but please, please take my little one.' Of course, I took the child. Most women were compelled to stand in the boats because they all wore the lifebelts, which made it almost impossible to sit down.

In our boat there were seven men, about 20 women, and several children. The night was dark. Twenty minutes after leaving the *Titanic* we heard an explosion and the vessel appeared to split in two and sank. Then a foreign woman in our boat began singing a hymn, and we all joined, although few knew the words. All around us we heard crying and sobbing for perhaps three minutes.

LIFEBOAT 1
Starboard Side, Launched 1.05 a.m.

Probably the most controversial lifeboat of the night, 'emergency' lifeboat No. 1, had a capacity of 40 but left with just 12 passengers, seven of whom were members of the crew.

The passengers were Sir Cosmo Duff-Gordon, Lady Lucy Duff-Gordon, Laura Mabel Francatelli, Abraham Solomon, and Charles Stengel.

The lifeboat was put under the command of Lookout George Symons, who had previously helped to launch lifeboats 5 and 3. First Officer Murdoch seems to have simply loaded whoever was nearby, and when Sir Cosmo Duff-Gordon asked if they could get in, he replied that he 'wished that they would'. The Duff-Gordons had already tried to get into lifeboats 7 and 3, the first of which was 'full' and the second of which would only take Lady Duff-Gordon.

It was perhaps inevitable that a lifeboat launched with so few passengers and a majority of men would result in some controversy, but the storm of media attention that eventually swept around the Duff-Gordons was extraordinary. A story soon circulated that Sir Cosmo had paid the lifeboat crew not to attempt to return and pick up survivors. In retrospect we can perhaps see that the Duff-Gordons were vilified as they represented the rigidity of class division in Edwardian society, which many believed resulted in some third class passengers unnecessarily losing their lives.

Lifeboat 1 was the second boat to reach the *Carpathia*, being picked up at approximately 4.30 a.m.

14
Lucy Duff-Gordon, First Class Passenger

Lucy Duff-Gordon was a well-know fashion designer, who after a previous divorce married Sir Cosmo Duff-Gordon in 1900. The first extract comes from her autobiography, *Discretions and Indiscretions*, published in 1932. Within this Duff-Gordon vividly describes her experience of providing testimony to the British Inquiry. I have also provided this inquiry testimony for you to make up your own mind.

Discretions and Indiscretions, Chapter 13 It is only now, after so long, that I can bring myself to look back to that terrible last night on board the doomed *Titanic*. For years the horror was too vivid to bear the searchlight of memory. I had only to close my eyes to see the rows of lighted portholes extinguished row by row, until they sank under the black waters – to hear in my ears the hideous clamour that arose, ringing out over the quiet sea. I remember thinking at the time, fantastically enough, how remote and indifferent the stars seemed. I looked up at them a few minutes later with tear-filled eyes, when all was still again, and thought how many scenes of human agony they must have witnessed, and it came to me then that the life and death of man were very unimportant things.

I had not meant to sail on the *Titanic*, although urgent business in New York forced me to take the first available boat. To this day I cannot explain my reluctance when the clerk at the White Star offices said: 'The only berths we have are on our new *Titanic*, which will be making her maiden voyage.'

'Oh, I should not care to cross on a new ship,' I told him. 'I should be nervous.'

He laughed at the idea of it.

'Of all things, I should imagine you could not possibly feel nervous on the *Titanic*,' he answered. 'Why the boat is unsinkable! Her watertight compartments would enable her to weather the fiercest sea, and she is the last word in comfort and luxury. This first voyage is going to make history in ocean travel.'

It was, but not in the way he expected.

In spite of his arguments I refused to book my berth and went home and told my husband of my fears. He laughed at me, but when he realised I was really in earnest he offered to come with me rather than let me go on the voyage alone. I consented willingly, little knowing that by so doing I was to expose him to a storm of censure and ridicule, that well-nigh broke his heart and ruined his life.

The first days of the crossing were uneventful. Like everyone else I was entranced with the beauty of the liner. I had never dreamt of travelling in such luxury. I remember being childishly pleased on finding strawberries on my breakfast table.

'Fancy strawberries in April, and in mid-ocean. The whole thing is positively uncanny,' I kept saying to my husband. 'Why you would think you were at the Ritz.'

My pretty little cabin, with its electric heater and pink curtains, delighted me, so that it was a pleasure to go to bed. Everything aboard this lovely ship reassured me from the captain, with his kindly, bearded face and genial manner, and his 25 years of experience as a White Star commander, to my merry Irish stewardess, with her soft brogue and tales of the timid ladies she had attended during hundreds of Atlantic crossings. And yet, in spite of ridicule, nothing could persuade me to completely undress at night, and my warm coat and wrap lay always ready at hand, and my jewel case, with a few of my most treasured possessions, was placed on a convenient table within reach. I have never been a psychic woman, and in all my life have never been to a séance or dabbled in the occult, so I am even now loath to call this feeling of acute fear which I experienced a premonition, yet the fact remains that, though I have crossed the Atlantic many times both before and since, I have never had it on any other occasion. Something warned me, some deep instinct, that all was not well.

The time passed happily enough. I had my secretary Miss Francatelli with me, as well as my husband, and we both found several friends on board. Mr and Mrs Thayer, the former was president of the Pennsylvania Railway, were among them.

The day of the disaster dawned calm and bright, the sea was exceptionally still, but as the day wore on the cold increased. The wind was the coldest I ever felt, but it died down towards night. As we walked round the deck I shivered in my furs.

'I have never felt so cold,' I said to Cosmo. 'Surely there must be icebergs about.'

He made fun of my ignorance and Captain Smith, who happened to be passing, assured me that we were right away from the ice zone.

Miss Francatelli, my secretary, and I went into my cabin and shut up all the portholes, and lit the electric stove to try to get warm, but it was no use, and when we all three went down to the restaurant we kept on our thick clothes instead of dressing for dinner.

I remember that last meal on the *Titanic* very well. We had a big vase of beautiful daffodils on the table, which were as fresh as if they had just been picked. Everybody was very gay and at neighbouring tables people were making bets on the probable time of this record-breaking run.

Bruce Ismay, chairman of the White Star Line, was dining with the ship's doctor next to our table and I remember that several men appealed to him as to how much longer we should be at sea. Various opinions were put forward, but none dreamed that the *Titanic* would make her harbour that night. Mr Ismay was most confident, and said that undoubtedly the ship would establish a record.

Further along the room the Wideners and the Thayers (multi-millionaires both of them) were dining with the captain and others, and there was a great deal of laughter and chatter from their table. It was the last time I saw them. At another table sat Colonel John Jacob Astor and his young bride. They were coming back to New York after a honeymoon in Europe, and I thought how much in love they were – poor things, it was the last few hours they were to have together. They were joined by Isidor Straus, the multi-millionaire and his wife. These two so openly adored one another that we used to call them 'Darby and Joan' on the ship. They told us laughingly that in their long years of married life they had never been separated for one day or night. Their bodies were found afterwards clasped in one another's arms, after Mrs Straus had hidden from the officers, who were trying to force her into one of the boats.

After dinner we went to the lounge where we met Mr and Mrs Edgar Meyer. I had my little autograph book with me and I got them to write in it. It was one of the 'confession' books, which were so popular just then. Mr Meyer filled in his 'Likes', 'Abominations', etc., and then came to the column marked 'Madnesses'. He laughed as he said, 'I have only one – to live,' and wrote it down. In less than two hours after he was drowned.

We went up to our cabins on A Deck. Cosmo went to bed early. Miss Francatelli and I sat chatting by the stove before we undressed.

I had been in bed, I suppose, for about an hour, and the lights were all out, when I was awakened by a funny rumbling noise. It was like nothing I had ever heard before. It seemed almost as if some giant hand had been playing bowls, rolling the great balls along. Then the boat stopped and immediately there was the frightful noise of escaping steam, and I heard people running outside my cabin, but they were laughing and gay.

'We must have hit an iceberg,' I heard one of them say. 'There is ice on the deck.'

'Don't be ridiculous,' he said. 'Even if we have grazed an iceberg it can't do serious damage with all these watertight compartments. The worst that can happen is that it will slow us down. Go back to bed and don't worry.'

However I went and looked over the side of the boat. I could see nothing and it was pitch black. Several other people hurried up on deck but on hearing from a ship's officer that it was 'nothing but temporary trouble' they went quietly back to bed. I think to this day that had it not been for this ill-advised reticence, hundreds more lives would have been saved. As it was, the appalling danger we were in was concealed from us until it was too late and in the ensuing panic many lifeboats were lowered half-filled because there was no time to fill them.

I went back to my cabin. Everything outside appeared as usual but I was uneasy and the roar of steam still continued to alarm me. Presently it stopped and there came an infinitely more frightening silence. The engines *had* stopped. Something in the cessation of that busy, homely sound filled me with panic. I rushed back to Cosmo.

'I beg you to go up on deck and see what has happened,' I cried, shaking him.

He got out of his warm bed rather unwillingly. In 10 minutes he was back looking rather grave.

'I have just been up to the bridge and seen Colonel Astor,' he said. 'He told me he was going to ask his wife to dress and I think you had better do the same.'

I hurriedly put on the warmest clothes I could find, covering them with a thick coat. As I was dressing, Miss Francatelli came into the room, very agitated: 'There is water down in my cabin and they are taking the covers off the lifeboats on deck.'

Just as she finished speaking a steward knocked at the door.

'Sorry to alarm you, madam, but the captain's orders are that all passengers are to put on lifebelts.'

He laughed and joked as he helped us don them.

'Wrap up warmly, for you may have a little trip for an hour or so in one of the lifeboats,' he said.

We followed him out of the cabin. Before the door closed I looked round it for a last time. I shall never forget that glimpse of the lovely little room with its beautiful lace quilt and pink cushions, photographs all around with a big basket of lilies of the valley that my 'Lucile' girls had given me when I left Paris, on the table. It all looked so homely and pretty, just like a bedroom on land, that it did not seem possible there could be any danger. But as if to give this reassuring thought the lie, at that moment a vase of flowers on the washstand slid off suddenly and fell with a crash to the floor.

We looked at one another.

On the port side was a scene of indescribable horror. Boat after boat was being lowered in a pandemonium of rushing figures fighting for places, tearing at each other, trampling women and children under foot. The Lascars from below deck had run amok and were battling like devils round the remaining boats. Over the confusion the voices of the ship's officer roared: 'Stand back! Women and children first!' and I heard the sharp bark of a revolver.

My legs shook so that I could hardly stand and if it had not been for my husband's arm, I should have fallen.

'Come, dear,' he said, 'I must get you to the boats.'

I clung to him with all my strength and although I could scarcely get out the words, I insisted nothing would make me leave him. He saw that I meant it and besides the crowd round the boats on that deck was so thick that it was useless to try to approach them.

While we stood there people rushed by us in a headlong dash to get anywhere away from the hell of that struggling, yelling mob, and there were heart-rending shrieks as one boat, too hurriedly launched, upset and its occupants were shot out into the black depths of water below.

'We will go round to the starboard side,' Cosmo said. 'It may be better there. It can't possibly be worse.'

It was better, for although there were crowds, there was no confusion. The lifeboats were being quietly filled with women, while officers and male passengers helped to launch them. Even in that terrible moment I was filled with wonder at the American wives who were leaving their husbands without a word of protest or regret, scarce of farewell. They have brought the cult of chivalry to such a pitch in the States that it comes as second nature to their men to sacrifice themselves and to women to let them to do it. But I had no such ideas about my husband and when two officers came up and tried to force me into one of the boats I refused. Cosmo pleaded with me while three or four boats were launched and the crowds round the side thinned. But I only said, 'Promise me that whatever you do you will not let them separate us,' and I clung to him until at last seeing there was no use resisting me he gave in, and we stood waiting there with Miss Francatelli, who refused to leave us.

Suddenly we saw that everyone in the vicinity had dispersed, except for some sailors who were launching a little boat. We found out afterwards that it was not a lifeboat but the captain's 'emergency' boat. The men who were to man it were all stokers with the exception of one seaman whom the officer placed in charge of it. Seeing nobody else about my husband asked the officer whether we might get into it and on receiving his permission we were helped in, followed by two American men who came up at the last moment. I shall never forget how black and deep the water looked below us, and how I hated leaving the big, homely ship for this frail little boat. Just beside us was a man sending off rockets and the ear-splitting noise added to the horror of being suspended in mid-air while one of the lowering ropes got caught and was only released after what seemed an interminable time.

The officer called out his last instructions to our crew: 'Pull away as quickly as possible, at least 200 yards [*c.* 182 metres]!'

Just as we touched the water I looked back. I could still see the man sending off rockets.

We rowed out into the darkness.

I have often noticed that on the heels of tragedy comes an absurd anticlimax. In my case it was deadly seasickness, which was nothing less than torture. To try to keep my mind off my physical suffering, I fixed my eyes on the ship. I could see her dark hull towering like a giant hotel, with light streaming from every cabin porthole. As I looked, one row of these shining windows was suddenly extinguished. I guessed the reason and turned shudderingly away. When I forced myself to look again, yet another row had disappeared. After what seemed long hours of misery a sharp exclamation from my husband roused me from the stupor into which I was sinking.

'My God! She is going now!' he cried.

I turned and saw the remaining lights of the *Titanic* burning with steady brilliance, but only for a moment and then they were gone. A dull explosion shook the air. From the doomed vessel there arose an indescribable clamour. I think that it was only at that moment that many of those poor souls on board realised their fate. A louder explosion followed and the stern of the great ship shot upwards out of the water. For a few seconds she stayed motionless while agonised cries from her decks grew in intensity, and then, with one downward rush, she plunged to her grave and the air was rent with those awful shrieks. Then silence, which I felt I could not bear; I felt my very reason tottering. Cosmo did his best to comfort me but I lapsed into a sort of unconsciousness, from which I was aroused by a dreadful paroxysm of seasickness, which persisted at intervals through the rest of the night. Between bouts of my horrible sickness I could see the dark shadows of icebergs surrounding us.

Chapter 14 On that night of horror when we rowed away from the place where we had seen the vast bulk of the *Titanic* sink slowly beneath the sea as though some relentless giant hand had drawn her under, we scarcely spoke to one another. Our ears were too full of those terrible cries of despair from the poor souls she had carried down with her for us to want to break the silence which succeeded them. There was only the splash of the oars as the men rowed, seeking perhaps to flee their thoughts, and now and then a muttered sentence as they strained their eyes into the gloom for some sign of the other boats.

But I noticed these things in a hazy, detached sort of way, for I had gone through too much in the hours since I left my cabin to think clearly, and to add to it I was enduring agonies of seasickness. Now anyone who has ever suffered from this unromantic and very distressing complaint will agree that there are few things more calculated to destroy one's morale and unfit one for mental effort. While some hundreds of yards away men and women were going to their deaths beneath the icy waters of the Atlantic, and one of the most appalling tragedies of a lifetime was being enacted, I lay stretched out along the side of the boat scarcely conscious of anything but my own physical suffering. Had I been pitched into the sea myself I should not have made the least resistance; in fact death would have been almost in the nature of a relief.

Once or twice during the night I revived a little and tried to talk to reassure Cosmo, who was very worried on my account for, as he told me afterwards, I appeared so ill that he feared I might die of exposure before we were rescued. The others followed my example and when the men rested on their oars for a few minutes we chatted of little unimportant things, as people do when they have been through a great mental strain. With one accord we avoided the tragic side of the wreck, for we did not trust ourselves to speak of it, but we tried to make feeble jokes about our present plight. I remember I teased Miss Francatelli about the weird assortment of clothes the poor girl had flung on before leaving the ship, for she was generally very fussy over her clothes.

'Just fancy, you actually left your beautiful nightdress behind you!' I told her and we laughed as though I had said something witty, though in our hearts we felt far from laughter.

'Never mind, madam, you were lucky to come away with your lives,' said one of the sailors. 'Don't you bother about anything you had to leave behind you.'

Another voice took up the tale: 'You people need not bother about losing your things for you can afford to buy new ones when you get ashore. What about us poor fellows? We have lost all our kit and our pay stops from the moment the ship went down.'

For the first time Cosmo came into the conversation. 'Yes, that's hard luck if you like,' he said. 'But don't worry, you will get another ship. At any rate I'll give you a fiver each towards getting a new kit.'

It was said with his characteristic impulsiveness and I don't think anybody thought much of it at the time, but I remember every word of that conversation for it had a tremendous bearing on our future. I little thought then that because of these few words we should be disgraced and branded as cowards in every corner of the civilised world.

The awful night wore on while we sat huddled in the boat, nearly dying of cold. I heard Cosmo, who was sitting behind me, rubbing his hands together to keep them from freezing, and every now and then when the men stopped rowing, Miss Francatelli would take their poor numbed hands in her lap and rub them with all her might to try and get a little warmth in them. Soon she, too, was overcome with the cold and lay down in the bottom of the boat. We had nothing to eat, but Cosmo found a few cigars in his pocket and broke them in half and shared them with the men. They had only two matches among them but somehow they managed to light them and the smoke was reassuring.

Towards morning the light wind, which had died down overnight, rose again and the sea began to get very rough; as the first faint streaks of dawn broke, we saw rows of 'white horses' racing towards us, beautiful but very alarming, for our frail little boat could never have lived long in a rough sea.

Fortunately we saw something else, or rather I did, for the others refused to believe me at first, when I told them I could see two lights far away on the horizon, too big and too steady to be stars. They insisted it was only my imagination, since nobody else in the boat could see anything although they all strained their eyes into the distance. But the lights grew gradually bigger until they resolved themselves into the outline of an approaching steamer, the *Carpathia*.

By this time it was daylight and the sun was rising. I shall never forget the beauty of that dawn stealing over the cold Atlantic, stretching crimson fingers across the gray of the sky, lighting up the icebergs till they looked like giant opals, as we threaded our way past them. The men were rowing now for all they were worth, and one of them began to sing. We were all nearly hysterical with the reaction from our miseries of the night, and as we saw other boats alongside of us we imagined most of our fellow passengers on the *Titanic* had been saved like us; not one of us guessed the appalling truth. As we drew up beside the *Carpathia* the wreck and the dreadful experiences we had gone through seemed to have passed away like a nightmare.

Miss Francatelli and I were so numb with cold that we could not possibly climb the rope ladder which they let down from the ship, and they had some difficulty getting us up on deck, but it was managed at last and oh, the joy of setting foot on the ship. We clung to each other like children, too exhausted to speak, only realising the blessed fact that we were saved.

I can never be grateful enough for the kindness shown to us on the *Carpathia*; from Captain Rostron and Mr Brown, the Purser, downwards, crew and passengers vied with one another in their attentions to us and to all the survivors. Everything that could possibly be done for our comfort had been thought of; preparations had gone on all night since first the ship's wireless picked up the *Titanic*'s message of distress. Bakers had been baking bread to feed three thousand, blankets had been heated and passengers doubled up with strangers anywhere and everywhere to offer their cabins to the survivors.

The moment I stepped on deck a motherly stewardess rushed up and flung a warm rug round my shoulders while another took charge of Miss Francatelli. We were taken below where we were given brandy and steaming hot coffee and offered changes of clothing. Cosmo and the two Americans, whose names we found out were Mr Stengel and Mr Salomon, were delivered into the care of a steward who prepared hot baths for them and served them with breakfast.

I felt too ill to eat anything and after being given a sedative I was put to bed in a beautiful cabin, which two passengers gave over to Cosmo and myself. There I lay for hours, too exhausted to rouse myself.

I did not wake until the following morning, when the sun was streaming in through the portholes and for the moment I completely forgot the events of the last 48 hours, and was surprised only by the unfamiliarity of the cabin. Then a stewardess came in with some tea and on seeing her instead of my Irish stewardess on the *Titanic*, suddenly everything swept over me in a tide of remembrance. I saw the *Titanic* as I had last seen her, plunging to her grave under the Atlantic, I heard again those heart-rending cries from her decks, and burying my face in the pillows I sobbed uncontrollably. It was the first time that the full realisation of the disaster came to me.

Later in the morning a kind American woman, who was in the next cabin, came in and helped me to dress and we went on deck together. Here we found numbers of fellow survivors, rescued like ourselves, grouped about the ship, discussing the tragedy. Each of them had some new story of horror to tell, many nearly distraught with anxiety over the fate of husbands or sons who had been left on the ship, of whom they could get no tidings.

One of the women I talked to was Mrs Tyrell Cavendish, the daughter of Mr Henry Siegel. She was heartbroken over the loss of her husband, who had put her into one of the first boats to leave the wreck, and had then gone back to save other women and children. The boat in which she had escaped had carried 24 women and only two sailors to row them. One of the men was so overcome by the cold that he had collapsed in the bottom of the boat, and the women had taken their turn at the oars, and somehow or other managed to get the boat alongside the *Carpathia*. Several of them had been almost frozen during the night for they were only half dressed and without shoes or stockings.

Another woman told me that one of the sailors in her boat had collapsed over his oar. She was sitting quite close to him and had tried to restore him until she realised he was dead. So she had propped him against her knee and had sat like that all the remainder of the night so that the other women in the boat should not be alarmed. A lovely little boy of two years old, the child of very rich American parents, had been brought away by his nurse, who was nearly distracted with grief. The child's mother had refused to leave her husband and both had gone down with the ship. In another cabin were a mother and her three daughters, hoping against hope for news of the father and two brothers who had packed them into one of the boats and waved 'goodbye' as they stood on the decks to wait for death together.

One of the saddest figures was an elderly woman shabbily dressed with a shawl over her head who had been landed from one of the boats and dumped on the first class deck. She ran hither and thither peering over the sides, ringing her hands and talking and moaning to herself in a language none of us could understand. We tried to speak to her in English, French, German, and Italian, but she only shook her head. In the end Captain Rostron saw her and sent for somebody from third class who could talk Russian, for he had guessed her nationality. A man and woman came and her joy at finding people who understood her was pathetic, although they had little enough comfort to give her and could only listen to her sad story. They told us that she was the only one left of an entire family which had been immigrating to the States. Her husband, her four children, and her brother and his wife and family had all gone down on the *Titanic*.

All that day and for the remainder of the voyage until we arrived in New York the *Carpathia* was a ship of sorrow as nearly all were grieving over the loss of somebody.

There were one or two little comedies, which came as a welcome relief. One of them was the escape of the *Titanic*'s baker, who had been extraordinarily lucky. After the ship struck the iceberg he had gone to his cabin and drunk half a bottle of brandy 'to steady his nerves'. As he set the bottle down the ship gave a dreadful lurch, though he attributed his loss of equilibrium to the effects of the brandy at the time. Then hearing the sound of scurrying feet as the crew rushed on deck, he decided to follow them. At the door of his cabin he looked back and the half-finished bottle of brandy caught his eye. It was a pity to waste it on the sea, he thought, so he drank it. When he eventually arrived on deck he was in an optimistic mood and indifferent as to his probable plight, which was fortunate for him as just then the ship settled down and he, with hundreds of others, was flung into the icy water. He was not in a state to offer much resistance and contented himself with swimming mechanically about, keeping himself afloat rather from a subconscious sense of self-preservation than from any consistent effort.

While he was doing this he came upon a raft rigged by others of a more energetic frame of mind and as there was a vacant place he was allowed to climb upon it. By that time he had been in the water for over an hour and was nearly frozen but after being taken aboard the *Carpathia* he recovered. The doctors who attended him said that without any doubt the whole bottle of brandy had saved his life for without it he could never have withstood the intense cold of the sea for so long. This is one of the very few comedies I ever heard of the loss of the *Titanic* although I fear it is one of which temperance advocates will not approve.

On our second day on the *Carpathia* Cosmo and I were discussing our terrible night in the boat when he said suddenly, 'Oh, by the way, I must not forget that I promised those poor fellows a fiver each towards getting a new kit if ever we were saved. I shall write them cheques and give them to them tomorrow.'

'Yes, indeed they deserve it for the way they kept their courage up,' I answered. 'I am going to ask them all to write their names on my lifebelt before we get ashore for I should like to keep it in memory of our wonderful escape.'

So Cosmo sent for Hendrickson, the fireman to whom he had first promised the money that night, and asked him to let him have a list of the men who had manned the boat, and later he came back to me with it.

'Just imagine, there was only one seaman, Symons, who was in charge of the boat among them,' he said to me as we looked at the list. 'All the rest were firemen.'

He sent for Miss Francatelli and, as he had no cheque book with him, she wrote out cheques on half sheets of notepaper which Cosmo signed. The Purser, Mr Brown, supplied stamps.

Then Cosmo sent for the men and they came up on the promenade deck where an informal little presentation took place. All the passengers who were there cheered as the men came forward rather sheepishly to receive the envelopes containing the cheques, and the ship's doctor, who was interested in photography, took a picture of them all. Then they came to say 'goodbye' to me and wrote their names on my lifebelt … 'Symons, Hendrickson, Taylor, Collins, Pusey, Sheath and Horswill.'

I have kept it ever since.

As we went back to our cabin I said to Cosmo, 'You know I think some of the other survivors might have done the same thing for the men in their boats and raised a collection among themselves. Of course one could not expect the third class passengers to do it but the first and second class could well afford it and it would have been only a small thing to do for these men who have lost far more by being shipwrecked than we have.'

Cosmo agreed with me. 'At all events I don't regret having done it,' he said. 'Probably the others did not think of it.'

Neither of us could have guessed that that simple act of kindness was forging a powerful link in the chain of evidence which was to be used with such force against us.

I shall never forget the night of our arrival in New York, nor, I think, will anyone else who was aboard the *Carpathia* and witnessed the harrowing scenes at the Cunard Line pier, where 10,000 men and women had waited for over two hours in a drizzling rain for news of friends and relatives who had been on the *Titanic*. Before the ship anchored we caught glimpses of white anxious faces with desperate eyes scanning our decks as the vast crowd waited silently. Women wrapped in costly furs and millionaires who had driven up in luxurious cars stood shoulder to shoulder with men and women from the slums, allied in a common sorrow, hoping the same forlorn hope that perhaps there had been some mistake after all, that perhaps the wireless's list of survivors' names had been incomplete. Most of the women were crying and the men stared straight ahead with set, white faces.

In one group I recognised Elsie de Wolfe, Miss Marbury, Bainbridge Colby, and Mr Merritt, the editor of the *Sunday American*. A few minutes later we were down the gangway and they were alternately laughing and crying over us. Only then did I begin to realise the agony of mind they were in while they waited for us for two hours. They had only been told we were among the survivors but had no confirmation of the news to depend on, and all those who were waiting for friends had been in terrible suspense when it became known that many of those rescued had died aboard the *Carpathia*. Nobody had dared to do more than hope for the best until they had actually seen the passengers disembarked.

We drove to the Ritz where we found a suite of rooms had been prepared for us. Elsie had filled them with flowers, and there were new clothes laid out for us. At dinner that night we were all very gay and drank champagne. Every few minutes the telephone would ring and I was kept busy answering the messages of congratulations while flowers and other presents were showered upon us. But I could not be quite happy even in the warmth of our welcome for I kept remembering the men and women who had sat at dinner that last night on board the *Titanic*. It seemed so long ago. I could scarcely believe that only four days had passed.

It was to escape from my thoughts that I flung myself with renewed energy into my work. I shut myself up in my studio and spent the whole day there, refusing to see anyone.

But I was not to be left in peace. About three days after our arrival in New York the first thunder clouds of the storm that was to break over our heads gathered up.

The most extraordinary reports began to be circulated about the wreck of the *Titanic* and as these passed from one to another they were magnified into fantastic stories without a shred of truth. The horror and grief which had shaken America resolved itself into a sort of hysteria. Everyone looked for a victim to blame for the tragedy, and class hatred ran high. The wildest rumours as to the 'scandalous conduct' of the 'millionaires' who had been passengers were put about and these were sedulously fanned by the agitators. The names of men who had been drowned were heaped with the vilest abuse, were proclaimed far and wide as cowards, and in some cases their relatives were booed and shouted at in the streets. Nobody knew exactly how these rumours started but they gained currency nonetheless.

It was said that Colonel Astor and George Widener had been shot aboard the *Titanic* while fighting with women to get into the lifeboats; that a boatful of women had been turned out to make room for the pet dogs and luggage of Mrs Astor; that any steerage passengers who had been saved had forced themselves on deck as Captain Smith and his officers had given orders that only first and second class were to be allowed to get into the boats; that the hatches had been fastened down on the third class compartments. It was said Captain Smith had been attending a noisy dinner party on the night of the accident and that he was so drunk that he was unable to take any part in the control of the ship; that the first officer had shot himself on the bridge; and that practically every man among the first class had tried to stampede for the boats, trampling women and children under foot.

I need not say how false these rumours were. Everyone knows now that Colonel Astor and George Widener died as did the rest of the men who went down with the ship, like brave men, having helped to load the boats with women and children; the memory of Captain Smith has been too abundantly established as a sailor and a gentleman to need any comment from me, and it is known that the proportion of third class passengers saved was actually higher than the proportion of first class.

The majority of the rumours were directed against Bruce Ismay, managing director of the White Star Line. It was stated that he was directly responsible for the accident, since he had caused the *Titanic* to deviate from her proper course. His picture was published all over the States with the caption that this was the man 'who so managed and directed the line that the *Titanic* disregarded all warnings, neglected all precautions, drove headlong into a known and definitely located sea of ice, killing 1,300 heroic men, while he, himself a coward, escaped in a lifeboat with the women and children, leaving some helpless woman in his place, to drown'.

Of course we heard all these reports – it was difficult not to for the papers were full of them – but we never connected them in any way with ourselves.

Then one morning we received a newspaper cutting which was sent by a friend, who felt we ought to defend ourselves from the terrible accusations being made against us and of which we had so far heard nothing. It was the account of an interview which a certain Robert Hopkins, a seaman on the *Titanic*, had given to the press. It had already appeared in several papers, we were told.

This man, Robert Hopkins, had stated that he could throw light on the mystery of the 'Millionaire's Boat' (we had already read amazing stories of this boat but had no idea they referred to us), which had been the first to leave the ship. It was occupied, he stated, by Sir Cosmo Duff-Gordon, Lady Duff-Gordon, and 11 others, only two of whom were women. A man, whom Hopkins asserted was an American millionaire, had promised the boat's crew to 'make it all right with them' if they 'would get right away from the ship', which they did. Each member of the crew, concluded Hopkins, received a cheque for five pounds upon Coutts' Bank when they were taken aboard the *Carpathia*

Naturally this tale loosed the whole of the 'yellow press' upon us, and every day the papers had some new addition to make. Hopkins was interviewed again and further drew on his inventive powers, the other seamen were asked to give their version, and our fellow passengers also made statements, which completely cleared Cosmo and should have put an end to the story then and there. All the men of our boat's crew indignantly denied the statement which Hopkins had made and explained the real circumstances in which the cheques had been promised. Hopkins, who had been in another boat, could not possibly have known what transpired in ours, but hearing of the presentation of the cheques on board the *Carpathia* he had put his own interpretation on the incident.

At first we were inclined to take no notice of the scurrilous attacks being made on us in New York.

'It is such a ridiculous story that it cannot possibly do us any harm,' Cosmo said. 'Nobody will believe a thing like that.'

But a lie that has a grain of truth in it is very difficult to refute. It was an undeniable fact that Cosmo had given each man in our boat a present of five pounds towards a new kit, though from a very different motive than the one imputed to him.

Then Mr Tweedie, our lawyer and very good friend, wired us from London that the stories, which had appeared in certain American papers, were being quoted in England. He advised us to return immediately and to insist on being present at the Board of Trade Inquiry on the loss of the *Titanic*, so that we might have a chance of personally refuting the abominable libels which were being circulated about us.

So although I had intended to stay several weeks in New York we sailed on the *Lusitania* on 7 May.

Chapter 15 Many years ago I promised my husband that one day I would tell the true story of the most tragic chapter in our lives and vindicate his honour, yet it is only now, after his death, that I am able to do so. For myself I would have been content enough to let it rest, for I do not altogether believe in uncovering old hurts, but he would have wished me to do it, and I owe it to the memory of one who was in every respect the bravest and most honourable of men.

I suppose the most terrible thing that can happen to a man is for him to be accused of cowardice, for however unjust the charge may be it leaves a stain which can never be wiped out, at least not in his lifetime, for we are more charitable in our judgement of the dead.

Now a man can be accused of all sorts of things and get away with them, and without losing the respect of other men, but call him a coward and you get back to something primitive, and his own kind will turn on him and make him feel it for the rest of his life. At least that is what happened in my husband's case. He never lived down the shame of the charges that were brought against him, and from that time he became a changed man. He never spoke much about it but I know his heart was broken.

I shall never forget his stricken face when we landed from the *Lusitania* and caught the boat train for London. All over the station were newspaper placards ... 'Duff-Gordon Scandal' ... 'Baronet and Wife Row Away from the Drowning' ... 'Sir Cosmo Duff-Gordon Safe and Sound While Women Go Down on *Titanic*'. Newsboys ran by us shouting, 'Read about the *Titanic* coward!'

My son-in-law, Lord Tiverton, met us and his loyalty was a great comfort to us both, but he looked rather grave as he spoke of the Court of Inquiry.

'You will have to give evidence,' he told us. 'It is only fair that you should. You must have a chance of showing how false these abominable stories are. Of course Esme and I know there is not a shade of foundation in them but they have given rise to a lot of nasty gossip.'

So we made the journey back to London feeling wretchedly dispirited. At the house in Lennox Gardens we found a stack of letters and telegrams waiting for us. Most of them were from old friends who were furiously indignant at the stories that had been circulated and wanted to assure us of their sympathy. Others were from complete strangers who had read of the case in the papers. These were generally written in the most abusive strain. Some contained offers of advice, more or less practical. Mrs Asquith wrote to tell me that she would be present at the hearings every day and that she was sure I would come out of the ordeal with flying colours. She advised me to take a stiff dose of brandy 'to buck me up', hardly a wise suggestion as preparation for the witness box, but fortunately I did not act on it.

I never realised until the day I attended the Court how absolutely alone we all are in our moments of sorrow. The Scottish Hall in Buckingham Gate, where it was held, was so crowded there was scarcely a vacant place anywhere. Looking at them all as I went in I recognised many who regarded themselves as my intimate friends, yet it came to me that they were rather enjoying the novelty of seeing two people standing in a moral pillory, watching for us to make some slip in our evidence.

Now looking back on it after all these years I think the real cause of the storm which raged round us was that public opinion had to be offered some sacrifice. In the squabble as to whether the Duff-Gordons had or had not acted in a cowardly manner the real issue of the inquiry was very much obscured, at least from the point of view of the man in the street.

Nobody can doubt that the wreck of the *Titanic* was, as the verdict of the court described it, 'an act of God'. But equally nobody can deny that had the ship been better equipped in the way of lifeboats, and better organised in the manning of them, far more lives would have been saved. I am writing simply from the point of view of a passenger without technical knowledge of the control of a ship, but I think the tragic reticence of the officers, which kept the majority of passengers in ignorance of the probable fate of the *Titanic* and so lost valuable time in which every boat could have been filled to its utmost capacity without confusion, was responsible for unnecessary loss of life.

I do not for a moment suggest that anyone was to blame for this. It is very easy to be wise after an emergency and say what ought, or ought not, to have been done. What actually happened at the time was that nobody believed this magnificent boat, the 'unsinkable' *Titanic*, as she had been proclaimed far and wide, could possibly go down. They trusted in her wonderful construction, her powerful pumps and watertight compartments, and but for one of those strange coincidences that sometimes happen in moments of tragedy, when it seems that fate takes a hand in the game and sweeps our cards off the table, they would have been justified.

The real tragedy of the wreck was that there was no need for a single life to have been lost, for the Leyland liner *Californian* was only 17 miles away when the *Titanic* was struck, and she could have taken aboard every man, woman, and child long before the ship sank, but the *Californian*'s wireless was incapacitated and she was deaf to the frantic calls so near to her.

Then again, had the *Titanic* struck the iceberg in almost any other fashion than the one in which she did strike it, her watertight compartments would have saved her. But she struck twice, each time on a bulkhead, knocking four compartments into one, the fine razor-like surface of the ice cutting its way through steel plating as though it had been so much paper.

But although there was no blame to attach to anyone for one of the most appalling tragedies of the sea, there had to be some outlet for the public's emotion and so the same thing happened in England as in America.

The Duff-Gordons were known to have escaped in a lifeboat which contained their secretary, two American gentlemen, and seven sailors. Therefore everybody immediately assumed that the story of their escape was one of flagrant cowardice and with one accord heaped mud upon the Duff-Gordons.

Lord Mersey, President of the Court, repeatedly emphasised the fact that the 'Duff-Gordon incident' had only a small bearing on the inquiry, but this fact was lost sight of by the general public, who were apparently disposed to regard us as criminals on trial. The spectacle of two people who had just come through the frightful ordeal of the wreck facing an infinitely worse ordeal was one that appealed to the popular imagination and they flocked to the court to appreciate it to the full.

The charge we had to face was a moral one. We could have incurred no legal penalties, nothing would have been demanded of us had it been proved, but the real issue at stake was to both of us infinitely more serious. As one of the papers put it: 'The audience was not to be cheated out of the smallest particle of what has become the scandal of the day in England.' It was a terrible spectacle, this man of old family, battling pale-faced, almost pleading, for something still dearer than life, fighting for honour and repute.

The accusation which was actually brought against us was one of incredible cowardice. It was based entirely on the statement of one man among our boat's crew, Charles Hendrickson, a Scandinavian fireman. Hendrickson stated that after the *Titanic* went down he had been the only one in the boat who wanted to return to the spot to try to pick up survivors, but that all the others had overruled him with their objections. I had been the one to offer the most resistance, he said, for I had protested that there was too great a danger of our being swamped, and that Cosmo had upheld my objections.

This story, coupled with the one Hopkins had spread in America of a five pounds bribe, was as terrible as it was untrue. Hendrickson admitted, as did all the men of the boat's crew, that there had been no foundation whatever to the story of the bribe, and the explanation which he gave of the cheques was the correct one – that they had been offered as a voluntary contribution towards a new kit for each man, and the offer had been made in the boat long after the sinking of the *Titanic*. But even so, the story had persisted and it was only after we had both been through a very searching cross-examination on the question of the cheques, and the other witnesses had also given their evidence, that we were completely cleared.

It was a lovely spring day, I remember, as we drove to the court, and it was difficult to believe that we were not going to some pleasant social function for there were such rows of cars outside. Inside the room too, there was little of the atmosphere of a court, in spite of the imposing array of counsel. All the women there seemed to have put on their prettiest spring frocks. I caught sight of the Duchess of Wellington, Lady Eileen Wellesley, and Margot Asquith, whose bright eyes followed every posture of the witnesses, Prince Maurice of Battenberg, Prince Albert of Schleswig-Holstein, the Russian Ambassador, and many other people who had been guests at our house; eager all of them to see what would happen.

As Cosmo stood up to give his evidence I thought suddenly that a court of law can sometimes be a substitute for the arena of the Old World. Once or twice I closed my eyes and tried to imagine I was far away from it all. When I opened them again I saw Lord Mersey and the row of counsel through a haze.

Sir Rufus Isaacs, the Attorney General, led for the Board of Trade. With him were Sir John Simon, Mr Butler Aspinall, Mr S. A. Rowlatt, and Mr Raymond Asquith.

Sir Robert Finlay, Mr F. Laing, Mr Maurice Hill, and Mr Norman Raeburn appeared for the White Star Line, and there were many more whose names I cannot remember.

H. E. Duke, who is now Lord Merrivale, and Vaughan Williams, who were appearing for us, looked a very small army against so many who were appearing against us, I thought dismally.

Our only defence was a complete denial of Hendrickson's story. There had of course been no such conversation in the boat, certainly none in which we took part. Nobody had suggested going back to rescue possible survivors because we were at far too great a distance from the ship when she went down to have been able to do so. When the *Titanic* disappeared we were left in our frail boat without a light of any sort, without even a compass and with no means of knowing where to search for people in the water. Miss Francatelli and I had been the only women in the boat simply because we had been the only women left on the starboard deck when it was launched. My husband and the two American men had only got into the boat because there was no one else there to do so and the officer superintending the loading of the boat had given them permission to get in. The crew of seven had been appointed to man the boat by this officer and they had acted on his instructions in pulling well away from the ship.

When the *Titanic* sank I was too seasick to have taken part in a discussion as to which direction we ought to follow even if I had wanted to do so and Cosmo, who had only been a passenger in the boat, had left the entire navigation to Symons, the seaman, whom the officer had placed in charge of her.

Symons in the course of his evidence stated on oath that he considered that to have returned to the place where the *Titanic* had sunk would have endangered the safety of all on board, as we should have more than probably been swamped. He also affirmed there had been no discussion whatever as to the advisability of returning and that neither Sir Cosmo nor I had made any suggestions on the point whatever. The story that we had deliberately rowed away and left the drowning to their fate was monstrous.

For over two hours, Cosmo was cross-examined by Sir Rufus Isaacs whilst the crowd of spectators lent forward, anxious not to miss one syllable of dialogue. Once when Sir Rufus lowered his voice, Margot Asquith called out impatiently, 'Speak up!' and other women echoed her. Several times there were bursts of applause, once especially, when Lord Mersey intervened to rule out a question put by another opposing counsel, Mr Harbinson.

Sir Rufus Isaacs was absolutely relentless in the way he pressed his questions; he was, in fact, thought extremely severe to my husband, as were several of the other counsel and their attitude evoked a great deal of criticism afterwards when we were dismissed from the case, Lord Mersey having announced that he proposed to take no notice whatever of the charge against Sir Cosmo Duff-Gordon.

Mr Ashmead Bartlett in an article published in *The Academy* under the title 'Inquiry or Star Chamber?' voiced, I think, the general opinion. He wrote:

Every fair-minded person must deplore what passed at the proceedings of the *Titanic* Court of Inquiry last week. The court was constituted by the Board of Trade, acting under pressure of public opinion, to inquire into the causes which brought about the disaster of the *Titanic* and the resulting heavy loss of life. It was surely never intended that it should resolve itself into a species of Court of Star Chamber to torture witnesses who were fortunate enough to survive and to cast the gravest reflections on their characters and conduct during those two tragic hours. Still less was the court constituted that efforts might be made to stir up class against class in order to prove that undue preference was shown to the aristocrat and the wealthy. Yet almost the whole of last week's evidence was taken up endeavouring to prove, by counsel on behalf of the Crown and by various other counsel representing Seaman's Unions, Stokers' Unions and the third class passengers, that Sir Cosmo and Lady Duff-Gordon were responsible for the fact that No. 1 lifeboat only contained 12 persons, instead of its full complement.

Torquemada never placed his victims more unfairly on the rack of the Inquisition than have Sir Cosmo and Lady Duff-Gordon been placed on the rack of cross-examination. Every counsel, from the Attorney General Sir Rufus Isaacs (from whom one at least expected some semblance of fair play), to Mr Harbinson, who put the climax on the proceedings with his scandalous question, has endeavoured to prove by the most skilful questioning, by *suggestio falsi*, and by every other weapon in the armoury of the cross-examiner, that Sir Cosmo induced the crew of No. 1 lifeboat to row away from the sinking ship by offering them five pounds apiece. There is not one tittle of evidence to support this derogatory aspersion. Hendrickson's evidence is not supported by a single other person in the boat. Able Seaman Symons, who was in charge of the lifeboat, assumed full responsibility for all that occurred and declared on oath that in his considered opinion it would have been most dangerous to have ventured into the drowning multitude, and that he refrained from doing so in order to preserve the lives of those on board.

On the subject of the five pound cheques, Mr Ashmead Bartlett continues:

Sir Cosmo, taking compassion on the unfortunate plight of these men, who had lost everything they possessed in the world, offered them five pounds apiece with which to purchase immediate necessities. Was there ever a more natural action for a gentleman to take? Would not anyone who had been almost miraculously preserved from a fate which had overwhelmed so many have adopted the same course? Yet on account of this harmless act of gratitude and charity Sir Cosmo has been held up to public vilification and every unworthy motive attributed to him. But all efforts of counsel have failed to prove that either Sir Cosmo or Lady Duff-Gordon ever said a single word against going back or that they attempted to induce the crew to row away from the scene of the disaster by offering them a monetary reward.

The scene in court on Friday will never be forgotten by those who witnessed it. There did not seem to be a single commonsense man of the world with any idea of fair play in court. Not one of the eminent KCs seemed to grasp the vast and essential difference between men's actions in a time of great emergency and as they appear weeks afterward at a Court of Inquiry when the danger is past and the setting is absolutely different. It was not an inspiring spectacle to watch the row of lawyers increasing the sufferings of those who have just passed through the most awful ordeal which a man or woman could be called upon to face.

I was immensely grateful to Mr Ashmead Bartlett for his warm championship of our cause at the time and I am still. Other writers were not so kind. George Bernard Shaw indulged his biting sarcasm at our expense. Referring to the cry of 'Women and Children First', which he described as a 'romantic formula'. He wrote:

> And never did the chorus of solemn delight at the strict observance of this formula by the British heroes on board the *Titanic* rise to sublimer strains than in the papers containing the first account of the wreck by a surviving witness, Lady Duff-Gordon. She described how she escaped in the captain's boat with only one other woman in it and 10 men, 12 all told. Chorus: 'Not once or twice in our rough island story, etc. etc.'

Someone cut this out and sent it to me. It hurt me and I was childishly pleased when the article was replied to by Mr Benedict Ginsburg, who wrote equally bitterly:

> For the sake of modern literature and especially the 20th-century drama I cordially trust that the Mr Shaw who signs this article is not the playwright of the same name … Mr Shaw must now be sorry that in his anxiety to be smart at other people's expense he failed to observe another old formula, 'Do not write of a matter while it is still *sub judice*.' Had he regarded that he would have waited and would have known something about the authenticity of Lady Duff-Gordon's observations and also why there were 10 men to two women in that particular boat.

T. P. O'Connor wrote with his usual kindness and tolerance:

> In the case of the Duff-Gordons. At first the story told against them was ghastly; it was that Sir Cosmo Duff-Gordon promised a number of sailors a five pound note each before they left the sinking *Titanic* and that they had secured preferential treatment by an appeal to greed. If the story had been true one might well stand aghast at such selfishness. But it is now distinctly proven there was not a word of truth in the story.

But despite our complete vindication before the inquiry and the generous championship we got from the press, a great deal of the mud that was flung stuck to us both. For years afterwards, I was quite used to hearing people who did not know me whisper: 'That is Lady Duff-Gordon, the woman who rowed away from the drowning.'

For myself I did not mind, for none of the people whose opinion I cared about believed such an outrageous story, but I minded very much for Cosmo's sake. To the end of his life he grieved at the slur which had been cast on his honour.

British Board of Trade Inquiry (inquiry question is followed immediately by witness's answer) Lady Duff-Gordon, you will remember on the night of this disaster to the *Titanic*, you were wakened, I think, by the collision? I was.

I only want you to tell me one thing before we get to the boat, had there been offers to you to go into any of the lifeboats? Oh, yes, they came and tried to drag me away.

You mean some of the sailors? The sailors. I was holding my husband's arm. They were very anxious that I should go.

And you refused to go? Absolutely.

Well, eventually you did go with your husband, as we know, in what has been called the emergency boat? Yes, I did.

Just tell us quite shortly – I do not want to go into it in any detail – but quite shortly, how it was you went into that boat. Do you remember? Oh, quite well.

Well, would you tell my Lord? After the three boats had gone down, my husband, Miss Franks [Francatelli] and myself were left standing on the deck. There were no other people on the deck at all visible and I had quite made up my mind that I was going to be drowned, and then suddenly we saw this little boat in front of us and we saw some sailors, and an officer apparently giving them orders and I said to my husband, 'Ought we not to be doing something?' He said, 'Oh, we must wait for orders,' and we stood there for quite some time while these men were fixing up things, and then my husband went forward and said, 'Might we get into this boat?' and the officer said in a very polite way indeed, 'Oh certainly; do; I will be very pleased.' Then somebody hitched me up from the deck and pitched me into the boat and then I think Miss Franks was pitched in. It was not a case of getting in at all. We could not have got in, it was quite high. They pitched us up in the sort of way into the boat and after we had been in a little while the boat was started to be lowered and one American gentleman got pitched in, and one American gentleman was pitched in while the boat was being lowered down.

Now you will remember when you got into the boat, and before the *Titanic* sank, did the men start rowing away from the *Titanic*? Oh, the moment we touched the water the men began rowing.

Had you heard any orders given? Yes.

Do you remember what they were? As far as I can remember, it was to row quickly away from the boat for about 200 yards [*c.* 182 metres].

And 'come back if called upon'? No.

You did not hear that? Oh, no.

I do not quite understand? I did not hear that.

As far as you knew all they had to do was to row out 200 yards [*c.* 182 metres]? Yes.

Then did the men commence doing that? At once.

And did you hear any conversation at all in the boat before the *Titanic* sank? No.

Let me ask you again. I am speaking to you of before the *Titanic* sank. You understand? Yes.

What I am asking you is: Before she sank did you hear the men saying anything in the boat? No.

Did you hear anything said about suction? Well, perhaps I may have heard it, but I was terribly sick, and I could not swear to it.

What? I was awfully sick; I do not think I could swear to it.

I am asking you about something which I only know from your statement to your solicitor. Did you hear a voice say, 'Let us get away'? Yes, I think so.

Did you hear it said, 'It is such an enormous boat; none of us know what the suction may be if she is a goner'? Yes, I heard them speaking of the enormous boat. It was the word 'suction' I was not sure of. I see what you mean.

It is not what I mean, Lady Duff-Gordon. It is what you are said to have said to your solicitor? Well, I may have said so.

'Such an enormous boat'; that is referring to the *Titanic*? Yes.

'None of us know what the suction may be if she is a goner'? That was, I am sure, long before the *Titanic* sank.

That is what I was asking you? Yes.

I put it to you, but I do not think you appreciated the question? No, I did not.

It was before the *Titanic* sank? Yes, it was before.

Now after the *Titanic* sank you still continued to be seasick, I understand? Yes, terribly.

I only want to ask you one question about that. Tell me first of all do you recollect very well what happened when you were in the boat? No.

Your mind is hazy about it? Very.

There may have been some talk which you would not recollect, I suppose? Well, I do not know.

You think you might? I think I would.

I will put to you definitely what is said with reference to yourself. Did you hear after the *Titanic* had sunk the cries of the people who were drowning? No; after the *Titanic* sank I never heard a cry.

You never heard anything? No, not after the *Titanic* sank.

Did not you hear cries at all? Yes, before she sank; terrible cries.

Before she sank? Yes.

Did you see her sink? I did.

You mean you heard nothing at all after that? My impression was that there was absolute silence.

Were your men rowing? Yes.

What, all the time? No, they began to row as soon as the boat went down.

Did you hear a proposal made that you should go back to where the *Titanic* was sunk? No.

Did you hear any shouting in your boat – it would be better if you would attend to me? I am listening.

Did you hear anybody shout out in the boat that you ought to go back? No.

With the object of saving people who were in the *Titanic*? No.

You knew there were people in the *Titanic*, did you not? No, I did not think so; I do not think I was thinking anything about it.

Did you say that it would be dangerous to go back, that you might get swamped? No.

Have you seen in the London *Daily News* what purports to be an article specially written by yourself in America? I have.

Did you write such an article? No.

It is an entire invention from beginning to end? *Witness answers:* Which article?

The one in the *Daily News* which appeared on the 20 April 1912? Yes, it is rather inventive. A man wrote it from what he thought he heard me saying.

Do you mean to say that somebody came to interview you? Oh, quantities of people came to interview me.

But this particular man from the *Daily News*? No, he did not; he was a friend having supper with us the night we arrived.

Will you kindly look at that article (hands the same to the witness)? *Witness answers:* What am I supposed to say?

If you will look at the heading of the second column on this side you will see that it is an article supposed to be specially written by you, and what purports to be your signature appears at the foot of the column. Are you looking at it now, Lady Duff-Gordon, for the first time? For the first time.

Do you mean to say you have never seen the *Daily News* with that article in it up to today? Never; this is the first time. The last little bit here is absolutely a story.

Absolutely what? A story.

Then if your signature appears there it is a forgery, is it? Oh, absolutely.

You say that a friend came and had supper with you, and you suggest he is responsible for what appears here? I know he is.

Some of it may be true and some of it may be false? *Witness answers:* Would you like me to tell you the story?

I should like you to answer the question. Is this true that you watched several women and children and some men climb into the lifeboats, and did an officer say, 'Lady Gordon, are you ready?' It is not true that the officer spoke to me, but I did see women and children being handed into the lifeboats.

Is it true that he said, 'Lady Gordon, are you ready?' It is untrue.

Is this true: 'I said to my husband, well, we might as well take a boat, although the trip will only be a little pleasure excursion until the morning'? Quite untrue.

That is untrue. Is it untrue that you said it was the captain's special boat, that five stokers got in and two Americans – Mr Salomon, of New York, and Mr Stengel, of Newark? I do not remember saying that.

It is true, is it not, that that number of persons did get in? It was Mr Salomon and Mr Stengel and Miss Franks [Francatelli], my husband and myself. We were the passengers.

'Besides those two passengers there were Sir Cosmo, myself, Miss Franks, an English girl.' Is it true you said that? I think that might easily be.

Is this true that you said this: 'Numbers of men standing nearby joked with us because we were going out on the ocean'? No, that is not true.

That is invention? Absolutely.

Is it true that you said that some of them said, 'The ship cannot sink,' and that one of them said, 'You will get your death of cold out there amid the ice.' Is that true? No, not true.

Is it true that you said you were slung off and cruised around for two hours, and it did not seem very cold? Quite untrue.

Is it true that you said, 'I suddenly clutched the sides of the lifeboat. I had seen the *Titanic* give a curious shiver.' That is invention, is it? Yes, quite.

Did you say, 'Everything could be clearly made out; there were no lights on the ship, save for a few lanterns'? No.

Is this true that you said this: 'We watched her – we were 200 yards [*c.* 182 metres] away – go down slowly, almost peacefully'? No.

Did you say then, 'An awful silence seemed to hang over everything, and then from the water all about where the *Titanic* had been arose a Bedlam of shrieks and cries'? No, I never said that.

That is entirely untrue? Absolutely.

Is this true that you said this: 'Women and men were clinging to bits of wreckage in the icy water'? No.

'And it was at least an hour before the awful chorus of shrieks ceased, gradually dying into a moan of despair'? No, I never said that.

Did you say this: 'I remember the very last cry; it was a man's voice calling loudly, 'My God, My God,' he cried monotonously, in a dull, hopeless way.' That is untrue? Absolutely untrue.

'And we waited gloomily in the boats through the rest of the night, the stokers rowing as hard as they could to keep themselves warm'? Quite untrue.

Do you write for any American papers at all? Yes, the *Sunday American*.

Did you supply an article to the *Evening Herald*? No.

When you were at New York you went to a hotel? Yes.

And that evening you had supper together with your husband? Several people – six ladies.

Did Mr Merritt [editor of the *Sunday American*] come there? Yes.

Was he a gentleman you had known? A great friend of ours.

Had you any idea of any publication of anything at that time? Yes.

What did he say to you? After he had left us about half an hour he telephoned to me, and he said, 'Mr Hurst has just rung me up, and must have your story of the *Titanic* wreck for tomorrow morning's newspaper.' He said, 'May I tell your story as I have heard it?'

What did you say? I said, 'Yes,' and he tells me afterwards that he telephoned to their head office all he knew about it, and then a clever reporter put all that into words and it appeared next morning in the *New York American*.

Your friend told some clever American reporter what he had heard? Yes.

And then you were advertised as having written and signed this false article? That is it.

And was that published in various papers, did you find? Oh, all over – everywhere.

But you had not seen this in the *Daily News* till when? Just now; here.

LIFEBOAT 6
Port Side, Launched 1.10 a.m.

Loaded and launched under the command of Second Officer Charles Lightoller, this lifeboat left with approximately 26 passengers, again, almost entirely first class female passengers. Mary Smith makes reference to the strict 'women and children first policy' in contrast with the starboard boats where at a similar time couples were being allowed to board. Major Peuchen's experience as a yachtsman probably saved his life; he was the only male passenger that Lightoller permitted (barring stowaways) to board a lifeboat all night.

The crew of lifeboat 6 included the Lookout Frederick Fleet, who was the first person to see the iceberg, calling down to the bridge with the cry 'iceberg right ahead'. Under the command of Quartermaster Hichens this boat was notable for disharmony – with Mary Smith, Major Peuchen and Margaret Brown having little positive to say about Hichens. There was certainly disagreement over whether the lifeboat should return to look for survivors. In contemporary newspaper accounts Hichens was portrayed as reluctant to return and reported as saying, 'We are to look out for ourselves now, and pay no attention to those stiffs'! When questioned about this, Hichens defends himself, denying newspaper reports. Exactly what happened we will never know, but it is these clashes that make this one of the most interesting lifeboats to leave the *Titanic*.

At this point in the night lifeboats were still proving difficult to fill, or at least to fill with women and children. Major Peuchen's testimony describes how stokers were sent back below deck when they looked like they were about to approach lifeboats. Upon launch there were at least 30 spaces left in this lifeboat.

Male crew: two; male passengers: two; women and children: 24; total for lifeboat: 28 (British Board of Inquiry).

15

Mary Smith, First Class Passenger

Mary Smith was an American from West Virginia. She was travelling on the *Titanic* with her new husband, Lucien P. Smith, who went down with the ship and didn't survive. Smith later married Robert Daniel, another *Titanic* survivor.

The criticism that Mary makes of Ismay's behaviour on board the *Carpathia* was echoed by other passengers. Bruce Ismay was the chair of the White Star Line. It is notable that in his own testimony Ismay is keen to describe himself as an ordinary passenger, to avoid being held responsible for the fate of the *Titanic*. But on board the *Carpathia* this ordinary passenger does seem to get extraordinary treatment. See the *Titanic*'s wireless operator Harold Bride's account (chapter 58) for an explanation of why some telegraphs from survivors weren't sent.

Mary shares her fellow passengers' view of Quartermaster Hichens, calling him a 'lazy, uncouth' man.

US Senate Inquiry Statement At 7.30 p.m., as usual, my husband and I went to dinner in the café. There was a dinner party going on, given by Mr Ismay to the captain and various other people on board ship. This was a usual occurrence of the evening, so we paid no attention to it. The dinner did not seem to be particularly gay; while they had various wines to drink, I am positive none were intoxicated at a quarter of nine o'clock, when we left the dining room. There was a coffee room directly outside of the café, in which people sat and listened to the music and drank coffee and cordials after dinner. My husband was with some friends just outside of what I know as the Parisian Café. I stayed up until 10.30 p.m., and then went to bed. I passed through the coffee room, and Mr Ismay and his party were still there. The reason I am positive about the different time is because I asked my husband at the three intervals what time it was. I went to bed, and my husband joined his friends. I was asleep when the crash came. It did not awaken me enough to frighten me; in fact, I went back to sleep again. Then I awakened again, because it seemed that the boat had stopped. About that time my husband came into the room. Still I was not frightened, but thought he had come in to go to bed. I asked him why the boat had stopped, and, in a leisurely manner, he said, 'We are in the north and have struck an iceberg. It does not amount to anything, but will probably delay us a day getting into New York. However, as a matter of form, the captain has ordered all ladies on deck.' That frightened me a little, but after being reassured there was no danger I took plenty of time in dressing – putting on all my heavy clothing, high shoes, and two coats, as well as a warm knit hood.

While I dressed, my husband and I talked of landing, not mentioning the iceberg. I started out, putting on my life preserver, when we met a steward, who was on his way to tell us to put on life preservers and come on deck. However, I returned to the room with the intention of bringing my jewellery, but my husband said not to delay with such trifles. However, I picked up two rings and went on deck. After getting to the top deck, the ladies were ordered on deck A without our husbands.

I refused to go; but, after being told by three or four officers, my husband insisted, and, along with another lady, we went down. After staying there some time with nothing seemingly going on, someone called saying they could not be lowered from that deck, for the reason it was enclosed in glass. That seemed to be the first time the officers and captain had thought of that, and hastened to order us all on the top deck again. There was some delay in getting lifeboats down: in fact, we had plenty of time to sit in the gymnasium and chat with another gentleman and his wife. I kept asking my husband if I could remain with him rather than go in a lifeboat. He promised me I could. There was no commotion, no panic, and no one seemed to be particularly frightened; in fact, most of the people seemed interested in the unusual occurrence, many having crossed 50 and 60 times. However, I noticed my husband was busy talking to any officer he came in contact with; still I had not the least suspicion of the scarcity of lifeboats, or I never should have left my husband.

When the first boat was lowered from the left-hand side I refused to get in, and they did not urge me particularly; in the second boat they kept calling for one more lady to fill it, and my husband insisted that I get in it, my friend having gotten in. I refused unless he would go with me. In the meantime Captain Smith was standing with a megaphone on deck. I approached him and told him I was alone, and asked if my husband might be allowed to go in the boat with me. He ignored me personally, but shouted again through his megaphone, 'Women and children first.' My husband said, 'Never mind Captain about that; I will see that she gets in the boat.' He then said, 'I never expected to ask you to obey, but this is one time you must; it is only a matter of form to have women and children first. The boat is thoroughly equipped, and everyone on her will be saved.' I asked him if that was absolutely honest, and he said, 'Yes.' I felt better then, because I had absolute confidence in what he said. He kissed me goodbye and placed me in the lifeboat with the assistance of an officer. As the boat was being lowered he yelled from the deck, 'Keep your hands in your pockets; it is very cold weather.' That was the last I saw of him, and now I remember the many husbands that turned their backs as the small boat was lowered, the women blissfully innocent of their husbands' peril, and said goodbye with the expectation of seeing them within the next hour or two. By that time our interest was centred on the lowering of the lifeboat, which occurred to me – although I know very little about it – to be a very poor way to lower one. The end I was in was almost straight up, while the lower end came near touching the water. Our seaman said, himself, at the time, that he did not know how to get the rope down, and asked for a knife. Some person in the boat happened to have a knife – a lady, I think – who gave it to him. He cut the rope, and we were about to hit bottom when someone spoke of the plug. After a few minutes excitement to find something to stop the hole in the bottom of the boat where the plug is, we reached the water all right. The Captain looked over to see us, I suppose, or something of the kind, and noticed there was only one man in the boat. Major Peuchen, of Canada, was then swung out to us as an experienced seaman. There was a small light on the horizon that we were told to row towards. Some people seemed to think it was a fishing smack or small boat of some description. However, we seemed to get no nearer the longer we rowed, and I am of the opinion it was a star.

Many people in our boat said they saw two lights. I could not until I had looked a long time; I think it was the way our eyes focused, and probably the hope for another boat. I do not believe it was anything but a star. There were 24 people in our boat – they are supposed to hold 50. During the night they looked for water and crackers and a compass, but they found none that night. We were some distance away when the *Titanic* went down. We watched with sorrow, and heard the many cries for help and pitied the Captain, because we knew he would have to stay with his ship. The cries we heard I thought were seamen, or possibly steerage, who had overslept, it not occurring to me for a moment that my husband and my friends were not saved. It was bitterly cold, but I did not seem to mind it particularly. I was trying to locate my husband in all the boats that were near us. The night was beautiful; everything seemed to be with us in that respect, and a very calm sea. The icebergs on the horizon were all watched with interest; some seemed to be as tall as mountains, and reminded me of the pictures I had studied in geography. Then there were flat ones, round ones also. I am not exactly sure what time, but think it was between 5 and 5.30 a.m. when we sighted the *Carpathia*. Our seaman suggested we drift and let them pick us up; however, the women refused and rowed toward it. Our seaman was Hichens, who refused to row, but sat in the end of the boat wrapped in a blanket that one of the women had given him. I am not of the opinion that he was intoxicated, but a lazy, uncouth man, who had no respect for the ladies, and who was a thorough coward. We made no attempt to return to the sinking *Titanic*, because we supposed it was thoroughly equipped. Such a thought never entered my head. Nothing of the sort was mentioned in the boat, having left the ship so early we were innocent of the poor equipment that we now know of. The sea had started to get fairly rough by the time we were taken on the *Carpathia*, and we were quite cold and glad for the shelter and protection. I have every praise for the *Carpathia's* captain and its crew, as well as the passengers aboard. They were kindness itself to each and every one of us, regardless of the position we occupied on boat. One lady very kindly gave me her berth, and I was as comfortable as can be expected under the circumstances until we arrived in New York. The ship's doctors were particularly nice to us. I know many women who slept on the floor in the smoking room while Mr Ismay occupied the best room on the *Carpathia*, being in the centre of the boat, with every attention, and a sign on the door: 'Please do not knock.' There were other men who were miraculously saved, and barely injured, sleeping on the engine room floor, and such places as that, as the ship was very crowded. The discipline coming into New York was excellent. We were carefully looked after in every way with the exception of a Marconigram I sent from the *Carpathia* on Monday morning, 15 April, to my friends. Knowing of their anxiety, I borrowed money from a gentleman and took this Marconigram myself and asked the operator to send it for me, and he promised he would. However, it was not received. Had it been sent, it would have spared my family, as well as Mr Smith's, the terrible anxiety which they went through for four days. This is the only complaint I have to make against the *Carpathia*. They did tell me they were near enough to land to send it, but would send it through other steamers, as they were cabling the list of the rescued that way. He also said it was not necessary to pay him, because the White Star Line was responsible. I insisted, however, because I thought that probably the money might have some weight with them, as the whole thing seemed to have been a moneyed accident.

16

Margaret 'Molly' Brown, First Class Passenger

Margaret featured as somewhat of a heroine in the film *Titanic* where she befriends Jack and Rose. Certainly Margaret emerges from accounts as a generous, practical women. Born to a poor family Margaret married a young miner, James Brown, in 1886. The couple suddenly found themselves rich when James developed a new gold mining technique with their lives changing overnight.

In this extract I have replicated the journalist's copy as well as direct quotes from Margaret. We can see that, just over a week after the disaster, heroes and villains had already been created.

New York Times, 20 April 1912 Mrs J. J. Brown, wife of a Denver mine owner, told yesterday afternoon to a reporter for the *Times* at the Ritz-Carlton the story of her seven-hour vigil in an open boat after leaving the *Titanic*.

Oftentimes it has been written that out of each great moment of history some man has emerged as master of the situation, someone's hand and mind has controlled where others held back. From verified statements and from circumstances explained by others the work of the women makes them the central figures in the great sea tragedy.

When seen at the Ritz-Carlton Mrs Brown wore the same dress in which she had gone over the side of the liner in a lifeboat. The black and white silk facing of the black velvet outer coat was discoloured, and her white-topped shoes were spotted with salt water in which her feet had rested.

'My hair? Oh, that I have not bothered with since Sunday,' she said.

'But this morning? Did you not rest last night?'

'No,' she said smilingly. 'Why should I? There was work to do. I left the *Carpathia* at three o'clock this morning. There were many women there whom I had to look out for.'

In the women's parlour of the Ritz-Carlton sat the Russian Consul and a young Russian woman, who had lost her husband and all of her money in the disaster. This woman had been brought to the hotel to meet the Consul by the tireless Mrs Brown, so that something could be done to assist her. The picture was as perfect a one of absolute democracy as could be obtained.

The woman, who was returning to her luxurious home in Denver after seven hours in an open boat, during which time she continually used an oar, after four days in watching over others and waiting on the sick, after remaining up practically all night Thursday night, sat holding the hand of the little brown-eyed, baby-faced Russian woman, and repeating to her in German time and again that everything was all right.

The grief of the young widow was of that profound kind which has passed the stage of tears. When the interview was over and she was to go, whither she knew not, in a land where she was penniless, where she knew no word of its language, she stood for a moment looking at the stronger woman, who had mastered the situation and had been the leader. Hesitatingly she held out her hand, and then turning her face up like a little child, she paid the only tribute she understood as she kissed the older woman on the cheek, and mutely walked away with the Consul leading her by the hand. It was the final tribute to fortitude combined with tenderness.

'The whole thing,' said Mrs Brown, 'was so formal that it was difficult for anyone to realise that it was a tragedy. Men and women stood in little groups and talked. Some laughed as the first boats went over the side. All the time the band was playing. After a little while I helped put some women into a boat. I remember the last woman. She was French. She was very excited. I spoke to her in French and helped to put her into the boat. Somehow I did not seem to care about the thing of being saved. We thought that the ship was so big that she could not go down for a day at any rate. The passengers had been stepping from the deck into the boat in which I put the French woman. Then they swung it out over the water. I had then gone to an upper deck and was looking down at it and watching the picture.

'I had noticed two men following me from place to place as I talked with the women here and there. These two men just then followed me to the upper deck and carried me down, and practically threw me into the boat with the words, "You are going, too." They were Edward P. Calderhead and James McGough, two American merchants. I owe my life to them, for there were no more boats, and I would be now with these who are at the bottom, for I had gone back upstairs, you see.

'We were lowered to the water as gently as if it were a boat drill. Our boat could have carried several more. I can still see the men up on the deck tucking in the women and bowing and smiling. It was a strange sight. It all seemed like a play, like a drama that was being enacted for entertainment. It did not seem real. Men would say, "After you," as they made some woman comfortable and stepped back. I afterward heard someone say that men went downstairs into the restaurant. Many of them smoked. Many of them walked up and down. For a while after we reached the water we watched the ship. We could hear the band. Every light was shining.

'The man in the back of the boat, a quartermaster they said he was, told us to row away from the big steamer. I was getting cold. I took off my lifebelt because I knew how cold the water was and I felt that if I were to be drowned I wanted it over quickly – they say it takes but two minutes. I did not wish to linger. I figured it all out, and then I got an oar. In this way I managed to keep warm.

'It was just midnight as we dropped down to the water, perhaps a minute or so after. It did not seem long before there was a great sweep of water which went over us all. A great wave rose once and then fell, and we knew that the steamer was gone. We could see as plainly as if it had been day. There may have been many swimming but we had rowed at least a mile and a half by the time the steamer went down, and I saw none of this. I saw no dead people.

'To me there was not one tragic, harrowing element near me. We were in a boat, we were safe and we were at work. I was simply fascinated. In a few moments the man in the back of the boat began to complain that we had no chance. There were only three men in the boat. For at least three hours he seemed to break the monotony of it.

'We stood him patiently, and then after he had told us that we had no chance, told us many times, and after he had explained that we had no food, no water, and no compass I told him to be still or he would go overboard. Then he was quiet. I rowed because I would have frozen to death. I made them all row. It saved their lives.

'Soon after the steamer went down we began to see the other boats. In the haze, with a sea as calm as glass, we talked to two boats which were near us. All of us, 16 boats in all, waved back and forth to each other in the growing dawn. A strange man sat in the back of the boat. He seemed to be a foreigner. He never moved his hands once. I wonder why he did not freeze to death. He had on kid gloves and a monocle, which he never once dropped out of his eye. We picked up one man and I put him to work rowing and put some of our clothes around him.

'A little while after the steamer dived down we saw plainly a fishing boat. We pulled hard to try to get near it, but it faded away in the mist. I think we rowed at least nine miles altogether in trying to reach this fishing boat, and in rowing back to where we believed we should wait for help. Then, suddenly, like a streak of lightning over the edge of the sky shot the searchlight of the *Carpathia*. I knew we were saved, and I began to look about me. She must have been 10 miles away then. I made them keep on rowing, for I knew they might even then freeze before we were reached.

'Then, knowing that we were safe at last, I looked about me. The most wonderful dawn I have ever seen came upon us. I have just returned from Egypt. I have been all over the world, but I have never seen anything like this. First the grey and then the flood of light. Then the sun came up in a ball of red fire.

'For the first time we saw where we were. Near us was open water, but on every side was ice. Ice 10 feet [*c.* three metres] high was everywhere, and to the right and left and back and front were icebergs. This sea of ice was 40 miles wide, they told me. Imagine some artist able to picture what we saw from that boat at dawn in that field of ice, with the red sun playing on those giant icebergs.

'We did not wait for the *Carpathia* to come to us. We rowed towards it. We were picked up at 7 a.m. We were lifted up in a sort of nice little sling that was lowered down to us. After that it was all over. The passengers of the *Carpathia* were so afraid that we would not have room enough that they gave us practically the whole ship to ourselves.

'I was hurrying here to see my son who is in Medford, Oregon. He was married very young and went out there to live. His baby is ill, and, of course, I had to get home to see what I could do. I left my daughter in Paris, and am going back in May. We are to visit friends in London. I have not been made afraid by my experience. I have no fear of water. I simply did what was to be done. For 15 years I have laboured in Denver with Judge Lindsey in rescue work, and when my time came I did what I could.'

It has been learned that the women passengers of the *Titanic* who were rescued refer to 'Lady Margaret', as they call Mrs Brown, as the strength of them all.

17

Arthur Peuchen, First Class Passenger

Major Peuchen was a Canadian army major. At this point in the night the boat deck seems still very much for first class passengers only; Peuchen describes with admiration how an officer drove a hundred stokers 'like a lot of sheep, right off the deck'. Working deep down in the ship's boiler rooms, stokers would fully understand that *Titanic* really was going to sink. By now it was almost an hour and a half after water had started pouring into the great ship's boiler rooms.

Peuchen accurately describes *Titanic's* near collision with the *New York* when leaving Southampton. This incident was later referred to by many survivors as a bad omen.

US Senate Inquiry (inquiry question is followed immediately by witness's answer) Major, I wish you would tell the committee in your own way, beginning from the time you boarded the ship, the *Titanic*, at Southampton, the condition of the weather on the voyage; whether or not any accident occurred before the collision where the boat was lost; whether there was any fire aboard the ship between Southampton and the place of the catastrophe; whether you saw any drill of officers or men; and as nearly as you can, in your own way, what took place from the time the *Titanic* sailed. You may proceed in your own way and take your own time, and you will not be interrupted until you finish. *Witness answers:* The day was a fine day. Shortly after leaving our pier our wash or suction caused some trouble at the head of the pier that we were going around, at which there were two or three boats of the same company as our boat. There was considerable excitement on those boats on account of the snapping of their mooring lines, but there was no excitement on ours, the *Titanic*. There was also excitement on the wharves when the larger ship commenced to snap one or two of her moorings. But I do not think there was any accident.

The smaller boat, I think, was the *New York*. She drifted away, not being under steam and having no control of herself. The result was that she was helpless. At first she drifted to our stern, and then afterwards she drifted along and got very near our bows. I think we stopped our boat and we were simply standing still. They got a tug or two to take hold of the *New York* and they moved her out of harm's way. I should think we were delayed probably three quarters of an hour by this trouble. Then we moved out of the harbour.

The weather up to the time of Sunday was pleasant. There was very little wind; it was quite calm. Everything seemed to be running very smoothly on the steamer, and there was nothing that occurred. There was no mention of fire in any way. In fact, it was a very pleasant voyage up to Sunday evening. We were all pleased with the way the new steamer was progressing and we had hopes of arriving in New York quite early on Wednesday morning. Do you wish me to go on further?

Go right along. I wish you to complete your statement, in your own way, up to the time you went on board the *Carpathia*. *Witness answers:* It would be a rather long story.

Well, I want it in the record, Major. *Witness answers:* Sunday evening I dined with my friends, Markleham Molson, Mr Allison, and Mrs Allison; and their daughter was there for a short time. The dinner was an exceptionally good dinner. It seemed to be a better bill of fare than usual, although they are all good. After dinner my friends and I went to the sitting-out room and had some coffee. I left the friends I had dined with about nine o'clock, I think, or a little later. I then went up to the smoking room and joined Mr Beatty, Mr McCaffry, and another English gentleman who was going to Canada. We sat chatting and smoking there until probably 20 minutes after 11, or it may have been a little later than that. I then bid them good night and went to my room. I probably stopped, going down, but I had only reached my room and was starting to undress when I felt as though a heavy wave had struck our ship. She quivered under it somewhat. If there had been a sea running I would simply have thought it was an unusual wave which had struck the boat; but knowing that it was a calm night and that it was an unusual thing to occur on a calm night, I immediately put my overcoat on and went up on deck. As I started to go through the grand stairway I met a friend, who said, 'Why, we have struck an iceberg.'

Give his name, if you can. *Witness answers:* I cannot remember his name. He was simply a casual acquaintance I had met. He said, 'If you will go up on the upper deck' or 'If you will go up on A deck, you will see the ice on the fore part of the ship.' So I did so. I went up there. I suppose the ice had fallen inside the rail, probably four to four and a half feet. It looked like shell ice, soft ice. But you could see it quite plainly along the bow of the boat. I stood on deck for a few minutes, talking to other friends, and then I went to see my friend, Mr Hugo Ross, to tell him that it was not serious; that we had only struck an iceberg. I also called on Mr Molson at his room, but he was out. I afterwards saw Mr Molson on deck and we chatted over the matter, and I suppose 15 minutes after that I met Mr Hays, his son-in-law, and I said to him, 'Mr Hays, have you seen the ice?' He said, 'No.' I said, 'If you care to see it I will take you up on the deck and show it to you.' So we proceeded from probably C deck to A deck and along forward, and I showed Mr Hays the ice forward. I happened to look and noticed the boat was listing, probably half an hour after my first visit to the upper deck. I said to Mr Hays, 'Why, she is listing; she should not do that, the water is perfectly calm, and the boat has stopped.' I felt that looked rather serious. He said, 'Oh, I don't know; you cannot sink this boat.' He had a good deal of confidence. He said, 'No matter what we have struck, she is good for eight or 10 hours.'

I hardly got back in the grand staircase – I probably waited around there 10 minutes more – when I saw the ladies and gentlemen all coming in off the deck looking very serious, and I caught up to Mr Beatty, and I said, 'What is the matter?' He said, 'Why the order is for lifebelts and boats.' I could not believe it at first, it seemed so sudden. I said, 'Will you tell Mr Ross?' He said, 'Yes; I will go and see Mr Ross.' I then went to my cabin and changed as quickly as I could from evening dress to heavy clothes. As soon as I got my overcoat on I got my life preserver and I came out of my cabin.

In the hallway I met a great many people, ladies and gentlemen, with their lifebelts on, and the ladies were crying, principally, most of them. It was a very serious sight, and I commenced to realise how serious matters were. I then proceeded up to the boat deck, and I saw that they had cleared away.

Pardon me one moment. Were you still on C deck? *Witness answers:* I was on C deck when I came out and saw the people standing in the corridor near the grand stairway. I then proceeded upstairs to the boat deck, which is the deck above A.

I saw the boats were all ready for action; that is, the covers had been taken off them, and the ropes cleared, ready to lower. This was on the port side. I was standing near by the Second Officer, and the Captain was standing there as well, at that time. The Captain said – I do not know whether it was the Captain or the Second Officer said – 'We will have to get these masts out of these boats, and also the sail.' He said, 'You might give us a hand,' and I jumped in the boat, and we got a knife and cut the lashings of the mast, which is a very heavy mast, and also the sail, and moved it out of the boat, saying it would not be required. Then there was a cry, as soon as that part was done, that they were ready to put the women in; so the women came forward one by one. A great many women came with their husbands.

Just a second, before you come to that. What number boat did you get into? I got into – I think it was – the first large boat forward on the port side, and I imagine, from the way they number those boats, the emergency boat is 2, and the first large one is 4, and the next one is 6. I am not sure about that.

Beginning to count from the forward end? From the forward end; from the bow.

On the port side? On the port side. This was the largest lifeboat – the first large lifeboat toward the bow on the port side. They would only allow women in that boat, and the men had to stand back.

Was there any order to that effect given? That was the order. The Second Officer stood there and he carried out that to the limit. He allowed no men except the sailors, who were manning the boat, but there were no passengers that I saw got into that boat.

How many sailors? I am not sure, but I imagine there were about four. As far as my memory serves me, there were about four. I was busy helping and assisting to get the ladies in. After a reasonable complement of ladies had got aboard, she was lowered, but I did not see one single passenger get in that first boat.

You mean male passenger? Yes; male passenger.

Did you see any attempt to get in? No; I never saw such order. It was perfect order. The discipline was splendid. The officers were carrying out their duty and I think the passengers behaved splendidly. I did not see a cowardly act by any man.

Was the boat safely lowered? The boat was loaded, but I think they could have taken more in this boat. They took, however, all the ladies that offered to get in at that point.

Was the boat safely lowered? Oh, very; the boat was safely lowered.

Who was in it that you know of? I should say about – I do not know – I imagine about 26 or 27. There was room for more. Then, as soon as that boat was lowered, we turned our attention to the next. I might say that I was rather surprised that the sailors were not at their stations, as I have seen fire drill very often on steamers where they all stand at attention, so many men at the bow and stern of these lifeboats. They seemed to be short of sailors around the lifeboats that were being lowered at this particular point. I do not know what was taking place in other parts of the steamer.

There was one act, sir, I would like to mention a little ahead of my story. When I came on deck first, on this upper deck, there were, it seems to me, about a hundred stokers came up with their dunnage bags, and they seemed to crowd this whole deck in front of the boats. One of the officers – I do not know which one, but a very powerful one – came along and drove these men right off that deck. It was a splendid act.

Off the boat deck? Off the boat deck. He drove them, every man, like a lot of sheep, right off the deck.

Where did they go? I do not know. He drove them right ahead of him, and they disappeared. I do not know where they went, but it was a splendid act. They did not put up any resistance. I admired him for it. I had finished with the lowering of the first boat from the port side. We then proceeded to boat No. 2 or No. 4 or No. 6; I do not know which it is called.

You had stepped into the boat to assist in lowering it? Yes; and then got out of it again.

And you stepped out of it? I only got into the boat to assist in taking out the mast and the sail.

I understand. Then you got out again? Then I got out again, and I assisted the ladies into the boat. We then went to the next boat and we did the same thing – got the mast and the sail out of that. There was a quartermaster in the boat, and one sailor, and we commenced to put the ladies in that boat. After that boat had got a full complement of ladies, there were no more ladies to get in, or if there were any other ladies to get in they did not wish to do so, because we were calling out for them – that is, speaking of the port side – but some would not leave their husbands.

Do you know who they were? I only saw one or two stand by who would not get in. Whether they afterwards left them I cannot say, but I saw one or two women refuse to get in on that account.

Did you see any woman get in and then get out because her husband was not with her? No, I do not think I did. I saw one lady where they had to sort of pull her away from her husband, he insisting upon her going to the boat and she did not want to go. The boat was then lowered down.

Pardon me a moment. How many were put into this second boat? I did not know at the time of the lowering, but as I happened to be a passenger later on, they were counted and there were exactly 20 women, one quartermaster, one sailor, and one stowaway that made his appearance after we had been out about an hour.

23 all together? 23 all together; before I was a passenger. After that the boat was lowered down some distance, I should imagine probably parallel with C deck, when the quartermaster called up to the officer and said, 'I cannot manage this boat with only one seaman.'

Where was this call from? As the boat was going down, I should think about the third deck. So he made this call for assistance, and the Second Officer leaned over and saw he was quite right in his statement, that he had only one man in the boat, so they said, 'We will have to have some more seamen here,' and I did not think they were just at hand, or they may have been getting the next boat ready. However, I was standing by the officer, and I said, 'Can I be of any assistance? I am a yachtsman, and can handle a boat with an average man.' He said, 'Why, yes. I will order you to the boat in preference to a sailor.'

Pardon me right there. Who was this man then in the boat? He was one of the quartermasters. The Captain was standing still by him at that time, and I think, although the officer ordered me to the boat, the Captain said, 'You had better go down below and break a window and get in through a window, into the boat.'

The Captain said that? Yes. That was his suggestion; and I said I did not think it was feasible, and I said I could get in the boat if I could get hold of a rope. However, we got hold of a loose rope in some way that was hanging from the davit, near the block anyway, and by getting hold of it I swung myself off the ship, and lowered myself into the boat.

How far did you have to swing yourself? The danger was jumping off from the boat. It was not after I got a straight line; it was very easy lowering. But I imagine it was opposite the C deck at the time. On getting into the boat I went aft in the lifeboat, and said to the quartermaster, 'What do you want me to do?' He said, 'Get down and put that plug in,' and I made a dive down for the plug, and the ladies pretty well aft, and I could not see at all. It was dark down there. I felt with my hands, and I said it would be better for him to do it and me do his work, and I said, 'Now, you get down and put in the plug, and I will undo the shackles,' that is, take the blocks off. So he dropped the blocks, and he got down, and he came rushing back to assist me, and he said, 'Hurry up.' He said, 'This boat is going to founder.' I thought he meant our lifeboat was going to founder. I thought he had had some difficulty in finding the plug, or he had not gotten it in properly. But he meant the large boat was going to founder, and that we were to hurry up and get away from it. So we got the rudder in, and he told me to go forward and take an oar. I went forward and got an oar on the port side of the lifeboat; the sailor was on my left, on the starboard side. But we were just opposite each other in rowing.

Who was the sailor? He was the man who gave evidence just before me.

Mr Fleet, from the lookout? From the lookout, yes; sitting next to me on my left. He told us to row as hard as possible away from the suction. Just as we got rowing out part of the way, this stowaway, an Italian ...

Pardon me. Did the officer say to row away, so as to get away from the suction? The quartermaster who was in charge of our boat told us to row as hard as we could to get away from this suction, and just as we got a short distance away this stowaway made his appearance. He was an Italian by birth, I should think, who had a broken wrist or arm, and he was of no use to us to row. He got an oar out, but he could not do much, so we got him to take the oar in.

Where did he make his appearance from, Major? Underneath; I think he was stowed away underneath. I should imagine if there was any room for him to get underneath the bow of the boat he would be there. I imagine that was where he came from. He was not visible when looking at the boat. There were only two men when she was lowered.

Would you know him if you should see him? No, it was dark. At daylight I was rowing very hard – in the morning – and I did not notice. As we rowed, pulled away from the *Titanic*, there was an officer's call of some kind. We stopped rowing.

A whistle? A sort of a whistle. Anyway, the quartermaster told us to stop rowing so he could hear it, and this was a call to come back to the boat. So we all thought we ought to go back to the boat. It was a call. But the quartermaster said, 'No, we are not going back to the boat.' He said, 'It is our lives now, not theirs,' and he insisted upon our rowing farther away.

Who made the rebellion against it? I think the rebellion was made by some of the married women that were leaving their husbands.

And did you join in that? I did not say anything. I knew I was perfectly powerless. He was at the rudder. He was a very talkative man. He had been swearing a great deal, and was very disagreeable. I had had one row with him. I asked him to come and row, to assist us in rowing, and let some woman steer the boat, as it was a perfectly calm night. It did not require any skill for steering. The stars were out. He refused to do it, and he told me he was in command of that boat, and I was to row.

Did he remain at the tiller? He remained at the tiller, and if we wanted to go back while he was in possession of the tiller, I do not think we could have done so. The women were in between the quartermaster and myself and the other seaman. The night was cold and we kept rowing on. Then he imagined he saw a light. I have done a good deal of yachting in my life, I have owned a yacht for six years and have been out on the Lakes, and I could not see these lights. I saw a reflection. He thought it was a boat of some kind. He thought probably it might be a buoy out there of some kind, and he called out to the next boat, which was within hearing, asking if he knew if there was any buoy around there. This struck me as being perfectly absurd, and showed me the man did not know anything about navigating, expecting to see a buoy in the middle of the Atlantic. However, he insisted upon us rowing. We kept on rowing toward this imaginary light and, after a while, after we had gone on a distance – I am ahead of my story. We commenced to hear signs of the breaking up of the boat.

Of the *Titanic*? Of the *Titanic*. At first I kept my eyes watching the lights, as long as possible.

From your position in the boat, did you face it? I was facing it at this time. I was rowing this way, and afterwards I changed to the other way. We heard a sort of a call for help after this whistle I described a few minutes ago. This was the officer calling us back. We heard a sort of a rumbling sound and the lights were still on at the rumbling sound, as far as my memory serves me; then a sort of an explosion, then another. It seemed to be one, two, or three rumbling sounds, then the lights went out. Then the dreadful calls and cries.

For help? We could not distinguish the exact cry for assistance; moaning and crying; frightful. It affected all the women in our boat whose husbands were among these; and this went on for some time, gradually getting fainter, fainter. At first it was horrible to listen to.

How far was it away? I think we must have been five eighths of a mile, I should imagine, when this took place. It was very hard to guess the distance. There were only two of us rowing a very heavy boat with a good many people in it, and I do not think we covered very much ground.

While these cries of distress were going on, did anyone in the boat urge the quartermaster to return? Yes; some of the women did. But, as I said before, I had had a row with him, and I said to the women, 'It is no use you arguing with that man, at all. It is best not to discuss matters with him.' He said it was no use going back there, there was only a lot of stiffs there, later on, which was very unkind, and the women resented it very much. I do not think he was qualified to be a quartermaster.

As a matter of fact, you did not return to the boat? We did not return to the boat.

After you left its side? No.

And when the boat went down, were you looking toward it? I was looking toward the boat; yes.

Did you see it? I saw it when the lights went out. You could not tell very much after the lights went out.

You were not close enough to recognise anyone aboard? Oh, no.

Could you see the outlines of the people on the deck? No; you could not. I could only see the outline of the boat, you might say.

Do you know how she went down? While the lights were burning, I saw her bow pointing down and the stern up; not in a perpendicular position, but considerable.

About what angle? I should think an angle of not as much as 45 degrees.

From what you saw, do you think the boat was intact, or had it broken in two? It was intact at that time. I feel sure that an explosion had taken place in the boat, because in passing the wreck the next morning – we steamed past it – I just happened to think of this, which may be of some assistance to this inquiry – I was standing forward, looking to see if I could see any dead bodies, or any of my friends, and to my surprise I saw the barber's pole floating. The barber's pole was on the C deck, my recollection is – the barber shop – and that must have been a tremendous explosion to allow this pole to have broken from its fastenings and drift with the wood.

Did you hear the explosions? Yes, sir; I heard the explosions.

How loud were they? Oh, a sort of a rumbling sound. It was not a sharp sound – more of a rumbling kind of a sound, but still sharp at the same time. It would not be as loud as a clap of thunder, or anything that way, or like a boiler explosion, I should not think.

Were these explosions evidently from under the water? I should think they were from above. I imagined that the decks had blown up with the pressure, pulling the boat down, bow on, this heavyweight, and the air between the decks; that is my theory of the explosion. I do not know whether it is correct or not, but I do not think it was the boilers. I think it was the pressure, that heavy weight shoving that down, the water rushing up, and the air coming between the decks; something had to go.

How many explosions did you hear? I am not absolutely certain of this, because there was a good deal of excitement at the time, but I imagine there were three, one following the other very quickly.

Did you see the Captain after he told you to go below and get through the window into the lifeboat? No; I never saw him after that.

From what you saw of the Captain, was he alert and watchful? He was doing everything in his power to get women in these boats, and to see that they were lowered properly. I thought he was doing his duty in regard to the lowering of the boats, sir.

Who was the officer with you on your side of the boat? The Second Officer.

Mr Lightoller? Yes, sir.

Had you seen the Captain before that night? I passed him in one of the companionways some place, just about dinner time.

What time? I cannot be very certain as to the hour; around seven o'clock, I imagine. I generally come out to dress about seven o'clock.

What time did you dine that night? I dined a little after seven; I think it was a quarter after.

In the main dining room? In the main dining room; yes.

Did the Captain dine in that room? I do not think so. I think he dined in the other – in the restaurant.

But you did not see him? I did not see him dining.

I wish you would say whether or not these lifeboats were equipped with food and water and lights. *Witness answers:* As far as I could tell, our boat was equipped with everything in that respect. I heard some talk that there was not proper food in some of the boats, and when I was on the *Carpathia* I made it my business to go down and look at one or two, and I found hard-tack in this sealed box.

In both of them? On the boat. I did not go all around the fleet.

You say you looked at one or two? One or two.

Did you find provisions and water in both? I did not examine the kegs, but I was assured by the sailors there was water in them.

Did you see lights in them? We had lights in our boat, but some of the other boats did not. I know there was a boat that hung near us that had not lights. Whether it was on account of not being able to light their lights I do not know.

You say there were 36 or 37 people in your boat? No, sir.

In the first boat that was lowered? No; I said I thought about 26 or 27.

In the first one? Yes; I think so.

And 23 in the second boat before you got in? Including the stowaway there would be 23. I made the 24th.

20 women? 20 women, yes; the quartermaster, one seaman, the stowaway, and then when I got in there were 24.

Any children? No; I do not think we had any children. Later on we tied up to another boat, toward morning, for a very short time – I think for about 15 minutes.

What boat was that? I do not know. Our quartermaster did not know the number of our boat. I do not know the other. I know they called out and asked the number of our boat and our quartermaster did not know which it was.

Did you hear the testimony given this morning by the Third Officer [Herbert Pitman, see chapter 5]? I heard part of it, sir. I was out in the hall while he was giving some of it.

Did you hear him say that a lifeboat was attached to his lifeboat for a while? Yes; but, then, let me see; did he not say he took some people off that boat?

I was going to come to that. *Witness answers:* No; that was not our boat.

He said he took three people out of his lifeboat. *Witness answers:* And put them into the one attached.

That was not done in your boat? No. The only thing that occurred with the boat we were tied up with was, we asked how many men they had in their boat, and this quartermaster said he had about seven sailors, or something like that – six or seven.

Then we said, 'Surely you can spare us one man, if you have so many,' and we got a fireman.

You got a fireman? One more man out of that boat.

They transferred one more man to you? Yes; one more man.

What did he do? He assisted in rowing on the starboard side of the lifeboat, and I rowed on the port side.

Did any of the women help with the oars? Yes; they did, very pluckily, too. We got the oars. Before this occurred we got a couple of women rowing aft, on the starboard side of our boat, and I got two women to assist on our side; but of course the woman with me got sick with the heavy work, and she had to give it up. But I believe the others kept on rowing quite pluckily for a considerable time.

Do you know who these women were at the oars? I know one of them. Miss M. E. A. Norton, Apsley Villa, Horn Lane, Acton, London.

Is that the only one of the women who handled the oars that you know by name? No; I think there is another.

The other two women who handled the oars you do not know? I do not know their names.

Do you know any other passengers on your lifeboat? There are several who put their names on the back of that card.

Can you read them? Mrs Walter Clark, 2155 West Adams Street, Los Angeles, Cal.; Miss E. Bowerman, Thorncliff, St Leonards-on-Sea, England; Mrs Lucien P. Smith, Huntington, W. Va.; Mrs Martin Rothschild, 753 West End Avenue, New York; Mrs Tyrell Cavendish, Driftwood, Monmouth; Mrs Edgar J. Mayer [Meyer], 158 West Eighty-Sixth Street, New York; Mrs Walter Douglas, Deepshaven, Mass.; Mrs J. J. Brown, Denver.

Major, at any time between leaving the side of the *Titanic* and reaching the *Carpathia*, did Mrs Douglas hold the tiller? I think the Quartermaster was at the tiller all the time, with the exception probably of a couple of minutes. I know he asked one of the ladies for some brandy, and he also asked for one of her wraps, which he got.

The officer did? The Quartermaster, not the officer.

Do you know Mrs Douglas? Yes.

Was her husband [Walter Douglas] lost? Yes, sir.

You say when the impact occurred, the ship shuddered? When the impact occurred, describing it I would say it would be like a wave striking it, a very heavy wave.

How soon after that did the boat begin to list? I should think about 25 minutes afterwards.

So far as you could observe, did the passengers have on lifebelts? They had.

Before you left the boat, so you can say from your own knowledge they had them on? I say if they had not them on, I think they could have gotten them all right. I did not hear of any shortage of life preservers, or of any complaints, rather.

Did you have any light on your lifeboat? Yes; we did.

What was the colour? Just an ordinary white light.

Not a green light? No.

But a white light? Yes.

Did you see other lights on lifeboats? Yes. We could see those different lifeboats that had lights. They were all over. They were not all staying together at all. Some of them were going east, west, north, and south, it seemed to me, but there was one boat that had a sort of an electric light, and one a sort of a bluish light, as well, which we thought at first was a steamer or something.

I believe you said you have had considerable experience as a mariner? Yes, sir.

Can you say whether the *Titanic* listed to the starboard or port side? She listed to the starboard side; the side she was struck on.

Did she go down by the bow or by the head? *Witness answers:* Eventually, you mean?

Yes. *Witness answers:* She was down by the bow.

Where was this impact on the bow of the ship? It was aft of the bow about 40 feet [*c.* 12 metres], I should imagine, on the starboard side – about 40 or 50 feet [*c.* 12–15 metres], I should imagine from where the ice started to come off the iceberg.

You say you saw some ice on the deck? Yes, sir.

Do you know of anyone being injured by ice on the deck? No; but I know a great many of the passengers were made afraid by this iceberg passing their portholes. The ship shoved past this ice, and a great many of them told me afterwards they could not understand this thing moving past them – those that were awakened at the time. In fact, it left ice on some of the portholes, they told me.

Do you know of your own knowledge whether any alarm was sounded to arouse the passengers from their rooms after the impact? There was no alarm sounded whatever. In fact, I talked with two young ladies who claimed to have had a very narrow escape. They said their stateroom was right near the Astors', I think almost next to it, and they were not awakened.

They were not awakened? They slept through this crash, and they were awakened by Mrs Astor. She was in rather an excited state, and their door being open – and I think the Astor door was open – they think that was the means of their being saved.

On what deck were they? I do not know, sir. It was only conversation told me on the *Carpathia*.

I think you said that from your judgement and from your own observation there was no general alarm given? No, I did not hear one. I was around the boat all the time.

After getting aboard the *Carpathia*, did you learn the latitude and longitude in which the boats were picked up? No, sir; I did not. All I know is that when I made inquiries for the nearest port, I was told it was 36 hours' sail to Halifax.

Did you see those lifeboats on the port side of the ship? Were you on the port side? I was on the port side.

Did you see them on the starboard side? No, sir. We heard afterwards that the officers on the starboard side were more generous in allowing the men in than on the port side. That is what I heard afterwards; that some of the officers on the starboard side had allowed some of the men into the boats.

You were on the same side with Mr Lightoller? That was the port side; yes.

And on that side they did not permit but two men to get into the first boat? I think there were four sailors in the first boat, sir.

Not more than four? I would not be certain about that, sir. They did not allow any male passengers; that is what I mean.

Did you see any lifeboat that was caught in the gear or tackle? No; the boats I saw lowered away very nicely, indeed, in a very short time.

Did you see any collapsible boat [lifeboats A, B, C & D] lowered? No; I think our boat left before they started to get those out.

Were those lifeboats taken aboard the *Carpathia*? I think two or three boats were allowed to drift. One, I think, had some dead bodies in it. I saw two, at least, drifting away. I was afraid they could not take care of more.

You saw two or three drifting away? That is, after they let them go.

Did you see any dead bodies in those drifting boats? No; I saw dead bodies in one of the boats that came up, lying in the bow. I do not know whether that was set adrift or not. I was told that one boat contained three bodies.

Did you see Mr Ismay that night? I saw him. I think I saw him standing for a moment without his hat on; just a moment, on the port side.

On the boat deck? On the boat deck; yes.

What time? I should say it would be probably an hour after we had struck the iceberg.

An hour after you struck the iceberg? I would not be certain. I think it was Mr Ismay. I think I saw him standing for a moment.

What was he doing; anything? Not at that time.

You did not see him after that? I did not see him after that except on coming aboard the *Carpathia*.

Did you see Mr Hays after he passed this word with you about the icebergs? Yes I saw him again on the upper deck just before I started to help with the boats.

That is the last time you saw him? Yes. I shook hands with him then and he said, 'This boat is good for eight hours. I have just been getting this from one of the best old seamen, Mr Crossley' – I think he mentioned his name – 'of Milwaukee,' and some person else; and he said, 'Before that time, we will have assistance.'

Did you know of the proximity of the *Titanic* to ice on Sunday? No, sir. All I know is that there was a big change in the temperature between the afternoon and the time I went on deck later on in the evening.

Did that indicate anything unusual to you? I had only had experience once before among icebergs, and it was cold, and a similar change took place in the weather.

What was the movement of the ship after the collision with the iceberg? After the collision it seemed to me, not immediately, but after a short space of time, it sounded as though we were reversing.

What effect did that have upon the progress of the ship, if you noticed? She still was going, even if they were reversing for a certain period.

Did you observe how long she continued to go ahead? No; I did not.

Did you form any idea as to how far she had gone beyond the iceberg, after striking it, before she stopped? No. I was really too much interested in changing my clothes and in my friends, and I really did not pay any attention to that.

Have you any idea how far you were away from the iceberg when you took to the lifeboat? We took to the lifeboat – I should imagine I was in the lifeboat probably an hour after we struck. We had been going ahead at a pretty good rate of speed, and then we had to reverse. I should imagine we would be three miles away from it, I think – at least two and a half miles, probably.

After you took to the lifeboat you proceeded to row in the direction in which the ship had been moving, westward? No; we started right off from the port side of the boat directly straight off from her about amidship, on the port side, right directly north, I think it would be, because the Northern Lights appeared where this light we had been looking at in that direction appeared shortly afterwards.

When did you first see an iceberg? Just after daybreak or just a little before daybreak.

Can you give us an idea of how far you probably were at that time from where the *Titanic* went down? I should imagine we would be probably two miles, and we kept on rowing for this imaginary light for some time.

How far away from you was this iceberg, and in what direction? There were several icebergs. There were at least three icebergs that you could see plainly. There was one toward the front, the way our boat was facing, and one on the west. I should think there was one toward the north and one toward the south. We seemed to be in a nest of icebergs, with some smaller ones, of course.

About how many, in all, that you can recall? I think you could see – at least to count, I think – five.

What were about the sizes of them? Two were large; another was sort of smaller in size. Some were jagged, but very high, and a number of them not so high.

These large ones you think were about what height above the water, and what width and length, if you can give us an idea? They were at least 100 feet [*c.* 30 metres] high, two of them, and of a width I should think of 300 feet [*c.* 91 metres] and 400 feet [*c.* 121 metres] long; somewhat like an island.

Major, do you mean for us to understand that at the time lifeboat No. 4 and lifeboat No. 6 on the port side of the ship were loaded and lowered every woman in sight was given an opportunity? Every woman on the port side was given an opportunity. In fact, we had not enough women to put into the boats. We were looking for them. I cannot understand why we did not take some men. The boats would have held more.

If there had been more women there they could have found room in those boats? Plenty of room.

Do you mean to say, too, that so far as you knew and heard and observed no general alarm was given throughout the ship, arousing the passengers, and advising them of their danger? I did not hear any alarm whatever.

Do you know what the method is of giving an alarm in an emergency of that kind? I have never had the experience of an accident at sea before.

Major, can you give us any idea why, if the passengers were equipped with lifebelts, and they were in good condition, those passengers would not float and live for four or five or six hours afterwards? That is something that astonished me very much. I was surprised, when we steamed through this wreckage very slowly after we left the scene of the disaster – we left the ground as soon as this other boat, the *Californian*, I understand, came along – that we did not see any bodies in the water. I understood the *Californian* was going to cruise around, and when she came we started off, and we went right by the wreckage. It was something like two islands, and was strewn along, and I was interested to see if I could see any bodies, and I was surprised to think that with all these deaths that had taken place we could not see one body;

I was very much surprised. I understand a life preserver is supposed to keep up a person, whether dead or alive.

You think the *Carpathia* passed in the immediate vicinity where the *Titanic* went down? No, I would not say the immediate vicinity, because there was a breeze started up at daybreak, and the wreckage would naturally float away from where she went down, somewhat. It might be that it had floated away, probably a mile or half a mile; probably not more than that, considering that the wind only sprang up at daybreak.

You heard sounds of people calling for help when you were, you say, about five eighths of a mile away, when the *Titanic* went down? Yes, sir.

And immediately you heard these cries and then you heard them gradually die out? Yes, sir.

Is it your idea that the water was so cold that a person could not live in it except for a short time? I feel quite sure that a person could not live in that water very long. Those who had been in the water had their feet frozen; that is, those who were standing up in a boat in the water. I happened to have the cabin with three of them who were rescued, and they said they sustained their life by punching each other during the two or three hours they stood up. The minute anyone got tired and sat down in the water, or at least very shortly thereafter, he floated off the raft, dead, I believe.

What was the temperature of the water, if you know? I do not know, sir.

You say people were frozen? Their feet were frozen; yes, sir.

Was that by exposure, after being taken out of the water on the boat? Yes, sir. A number of them swam, I know of three cases, at least, where they jumped from the big boat and swam and got on to a raft which was partly submerged in the water, and they stood up in the raft, and those are the ones whose feet were badly swollen or frozen.

You assume from that that the water was very cold? I am sure it was.

Was it below the freezing point? It must have been very near the freezing point, anyway. It probably would not be quite freezing; but it being salt water, of course it would not freeze very readily.

Was there any floating ice, aside from these icebergs? Oh, yes; when we started to steam away we passed a lot of floating ice, I suppose several miles long.

You mean the *Carpathia* steamed through the ice? Yes.

Did you come into contact with floating ice while you were on the lifeboat? No, sir; we did not.

Have you any idea as to how long a person could live in water like that? It depends on his constitution, but I should imagine that if a person could stay in the water a half an hour he would be doing very well.

Would not the effort to swim, and exercise, prevent one getting numb for several hours? Up to a certain point; yes. But I do not think a man could live an hour in that water.

Did you observe in this wreckage any broken pieces of life preservers, corks, and things of that sort? There was a very large quantity of floating cork. I am at a loss to understand where it came from. There were a great many chairs in the water; all the steamer chairs were floating and pieces of wreckage; but there was a particularly large quantity of cork.

What was the appearance of the cork? Did it look as if it had come from life preservers? *Witness answers:* I was not near enough to tell that. I would not like to pass an opinion, but it looked like cork to me.

You said, I believe, that there seemed to be a lack of competent sailors to take charge of the lifeboats? I would not like to say that, sir. I said that they were not at their stations, ready to man the boats. I imagine this crew was what we would call in yachting terms a scratch crew, brought from different vessels. They might be the best, but they had not been accustomed to working together.

Did you see any other boats filled – that is, loaded – and lowered? Those were the only two I saw filled and lowered.

Did you see the boats as the *Carpathia* reached them? Did the boats come to the *Carpathia* or did the *Carpathia* go around and pick up the boats? *Witness answers:* I do not know whether she came to anchor; I think probably she did. However, she was in the lee of all the boats. That is, we had all come down; we were to the weather of the *Carpathia*, and so she stayed there until we all came down on her.

Did you observe in what manner these boats reached the *Carpathia*? What position was your boat in, for instance, among the first or the last? *Witness answers:* I think there were about two or three after us. We were almost the last. We were about the last, with the exception of two or three.

Did you observe the condition of those boats, as to whether they were all loaded to their capacity or not at that time, at the time you saw them unloaded? I saw some of the boats come in; one boat particularly was very full, had a large number of passengers. She seemed to be crowded right down. Whether they had taken on more in the water, I do not know.

Do you know what boat that was – the number of it, or the officer in charge? No, sir; there seemed to be a lot of steerage or second class passengers on that boat; but still, I did not know them by sight.

Was it a collapsible boat [lifeboats A, B, C & D]? No; that was one of the regular lifeboats.

The boat you were in, you say, could have carried how many more people than you had? Well, I made inquiries, and I was told that those boats were capable of holding from 60 to 65, I suppose according to how they were stowed and how the boat was trimmed and the weight of the passengers; but I should imagine they ought to hold a good number. They seemed very solid and strong boats. I was told by the Second Officer, though, that they could not lower those boats filled to the full capacity. That was the capacity with them floating, according to the figures given.

And the idea was to fill them after they reached the water? It struck me that those boats ought to have a certain capacity on the hooks, and then be loaded up to that capacity; and then they should have some means of filling them in the water.

There were none attempted to be loaded except from the rail? That is the only place I saw any boats loaded, sir.

Referring to that light that you observed, that you said you thought was a hallucination, did that disappear after a while? Yes; it disappeared; but I did not think, from my knowledge of yachting, that it was a boat light. I think it was one of those reflected lights. The Northern Lights were very strong that night. It might have been some reflection on ice. I was not satisfied it was the light of a steamer, by any means.

You could not tell, then, of course, whether it might be a stern light or what sort of a light it might be on a steamer? It was a glare. It was not a distinct light, it was a glare.

Was it as clear a night while you were on the water in this boat as it was prior to the catastrophe? Yes; it was a beautiful night. It was a dark night, but starlit. We could see some distance. We could see another boat without a light, some distance away, by the shadow.

You were how many hours on the water, do you think? I think we were rather late in getting to the *Carpathia*. I imagine that we were at least eight hours on the water.

About what time did you get on the *Carpathia*? It was after eight o'clock that I looked at my watch; it was something after eight o'clock that we got on.

What time did the dawn come? We could just commence to distinguish light, I think, about near four o'clock.

Prior to four o'clock, while you were drifting in the water, did you see any icebergs? No, we did not drift near anything.

When the dawn came, did you find yourself near icebergs? We found that there was a sort of a field of icebergs. There were icebergs in one direction, probably a mile away, and another iceberg in another direction, probably half a mile away, and another iceberg over here, probably five miles away.

Were there any icefields? I did not notice any in the morning. I was busy rowing, because I rowed all the time. But when we started to steam away on the *Carpathia*, I could see this icefield four miles long.

Did you observe any of these icefields before you got on the *Carpathia*? No, I did not. Well, I could see something like an island at a distance, but not as clear as when we got on the *Carpathia*.

But you think when the dawn came the nearest iceberg was about half a mile away? It was farther than that. In rowing the boat I know we thought at first we would have to row close to the iceberg, and we were then about five miles off, at least. It was a question whether we were going to get very close to this island of ice or not. The iceberg was between our boat and the *Carpathia*.

All the icebergs were not between you and the *Carpathia*? No; this was the only one.

And the others were in different directions? Yes.

At all points of the compass? Yes.

How do you account for the fact that you were not able to see any of these icebergs when you were in the water before the dawn and you were able to see a boat? Well, they were a little farther away than the boat; but we picked these icebergs out pretty early in the morning, before dawn. They were dark objects; in fact, we did not know what they were at that time.

Is it your observation that on a night of that kind glasses enable one to get a wider range of vision? Yes; we use glasses at night, especially when the night is bright. There is such a difference in the human eye. Take 12 men on a yacht and one man will see twice as far as another.

Without glasses? Yes, sir.

I mean at night, such a night as you had that night, would glasses add very much to the range of your vision? I think they would. I can see better with glasses at night than I can with my naked eye.

Have you any idea how much they add to the range? For instance, if you look at the moon at night with a glass you can see everything distinctly, and with the naked eye you cannot.

How is it with reference to objects on the sea? I think glasses assist you, provided it is bright enough.

And you think that night was bright enough? I think it would assist. I really think if we had had a searchlight, though, we would have saved the ship.

You say the Second Officer told you that he could not lower the lifeboats safely if they were filled to their capacity? The Second Officer [of the *Carpathia*, James Bisset] sent for me on board the *Carpathia*, as he had heard some complaints from the ladies about this quartermaster [Hichens], and while there I asked him regarding the loading of these boats, and he stated that those boats were filled just nicely for lowering from the height of the deck.

He told you this after the *Titanic* had gone down? Yes. I cannot understand why they have such very heavy block and tackle, if they can only put in such a small number of people, because the tonnage of 24 people is only about a ton and a half, English tons.

Well, Major, some of these boats contained many more people than were in your boat? Yes; but whether they were picked up afterwards or not, I do not know.

Or whether they were lowered from the *Titanic*, you do not know? No, sir.

You heard nothing of that kind while these two boats were being lowered? *Witness answers:* Heard what?

Did you hear the Second Officer say that they could only be partially filled and lowered with safety? No; he made no remark of that kind, sir. I think it was a case that we had no more ladies to put in there.

You had no more ladies to put in, and they were to be lowered without being filled? I do not know exactly what 'filled' means in that sense – filled from the deck. I spoke to the officer about it a couple of days afterwards, and he told me that was the reason they were not filled, that they were just comfortably filled for lowering that distance.

Did you see any rockets fired on the *Titanic* during the 15 or 20 or 30 minutes before her sinking? I do not know as to that time before sinking, but while we were lowering the boat they were sending up rockets.

Sending them from your deck? From the bridge, I should say.

What coloured rockets – red and all colours? A good deal like an ordinary skyrocket, going up and breaking, and the different colours flying down.

Do you know why they were being exploded? Because we wanted assistance.

Did you know that any assistance was available? No. I think if there was any assistance available we should have been told of it when we left the boat. We were rowing around there, and if we had known that some ship was coming we would not have started off rowing for an imaginary light, trying to make a great many miles. I do not know whether they had that information or not.

Did you hear the testimony that there was a light sighted, or a boat sighted about five miles ahead of the *Titanic*, after the collision? I read in the morning paper that some evidence was given yesterday in regard to that.

But you did not hear anything about that on the *Carpathia*? No; and I did not see it.

When you and Mr Hays went forward to look at the ice, how much of it could you see? I should think about four and a half feet [*c.* 1.37 metres] of ice, probably one and a half to two inches [*c.* 4–5 cm] thick. That is, it would be thicker on the rail than it would be on the bow, I heard the men walking over it, and it would crunch under their feet.

Do you mean to be understood as saying that you saw that part of the berg that was sloughed off by the impact? Yes; sort of shaken off. As we went past, this would scrape off.

Did you look at the iceberg itself? Oh, I did not see that; it had passed.

Did you talk with Mr Fleet, the man in the lookout, who was in your lifeboat about this iceberg? Yes. I spoke to him about it.

What did you say to him about it? I was interested when I found he was in the crow's nest, and I said, 'What occurred?' In the conversation he said he rang three bells, and then he signalled to the bridge.

Did he say how far off the iceberg was when he first sighted it? No; he did not tell me that.

Did he say what it looked like when he first saw it? No; he did not go into that. The only thing he said was that he did not get any reply from the bridge.

From the telephone? I heard afterwards that really the officers were not required to reply.

That is, the information is imparted from the crow's nest to the officer at the bridge, and that is the end of that information? I spoke to the Second Officer [Lightoller] on the boat regarding the conversation; and he told me it is simply a matter of whether the officer wishes to reply or not. He gets the information, probably, and acts right on it without attempting to reply to the crow's nest.

Did he tell you anything more about the iceberg and the collision than you have stated? That is all. They had some conversation – the quartermaster was asking them who was on the bridge and they were calling over, and they did not know which officer was on the bridge, and the quartermaster called out to another boat, to the quartermaster or whoever was in charge of the other boat.

Another lifeboat? Yes, sir.

From your boat? Yes, sir; they were not far off.

What did he say? I did not catch the answer.

No; I mean what did the quartermaster say? He said, 'You know one officer was on duty on the bridge at the time we struck.' So far as I could gather, the officer was in command of the other boat. He did not know; he might not have been on duty.

And the lookout in the crow's nest did not seem to know? No.

I would like to ask whether, from what you observed, in your opinion, there was proper discipline on the part of the crew in loading the lifeboats, whether they were loaded systematically and with care, and with consideration for the lives of the passengers, and considering the peril in which they were placed. *Witness answers:* Among those of the crew that I saw working, such as loading the boats, lowering the boats, and filling the boats, the discipline could not have been better.

The discipline could not have been better? No, sir; but there were too few.

Too few of them? Too few, yes. That is, I am only speaking now of the port side of the boat, where I happened to be. I cannot speak of all over the boat.

No. I said from your observation. *Witness answers:* Yes, just from that. I was surprised not to see more sailors at their stations. I was also surprised that the boats were not filled with more people.

Each boat constitutes a station? Yes, that is what I understand.

Each lifeboat? Yes.

And from your observation, do I understand you to say that there was not a sailor at each station? Oh, I do not say that there was not a sailor at each station, but there was not a full complement.

There was not the full complement? No, sir. From what I gathered I understand that these men had been told off; that is, that each man had been assigned to his station, but they had had no practice, from what I learned from talking with the crew.

Did you see any drill yourself? Oh, no; there was no drill. As a rule Sunday is the day they do some drilling; but I did not see any drilling on Sunday.

Would you have been likely to see it if it had occurred? Yes. It is very interesting and I always like to see it. There is always the bugle sounding the call. I have seen it, crossing, many times, the fire drill and the boat drill.

Did you, before or after the *Titanic* struck, learn that it was officially known to the ship, on Sunday, that there were icebergs on or near her track? I heard it afterwards, but not before.

Not before Sunday? I heard, on the *Carpathia*, that they were expecting icebergs or ice.

From whom did you hear it? I heard the Third Officer [Pitman] just mention it, casually, to two or three of them, that they knew that there was ice; that they were approaching ice.

What time of day was this? I do not know. It was on the fore part of the *Carpathia*.

The fore part of the journey on the *Carpathia*? Yes.

Did they seem to be quite agreed that that was the case, or was there some dispute about it? No; there was no dispute. This was just a casual remark that was made.

I think that is all, Major. *Witness answers:* Could I make just a little statement, sir? It will not be very long. I have been quoted as making a great many statements or as saying several things, and I would like to just put this straight. I do not criticise Captain Smith, but I do criticise the policy and methods pursued by the company, for I feel sure that in this case caution would have been of every virtue and would have averted the terrible calamity. I have been given the credit of saying many things which are absolutely untrue and I wish to state that I have not said any personal or unkind thing about Captain Smith. I have been quoted as saying some very unkind things about the late captain, but I assure you I have never made any statement of that kind.

Did you ever sail with him before? No, sir.

Is that all you care to say, Major? That is all. I am here, sir, more on account of the poor women that came off our boat. They asked me if I would come and tell this court of inquiry what I had seen, and when you wired me, sir, I came at once, without being pressed in any way, simply to carry out my promise to the poor women on our boat.

18
Robert Hichens, Quartermaster

Quartermasters were experienced sailors who assisted the ship's officers on the bridge. Hichens was at the wheel when *Titanic* struck the iceberg and responded to First Officer Murdoch's order to turn 'Hard astarboard'.

Hichens came under criticism from the other occupants of lifeboat 6. Mary Smith's statement describes Hichens as having 'little respect for the ladies' and being a 'thorough coward'. Major Peuchen describes him as 'a very talkative man … swearing a great deal, and … very disagreeable'. In this extract Hichens takes the opportunity to directly respond to personal criticism of him made by Mrs Leila Meyer (not Mayer as incorrectly transcribed), a passenger in lifeboat 6.

Hichens died of natural causes in 1940 aged 58. The later years of his life were difficult, with a spell in prison, a broken marriage, unemployment and alcohol abuse. Relatives described him as being 'racked with guilt' over his part in the sinking, and upset by the criticism he received in the press over his command of lifeboat 6 and refusal to go back to search for survivors.

US Senate Inquiry (inquiry question is followed immediately by witness's answer) I wish you would tell now, in your own way, what occurred that night from the time you went on watch until the collision occurred. *Witness answers:* I went on watch at eight o'clock. The officers on the watch were the second officer, Mr Lightoller, senior in command; the Fourth Officer, Mr Boxhall; and the Sixth Officer, Mr Moody. My first orders when I got on the bridge was to take the Second Officer's compliments down to the ship's carpenter and inform him to look to his fresh water; that it was about to freeze. I did so. On the return to the bridge, I had been on the bridge about a couple of minutes when the carpenter came back and reported the duty carried out. Standing by waiting for another message – it is the duty of the quartermaster to strike the bell every half hour – as the standby quartermaster, sir, I heard the second officer repeat to Mr Moody, the Sixth Officer, to speak through the telephone, warning the lookout men in the crow's nest to keep a sharp lookout for small ice until daylight and pass the word along to the other lookout men. The next order I received from the Second Officer was to go and find the Deck Engineer and bring him up with a key to open the heaters up in the corridor of the officers quarters, also the wheelhouse and the chart room, on account of the intense cold. At a quarter to 10 I called the First Officer, Mr Murdoch, to let him know it was one bell, which is part of our duty; also took the thermometer and barometer, the temperature of the water, and the log. At 10 o'clock I went to the wheel, sir. Mr Murdoch came up to relieve Mr Lightoller. I had the course given me from the other quartermaster, north 71 west, which I repeated to him, and he went and reported it to the First Officer or the Second Officer in charge, which he repeated back – the course, sir. All went along very well until 20 minutes to 12, when three gongs came from the lookout, and immediately afterwards a report on the telephone, 'Iceberg right ahead.' The Chief Officer rushed from the wing to the bridge, or I imagine so, sir. Certainly I am enclosed in the wheelhouse, and I cannot see, only my compass. He rushed to the engines. I heard the telegraph bell ring; also give the order 'Hard astarboard' with the Sixth Officer standing by me to see the duty carried out and the Quartermaster standing by my left side. Repeated the order, 'Hard astarboard. The helm is hard over, sir.'

Who gave the first order? Mr Murdoch, the First Officer, sir; the officer in charge. The Sixth Officer repeated the order, 'The helm is hard astarboard, sir.' But, during the time, she was crushing the ice, or we could hear the grinding noise along the ship's bottom. I heard the telegraph ring, sir. The skipper came rushing out of his room – Captain Smith – and asked, 'What is that?' Mr Murdoch said, 'An iceberg.' He said, 'Close the emergency doors.'

Who said that, the Captain? Captain Smith, sir, to Mr Murdoch; 'Close the emergency doors.' Mr Murdoch replied, 'The doors are already closed.' The Captain sent then for the carpenter to sound the ship. He also came back to the wheelhouse and looked at the commutator in front of the compass, which is a little instrument like a clock to tell you how the ship is listing. The ship had a list of 5° to the starboard.

How long after the impact, or collision? I could hardly tell you, sir. Judging roughly, about five minutes; about five to 10 minutes. I stayed to the wheel, then, sir, until 23 minutes past 12. I do not know whether they put the clock back or not. The clock was to go back that night 47 minutes, 23 minutes in one watch and 24 in the other.

Had the clock been set back up to the time you left the wheel? I do not know, sir. I did not notice it.

When do you say you left the wheel, at 20 minutes after 12? I left the wheel at 23 minutes past 12, sir. I was relieved by Quartermaster Perkis. He relieved me at 23 minutes past 12. I think the First Officer, or one of the officers said, 'That will do with the wheel; get the boats out.' I went out to get the boats out on the port side. I think I got in No. 6 boat, sir; put in charge of her by the Second Officer, Mr Lightoller. We lowered away from the ship, sir, and were told to 'pull toward that light', which we started to do, to pull for that light. I had 38 women in the boat, sir, one seaman [Fleet] and myself, with two male passengers, one Italian boy and a Canadian major [Peuchen], who testified here yesterday.

Were you in charge of the boat? I was; yes, sir. Everybody seemed in a very bad condition in the boat, sir. Everybody was quite upset, and I told them somebody would have to pull; there was no use stopping there alongside of the ship, and the ship gradually going by the head. We were in a dangerous place, so I told them to man the oars, ladies and all, 'All of you do your best.' We got away about a mile, I suppose, from the ship, going after this light, which we expected to be a 'cod banker', a schooner that comes out on the Banks.

A fisherman's boat? Yes, sir; we expected her to be that, sir; but we did not get any nearer the light. There were several other boats around us at this time and one boat that had no light came close up to us. He had four to six men in his boat and I borrowed one fireman from him to put in my boat, to enable me to pull. We did not seem to get any nearer the light, so we conversed together, and we tied our boats side by side. We stopped there until we saw the *Carpathia* heave in sight about daybreak. The wind had sprung up a bit then, and it got very choppy. I relieved one of the young ladies with the oar, and told her to take the tiller. She immediately let the boat come athwart, and the ladies in the boat got very nervous. So I took the tiller back again and told them to manage the best way they could.

Do you know who that woman was? I do not, sir. They were all entire strangers to me, sir. But the lady I refer to, Mrs Mayer [Meyer], she was rather vexed with me in the boat and I spoke rather straight to her, and she accused me of wrapping myself up in the blankets in the boat, using bad language, and drinking all the whisky, which I deny, sir. I was standing to attention, exposed, steering the boat all night, which is a very cold billet. I would rather be pulling the boat than be steering. But I seen no one there to steer, so I thought, being in charge of the boat, it was the best way to steer myself, especially when I seen the ladies get very nervous with the nasty tumble on. We got down to the *Carpathia* and I seen every lady and everybody out of the boat, and I seen them carefully hoisted on board the *Carpathia*, and I was the last man to leave the boat. That is all I can tell you.

I want to ask you a few questions. I would like to ask you whether you had any trouble with the major, between the *Titanic* and the *Carpathia*? I had no trouble with him at all, sir, only once. He was not in the boat more than 10 minutes before he wanted to come and take charge of the boat.

What did you say to him? I told him, 'I am put here in charge of the boat.' I said, 'You go and do what you are told to do.'

Did he say anything more to you? He did not answer me, sir, but sat down; went forward on the starboard bow, alongside of Seaman Fleet [one of the lookouts], who was working very hard. He done most of the work himself; Fleet was doing most of the work.

Did you lie on your oars off the *Titanic* at any time before the *Titanic* went down? Yes, sir.

How long? Well, we had no time, sir; I could hardly tell you.

About how long? That I could hardly tell you, sir, because our minds was thinking of other things, sir. I do know we did it, sir.

How far were you from the *Titanic* at the time she went down? When we sighted the *Carpathia* we were about a mile from her.

No; when you were lying on your oars? About one mile, sir.

About a mile from the *Titanic*? Yes, sir.

Could you see the *Titanic*? I could not see her; not after the lights went out; no, sir.

You could see the lights? We could see the lights go out; yes, sir.

And you knew the location of the boat? We heard the cries for an interval of about two or three minutes.

As the ship disappeared? As the ship disappeared; yes, sir.

The major [Peuchen], who was in that boat with you, said yesterday that you were lying on your oars, drifting, and before the *Titanic* went down you heard cries of distress, and for help. Is that true? I did not hear any cries as regarding distress. We heard a lot of crying and screaming. At one time we were made fast to another boat.

We were not lying on our oars at all.

You made fast to another boat. What boat? The boat the master-at-arms was in, sir. I think it was No. 8 boat. He left about the same time as we did [lifeboat 16 was the boat that Joseph Bailey, the only surviving master-at-arms, was in].

You had 38 women in your boat? Yes, sir; I counted them, sir.

And how many men? I had Fleet, myself ...

Fleet, the major, and yourself? And an Italian boy, sir.

That is four men? Four, sir. But the Italian boy had a broken arm, sir.

Was he the one who was hid away? I do not know how he managed to get on the boat at all, sir; I do not know.

Was he dressed in woman's clothing? No; I do not think so, sir.

During the time that you were lying off your oars, and before the *Titanic* sank, did the women in your boat urge you to go toward the *Titanic*? Not that I remember, sir. I am not aware of it.

Did they urge you not to go toward the *Titanic*? Not that I am aware of, sir.

So far as you can recollect, did the women say nothing either one way or the other about it? No, sir; not that I remember. In fact, under the conditions, with one seaman in the boat and myself to pull a big boat like that, and being a mile away from the *Titanic* – I did not know what course to take, we had no compass in the boat – it seemed impossible, sir.

The major said yesterday when you were asked to return to the source from which these distress cries came ... *Witness answers:* I read it in the paper, but that is continually false, sir.

That you said, 'We are to look out for ourselves now, and pay no attention to those stiffs.' *Witness answers:* I never made use of that word, never since I have been born, because I use other words in preference to that.

Did you say anything about it? Not that I am aware of, sir.

And you wish the committee to understand that you did not refuse to go to the relief of people in the water, either before or after the *Titanic* disappeared? I could not, sir. I was too far away, and I had no compass to go back, to enable me to find where the cries came from. The cries I heard lasted about two minutes, and some of them were saying, 'It is one boat aiding the other.' There was another boat aside of me, the boat the master-at-arms was in, full right up.

How long after you were lying on your oars was it that the *Titanic* went down? I could hardly tell you, sir.

Did you instruct the men in your boat to row away from the *Titanic* after it went down? I did, sir.

Why did you not row toward the scene of the *Titanic*? The suction of the ship would draw the boat, with all her occupants, under water, I thought, sir.

Is that the sole reason you did not go toward the *Titanic*? I did not know which way to go back to the *Titanic*. I was looking at all the other boats; I was among all the other boats.

What other boats; the lifeboats? We were all together; yes, sir.

Why were you looking at the lifeboats? We were looking at each other's lights.

Did you have a light? I did; yes, sir. We all had lights and were showing them to one another.

The lifeboats all had lights? Most all of us. We kept all showing our lights now and then to let them know where we were, too.

Do you mean to tell me you would pass your time in showing one another your own lights, but did not go toward the *Titanic*? Yes; but before the *Titanic* sank we were all pulling for a light which we thought was to be a cod banker. We all made for this light.

You made up your mind it was not the boat you thought it was? You thought it was a fishing boat? *Witness answers:* We all thought so, and all pulled for that light.

You then pulled for that light, and finally discovered you were making no progress toward it? Yes, sir.

And you stopped? We stopped then; yes, sir.

And at that time you were a mile away from the *Titanic*? Yes, sir; a mile or more, sir.

And was the *Titanic* still afloat? The *Titanic* was still afloat, sir, and her lights all showing.

How long after that did you see her go down? I could hardly tell you. Probably 10 minutes after that her lights disappeared, but I did not see her go down.

You, yourself, did not see her disappear? No, sir.

Was your back toward her? We could not see her at all. When I seen the lights disappear, that was all I could see, because it was very dark.

You sat at the tiller? I was standing at the tiller.

With your back to the ship? Yes, sir.

And you did not see her go down? No, sir.

After the lights disappeared and went out, did you then hear cries of distress? We did hear cries of distress, or I imagined so, sir, for two or three minutes. Some of the men in the boat said it was the cries of one boat hailing the other. I suppose the reason they said this was not to alarm the women – the ladies in the boat.

Did the Italian say that? The Italian could not speak. I am not talking of our own men, but the boat close, nearby.

Some other boat? Yes, sir; we were having conversation with them and the master-at-arms.

You desire the committee to understand that you kept a safe distance from the *Titanic* after you got into the lifeboat; you made fast to the other lifeboat; you went away from the *Titanic* about a mile; you lay there on your oars; you saw the *Titanic* go down, or saw the lights go out, and you did not go in that direction at all? We did not know what direction to go, sir.

Did you, after the lights went out, go in the direction in which the lights were? When the lights were gone out, we were still heading toward this cod banker, all of us.

That fishing boat was away from the *Titanic*'s position? Yes, sir; a good ways, sir.

You were heading for that? Yes, sir.

When you left the *Titanic* in the lifeboat, did anyone tell you to take that load off and come back to the *Titanic*? Yes, sir.

Who told you that? I think it was the First Officer or the Second Officer. I am not sure which officer it was.

Mr Murdoch or Mr Lightoller? One of them; I am not sure which.

What did you say? All right, we was willing to pull away for this light; but when we got down we told him we had to have one more man in the boat.

You wanted another man? We wanted two or three more men if we could get them.

But you did not get them? No, sir; only this major; he came down. He got in then, and that is all.

He swung himself out and got in, didn't he? Yes, sir.

Did that call come back before the major got into the boat, or was it when you were away from the ship and rowing away? When I got down to the bottom, when we were lowered down in the water, we only had one man there, one seaman besides myself.

Then you say it was the First or Second Officer called you to come back? He told us to go away and make for the light. We had them orders before we went down below. We had no orders when we got to the water at all; we couldn't hear then.

The orders you got were to take that boat to the water? To that light.

To the light and return? Yes, sir, that is right.

And that order was given to you by the First or Second Officer? Yes, sir.

Was your lifeboat lowered from the port or from the starboard side? The port, sir.

You did not carry out that order? Yes; I did, sir.

What did you do? I pulled for that light – this imaginary light. We were pulling for it all the time.

You pulled for this imaginary light? Yes, sir.

And never returned to the side of the *Titanic*? We could not return, sir.

I think I understand you. I want you to tell the committee, if you can, why you put the ship to starboard, which I believe you said you did, just before the collision with the iceberg? I do not quite understand you, sir.

You said that when you were first apprised of the iceberg, you did what? Put the helm to starboard, sir. That is the order I received from the Sixth Officer.

What was the effect of that? The ship minding the helm as I put her to starboard.

But suppose you had gone bows on against that object? I don't know nothing about that. I am in the wheelhouse, and, of course, I couldn't see nothing.

You could not see where you were going? No, sir; I might as well be packed in ice. The only thing I could see was my compass.

The officer gave you the necessary order? Gave me the order, 'Hard astarboard.'

Hard astarboard? Yes, sir.

You carried it out immediately? Yes, sir; immediately, with the Sixth Officer behind my back, with the junior officer behind my back, to see whether I carried it out – one of the junior officers.

Is that the only order you received before the collision, or impact? That is all, sir. Then the First Officer told the other quartermaster standing by to take the time, and told one of the junior officers to make a note of that in the logbook. That was at 20 minutes of 12; sir.

You said it was pretty cold that night? Very intense cold, sir.

What did that indicate to you – that you were in the vicinity of the Great Banks of Newfoundland? I do not know, sir. In the morning, when it turned daybreak, we could see icebergs everywhere; also a field of ice about 20 to 30 miles long, which it took the *Carpathia* two miles to get clear from when it picked the boats up. The icebergs was up on every point of the compass, almost.

It was very cold? Very cold, sir.

Freezing, I believe you said. *Witness answers:* Yes, sir.

Did you yourself take the temperature of the air or water that night? Yes, sir.

Where and when? About 10 minutes before I went to the wheel, sir.

How did you take the temperature of the air? We have a bucket, sir, attached to a piece of line about 20 fathoms long, which we put over the lee side of the ship, and draw just sufficient water to put the instrument in to cover the mercury to make its temperature rise.

Is that a dipper or pail? A small bucket, leaded at the bottom.

What is attached to it, a rope or chain? A piece of line about as thick as your black lead pencil.

Did you take that line and lower this bucket yourself? Yes, sir; when it was my duty to do so I did it.

You did it that night just before going to the wheel? Yes, sir.

The bucket reached the water, did it? Certainly, sir.

You took the temperature? Yes.

What was it? I could not tell at the present, sir. We have to enter it up in the log book.

Did you enter it? I did, sir.

But you cannot remember what it was? I cannot remember; no, sir.

Whether it was zero? No, sir; I know it was not zero.

You cannot give us any idea about it? No, sir.

Had you heard you were in the vicinity of ice? I heard by the Second Officer when he repeated it. He sent me with his compliments to the ship's carpenter to look out for the ship's water, that it was freezing, at eight o'clock. Then I knew. I didn't know before, but I heard the second officer distinctly tell Mr Moody, the Sixth Officer to repeat through the telephone, to keep a sharp lookout for small ice until daylight, and to pass the word along for the other lookout men.

You heard no officer say anything about icebergs, or an icefield, or growlers, or whatever they call these things, except what you have described, when he said it was freezing? Yes.

You left the wheelhouse that Sunday night at ... *Witness answers:* 23 minute past 12.

Were you relieved at the wheelhouse? I was relieved at the wheel by Quartermaster Perkis. He took the wheel from me.

Did he survive? Yes, all the quartermasters survived, sir, having charge of boats.

Your watch had not expired? My watch had expired; yes.

When he relieved you? Yes, sir. It was my watch to go below then.

Did you have daily drills with the lifeboats? Yes, sir.

Fire drills and lifeboat drills every day; is that customary? I did not see them. The only thing I saw was the emergency boat. There is one emergency boat on each side of the bridge, just abaft the bridge, which is kept, in case of accident always swung out.

There was a daily drill for the emergency boat? Yes, at six o'clock in the evening, usually.

You know, do you not, that the Second Officer and other officers say that there were no daily drills; that the only drill took place at Southampton, when two lifeboats were lowered? Yes; as regards drilling, that is true, sir; but what I am talking about is the emergency boat. They mustered the men every night at six o'clock, in case of emergency, in case they should want the emergency boat on account of a man falling overboard or anything else.

Do they muster these men every night at six o'clock? Yes, sir.

Where? On the bridge; they muster them there with an officer.

And what do they do – lower the boat? No; I have never seen them do that. I have been in the wheelhouse at the time.

You did not see them? No; but I have heard the report, and I have seen the officer as I was going to the wheelhouse; and one evening I might be on the dogwatch, from six to eight o'clock.

But you do not know what they did – whether they lowered the boat to the water? No, sir.

And that is the drill you referred to? No; I am not referring to any drill; I am only referring to the mustering of the men at six o'clock.

How many men are mustered? About eight, I think; six seamen and the quartermaster and an officer.

Every night at six o'clock? Yes, sir.

But they go to those two boats, one on the port and one on the starboard side? Yes, sir.

And what they do when they get there you do not know of your own knowledge? No, sir; the boat is always kept in readiness to be gotten out at a moment's notice in case of accident.

It seems to be the judgement of my associates that you should be permitted to go. Is there anything further you would like to say? I would like to make a little statement as regarding Mrs Mayer's [Meyer] statement in the newspapers about my drinking the whisky sir, and about the blankets. I was very cold, sir, and I was standing up in the boat. I had no hat on. A lady had a flask of whisky or brandy, or something of that description, given her by some gentleman on the ship before she left, and she pulled it out and gave me about a tablespoonful and I drank it. Another lady, who was lying in the bottom of the boat, in a rather weak condition, gave me a half wet and half dry blanket to try to keep myself a little warm, as I was half frozen. I think it was very unkind of her, sir, to make any statement criticising me. When we got to the ship I handled everyone as carefully as I could, and I was the last one to leave the boat, and I do not think I deserve anything like that to be put in the papers. That is what upset me and got on my nerves.

LIFEBOAT 16
Port Side, Launched 1.20 a.m.

Sixth Officer James Moody loaded this lifeboat. Moody was the only junior officer who didn't survive the disaster and was last seen attempting to launch collapsible lifeboat A off the deck.

Male crew: six; male passengers: 0; women and children: 50; total for lifeboat: 56 (British Board of Inquiry).

19
Annie Kelly, Third Class Passenger

Annie Kelly was part of a large party travelling to the US from County Mayo in Ireland. Annie settled in the US and became a nun. This extract is taken from the *Story of the Wreck of the Titanic* by Marshall Everett.

When there was only one seat left in the last lifeboat of the *Titanic*, had Mrs John Burke taken it the chances are that Miss Annie Kelly, a 17-year-old Chicago girl, might be at the bottom of the sea. So she told friends who gathered at her home to celebrate her lucky escape when the ship sank.

Miss Kelly told in a graphic manner the conditions in the steerage at the time the ship struck the iceberg and also how she was pushed into the last seat in the last boat.

With Miss Kelly when she arrived in Chicago was 15-year-old Annie McGowan, niece of Thomas McDermott, of Chicago, whose aunt, Miss Kate McGowan, perished in the lost ship. The girl was wrenched from her aunt's side and thrust into a boat, which pushed away from the ship. She never saw her relative again.

Annie Kelly and Annie McGowan embarked in the third cabin of the *Titanic* with the Burke family, which consisted of Mr and Mrs John Burke, who were coming to Chicago on their honeymoon; and Catherine and Margaret Burke, cousins of John and Margaret Manion, who were bound for Chicago to join their brother, Edward Manion.

'I should not have been saved except for Mrs Burke's refusal to leave her husband and the Misses Burke saying they would not go if their uncle and aunt could not go with them,' said Miss Kelly. 'I went in the very last boat and I was the very last passenger. The officer said there was room for just one more.

'I was aroused by the call of the stewardess, who told us all to dress as quickly as we could, though she did not explain what was the trouble. I dressed and went up on the second deck. Annie McGowan was with me when I was going up the stairs. But she became separated from me at the head of the stairway, and was carried by the throng over to the other side of the ship. I did not see her again until I was on the *Carpathia*.

'On the side where I was carried, some wild-looking men were trying to rush into the boats, and the officers and crew fired at them. Some of the men fell. Others were beaten back by the officers, who used pistols on them.'

20

Mary Sloan, Stewardess

This is a letter from the young stewardess Mary Sloan to her sister two weeks after the sinking. It was sent from the SS *Lapland*, a ship used to carry many of the *Titanic*'s crew back to the UK following the US inquiry.

My dear Maggie,

I expect that you will be glad to hear from me once more and to know I am still in the land of the living. Did you manage to keep the news from mother? I trust she is well. Well, we are now nearing England in the *Lapland*. They are very good to us here, and we have had a lovely passage home. About that dreadful night, I won't go into details now. I shall tell you all when I see you. I hope you got the cablegram all right. I shall never forget Mr Shannon's friends in New York. They, I mean Mrs M'Williams, came on board the *Lapland* on Friday morning accompanied by a Mr Robb, president of the telephone in NY. Mr Robb sent off the cable, and Mrs M'Williams took me to Brooklyn, gave me money and clothes. Mr and Mrs Robb came at night and Mr Robb made me take a 10 dollar bill. Young Mr Bryans a five dollar bill. Did you ever hear of such kindness from strangers? Of course I took them on condition that I would pay them back again. You must write to them and thank them as I will also. The ladies of New York Relief Committee came on board the *Lapland* with changes of underclothing, but I was at Brooklyn. You will be glad to know that dreadful night I never lost my head once. When she struck at a quarter to 12 and the engines stopped I knew very well something was wrong. Doctor Simpson came and told me the mails were afloat. I knew things were pretty bad. He brought Miss Marsden and I into his room and gave us a little whisky and water. I laughed and asked him if he thought we needed it, and he said we should. Miss Marsden was crying; he was cross with her. He asked me if I was afraid; I replied I was not. He said well spoken like a true Ulster girl. He had to hurry away to see if anyone was hurt. We helped him on with his greatcoat. I never saw him again. I felt better after. Then I saw our dear old Doctor Laughlin; I asked him to tell me the worst. He said, child, things are very bad. I indeed got a lifebelt and got on deck. I went round my rooms to see if my passengers were all up and to see if they had lifebelts on. Poor Mr Andrews came along; I read in his face all I wanted to know. He saw me knocking at some of the passengers' doors; he said that was right, told me to see if they had lifebelts on and to get one for myself and go on deck. He was a brave man. Last time I saw and heard him was about an hour later helping to get the women and children into the boats, imploring them not to hesitate, but to go when asked as there was no time to be lost; so Mr Andrews met his fate like a true hero realising his great danger, and gave up his life to save the women and children of the *Titanic*. They will find it hard to replace him, and I myself am terribly cut up about him. I was talking to him on the Friday night previous as he was going into dinner. The dear old doctor was waiting for him on the stair landing, and calling him by his Christian name, Tommy. Mr Andrews seemed loth to go, he wanted to talk about home, he was telling me his father was ill, and Mrs A was not so well. I was congratulating him on the beauty and perfection of the ship. He said the part he did not like the *Titanic* was taking us further away from home every hour. I looked at him and his face struck me at the time as having a very sad expression. He is one of the many who can be ill spared. Well, I got away from all the others and intended to go back to my room for some of my jewellery, but I had not time at the last. I went on deck the second time; one of our little bill boys recognised me, and pointing to a crowded boat said, Miss Sloan, that's your boat No. 12. I said, child, how do you know, I will wait for another, so it pushed off without me. I was still standing when I saw Captain Smith getting excited. Passengers would not have noticed; I did. I knew then we were soon going; the distress signals then were going every second, so I thought if anyone asked me again to go I should do so. There was a big crush from behind me. At last they realised their danger, so I was pushed into the boat. I believe it was one of the last boats to leave. We had scarcely got clear when she began sinking rapidly. The rest is too awful to write about. We were in the boats all night. I took a turn to row. The women said I encouraged them; I was pleased. We picked up 30 men, standing on an upturned boat; among them was one of our officers, Mr Lightoller. We then took charge until the *Carpathia* picked us up about seven in the morning. I only hope I shall never have a like experience again. Mr Lightoller paid me the compliment of saying I was a sailor. We were arriving about midnight on Sunday night. I don't know what the White Star people are going to do with us. I shall wait and see. I have lost everything. I will stay in Marland Terrace, so you can write me there.

Should love to see you all and talk to you.

We are arriving on the *Lapland*. I think I told you this before. Trusting this will find you all safe and well.

Your loving Sister,

Mary

Give my love to Mrs Brown, Willie and Joe. Let Lizzie read this as the paper is short here.

21

Margaret Murphy, Third Class Passenger

From Foster, County Longford, in Ireland. Margaret vividly describes how third class passengers were kept from reaching the boat decks.

Irish Independent, 9 May 1912 'Before all the steerage passengers had even had a chance for their lives the *Titanic*'s sailors fastened the doors and companionways leading up from the third class section. That meant certain death to all who remained below. And while the sailors were beating back the steerage passengers, lifeboats were putting away, some of them not half filled.'

Having related how a brave young Irishman, John Kiernan, who was lost, gave her his lifebelt, she said, 'A crowd of men were trying to get up to a higher deck and were fighting the sailors; all striking and scuffling and swearing. Women and some children were there praying and crying. Then the sailors fastened down the hatchways leading to the third class section. They said they wanted to keep the air down there so the vessel would stay up longer. It meant all hope was gone for those still down there.'

John Kiernan, she said, helped her into the boat and said 'Goodbye' as he had said it a hundred times at the door of her father's store. She knew he did not intend to get in himself, but the sailors drove him away. She added, 'Just as the davits were being swung outward a Chinaman pushed a woman out of the boat and took her place. Sailors grabbed him and handed him back to the deck. Then someone shot him and his body tumbled into the water. It was terrible.'

LIFEBOAT 14
Port Side, Launched 1.25 a.m.

This lifeboat was loaded by Fifth Officer Lowe. By now the atmosphere was becoming increasingly frantic, with Lowe firing two or three shots from his revolver to assert his authority and control the crowds.

This was the lifeboat used by Lowe to go back to look for survivors in the water after the *Titanic* took its final plunge. Its original passengers were divided up amongst lifeboats 10, 12, 14 and D. By the time Lowe and his hastily assembled crew had returned to the scene it was after 3 a.m. Only four survivors were picked up and one of these died shortly afterwards

Male crew: eight; male passengers: two; women and children: 53; total for lifeboat: 63 (British Board of Inquiry).

22
Charlotte Collyer, Second Class Passenger

An Englishwoman from Bishopstoke, near Southampton, Charlotte, her husband Harvey, and their eight-year-old daughter Marjorie were immigrating to the USA. Only Charlotte and her daughter ever reached New York. This account was given in May 1912 to *The Semi Monthly Magazine*.

The next morning, we went to Southampton; and there my husband drew from the bank all his money, including the sum we had received for our store. It came to several thousand dollars in American money, and he took it all in bank notes. The clerk asked him if he did not want a draft; but he shook his head and put the notes in a wallet which he kept, to the end, in the inside breast pocket of his coat. We had already sent forward the few personal treasures that we had kept from our old home; so that, when we went on board the *Titanic*, our every earthly possession was with us.

We were travelling second cabin, and from our deck, which was situated well forward, we saw the great send off that was given to the boat. I do not think there had ever been so large a crowd in Southampton and I am not surprised that it should have come together. The *Titanic* was wonderful, far more splendid and huge than I had dreamed of. The other craft in the harbour were like cockleshells beside her, and they, mind you, were the boats of the American and other lines that a few years ago were thought enormous. I remember a friend said to me, just before visitors were ordered ashore, 'Aren't you afraid to venture on the sea?' But now it was I who was confident. 'What, on this boat!' I answered. 'Even the worst storm couldn't harm her.' Before we left the harbour, I saw the accident to the *New York*, the liner that was dragged from her moorings and swept against us in the channel. It did not frighten anyone, as it only seemed to prove how powerful the *Titanic* was.

I don't remember very much about the first few days of the voyage. I was a bit seasick, and kept to my cabin most of the time. But on Sunday 14 April, I was up and about. At dinnertime I was at my place in the saloon, and enjoyed the meal, though I thought it too heavy and rich. No effort had been spared to serve even to the second class passengers on the Sunday the best dinner that money could buy. After I had eaten, I listened to the orchestra for a while; then, at perhaps nine o'clock, or half past nine, I went to my cabin.

I had just climbed into my berth when a stewardess came in. She was a sweet woman, who had been very kind to me. I take this opportunity to thank her; for I shall never see her again. She went down with the *Titanic*.

'Do you know where we are?' she said pleasantly. 'We are in what is called The Devil's Hole.'

'What does that mean?' I asked.

'That is the dangerous part of the ocean,' she answered. 'Many accidents have happened near here. They say that icebergs drift down as far as this. It's getting to be very cold on deck, so perhaps there's ice around us now!'

She left the cabin, and I soon dropped off to sleep. Her talk about icebergs had not frightened me; but it shows that the crew were awake to the danger. As far as I can tell, we had not slackened our speed in the least.

It must have been a little after 10 o'clock when my husband came in and woke me up. He sat about and talked to me, for how long I do not know, before he began to make ready to go to bed.

And then, the crash!

The sensation, to me, was as if the ship had been seized by a giant hand and shaken once, twice; then stopped dead in its course. That is to say, there was a long backward jerk, followed by a shorter forward one. I was not thrown out of my berth, and my husband staggered on his feet only slightly. We heard no strange sounds, no rending of plates and woodwork; but we noticed that the engines had ceased running. They tried to start the engines a few minutes later; but, after some coughing and rumbling, there was silence once more. Our cabin was so situated that we could follow this clearly.

My husband and I were not alarmed. He said that there must have been some slight accident in the engine room, and at first he did not intend to go on deck. Then he changed his mind, put on his coat and left me. I lay quietly in my berth with my little girl, and almost fell asleep again.

In what seemed a very few moments, my husband returned. He was a bit excited then. 'What do you think?' he exclaimed. 'We have struck an iceberg, a big one; but there is no danger. An officer just told me so.'

I could hear the footsteps of people on the deck above my head. There was some stamping, and queer noises as if ship's tackle was being pulled about.

'Are the people frightened?' I asked quietly.

'No,' he replied; 'I don't thing the shock waked up many in the second cabin, and a few of those in the saloons have troubled to go on deck. I saw five professional gamblers playing with some of the passengers, as I went by. Their cards had been jerked off the table when the boat struck; but they were gathering them up, and had started their game again before I left the saloon.'

This story reassured me. If those people at their cards were not worried, why should I be? I think my husband would have retired to his berth without asking any more questions about the accident; but suddenly we heard hundreds of people running along the passageway in front of our door. They did not cry out; but the pattering of their feet reminded me of rats scurrying through an empty room.

I could see my face in a mirror opposite, and it had grown very white. My husband, too, was pale; and he stammered when he spoke to me.

'We had better go on deck, and see what's wrong,' he said.

I jumped out of bed, and put over my nightdress, a dressing gown and then an Ulster. My hair was down, but I hurriedly tied it back with a ribbon. By progress, it seemed to have tilted forward a little. I caught up my daughter, Marjorie, just as she was in her nightgown, wrapped a White Star cabin blanket around her, and started out of the door. My husband followed immediately behind. Neither of us took any of our belongings from the cabin; and I remember that he even left his watch lying on his pillow. We did not doubt for an instant that we would return.

When we reached the second cabin promenade deck, we found a great many people there. Some officers were walking up and down, and shouting, 'There is no danger, no danger whatever!' It was a clear starlight night, but very cold. There was not a ripple on the sea. A few of the passengers were standing by the rail, and looking down; but I want to say that, at that time, no one was frightened.

My husband stepped over to an officer – it was either Fifth Officer Harold Lowe or First Officer Murdoch – and asked him a question. I heard him shout back, 'No we have no searchlight; but we have a few rockets on board. Keep calm! There is no danger!'

Our party of three stood close together. I did not recognise any of the other faces about me, probably because of the excitement. I never went near the first cabin promenade deck, so did not see any of the prominent people on board.

Suddenly there was a commotion near one of the gangways, and we saw a stoker come climbing up from below. He stopped a few feet away from us. All the fingers of one hand had been cut off. Blood was running from the stumps, and blood was splattered over his face and over his clothes. The red marks showed very clearly against the coal dust with which he was covered.

I started over and spoke to him. I asked if there was any danger.

'Danger!' he screamed, at the top of his voice. 'I should just say so! It's 'ell down below. Look at me! This boat'll sink like a log in 10 minutes!'

He staggered away, and lay down, fainting with his head on a coil of rope. And at that moment I got my first grip of fear – awful, sickening fear. That poor man, with his bleeding hand and his speckled face, brought up a picture of smashed engines and mangled human bodies. I hung on to my husband's arm, and although he was very brave and was not trembling, I saw that his face was as white as paper. We realised that the accident was much worse than we had supposed; but even then I, and all the others about me of whom I have any knowledge, did not believe that the *Titanic* could go down.

The officers now were running to and fro, and shouting orders. I have no clear idea of what happened during the next quarter of an hour. The time seems much shorter; but it must have been between 10 and 15 minutes. I saw First Officer Murdoch place guards by the gangways, to prevent others like the wounded stoker from coming on deck. How many unhappy men were shut off in that way from their one chance of safety I do not know; but Mr Murdoch was probably right. He was a masterful man, astoundingly brave and cool. I had met him the day before, when he was inspecting the second cabin quarters, and thought him a bulldog of a man who would not be afraid of anything. This proved to be true; he kept order to the last, and died at his post. They say he shot himself. I do not know.

Those in charge must have herded us toward the nearest boat deck; for that is where I presently found myself, still clinging to my husband's arm, and with little Marjorie beside me. Many women were standing with their husbands, and there was no confusion.

Then, above the clamour of people asking questions of each other, there came the terrible cry: 'Lower the boats. Women and children first! Women and children first!' They struck utter terror into my heart, and now they will ring in my ears until I die. They meant my own safety; but they also meant the greatest loss I have ever suffered – the life of my husband.

The first lifeboat was quickly filled and lowered away. Very few men went in her, only five or six members of the crew, I should say. The male passengers made no attempt to save themselves. I never saw such courage, or believe it possible. How the people in the first cabin and the steerage may have acted, I do not know; but our second cabin men were heroes. I want to tell that to every reader of this article.

The lowering of the second boat took more time. I think all those women who were really afraid and eager to go had got into the first. Those who remained were wives who did not want to leave their husbands, or daughters who would not leave their parents. The officer in charge was Harold Lowe. First Officer Murdoch had moved to the other end of the deck. I was never close to him again.

Mr Lowe was very young and boyish-looking; but, somehow, he compelled people to obey him. He rushed among the passengers and ordered the women into the boat. Many of them following him in a dazed kind of way; but others stayed by their men. I could have had a seat in that second boat; but I refused to go. It was filled at last, and disappeared over the side with a rush.

There were two more lifeboats at that part of the deck. A man in plain clothes was fussing about them and screaming out instructions. I saw Fifth Officer Lowe order him away. I did not recognise him; but from what I have read in the newspapers, it must have been Bruce Ismay, the managing director of the line.

The third boat was about half full when a sailor caught Marjorie, my daughter, in his arms, tore her away from me and threw her into the boat. She was not even given a chance to tell her father goodbye!

'You too!' a man yelled close to my ear. 'You're a woman. Take a seat in that boat, or it will be too late!'

The deck seemed to be slipping under my feet. It was leaning at a sharp angle; for the ship was then sinking fast, bows down. I clung desperately to my husband. I do not know what I said; but I shall always be glad to think that I did not want to leave him.

A man seized me by the arm. Then, another threw both his arms about my waist and dragged me away by main strength. I heard my husband say, 'Go, Lottie! For God's sake be brave and go! I'll get a seat in another boat.'

The men who held me rushed me bodily into the lifeboat. I landed on one shoulder and bruised it badly. Other women were crowding behind me; but I stumbled to my feet and saw over their heads my husband's back, as he walked steadily down the deck and disappeared among the men. His face was turned away, so that I never saw it again; but I know that he went unafraid to his death.

His last words, when he said that he would get a seat in another boat, buoyed me up until every vestige of hope was gone. Many women were strengthened by the same promise, or they must have gone mad and leaped into the sea. I let myself be saved, because I believed that he, too, would escape; but I sometimes envy those whom no earthly power could tear from their husband's arms. There were several such among those brave second cabin passengers. I saw them standing beside their loved ones to the last; and when the roll was called the next day on board the *Carpathia*, they did not answer.

The boat was practically full, and no more women were anywhere near it when Fifth Officer Lowe jumped in and ordered it lowered. The sailors on deck had started to obey him, when a very sad thing happened. A young lad, hardly more than a schoolboy, a pink-cheeked lad, almost small enough to be counted as a child, was standing close to the rail. He had made no attempt to force his way into the boat, though his eyes had been fixed piteously on the officer. Now, when he realised that he was really to be left behind, his courage failed him. With a cry, he climbed upon the rail and leaped down into the boat. He fell among us women, and crawled under a seat. I and another women covered him up with our skirts. We wanted to give the poor lad a chance; but the officer dragged him to his feet and ordered him back upon the ship.

He begged for his life. I remember him saying that he would not take up much room; but the officer drew his revolver, and thrust it into his face. 'I give you just 10 seconds to get back on to that ship before I blow your brains out!' he shouted. The lad only begged the harder and I thought I should see him shot as he stood. But the officer suddenly changed his tone. He lowered his revolver, and looked the boy squarely in the eyes. 'For God's sake, be a man!' he said gently. 'We've got women and children to save. We must stop at the decks lower down and take on women and children.'

The little lad turned round and climbed back over the rail, without a word. He took a few uncertain steps, then lay face down upon the deck, his head beside a coil of rope. He was not saved.

All the women about me were sobbing; and I saw my little Marjorie take the officer's hand. 'Oh. Mr Man, don't shoot. Please don't shoot the poor man!' she was saying; and he spared the time to shake his head and smile.

He screamed another order for the boat to be lowered; but just as we were getting away, a steerage passenger, an Italian, I think, came running the whole length of the deck and hurled himself into the boat. He fell upon a young child, I found out afterward, and injured her internally. The officer seized him by the collar, and by sheer brute strength pushed him back on to the *Titanic*. As we shot down toward the sea, I caught a glimpse of this coward. He was in the hands of about a dozen men of the second cabin. They were driving their fists into his face, and he was bleeding from the nose and mouth.

As a matter of fact we did not stop at any other deck to take on other women and children. It would have been impossible, I suppose. The bottom of our boat slapped the ocean, as we came down, with a force that I thought must shock us all overboard. We were drenched with ice-cold spray; but we hung on, and the men at the oars rowed us rapidly away from the wreck.

It was then that I saw for the first time the iceberg that had done such terrible damage. It loomed up in the clear starlight, a bluish-white mountain quite near to us. Two other icebergs lay close together, like twin peaks. Later, I thought I saw three or four more; but I cannot be sure. Loose ice was floating in the water. It was very cold.

We had gone perhaps half a mile when the officer ordered the men to cease rowing. No other boats were in sight, and we did not even have a lantern to signal with. We lay there in silence and darkness on that utterly calm sea.

I shall never forget the terrible beauty of the *Titanic* at that moment. She was tilted forward, head down, with her first funnel partly under water. To me she looked like an enormous glow worm; for she was alight from the rising waterline, clear to her stern – electric lights blazing in every cabin, lights on all the decks and lights at her mast heads. No sound reached us, except the music of the band, which I seemed, strange to say, to be aware of for the first time. Oh, those brave musicians! They were playing lively tunes, ragtime, and they kept it up to the very end. Only the engulfing ocean had power to drown them into silence.

At that distance, it was impossible to recognise anyone on board. But I could make out groups of men on every deck. They were standing with arms crossed, upon their chests, and with lowered heads. I am sure that they were in prayer. On the boat deck that I had just left, perhaps 50 men had come together. In the midst of them was a tall figure. This man had climbed on a chair, or a coil of rope so that he was raised far above the rest. His hands were stretched out, as if he were pronouncing a blessing. During the day, a priest, a certain Father Byles, had held services in the second cabin saloon; and I think it must have been he who stood there, leading those doomed men in prayer. The band was playing 'Nearer My God to Thee'. I could hear it very distinctly. The end was very close.

It came with a deafening roar that stunned me. Something in the very bowels of the *Titanic* exploded, and millions of sparks shot up to the sky, like rockets in a park on the night of a summer holiday. This red spurt was fan-shaped as it went up; but the sparks descended in every direction, in the shape of a fountain of fire. Two other explosions followed, dull and heavy, as if below the surface. The *Titanic* broke in two before my eyes. The fore part was already partly under the water. It wallowed over and disappeared instantly. The stern reared straight on end, and stood poised on the ocean for many seconds – they seemed minutes to me.

It was only then that the electric lights on board went out. Before the darkness came, I saw hundreds of human bodies clinging to the wreck, or leaping into the water. The *Titanic* was like a swarming beehive; but the bees were men; and they had broken their silence now. Cries more terrible than I had ever heard rang in my ears. I turned my face away; but looked round the next instant and saw the second half of the great boat slip below the surface as easily as a pebble in a pond. I shall always remember that last moment as the most hideous of the whole disaster.

Many calls for help came from the floating wreckage, but Fifth Officer Lowe told some women who asked him to go back that it would certainly result in our being swamped. I believe that some of the boats picked up survivors at this time; and I was told afterward by more than one trustworthy person that Captain E. J. Smith of the *Titanic* was washed against a collapsible boat and held on to it for a few moments. A member of the crew assured me that he tried to pull the captain on board, but that he shook his head, cast himself off, and sunk out of sight.

For our part, we went in search of other lifeboats that had escaped. We found four or five, and Mr Lowe took command of the little fleet. He ordered that the boats should be linked together with ropes, so as to prevent any one of them from drifting away and losing itself in the darkness. This proved to be a very good plan, and made our rescue all the more certain when the *Carpathia* came.

He then, with great difficultly, distributed most of the women in our boat among the other craft. This took perhaps half an hour. It gave him an almost empty boat, and as soon as possible he cut loose, and we went in search of survivors.

I had no idea of the passage of time during the balance of that awful night. Someone gave me a ship's blanket, which served to protect me from the bitter cold; and Marjorie had the cabin blanket that I had wrapped around her. But we were sitting with our feet in several inches of icy water. The salt spray had made us terribly thirsty, and there was no food of any kind on board the boat. The suffering of most of the women, from these various causes, was beyond belief. The worst thing that happened to me was when I fell over, half fainting, against one of the men at the oars. My loose hair was caught in the rowlock, and half of it was torn out by the roots.

I know that we rescued a large number of men from the wreckage, but I can recall clearly only two incidents.

Not far from where the *Titanic* went down, we found a lifeboat floating bottom up. Along its keel were lying about 20 men. They were packed closely together, and were hanging on desperately; but even the strongest were so badly frozen that, in a few moments more, they must have slipped into the ocean. We took them on board, one by one, and found that of the number four were already corpses. The dead men were cast into the sea. The living grovelled in the bottom of our boat, some of them babbling like maniacs.

A little further on, we saw a floating door that must have been torn loose when the ship went down. Lying upon it, face downwards, was a small Japanese. He had lashed himself with a rope to his frail raft, using the broken hinges to make knots secure. As far as we could see, he was dead. The sea washed over him every time the door bobbed up and down, and he was frozen stiff. He did not answer when he was hailed, and the officer hesitated about trying to save him.

'What's the use?' said Mr Lowe. 'He's dead, likely, and if he isn't there's others better worth saving than a Jap!'

He had actually turned our boat around, but he changed his mind and went back. The Japanese was hauled on board, and one of the women rubbed his chest, while others chafed his hands and feet. In less time than it takes to tell, he opened his eyes. He spoke to us in his own tongue; then seeing that we did not understand, he struggled to his feet, and in five minutes or so had almost recovered his strength. One of the sailors near to him was so tired that he could hardly pull his oar. The Japanese bustled over, pushed him from his seat, took the oar, and worked like a hero until we were finally picked up. I saw Mr Lowe watching him in open-mouthed surprise.

'By Jove!' muttered the officer. 'I am ashamed of what I said about the little blighter. I'd save the likes o' him six times over, if I got the chance.'

After this rescue all my memories are hazy until the *Carpathia* arrived at down. She stopped maybe four miles away from us, and the task of rowing over to her was one of the hardest that our poor frozen men, and women, too, had had to face. Many women helped at the oars; and one by one the boats crawled over the ocean to the side of the waiting liner. They let down rope ladders to us; but the women were so weak that it is a marvel that some of them did not lose their hold and drop back into the water.

When it came to saving the babies and young children, the difficulty was even greater, as no one was strong enough to risk carrying a living burden. One of the mail clerks on the *Carpathia* solved the problem. He let down empty United States mail bags. The little mites were tumbled in, the bags locked, and so they were hauled up to safety.

We all stood at last upon the deck of the *Carpathia*, more than 670 of us; and the tragedy of the scene that followed is too deep for words. There was scarcely anyone who had not been separated from husband, child or friend. Was the lost one among this handful saved? We could only rush frantically from group to group, searching the haggard faces, crying out names and endless questions.

No survivor knows better than I the bitter cruelty if disappointment, and despair. I had a husband to search for, a husband whom, in the greatness of my faith, I had believed would be found in one of the boats.

He was not there; and it is with these words that I can best end my story of the *Titanic*. There are hundreds of others who can tell, and have already told, of that sad journey on the *Carpathia* to New York.

23

Daisy Minahan, First Class Passenger

Daisy Minahan was a 33-year-old school teacher returning from a holiday in Europe. Daisy's brother William did not survive the sinking but her sister-in-law Lillian was also saved in lifeboat 14.

United States Senate Inquiry Affidavit I was asleep in stateroom C-78; the crying of a woman in the passageway awakened me. I roused my brother and his wife, and we began at once to dress. No one came to give us warning. We spent five minutes in dressing and went on deck to the port side. The frightful slant of the deck toward the bow of the boat gave us our first thought of danger. An officer came and commanded all women to follow, and he led us to the boat deck on the starboard side. He told us there was no danger, but to get into a lifeboat as a precaution only. After making three attempts to get into boats, we succeeded in getting into lifeboat No. 14. The crowd surging around the boats was getting unruly.

Officers were yelling and cursing at men to stand back and let the women get into the boats. In going from one lifeboat to another we stumbled over huge piles of bread lying on the deck.

When the lifeboat was filled there were no seamen to man it. The officer in command of No. 14 called for volunteers in the crowd who could row. Six men offered to go. At times when we were being lowered we were at an angle of 45° and expected to be thrown into the sea. As we reached the level of each deck men jumped into the boat until the officer threatened to shoot the next man who jumped. We landed in the sea and rowed to a safe distance from the sinking ship. The officer counted our number and found us to be 48. The officer commanded everyone to feel in the bottom of the boat for a light. We found none. Nor was there bread or water in the boat. The officer, whose name I learned afterwards to be Lowe, was continually making remarks such as, 'A good song to sing would be "Throw Out the Life Line",' and 'I think the best thing for you women to do is to take a nap.'

The *Titanic* was fast sinking. After she went down the cries were horrible. This was at 2.20 a.m. by a man's watch who stood next to me. At this time three other boats and ours kept together by being tied to each other. The cries continued to come over the water. Some of the women implored Officer Lowe, of No. 14, to divide his passengers among the three other boats and go back to rescue. His first answer to those requests was, 'You ought to be damn glad you are here and have got your own life.' After some time he was persuaded to do as he was asked. As I came up to him to be transferred to the other boat he said, 'Jump, God damn you, jump.' I had showed no hesitancy and was waiting only my turn. He had been so blasphemous during the two hours we were in his boat that the women at my end of the boat all thought he was under the influence of liquor. Then he took all of the men who had rowed No. 14, together with the men from the other boats, and went back to the scene of the wreck. We were left with a steward and a stoker to row our boat, which was crowded. The steward did his best, but the stoker refused at first to row, but finally helped two women, who were the only ones pulling on that side. It was just four o'clock when we sighted the *Carpathia*, and we were three hours getting to her. On the *Carpathia* we were treated with every kindness and given every comfort possible.

A stewardess who had been saved told me that after the *Titanic* left Southampton there were a number of carpenters working to put the doors of the airtight compartments in working order. They had great difficulty in making them respond, and one of them remarked that they would be of little use in case of accident, because it took so long to make them work.

I have given you my observations and experiences after the disaster, but want to tell you of what occurred on Sunday night, 14 April.

My brother, his wife, and myself went to the café for dinner at about 7.15 p.m. (ship's time). When we entered there was a dinner party already dining, consisting of perhaps a dozen men and three women. Captain Smith was a guest, as also were Mr and Mrs Widener, Mr and Mrs Blair, and Major Butt. Captain Smith was continuously with his party from the time we entered until between 9.25 and 9.45, when he bid the women good night and left. I know this time positively, for at 9.25 my brother suggested my going to bed. We waited for one more piece of the orchestra, and it was between 9.25 and 9.45 (the time we departed) that Captain Smith left.

Sitting within a few feet of this party were also Sir Cosmo and Lady Duff-Gordon, a Mrs Meyers of New York, and a Mrs Smith of Virginia. Mr and Mrs Harris also were dining in the café at the same time.

I had read testimony before your committee stating that Captain Smith had talked to an officer on the bridge from 8.45 to 9.25. This is positively untrue, as he was having coffee with these people during this time. I was seated so close to them that I could hear bits of their conversation.

24

Esther & Eva Hart, Second Class Passengers

The Hart family was immigrating to Canada where Benjamin Hart was planning to open a tobacconist. Benjamin's wife Esther was one of several passengers who later claimed to have had premonitions of the disaster.

Just seven at the time of the sinking Eva Hart later published her memoirs in a book called *A Girl Aboard The Titanic*.

Ilford Graphic, 12 May 1912 I can honestly say that from the moment the journey to Canada was mentioned, till the time we got aboard the *Titanic*, I never contemplated with any other feelings but those of dread and uneasiness. It was all done in a hurry. My husband of late had not been successful in business and things looked like going from bad to worse.

He was a very clever carpenter and his chest of tools was considered to be as perfect and expensive as any carpenter could wish for. At any rate he valued them at £100. He was going out to start building with a Mr Wire at Winnipeg. Mr Wire has since written to me expressing his deep regret at Ben's untimely loss, and adding, 'There were five Winnipeg men lost on the *Titanic* and I might have been one of them.'

The idea seized on Ben's imagination. 'I'll go out to a new country,' he said, 'where I'll either sink or swim.' In fact, during the time prior to our leaving Ilford, the latter statement was always in his mouth. I little knew then how sadly prophetic it was to turn out for my poor dear.

I said at the commencement that I viewed the journey with dread and uneasiness, but in saying that I do not wish anyone to think that I ever imagined anything so dreadful would happen as did happen. You see I was leaving my father and mother when they were at fairly advanced age, and neither of them in the best of health and I knew that in saying goodbye, I was saying goodbye forever: but it has pleased God to take my husband and send me back to them. Then I was leaving all the friends I had known in Ilford for so many years: and lastly, I dreaded the sea: the idea of being on the sea at night was bad enough, but for six or seven, I could not contemplate it, it was a nightmare to me.

Well, we said all our 'Goodbyes' and reached Southampton, and almost the first thing Ben did was take me to see the *Titanic*. He was always an enthusiastic in anything he was interested in: and he could not have been more enthusiastic over the *Titanic* had he been a part proprietor of it. 'There, old girl,' he said, 'there's a vessel for you! You're not afraid now.' I tried to share his confidence, but my heart quite failed me when we got aboard and I counted the number of boats there were. I said, 'Ben, we are carrying over 2,000 people and there are not enough boats for half of them if anything happens.' He laughed at my fears and said that beyond boat drills he did not expect the boats would come off the davits. But from that moment I made up my mind to one thing, till we were safe on land at New York. Nothing should ever persuade me to undress, and nothing did, although Ben at times got very cross with me. So each night I simply rested in my bunk, fully dressed and fully prepared, God knows why, for the worst.

We were fortunate in having some very nice people at our table. We were in parties of eight in the second saloon, and our party included a lady and gentleman from the Cape, Mr and Mrs Brown and their daughter, who were on their way to Vancouver. Mr Guggenheim's (a millionaire) chauffeur (both Mr and Mrs Guggenheim and he were drowned), a lady named Mrs Mary Mack, whose body has since been recovered, and Mr Hart, myself, and baby.

Mr Brown and Ben got on capitally together. They were the exact opposite of each other. Mr Brown was a quiet, reserved man who scarcely ever spoke, and Ben was fond of talking and so they got on well, promenaded the deck together, had their midday 'Bass' together, and smoked their pipes together. Indeed, Mrs Brown said that she had never seen her husband 'take' to anyone like he had to my Ben.

Oh dear! Oh dear! To think that, of the eight at the table, four were taken and four were left. I can see their bright, happy faces now as we sat round that table at meal times, talking of the future; they were all so confident, so looking forward to a new life in a new land, and well they found it, but in God's way, not theirs.

Now a very curious thing happened on the Saturday night. We had made splendid progress, and although I was still far from easy in my mind, I was as content as I could be off the land. I heard someone remark with glee that we were making a beeline for New York. I knew we were going at a tremendous speed, and it was the general talk – I cannot say what truth there was in it – that the captain and officers were 'on' something good if we broke the record.

But on the Saturday night I was resting in my bunk and my husband was sound asleep above me. Everything was quiet, except the throb of the screw and a strange straining and creaking of everything in the cabin, which I had noticed all the voyage. I may have just dozed off when I was awakened by a feeling as if some gigantic force had given the ship a mighty push behind. I could even hear the swirl of the waters which such a push to such a vessel would cause. I sat up, no doubt as to my being wide awake, again came the push and the swirl, and yet again a third time. For a few minutes I was dazed, frozen with terror of I know not what. Then I stood up and shook my husband, who was still sleeping soundly. 'Ben,' I said, 'Ben, wake up, get up, something dreadful has happened or is going to happen.' He was a little cross, as a man naturally is when he is woken from a sound sleep by the ungrounded fears (as he thinks) of a woman, but he saw that I was upset, and so he got up and partly dressed, and went up on the hurricane deck, and soon returned and assured me that the sea was calm and that the ship was travelling smoothly.

The next morning at breakfast, he laughingly told our table about it, and said what he was going to do that (Sunday) night to keep me quiet. He was going to insist upon my having a strong glass of hot grog to make me sleep. Mr Brown explained the creaking and straining by saying that as it was a new vessel everything was settling down into its proper place. 'Why,' he said. 'When we get to New York, it's more than likely that a lot of the paint will have come away, a lot of the joints have started,' and so on. 'That's all very well,' I said, 'but what about those awful jerks one after the other?' That he could not explain, nor anybody else. I say it was a warning from God to me, for I think that perhaps I was the only one of the 2,000 odd about who went in daily and nightly dread of the unforeseen. But had I told it to those in authority! Would anyone have listened to a silly, weak woman's superstitious fears? Would they have gone one hair's breadth out of their course? Would they have ordered one revolution less per minute of the screw? So I could only do what women have had to do from the beginning, eat my heart out with fear and wait.

Now if I had known that just at this time of the year the icebergs get across the track of the Atlantic liners, a little incident which occurred on this Sunday would have sent me straight to the captain, even if I'd have had to climb on to his bridge. But the simple things we ought to know we are never told. My husband was always a man who could bear extremes of heat and cold better than anyone I have ever met. All through those trying days of heat last year, when everyone else was melting and parched, he never once grumbled, but kept as cool as a cucumber. And the same with the cold. I have known him, when other people have been hanging over the fires, in and out of the house with his coat off, laughing at the poor shivering ones. And yet at midday on this fatal Sunday, he suddenly came up to baby and myself, and said rubbing his hands, 'How cold it has turned. I feel as if there was not a warm drop of blood in my body. Come and have a romp with daddy,' he said to baby, and together they went off and ran and romped on the hurricane desk.

We were in the iceberg region and the Almighty sent a warning to my husband – the man who was never cold before now shivered and shook like one stricken with ague.

But, beyond thinking it a curious thing, we took no heed.

And now, I come to a part of my story that I shrink from telling. Indeed, I think I have lingered over the first part because I dread relating the events of that awful night. I have read somewhere of people living a whole lifetime in a few hours. I know now that I have done so. To have gone through what I went through, to have suffered what I have suffered, to have seen what I have seen, to know what I know, and still to be alive, and above all – thank the Lord – to still preserve my reason, is a great and a growing marvel to me.

We had retired to our cabin about 10, and my husband, who thoroughly enjoyed the life aboard ship and drank his fill of the ozone – he could never get enough of it – was soon undressed and fast asleep in his bunk. My little Eva too was sound asleep, and I was sitting on my portmanteau with my head resting on the side of my bunk. And then all of a sudden there came the most awful sound I have ever heard in my life, a dreadful tearing and ripping sound – how any people who were awake at the time can say they scarcely felt a shock I cannot understand – the sound of great masses of steel and iron being violently torn, rent and cut asunder.

I was on my feet in an instant, for I knew something dreadful had happened. I shook Ben, and he awoke. 'Daddy,' I said, 'get up at once. We have hit something I am sure and it's serious.' Poor dear Ben! He was partly asleep still, and he said, 'Oh woman – again! I really don't know what I shall do with you?' 'Ben,' I said, not loudly, but with a quiet insistence which influenced him far more, 'something has happened; go up on deck and find out what it is.' He went up in his nightshirt and bare feet; in a few moments he was back again. He said, 'All the men are at the lifeboats – it's only a lifeboat drill.' I said, 'They don't have lifeboat drills at 11 at night. I tell you something has happened – dress quickly and let us dress the baby.' So he hurriedly put on his pants and his overcoat, put his big motor coat over me and then dressed the sleeping little girl. Just then a stewardess, with whom I was on friendly terms, came along and said she would soon find out all about it. She knew the Marconi operator and would ask him. So she went away and quickly came back saying that everything was all right. But I said, 'Everything is not all right, we have struck something and the water is coming in.' I think by this time Ben had realised, although he would not say so, that danger was ahead, for when he got up on B deck, he turned away for a few moments, and said his Jewish prayers. The next few minutes were so crowded with events, so fraught with all that matters in this world – life to a few of us, death to the majority of us – that I have no coherent recollection of what happened.

I know that there was a cry of 'She's sinking'. I heard hoarse shouts of 'Women and children first', and then from boat to boat we were hurried, only to be told, 'Already full.' Four boats we tried and at the fifth there was room. Eva was thrown in first, and I followed her. Just then, a man who had previously tried to get in succeeded in doing so, but was ordered out, and the officer fired his revolver into the air to let everyone see it was loaded, and shouted out, 'Stand back! I say, stand back! The next man who puts his foot in this boat, I will shoot him down like a dog.' Ben, who had been doing what he could to help the women and children, said quietly, 'I'm not going in, but for God's sake look after my wife and child.' And little Eva called out to the officer with the revolver, 'Don't shoot my daddy. You shan't shoot my daddy.' What an experience for a little child to go through! At the age of seven to have passed through the valley of the shadow of death. I wonder if she will ever forget it? I know I shan't, if I live for a hundred years.

So that was the last I saw of my poor lost dear – no farewell kiss, no fond word – but in a moment he had gone and we were hanging over the sea, 50 or 60 feet [*c.* 15–18 metres] above it, and then there were two or three horrible jerks as the boat was lowered from the davits and we were in the water, so crowded that we could scarcely move.

In the midst of all these stunning blows one despairing tact alone seized my thoughts: I knew, and a woman is never wrong in such matters, that I had seen the last of my Ben, and that I had lost the best and truest friend, the kindest and most thoughtful husband that ever woman had.

The officer in charge of our boat was standing on that raised part of it right at the end. We were all women and children aboard (at least I thought so then, but we were not, as I will presently tell you) and we were all crying and sobbing; and the officer said, not roughly, but I think with a kindly desire to keep our minds off the terrible time we had gone through. 'Don't cry, please don't cry. You'll have something else to do than cry; some of you will have to handle the oars. For God's sake stop crying. If I had not the responsibility of looking after you I would put a bullet through my brain.' So we got away from the ship for a safe distance, for there was no doubt now about her sinking. The front portion of her was pointing downwards and she appeared to be breaking in halves. Then with a mighty and tearing sob, as of some gigantic thing instinct with life, the front portion of her dived, for that is the only word I can use properly to describe it, dived into the sea, and the after part with a heavy list, also disappeared. And then a wonderful thing happened. Apart from the swirl of the water close to the vessel, caused by such a mass sinking, the sea was as smooth as glass; it seemed as if the Almighty, in order that as many should be saved as possible, had, with a merciful hand, smoothed and calmed the waters. For a few moments we could see everything that was happening, for, as the vessel sank, millions and millions of sparks flew up and lit everything around us. And in an instant the sea was alive with wreckage, with chairs, pillows, and rugs, benches, tables, cushions, and, strangely enough, black with an enormous mass of coffee beans. And the air was full of the awful and despairing cries of drowning men. And we were helpless to help, for we dared not go near them.

Our officer was busy shouting out till he was hoarse, 'Let all the boats keep as near together as possible. That's our only chance of being picked up. If we separate we are lost. Keep together.' An inky blackness now settled over us, and not a soul in our boat had a match; but the officer found in his pockets an electric torch, which he kept flashing, shouting out all the time, 'Keep together – it's our only chance.' The duty that the officer allotted to me was to bale the water out of the boat. While sitting there I had the impression that there was somebody near me who ought not to be there. So, when I could get my elbows free I put my hand down under the seat and touched a human form. It was a poor wretch of a man who had smuggled himself into the boat, and had sat there during all that awful time, under the seat in about six inches [*c.* 15 cm] of water. When we got him out he was so stiff he could scarcely move.

It had got a little lighter now, and our officer had collected nearly all the boats together; and he called from one to the other, 'How many in yours – how many in yours?' and then he discovered that there was room in those other boats to put the whole of our 55 in, so we were transferred to them, and the officer now collected a few seamen in his now empty boat and rowed away to see what he could find. So, with proper management another 55 people could easily have been saved. I cannot understand why, in the midst of such terrible doings, these boats left the ship without their full number of passengers; 55 precious lives lost either through selfishness or carelessness, I know not which.

It was no easy matter for me to get from one boat to the other. I am no light weight at the best of times, but now I was weak from want of sleep – weak with the terror of the night – and laden with Ben's heavy motor coat. Eva had been handed in, and I shall never forget my feelings when I saw her leave, and found myself unable to get a footing on the boat she was in. At last I managed it, how I could not tell. Eva was suffering from a violent attack of vomiting: for, when they had thrown her into the first boat from the *Titanic* she had hit her stomach on the edge of the boat. And there the poor little thing was, and I could not get near her to wipe her mouth. So there we sat the weary night through until, at eight in the morning, the *Carpathia* came on the scene. I always thought that these ship boats had to be provisioned beforehand, in view of possible accidents, but there was no water, nor were there biscuits in the boat. An oversight I suppose, but one fraught with terrible consequences had not the *Carpathia* arrived in good time.

Gradually the welcome dawn broke; and as the sun rose and we looked at where the sky and sea met, we saw one of the most wonderful sights that could be imagined. Right away there, stretching for miles and miles, there appeared what seemed to us an enormous fleet of yachts, with their glistening sails all spread. As the sun grew brighter they seemed to sparkle with innumerable diamonds. They were icebergs; and, moving slowly and majestically along all by itself, a mile or so in length, in form like the pictures of Gibraltar I have seen, was the monster iceberg, the cause of all our trouble.

And now about eight o'clock the *Carpathia* came into sight and we were all aboard by 8.30. I cannot say much of my life on board this vessel. It was no matter for a ship to take on another 700 people, many of them but lightly clad, most of them ill, and all suffering severely from shock; all was done for us that could be done, but I could neither rest nor sleep. My little Eva was still suffering from her vomiting attack and I found my hands full in nursing her; but when at night she was asleep, I could do nothing but walk the corridor, up and down, up and down, and thinking, thinking all the time. So much did I walk about at night that the kind-hearted sailors christened me The Lady of the Watch.

Well, eventually we arrived at New York. And what can I say of the kindness of the 'Women's Relief Committee', and the help they rendered us poor stranded souls. Kindness! That's but a poor word; and yet I can find no other for their intensely practical sympathy. No formulas, no questions. We had got to be helped and that quickly, and quickly they did it. In a short space of time with a speed that seemed incredible, there was a sufficiency of clothing for every destitute woman and child – my women readers will understand me when I say that everything a woman needed was there in abundance – from a blouse to a safety pin, underclothing, stays, stockings, garters, suspenders, hair pins, boots of all sizes, each pair with laces or a button hook in them as was necessary. I have never heard of such foresight. I have never experienced such real kindness. God bless the ladies of the 'Women's Relief Committee of New York', say I heartily and fervently. Why, Mrs Satterlee actually drove me in her beautiful car to the hotel where I was to stay pending my return to England, and wanted me to go to lunch with her in her house, but my heart was too full for that. She knew the reason and appreciated it like the lady she is. One touching little incident occurred before I sailed for home on the *Celtic*, and that was the receipt of a letter from little children in New Jersey. They had heard of my Eva and they sent her a dollar bill with a beautiful little letter. I don't think that bill will ever be changed, for both it and the letter will be framed.

There is but little to add. I returned on the *Celtic* with five other ladies from the *Titanic*, including Mrs Ada Clarke, of Southampton. We were treated with every kindness and consideration. A lady in the first saloon sent out word that whatever we wanted in the way of fruit, or any other delicacies not included in our menu, we were to have.

And now I have only one object in life, and that is the future of my little Eva. My lost Ben had such dreams of her future; he meant to do such things for her; and, whatever money I get, apart from the bare cost of the necessities of life, shall be devoted to her upbringing in such a way as shall realise, as far as my endeavours and finances can go, his wishes with regard to her.

25

Joseph Scarrott, Able Seaman

Joseph Scarrott was 33 and from Southampton. Initially in charge of this boat it was Scarrott who told Lowe (the Fifth Officer, not Chief Officer as Scarrott describes him) of the difficulties in maintaining order, resulting in Lowe firing his revolver.

Scarrott describes going back with Fifth Officer Lowe to find survivors. Four survivors were picked up, one of whom, William Hoyt, died shortly afterwards.

British Board of Trade Inquiry (inquiry question is followed immediately by witness's answer) Was it your watch from 8 to 12 on the Sunday night? Yes.

What were your duties during that watch? To stand by for a call in case I was wanted for anything whatever.

Shortly before the ship struck the iceberg did you hear the bell strike in the crow's nest? Yes.

What did you hear? Three bells.

Do you know what time that was? Not to be exact I do not, but it was round about half past 11.

Shortly after that did you feel anything? Yes.

What did you feel? Well, I did not feel any direct impact, but it seemed as if the ship shook in the same manner as if the engines had been suddenly reversed to full speed astern, just the same sort of vibration, enough to wake anybody up if they were asleep.

Did you feel anything besides that? No.

Did you feel the ship strike anything? No, not directly.

'Not directly,' you say? Not as if she hit anything straight on – just a trembling of the ship.

How soon did you feel this vibration after you heard the three strikes on the gong? As I did not take much notice of the three strikes on the gong, I could hardly recollect the time; but I should think it was – well, we will say about five or eight minutes; it seemed to me about that time.

Where were you at the time? Just about the forecastle head.

Did you remain there? No.

Where did you go? I rushed down to tell my mate, who was in the bathroom just at the bottom of the ladder. He asked me to give him a call if anything was doing.

What did you do after that? Rushed on deck with the remainder of those that were in the forecastle. The shock caused everybody to turn out, and we came on deck to see what was the cause of the vibration.

Did the boatswain give any orders to the hands? Yes.

What was his order? 'All hands on deck; turn out the boats and take the covers off and place the covers amidships.'

When you got on deck did you see anything; did you see any ice or iceberg? Oh, yes, when we first came up.

Tell me what you saw. *Witness answers:* When we came up, that was before the boatswain's call, we saw a large quantity of ice on the starboard side on the fore well deck, and I went and looked over the rail there and I saw an iceberg that I took it we had struck. It would be abaft the beam then – abaft the starboard beam.

Was it close to? No, it seemed the ship was acting on her helm and we had swung clear of the iceberg.

But how far away from your beam was the iceberg, a ship's length or two ships' length? Not a ship's length.

You speak of this ship as if answering her helm – as if answering under which helm? Under the starboard helm – under the port helm.

Get it right? Under port helm. Her stern was slewing off the iceberg. Her starboard quarter was going off the icebergs, and the starboard bow was going as if to make a circle round it.

What was the shape of this iceberg? Well, it struck me at the time that it resembled the Rock of Gibraltar looking at it from Europa Point. It looked very much the same shape as that, only much smaller.

Like a lion couchant? As you approach Gibraltar – it seemed that shape. The highest point would be on my right, as it appeared to me.

You received the words, 'Uncover and turn out the boats'? Yes.

Now which was your boat? No. 14.

On which side was she? The port side.

And was she well aft on the port side? In the after section.

Did you go to that boat? No.

Did you go to any other boat? I went to 14 boat finally, but not at first.

Not at first? No, not at the first order.

Which boat did you go to first? The first boat on the port side – not the emergency boat. The first boat was the first boat to uncover. You understand we started on the port side and got those boats uncovered and cleared and turned them out, falls all ready for lowering, and then worked with the starboard boats. At the time we were working at the starboard boat – I think I was at boat 13 – the Chief Officer came along and asked me whether it was my right boat. I said, 'No, we are all assisting here.' He said, 'All right, go to your own boat,' and then I went to No. 14 boat.

Then how comes it that you did not go to your own boat in the first instance? Acting on the boatswain's orders.

Which boat did you go to first – what number? I think it is 4, the first boat abaft the emergency boat on the port side [it would be lifeboat 4].

How many boats did you assist in getting out and down to the water before you went to your own boat? I think I assisted in getting four out ready for lowering, but not down to the water. I was at my own station then. By the time the order was passed for women and children first, by Mr Wilde, I assisted to get them all out ready for lowering. I personally helped at four boats.

Was there any difficulty or not in getting them out? There was in one or two cases, but the difficulty was not great. It merely wanted a kick of the foot just to clear the chock.

That is a small difficulty, if it is a difficulty at all. It has always got to be done? Yes, you have to watch for that. That is common. That is a thing which is likely to happen at any time.

Apart from the difficulty, if it can be called a difficulty, the boats were got out readily and easily? Yes.

What is the number of your boat? 14.

Then, later, having assisted at the other boats, you got to your own boat? Yes.

Does that boat belong to any particular officer? Whether it does or not I do not know.

Who was taking charge of that boat when you got there – was there anybody? When I got there I put myself in charge as the only sailorman there. I was afterwards relieved by the Fifth Officer, Mr Lowe.

Later? Yes.

Yes, we will come to that. Now, having got to boat 14, which was your boat, what was done about that? Directly I got to my boat I jumped in, saw the plug in, and saw my dropping ladder was ready to be worked at a moment's notice; and then Mr Wilde, the Chief Officer, came along and said, 'All right; take the women and children,' and we started taking the women and children. There would be 20 women got into the boat, I should say, when some men tried to rush the boats, foreigners they were, because they could not understand the order which I gave them, and I had to use a bit of persuasion. The only thing I could use was the boat's tiller.

When you say that foreigners tried to rush the boat, were they passengers? By their dress I should say yes, my Lord.

Did the Fifth Officer assist you in this persuasion? He was not there then.

Did you get these men out of your boat, or prevent them getting in? Yes, I prevented five getting in. One man jumped in twice and I had to throw him out the third time.

Did you succeed in getting all the women and children that were about into your boat? Yes, when Mr Lowe came and took charge he asked me how many were in the boat; I told him as far as I could count there were 54 women and four children, one of those children being a baby in arms. It was a very small baby which came under my notice more than anything, because of the way the mother was looking after it, being a very small child.

How many women did you say? 54.

And four children? Yes.

Were there any other passengers in that boat? Not passengers; no, sir.

Who else was in that boat? Myself, two firemen, and three or four stewards. I will not be certain as regards the exact number of stewards, but there were not more than four.

Was Mr Lowe, the Fifth Officer, also in the boat? We were practically full up. I was taking the women in when Mr Lowe came. There was another officer with him on the boat deck, but I do not know which one that was, and he said to this other officer, 'All right, you go in that boat and I will go in this.' That would mean No. 16 boat; she was abaft us, the next boat. Mr Lowe came in our boat. I told him that I had had a bit of trouble through the rushing business, and he said, 'All right.' He pulled out his revolver and he fired two shots between the ship and the boat's side, and issued a warning to the remainder of the men that were about there. He told them that if there was any more rushing he would use it. When he fired the two shots he fired them into the water. He asked me, 'How many got into the boat?' I told him as near as I could count that that was the number, and he said to me, 'Do you think the boat will stand it?' I said, 'Yes, she is hanging all right.' 'All right,' he said. 'Lower away 14.'

Was she then lowered to the water? Yes.

And having been lowered to the water, was she disengaged? No, she hung up. The forward fall lowered all right, sufficiently far enough that the fore part of the boat was afloat and the forward fall slack. Her after fall then would be about 10 feet [c. three metres] – we had about 10 feet to go on the after fall. Our boat was at an angle of pretty well 45 degrees. I called Mr Lowe's attention to it. He said, 'Why don't they lower away aft?' I know the man that was lowering the after fall; it was McGough. I looked overhead naturally enough, seeing the boat did not come down, and the fall was twisted. It resembled more a cable hawser than a fall, and would not render at all. I called Mr Lowe's attention to the fact. He said, 'What do you think is best to be done?' I said, 'I can case it. I will cut one part of the fall, and it will come easy. I have not the least doubt but what she will come away with her releasing gear.' He said, 'Do not you think the distance rather too much?' I said, 'No; she might start a plug, but I will look out for that.' We dropped her by the releasing gear, and when she was clear I jumped to the plug to see if the impact of the water had started it, but it remained fast. After that we got clear of the ship.

Now you are clear of the ship? Yes.

Now, having got clear of the ship, what was done with that boat? Where did it go to? We just rowed clear of the ship. I suppose Mr Lowe used his discretion to get clear of the suction which was likely to take place, and we saw four other boats then. 16 was the nearest boat. She had just got clear a little previous to us.

On which side of the *Titanic*? On the port side.

How many were rowing? Four.

Do you know who they were – were they seamen? I can only account for two as regards their rating. I was pulling the after-oar on the port side of the boat, and on my left was a fireman; but as regards the other two that were further forward on the boat, I cannot say what they were as regards their rating.

I thought you said they were stewards. *Witness answers:* I do not know whether those stewards were rowing. There were more than four men in the boat.

Am I right in supposing that in your boat, No. 14, there were yourself, two firemen, three or four stewards, and Lowe? There is a correction there, my Lord. There was one man in that boat that we had been under the impression – when I say 'we', I mean the watch of sailors – that he was a sailorman. That man was not a sailor at all, though acting in the capacity of sailor. That was another man that was in the boat.

What was he? A window cleaner; he was supposed to be in the ship as a window cleaner [William Harder].

Who was steering your boat? Mr Lowe, the Fifth Officer.

How far off from the *Titanic* was your boat rowed? I should judge about 150 yards [*c.* 137 metres].

Then did she lie there? She lay there with the remainder of the other boats – with the four other boats that we saw when we got clear of the ship.

Did you see four other boats there? Yes.

Did you speak to them? Yes.

And was anything done with the other boats? Mr Lowe asked them who was in charge of the boats, what officers were there, and we got a reply from each boat individually to say they had no officer in the boat. He said, 'All right, consider the whole of you are under my orders; remain with me,' and when the ship sank, when there was nothing left of her above the water, he waited, I suppose, about a couple of minutes, not more, and ordered all our boats to row where we last saw the ship to see if we could pick up anybody.

You have gone on a little too fast. You spoke of four other boats? Yes.

And you remained there? Yes.

Now what was happening as far as you could see, on the *Titanic* while you were lying off; was she sinking by the head, or what? She was sinking by the head.

You could see that? Yes.

Was she sinking at first fast or slow? Very slow it appeared to be.

As time went on did she sink faster? As the water seemed to get above the bridge she increased her rate of going down.

Going down head first? Head first.

I should have thought that when the water got to the bridge the boat would go to the bottom at once. *Witness answers:* She was right up on end then.

Do you say the water got to the bridge? Yes, I am judging from what I saw. When the port bow light disappeared she seemed to go faster. That light is seen about level with the bridge, the port bow light.

Is it level with the bridge? Is not the bridge above it? The bridge would be above it, yes.

You said *Titanic* was standing end on. What do you mean by that? This part of the ship was right up in the air. You could see her propeller right clear, and you could see underneath the keel; you could see part of her keel.

You saw the port light disappear? Yes.

And then after that the ship went? Yes, she seemed to go with a rush then.

How soon after you saw the bridge level with the water did the ship disappear?

Well, I cannot say as regards the time, but when it got there the ship went with a rush, and you could hear the breaking up of things in the ship, and then followed four explosions. To the best of my recollection that is the number of the explosions.

As soon as the ship went down, what was done with your boat? Did she remain where she was for a little time, or did she row in to where the ship had sunk? She rowed in in company with the four other boats, under the orders of Mr Lowe, to see if we could pick up anybody from the wreckage.

The whole five of you rowed in? The whole five of us.

Was there much wreckage? No, not so much as you would expect from a big ship like that.

Did you see many people in the water? Later on, but not then. We did not see many then when we got right over the top of the ship. There did not appear to be many people in the water at all.

Did you hear cries? Yes.

Much? Yes, rather a great deal.

Now did you succeed in rescuing anybody? Not our boat individually, but the other boats in our charge did get somebody, but how many I cannot say.

You mean people who had dropped from the vessel into the water? I take it that is where they came from.

Your boat got none of them? We got none of them. The boats that got them were the boats away to our right; they would be to leeward, where the wreckage would drift.

Did you see anything of a raft or rafts in the water? Later on in the morning we saw one.

That was not till later on? No.

You succeeded in rescuing no passengers? No.

Now, after seeing there was no chance of rescuing passengers, what did you do; did you remain there or did you sail away in any direction, or row, or what? Mr Lowe ordered four of the boats to tie together by the painters. He told the men that were in charge of them, the seamen there, what the object was. He said, 'If you are tied together and keep all together, if there is any passing steamer they will see a large object like that on the water quicker than they would a small one.' During the time that was going on – we intended to make fast ourselves, of course, with the four – we heard cries coming from another direction. Mr Lowe decided to transfer the passengers that we had, so many in each boat, and then make up the full crew; it did not matter whether it was sailors or anything, and go in the direction of those cries and see if we could save anybody else. The boats were made fast and the passengers were transferred, and we went away and went among the wreckage. When we got to where the cries were we were amongst hundreds, I should say, of dead bodies floating in lifebelts.

Was it dark then? Yes.

Still dark? Yes, and the wreckage and bodies seemed to be all hanging in one cluster. When we got up to it we got one man, and we got him in the stern of the boat – a passenger it was, and he died shortly after we got him into the boat. One of the stewards that was in the boat tried means to restore life to the man; he loosed him and worked his limbs about and rubbed him; but it was of no avail at all, because the man never recovered after we got him into the boat. We got two others then as we pushed our way towards the wreckage, and as we got towards the centre we saw one man there. I have since found out he was a storekeeper; he was on top of a staircase; it seemed to be a large piece of wreckage anyhow which had come from some part of the ship. It was wood anyhow. It looked like a staircase. He was kneeling there as if he was praying, and at the same time he was calling for help. When we saw him we were about from here to that wall away from him, and the boats, the wreckage were that thick – and I am sorry to say there were more bodies than there was wreckage – it took us a good half-hour to get that distance to that man to get through the bodies. We could not row the boat; we had to push them out of the way and force our boat up to this man. But we did not get close enough to get him right off – only just within the reach of an oar. We put out an oar on the fore part of the boat, and he got hold of it, and he managed to hold on, and we got him into the boat. Those three survived. There was one dead in our boat, and that was the passenger, the first one we picked up.

You got four on board, one of whom died – is that it? Yes, that is correct.

What did you do after that? We made sail and sailed back to take our other boats in tow that could not manage themselves at all. We made sail then, but just as we were getting clear of the wreckage we sighted the *Carpathia*'s lights.

Then what did you do; did you go back to the four other boats? Yes, we went back to the four other boats. On our way back we saw one of our patent rafts.

What is a patent raft? I can give the details of the construction of it. These are air boxes with a seat construction on them, and on the top of them there is a sort of canvas bulwark. It is not a Berthon boat at all; it is not collapsible. It is constructed, and there is a canvas bulwark to it. This one we saw was awash. There seemed to be about 18 or 20 people on it. I particularly took notice of two women that were there, and we made straight for them first and got them off and got them into our boat.

How many? I will not be exact to the number, but I think there would be about 20, because we were under sail at the time. My attention was directed to the sail while the officer manoeuvred the boat alongside this raft.

How many on the raft were women? I only noticed two.

26
Harold Lowe, Fifth Officer

Notable as the only officer to return to the scene of the sinking to look for survivors, Fifth Officer Lowe was from Wales and at 29 years old was a relatively young officer. Whilst loading lifeboat 5 Lowe argued with the managing director of the White Star Line, Bruce Ismay, who was trying to assist with loading. Lowe didn't recognise Ismay at the time, only later realising who he had been dealing with. 'Foreigners' get a bad press from Lowe, who claimed that one passenger, an Italian, had 'sneaked in dressed like a women' with a 'shawl over his head'. Later

Lowe didn't want to help a Japanese survivor struggling on a makeshift raft. During the British Inquiry the Italian ambassador asked for and received a retraction of a statement by Fifth Officer Lowe which describes 'Italians' jumping into his boat and needing to be scared off by gunshots.

British Board of Trade Inquiry (inquiry question is followed immediately by witness's answer) Were you asleep at the time of the collision? I was.

Just tell us what woke you up? I was half awakened by hearing voices in our quarters, because it is an unusual thing, and it woke me up. I suppose I lay down there for a little while until I fully realised, and then I jumped out of bed and opened my door a bit and looked out, and I saw ladies in our quarters with lifebelts on.

When you first looked out people had got their lifebelts on? They had.

Do you know the time? I do not. I have not the remotest idea of the time right throughout.

Were the boats being attended to? As soon as I looked out through the door I jumped back and got dressed and went out on deck, and the boats were being cleared.

Did you go to the starboard side first? I had to go round the port side first; that is on my way to the starboard.

As you were round the port side, the boats there were being cleared, were they? Yes.

Did you take any part in clearing the boats there or have anything to do in connection with them on the port side? No.

You got to the starboard side? I got to the starboard side.

What boat did you get to? The first boat I went to was No. 7.

Why did you go round to No. 7? Because the people were there.

What was being done at No. 7? Loading it with women and children.

Did you assist there? I did.

Did you see that boat lowered? I did; I assisted in lowering it.

Then did you go to No. 5? I went to No. 5.

Did you see that lowered? I did.

Did you assist? I did.

When you say you assisted, did you take charge of the operations? I assisted; that is to say, Mr Murdoch was superintending.

Then was No. 5 lowered after No. 7? No. 5 was lowered after No. 7.

Did you then go to No. 3? I then went to No. 3.

Was that lowered? That was lowered.

And did you then go to the emergency boat? I went to No. 1, the emergency boat.

Was that lowered? Yes.

When your boat was lowered that lot of boats were finished with. Did you notice any list? No.

Was the vessel down by the head? Yes.

You noticed that? Yes, of course I did. I noticed that as soon as I got up.

Did you look for any lights at this time at all? As I was getting the emergency boat ready, No. 1, Mr Boxhall was firing the detonators, the distress signals, and somebody mentioned something about a ship on the port bow, and I glanced over in that direction casually and I saw a steamer there.

What did you see of her? I saw her two masthead and her red sidelights.

Where did you go then? I then went to No. 14.

That is right aft on the other side, is it not? That would be the second forward boat of the after section, and the second boat from aft of the after section.

Why did you go to her in particular? Because they seemed to be busy there.

Did you go to assist there? I did.

Who was in charge there? I do not know who was in charge there. I finished up loading No. 14, and Mr Moody was finishing up loading No. 16.

You were loading No. 14 and he was loading No. 16? Yes.

Did you see anything about No. 12? Numbers 12, 14 and 16 went down pretty much at the same time.

You went in No. 14, did not you? Yes.

Did you go by anybody's orders? I did not. I saw five boats go away without an officer, and I told Mr Moody on my own that I had seen five boats go away, and an officer ought to go in one of these boats. I asked him who it was to be: him or I – and he told me, 'You go; I will get in another boat.'

I forget where he comes in order of seniority; is he senior to you or junior to you? No, he was junior.

Were you lowered in that boat? I was lowered in No. 14.

I want to ask you a little about that. Was there any difficulty in lowering when you got near the water? Yes, I slipped her.

Did the falls go wrong? Something got wrong and I slipped her.

That means to say, you threw off the lever when you were some way from the water? I should say I dropped her about five feet [*c.* one and a half metres].

No doubt you dealt with the situation quite rightly, but I want to know what caused the situation. Was it because the rope would not run any further? I do not know, because, you must understand, that the lowering away was being carried out on deck, and I must have been about 64 feet [*c.* 19.5 metres] below that deck, and I could not see it.

Did you look up? Yes.

Could you tell me why you were not being lowered further? No.

One of the men in your boat has given evidence, and he says he looked up and saw the rope of the falls twisted? No; I looked up and I could not see anything.

Just let me ask you this, because it is fair to ask you it. Could they twist? I suppose they could.

Can the blocks revolve at the top? Oh, yes, the blocks are movable in the davits; they are swivelled; both are swivelled, the top and bottom blocks.

Then you got to the water and you slipped her, as you say? Yes.

Did you take command of the boat? Yes.

What did you do with her? I took, I think it was, No. 12 to a distance of about 150 yards [*c.* 137 metres] from the ship, and told him to stay there until I gave him orders to go away or any other orders. I then came back to the ship and escorted another boat, and so on, until I had five boats there.

You gathered five boats together? Yes.

There is just another thing I want to ask you. Did you use a revolver at all? I did.

How was that? It was because while I was on the boat deck, just as they had started to lower, two men jumped into my boat. I chased one out and to avoid another occurrence of that sort I fired my revolver as I was going down each deck, because the boat would not stand a sudden jerk. She was loaded already I suppose with about 64 people on her, and she would not stand any more.

You were afraid of the effect of any person jumping in the boat through the air? Certainly, I was.

In your judgement had she enough in her to lower safely? She had too many in her as far as that goes. I was taking risks.

You say you collected these four boats together at a distance of about 150 yards [*c*. 137 metres]? Yes.

Can you judge how long that was before the ship went down? I have not the remotest idea of time from the time she went down until we boarded the *Carpathia*. All I know is that when we boarded the *Carpathia* in the morning it was six o'clock, and that is the only time I know of.

You could not give me any idea? I could not; it is no good my trying.

What did you do after you got the four boats out there? I tied them together in a string, and made them step their masts.

What was that for? In case it came on to blow, and then they would be ready.

Did you transfer any of your passengers? Yes, I transferred all of them.

Among the other boats? Into the other four boats.

Why did you do that? So as to have an empty boat to go back.

To do what? To go back to the wreck.

Was that before the *Titanic* foundered or after? No, that was after she went down.

Having got an empty boat, did you go back to the wreckage? I did.

Was there much wreckage? No, very little.

Am I to understand that you were alone in the boat? No.

You were there with your crew? Yes.

How many men had you in the boat? I do not know; I should say seven.

Including yourself? Yes, I should say six and myself.

Did you row six oars back to the wreck? No, five oars, I think, and I had a man on the lookout.

I understand what you say is that you got rid of the passengers. You got rid of the people who could not do anything, and went back with a working crew to look for people who were drowning; that is what you mean? Yes; it would be no good me going back with a load of people.

Certainly; I am not complaining; I am only trying to bring it out in your favour, if I may say so. You rescued some people, did not you? I picked up four.

I think one died in the boat, did he not? One died, a Mr Hoyt, of New York.

Were they men? Four men.

Did you see any other people alive? Not one, or else I should have picked them up.

Did you see bodies? Yes.

After that did you come across the submerged collapsible of which we have heard? Yes.

It was you who took the people off that, was it? I did.

Was it the one with Mr Lightoller on board? No, it was not.

Another one? Another one.

Were there two submerged collapsibles? I do not know – I did not know at the time, but, of course, I know now. The one that I picked up, I reckon, had been pierced, but I do not know. She was right side up and all that [collapsible lifeboat A].

Was she extended, or whatever you call it, opened out; were the collapsible sides pulled up? No, the sides had dropped somehow or other.

She was flat? She was right side up.

Can you give us any idea of who were on board of her – you do not know? No. I can only give you one, and that was the lady that was on board there.

The lady? Yes.

Can you tell me how many collapsibles got to the *Carpathia*, because we cannot account for the collapsibles? I abandoned one, and then I towed another one while I was under sail to the *Carpathia*; that is two; then the one that Mr Lightoller was on, that is three. I do not know where the fourth is.

So far as you know there were only three ever got away from the wreck in any shape? As far as I know.

You stated in giving evidence in America that a crowd went down to the gangway doors to get them open, and that you were going to load the boats and take passengers in from these gangway doors? I did.

It has come out in the evidence that a number of women and children perished on the *Titanic*. I believe that is a fact. May it be that in the expectation of this method being carried out, a number of the women and children were directed down to these gangways? No, it is not.

Were you giving directions as to the filling of boat No. 1? I was.

And the lowering of her? And the lowering of her.

She was loaded with a very small number of passengers – five? I do not know how many there were. I took everybody that was there; that is all I know.

You took what? I cleared the deck, my Lord.

You mean to say that when you took the people into No. 1 there were no people left on the deck? There were no people left on the starboard deck.

At that time what search did you have made for people – for passengers? I did not make any search.

You did not, for instance, send over to the port side to find if there were any women or children? No, because I wanted to get the boats away. I did not have any time to waste.

And you did not send down to any of the lower decks? There was nobody on the next deck. I stopped the boat there and asked them to look.

Or on any of the lower decks? I do not know about that. I stopped the lowering of the boat at A deck, and told the men to have a look there, and they saw nobody.

There was no particular reason why that boat should have been lowered with only five passengers? No particular reason why the boat should be lowered with only five people.

At the time that boat No. 1 was lowered there were still other boats on the starboard side? That I am not prepared to answer; I do not know.

I mean boats were lowered after No. 1? I say I do not know.

Is it not the function of lifeboats on a steamer, as far as possible, to take away the full complement of passengers? Yes; but I was working on the idea that the gangway doors were going to be opened and take people from there.

And that was why you lowered the boats from the boat deck when they were not altogether full? Certainly; we were not going to load the boat with its floating capacity from the davits.

What grounds or evidence had you for the opinion you formed that there were going to be additional people put in the lifeboats from the gangways? I really forget now. I must have overheard it.

Do you remember whom you overheard saying it? I do not.

Did you hear any instructions given? No; but as I say, I overheard a conversation somewhere referring to the gangway doors being opened, and that the boatswain and a crowd of men had been sent down there.

With reference to these boats that were lowered on your side at which you assisted, did you, after they had been lowered, take any means of communicating with those on board in order to have them filled up through the gangways? Yes. I told them to haul off from the ship's side, but to remain within hail. That is what I told each of them with the exception of the boat that Mr Pitman went in.

What I want to get at is this: you having formed the impression that the boats were going to be filled to their full complement from the gangways, did you take any steps to have the gangway doors opened or in any way to have passengers brought to the gangways? *Witness answers:* Haven't I told you that the order had been given to open the gangway doors by somebody else?

Were there people collected, do you know, at the gangway doors that had been opened? I do not, because that was in the hands of the senior officers, and I was a junior.

Beyond lowering these boats and forming that impression, you did nothing to open up communication with the gangways and have the people brought there and lowered into these boats? No, I did not.

You just mentioned one fact that I would like to put to you. You say you saw five boats go away without an officer? I did.

Were there any officers there to take control of the boats? *Witness answers:* How do you mean, were there any officers there?

Why did these five boats go away without an officer? Because I suppose the officers were busy working elsewhere.

In your opinion would it have been better organisation if on this occasion there had been more officers on board to look after the boats? No.

Do you think that more officers on the *Titanic* would have been necessary? No.

Why not? For the simple reason that men, as long as there is somebody to look after a bunch of them, are all right.

Do you think it was a proper system of organisation that would allow five boats to be lowered without any officer in control? Certainly.

Who was in control of each of those five boats? I do not know who was in control of them.

Do you know if anybody was in control? Certainly; there were men in charge of them.

Did it take half an hour to launch these boats? I do not know. It was not the launching of the boats that took the time. We got the whole boat out and in the water in less than 10 minutes. It was getting the people together that took the time.

Did you hear any orders given to the people brought up to the boat deck? Yes. I forget now who I heard, but I heard the order given anyhow, 'Everybody on the boat deck.'

Do you think there were sufficient seamen on board the *Titanic* adequately to carry out the operation of launching the boats? Certainly, they did so.

Did they take what you consider a normal time or an abnormal time to do it? It depends upon what you mean by 'an abnormal time'; less time or more time?

Do you think it would have been done quicker if there had been more men? No. The thing was done as I do not suppose any other ship could do it.

In the same time? No ship could have done it in better time, and better in all respects – in every respect.

How do you account for it that when you went back you were only able to pick up four people? I do not know.

When you began to return with your empty boat how far had you to row to the place? About 150 yards [*c.* 137 metres]

And there were five of you rowing? Yes, five I think, and there was one on the lookout, and myself steering.

Did you return to the wreckage immediately after the *Titanic* had disappeared? I did not.

Had you any reason for not doing so? I had.

Would you mind telling me what it was? Because it would have been suicide to go back there until the people had thinned out.

Your boat at that time was empty except for the crew? It was.

And it was one of the ordinary lifeboats, with the gunwale a considerable distance above the water? Yes.

I put it to you, as an experienced seaman, would not it be impossible for people who were struggling in the water to get into the boat without the assistance of those who were in the boat? No, it would not.

They could not get in without help? Yes.

Therefore if you had gone back to where the *Titanic* had sunk, it would have been impossible for these people who were floating about to have swamped your boat, because you could have detached them? *Witness answers:* How could you detach them?

How could they get into the boat without you helped them in? *Witness answers:* Could not a man hold his weight on the side like that without help from me?

About what height would the gunwale of the boat be above the water? There are lifelines round the lifeboat too and they could get hold of those and hang on the rail.

Do not you think it would have been possible for the crew of your boat to have got a considerable number of people out of the water? No, it would have been useless to try it, because a drowning man clings at anything.

Is it a fact that the same falls that lower No. 1 boat are also required to lower the collapsible boat underneath it? Yes.

And that would be an additional reason for wanting to get No. 1 into the water as quickly as possible? Yes, it would be.

Did you know Sir Cosmo and Lady Duff-Gordon by sight? I did not. I did not know a soul on board.

Did you ever say to Lady Duff-Gordon, 'Come along, Lady Duff-Gordon'? I said nothing to her. I simply bundled her into the boat.

I think after you had got rid of your passengers and went back with the crew you spent a considerable time in rescuing one man from some wreckage? Yes, it was rather awkward to get in amongst it, because you could not row, because of the bodies. You had to push your way through.

And that would account, perhaps, for the time you took to take one man off? Certainly it would.

Did the wind get up after that? Yes, a breeze sprang up then.

Did you put up your sail? Yes.

Did you keep your sail up and tow the other boat while you were sailing? I kept the sail up from then until I got alongside the *Carpathia*, and towed the collapsible and picked up the other collapsible – the sinking one.

Have you any suggestion to make as to the sail that you had in the boat? Was it a suitable sail for the occasion? The sail might be improved.

When did you use the sail? I used the sail from the time I got to the wreck until I got on board the *Carpathia*.

Then you were using it for several hours? I do not know about several hours. I suppose it was about two and a half hours.

What is your suggestion? That they be made without a dipping tack – that the tack be lashed abaft the mast, the same as ordinary lugsails.

Did you find it difficult to manoeuvre it with passengers in your boat? Besides that you want a man that knows something about dipping tack. You have to lower the sail and slacken the sheet before you can dip it.

Can you tell us the last you saw of Mr Moody on the *Titanic*? When I had that conversation with him. That is the last I saw of him.

Did you see whether he actually got into any other boat? No, I did not.

Do you remember being at No. 5 boat with Mr Murdoch? Yes.

Do you remember meeting a gentleman there who was interfering with the work? Yes.

Who was it? I afterwards learned it was Mr Bruce Ismay.

What did he say to you or say to anybody; was he giving orders? No, he was trying all in his power to help the work, and he was getting a little bit excited.

What was he doing to help the work? He was going like this, 'Lower away, lower away'.

Did you see Mr Ismay go into any boat? No. I told the men to go ahead clearing No. 3 boat, and Mr Ismay went there and helped them.

You did not see him go into a boat afterwards? No.

Did Mr Ismay do all he could to help? He did everything in his power to help.

You have told us how you tied the boats under your command together and went back with your boat with only the crew to help? Yes.

Did you approach as soon as you thought you could do so with reasonable safety? I did. I had to wait until I could be of some use. It was no good going back there to be swamped.

And you saved some. Then coming back you were under sail, if I rightly understand? I was.

And you took your own collapsible in tow? That was the collapsible that I had in the string of boats, yes.

And then you met another collapsible? I did not meet her. It was a good way off and I sailed down to her.

I want you to tell me a little particularly about that collapsible. How many people were on her? I do not know. I do not want to appear sarcastic, or anything like that, but you do not count people in a case like this. I should say, roughly, about 20 men and one woman.

And you took them off her? Yes.

She was in a bad way rather? Yes.

Did you leave anyone on that collapsible? I did. I left three bodies.

Are you certain that the three bodies that you left were the bodies of dead people? Absolutely certain.

Did you satisfy yourself about that? I made the men on that collapsible turn those bodies over before I took them into my boat. I said, 'Before you come on board here you turn those bodies over and make sure they are dead,' and they did so.

Is there the slightest doubt in your own mind that they were dead? Not the slightest doubt.

Do you see any reason why the lifeboats should not have been lowered full of people? Yes, I do.

Did you see any one of them lowered full of people – I mean with about 60 in the boat? No, sir. I could not say that I did.

What in your opinion is the reason why the boat should not be lowered full of people? The reason, my Lord, is that the boat is suspended from both ends, and all the weight is in the middle, and that being so the boat is apt to buckle, that is, break in the middle, and both ends buckle up and shoot the whole lot out of her.

At all events you would not think it safe to do it? No.

How many were in your boat when it was lowered? I mustered them when I got away from the ship and there were 58 passengers – that would be 65 altogether.

That was lowered without buckling? Yes, but I said I was taking on risks, sir.

Did you see the *Titanic* sink? I did.

Can you tell me anything about this righting of the after end of the vessel; did you see that? No, I did not see her right at all – you mean to say that she evened up on her keel?

Yes, the after part of her? No, my Lord, I did not.

Did you see her actually go down? I did.

If she had righted herself in that way would you have seen it? Yes, because I was within 150 yards [*c.* 137 metres] of her.

And you did not see that? I did not.

LIFEBOAT 12
Port Side, Launched 1.30 a.m.

Second Officer Charles Lightoller supervised the loading of this lifeboat, which took almost exclusively second class women. Archibald Gracie notices a 'Frenchman' jump from the deck as the boat is lowered. Imantita Shelley also describes a 'crazed Italian' jumping into the boat, showing the casual racism notable in many of the survivors' stories.

This lifeboat took a large number of passengers from collapsible lifeboats D and B later on in the night, arriving at the *Carpathia* at capacity. Being the last boat to reach the *Carpathia*, at 8.30 a.m. lifeboat 12 had been drifting in the North Atlantic for approximately seven hours before rescue.

Male crew: two; male passengers: one (?); women and children: 40; total for lifeboat: 43 (British Board of Inquiry).

27
Imantita Shelley, Second Class Passenger

Returning to the US with her mother was 25-year-old Imantita Shelley. In her affidavit Shelley refers to Ida and Isidor Straus. Isidor Straus owned Macy's department store in New York and the couple were known to many on board. The Strauses had a happy marriage and it seems that they were rarely apart. The story of their death is often romanticised. Ida refused to board a lifeboat without her husband and witnesses later described their last moments on the deck of the *Titanic* sitting on deckchairs awaiting their fate.

United States Senate Inquiry Affidavit That her mother, Mrs Lutie Davis Parrish, of Woodford County, Ky., and herself embarked on the White Star steamship *Titanic* at Southampton, England, upon the 10th day of April, 1912, having purchased the best second class accommodation sold by said company.

That instead of being assigned to the accommodation purchased, were taken to a small cabin many decks down in the ship, which was so small that it could only be called a cell. It was impossible to open a regulation steamer trunk in said cabin. It was impossible for a third person to enter said cabin unless both occupants first of all crawled into their bunks.

That the stewardess was sent to the chief purser demanding transfer to accommodation purchased. That he replied he could do nothing until the boat had left Queenstown, Ireland, when he would check up all tickets and find out if there was any mistake.

That after leaving Queenstown Mrs L. D. Parrish made 11 trips herself to the purser asking for transfer, only to be put off with promises. That at nine o'clock p. m., no one having come to take them to better quarters, Mrs Shelley wrote a note to the purser to the effect that she had paid for the best second class accommodation on the ship and had the receipts to prove it; that she was very ill and, owing to that freezing cold of the cabin, was in great danger; that if he, the purser, refused to act she, Mrs Shelley, would appeal to the captain; that if neither would act she realised she would have to wait until reaching America for redress, but most assuredly would claim damages if she lived to reach her native land.

That the result of this letter was the arrival of four stewards to carry her to the room paid for, who offered apology after apology.

That the stewardess, on being asked what the purser had said on reading the note, replied, 'He asked first if you were really so very sick, to which I answered there was no doubt about that. Then the purser asked me if there was such a cabin on board the *Titanic*, where a cabin trunk could not be opened; to which I replied in the affirmative. I also told him that the cabin was entirely too small for two women, and that two men could not hardly fit in; that it was impossible for myself or the steward to enter the cabin and to wait upon the occupants unless both of them first climbed into their berths. The purser then told me that he would have to act at once, or the company would get into trouble.'

That after being transferred to this new cabin the second class physician, Dr Simpson, called from three to four times a day; that he feared the attack of tonsillitis brought on by the chill would become diphtheritic and ordered Mrs Shelley to remain in her cabin.

That this cabin, though large and roomy, was not furnished in the comfortable manner as the same accommodation procured on the Cunard and other lines; that it looked in a half-finished condition; that this room was just as cold as the cell from which we had just been removed, and on asking the steward to have the heat turned on, he answered that it was impossible, as the heating system for the second class cabins refused to work. That of all the second class cabins, only three – the three first cabins to be reached by the heat – had any heat at all, and that the heat was so intense there that the occupants had complained to the purser, who had ordered the heat shut off entirely; consequently the rooms were like ice houses all of the voyage, and Mrs L. D. Parrish, when not waiting on her sick daughter, was obliged to go to bed to keep warm.

That afterwards, when on board the *Carpathia*, Mrs Shelley took pains to inquire of steerage passengers as to whether or not they had heat in the steerage of the *Titanic* and received the answer that there was the same trouble with their heating plant, too.

That although the servants on board were most willing, they had a hard time to do their work; that the stewardess could not even get a tray to serve Mrs Shelley's meals and had to bring the plates and dishes one at a time in her hands, making the service very slow and annoying. The food, though good and plentiful, was ruined by this trouble in serving. That although both steward and stewardess appealed time and time again to the heads of their departments, no relief was obtained: there seemed to be no organisation at all. That in the ladies toilet room only part of the fixtures had been installed, some of the said fixtures being still in crates.

That in the early evening of the night of the accident the temperature had fallen considerably, so that all on board realised we were in the ice belt. There were rumours of wireless messages from other ships warning of icebergs close at hand. It was also reported that certain first class passengers had asked if the ship was to slow down whilst going through the ice belts and had been told by the captain that, on the contrary, the ship would be speeded through.

That at the moment of the collision we were awakened out of sleep by the shock, and especially by the stopping of the engines. That excited voices were heard outside in the passage, saying that an iceberg had been run into. That after continued ringing of the steward bell a steward, but not the regular one, came and insisted that all was well and for all passengers to go back to bed. Afterwards, on board the *Carpathia*, a first cabin passenger, a Mrs Baxter, of Montréal, Canada, told Mrs Shelley that she had sent her son to the captain at the time of the collision to find out what to do. That her son had found the captain in a card game, and he had laughingly assured him that there was no danger and to advise his mother to go back to bed.

That about three quarters of an hour after returning to their berths a steward came running down the passage bursting open the cabin doors and calling, 'All on deck with lifebelts on.' That this steward brought Mrs Parrish and Mrs Shelley each a lifebelt and showed them how to tie them on. That they were told to go up to the top deck, the boat deck. That as Mrs Shelley was very weak, it took several minutes to reach the upper deck. That Mr and Mrs Isidor Straus, who had known of Mrs Shelley being so ill, met them on the way and helped them to the upper deck, where they found a chair for her and made her sit down.

That owing to the great number of persons on the deck Mrs Shelley was not able to see anything of the handling of boats except the one she herself was placed in. There was practically no excitement on the part of anyone during this time, the majority seeming to think that the big boat could not sink altogether, and that it was better to stay on the steamer than trust to the lifeboats. After sitting on the chair for about five minutes one of the sailors ran to Mrs Shelley and implored her to get in the lifeboat that was then being launched. He informed Mrs Shelley that it was the last boat on the ship, and that unless she got into that one she would have to take her chances on the steamer, and that as she had been so sick she ought to take to the boat and make sure. Mrs Straus advised taking to the boats, and, pushing her mother toward the sailor, Mrs Shelley made for the davits where the boat hung. It was found impossible to swing the davits in, which left a space of between four and five feet [*c.* one and a half metres] between the edge of the deck and the suspended boat. The sailor picked up Mrs Parrish and threw her bodily into the boat. Mrs Shelley jumped and landed safely. That two men of the ship's crew manned this boat at the time of launching, one of whom said he was a stoker and the other a ship's baker.

That at the time of launching these were the only men in the boat. That at the time of lowering the boat it seemed to be as full of passengers as the seating capacity called for, but owing to the excitement no thought of numbers entered Mrs Shelley's head. The boat appeared to be filled with as many as could get in without overcrowding, all of them women and children, with the exception of the two mentioned above.

That on trying to lower the boat the tackle refused to work and it took considerable time, about five minutes, it is believed, to reach the water. That on reaching the water the casting off apparatus would not work and the ropes had to be cut.

That just as they reached the water a crazed Italian jumped from the deck into the lifeboat, landing on Mrs Parrish, severely bruising her right side and leg. This gave them one extra man.

After coming loose from the ship the orders were to pull out toward the other boats and get as far away from the probable suction which would ensue if the steamer should sink. Orders were also given to keep in sight of the green light of the ship's [emergency] boat [No. 2] which had been sent out ahead to look for help. That on reaching a distance of about 100 yards [*c.* 91 metres] from the *Titanic* a loud explosion or noise was heard, followed closely by another, and the sinking of the big vessel began.

Throughout the entire period from the striking of the icebergs and taking to the boats the ship's crew behaved in an ideal manner. Not a man tried to get into a boat unless ordered to, and many were seen to strip off their clothing and wrap around the women and children who came up half clad from their beds. Mrs Shelley feels confident that she speaks the truth when she says that with the exception of those few men ordered to man the boats all other sailors saved had gone down with the ship and were miraculously saved afterwards. Mrs Shelley says that no crew could have behaved in a more perfect manner and that they proved themselves men in every sense of the word. That after the sinking of the ship the boat they were in picked up several struggling in the water and were fortunate enough to rescue 30 sailors who had gone down with the ship, but who had been miraculously blown out of the water after one of the explosions and been thrown near a derelict collapsible boat to which they had managed to cling. That after taking all those men on board the boat was so full that many feared they would sink, and it was suggested that some of the other boats should take some of these rescued ones on board; but they refused, for fear of sinking.

Mrs Shelley states that she does not know what the official number of her lifeboat was, nor the official numbers of the boats finally rescued by the *Carpathia*: that on conversing with members of the crew and other survivors on board the *Carpathia* it was told Mrs Shelley that 13 boats had been picked up; that the first boat to be picked up by the *Carpathia* was what was called the signal boat – the one with the green light – which all followed as a guide and which had been picked up about three or half past three in the morning; that the boat Mrs Shelley was in was picked up shortly after eight o'clock in the morning.

That as to equipment of the lifeboats there was none in her boat except four oars and a mast, which latter was useless; there was no water nor any food; that there was neither compass nor binnacle light nor any kind of lantern; that on questioning occupants of other lifeboats they told her the same story – lack of food, water, compass, and lights, and that several boats had no oars or only two or three.

That one of that *Titanic*'s crew who was saved told that no positions had been assigned to any of the crew in regard to lifeboat service, as is the rule, and that that was one of the reasons of the confusion in assigning men to manage the lifeboats when the accident did occur.

That right after the *Titanic* began to sink a steamer was sighted about two miles away, and all were cheered up; as it was figured that they would all be picked up inside an hour or so; that, however, their hopes were blighted when the steamer's lights suddenly disappeared.

28
Laura Mae Cribb, Third Class Passenger

In this article Laura Cribb attributes her survival to her father's contacts as a butler and knowledge of the ship. Many survivors attribute their survival to personal contacts and this contributed towards the higher survival rates for first class passengers. First class passengers had often formed a bond with the stewards responsible for them and these stewards in turn felt a personal responsibility to ensure their passengers were safe. This bond was looser in third class where one steward might have upwards of 50 passengers in their charge. Laura eventually settled in the US.

Newark Star, 20 April 1912 To the rare presence of mind of her father, John H. Cribb, who lost his life when the *Titanic* sank, Miss Lillian M. Cribb, 17 years old, believes she owes her life. Controlling her overtaxed nerves as best she could upon her arrival at the home of her uncle, John W. Welch, at 106 Pennington Street, last night, she recited the incidents attending her rescue aboard the *Carpathia*.

'It was such a beautifully clear night, with the stars lighting the sky, that but few of the third cabin passengers had retired. I myself had been asleep only a few minutes when the alarm was sounded, and hardly realising any danger, I dressed and went out. I found my father waiting for me. He grasped me by the hand and almost dragged me to the deck above by a passageway which was known only to persons familiar with the ship.

'As a butler in prominent homes around New York he had acquired friendships which gave him entry to circles of that vocation, and some of those acquaintances renewed on board the *Titanic* stood him in good stead at this time, for we were permitted to mount to the upper decks by this stairway, used ordinarily only by employees. He escorted me to a lifeboat and, placing me in one which was about to be lowered, he bade me goodbye, saying that he would get into another and meet me in a short while.

'I did not see him again. But, oh, the awfulness of it all did not come to me until long afterward. I didn't think it was so serious. I kept hearing them say over and over, "Women and children first," and I permitted myself to be placed into a lifeboat, but I could not realise that it was anything but a sort of a dream. There were 35 people in our boat, which was the fourth to leave the *Titanic*, and all but five, who were sailors sent to man the boat, were women.

'We pushed away and the men rowed as hard as they could, so, as they said, we would not be caught in the suction when the vessel should go down. I saw the big iceberg which we struck and it looked as though the ship was stuck fast into it. The lights were lit for perhaps a half-hour after we left the ship and they disappeared and we did not see the ship or the iceberg again. After drifting about until daylight we discerned a wide field of ice with several high icebergs protruding, but I could not say that any one of them was that which we had struck.

'When we were taken aboard the *Carpathia* we were asked to what class we belonged. I, of course, told them I was of the third class, as did others, but immediately we became aware that there was a difference between the accommodations of the two ships for the same classification of passengers. Such things as table linens and other homelike features were missing in our new habitations, we found. But eventually foreigners of a certain class were relegated to another part of the ship and we were given what was probably more attention than was usual for that grade of passengers. In fact, there was one of my father's old friends who saw that I and some of my new acquaintances got some of the things on the bill of fare that the second class passengers got, and so we did not fare so badly after all, so far as eating was concerned.'

Miss Cribb is decidedly English in her speech and manner, but by birth she is an American, having been born in Newark 17 years ago. The last eight years she has lived in Bournemouth, England, where her mother and two brothers and a sister still remain. She and her father had preceded the rest of the family on what was to have been their return to this country for the purpose of making their home.

Mr Cribb was for several years assistant steward of the Essex Club of this city and he was later butler for Herbert Ballentine. In a similar capacity he was in the employ of Frank Gould on the yacht *Helenita*, and until last September was butler at the home of E. S. Repello, 841 Madison Venue, New York. It was to the last mentioned place to which he had expected to return on his arrival upon the *Titanic*.

LIFEBOAT 9
Starboard Side, Launched 1.30 a.m.

First Officer Murdoch supervised the loading of lifeboat 9 and put boatswain's mate Albert Hains in charge. Second class female passengers were the largest contingent. But a significant number of men were allowed to climb in when no more women were forthcoming. This included some industrious third class men who had managed to negotiate their way to the boat deck and several crew members. There were also a handful of lucky second class men. Statistically, second class male passengers had the worst survival rates with less than one in 10 surviving.

Male crew: eight; male passengers: six; women and children: 42; total for lifeboat: 56 (British Board of Inquiry).

29
Berk Pickard, Third Class Passenger

There was much debate immediately after the sinking and for many years to come about class discrimination in loading the *Titanic* lifeboats. It is certainly true that first class passengers had a better chance of survival, but the British inquiry's conclusion was that there was no discrimination. In this extract Berk Pickard states that the steerage passengers 'were not prevented from getting up to the upper decks by anybody, or by closed doors, or anything else'. However, it also becomes clear that he had to navigate the unfamiliar second class accommodation and climb a ladder to get to the boat deck, and on such a large ship this was no easy task.

US Senate Inquiry Affidavit At the time I took passage on the *Titanic* I came from London. I am 32 years old. I am a leather worker; a bag maker. I was born in Russia, in Warsaw. My name was Berk Trembisky. I was for a long time in France and I assumed a French name. As regards private business, I am Pickard.

I was one of the third class passengers on the *Titanic*. My cabin was No. 10 in the steerage, at the stern. I first knew of the collision when it happened, about 10 minutes to 12. We had all been asleep, and all of a sudden we perceived a shock. We did not hear such a very terrible shock, but we knew something was wrong, and we jumped out of bed and we dressed ourselves and went out, and we could not get back again. I wanted to go back to get my things but I could not. The stewards would not allow us to go back. They made us all go forward on the deck. There were no doors locked to prevent us from going back. I did not take much notice of it, and I went to the deck. The other passengers started in arguing. One said that it was dangerous and the other said that it was not; one said white and the other said black. Instead of arguing with those people, I instantly went to the highest spot.

I said to myself that if the ship had to sink, I should be one of the last. That was my first idea, which was the best. I went and I found the door. There are always a few steps from this third class, with a movable door, and it is marked there second class passengers have no right to penetrate there. I found this door open so that I could go into the second class, where I did not find any people, only a few that climbed on the ladder and went into the first class, which I did. I found there only a few men and about two ladies. They had been putting them into lifeboats and as no women were there; we men sprang in the boat. We had only one woman and another young girl. There were two women. They just stood in front of me. We were lowered down, and when I was lowered down I saw the whole ship, as big as she was, the right side a little bit sinking, and I was far from imagining that it was the beginning of the end. When I was going away from the ship, of course I was rather frightened; I was sorry at not being on the ship, and I said to the seaman, 'I would rather be on the ship.' He was laughing at me, and he said, 'Do you not see we are sinking?' I was rather excited, and I said, 'It is fortunate that the sea is nice, but perhaps in five minutes we will be turned over.' So I was in the boat until five o'clock in the morning.

In regard to the ship, I saw the ship very quickly started sinking, and one rail went under and then another, until in a half an hour, from my point of view, the ship sank altogether.

The steerage passengers, so far as I could see, were not prevented from getting up to the upper decks by anybody, or by closed doors, or anything else. While I was on the ship no one realised the real danger, not even the stewards. If the stewards knew, they were calm. It was their duty to try to make us believe there was nothing serious. Nobody was prevented from going up. They tried to keep us quiet. They said, 'Nothing serious is the matter.' Perhaps they did not know themselves. I did not realise it, the whole time, even to the last moment. Of course, I would never believe such a thing could happen.

The lifeboat I got into was an ordinary lifeboat. I do not know what number it was; I am sorry to say I did not look at it. There was some seaman in charge of it, who belonged to the ship. What kind of employment the seamen were in I do not know, but they belonged to the ship.

The only warning given to the steerage passengers after the collision was that we were ordered to take our lifebelts and go to the deck. There was no water in the steerage when I left.

That is all I know about it. I was one of the first to go. Of course, if I had stayed until a little bit later, I would have seen a little bit more. I was one of the luckiest ones, I think.

LIFEBOAT 11
Starboard Side, Launched 1.35 a.m.

Supervised by First Officer Murdoch, lifeboat 11 was one of the few lifeboats to be launched at capacity. Filled from both the boat deck and A deck, it was placed under the charge of Quartermaster Humphreys. A number of stewards, both male and females, got away in this lifeboat.

Male crew: nine; male passengers: one; women and children: 60; total for lifeboat: 70 (British Board of Inquiry).

30
Annie Robinson, Stewardess

Annie Robinson was a 40-year-old stewardess from Southampton. Robinson refers to a meeting with Thomas Andrews. As the ship's builder and one of the first to investigate the damage caused by the iceberg, Andrews was well aware of the genuine danger they were in. In 1914 Annie Robinson committed suicide. She jumped overboard whilst travelling across the Atlantic on board the *Devonian*. Newspaper accounts report that Annie was in 'a high state of excitement because of the fog and the sounding of the fog horn'. For many survivors the *Titanic* disaster loomed large for the rest of their lives.

British Board of Trade Inquiry (inquiry question is followed immediately by witness's answer) And at the time the ship struck the iceberg I think you were in bed? I was.

Did you get up and dress? I did.

And did you afterwards go in the direction of the mail room? Yes.

What deck were you on? E deck.

When you got to the top of the stairs which lead down to the mail room what did you see? I saw two mail bags and a man's Gladstone bag, and on looking down the staircase I saw water within six steps of coming on to E deck.

That would mean that it had gone up to the top of the mail room and into the compartment above that? Certainly.

Are the stairs you are speaking of the ones by the side of the squash racquets court? Yes [see illustration 58 for position of the squash court and mail room. The mail room is to the left of the court].

About what time was this? About half an hour after she struck.

Did you see the captain and Mr Andrews about this time? The mail man passed along first and he returned with Mr McElroy and the Captain and they went in the direction of the mail room, but that was before.

It was seeing the Captain and Mr Andrews going to the mail room that made you go there? I followed after they had come back.

When you saw the water there I suppose you realised that things were rather serious? I did.

Did you go and look after your ladies? I did.

How many ladies were under your charge? Seven ladies and one maid and a governess.

Did you see other stewardesses doing the same thing, looking after their passengers? The stewardess on my deck was doing exactly the same thing.

Did you then go upstairs on to A deck? I had to call a stewardess I had met on the boat on A deck.

Were you told by a steward there to put on your coat and lifebelt? Mr Andrews told me first.

Did Mr Andrews tell you anything else? Yes. Mr Andrews told me to put my lifebelt on after I had been on E deck.

Did he say something to you about blankets? We had already got the blankets and the lifebelts out of the rooms which were unoccupied at the foot of the staircase. Mr Andrews said to me, 'Put your lifebelt on and walk about and let the passengers see you.' I said to him, 'It looks rather mean,' and he said, 'No, put it on,' and then after that he said to me, 'Well, if you value your life put your belt on.'

Did you put your belt on and walk about in it? I did.

Did he say anything to you about Mr Ismay? No, Mr Ismay's name was never mentioned in my hearing.

So far as you know were all the ladies on E deck warned by the stewardesses whose business it was to look after them? Yes, and they were all saved, too.

You told us you were responsible for seven or eight ladies; were they all saved? They were.

Eventually you were put into boat No. 11? Yes.

I will not ask you about what happened in the boat, but there is one thing I should have asked you about what happened before; did you see the carpenter? I did; he was the first man I saw. He came along when I was looking down at the water, and he had the lead line in his hand.

Had he taken a sounding, do you know? I could not tell you that.

Did he say anything to you? No, the man looked absolutely bewildered, distracted. He did not speak.

You think he looked alarmed? He certainly was.

Can you remember at all what time it was when your boat left? Well, I looked at my watch when the ship went down and it was 20 minutes to 2. That was by altered time when we were in the boat, and I do not think we were in the boat more than three quarters of an hour.

You left about three quarters of an hour before the ship went down? Yes.

Can you state at what time it was when Mr Andrews said to you, 'If you value your life put your lifebelt on'? It was about half an hour when I saw the water on the deck, and I should say it would be about a quarter of an hour after that.

About three quarters of an hour after the collision you mean? Yes.

Have you ever been in a collision before? Yes.

What ship was that? The *Lake Champlain*? Yes.

Also an iceberg? Yes.

So that you knew exactly what to do on this occasion? Yes.

Did the people get into the boat in an orderly way? Yes.

Did you hear the band playing? Yes.

Was it still playing when you left the ship? Yes it was. It was playing when I went up to A deck to call the other stewardess, and when I left the ship it was still playing.

31

Marie Jerwan, Second Class Passenger

Originally from Switzerland, Marie Jerwan had immigrated to the US a few years previously. Marie is another woman who is reported as taking care of a baby in the lifeboats. The Mrs Balls referred to is Ada Ball, Jerwan's cabin-mate.

New York Times, 19 April 1912 When the ship struck the iceberg it was a tremendous shock that made me think that the boilers had blown up. I had not retired, although it was late, and ran out. I asked one of the officers what had happened and he said it was nothing of consequence. Some of the women who had been awakened and who ran out were told the same and went back to bed. I did not, and about 20 minutes later the officers came around telling us to put on lifebelts. Mrs Balls had not even been awakened by the shock and had no time to dress when we went on deck.

There was only a slight slope to the deck for about half an hour, but by the time they were launching the small boats the ship had begun to go down by the head rapidly. Still we had no idea that there was any danger of her sinking. Everything was done without the slightest disorder. No one got hysterical and there was no confusion except when a child would be put in a boat and the mother told to wait for another one. I saw several instances of this. The crew and the men passengers all behaved as if everything would turn out all right and we women thought it would.

When I got in one of the boats I found a baby in my possession without the least idea whom it belonged to. I never found out. When we were picked up by the *Carpathia* the baby was taken on board in a net and I never saw it again. I suppose it was found by the mother.

Before we had been in the boat very long we saw the *Titanic* go down. Then we knew that all the people we had left behind were lost. We saw it go plainly, although it was night. The stars were bright and we could see the lights of the ship. Suddenly those in the bow seemed to go out, and then quickly the same thing happened to those in the stern. The band was in the stern and went down playing. We could hear the screams of those on board and cries of 'Save us' but of course we could do nothing.

Everybody on the ship blamed the Captain. The sailor who rowed our boat told me that he had followed the sea for 45 years and had never been in any kind of accident before, except on the *Olympic* when she rammed into the *Hawke*. 'That was under the same Captain,' he said, 'and now I am having my second experience under him.'

There was no food nor drinking water in the boat, but we found some oil. We dipped our handkerchiefs in this and burned them for signals. On one of the boats we heard four or five pistol shots, probably for signals. We were told that some of the boats would carry 80 each, but some had less that 50 and some a little more.

It was about seven in the morning when we were picked up. We had been in the boat nearly seven hours. All though the night we kept thinking we saw the lights of a ship, but it was only the stars that deceived us. When we finally did see the *Carpathia* approaching we could hardly believe it was not another mistake. On the *Carpathia* we saw an iceberg that they said was 20 miles across, and we saw some when in the small boat, but of course there was no way of telling which of these sank the *Titanic*. While we were on the *Titanic* we could see nothing of the iceberg we had struck.

LIFEBOAT 13
Starboard Side, Launched 1.40 a.m.

Loaded by First Officer Murdoch and Sixth Officer Moody, this lifeboat contained some of the passengers that John Hart, a third class steward, had led up to the boat deck. This lifeboat had a lucky escape when lifeboat 15 was launched on top of it. The occupants in lifeboat 13 only just raised the alarm in time. Stoker Frederick Barrett was in charge of this boat. Male crew: five; male passengers: 0; women and children: 59; total for lifeboat: 64 (British Board of Inquiry).

32
Lawrence Beesley, Second Class Passenger

Lawrence Beesley was a 34-year-old science teacher. A Cambridge University graduate, Beesley wrote one of the more considered and authoritative eyewitness accounts of the disaster. *The Loss of the SS Titanic, its Story and its Lessons* was first published just nine weeks after the disaster. No *Titanic* collection would be complete without Beesley, and it is for this reason that I have included a major extract. I would like to thank Nicholas Wade, Lawrence Beesley's grandson, for permission to reproduce this extract. As with many accounts, some of Beesley's timings are a little off. His estimate of when lifeboat 13 was launched is earlier than the time now accepted.

Contemporary reviews of the book include: 'The best first-hand account of a passenger's experiences ... a first-rate piece of descriptive writing' *The Guardian*; 'Remarkable for its vividness and completeness' *The Daily Express*; 'The clearest account given by any survivor of the disaster' *The Daily Mail*.

Preface
The circumstances in which this book came to be written are as follows. Some five weeks after the survivors from the *Titanic* landed in New York, I was the guest at

luncheon of Hon. Samuel J. Elder and Hon. Charles T. Gallagher, both well-known lawyers in Boston. After luncheon I was asked to relate to those present the experiences of the survivors in leaving the *Titanic* and reaching the *Carpathia*.

When I had done so, Mr Robert Lincoln O'Brien, the editor of the *Boston Herald*, urged me as a matter of public interest to write a correct history of the *Titanic* disaster, his reason being that he knew several publications were in preparation by people who had not been present at the disaster, but from newspaper accounts were piecing together a description of it. He said that these publications would probably be erroneous, full of highly coloured details, and generally calculated to disturb public thought on the matter. He was supported in his request by all present, and under this general pressure I accompanied him to Messrs Houghton Mifflin Company, where we discussed the question of publication.

Messrs Houghton Mifflin Company took at that time exactly the same view that I did, that it was probably not advisable to put on record the incidents connected with the *Titanic*'s sinking: it seemed better to forget details as rapidly as possible.

However, we decided to take a few days to think about it. At our next meeting we found ourselves in agreement again – but this time on the common ground that it would probably be a wise thing to write a history of the *Titanic* disaster as correctly as possible. I was supported in this decision by the fact that a short account, which I wrote at intervals on board the *Carpathia*, in the hope that it would calm public opinion by stating the truth of what happened as nearly as I could recollect it, appeared in all the American, English and Colonial papers and had exactly the effect it was intended to have. This encourages me to hope that the effect of this work will be the same.

Another matter aided me in coming to a decision – the duty that we, as survivors of the disaster, owe to those who went down with the ship, to see that the reforms so urgently needed are not allowed to be forgotten.

Whoever reads the account of the cries that came to us afloat on the sea from those sinking in the ice-cold water must remember that they were addressed to him just as much as to those who heard them, and that the duty, of seeing that reforms are carried out devolves on everyone who knows that such cries were heard in utter helplessness the night the *Titanic* sank.

Chapter 1 Construction & Preparations for the First Voyage

The history of the RMS *Titanic*, of the White Star Line, is one of the most tragically short it is possible to conceive. The world had waited expectantly for its launching and again for its sailing; had read accounts of its tremendous size and its unexampled completeness and luxury; had felt it a matter of the greatest satisfaction that such a comfortable, and above all such a safe boat had been designed and built – the 'unsinkable lifeboat' – and then in a moment to hear that it had gone to the bottom as if it had been the veriest tramp steamer of a few hundred tons; and with it 1,500 passengers, some of them known the world over! The improbability of such a thing ever happening was what staggered humanity.

If its history had to be written in a single paragraph it would be somewhat as follows:

The RMS *Titanic* was built by Messrs Harland & Wolff at their well-known shipbuilding works at Queen's Island, Belfast, side by side with her sister ship the *Olympic*. The twin vessels marked such an increase in size that specially laid-out joiner and boiler shops were prepared to aid in their construction, and the space usually taken up by three building slips was given up to them. The keel of the *Titanic* was laid on 31 March 1909, and she was launched on 31 May 1911; she passed her trials before the Board of Trade officials on 31 March 1912, at Belfast, arrived at Southampton on 4 April and sailed the following Wednesday, 10 April, with 2,208 passengers and crew, on her maiden voyage to New York. She called at Cherbourg the same day, Queenstown Thursday, and left for New York in the afternoon, expecting to arrive the following Wednesday morning. But the voyage was never completed. She collided with an iceberg on Sunday at 11.45 p.m. in Lat. 41° 46' N and Long. 50° 14' W, and sank two hours and a half later; 815 of her passengers and 688 of her crew were drowned and 705 rescued by the *Carpathia*.

Such is the record of the *Titanic*, the largest ship the world had ever seen – she was three inches [*c.* seven and a half cm] longer than the *Olympic* and 1,000 tons more in gross tonnage – and her end was the greatest maritime disaster known. The whole civilised world was stirred to its depths when the full extent of loss of life was learned, and it has not yet recovered from the shock. And that is without doubt a good thing. It should not recover from it until the possibility of such a disaster occurring again has been utterly removed from human society, whether by separate legislation in different countries or by international agreement. No living person should seek to dwell in thought for one moment on such a disaster except in the endeavour to glean from it knowledge that will be of profit to the whole world in the future. When such knowledge is practically applied in the construction, equipment, and navigation of passenger steamers – and not until then – will be the time to cease to think of the *Titanic* disaster and of the hundreds of men and women so needlessly sacrificed.

A few words on the ship's construction and equipment will be necessary in order to make clear many points that arise in the course of this book. A few figures have been added which it is hoped will help the reader to follow events more closely than he otherwise could.

The considerations that inspired the builders to design the *Titanic* on the lines on which she was constructed were those of speed, weight of displacement, passenger and cargo accommodation. High speed is very expensive, because the initial cost of the necessary powerful machinery is enormous, the running expenses entailed very heavy, and passenger and cargo accommodation have to be fined down to make the resistance through the water as little as possible and to keep the weight down. An increase in size brings a builder at once into conflict with the question of dock and harbour accommodation at the ports she will touch: if her total displacement is very great while the lines are kept slender for speed, the draught limit may be exceeded. The *Titanic*, therefore, was built on broader lines than the ocean racers, increasing the total displacement; but because of the broader build, she was able to keep within the draught limit at each port she visited. At the same time she was able to accommodate more passengers and cargo, and thereby increase largely her earning capacity. A comparison between the *Mauretania* and the *Titanic* illustrates the difference in these respects:

	Displacement	Horse power	Speed in knots
Mauretania	44,640	70,000	26
Titanic	60,000	46,000	21

The vessel when completed was 883 feet [*c.* 269 metres] long, 92½ feet [*c.* 28 metres] broad; her height from keel to bridge was 104 feet [*c.* 32 metres]. She had eight steel decks, a cellular double bottom, 5¼ feet [*c.* 1.6 metres] through (the inner and outer 'skins' so called), and with bilge keels projecting 2 feet [*c.* 60 cm] for 300 feet [*c.* 91 metres] of her length amidships. These latter were intended to lessen the tendency to roll in a sea; they no doubt did so very well, but, as it happened, they proved to be a weakness, for this was the first portion of the ship touched by the iceberg and it has been suggested that the keels were forced inwards by the collision and made the work of smashing in the two 'skins' a more simple matter. Not that the final result would have been any different.

Her machinery was an expression of the latest progress in marine engineering, being a combination of reciprocating engines with Parsons's low-pressure turbine engine – a combination which gives increased power with the same steam consumption, an advance on the use of reciprocating engines alone. The reciprocating engines drove the wing-propellers and the turbine a mid-propeller, making her a triple-screw vessel. To drive these engines she had 29 enormous boilers and 159 furnaces. Three elliptical funnels, 24 feet 6 inches [*c.* 7.5 metres] in the widest diameter, took away smoke and water gases; the fourth one was a dummy for ventilation.

She was fitted with 16 lifeboats 30 feet [*c.* nine metres] long, swung on davits of the Welin double-acting type. These davits are specially designed for dealing with two and, where necessary, three, sets of lifeboats – i.e. 48 altogether; more than enough to have saved every soul on board on the night of the collision. She was divided into 16 compartments by 15 transverse watertight bulkheads reaching from the double bottom to the upper deck in the forward end and to the saloon deck in the after end, in both cases well above the waterline. Communication between the engine rooms and boiler rooms was through watertight doors, which could all be closed instantly from the captain's bridge: a single switch, controlling powerful electromagnets, operated them. They could also be closed by hand with a lever, and in case the floor below them was flooded by accident, a float underneath the flooring shut them automatically. These compartments were so designed that if the two largest were flooded with water – a most unlikely contingency in the ordinary way – the ship would still be quite safe. Of course, more than two were flooded the night of the collision, but exactly how many is not yet thoroughly established.

Her crew had a complement of 860, made up of 475 stewards, cooks, etc., 320 engineers, and 65 engaged in her navigation. The machinery and equipment of the *Titanic* was the finest obtainable and represented the last word in marine construction. All her structure was of steel, of a weight, size, and thickness greater than that of any ship yet known: the girders, beams, bulkheads, and floors all of exceptional strength. It would hardly seem necessary to mention this, were it not that there is an impression among a portion of the general public that the provision of Turkish baths, gymnasiums, and other so-called luxuries involved a sacrifice of some more essential things, the absence of which was responsible for the loss of so many lives. But this is quite an erroneous impression. All these things were an additional provision for the comfort and convenience of passengers, and there is no more reason why they should not be provided on these ships than in a large hotel. There were places on the *Titanic*'s deck where more boats and rafts could have been stored without sacrificing these things. The fault lay in not providing them, not in designing the ship without places to put them. On whom the responsibility must rest for their not being provided is another matter and must be left until later.

When arranging a tour round the United States, I had decided to cross in the *Titanic* for several reasons – one, that it was rather a novelty to be on board the largest ship yet launched, and another that friends who had crossed in the *Olympic* described her as a most comfortable boat in a sea way, and it was reported that the *Titanic* had been still further improved in this respect by having 1,000 tons more built in to steady her. I went on board at Southampton at 10 a.m. Wednesday 10 April, after staying the night in the town. It is pathetic to recall that as I sat that morning in the breakfast room of a hotel, from the windows of which could be seen the four huge funnels of the *Titanic* towering over the roofs of the various shipping offices opposite, and the procession of stokers and stewards wending their way to the ship, there sat behind me three of the *Titanic*'s passengers discussing the coming voyage and estimating, among other things, the probabilities of an accident at sea to the ship. As I rose from breakfast, I glanced at the group and recognised them later on board, but they were not among the number who answered to the roll call on the *Carpathia* on the following Monday morning.

Between the time of going on board and sailing, I inspected, in the company of two friends who had come from Exeter to see me off, the various decks, dining saloons and libraries; and so extensive were they that it is no exaggeration to say that it was quite easy to lose one's way on such a ship. We wandered casually into the gymnasium on the boat deck, and were engaged in bicycle exercise when the instructor came in with two photographers and insisted on our remaining there while his friends – as we thought at the time – made a record for him of his apparatus in use. It was only later that we discovered that they were the photographers of one of the illustrated London papers. More passengers came in, and the instructor ran here and there, looking the very picture of robust, rosy-cheeked health and 'fitness' in his white flannels, placing one passenger on the electric 'horse', another on the 'camel', while the laughing group of onlookers watched the inexperienced riders vigorously shaken up and down as he controlled the little motor which made the machines imitate so realistically horse and camel exercise.

It is related that on the night of the disaster, right up to the time of the *Titanic*'s sinking, while the band grouped outside the gymnasium doors played with such supreme courage in face of the water which rose foot by foot before their eyes, the instructor was on duty inside, with passengers on the bicycles and the rowing machines, still assisting and encouraging to the last. Along with the bandsmen it is fitting that his name, which I do not think has yet been put on record – it is McCawley – should have a place in the honourable list of those who did their duty faithfully to the ship and the line they served.

Chapter 2 From Southampton to the Night of the Collision

Soon after noon the whistles blew for friends to go ashore, the gangways were withdrawn, and the *Titanic* moved slowly down the dock, to the accompaniment of last messages and shouted farewells of those on the quay. There was no cheering or hooting of steamers' whistles from the fleet of ships that lined the dock, as might seem probable on the occasion of the largest vessel in the world putting to sea on her maiden voyage; the whole scene was quiet and rather ordinary, with little of the picturesque and interesting ceremonial which imagination paints as usual in such circumstances. But if this was lacking, two unexpected dramatic incidents supplied a thrill of excitement and interest to the departure from dock. The first of these occurred just before the last gangway was withdrawn – a knot of stokers ran along the quay, with their kit slung over their shoulders in bundles, and made for the gangway with the evident intention of joining the ship. But a petty officer guarding the shore end of the gangway firmly refused to allow them on board; they argued, gesticulated, apparently attempting to explain the reasons why they were late, but he remained obdurate and waved them back with a determined hand; the gangway was dragged back amid their protests, putting a summary ending to their determined efforts to join the *Titanic*. Those stokers must be thankful men today that some circumstance, whether their own lack of punctuality or some unforeseen delay over which they had no control, prevented their being in time to run up that last gangway! They will have told – and will no doubt tell for years – the story of how their lives were probably saved by being too late to join the *Titanic*.

The second incident occurred soon afterwards, and while it has no doubt been thoroughly described at the time by those on shore, perhaps a view of the occurrence from the deck of the *Titanic* will not be without interest. As the *Titanic* moved majestically down the dock, the crowd of friends keeping pace with us along the quay, we came together level with the steamer *New York* lying moored to the side of the dock along with the *Oceanic*, the crowd waving 'goodbyes' to those on board as well as they could for the intervening bulk of the two ships. But as the bows of our ship came about level with those of the *New York*, there came a series of reports like those of a revolver, and on the quay side of the *New York* snaky coils of thick rope flung themselves high in the air and fell backwards among the crowd, which retreated in alarm to escape the flying ropes. We hoped that no one was struck by the ropes, but a sailor next to me was certain he saw a woman carried away to receive attention. And then, to our amazement the *New York* crept towards us, slowly and stealthily, as if drawn by some invisible force which she was powerless to withstand. It reminded me instantly of an experiment I had shown many times to a form of boys learning the elements of physics in a laboratory, in which a small magnet is made to float on a cork in a bowl of water and small steel objects placed on neighbouring pieces of cork are drawn up to the floating magnet by magnetic force. It reminded me, too, of seeing in my little boy's bath how a large celluloid floating duck would draw towards itself, by what is called capillary attraction, smaller ducks, frogs, beetles, and other animal folk, until the menagerie floated about as a unit, oblivious of their natural antipathies and reminding us of the 'happy families' one sees in cages on the seashore. On the *New York* there was shouting of orders, sailors running to and fro, paying out ropes and putting mats over the side where it seemed likely we should collide; the tug which had a few moments before cast off from the bows of the *Titanic* came up around our stern and passed to the quay side of the *New York's* stern, made fast to her and started to haul her back with all the force her engines were capable of; but it did not seem that the tug made much impression on the *New York*. Apart from the serious nature of the accident, it made an irresistibly comic picture to see the huge vessel drifting down the dock with a snorting tug at its heels, for all the world like a small boy dragging a diminutive puppy down the road with its teeth locked on a piece of rope, its feet splayed out, its head and body shaking from side to side in the effort to get every ounce of its weight used to the best advantage. At first all appearance showed that the sterns of the two vessels would collide; but from the stern bridge of the *Titanic* an officer directing operations stopped us dead, the suction ceased, and the *New York* with her tug trailing behind moved obliquely down the dock, her stern gliding along the side of the *Titanic* some few yards away. It gave an extraordinary impression of the absolute helplessness of a big liner in the absence of any motive power to guide her. But all excitement was not yet over: the *New York* turned her bows inward towards the quay, her stern swinging just clear of and passing in front of our bows, and moved slowly head on for the *Teutonic* lying moored to the side; mats were quickly got out and so deadened the force of the collision, which from where we were seemed to be too slight to cause any damage. Another tug came up and took hold of the *New York* by the bows; and between the two of them they dragged her round the corner of the quay, which just here came to an end on the side of the river.

We now moved slowly ahead and passed the *Teutonic* at a creeping pace, but notwithstanding this, the latter strained at her ropes so much that she heeled over several degrees in her efforts to follow the *Titanic*: the crowd were shouted back, a group of gold-braided officials, probably the harbour master and his staff, standing on the sea side of the moored ropes, jumped back over them as they drew up taut to a rigid line, and urged the crowd back still farther. But we were just clear, and as we slowly turned the corner into the river I saw the *Teutonic* swing slowly back into her normal station, relieving the tension alike of the ropes and of the minds of all who witnessed the incident.

Unpleasant as this incident was, it was interesting to all the passengers leaning over the rails to see the means adopted by the officers and crew of the various vessels to avoid collision, to see on the *Titanic*'s docking bridge (at the stern) an officer and seamen telephoning and ringing bells, hauling up and down little red and white flags, as danger of collision alternately threatened and diminished. No one was more interested than a young American kinematograph photographer, who, with his wife, followed the whole scene with eager eyes, turning the handle of his camera with the most evident pleasure as he recorded the unexpected incident on his films. It was obviously quite a windfall for him to have been on board at such a time. But neither the film nor those who exposed it reached the other side, and the record of the accident from the *Titanic*'s deck has never been thrown on the screen.

As we steamed down the river, the scene we had just witnessed was the topic of every conversation: the comparison with the *Olympic–Hawke* collision was drawn in every little group of passengers, and it seemed to be generally agreed that this would confirm the suction theory which was so successfully advanced by the cruiser *Hawke* in the law courts, but which many people scoffed at when the British Admiralty first suggested it as the explanation of the cruiser ramming the *Olympic*. And since this is an attempt to chronicle facts as they happened on board the *Titanic*, it must be recorded that there were among the passengers and such of the crew as were heard to speak on the matter, the direst misgivings at the incident we had just witnessed. Sailors are proverbially superstitious; far too many people are prone to follow their lead, or, indeed, the lead of anyone who asserts a statement with an air of conviction and the opportunity of constant repetition; the sense of mystery that shrouds a prophetic utterance, particularly if it be an ominous one (for so constituted apparently is the human mind that it will receive the impress of an evil prophecy far more readily than it will that of a beneficent one, possibly through subservient fear to the thing it dreads, possibly through the degraded, morbid attraction which the sense of evil has for the innate evil in the human mind), leads many people to pay a certain respect to superstitious theories. Not that they wholly believe in them or would wish their dearest friends to know they ever gave them a second thought; but the feeling that other people do so and the half conviction that there 'may be something in it, after all,' sways them into tacit obedience to the most absurd and childish theories. I wish in a later chapter to discuss the subject of superstition in its reference to our life on board the *Titanic*, but will anticipate events here a little by relating a second so-called 'bad omen' which was hatched at Queenstown. As one of the tenders containing passengers and mails neared the *Titanic*, some of those on board gazed up at the liner towering above them, and saw a stoker's head, black from his work in the stokehold below, peering out at them from the top of one of the enormous funnels – a dummy one for ventilation – that rose many feet above the highest deck. He had climbed up inside for a joke, but to some of those who saw him there the sight was seed for the growth of an 'omen', which bore fruit in an unknown dread of dangers to come. An American lady – may she forgive me if she reads these lines! – has related to me with the deepest conviction and earnestness of manner that she saw the man and attributes the sinking of the *Titanic* largely to that. Arrant foolishness, you may say! Yes, indeed, but not to those who believe in it; and it is well not to have such prophetic thoughts of danger passed round among passengers and crew: it would seem to have an unhealthy influence.

We dropped down Spithead, past the shores of the Isle of Wight looking superbly beautiful in new spring foliage, exchanged salutes with a White Star tug lying to in wait for one of their liners inward bound, and saw in the distance several warships with attendant black destroyers guarding the entrance from the sea. In the calmest weather we made Cherbourg just as it grew dusk and left again about 8.30 p.m., after taking on board passengers and mails. We reached Queenstown about 12 noon on Thursday, after a most enjoyable passage across the Channel, although the wind was almost too cold to allow of sitting out on deck on Thursday morning.

The coast of Ireland looked very beautiful as we approached Queenstown harbour, the brilliant morning sun showing up the green hillsides and picking out groups of dwellings dotted here and there above the rugged grey cliffs that fringed the coast. We took on board our pilot, ran slowly towards the harbour with the sounding-line dropping all the time, and came to a stop well out to sea, with our screws churning up the bottom and turning the sea all brown with sand from below. It had seemed to me that the ship stopped rather suddenly, and in my ignorance of the depth of the harbour entrance, that perhaps the sounding-line had revealed a smaller depth than was thought safe for the great size of the *Titanic*: this seemed to be confirmed by the sight of sand churned up from the bottom – but this is mere supposition. Passengers and mails were put on board from two tenders, and nothing could have given us a better idea of the enormous length and bulk of the *Titanic* than to stand as far astern as possible and look over the side from the top deck, forwards and downwards to where the tenders rolled at her bows, the merest cockleshells beside the majestic vessel that rose deck after deck above them. Truly she was a magnificent boat! There was something so graceful in her movement as she rode up and down on the slight swell in the harbour, a slow, stately dip and recover, only noticeable by watching her bows in comparison with some landmark on the coast in the near distance; the two little tenders tossing up and down like corks beside her illustrated vividly the advance made in comfort of motion from the time of the small steamer.

Presently the work of transfer was ended, the tenders cast off, and at 1.30 p.m., with the screws churning up the sea bottom again, the *Titanic* turned slowly through a quarter circle until her nose pointed down along the Irish coast, and then steamed rapidly away from Queenstown, the little house on the left of the town gleaming white on the hillside for many miles astern. In our wake soared and screamed hundreds of gulls, which had quarrelled and fought over the remnants of lunch pouring out of the waste pipes as we lay to in the harbour entrance; and now they followed us in the expectation of further spoil. I watched them for a long time and was astonished at the ease with which they soared and kept up with the ship with hardly a motion of their wings: picking out a particular gull, I would keep him under observation for minutes at a time and see no motion of his wings downwards or upwards to aid his flight. He would tilt all of a piece to one side or another as the gusts of wind caught him, rigidly unbendable, as an aeroplane tilts sideways in a puff of wind. And yet with graceful ease he kept pace with the *Titanic* forging through the water at 20 knots: as the wind met him he would rise upwards and obliquely forwards, and come down slantingly again, his wings curved in a beautiful arch and his tail feathers outspread as a fan. It was plain that he was possessed of a secret we are only just beginning to learn – that of utilising air currents as escalators up and down which he can glide at will with the expenditure of the minimum amount of energy, or of using them as a ship does when it sails within one or two points of a head wind. Aviators, of course, are imitating the gull, and soon perhaps we may see an aeroplane or a glider dipping gracefully up and down in the face of an opposing wind and all the time forging ahead across the Atlantic Ocean. The gulls were still behind us when night fell, and still they screamed and dipped down into the broad wake of foam which we left behind; but in the morning they were gone: perhaps they had seen in the night a steamer bound for their Queenstown home and had escorted her back.

All afternoon we steamed along the coast of Ireland, with grey cliffs guarding the shores, and hills rising behind gaunt and barren; as dusk fell, the coast rounded away from us to the north-west, and the last we saw of Europe was the Irish mountains dim and faint in the dropping darkness. With the thought that we had seen the last of land until we set foot on the shores of America, I retired to the library to write letters, little knowing that many things would happen to us all – many experiences, sudden, vivid and impressive to be encountered, many perils to be faced, many good and true people for whom we should have to mourn – before we saw land again.

There is very little to relate from the time of leaving Queenstown on Thursday to Sunday morning. The sea was calm – so calm, indeed, that very few were absent from meals; the wind westerly and south-westerly – 'fresh' as the daily chart described it – but often rather cold, generally too cold to sit out on deck to read or write, so that many of us spent a good part of the time in the library, reading and writing. I wrote a large number of letters and posted them day by day in the box outside the library door: possibly they are there yet.

Each morning the sun rose behind us in a sky of circular clouds, stretching round the horizon in long, narrow streaks and rising tier upon tier above the skyline, red and pink and fading from pink to white, as the sun rose higher in the sky. It was a beautiful sight to one who had not crossed the ocean before (or indeed been out of sight of the shores of England) to stand on the top deck and watch the swell of the sea extending outwards from the ship in an unbroken circle until it met the skyline with its hint of infinity: behind, the wake of the vessel white with foam where, fancy suggested, the propeller blades had cut up the long Atlantic rollers and with them made a level white road bounded on either side by banks of green, blue, and blue-green waves that would presently sweep away the white road, though as yet it stretched back to the horizon and dipped over the edge of the world back to Ireland and the gulls, while along it the morning sun glittered and sparkled. And each night the sun sank right in our eyes along the sea, making an undulating, glittering pathway, a golden track charted on the surface of the ocean which our ship followed unswervingly until the sun dipped below the edge of the horizon, and the pathway ran ahead of us faster than we could steam and slipped over the edge of the skyline – as if the sun had been a golden ball and had wound up its thread of gold too quickly for us to follow.

From 12 noon Thursday to 12 noon Friday we ran 386 miles, Friday to Saturday 519 miles, Saturday to Sunday 546 miles. The second day's run of 519 miles was, the purser told us, a disappointment, and we should not dock until Wednesday morning instead of Tuesday night, as we had expected; however, on Sunday we were glad to see a longer run had been made, and it was thought we should make New York, after all, on Tuesday night. The purser remarked, 'They are not pushing her this trip and don't intend to make any fast running: I don't suppose we shall do more than 546 now; it is not a bad day's run for the first trip.' This was at lunch, and I remember the conversation then turned to the speed and build of Atlantic liners as factors in their comfort of motion: all those who had crossed many times were unanimous in saying the *Titanic* was the most comfortable boat they had been on, and they preferred the speed we were making to that of the faster boats, from the point of view of lessened vibration as well as because the faster boats would bore through the waves with a twisted, screw-like motion instead of the straight up-and-down swing of the *Titanic*. I then called the attention of our table to the way the *Titanic* listed to port (I had noticed this before), and we all watched the skyline through the portholes as we sat at the purser's table in the saloon: it was plain she did so, for the skyline and sea on the port side were visible most of the time and on the starboard only sky. The purser remarked that probably coal had been used mostly from the starboard side. It is no doubt a common occurrence for all vessels to list to some degree, but in view of the fact that the *Titanic* was cut open on the starboard side and before she sank listed so much to port that there was quite a chasm between her and the swinging lifeboats, across which ladies had to be thrown or to cross on chairs laid flat, the previous listing to port may be of interest.

Returning for a moment to the motion of the *Titanic*, it was interesting to stand on the boat deck, as I frequently did, in the angle between lifeboats 13 and 15 on the starboard side (two boats I have every reason to remember, for the first carried me in safety to the *Carpathia*, and it seemed likely at one time that the other would come down on our heads as we sat in 13 trying to get away from the ship's side), and watch the general motion of the ship through the waves resolve itself into two motions – one to be observed by contrasting the docking-bridge, from which the log-line trailed away behind in the foaming wake, with the horizon, and observing the long, slow heave as we rode up and down. I timed the average period occupied in one up-and-down vibration, but do not now remember the figures. The second motion was a side-to-side roll, and could be calculated by watching the port rail and contrasting it with the horizon as before. It seems likely that this double motion is due to the angle at which our direction to New York cuts the general set of the Gulf Stream sweeping from the Gulf of Mexico across to Europe; but the almost clock-like regularity of the two vibratory movements was what attracted my attention: it was while watching the side roll that I first became aware of the list to port. Looking down astern from the boat deck or from B deck to the steerage quarters, I often noticed how the third class passengers were enjoying every minute of the time: a most uproarious skipping game of the mixed-double type was the great favourite, while 'in and out and roundabout' went a Scotchman with his bagpipes playing something that Gilbert says 'faintly resembled an air'. Standing aloof from all of them, generally on the raised stern deck above the 'playing field', was a man of about 20 to 24 years of age, well-dressed, always gloved and nicely groomed, and obviously quite out of place among his fellow passengers: he never looked happy all the time. I watched him, and classified him at hazard as the man who had been a failure in some way at home and had received the proverbial shilling plus third class fare to America: he did not look resolute enough or happy enough to be working out his own problem. Another interesting man was travelling steerage, but had placed his wife in the second cabin: he would climb the stairs leading from the steerage to the second deck and talk affectionately with his wife across the low gate which separated them. I never saw him after the collision, but I think his wife was on the *Carpathia*. Whether they ever saw each other on the Sunday night is very doubtful: he would not at first be allowed on the second class deck, and if he were, the chances of seeing his wife in the darkness and the crowd would be very small, indeed. Of all those playing so happily on the steerage deck I did not recognise many afterwards on the *Carpathia*.

Coming now to Sunday, the day on which the *Titanic* struck the iceberg, it will be interesting, perhaps, to give the day's events in some detail, to appreciate the general attitude of passengers to their surroundings just before the collision. Service was held in the saloon by the purser in the morning, and going on deck after lunch we found such a change in temperature that not many cared to remain to face the bitter wind – an artificial wind created mainly, if not entirely, by the ship's rapid motion through the chilly atmosphere. I should judge there was no wind blowing at the time, for I had noticed about the same force of wind approaching Queenstown, to find that it died away as soon as we stopped, only to rise again as we steamed away from the harbour.

Returning to the library, I stopped for a moment to read again the day's run and observe our position on the chart; the Revd Mr Carter, a clergyman of the Church of England, was similarly engaged, and we renewed a conversation we had enjoyed for some days: it had commenced with a discussion of the relative merits of his university – Oxford – with mine – Cambridge – as worldwide educational agencies, the opportunities at each for the formation of character apart from mere education as such, and had led on to the lack of sufficiently qualified men to take up the work of the Church of England (a matter apparently on which he felt very deeply) and from that to his own work in England as a priest. He told me some of his parish problems and spoke of the impossibility of doing half his work in his church without the help his wife gave. I knew her only slightly at that time, but meeting her later in the day, I realised something of what he meant in attributing a large part of what success he had as a vicar to her. My only excuse for mentioning these details about the Carters – now and later in the day – is that, while they have perhaps not much interest for the average reader, they will no doubt be some comfort to the parish over which he presided and where I am sure he was loved. He next mentioned the absence of a service in the evening and asked if I knew the purser well enough to request the use of the saloon in the evening where he would like to have a 'hymn sing-song'; the purser gave his consent at once, and Mr Carter made preparations during the afternoon by asking all he knew – and many he did not – to come to the saloon at 8.30 p.m.

The library was crowded that afternoon, owing to the cold on deck, but through the windows we could see the clear sky with brilliant sunlight that seemed to augur a fine night and a clear day tomorrow, and the prospect of landing in two days, with calm weather all the way to New York, was a matter of general satisfaction among us all. I can look back and see every detail of the library that afternoon – the beautifully furnished room, with lounges, armchairs, and small writing- or card-tables scattered about, writing-bureaus round the walls of the room, and the library in glass-cased shelves flanking one side – the whole finished in mahogany relieved with white fluted wooden columns that supported the deck above. Through the windows there is the covered corridor, reserved by general consent as the children's playground, and here are playing the two Navatril children with their father – devoted to them, never absent from them. Who would have thought of the dramatic history of the happy group at play in the corridor that afternoon! The abduction of the children in Nice, the assumed name, the separation of father and children in a few hours, his death and their subsequent union with their mother after a period of doubt as to their parentage! How many more similar secrets the *Titanic* revealed in the privacy of family life, or carried down with her untold, we shall never know.

In the same corridor is a man and his wife with two children, and one of them he is generally carrying: they are all young and happy: he is dressed always in a grey knickerbocker suit – with a camera slung over his shoulder. I have not seen any of them since that afternoon.

Close beside me – so near that I cannot avoid hearing scraps of their conversation – are two American ladies, both dressed in white, young, probably friends only: one has been to India and is returning by way of England, the other is a school teacher in America, a graceful girl with a distinguished air heightened by a pair of *pince-nez*. Engaged in conversation with them is a gentleman whom I subsequently identified from a photograph as a well-known resident of Cambridge, Massachusetts, genial, polished, and with a courtly air towards the two ladies, whom he has known but a few hours; from time to time as they talk, a child acquaintance breaks in on their conversation and insists on their taking notice of a large doll clasped in her arms; I have seen none of this group since then. In the opposite corner are the young American kinematograph photographer and his young wife, evidently French, very fond of playing patience, which she is doing now, while he sits back in his chair watching the game and interposing from time to time with suggestions. I did not see them again. In the middle of the room are two Catholic priests, one quietly reading – either English or Irish, and probably the latter – the other, dark, bearded, with broad-brimmed hat, talking earnestly to a friend in German and evidently explaining some verse in the open Bible before him; near them a young fire engineer on his way to Mexico, and of the same religion as the rest of the group. None of them were saved. It may be noted here that the percentage of men saved in the second class is the lowest of any other division – only eight per cent.

Many other faces recur to thought, but it is impossible to describe them all in the space of a short book: of all those in the library that Sunday afternoon, I can remember only two or three persons who found their way to the *Carpathia*. Looking over this room, with his back to the library shelves, is the library steward, thin, stooping, sad-faced, and generally with nothing to do but serve out books; but this afternoon he is busier than I have ever seen him, serving out baggage declaration forms for passengers to fill in. Mine is before me as I write: 'Form for nonresidents in the United States. Steamship *Titanic*: No. 31444, D', etc. I had filled it in that afternoon and slipped it in my pocketbook instead of returning it to the steward. Before me, too, is a small cardboard square: 'White Star Line. RMS *Titanic*. 208. This label must be given up when the article is returned. The property will be deposited in the Purser's safe. The Company will not be liable to passengers for the loss of money, jewels, or ornaments, by theft or otherwise, not so deposited.' The 'property deposited' in my case was money, placed in an envelope, sealed, with my name written across the flap, and handed to the purser; the 'label' is my receipt. Along with other similar envelopes it may be still intact in the safe at the bottom of the sea, but in all probability it is not, as will be seen presently.

After dinner, Mr Carter invited all who wished to the saloon, and with the assistance at the piano of a gentleman who sat at the purser's table opposite me (a young Scotch engineer going out to join his brother fruit-farming at the foot of the Rockies), he started some hundred passengers singing hymns. They were asked to choose whichever hymn they wished, and with so many to choose, it was impossible for him to do more than have the greatest favourites sung. As he announced each hymn, it was evident that he was thoroughly versed in their history: no hymn was sung but that he gave a short sketch of its author and in some cases a description of the circumstances in which it was composed. I think all were impressed with his knowledge of hymns and with his eagerness to tell us all he knew of them. It was curious to see how many chose hymns dealing with dangers at sea. I noticed the hushed tone with which all sang the hymn 'For those in peril on the Sea'.

The singing must have gone on until after 10 o'clock, when, seeing the stewards standing about waiting to serve biscuits and coffee before going off duty, Mr Carter brought the evening to a close by a few words of thanks to the purser for the use of the saloon, a short sketch of the happiness and safety of the voyage hitherto, the great confidence all felt on board this great liner with her steadiness and her size, and the happy outlook of landing in a few hours in New York at the close of a delightful voyage; and all the time he spoke, a few miles ahead of us lay the 'peril on the sea' that was to sink this same great liner with many of those on board who listened with gratitude to his simple, heartfelt words. So much for the frailty of human hopes and for the confidence reposed in material human designs.

Think of the shame of it, that a mass of ice of no use to anyone or anything should have the power fatally to injure the beautiful *Titanic*! That an insensible block should be able to threaten, even in the smallest degree, the lives of many good men and women who think and plan and hope and love – and not only to threaten, but to end their lives. It is unbearable! Are we never to educate ourselves to foresee such dangers and to prevent them before they happen? All the evidence of history shows that laws unknown and unsuspected are being discovered day by day: as this knowledge accumulates for the use of man, is it not certain that the ability to see and destroy beforehand the threat of danger will be one of the privileges the whole world will utilise? May that day come soon. Until it does, no precaution too rigorous can be taken, no safety appliance, however costly, must be omitted from a ship's equipment.

After the meeting had broken up, I talked with the Carters over a cup of coffee, said goodnight to them, and retired to my cabin at about quarter to 11. They were good people and this world is much poorer by their loss.

It may be a matter of pleasure to many people to know that their friends were perhaps among that gathering of people in the saloon, and that at the last the sound of the hymns still echoed in their ears as they stood on the deck so quietly and courageously. Who can tell how much it had to do with the demeanour of some of them and the example this would set to others?

Chapter 3 The Collision & Embarkation in Lifeboats

I had been fortunate enough to secure a two-berth cabin to myself – D56 – quite close to the saloon and most convenient in every way for getting about the ship; and on a big ship like the *Titanic* it was quite a consideration to be on D deck, only three decks below the top or boat deck. Below D again were cabins on E and F decks, and to walk from a cabin on F up to the top deck, climbing five flights of stairs on the way, was certainly a considerable task for those not able to take much exercise. The *Titanic* management has been criticised, among other things, for supplying the boat with lifts: it has been said they were an expensive luxury and the room they took up might have been utilised in some way for more lifesaving appliances. Whatever else may have been superfluous, lifts certainly were not: old ladies, for example, in cabins on F deck, would hardly have got to the top deck during the whole voyage had they not been able to ring for the lift-boy. Perhaps nothing gave one a greater impression of the size of the ship than to take the lift from the top and drop slowly down past the different floors, discharging and taking in passengers just as in a large hotel. I wonder where the lift-boy was that night. I would have been glad to find him in our boat, or on the *Carpathia* when we took count of the saved. He was quite young – not more than 16, I think – a bright-eyed, handsome boy, with a love for the sea and the games on deck and the view over the ocean – and he did not get any of them. One day, as he put me out of his lift and saw through the vestibule windows a game of deck quoits in progress, he said, in a wistful tone, 'My! I wish I could go out there sometimes!' I wished he could, too, and made a jesting offer to take charge of his lift for an hour while he went out to watch the game; but he smilingly shook his head and dropped down in answer to an imperative ring from below. I think he was not on duty with his lift after the collision, but if he were, he would smile at his passengers all the time as he took them up to the boats waiting to leave the sinking ship.

After undressing and climbing into the top berth, I read from about quarter past 11 to the time we struck, about quarter to 12. During this time I noticed particularly the increased vibration of the ship, and I assumed that we were going at a higher speed than at any other time since we sailed from Queenstown. Now I am aware that this is an important point, and bears strongly on the question of responsibility for the effects of the collision; but the impression of increased vibration is fixed in my memory so strongly that it seems important to record it. Two things led me to this conclusion – first, that as I sat on the sofa undressing, with bare feet on the floor, the jar of the vibration came up from the engines below very noticeably; and second, that as I sat up in the berth reading, the spring mattress supporting me was vibrating more rapidly than usual: this cradle-like motion was always noticeable as one lay in bed, but that night there was certainly a marked increase in the motion. Referring to the plan, it will be seen that the vibration must have come almost directly up from below, when it is mentioned that the saloon was immediately above the engines as shown in the plan, and my cabin next to the saloon. From these two data, on the assumption that greater vibration is an indication of higher speed – and I suppose it must be – then I am sure we were going faster that night at the time we struck the iceberg than we had done before, i.e. during the hours I was awake and able to take note of anything.

And then, as I read in the quietness of the night, broken only by the muffled sound that came to me through the ventilators of stewards talking and moving along the corridors, when nearly all the passengers were in their cabins, some asleep in bed, others undressing, and others only just down from the smoking room and still discussing many things, there came what seemed to me nothing more than an extra heave of the engines and a more than usually obvious dancing motion of the mattress on which I sat. Nothing more than that – no sound of a crash or of anything else, no sense of shock, no jar that felt like one heavy body meeting another. And presently the same thing repeated with about the same intensity. The thought came to me that they must have still further increased the speed. And all this time the *Titanic* was being cut open by the iceberg and water was pouring in her side, and yet no evidence that would indicate such a disaster had been presented to us. It fills me with astonishment now to think of it. Consider the question of list alone. Here was this enormous vessel running starboard-side on to an iceberg, and a passenger sitting quietly in bed, reading, felt no motion or list to the opposite or port side, and this must have been felt had it been more than the usual roll of the ship – never very much in the calm weather we had all the way. Again, my bunk was fixed to the wall on the starboard side, and any list to port would have tended to fling me out on the floor: I am sure I should have noted it had there been any. And yet the explanation is simple enough: the *Titanic* struck the berg with a force of impact of over a million foot-tons; her plates were less than an inch thick, and they must have been cut through as a knife cuts paper: there would be no need to list; it would have been better if she had listed and thrown us out on the floor, for it would have been an indication that our plates were strong enough to offer, at any rate, some resistance to the blow, and we might all have been safe today.

And so, with no thought of anything serious having happened to the ship, I continued my reading; and still the murmur from the stewards and from adjoining cabins, and no other sound: no cry in the night; no alarm given; no one afraid – there was then nothing which could cause fear to the most timid person. But in a few moments I felt the engines slow and stop; the dancing motion and the vibration ceased suddenly after being part of our very existence for four days, and that was the first hint that anything out of the ordinary had happened. We have all 'heard' a loud-ticking clock stop suddenly in a quiet room, and then have noticed the clock and the ticking noise, of which we seemed until then quite unconscious. So in the same way the fact was suddenly brought home to all in the ship that the engines – that part of the ship that drove us through the sea – had stopped dead. But the stopping of the engines gave us no information: we had to make our own calculations as to why we had stopped. Like a flash it came to me: 'We have dropped a propeller blade: when this happens the engines always race away until they are controlled, and this accounts for the extra heave they gave'; not a very logical conclusion when considered now, for the engines should have continued to heave all the time until we stopped, but it was at the time a sufficiently tenable hypothesis to hold. Acting on it, I jumped out of bed, slipped on a dressing gown over pyjamas, put on shoes, and went out of my cabin into the hall near the saloon. Here was a steward leaning against the staircase, probably waiting until those in the smoke-room above had gone to bed and he could put out the lights. I said, 'Why have we stopped?' 'I don't know, sir,' he replied, 'but I don't suppose it is anything much.' 'Well,' I said, 'I am going on deck to see what it is,' and started towards the stairs. He smiled indulgently at me as I passed him, and said, 'All right, sir, but it is mighty cold up there.' I am sure at that time he thought I was rather foolish to go up with so little reason, and I must confess I felt rather absurd for not remaining in the cabin: it seemed like making a needless fuss to walk about the ship in a dressing gown. But it was my first trip across the sea; I had enjoyed every minute of it and was keenly alive to note every new experience; and certainly to stop in the middle of the sea with a propeller dropped seemed sufficient reason for going on deck. And yet the steward, with his fatherly smile, and the fact that no one else was about the passages or going upstairs to reconnoitre, made me feel guilty in an undefined way of breaking some code of a ship's regime – an Englishman's fear of being thought 'unusual', perhaps!

I climbed the three flights of stairs, opened the vestibule door leading to the top deck, and stepped out into an atmosphere that cut me, clad as I was, like a knife. Walking to the starboard side, I peered over and saw the sea many feet below, calm and black; forward, the deserted deck stretching away to the first class quarters and the captain's bridge; and behind, the steerage quarters and the stern bridge; nothing more: no iceberg on either side or astern as far as we could see in the darkness. There were two or three men on deck, and with one – the Scotch engineer who played hymns in the saloon – I compared notes of our experiences. He had just begun to undress when the engines stopped and had come up at once, so that he was fairly well-clad; none of us could see anything, and all being quiet and still, the Scotchman and I went down to the next deck. Through the windows of the smoking room we saw a game of cards going on, with several onlookers, and went in to enquire if they knew more than we did. They had apparently felt rather more of the heaving motion, but so far as I remember, none of them had gone out on deck to make any enquiries, even when one of them had seen through the windows an iceberg go by towering above the decks. He had called their attention to it, and they all watched it disappear, but had then at once resumed the game. We asked them the height of the berg and some said 100 feet [*c.* 30 metres], others, 60 feet [*c.* 18 metres]; one of the onlookers – a motor engineer travelling to America with a model carburettor (he had filled in his declaration form near me in the afternoon and had questioned the library steward how he should declare his patent) – said, 'Well, I am accustomed to estimating distances and I put it at between 80 and 90 feet [*c.* 24–27 metres].' We accepted his estimate and made guesses as to what had happened to the *Titanic*: the general impression was that we had just scraped the iceberg with a glancing blow on the starboard side, and they had stopped as a wise precaution, to examine her thoroughly all over. 'I expect the iceberg has scratched off some of her new paint,' said one, 'and the captain doesn't like to go on until she is painted up again.' We laughed at his estimate of the captain's care for the ship. Poor Captain Smith! He knew by this time only too well what had happened.

One of the players, pointing to his glass of whisky standing at his elbow, and turning to an onlooker, said, 'Just run along the deck and see if any ice has come aboard: I would like some for this.' Amid the general laughter at what we thought was his imagination – only too realistic, alas, for when he spoke the forward deck was covered with ice that had tumbled over – and seeing that no more information was forthcoming, I left the smoking room and went down to my cabin, where I sat for some time reading again. I am filled with sorrow to think I never saw any of the occupants of that smoking room again: nearly all young men full of hope for their prospects in a new world; mostly unmarried; keen, alert, with the makings of good citizens. Presently, hearing people walking about the corridors, I looked out and saw several standing in the hall talking to a steward – most of them ladies in dressing gowns; other people were going upstairs, and I decided to go on deck again, but as it was too cold to do so in a dressing gown, I dressed in a Norfolk jacket and trousers and walked up. There were now more people looking over the side and walking about, questioning each other as to why we had stopped, but without obtaining any definite information. I stayed on deck some minutes, walking about vigorously to keep warm and occasionally looking downwards to the sea as if something there would indicate the reason for delay. The ship had now resumed her course, moving very slowly through the water with a little white line of foam on each side. I think we were all glad to see this: it seemed better than standing still. I soon decided to go down again, and as I crossed from the starboard to the port side to go down by the vestibule door, I saw an officer climb on the last lifeboat on the port side – No. 16 – and begin to throw off the cover, but I do not remember that anyone paid any particular attention to him. Certainly no one thought they were preparing to man the lifeboats and embark from the ship. All this time there was no apprehension of any danger in the minds of passengers, and no one was in any condition of panic or hysteria; after all, it would have been strange if they had been, without any definite evidence of danger.

As I passed to the door to go down, I looked forward again and saw to my surprise an undoubted tilt downwards from the stern to the bows: only a slight slope, which I don't think anyone had noticed – at any rate, they had not remarked on it. As I went downstairs a confirmation of this tilting forward came in something unusual about the stairs, a curious sense of something out of balance and of not being able to put one's feet down in the right place: naturally, being tilted forward, the stairs would slope downwards at an angle and tend to throw one forward. I could not see any visible slope of the stairway: it was perceptible only by the sense of balance at this time.

On D deck were three ladies – I think they were all saved, and it is a good thing at least to be able to chronicle meeting someone who was saved after so much record of those who were not – standing in the passage near the cabin. 'Oh! why have we stopped?' they said. 'We did stop,' I replied, 'but we are now going on again.' 'Oh, no,' one replied; 'I cannot feel the engines as I usually do, or hear them. Listen!' We listened, and there was no throb audible. Having noticed that the vibration of the engines is most noticeable lying in a bath, where the throb comes straight from the floor through its metal sides – too much so ordinarily for one to put one's head back with comfort on the bath – I took them along the corridor to a bathroom and made them put their hands on the side of the bath: they were much reassured to feel the engines throbbing down below and to know we were making some headway. I left them and on the way to my cabin passed some stewards standing unconcernedly against the walls of the saloon: one of them, the library steward again, was leaning over a table, writing. It is no exaggeration to say that they had neither any knowledge of the accident nor any feeling of alarm that we had stopped and had not yet gone on again full speed: their whole attitude expressed perfect confidence in the ship and officers.

Turning into my gangway (my cabin being the first in the gangway), I saw a man standing at the other end of it fastening his tie. 'Anything fresh?' he said. 'Not much,' I replied; 'we are going ahead slowly and she is down a little at the bows, but I don't think it is anything serious.' 'Come in and look at this man,' he laughed; 'he won't get up.' I looked in, and in the top bunk lay a man with his back to me, closely wrapped in his bedclothes and only the back of his head visible. 'Why won't he get up? Is he asleep?' I said. 'No,' laughed the man dressing, 'he says –' But before he could finish the sentence the man above grunted: 'You don't catch me leaving a warm bed to go up on that cold deck at midnight. I know better than that.' We both told him laughingly why he had better get up, but he was certain he was just as safe there and all this dressing was quite unnecessary; so I left them and went again to my cabin. I put on some underclothing, sat on the sofa, and read for some 10 minutes, when I heard through the open door, above, the noise of people passing up and down, and a loud shout from above: 'All passengers on deck with lifebelts on.'

I placed the two books I was reading in the side pockets of my Norfolk jacket, picked up my lifebelt (curiously enough, I had taken it down for the first time that night from the wardrobe when I first retired to my cabin) and my dressing gown, and walked upstairs tying on the lifebelt. As I came out of my cabin, I remember seeing the purser's assistant, with his foot on the stairs about to climb them, whisper to a steward and jerk his head significantly behind him; not that I thought anything of it at the time, but I have no doubt he was telling him what had happened up in the bows, and was giving him orders to call all passengers.

Going upstairs with other passengers – no one ran a step or seemed alarmed – we met two ladies coming down: one seized me by the arm and said, 'Oh! I have no lifebelt; will you come down to my cabin and help me to find it?' I returned with them to F deck – the lady who had addressed me holding my arm all the time in a vice-like grip, much to my amusement – and we found a steward in her gangway who took them in and found their lifebelts. Coming upstairs again, I passed the purser's window on F deck, and noticed a light inside; when halfway up to E deck, I heard the heavy metallic clang of the safe door, followed by a hasty step retreating along the corridor towards the first class quarters. I have little doubt it was the purser, who had taken all valuables from his safe and was transferring them to the charge of the first class purser, in the hope they might all be saved in one package. That is why I said above that perhaps the envelope containing my money was not in the safe at the bottom of the sea: it is probably in a bundle, with many others like it, waterlogged at the bottom.

Reaching the top deck, we found many people assembled there – some fully dressed, with coats and wraps, well prepared for anything that might happen; others who had thrown wraps hastily round them when they were called or heard the summons to equip themselves with lifebelts – not in much condition to face the cold of that night. Fortunately there was no wind to beat the cold air through our clothing: even the breeze caused by the ship's motion had died entirely away, for the engines had stopped again and the *Titanic* lay peacefully on the surface of the sea – motionless, quiet, not even rocking to the roll of the sea; indeed, as we were to discover presently, the sea was as calm as an inland lake save for the gentle swell which could impart no motion to a ship the size of the *Titanic*. To stand on the deck many feet above the water lapping idly against her sides, and looking much farther off than it really was because of the darkness, gave one a sense of wonderful security: to feel her so steady and still was like standing on a large rock in the middle of the ocean. But there were now more evidences of the coming catastrophe to the observer than had been apparent when on deck last: one was the roar and hiss of escaping steam from the boilers, issuing out of a large steam pipe reaching high up one of the funnels: a harsh, deafening boom that made conversation difficult and no doubt increased the apprehension of some people merely because of the volume of noise: if one imagines 20 locomotives blowing off steam in a low key it would give some idea of the unpleasant sound that met us as we climbed out on the top deck.

But after all it was the kind of phenomenon we ought to expect: engines blow off steam when standing in a station, and why should not a ship's boilers do the same when the ship is not moving? I never heard anyone connect this noise with the danger of boiler explosion, in the event of the ship sinking with her boilers under a high pressure of steam, which was no doubt the true explanation of this precaution. But this is perhaps speculation; some people may have known it quite well, for from the time we came on deck until boat 13 got away, I heard very little conversation of any kind among the passengers. It is not the slightest exaggeration to say that no signs of alarm were exhibited by anyone: there was no indication of panic or hysteria; no cries of fear, and no running to and fro to discover what was the matter, why we had been summoned on deck with lifebelts, and what was to be done with us now we were there. We stood there quietly looking on at the work of the crew as they manned the lifeboats, and no one ventured to interfere with them or offered to help them. It was plain we should be of no use; and the crowd of men and women stood quietly on the deck or paced slowly up and down waiting for orders from the officers.

Now, before we consider any further the events that followed, the state of mind of passengers at this juncture, and the motives which led each one to act as he or she did in the circumstances, it is important to keep in thought the amount of information at our disposal. Men and women act according to judgement based on knowledge of the conditions around them, and the best way to understand some apparently inconceivable things that happened is for anyone to imagine himself or herself standing on deck that night. It seems a mystery to some people that women refused to leave the ship, that some persons retired to their cabins, and so on; but it is a matter of judgement, after all.

So that if the reader will come and stand with the crowd on deck, he must first rid himself entirely of the knowledge that the *Titanic* has sunk – an important necessity, for he cannot see conditions as they existed there through the mental haze arising from knowledge of the greatest maritime tragedy the world has known: he must get rid of any foreknowledge of disaster to appreciate why people acted as they did. Secondly, he had better get rid of any picture in thought painted either by his own imagination or by some artist, whether pictorial or verbal, 'from information supplied'. Some are most inaccurate (these, mostly word-pictures), and where they err, they err on the highly dramatic side. They need not have done so: the whole conditions were dramatic enough in all their bare simplicity, without the addition of any high colouring.

Having made these mental erasures, he will find himself as one of the crowd faced with the following conditions: a perfectly still atmosphere; a brilliantly beautiful starlight night, but no moon, and so with little light that was of any use; a ship that had come quietly to rest without any indication of disaster – no iceberg visible, no hole in the ship's side through which water was pouring in, nothing broken or out of place, no sound of alarm, no panic, no movement of anyone except at a walking pace; the absence of any knowledge of the nature of the accident, of the extent of damage, of the danger of the ship sinking in a few hours, of the numbers of boats, rafts, and other lifesaving appliances available, their capacity, what other ships were near or coming to help – in fact, an almost complete absence of any positive knowledge on any point. I think this was the result of deliberate judgement on the part of the officers, and perhaps it was the best thing that could be done. In particular, he must remember that the ship was a sixth of a mile long, with passengers on three decks open to the sea, and port and starboard sides to each deck: he will then get some idea of the difficulty presented to the officers of keeping control over such a large area, and the impossibility of anyone knowing what was happening except in his own immediate vicinity. Perhaps the whole thing can be summed up best by saying that, after we had embarked in the lifeboats and rowed away from the *Titanic*, it would not have surprised us to hear that all passengers would be saved: the cries of drowning people after the *Titanic* gave the final plunge were a thunderbolt to us. I am aware that the experiences of many of those saved differed in some respects from the above: some had knowledge of certain things, some were experienced travellers and sailors, and therefore deduced more rapidly what was likely to happen; but I think the above gives a fairly accurate representation of the state of mind of most of those on deck that night.

All this time people were pouring up from the stairs and adding to the crowd: I remember at that moment thinking it would be well to return to my cabin and rescue some money and warmer clothing if we were to embark in boats, but looking through the vestibule windows and seeing people still coming upstairs, I decided it would only cause confusion passing them on the stairs, and so remained on deck.

I was now on the starboard side of the top boat deck; the time about 12.20. We watched the crew at work on the lifeboats, numbers 9, 11, 13, 15, some inside arranging the oars, some coiling ropes on the deck – the ropes which ran through the pulleys to lower to the sea – others with cranks fitted to the rocking arms of the davits. As we watched, the cranks were turned, the davits swung outwards until the boats hung clear of the edge of the deck. Just then an officer came along from the first class deck and shouted above the noise of escaping steam, 'All women and children get down to deck below and all men stand back from the boats.' He had apparently been off duty when the ship struck, and was lightly dressed, with a white muffler twisted hastily round his neck. The men fell back and the women retired below to get into the boats from the next deck. Two women refused at first to leave their husbands, but partly by persuasion and partly by force they were separated from them and sent down to the next deck. I think that by this time the work on the lifeboats and the separation of men and women impressed on us slowly the presence of imminent danger, but it made no difference in the attitude of the crowd: they were just as prepared to obey orders and to do what came next as when they first came on deck. I do not mean that they actually reasoned it out: they were the average Teutonic crowd, with an inborn respect for law and order and for traditions bequeathed to them by generations of ancestors: the reasons that made them act as they did were impersonal, instinctive, hereditary.

But if there were anyone who had not by now realised that the ship was in danger, all doubt on this point was to be set at rest in a dramatic manner. Suddenly a rush of light from the forward deck, a hissing roar that made us all turn from watching the boats, and a rocket leapt upwards to where the stars blinked and twinkled above us. Up it went, higher and higher, with a sea of faces upturned to watch it, and then an explosion that seemed to split the silent night in two, and a shower of stars sank slowly down and went out one by one. And with a gasping sigh one word escaped the lips of the crowd: 'Rockets!' Anybody knows what rockets at sea mean. And presently another, and then a third. It is no use denying the dramatic intensity of the scene: separate it if you can from all the terrible events that followed, and picture the calmness of the night, the sudden light on the decks crowded with people in different stages of dress and undress, the background of huge funnels and tapering masts revealed by the soaring rocket, whose flash illumined at the same time the faces and minds of the obedient crowd, the one with mere physical light, the other with a sudden revelation of what its message was. Everyone knew without being told that we were calling for help from anyone who was near enough to see.

The crew were now in the boats, the sailors standing by the pulley ropes let them slip through the cleats in jerks, and down the boats went till level with B deck; women and children climbed over the rail into the boats and filled them; when full, they were lowered one by one, beginning with number 9, the first on the second class deck, and working backwards towards 15. All this we could see by peering over the edge of the boat deck, which was now quite open to the sea, the four boats which formed a natural barrier being lowered from the deck and leaving it exposed.

About this time, while walking the deck, I saw two ladies come over from the port side and walk towards the rail separating the second class from the first class deck. There stood an officer barring the way. 'May we pass to the boats?' they said. 'No, madam,' he replied politely, 'your boats are down on your own deck,' pointing to where they swung below. The ladies turned and went towards the stairway, and no doubt were able to enter one of the boats: they had ample time. I mention this to show that there was, at any rate, some arrangement – whether official or not – for separating the classes in embarking in boats; how far it was carried out, I do not know, but if the second class ladies were not expected to enter a boat from the first class deck, while steerage passengers were allowed access to the second class deck, it would seem to press rather hardly on the second class men, and this is rather supported by the low percentage saved. (While steerage passengers did find their way to other decks than their own, there is good evidence that some means were adopted to prevent them wandering at will to every part of the ship. An officer was stationed at the head of the stairs leading from the steerage deck to prevent steerage passengers climbing up to decks above – perhaps to lessen the possibility of a rush for the boats. Presently the boat to which he was assigned was being filled, and seeing it ready to go down, he said, 'There goes my boat! But I can't be in two places at the same time, and I have to keep this crowd back.')

Almost immediately after this incident, a report went round among men on the top deck – the starboard side – that men were to be taken off on the port side; how it originated, I am quite unable to say, but can only suppose that as the port boats, numbers 10 to 16, were not lowered from the top deck quite so soon as the starboard boats (they could still be seen on deck), it might be assumed that women were being taken off on one side and men on the other; but in whatever way the report started, it was acted on at once by almost all the men, who crowded across to the port side and watched the preparation for lowering the boats, leaving the starboard side almost deserted. Two or three men remained, however: not for any reason that we were consciously aware of; I can personally think of no decision arising from reasoned thought that induced me to remain rather than to cross over. But while there was no process of conscious reason at work, I am convinced that what was my salvation was a recognition of the necessity of being quiet and waiting in patience for some opportunity of safety to present itself.

Soon after the men had left the starboard side, I saw a bandsman – the cellist – come round the vestibule corner from the staircase entrance and run down the now deserted starboard deck, his cello trailing behind him, the spike dragging along the floor. This must have been about 12.40 a.m. I suppose the band must have begun to play soon after this and gone on until after 2 a.m. Many brave things were done that night, but none more brave than by those few men playing minute after minute as the ship settled quietly lower and lower in the sea and the sea rose higher and higher to where they stood; the music they played serving alike as their own immortal requiem and their right to be recorded on the rolls of undying fame.

Looking forward and downward, we could see several of the boats now in the water, moving slowly one by one from the side, without confusion or noise, and stealing away in the darkness which swallowed them in turn as the crew bent to the oars. An officer – I think First Officer Murdoch – came striding along the deck, clad in a long coat, from his manner and face evidently in great agitation, but determined and resolute; he looked over the side and shouted to the boats being lowered: 'Lower away, and when afloat, row around to the gangway and wait for orders.' 'Aye, aye, sir,' was the reply; and the officer passed by and went across the ship to the port side.

Almost immediately after this, I heard a cry from below of, 'Any more ladies?' and looking over the edge of the deck, saw boat 13 swinging level with the rail of B deck, with the crew, some stokers, a few men passengers and the rest ladies – the latter being about half the total number; the boat was almost full and just about to be lowered. The call for ladies was repeated twice again, but apparently there were none to be found. Just then one of the crew looked up and saw me looking over. 'Any ladies on your deck?' he said. 'No,' I replied. 'Then you had better jump.' I sat on the edge of the deck with my feet over, threw the dressing gown (which I had carried on my arm all of the time) into the boat, dropped, and fell in the boat near the stern.

As I picked myself up, I heard a shout: 'Wait a moment, here are two more ladies,' and they were pushed hurriedly over the side and tumbled into the boat, one into the middle and one next to me in the stern. They told me afterwards that they had been assembled on a lower deck with other ladies, and had come up to B deck not by the usual stairway inside, but by one of the vertically upright iron ladders that connect each deck with the one below it, meant for the use of sailors passing about the ship. Other ladies had been in front of them and got up quickly, but these two were delayed a long time by the fact that one of them – the one that was helped first over the side into boat 13 near the middle – was not at all active: it seemed almost impossible for her to climb up a vertical ladder. We saw her trying to climb the swinging rope ladder up the *Carpathia*'s side a few hours later, and she had the same difficulty.

As they tumbled in, the crew shouted, 'Lower away,' but before the order was obeyed, a man with his wife and a baby came quickly to the side: the baby was handed to the lady in the stern, the mother got in near the middle and the father at the last moment dropped in as the boat began its journey down to the sea many feet below.

Chapter 4 The Sinking of the *Titanic* Seen From a Lifeboat

Looking back now on the descent of our boat down the ship's side, it is a matter of surprise, I think, to all the occupants to remember how little they thought of it at the time. It was a great adventure, certainly: it was exciting to feel the boat sink by jerks, foot by foot, as the ropes were paid out from above and shrieked as they passed through the pulley blocks, the new ropes and gear creaking under the strain of a boat laden with people, and the crew calling to the sailors above as the boat tilted slightly, now at one end, now at the other, 'Lower aft!' 'Lower stern!' and 'Lower together!' as she came level again – but I do not think we felt much apprehension about reaching the water safely. It certainly was thrilling to see the black hull of the ship on one side and the sea, 70 feet [*c.* 21 metres] below, on the other, or to pass down by cabins and saloons brilliantly lighted; but we knew nothing of the apprehension felt in the minds of some of the officers whether the boats and lowering gear would stand the strain of the weight of our 60 people. The ropes, however, were new and strong, and the boat did not buckle in the middle as an older boat might have done. Whether it was right or not to lower boats full of people to the water – and it seems likely it was not – I think there can be nothing but the highest praise given to the officers and crew above for the way in which they lowered the boats one after the other safely to the water; it may seem a simple matter, to read about such a thing, but any sailor knows, apparently, that it is not so. An experienced officer has told me that he has seen a boat lowered in practice from a ship's deck, with a trained crew and no passengers in the boat, with practised sailors paying out the ropes, in daylight, in calm weather, with the ship lying in dock – and has seen the boat tilt over and pitch the crew headlong into the sea. Contrast these conditions with those obtaining that Monday morning at 12.45 a.m., and it is impossible not to feel that, whether the lowering crew were trained or not, whether they had or had not drilled since coming on board, they did their duty in a way that argues the greatest efficiency. I cannot help feeling the deepest gratitude to the two sailors who stood at the ropes above and lowered us to the sea: I do not suppose they were saved.

Perhaps one explanation of our feeling little sense of the unusual in leaving the *Titanic* in this way was that it seemed the climax to a series of extraordinary occurrences: the magnitude of the whole thing dwarfed events that in the ordinary way would seem to be full of imminent peril. It is easy to imagine it – a voyage of four days on a calm sea, without a single untoward incident; the presumption, perhaps already mentally half realised, that we should be ashore in 48 hours and so complete a splendid voyage – and then to feel the engine stop, to be summoned on deck with little time to dress, to tie on a lifebelt, to see rockets shooting aloft in call for help, to be told to get into a lifeboat – after all these things, it did not seem much to feel the boat sinking down to the sea: it was the natural sequence of previous events, and we had learned in the last hour to take things just as they came. At the same time, if anyone should wonder what the sensation is like, it is quite easy to measure 75 feet [*c.* 23 metres] from the windows of a tall house or a block of flats, look down to the ground and fancy himself with some 60 other people crowded into a boat so tightly that he could not sit down or move about, and then picture the boat sinking down in a continuous series of jerks, as the sailors pay out the ropes through cleats above. There are more pleasant sensations than this! How thankful we were that the sea was calm and the *Titanic* lay so steadily and quietly as we dropped down her side. We were spared the bumping and grinding against the side which so often accompanies the launching of boats: I do not remember that we even had to fend off our boat while we were trying to get free.

As we went down, one of the crew shouted, 'We are just over the condenser exhaust: we don't want to stay in that long or we shall be swamped; feel down on the floor and be ready to pull up the pin which lets the ropes free as soon as we are afloat.' I had often looked over the side and noticed this stream of water coming out of the side of the *Titanic* just above the waterline: in fact so large was the volume of water that as we ploughed along and met the waves coming towards us, this stream would cause a splash that sent spray flying. We felt, as well as we could in the crowd of people, on the floor, along the sides, with no idea where the pin could be found – and none of the crew knew where it was, only of its existence somewhere – but we never found it. And all the time we got closer to the sea and the exhaust roared nearer and nearer – until finally we floated with the ropes still holding us from above, the exhaust washing us away and the force of the tide driving us back against the side – the latter not of much account in influencing the direction, however. Thinking over what followed, I imagine we must have touched the water with the condenser stream at our bows, and not in the middle as I thought at one time: at any rate, the resultant of these three forces was that we were carried parallel to the ship, directly under the place where boat 15 would drop from her davits into the sea. Looking up we saw her already coming down rapidly from B deck: she must have filled almost immediately after ours. We shouted up, 'Stop lowering 14,' (in an account which appeared in the newspapers of 19 April I have described this boat as 14, not knowing they were numbered alternately) and the crew and passengers in the boat above, hearing us shout and seeing our position immediately below them, shouted the same to the sailors on the boat deck; but apparently they did not hear, for she dropped down foot by foot – 20 feet, 15, 10 – and a stoker and I in the bows reached up and touched her bottom swinging above our heads, trying to push away our boat from under her. It seemed now as if nothing could prevent her dropping on us, but at this moment another stoker sprang with his knife to the ropes that still held us and I heard him shout 'One! Two!' as he cut them through. The next moment we had swung away from underneath 15, and were clear of her as she dropped into the water in the space we had just before occupied. I do not know how the bow ropes were freed, but imagine that they were cut in the same way, for we were washed clear of the *Titanic* at once by the force of the stream and floated away as the oars were got out.

I think we all felt that that was quite the most exciting thing we had yet been through, and a great sigh of relief and gratitude went up as we swung away from the boat above our heads; but I heard no one cry aloud during the experience – not a woman's voice was raised in fear or hysteria. I think we all learnt many things that night about the bogey called 'fear', and how the facing of it is much less than the dread of it.

The crew was made up of cooks and stewards, mostly the former, I think; their white jackets showing up in the darkness as they pulled away, two to an oar: I do not think they can have had any practice in rowing, for all night long their oars crossed and clashed; if our safety had depended on speed or accuracy in keeping time it would have gone hard with us. Shouting began from one end of the boat to the other as to what we should do, where we should go, and no one seemed to have any knowledge how to act. At last we asked, 'Who is in charge of this boat?' but there was no reply. We then agreed by general consent that the stoker who stood in the stern with the tiller should act as captain, and from that time he directed the course, shouting to other boats and keeping in touch with them. Not that there was anywhere to go or anything we could do. Our plan of action was simple: to keep all the boats together as far as possible and wait until we were picked up by other liners. The crew had apparently heard of the wireless communications before they left the *Titanic*, but I never heard them say that we were in touch with any boat but the *Olympic*: it was always the *Olympic* that was coming to our rescue. They thought they knew even her distance, and making a calculation, we came to the conclusion that we ought to be picked up by her about two o'clock in the afternoon. But this was not our only hope of rescue: we watched all the time the darkness lasted for steamers' lights, thinking there might be a chance of other steamers coming near enough to see the lights which some of our boats carried. I am sure there was no feeling in the minds of anyone that we should not be picked up next day: we knew that wireless messages would go out from ship to ship, and as one of the stokers said, 'The sea will be covered with ships tomorrow afternoon: they will race up from all over the sea to find us.' Some even thought that fast torpedo boats might run up ahead of the *Olympic*. And yet the *Olympic* was, after all, the farthest away of them all; eight other ships lay within 300 miles of us.

How thankful we should have been to know how near help was, and how many ships had heard our message and were rushing to the *Titanic*'s aid. I think nothing has surprised us more than to learn so many ships were near enough to rescue us in a few hours.

Almost immediately after leaving the *Titanic* we saw what we all said was a ship's lights down on the horizon on the *Titanic*'s port side: two lights, one above the other, and plainly not one of our boats; we even rowed in that direction for some time, but the lights drew away and disappeared below the horizon.

But this is rather anticipating: we did none of these things first. We had no eyes for anything but the ship we had just left. As the oarsmen pulled slowly away we all turned and took a long look at the mighty vessel towering high above our midget boat, and

I know it must have been the most extraordinary sight I shall ever be called upon to witness; I realise now how totally inadequate language is to convey to some other person who was not there any real impression of what we saw.

But the task must be attempted: the whole picture is so intensely dramatic that, while it is not possible to place on paper for eyes to see the actual likeness of the ship as she lay there, some sketch of the scene will be possible. First of all, the climatic conditions were extraordinary. The night was one of the most beautiful I have ever seen: the sky without a single cloud to mar the perfect brilliance of the stars, clustered so thickly together that in places there seemed almost more dazzling points of light set in the black sky than background of sky itself; and each star seemed, in the keen atmosphere, free from any haze, to have increased its brilliance tenfold and to twinkle and glitter with a staccato flash that made the sky seem nothing but a setting made for them in which to display their wonder. They seemed so near, and their light so much more intense than ever before, that fancy suggested they saw this beautiful ship in dire distress below and all their energies had awakened to flash messages across the black dome of the sky to each other; telling and warning of the calamity happening in the world beneath. Later, when the *Titanic* had gone down and we lay still on the sea waiting for the day to dawn or a ship to come, I remember looking up at the perfect sky and realising why Shakespeare wrote the beautiful words he puts in the mouth of Lorenzo:

Jessica, look how the floor of heaven
Is thick inlaid with patines of bright gold.
There's not the smallest orb which thou behold'st
But in his motion like an angel sings,
Still quiring to the young-eyed cherubims;
Such harmony is in immortal souls;
But whilst this muddy vesture of decay
Doth grossly close it in, we cannot hear it.

But it seemed almost as if we could – that night: the stars seemed really to be alive and to talk. The complete absence of haze produced a phenomenon I had never seen before: where the sky met the sea the line was as clear and definite as the edge of a knife, so that the water and the air never merged gradually into each other and blended to a softened rounded horizon, but each element was so exclusively separate that where a star came low down in the sky near the clear-cut edge of the waterline, it still lost none of its brilliance. As the earth revolved and the water edge came up and covered partially the star, as it were, it simply cut the star in two, the upper half continuing to sparkle as long as it was not entirely hidden, and throwing a long beam of light along the sea to us.

In the evidence before the United States Senate Committee the captain of one of the ships near us that night said the stars were so extraordinarily bright near the horizon that he was deceived into thinking that they were ships' lights: he did not remember seeing such a night before. Those who were afloat will all agree with that statement: *we* were often deceived into thinking they were lights of a ship.

And next the cold air! Here again was something quite new to us: there was not a breath of wind to blow keenly round us as we stood in the boat, and because of its continued persistence to make us feel cold; it was just a keen, bitter, icy, motionless cold that came from nowhere and yet was there all the time; the stillness of it – if one can imagine 'cold' being motionless and still – was what seemed new and strange.

And these – the sky and the air – were overhead; and below was the sea. Here again something uncommon: the surface was like a lake of oil, heaving gently up and down with a quiet motion that rocked our boat dreamily to and fro. We did not need to keep her head to the swell: often I watched her lying broadside on to the tide, and with a boat loaded as we were, this would have been impossible with anything like a swell. The sea slipped away smoothly under the boat, and I think we never heard it lapping on the sides, so oily in appearance was the water. So when one of the stokers said he had been to sea for 26 years and never yet seen such a calm night, we accepted it as true without comment. Just as expressive was the remark of another – 'It reminds me of a bloomin' picnic!' It was quite true; it did: a picnic on a lake, or a quiet inland river like the Cam, or a backwater on the Thames.

And so in these conditions of sky and air and sea, we gazed broadside on the *Titanic* from a short distance. She was absolutely still – indeed from the first it seemed as if the blow from the iceberg had taken all the courage out of her and she had just come quietly to rest and was settling down without an effort to save herself, without a murmur of protest against such a foul blow. For the sea could not rock her: the wind was not there to howl noisily round the decks, and make the ropes hum; from the first what must have impressed all as they watched was the sense of stillness about her and the slow, insensible way she sank lower and lower in the sea, like a stricken animal.

The mere bulk alone of the ship viewed from the sea below was an awe-inspiring sight. Imagine a ship nearly a sixth of a mile long, 75 feet [c. 23 metres] high to the top decks, with four enormous funnels above the decks, and masts again high above the funnels; with her hundreds of portholes, all her saloons and other rooms brilliant with light, and all round her, little boats filled with those who until a few hours before had trod her decks and read in her libraries and listened to the music of her band in happy content; and who were now looking up in amazement at the enormous mass above them and rowing away from her because she was sinking.

I had often wanted to see her from some distance away, and only a few hours before, in conversation at lunch with a fellow passenger, had registered a vow to get a proper view of her lines and dimensions when we landed at New York: to stand some distance away to take in a full view of her beautiful proportions, which the narrow approach to the dock at Southampton made impossible. Little did I think that the opportunity was to be found so quickly and so dramatically. The background, too, was a different one from what I had planned for her: the black outline of her profile against the sky was bordered all round by stars studded in the sky, and all her funnels and masts were picked out in the same way: her bulk was seen where the stars were blotted out. And one other thing was different from expectation: the thing that ripped away from us instantly, as we saw it, all sense of the beauty of the night, the beauty of the ship's lines, and the beauty of her lights – and all these taken in themselves were intensely beautiful – that thing was the awful angle made by the level of the sea with the rows of porthole lights along her side in dotted lines, row above row. The sea level and the rows of lights should have been parallel – should never have met – and now they met at an angle inside the black hull of the ship. There was nothing else to indicate she was injured; nothing but this apparent violation of a simple geometrical law – that parallel lines should 'never meet even if produced ever so far both ways'; but it meant the *Titanic* had sunk by the head until the lowest portholes in the bows were under the sea, and the portholes in the stern were lifted above the normal height. We rowed away from her in the quietness of the night, hoping and praying with all our hearts that she would sink no more and the day would find her still in the same position as she was then. The crew, however, did not think so. It has been said frequently that the officers and crew felt assured that she would remain afloat even after they knew the extent of the damage. Some of them may have done so – and perhaps, from their scientific knowledge of her construction, with more reason at the time than those who said she would sink – but at any rate the stokers in our boat had no such illusion. One of them – I think he was the same man that cut us free from the pulley ropes – told us how he was at work in the stokehole, and in anticipation of going off duty in quarter of an hour – thus confirming the time of the collision as 11.45 – had near him a pan of soup keeping hot on some part of the machinery; suddenly the whole side of the compartment came in, and the water rushed him off his feet. Picking himself up, he sprang for the compartment doorway and was just through the aperture when the watertight door came down behind him, 'like a knife,' as he said; 'they work them from the bridge.' He had gone up on deck but was ordered down again at once and with others was told to draw the fires from under the boiler, which they did, and were then at liberty to come on deck again. It seems that this particular knot of stokers must have known almost as soon as anyone of the extent of injury. He added mournfully, 'I could do with that hot soup now' – and indeed he could: he was clad at the time of the collision, he said, in trousers and singlet, both very thin on account of the intense heat in the stoke-hole; and although he had added a short jacket later, his teeth were chattering with the cold. He found a place to lie down underneath the tiller on the little platform where our captain stood, and there he lay all night with a coat belonging to another stoker thrown over him and I think he must have been almost unconscious. A lady next to him, who was warmly clad with several coats, tried to insist on his having one of hers – a fur-lined one – thrown over him, but he absolutely refused while some of the women were insufficiently clad; and so the coat was given to an Irish girl with pretty auburn hair standing near, leaning against the gunwale – with an 'outside berth' and so more exposed to the cold air. This same lady was able to distribute more of her wraps to the passengers, a rug to one, a fur boa to another; and she has related with amusement that at the moment of climbing up the *Carpathia*'s side, those to whom these articles had been lent offered them all back to her; but as, like the rest of us, she was encumbered with a lifebelt, she had to say she would receive them back at the end of the climb. I had not seen my dressing gown since I dropped into the boat, but some time in the night a steerage passenger found it on the floor and put it on.

It is not easy at this time to call to mind who were in the boat, because in the night it was not possible to see more than a few feet away, and when dawn came we had eyes only for the rescue ship and the icebergs; but so far as my memory serves the list was as follows: no first class passengers; three women, one baby, two men from the second cabin; and the other passengers steerage – mostly women; a total of about 35 passengers. The rest, about 25 (and possibly more), were crew and stokers. Near to me all night was a group of three Swedish girls, warmly clad, standing close together to keep warm, and very silent; indeed there was very little talking at any time.

One conversation took place that is, I think, worth repeating: one more proof that the world after all is a small place. The 10 months' old baby which was handed down at the last moment was received by a lady next to me – the same who shared her wraps and coats. The mother had found a place in the middle and was too tightly packed to come through to the child, and so it slept contentedly for about an hour in a stranger's arms; it then began to cry and the temporary nurse said, 'Will you feel down and see if the baby's feet are out of the blanket! I don't know much about babies but I think their feet must be kept warm.' Wriggling down as well as I could, I found its toes exposed to the air and wrapped them well up, when it ceased crying at once: it was evidently a successful diagnosis! Having recognised the lady by her voice – it was much too dark to see faces – as one of my vis-à-vis at the purser's table, I said, 'Surely you are Miss — ?' 'Yes,' she replied, 'and you must be Mr Beesley; how curious we should find ourselves in the same boat!' Remembering that she had joined the boat at Queenstown, I said, 'Do you know Clonmel? A letter from a great friend of mine who is staying there at — [giving the address] came aboard at Queenstown.' 'Yes, it is my home: and I was dining at — just before I came away.' It seemed that she knew my friend, too; and we agreed that of all places in the world to recognise mutual friends, a crowded lifeboat afloat in mid-ocean at 2 a.m. 1,200 miles from our destination was one of the most unexpected.

And all the time, as we watched, the *Titanic* sank lower and lower by the head and the angle became wider and wider as the stern porthole lights lifted and the bow lights sank, and it was evident she was not to stay afloat much longer. The captain-stoker now told the oarsmen to row away as hard as they could. Two reasons seemed to make this a wise decision: one that as she sank she would create such a wave of suction that boats, if not sucked under by being too near, would be in danger of being swamped by the wave her sinking would create – and we all knew our boat was in no condition to ride big waves, crowded as it was and manned with untrained oarsmen. The second was that an explosion might result from the water getting to the boilers, and debris might fall within a wide radius. And yet, as it turned out, neither of these things happened.

At about 2.15 a.m. I think we were any distance from a mile to two miles away. It is difficult for a landsman to calculate distance at sea but we had been afloat an hour and a half, the boat was heavily loaded, the oarsmen unskilled, and our course erratic: following now one light and now another, sometimes a star and sometimes a light from a port lifeboat which had turned away from the *Titanic* in the opposite direction and lay almost on our horizon; and so we could not have gone very far away.

About this time, the water had crept up almost to her sidelight and the captain's bridge, and it seemed a question only of minutes before she sank. The oarsmen lay on their oars, and all in the lifeboat were motionless as we watched her in absolute silence – save some who would not look and buried their heads on each others' shoulders. The lights still shone with the same brilliance, but not so many of them: many were now below the surface. I have often wondered since whether they continued to light up the cabins when the portholes were under water; they may have done so.

And then, as we gazed awestruck, she tilted slowly up, revolving apparently about a centre of gravity just astern of amidships, until she attained a vertically upright position; and there she remained – motionless! As she swung up, her lights, which had shone without a flicker all night, went out suddenly, came on again for a single flash, then went out altogether. And as they did so, there came a noise which many people, wrongly I think, have described as an explosion; it has always seemed to me that it was nothing but the engines and machinery coming loose from their bolts and bearings, and falling through the compartments, smashing everything in their way. It was partly a roar, partly a groan, partly a rattle, and partly a smash, and it was not a sudden roar as an explosion would be: it went on successively for some seconds, possibly 15 to 20, as the heavy machinery dropped down to the bottom (now the bows) of the ship: I suppose it fell through the end and sank first, before the ship. But it was a noise no one had heard before, and no one wishes to hear again: it was stupefying, stupendous, as it came to us along the water. It was as if all the heavy things one could think of had been thrown downstairs from the top of a house, smashing each other and the stairs and everything in the way.

Several apparently authentic accounts have been given, in which definite stories of explosions have been related – in some cases even with wreckage blown up and the ship broken in two; but I think such accounts will not stand close analysis. In the first place the fires had been withdrawn and the steam allowed to escape some time before she sank, and the possibility of explosion from this cause seems very remote. Then, as just related, the noise was not sudden and definite, but prolonged – more like the roll and crash of thunder. The probability of the noise being caused by engines falling down will be seen by referring to illustration 57, where the engines are placed in compartments 3, 4 and 5. As the *Titanic* tilted up they would almost certainly fall loose from their bed and plunge down through the other compartments.

No phenomenon like that pictured in some American and English papers occurred – that of the ship breaking in two, and the two ends being raised above the surface. I saw these drawings in preparation on board the *Carpathia*, [probably illustrations 52, 53, 86, 90, 91 & 92] and said at the time that they bore no resemblance to what actually happened.

When the noise was over the *Titanic* was still upright like a column: we could see her now only as the stern and some 150 feet [*c.* 45 metres] of her stood outlined against the star-specked sky, looming black in the darkness, and in this position she continued for some minutes – I think as much as five minutes, but it may have been less. Then, first sinking back a little at the stern, I thought, she slid slowly forwards through the water and dived slantingly down; the sea closed over her and we had seen the last of the beautiful ship on which we had embarked four days before at Southampton.

And in place of the ship on which all our interest had been concentrated for so long and towards which we looked most of the time because it was still the only object on the sea which was a fixed point to us – in place of the *Titanic*, we had the level sea now stretching in an unbroken expanse to the horizon: heaving gently just as before, with no indication on the surface that the waves had just closed over the most wonderful vessel ever built by man's hand; the stars looked down just the same and the air was just as bitterly cold.

There seemed a great sense of loneliness when we were left on the sea in a small boat without the *Titanic*: not that we were uncomfortable (except for the cold) nor in danger: we did not think we were either, but the *Titanic* was no longer there.

We waited head on for the wave which we thought might come – the wave we had heard so much of from the crew and which they said had been known to travel for miles – and it never came. But although the *Titanic* left us no such legacy of a wave as she went to the bottom, she left us something we would willingly forget forever, something which it is well not to let the imagination dwell on – the cries of many hundreds of our fellow passengers struggling in the ice-cold water.

I would willingly omit any further mention of this part of the disaster from this book, but for two reasons it is not possible – first, that as a matter of history it should be put on record; and secondly, that these cries were not only an appeal for help in the awful conditions of danger in which the drowning found themselves – an appeal that could never be answered – but an appeal to the whole world to make such conditions of danger and hopelessness impossible ever again; a cry that called to the heavens for the very injustice of its own existence; a cry that clamoured for its own destruction.

We were utterly surprised to hear this cry go up as the waves closed over the *Titanic*: we had heard no sound of any kind from her since we left her side; and, as mentioned before, we did not know how many boats she had or how many rafts. The crew may have known, but they probably did not, and if they did, they never told the passengers; we should not have been surprised to know all were safe on some lifesaving device.

So that unprepared as we were for such a thing, the cries of the drowning floating across the quiet sea filled us with stupefaction: we longed to return and rescue at least some of the drowning, but we knew it was impossible. The boat was filled to standing room, and to return would mean the swamping of us all, and so the captain-stoker told his crew to row away from the cries. We tried to sing to keep all from thinking of them; but there was no heart for singing in the boat at that time.

The cries, which were loud and numerous at first, died away gradually one by one, but the night was clear, frosty and still, the water smooth, and the sounds must have carried on its level surface free from any obstruction for miles, certainly much farther from the ship than we were situated. I think the last of them must have been heard nearly 40 minutes after the *Titanic* sank. Lifebelts would keep the survivors afloat for hours; but the cold water was what stopped the cries.

There must have come to all those safe in the lifeboats, scattered round the drowning at various distances, a deep resolve that, if anything could be done by them in the future to prevent the repetition of such sounds, they would do it – at whatever cost of time or other things. And not only to them are those cries an imperative call, but to every man and woman who has known of them. It is not possible that ever again can such conditions exist; but it is a duty imperative on one and all to see that they do not. Think of it! A few more boats, a few more planks of wood nailed together in a particular way at a trifling cost, and all those men and women whom the world can so ill afford to lose would be with us today, there would be no mourning in thousands of homes which now are desolate, and these words need not have been written.

Chapter 5 The Rescue

All accounts agree that the *Titanic* sank about 2.20 a.m.: a watch in our boat gave the time as 2.30 a.m. shortly afterwards. We were then in touch with three other boats: one was 15, on our starboard quarter, and the others I have always supposed were 9 and 11, but I do not know definitely. We never got into close touch with each other, but called occasionally across the darkness and saw them looming near and then drawing away again; we called to ask if any officer were aboard the other three, but did not find one. So in the absence of any plan of action, we rowed slowly forward – or what we thought was forward, for it was in the direction the *Titanic*'s bows were pointing before she sank. I see now that we must have been pointing north-west, for we presently saw the Northern Lights on the starboard, and again, when the *Carpathia* came up from the south, we saw her from behind us on the south-east, and turned our boat around to get to her. I imagine the boats must have spread themselves over the ocean fanwise as they escaped from the *Titanic*: those on the starboard and port sides forward being almost dead ahead of her and the stern boats being broadside from her; this explains why the port boats were so much longer in reaching the *Carpathia* – as late as 8.30 a.m. – while some of the starboard boats came up as early as 4.10 a.m. Some of the port boats had to row across the place where the *Titanic* sank to get to the *Carpathia*, through the debris of chairs and wreckage of all kinds.

None of the other three boats near us had a light – and we missed lights badly: we could not see each other in the darkness; we could not signal to ships which might be rushing up full speed from any quarter to the *Titanic*'s rescue; and now we had been through so much it would seem hard to have to encounter the additional danger of being in the line of a rescuing ship. We felt again for the lantern beneath our feet, along the sides, and I managed this time to get down to the locker below the tiller platform and open it in front by removing a board, to find nothing but the zinc air tank which renders the boat unsinkable when upset. I do not think there was a light in the boat. We felt also for food and water, and found none, and came to the conclusion that none had been put in; but here we were mistaken. I have a letter from Second Officer Lightoller in which he assures me that he and Fourth Officer Pitman examined every lifeboat from the *Titanic* as they lay on the *Carpathia*'s deck afterwards and found biscuits and water in each. Not that we wanted any food or water then: we thought of the time that might elapse before the *Olympic* picked us up in the afternoon.

Towards 3 a.m. we saw a faint glow in the sky ahead on the starboard quarter, the first gleams, we thought, of the coming dawn. We were not certain of the time and were eager perhaps to accept too readily any relief from darkness – only too

The SINKING of the
TITANIC
and GREAT
SEA DISASTERS

THRILLING STORIES of SURVIVORS
WITH PHOTOGRAPHS & SKETCHES

WHITE STAR LINE
TRIPLE SCREW STEAMER
"OLYMPIC"

882½ FT.
LONG

46,359
TONS

Opposite: 2. *Titanic* was the second of the trio of *Olympic*-class ocean liners built by the Harland & Wolff shipyard for the White Star Line. *Olympic*, pictured, was her virtually identical sister ship. This is an illustration of *Olympic* produced after the *Titanic* sank. Notice the continuous row of lifeboats on the boat deck. Additional lifeboats were added as a result of the *Titanic* disaster.

3. *Titanic* proceeding down Southampton Water on its maiden voyage, 10 April 1912. Although *Titanic* was the most luxurious ship in the world she only carried 20 lifeboats, enough for 1,178 passengers. On her maiden voyage to New York she was carrying over 2,200 people.

4. At 45,000 grt *Titanic* was easily the largest ocean liner in the world.

Page 1 image: 1. Front cover of the first anthology of survivor accounts, *The Sinking of the Titanic*, by journalist Logan Marshall. An 'instant book', it was sold door-to-door across America in the months following the sinking of the *Titanic*.

5. Contemporary depiction of the *Titanic* sinking and the survivors on the lifeboats looking back in horror. In reality there was no huge iceberg nearby. Survivor Esther Hart, lifeboat 14: 'The air was full of the awful and despairing cries of drowning men. And we were helpless to help, for we dared not go near them.'

Above: 6. View from *Carpathia* of the iceberg which sank the *Titanic*. Captain Rostron of the *Carpathia*: 'It was a beautiful morning, a clear sun burning on sea and glistening on the icebergs. On every side there were dozens of these monsters so wonderful to look at, so dreadful to touch.'

Left: 7. c. A view of the bridge & crow's nest.

7.a. A graphic depiction of the *Titanic* striking the iceberg. From a French journal, April 1912.

7.b. 'As I was put into the boat he cried to me "It's alright little girl. You go. I will stay." As our boat shoved off he threw me a kiss, and that was the last I saw of him.' Mary Marvin, lifeboat 10, who was on her honeymoon and pregnant when her husband was lost.

8.a. Heartbreaking farewells. Romanticised view of the scene on the boat deck as husbands and wives were parted. Some women chose to remain with their men folk, including Rosalie Ida Straus, who drowned with her husband Isidor Straus. 'Mrs Strauss had hidden from the officers, who were trying to force her into one of the boats.' Lucy Duff-Gordon (lifeboat 1).

8.b. Loading of passengers into the lifeboats. It is easy to understand why the accounts of different eyewitnesses often differ so radically when it is remembered that the *Titanic* was over 260 metres in length and that the lifeboats were leaving from widely separated points. Margaret 'Molly' Brown, lifeboat 6: 'It was a strange sight. It all seemed like a play, like a drama that was being enacted for entertainment. It did not seem real. Men would say, 'After you,' as they made some woman comfortable and stepped back. I afterward heard some one say that men went downstairs into the restaurant. Many of them smoked. Many of them walked up and down. For a while after we reached the water we watched the ship. We could hear the band. Every light was shining.'

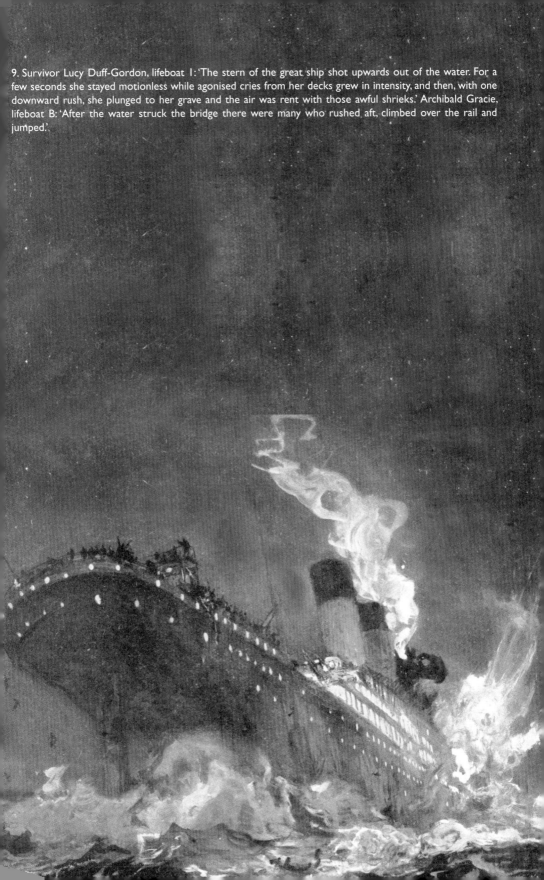

9. Survivor Lucy Duff-Gordon, lifeboat 1: 'The stern of the great ship shot upwards out of the water. For a few seconds she stayed motionless while agonised cries from her decks grew in intensity, and then, with one downward rush, she plunged to her grave and the air was rent with those awful shrieks.' Archibald Gracie, lifeboat B: 'After the water struck the bridge there were many who rushed aft, climbed over the rail and jumped.'.

Opposite: 10. 41° 16' N; 50° 14' W by Norman Wilkinson. This painting was commissioned as a frontispiece by the publisher of Filson Young's 1912 account of the sinking, *Titanic*, published in London just 37 days after the disaster. Over the years it has been much criticised for apparent inaccuracies but when *Titanic* survivor Eva Hart (lifeboat 14) was shown the image she said 'That's exactly how it was'.

Above: 11. *Titanic* survivors in one of the lifeboats approaching the *Carpathia*. Possibly lifeboat 6, as Quartermaster Hichens wore a blanket and was at the tiller. The number of occupants appear to match lifeboat 6 too.

Below: 12. Lifeboat 14 towing collapsible lifeboat D. Lifeboat 14, as it left the *Titanic* (some survivors were transferred to another lifeboat mid-Atlantic), included Charlotte Collyer and her daughter, Daisy Minahan, Esther Hart and her daughter Eva, Joseph Scarrott and Harold Lowe. Daisy: 'Some of the women implored Officer Lowe, of No. 14, to divide his passengers among the three other boats and go back to rescue. His first answer to those requests was, "You ought to be damn glad you are here and have got your own life."'

Opposite top: 13. *Titanic* survivors in collapsible lifeboat D, one of the last to be launched at *c.* 2.05 a.m. Hugh Woolner: 'We hopped up onto the gunwale preparing to jump out into the sea, because if we had waited a minute longer we should have been boxed in against the ceiling. And as we looked out we saw this collapsible, the last boat on the port side, being lowered right in front of our faces.'

16. *Titanic* passengers coming aboard the *Carpathia*. Helen Bishop (lifeboat 7): 'After we had pulled alongside of the rescue ship, many of the women were lifted aboard in chairs, tied to a rope. I was sufficiently composed to climb the ladder alongside to the deck. When the last of the survivors were taken on, the recounting of the experience began.'

17. Captain Rostron of the *Carpathia*: 'They started climbing aboard. Obviously they had got away in a hurry, for there were only twenty-five of them whereas the capacity of the boat was fully forty.'

Opposite, clockwise from centre: 14. *Titanic* survivors in a lifeboat. Mary Hewlett, lifeboat 13: 'We were alone on the calm sea. It seemed much longer than it really was before we saw the *Carpathia*.' 15.a. & 15.b. A view of one of the *Titanic* lifeboats alongside the *Carpathia* showing that some were far from full. Survivor Helen Bishop, lifeboat 7: 'It was then almost impossible to get people to venture into them…The officers implored people to get aboard, but they seemed to fear hanging out over the water at a height of 75 feet, and the officers ordered the boat lowered away with only a small portion of what it could carry.'

Opposite: 18. *Luxuries versus lifeboats.* Cartoon from American periodical, 8 May 1912. A common theme in the reaction to the sinking of *Titanic. Above:* 19. George Harder and his wife Dorothy Harder (first class passengers, both rescued on lifeboat 5). The Harders were a honeymoon couple saved from the *Titanic.* The woman weeping, with hand to her face, is Clara Hays (lifeboat 3). Her husband Charles M. Hays perished. When the cry came to get in the lifeboats the Harders, thinking there was no danger, jumped in one of the first boats lowered. *Centre:* 20. Group of survivors of the *Titanic* disaster aboard the *Carpathia* after being rescued. Howard Chapin, *Carpathia* passenger: 'Practically everyone was quiet and subdued, apparently stunned by the shock and the cold.' *Right:* 21. Howard Chapin, *Carpathia* passenger: 'Nearly all had on heavy garments, although very few were entirely dressed. Many men had on evening clothes.'

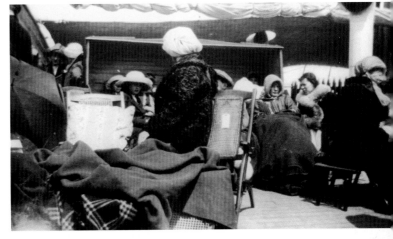

Above: 22. *Speed! The new terror of the sea*. Front-cover cartoon from an American periodical 1 May 1912. The satire is obvious. *Below*: 23. Photo taken before the 'orphans' of the *Titanic* were correctly identified and returned to their mother. The boys are French brothers Michel (age four) and Edmond Navratil (age two). They escaped the sinking ship in lifeboat D; their father perished. To board the ship (in second class), their father assumed the name Louis Hoffman and used their nicknames, Lolo and Mamon. Margaret Hays (lifeboat 7) volunteered once on board *Carpathia* to care for the 'orphans' as she could speak fluent French.

Opposite page, bottom left: 26. Eva Hart, her mother Esther and father Ben. Esther and her daughter survived in lifeboat 14. Ben drowned. Eva was one of the longest-surviving survivors and died in 1996. *Opposite page, bottom right*: 27. First class passenger Madeleine Astor (lifeboat 4) the 18-year-old bride of the millionaire John Astor who went down with the *Titanic*. She was pregnant at the time of the sinking and went on to give birth to a son in August 1912. At one stage whilst waiting on the boat deck, the Astors retired to the gym and sat on the mechanical horses.

Above left: 24. Left to right: Chief Officer Henry Wilde, Fourth Officer Joseph Boxhall and Captain Edward Smith. Henry Wilde took charge of the even-numbered boats, those on the port side, though he is not referred to very much in the survivor accounts of the sinking. He died in the disaster and was last reported attempting to free the lifeboats A and B. Boxhall survived on lifeboat 2 and decided against returning to pick up survivors in the water. *Above right:* 25. Ida Hippach and her daughter Gertrude, first class passengers, who survived the *Titanic* disaster in lifeboat 4. They explained their escape to the *New York Times:* 'We saw Colonel Astor place Mrs Astor in a boat and heard him assure her that he would follow later. He turned to us with a smile and said, "Ladies, you are next." The officer in charge of the boat protested that the craft was full and the seamen started to lower it. Colonel Astor exclaimed, "Hold that boat," in the voice of a man to be obeyed, and the men did as he ordered. The boat had been ordered past the upper deck, and the Colonel took us to the next deck below and put us in the boat, one after the other, through a porthole.'

Above left: 28. Archibald Gracie was one of the few passengers to have survived in the freezing waters before scrambling onto the upturned lifeboat B. He describes vividly how he went down with the ship: 'I was in a whirlpool of water, swirling round and round, as I still tried to cling to the railing as the ship plunged to the depths below. Down, down, I went'. *Above centre*: 29. Eleanor Widener (first class passenger, lifeboat 4), who left her husband, George, behind on the sinking ship. *Above right*: 30. Marian Thayer (first class passenger, lifeboat 4), mother of Jack Thayer (first class passenger, lifeboat B). They were reunited on board *Carpathia*. Jack, like Gracie, survived in the water and described the moment the *Titanic* went down just metres away from the upturned lifeboat B: '[*Titanic*] pivoting and moving in an almost perpendicular position, was sticking up in the air almost 300 feet. The ship then corkscrewed around so that the propeller, rudder and all seemed to go right over the heads of us on the upturned boat. Of course the lights now were all out. The ship seemed to hang in this position for minutes. Then with a dive and final plunge, the *Titanic* went under the water with very little apparent suction or noise.'

Above left: 31. Margaret Brown (first class passenger, lifeboat 6), better known as the unsinkable Molly Brown. Molly is remembered for her presence of mind when her fellow lifeboat passengers despaired: 'I rowed because I would have frozen to death. I made them all row. It saved their lives.' Lifeboat 6 was one of the last to be picked up by *Carpathia* at around 7 a.m. *Above centre*: 32. Eloise Smith (first class passenger, lifeboat 6), one of the first class passengers who was widowed by the *Titanic*. Eloise and her husband Lucien had only been married a few months. *Above right*: 33. Charlotte Collyer and her daughter Marjorie (second class passengers, lifeboat 14). Charlotte's account is the fullest we have from a female survivor: 'Something in the very bowels of the *Titanic* exploded... two other explosions followed, dull and heavy, as if below the surface. The *Titanic* broke in two before my eyes. The fore part was already partly under the water. It wallowed over and disappeared instantly. The stern reared straight on end, and stood poised on the ocean for many seconds – they seemed minutes to me.'

Above: 34. *Titanic* under construction in Belfast c. May 1911.

Right: 35. Sister ships *Olympic* and *Titanic*. View of bows in shipyard construction scaffolding Belfast c. May 1911. The *Olympic* was almost identical to *Titanic*, and many more press photographs were taken of *Olympic* than *Titanic* and hence many of the views of the two ships (including those captioned *Titanic* in 1911 and 1912) are actually of the *Olympic*.

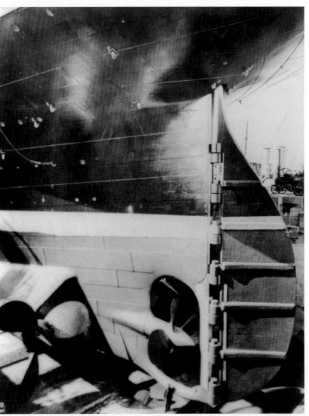

Above: 36. View of one of *Titanic*'s huge propellers, with shipyard workers in the background just prior to *Titanic*'s launch 31 May 1911.

Left: 37. View of the stern and rudder of the *Titanic* in dry dock.

38. The funnel-less *Titanic* in May 1911 just after her launch.
39. The *Titanic*. Seven-year-old survivor, Eva Hart (lifeboat 14), described her thoughts when she first saw the ship: 'I had never seen a ship before... it looked very big... everybody was very excited.'

40. Filson Young, author of one of the first accounts of the disaster, went to Southampton following the *Titanic* disaster to see her sister ship the *Olympic* leave for America. Having walked around on board he explained later in his book how he could understand the feeling of unsinkability that had given such false confidence to the passengers and crew aboard the *Titanic*.

41. *Titanic*'s sister ship, the *Olympic*.

42. First class suite bedroom (B59). Lucy Duff-Gordon (lifeboat 1): 'I had been in bed, I suppose, for about an hour, and the lights were all out, when I was awakened by a funny rumbling noise. It was like nothing I had ever heard before. It seemed almost as if some giant hand had been playing bowls, rolling the great balls along. Then the boat stopped and immediately there was the frightful noise of escaping steam, and I heard people running outside my cabin, but they were laughing and gay. "We must have hit an iceberg," I heard one of them say. "There is ice on the deck." '

43. Another opulent first class cabin bedroom.

Above: 44. Sitting room of a first class suite aboard *Titanic*. This cabin had a view onto the boat deck.

Left: 45. Lawrence Beesley (lifeboat 13): 'On the night of the disaster, right up to the time of the *Titanic*'s sinking, while the band grouped outside the gymnasium doors played with such supreme courage in face of the water which rose foot by foot before their eyes, the [gym] instructor was on duty inside, with passengers on the bicycles and the rowing-machines, still assisting and encouraging to the last. Along with the bandsmen it is fitting that his name, which I do not think has yet been put on record – it is [Thomas] McCawley – should have a place in the honourable list of those who did their duty faithfully to the ship and the line they served.'

46. *Titanic* passing through Belfast Lough en route to the Irish Sea for her trials, 2 April 1912.

47. *Titanic*'s near miss with the SS *New York* shortly after departing from Southampton on her maiden voyage, noon Wednesday 10 April.

Above: 48. The *Titanic* ablaze with lights heading out of Cherbourg harbour on Wednesday 10 April 1912. Lawrence Beesley (lifeboat 13): 'In the calmest weather we made Cherbourg just as it grew dusk and left again about 8.30 p.m. after taking on board passengers and mails.'

Left: 49. One of several candidates photographed in the immediate aftermath of the sinking for 'iceberg that sunk the *Titanic*'. These photographs were reproduced around the world in newspapers and books. This one was photographed near the scene of the sinking.

The following text appears within the top illustration:

The **TITANIC** WAS **175** FEET ABOVE WATER LINE

The **ICEBERG** INTO WHICH SHE CRASHED WAS ABOUT **100** FT AT THE HIGHEST PEAK

The **TITANIC** WAS **882** FT IN LENGTH

The LENGTH OF THE **BERG** IS ESTIMATED TO BE **500** FT.

The **TITANIC** WAS ABOUT **40** FT BELOW WATER LINE

The **ICEBERG** WAS BETWEEN **500** AND **700** FEET DEEP BELOW WATER LINE

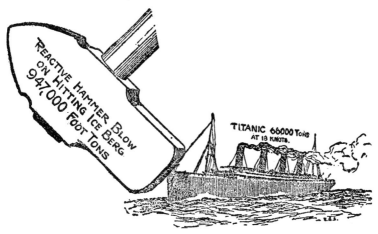

The following text appears within the lower diagram:

REACTIVE HAMMER BLOW ON HITTING ICE BERG. 947,000 FOOT TONS

TITANIC 66000 TONS AT 18 KNOTS.

Top: 50. A contemporary newspaper depiction of the iceberg alongside the *Titanic* based on a siting of an iceberg in the vicinity by Captain Wood of the *Etonian*.

Above: 51. Diagram showing the force of the *Titanic* hitting the iceberg. The iceberg punched along the ship's starboard side over c. 10 seconds, buckling the hull in several places below the waterline over c. 90 metres. This opened the first six compartments (the forward peak tank, the three forward holds and boiler rooms 5 and 6) to the sea. While the ship was designed to remain afloat with the first four compartments flooded, the collision caused flooding of the six forward compartments.

STRIKES STARBOARD BOW -12 ft AFT

52. Sunday 14 April 1912, '11.45 p.m. *Titanic* strikes an iceberg with its starboard bow, 12 feet aft.' Jack Thayer (first class passenger, lifeboat B) was one of a number of survivors to describe the ship breaking in two as she sank. This is the first in a series of six illustrations drawn aboard *Carpathia* that show the ship in her dying minutes and clearly show the two halves. It would be over 70 years before Thayer was proved right when the wreck was discovered resting on the seabed in two halves. Series of sketches executed on board *Carpathia* by Lewis Skidmore (a young art teacher), based on conversations with Jack Thayer following the rescue. The timings listed in this series of illustrations have since 1912 been revised.

SETTLES BY HEAD · BOATS ORDERED OUT

53. Monday 15 April 1912, '12.05 a.m. *Titanic* settles by head, boats ordered out.'
Opposite: 54. A chart from a 1912 edition of magazine *The Sphere* showing the ships too far away to help the *Titanic*. Note that the *Californian* is said to be 19½ miles away and there is a mystery ship between her and the stricken liner.

ICE FLOES

"VIRGINIAN"

PARISIAN
150 MILES
FROM TITANIC

COURSE OF
"PARISIAN"

ICE FLOES
& DOZENS OF LARGE ICEBERGS

ME RANGE OF
SS INSTRUMENTS
TITANIC

19½ MILES FROM WRECK
"CALIFORNIAN" SURROUNDED
BY ICE WITH
HER WIRELESS
NOT WORKING

THE MYSTERY
AS REPORTED
THE CAPTAIN
OF THE "CALI

MYSTERIOUS
SCHOONER
REPORTED BY
MOUNT TEMPLE

ICE FLOE
69 MILES LONG
12 MILES WIDE

ENORMOUS ICEBERGS
NORTH EASTERLY
SIDE OF FLOE

"MOUNT
TEMPLE"
50 MILES FROM TITANIC
(SEPERATED BY ICE FLOE)

COURSE OF
MOUNT TEMPLE

OF
WIRELESS TELEGRAPHY

TITANIC
SINKING

COURSE OF BIRMA

CARPATHIA 58 MILES FROM TITANIC
WIRELESS OF SAME POWER
AS "MOUNT TEMPLE"

SOUTHERN LIMIT
OF BERGS

RANGE OF WIRELESS PLANT OF THE
BIRMA"

"BIRMA"
100 MILES
SOUTH WEST
OF SINKING SHIP

COURSE OF FRANKFURT

"FRANKFURT"
WIRELESS SAME POWER
AS "VIRGINIAN"

DARKER SHADOW
IN THE WATER
REPRESENTS
DRIFT OF
THE CURRENT
SOUTH

Top: 55. Cutaway drawing of *Titanic* reproduced in newspapers in late April 1912 showing the suspected section (heavy black line) 'torn out' by the collision with the iceberg. Since the discovery of the wreck, scientists have used sonar to examine the area and discovered the iceberg had caused the hull to buckle, allowing water to enter *Titanic* between her steel plates. The illustration also shows much of the layout of the ship.

Bottom: 56. Longitudinal section of the *Titanic* from the Harland & Wolff blueprints *c*.1911. Bridge deck B through to lower deck G are marked.

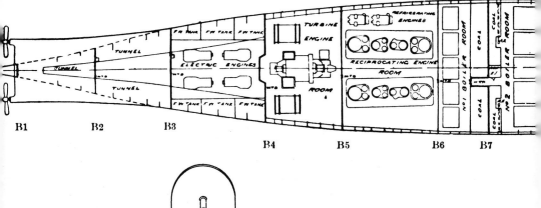

B1   B2   B3   B4   B5   B6   B7

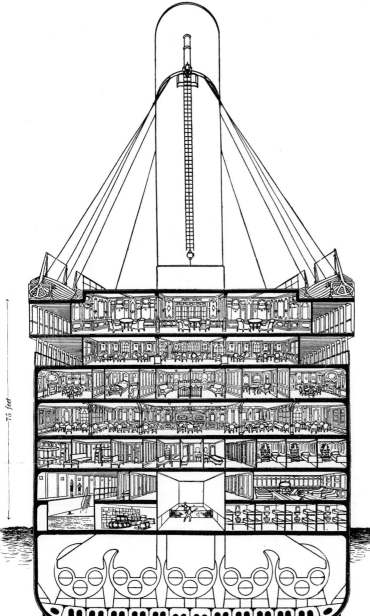

Top: 57. Plan of
the Tank Top of the
Titanic showing the 15
transverse bulkheads
of the ship's hull which
created 16 compartments,
each of which could be
isolated from the adjoining
compartment by a
watertight door. Note the
forward peak tank, three
forward holds and boiler
rooms 5 and 6 marked in
this plan.
Left: 58. Transverse amidship
section through the *Titanic*
showing the various decks
of the ship, the indoor
squash court, swimming
pool and third class living
quarters. The *Titanic*
consisted of ten decks, in
order, descending: Boat
Deck, Promenade Deck [A],
Bridge Deck [B], Shelter
Deck [C], Saloon Deck [D],
Upper Deck [E], Middle
Deck [F], Lower Deck [G],
Orlop Deck (the deck the
stokers stood on) and Tank
Top (the plating forming the
inner bottom of a ship hull).

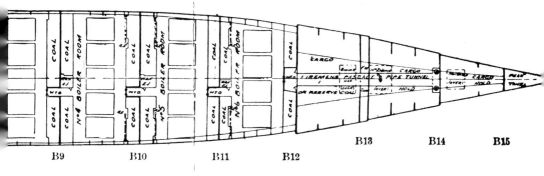

B9 B10 B11 B12 B13 B14 B15

59. A typical wireless room of an ocean liner of the period. Junior Wireless Operator Harold Bride (lifeboat B) relates the last few minutes in the wireless room with his Senior Wireless Operator Jack Phillips: 'Then came the Captain's voice: "Men, You have done your full duty. You can do no more. Abandon your cabin. Now it is every man for themselves. You look out for yourselves. I release you." I looked out. The boat deck was awash. Phillips clung on sending and sending. He clung on for about 10 minutes or maybe fifteen minutes after the Captain had released him. The water was then coming into our cabin.'

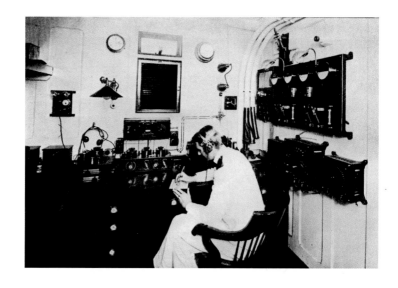

60. The wireless station at Cape Race was the first to hear *Titanic* transmit CQD, the distress signal, at 10.25 p.m. New York time simultaneously with the ships *La Touraine* and *Mount Temple*.

Left: 61. The first class gym on board *Titanic*.

Below left: 62. The first class Café Parisien was a favourite with the ship's younger set. Situated on the starboard side B deck, aft of the fourth funnel and outside the first class À la Carte Restaurant. The café's large picture windows gave diners a view of the sea while dining. Alfred Fernand Omont, a Frenchman, was playing cards in the Café Parisien with Pierre Maréchal, Paul Chevré and Lucien P. Smith when the collision took place. Chevré, Maréchal and Omont were all rescued in lifeboat 7. Omont: 'At about 11.40 p.m. there was a shock. I have crossed the Atlantic 13 times, and the shock was not a great one, and I thought it was caused by a wave... When the shock had happened, we saw something white through the portholes, and we saw water on the ports. When the waiter opened the porthole we saw nothing except a clear night.'

glad to be able to look each other in the face and see who were our companions in good fortune; to be free from the hazard of lying in a steamer's track, invisible in the darkness. But we were doomed to disappointment: the soft light increased for a time, and died away a little; glowed again, and then remained stationary for some minutes! The Northern Lights! It suddenly came to me, and so it was: presently the light arched fanwise across the northern sky, with faint streamers reaching towards the Polestar. I had seen them of about the same intensity in England some years ago and knew them again. A sigh of disappointment went through the boat as we realised that the day was not yet; but had we known it, something more comforting even than the day was in store for us. All night long we had watched the horizon with eager eyes for signs of a steamer's lights; we heard from the captain-stoker that the first appearance would be a single light on the horizon, the masthead light, followed shortly by a second one, lower down, on the deck; if these two remained in vertical alignment and the distance between them increased as the lights drew nearer, we might be certain it was a steamer. But what a night to see that first light on the horizon! We saw it many times as the earth revolved, and some stars rose on the clear horizon and others sank down to it: there were 'lights' on every quarter. Some we watched and followed until we saw the deception and grew wiser; some were lights from those of our boats that were fortunate enough to have lanterns, but these were generally easily detected, as they rose and fell in the near distance. Once they raised our hopes, only to sink them to zero again. Near what seemed to be the horizon on the port quarter we saw two lights close together, and thought this must be our double light; but as we gazed across the miles that separated us, the lights slowly drew apart and we realised that they were two boats' lanterns at different distances from us, in line, one behind the other. They were probably the forward port boats that had to return so many miles next morning across the *Titanic*'s graveyard.

But notwithstanding these hopes and disappointments, the absence of lights, food and water (as we thought), and the bitter cold, it would not be correct to say we were unhappy in those early morning hours: the cold that settled down on us like a garment that wraps close around was the only real discomfort, and that we could keep at bay by not thinking too much about it as well as by vigorous friction and gentle stamping on the floor (it made too much noise to stamp hard!). I never heard that anyone in boat 13 had any after effects from the cold – even the stoker who was so thinly clad came through without harm. After all, there were many things to be thankful for: so many that they made insignificant the temporary inconvenience of the cold, the crowded boat, the darkness and the hundred and one things that in the ordinary way we might regard as unpleasant. The quiet sea, the beautiful night (how different from two nights later when flashes of lightning and peals of thunder broke the sleep of many on board the *Carpathia*!), and above all the fact of being in a boat at all when so many of our fellow passengers and crew – whose cries no longer moaned across the water to us – were silent in the water. Gratitude was the dominant note in our feelings then. But grateful as we were, our gratitude was soon to be increased a hundred fold. About 3.30 a.m., as nearly as I can judge, someone in the bow called our attention to a faint faraway gleam in the south-east. We all turned quickly to look and there it was certainly: streaming up from behind the horizon like a distant flash of a warship's searchlight; then a faint boom like guns afar off, and the light died away again. The stoker who had lain all night under the tiller sat up suddenly as if from a dream, the overcoat hanging from his shoulders. I can see him now, staring out across the sea, to where the sound had come from, and hear him shout, 'That was a cannon!' But it was not: it was the *Carpathia*'s rocket, though we did not know it until later. But we did know now that something was not far away, racing up to our help and signalling to us a preliminary message to cheer our hearts until she arrived.

With every sense alert, eyes gazing intently at the horizon and ears open for the least sound, we waited in absolute silence in the quiet night. And then, creeping over the edge of the sea where the flash had been, we saw a single light, and presently a second below it, and in a few minutes they were well above the horizon and they remained in line! But we had been deceived before, and we waited a little longer before we allowed ourselves to say we were safe. The lights came up rapidly: so rapidly it seemed only a few minutes (though it must have been longer) between first seeing them and finding them well above the horizon and bearing down rapidly on us. We did not know what sort of a vessel was coming, but we knew she was coming quickly, and we searched for paper, rags – anything that would burn (we were quite prepared to burn our coats if necessary). A hasty paper torch was twisted out of letters found in someone's pocket, lighted, and held aloft by the stoker standing on the tiller platform. The little light shone in flickers on the faces of the occupants of the boat, ran in broken lines for a few yards along the black oily sea (where for the first time I saw the presence of that awful thing which had caused the whole terrible disaster – ice – in little chunks the size of one's fist, bobbing harmlessly up and down), and spluttered away to blackness again as the stoker threw the burning remnants of paper overboard. But had we known it, the danger of being run down was already over, one reason being that the *Carpathia* had already seen the lifeboat which all night long had shown a green light, the first indication the *Carpathia* had of our position. But the real reason is to be found in the *Carpathia*'s log: 'Went full speed ahead during the night; stopped at 4 a.m. with an iceberg dead ahead.' It was a good reason.

With our torch burnt and in darkness again we saw the headlights stop, and realised that the rescuer had hove to. A sigh of relief went up when we thought no hurried scramble had to be made to get out of her way, with a chance of just being missed by her, and having to meet the wash of her screws as she tore by us. We waited and she slowly swung round and revealed herself to us as a large steamer with all her portholes alight. I think the way those lights came slowly into view was one of the most wonderful things we shall ever see. It meant deliverance at once: that was the amazing thing to us all. We had thought of the afternoon as our time of rescue, and here only a few hours after the *Titanic* sank, before it was yet light, we were to be taken aboard. It seemed almost too good to be true, and I think everyone's eyes filled with tears, men's as well as women's, as they saw again the rows of lights one above the other shining kindly to them across the water, and 'Thank God!' was murmured in heartfelt tones round the boat. The boat swung round and the crew began their long row to the steamer; the captain called for a song and led off with

'Pull for the shore, boys'. The crew took it up quaveringly and the passengers joined in, but I think one verse was all they sang. It was too early yet, gratitude was too deep and sudden in its overwhelming intensity, for us to sing very steadily. Presently, finding the song had not gone very well, we tried a cheer, and that went better. It was more easy to relieve our feelings with a noise, and time and tune were not necessary ingredients in a cheer.

In the midst of our thankfulness for deliverance, one name was mentioned with the deepest feeling of gratitude: that of Marconi. I wish that he had been there to hear the chorus of gratitude that went out to him for the wonderful invention that spared us many hours, and perhaps many days, of wandering about the sea in hunger and storm and cold. Perhaps our gratitude was sufficiently intense and vivid to 'Marconi' some of it to him that night.

All around we saw boats making for the *Carpathia* and heard their shouts and cheers. Our crew rowed hard in friendly rivalry with other boats to be among the first home, but we must have been eighth or ninth at the side. We had a heavy load aboard, and had to row round a huge iceberg on the way.

And then, as if to make everything complete for our happiness, came the dawn. First a beautiful, quiet shimmer away in the east, then a soft golden glow that crept up stealthily from behind the skyline as if it were trying not to be noticed as it stole over the sea and spread itself quietly in every direction – so quietly, as if to make us believe it had been there all the time and we had not observed it. Then the sky turned faintly pink and in the distance the thinnest, fleeciest clouds stretched in thin bands across the horizon and close down to it, becoming every moment more and more pink. And next the stars died, slowly – save one which remained long after the others just above the horizon; and nearby, with the crescent turned to the north, and the lower horn just touching the horizon, the thinnest, palest of moons.

And with the dawn came a faint breeze from the west, the first breath of wind we had felt since the *Titanic* stopped her engines. Anticipating a few hours – as the day drew on to 8 a.m., the time the last boats came up – this breeze increased to a fresh wind which whipped up the sea, so that the last boat laden with people had an anxious time in the choppy waves before they reached the *Carpathia*. An officer remarked that one of the boats could not have stayed afloat another hour: the wind had held off just long enough.

The captain shouted along our boat to the crew, as they strained at the oars – two pulling and an extra one facing them and pushing to try to keep pace with the other boats – 'A new moon! Turn your money over, boys! That is, if you have any!' We laughed at him for the quaint superstition at such a time, and it was good to laugh again, but he showed his disbelief in another superstition when he added, 'Well, I shall never say again that 13 is an unlucky number. Boat 13 is the best friend we ever had.'

If there had been among us – and it is almost certain that there were, so fast does superstition cling – those who feared events connected with the number 13, I am certain they agreed with him, and never again will they attach any importance to such a foolish belief. Perhaps the belief itself will receive a shock when it is remembered that boat 13 of the *Titanic* brought away a full load from the sinking vessel, carried them in such comfort all night that they had not even a drop of water on them, and landed them safely at the *Carpathia*'s side, where they climbed aboard without a single mishap. It almost tempts one to be the 13th at table, or to choose a house numbered 13 fearless of any croaking about flying in the face of what is humorously called 'providence'.

Looking towards the *Carpathia* in the faint light, we saw what seemed to be two large fully rigged sailing ships near the horizon, with all sails set, standing up near her, and we decided that they must be fishing vessels off the Banks of Newfoundland which had seen the *Carpathia* stop and were waiting to see if she wanted help of any kind. But in a few minutes more the light shone on them and they stood revealed as huge icebergs, peaked in a way that readily suggested a ship. When the sun rose higher, it turned them pink, and sinister as they looked towering like rugged white peaks of rock out of the sea, and terrible as was the disaster one of them had caused, there was an awful beauty about them which could not be overlooked. Later, when the sun came above the horizon, they sparkled and glittered in its rays; deadly white, like frozen snow rather than translucent ice.

As the dawn crept towards us there lay another almost directly in the line between our boat and the *Carpathia*, and a few minutes later, another on her port quarter, and more again on the southern and western horizons, as far as the eye could reach: all differing in shape and size and tones of colour according as the sun shone through them or was reflected directly or obliquely from them.

We drew near our rescuer and presently could discern the bands on her funnel, by which the crew could tell she was a Cunarder; and already some boats were at her side and passengers climbing up her ladders. We had to give the iceberg a wide berth and make a detour to the south: we knew it was sunk a long way below the surface with such things as projecting ledges – not that it was very likely there was one so near the surface as to endanger our small boat, but we were not inclined to take any risks for the sake of a few more minutes when safety lay so near.

Once clear of the berg, we could read the Cunarder's name – *C A R P A T H I A* – a name we are not likely ever to forget. We shall see her sometimes, perhaps, in the shipping lists – as I have done already once when she left Genoa on her return voyage – and the way her lights climbed up over the horizon in the darkness, the way she swung and showed her lighted portholes, and the moment when we read her name on her side will all come back in a flash; we shall live again the scene of rescue, and feel the same thrill of gratitude for all she brought us that night.

We rowed up to her about 4.30, and sheltering on the port side from the swell, held on by two ropes at the stern and bow. Women went up the side first, climbing rope ladders with a noose round their shoulders to help their ascent; men passengers scrambled next, and the crew last of all. The baby went up in a bag with the opening tied up: it had been quite well all the time, and never suffered any ill effects from its cold journey in the night. We set foot on deck with very thankful hearts, grateful beyond the possibility of adequate expression to feel a solid ship beneath us once more.

Chapter 6 The Sinking of the *Titanic* Seen From Her Deck

The two preceding chapters have been to a large extent the narrative of a single eyewitness and an account of the escape of one boat only from the *Titanic*'s side. It will be well now to return to the *Titanic* and reconstruct a more general and complete account from the experiences of many people in different parts of the ship. A considerable part of these experiences was related to the writer first hand by survivors, both on board the *Carpathia* and at other times, but some are derived from other sources which are probably as accurate as first-hand information. Other reports, which seemed at first sight to have been founded on the testimony of eyewitnesses, have been found on examination to have passed through several hands, and have therefore been rejected. The testimony even of eyewitnesses has in some cases been excluded when it seemed not to agree with direct evidence of a number of other witnesses or with what reasoned judgement considered probable in the circumstances. In this category are the reports of explosions before the *Titanic* sank, the breaking of the ship in two parts, the suicide of officers. It would be well to notice here that the *Titanic* was in her correct course, the southerly one, and in the position which prudence dictates as a safe one under the ordinary conditions at that time of the year: to be strictly accurate she was 16 miles south of the regular summer route which all companies follow from January to August.

Perhaps the real history of the disaster should commence with the afternoon of Sunday, when Marconigrams were received by the *Titanic* from the ships ahead of her, warning her of the existence of icebergs. In connection with this must be taken the marked fall of temperature observed by everyone in the afternoon and evening of this day as well as the very low temperature of the water. These have generally been taken to indicate that without any possibility of doubt we were near an iceberg region, and the severest condemnation has been poured on the heads of the officers and captain for not having regard to these climatic conditions; but here caution is necessary. There can be little doubt now that the low temperature observed can be traced to the icebergs and icefield subsequently encountered, but experienced sailors are aware that it might have been observed without any icebergs being near. The cold Labrador current sweeps down by Newfoundland across the track of Atlantic liners, but does not necessarily carry icebergs with it; cold winds blow from Greenland and Labrador and not always from icebergs and icefields. So that falls in temperature of sea and air are not prima facie evidence of the close proximity of icebergs. On the other hand, a single iceberg separated by many miles from its fellows might sink a ship, but certainly would not cause a drop in temperature either of the air or water. Then, as the Labrador current meets the warm Gulf Stream flowing from the Gulf of Mexico across to Europe, they do not necessarily intermingle, nor do they always run side by side or one on top of the other, but often interlaced, like the fingers of two hands. As a ship sails across this region the thermometer will record within a few miles temperatures of $34°, 58°, 35°, 59°$, and so on.

It is little wonder then that sailors become accustomed to place little reliance on temperature conditions as a means of estimating the probabilities of encountering ice in their track. An experienced sailor has told me that nothing is more difficult to diagnose than the presence of icebergs, and a strong confirmation of this is found in the official sailing directions issued by the Hydrographic Department of the British Admiralty. 'No reliance can be placed on any warning being conveyed to the mariner, by a fall in temperature, either of sea or air, of approaching ice. Some decrease in temperature has occasionally been recorded, but more often none has been observed.'

But notification by Marconigram of the exact location of icebergs is a vastly different matter. I remember with deep feeling the effect this information had on us when it first became generally known on board the *Carpathia*. Rumours of it went round on Wednesday morning, grew to definite statements in the afternoon, and were confirmed when one of the *Titanic* officers admitted the truth of it in reply to a direct question. I shall never forget the overwhelming sense of hopelessness that came over some of us as we obtained definite knowledge of the warning messages. It was not then the unavoidable accident we had hitherto supposed: the sudden plunging into a region crowded with icebergs which no seaman, however skilled a navigator he might be, could have avoided! The beautiful *Titanic* wounded too deeply to recover, the cries of the drowning still ringing in our ears and the thousands of homes that mourned all these calamities – none of all these things need ever have been!

It is no exaggeration to say that men who went through all the experiences of the collision and the rescue and the subsequent scenes on the quay at New York with hardly a tremor were quite overcome by this knowledge and turned away, unable to speak; I, for one, did so, and I know others who told me they were similarly affected.

I think we all came to modify our opinions on this matter, however, when we learnt more of the general conditions attending transatlantic steamship services. The discussion as to who was responsible for these warnings being disregarded had perhaps better be postponed to a later chapter. One of these warnings was handed to Mr Ismay by Captain Smith at 5 p.m. and returned at the latter's request at 7 p.m., that it might be posted for the information of officers; as a result of the messages they were instructed to keep a special lookout for ice. This, Second Officer Lightoller did until he was relieved at 10 p.m. by First Officer Murdoch, to whom he handed on the instructions. During Mr Lightoller's watch, about 9 p.m., the captain had joined him on the bridge and discussed 'the time we should be getting up towards the vicinity of the ice, and how we should recognise it if we should see it, and refreshing our minds on the indications that ice gives when it is in the vicinity'. Apparently, too, the officers had discussed among themselves the proximity of ice and Mr Lightoller had remarked that they would be approaching the position where ice had been reported during his watch. The lookouts were cautioned similarly, but no ice was sighted until a few minutes before the collision, when the lookout man saw the iceberg and rang the bell three times, the usual signal from the crow's nest when anything is seen dead ahead.

By telephone he reported to the bridge the presence of an iceberg, but Mr Murdoch had already ordered Quartermaster Hichens at the wheel to starboard the helm, and the vessel began to swing away from the berg. But it was far too late at the speed she was going to hope to steer the huge *Titanic*, over a sixth of a mile long, out of reach of danger. Even if the iceberg had been visible half a mile away it is doubtful whether some portion of her tremendous length would not have been touched, and it is in the highest degree unlikely that the lookout could have seen the berg half a mile away in the conditions that existed that night, even with glasses. The very smoothness of the water made the presence of ice a more difficult matter to detect. In ordinary conditions the dash of the waves against the foot of an iceberg surrounds it with a circle of white foam visible for some distance, long before the iceberg itself; but here was an oily sea sweeping smoothly round the deadly monster and causing no indication of its presence.

There is little doubt, moreover, that the crow's nest is not a good place from which to detect icebergs. It is proverbial that they adopt to a large extent the colour of their surroundings; and seen from above at a high angle, with the black, foam-free sea behind, the iceberg must have been almost invisible until the *Titanic* was close upon it. I was much struck by a remark of Sir Ernest Shackleton on his method of detecting icebergs – to place a lookout man as low down near the waterline as he could get him. Remembering how we had watched the *Titanic* with all her lights out, standing upright like 'an enormous black finger,' as one observer stated, and had only seen her thus because she loomed black against the sky behind her, I saw at once how much better the sky was than the black sea to show up an iceberg's bulk.

And so in a few moments the *Titanic* had run obliquely on the berg, and with a shock that was astonishingly slight – so slight that many passengers never noticed it – the submerged portion of the berg had cut her open on the starboard side in the most vulnerable portion of her anatomy – the bilge. The most authentic accounts say that the wound began at about the location of the foremast and extended far back to the stern, the brunt of the blow being taken by the forward plates, which were either punctured through both bottoms directly by the blow, or through one skin only, and as this was torn away it ripped out some of the inner plates. The fact that she went down by the head shows that probably only the forward plates were doubly punctured, the stern ones being cut open through the outer skin only. After the collision, Murdoch had at once reversed the engines and brought the ship to a standstill, but the iceberg had floated away astern. The shock, though little felt by the enormous mass of the ship, was sufficient to dislodge a large quantity of ice from the berg: the forecastle deck was found to be covered with pieces of ice.

Feeling the shock, Captain Smith rushed out of his cabin to the bridge, and in reply to his anxious enquiry was told by Murdoch that ice had been struck and the emergency doors instantly closed. The officers roused by the collision went on deck: some to the bridge; others, while hearing nothing of the extent of the damage, saw no necessity for doing so. Captain Smith at once sent the carpenter below to sound the ship, and Fourth Officer Boxhall to the steerage to report damage. The latter found there a very dangerous condition of things and reported to Captain Smith, who then sent him to the mail room; and here again, it was easy to see, matters looked very serious. Mail bags were floating about and the water rising rapidly. All this was reported to the captain, who ordered the lifeboats to be got ready at once. Mr Boxhall went to the chartroom to work out the ship's position, which he then handed to the Marconi operators for transmission to any ship near enough to help in the work of rescue.

Reports of the damage done were by this time coming to the captain from many quarters, from the chief engineer, from the designer – Mr Andrews – and in a dramatic way from the sudden appearance on deck of a swarm of stokers who had rushed up from below as the water poured into the boiler rooms and coal bunkers: they were immediately ordered down below to duty again. Realising the urgent heed of help, he went personally to the Marconi room and gave orders to the operators to get into touch with all the ships they could and to tell them to come quickly. The assistant operator Bride had been asleep, and knew of the damage only when Phillips, in charge of the Marconi room, told him ice had been encountered. They started to send out the well-known 'CQD' message – which interpreted means: CQ 'all stations at tend', and D, 'distress', the position of the vessel in latitude and longitude following. Later, they sent out 'SOS', an arbitrary message agreed upon as an international code-signal.

Soon after the vessel struck, Mr Ismay had learnt of the nature of the accident from the captain and chief engineer, and after dressing and going on deck had spoken to some of the officers not yet thoroughly acquainted with the grave injury done to the vessel. By this time all those in any way connected with the management and navigation must have known the importance of making use of all the ways of safety known to them – and that without any delay. That they thought at first that the *Titanic* would sink as soon as she did is doubtful; but probably as the reports came in they knew that her ultimate loss in a few hours was a likely contingency. On the other hand, there is evidence that some of the officers in charge of boats quite expected the embarkation was a precautionary measure and they would all return after daylight. Certainly the first information that ice had been struck conveyed to those in charge no sense of the gravity of the circumstances: one officer even retired to his cabin and another advised a steward to go back to his berth as there was no danger.

And so the order was sent round, 'All passengers on deck with lifebelts on'; and in obedience to this a crowd of hastily dressed or partially dressed people began to assemble on the decks belonging to their respective classes (except the steerage passengers, who were allowed access to other decks), tying on lifebelts over their clothing. In some parts of the ship women were separated from the men and assembled together near the boats, in others men and women mingled freely together, husbands helping their own wives and families and then other women and children into the boats. The officers spread themselves about the decks, superintending the work of lowering and loading the boats, and in three cases were ordered by their superior officers to take charge of them. At this stage great difficulty was experienced in getting women to leave the ship, especially where the order was so rigorously enforced, 'Women and children only.' Women in many cases refused to leave their husbands, and were actually forcibly lifted up and dropped in the boats. They argued with the officers, demanding reasons, and in some cases even when induced to get in were disposed to think the whole thing a joke, or a precaution which it seemed to them rather foolish to take. In this they were encouraged by the men left behind, who, in the same condition of ignorance, said goodbye to their friends as they went down, adding that they would see them again at breakfast-time. To illustrate further how little danger was apprehended – when it was discovered on the first class deck that the forward lower deck was covered with small ice, snowballing matches were arranged for the following morning, and some passengers even went down to the deck and brought back small pieces of ice which were handed round.

Below decks too was additional evidence that no one thought of immediate danger. Two ladies walking along one of the corridors came across a group of people gathered round a door which they were trying vainly to open, and on the other side of which a man was demanding in loud terms to be let out. Either his door was locked and the key not to be found, or the collision had jammed the lock and prevented the key from turning. The ladies thought he must be afflicted in some way to make such a noise, but one of the men was assuring him that in no circumstances should he be left, and that his (the bystander's) son would be along soon and would smash down his door if it was not opened in the meantime. 'He has a stronger arm than I have,' he added. The son arrived presently and proceeded to make short work of the door: it was smashed in and the inmate released, to his great satisfaction and with many expressions of gratitude to his rescuer. But one of the head stewards who came up at this juncture was so incensed at the damage done to the property of his company, and so little aware of the infinitely greater damage done the ship, that he warned the man who had released the prisoner that he would be arrested on arrival in New York.

It must be borne in mind that no general warning had been issued to passengers: here and there were experienced travellers to whom collision with an iceberg was sufficient to cause them to make every preparation for leaving the ship, but the great majority were never enlightened as to the amount of damage done, or even as to what had happened. We knew in a vague way that we had collided with an iceberg, but there our knowledge ended, and most of us drew no deductions from that fact alone. Another factor that prevented some from taking to the boats was the drop to the water below and the journey into the unknown sea: certainly it looked a tremendous way down in the darkness, the sea and the night both seemed very cold and lonely; and here was the ship, so firm and well lighted and warm.

But perhaps what made so many people declare their decision to remain was their strong belief in the theory of the *Titanic*'s unsinkable construction. Again and again was it repeated, 'This ship cannot sink; it is only a question of waiting until another ship comes up and takes us off.' Husbands expected to follow their wives and join them either in New York or by transfer in mid-ocean from steamer to steamer. Many passengers relate that they were told by officers that the ship was a lifeboat and could not go down; one lady affirms that the captain told her the *Titanic* could not sink for two or three days; no doubt this was immediately after the collision.

It is not any wonder, then, that many elected to remain, deliberately choosing the deck of the *Titanic* to a place in a lifeboat. And yet the boats had to go down, and so at first they went half full: this is the real explanation of why they were not as fully loaded as the later ones. It is important then to consider the question how far the captain was justified in withholding all the knowledge he had from every passenger. From one point of view he should have said to them, 'This ship will sink in a few hours: there are the boats, and only women and children can go to them.' But had he the authority to enforce such an order? There are such things as panics and rushes which get beyond the control of a handful of officers, even if armed, and where even the bravest of men get swept off their feet – mentally as well as physically.

On the other hand, if he decided to withhold all definite knowledge of danger from all passengers and at the same time persuade – and if it was not sufficient, compel – women and children to take to the boats, it might result in their all being saved. He could not foresee the tenacity of their faith in the boat: there is ample evidence that he left the bridge when the ship had come to rest and went among passengers urging them to get into the boat and rigorously excluding all but women and children. Some would not go. Officer Lowe testified that he shouted, 'Who's next for the boat?' and could get no replies. The boats even were sent away half loaded – although the fear of their buckling in the middle was responsible as well for this – but the captain with the few boats at his disposal could hardly do more than persuade and advise in the terrible circumstances in which he was placed.

How appalling to think that with a few more boats – and the ship was provided with that particular kind of davit that would launch more boats – there would have been no decision of that kind to make! It could have been stated plainly, 'This ship will sink in a few hours: there is room in the boats for all passengers, beginning with women and children.'

Poor Captain Smith! I care not whether the responsibility for such speed in iceberg regions will rest on his shoulders or not: no man ever had to make such a choice as he had that night, and it seems difficult to see how he can be blamed for withholding from passengers such information as he had of the danger that was imminent.

When one reads in the press that lifeboats arrived at the *Carpathia* half full, it seems at first sight a dreadful thing that this should have been allowed to happen; but it is so easy to make these criticisms afterwards, so easy to say that Captain Smith should have told everyone of the condition of the vessel. He was faced with many conditions that night which such criticism overlooks. Let any fair-minded person consider some few of the problems presented to him – the ship was bound to sink in a few hours; there was lifeboat accommodation for all women and children and some men; there was no way of getting some women to go except by telling them the ship was doomed, a course he deemed it best not to take; and he knew the danger of boats buckling when loaded full. His solution of these problems was apparently the following: to send the boats down half full, with such women as would go, and to tell the boats to stand by to pick up more passengers passed down from the cargo ports. There is good evidence that this was part of the plan: I heard an officer give the order to four boats and a lady in No. 4 boat on the port side tells me the sailors were so long looking for the port where the captain personally had told them to wait that they were in danger of being sucked under by the vessel. How far any systematic attempt was made to stand by the ports, I do not know: I never saw one open or any boat standing near on the starboard side; but then, boats 9 to 15 went down full, and on reaching the sea rowed away at once. There is good evidence, then, that Captain Smith fully intended to load the boats full in this way. The failure to carry out the intention is one of the things the whole world regrets, but consider again the great size of the ship and the short time to make decisions, and the omission is more easily understood. The fact is that such a contingency as lowering away boats was not even considered beforehand, and there is much cause for gratitude that as many as 705 people were rescued. The whole question of a captain's duties seems to require revision. It was totally impossible for any one man to attempt to control the ship that night, and the weather conditions could not well have been more favourable for doing so. One of the reforms that seem inevitable is that one man shall be responsible for the boats, their manning, loading and lowering, leaving the captain free to be on the bridge to the last moment.

But to return for a time to the means taken to attract the notice of other ships. The wireless operators were now in touch with several ships, and calling to them to come quickly for the water was pouring in and the *Titanic* beginning to go down by the head. Bride testified that the first reply received was from a German boat, the *Frankfurt*, which was 'All right: stand by', but not giving her position. From comparison of the strength of signals received from the *Frankfurt* and from other boats, the operators estimated the *Frankfurt* was the nearest; but subsequent events proved that this was not so. She was, in fact, 140 miles away and arrived at 10.50 a.m. next morning, when the *Carpathia* had left with the rescued. The next reply was from the *Carpathia*, 58 miles away on the outbound route to the Mediterranean, and it was a prompt and welcome one – 'Coming hard', followed by the position. Then followed the *Olympic*, and with her they talked for some time, but she was 560 miles away on the southern route, too far to be of any immediate help. At the speed of 23 knots she would expect to be up about 1 p.m. next day, and this was about the time that those in boat 13 had calculated. We had always assumed in the boat that the stokers who gave this information had it from one of the officers before they left; but in the absence of any knowledge of the much nearer ship, the *Carpathia*, it is more probable that they knew in a general way where the sister ship, the *Olympic*, should be, and had made a rough calculation.

Other ships in touch by wireless were the *Mount Temple*, 50 miles; the *Birma*, 100 miles; the *Parisian*, 150 miles; the *Virginian*, 150 miles; and the *Baltic*, 300 miles. But closer than any of these – closer even than the *Carpathia* – were two ships: the *Californian*, less than 20 miles away, with the wireless operator off duty and unable to catch the 'CQD' signal which was now making the air for many miles around quiver in its appeal for help – immediate, urgent help – for the hundreds of people who stood on the *Titanic*'s deck.

The second vessel was a small steamer some few miles ahead on the port side, without any wireless apparatus, her name and destination still unknown; and yet the evidence for her presence that night seems too strong to be disregarded. Mr Boxhall states that he and Captain Smith saw her quite plainly some five miles away, and could distinguish the masthead lights and a red port light. They at once hailed her with rockets and Morse electric signals, to which Boxhall saw no reply, but Captain Smith and stewards affirmed they did. The second and third officers saw the signals sent and her lights, the latter from the lifeboat of which he was in charge. Seaman Hopkins testified that he was told by the captain to row for the light; and we in boat 13 certainly saw it in the same position and rowed towards it for some time. But notwithstanding all the efforts made to attract its attention, it drew slowly away and the lights sank below the horizon.

The pity of it! So near, and so many people waiting for the shelter its decks could have given so easily. It seems impossible to think that this ship ever replied to the signals: those who said so must have been mistaken. The United State Senate Committee in its report does not hesitate to say that this unknown steamer and the *Californian* are identical, and that the failure on the part of the latter to come to the help of the *Titanic* is culpable negligence. There is undoubted evidence that some of the crew on the *Californian* saw our rockets; but it seems impossible to believe that the captain and officers knew of our distress and deliberately ignored it. Judgement on the matter had better be suspended until further information is forthcoming. An engineer who has served in the transatlantic service tells me that it is a common practice for small boats to leave the fishing smacks to which they belong and row away for miles; sometimes even being lost and wandering about among icebergs, and even not being found again. In these circumstances, rockets are part of a fishing smack's equipment, and are sent up to indicate to the small boats how to return. Is it conceivable that the *Californian* thought our rockets were such signals, and therefore paid no attention to them?

Incidentally, this engineer did not hesitate to add that it is doubtful if a big liner would stop to help a small fishing boat sending off distress signals, or even would turn about to help one which she herself had cut down as it lay in her path without a light. He was strong in his affirmation that such things were commonly known to all officers in the transatlantic service.

With regard to the other vessels in wireless communication, the *Mount Temple* was the only one near enough from the point of distance to have arrived in time to be of help, but between her and the *Titanic* lay the enormous ice-floe, and icebergs were near her in addition.

The seven ships which caught the message started at once to her help but were all stopped on the way (except the *Birma*) by the *Carpathia*'s wireless announcing the fate of the *Titanic* and the people aboard her. The message must have affected the captains of these ships very deeply: they would understand far better than the travelling public what it meant to lose such a beautiful ship on her first voyage.

The only thing now left to be done was to get the lifeboats away as quickly as possible, and to this task the other officers were in the meantime devoting all their endeavours. Mr Lightoller sent away boat after boat: in one he had put 24 women and children, in another 30, in another 35; and then, running short of seamen to man the boats he sent Major Peuchen, an expert yachtsman, in the next, to help with its navigation. By the time these had been filled, he had difficulty in finding women for the fifth and sixth boats for the reasons already stated. All this time the passengers remained – to use his own expression – 'as quiet as if in church'. To man and supervise the loading of six boats must have taken him nearly up to the time of the *Titanic*'s sinking, taking an average of some 20 minutes to a boat. Still at work to the end, he remained on the ship till she sank and went down with her. His evidence before the United States Committee was as follows: 'Did you leave the ship?' 'No, sir.' 'Did the ship leave you?' 'Yes, sir.'

It was a piece of work well and cleanly done, and his escape from the ship, one of the most wonderful of all, seems almost a reward for his devotion to duty.

Captain Smith, Officers Wilde and Murdoch were similarly engaged in other parts of the ship, urging women to get in the boats, in some cases directing junior officers to go down in some of them – Officers Pitman, Boxhall, and Lowe were sent in this way – in others placing members of the crew in charge. As the boats were lowered, orders were shouted to them where to make for: some were told to stand by and wait for further instructions, others to row for the light of the disappearing steamer.

It is a pitiful thing to recall the effects of sending down the first boats half full. In some cases men in the company of their wives had actually taken seats in the boats – young men, married only a few weeks and on their wedding trip – and had done so only because no more women could then be found; but the strict interpretation by the particular officer in charge there of the rule of 'Women and children only' compelled them to get out again. Some of these boats were lowered and reached the *Carpathia* with many vacant seats. The anguish of the young wives in such circumstances can only be imagined. In other parts of the ship, however, a different interpretation was placed on the rule, and men were allowed and even invited by officers to get in – not only to form part of the crew, but even as passengers. This, of course, in the first boats and when no more women could be found.

The varied understanding of this rule was a frequent subject of discussion on the *Carpathia* – in fact, the rule itself was debated with much heart-searching. There were not wanting many who doubted the justice of its rigid enforcement, who could not think it well that a husband should be separated from his wife and family, leaving them penniless, or a young bridegroom from his wife of a few short weeks, while ladies with few relatives, with no one dependent upon them, and few responsibilities of any kind, were saved. It was mostly these ladies who pressed this view, and even men seemed to think there was a good deal to be said for it. Perhaps there is, theoretically, but it would be impossible, I think, in practice. To quote Mr Lightoller again in his evidence before the United States Senate Committee – when asked if it was a rule of the sea that women and children be saved first, he replied, 'No, it is a rule of human nature.' That is no doubt the real reason for its existence.

But the selective process of circumstances brought about results that were very bitter to some. It was heart-rending for ladies who had lost all they held dearest in the world to hear that in one boat was a stoker picked up out of the sea so drunk that he stood up and brandished his arms about, and had to be thrown down by ladies and sat upon to keep him quiet. If comparisons can be drawn, it did seem better that an educated, refined man should be saved than one who had flown to drink as his refuge in time of danger.

These discussions turned sometimes to the old enquiry – 'What is the purpose of all this? Why the disaster? Why this man saved and that man lost? Who has arranged that my husband should live a few short happy years in the world, and the happiest days in those years with me these last few weeks, and then be taken from me?' I heard no one attribute all this to a Divine Power who ordains and arranges the lives of men, and as part of a definite scheme sends such calamity and misery in order to purify, to teach, to spiritualise. I do not say there were not people who thought and said they saw Divine Wisdom in it all, so inscrutable that we in our ignorance saw it not; but I did not hear it expressed, and this book is intended to be no more than a partial chronicle of the many different experiences and convictions.

There were those, on the other hand, who did not fail to say emphatically that indifference to the rights and feelings of others, blindness to duty towards our fellow men and women, was in the last analysis the cause of most of the human misery in the world. And it should undoubtedly appeal more to our sense of justice to attribute these things to our own lack of consideration for others than to shift the responsibility on to a power whom we first postulate as being all wise and all loving.

All the boats were lowered and sent away by about 2 a.m., and by this time the ship was very low in the water, the forecastle deck completely submerged, and the sea creeping steadily up to the bridge and probably only a few yards away.

No one on the ship can have had any doubt now as to her ultimate fate, and yet the 1,500 passengers and crew on board made no demonstration, and not a sound came from them as they stood quietly on the decks or went about their duties below. It seems incredible, and yet if it was a continuation of the same feeling that existed on deck before the boats left – and I have no doubt it was – the explanation is straightforward and reasonable in its simplicity. An attempt is made in the last chapter to show why the attitude of the crowd was so quietly courageous. There are accounts which picture excited crowds running about the deck in terror, fighting and struggling, but two of the most accurate observers, Colonel Gracie and Mr Lightoller, affirm that this was not so, that absolute order and quietness prevailed. The band still played to cheer the hearts of all near; the engineers and their crew – I have never heard anyone speak of a single engineer being seen on deck – still worked at the electric light engines, far away below, keeping them going until no human being could do so a second longer, right until the ship tilted on end and the engines broke loose and fell down. The light failed then only because the engines were no longer there to produce light, not because the men who worked them were not standing by them to do their duty. To be down in the bowels of the ship, far away from the deck where at any rate there was a chance of a dive and a swim and a possible rescue; to know that when the ship went – as they knew it must soon – there could be no possible hope of climbing up in time to reach the sea; to know all these things and yet to keep the engines going that the decks might be lighted to the last moment, required sublime courage.

But this courage is required of every engineer and it is not called by that name: it is called 'duty'. To stand by his engines to the last possible moment is his duty. There could be no better example of the supremest courage being but duty well done than to remember the engineers of the *Titanic* still at work as she heeled over and flung them with their engines down the length of the ship. The simple statement that the lights kept on to the last is really their epitaph, but Lowell's words would seem to apply to them with peculiar force:

> The longer on this earth we live
> And weigh the various qualities of men –
> The more we feel the high, stern-featured beauty
> Of plain devotedness to duty.
> Steadfast and still, nor paid with mortal praise,
> But finding amplest recompense
> For life's ungarlanded expense
> In work done squarely and unwasted days.

For some time before she sank, the *Titanic* had a considerable list to port, so much so that one boat at any rate swung so far away from the side that difficulty was experienced in getting passengers in. This list was increased towards the end, and Colonel Gracie relates that Mr Lightoller, who has a deep, powerful voice, ordered all passengers to the starboard side. This was close before the end. They crossed over, and as they did so a crowd of steerage passengers rushed up and filled the decks so full that there was barely room to move. Soon afterwards the great vessel swung slowly, stern in the air, the lights went out, and while some were flung into the water and others dived off, the great majority still clung to the rails, to the sides and roofs of deck structures, lying prone on the deck. And in this position they were when, a few minutes later, the enormous vessel dived obliquely downwards. As she went, no doubt many still clung to the rails, but most would do their best to get away from her and jump as she slid forwards and downwards. Whatever they did, there can be little question that most of them would be taken down by suction, to come up again a few moments later and to fill the air with those heart-rending cries which fell on the ears of those in the lifeboats with such amazement. Another survivor, on the other hand, relates that he had dived from the stern before she heeled over, and swam round under her enormous triple screws lifted by now high out of the water as she stood on end. Fascinated by the extraordinary sight, he watched them up above his head, but presently realising the necessity of getting away as quickly as possible, he started to swim from the ship, but as he did she dived forward, the screws passing near his head. His experience is that not only was no suction present, but even a wave was created which washed him away from the place where she had gone down.

Of all those 1,500 people, flung into the sea as the *Titanic* went down, innocent victims of thoughtlessness and apathy of those responsible for their safety, only a very few found their way to the *Carpathia*. It will serve no good purpose to dwell any longer on the scene of helpless men and women struggling in the water. The heart of everyone who has read of their helplessness has gone out to them in deepest love and sympathy; and the knowledge that their struggle in the water was in most cases short and not physically painful because of the low temperature – the evidence seems to show that few lost their lives by drowning – is some consolation.

If everyone sees to it that his sympathy with them is so practical as to force him to follow up the question of reforms personally, not leaving it to experts alone, then he will have at any rate done something to atone for the loss of so many valuable lives.

We had now better follow the adventures of those who were rescued from the final event in the disaster. Two accounts – those of Colonel Gracie and Mr Lightoller – agree very closely. The former went down clinging to a rail, the latter dived before the ship went right under, but was sucked down and held against one of the blowers. They were both carried down for what seemed a long distance, but Mr Lightoller was finally blown up again by a 'terrific gust' that came up the blower and forced him clear. Colonel Gracie came to the surface after holding his breath for what seemed an eternity, and they both swam about holding on to any wreckage they could find. Finally they saw an upturned collapsible boat and climbed on it in company with 20 other men, among them Bride, the Marconi operator. After remaining thus for some hours, with the sea washing them to the waist, they stood up as day broke, in two rows, back to back, balancing themselves as well as they could, and afraid to turn lest the boat should roll over. Finally a lifeboat saw them and took them off, an operation attended with the greatest difficulty, and they reached the *Carpathia* in the early dawn.

Not many people have gone through such an experience as those men did, lying all night on an overturned, ill-balanced boat, and praying together, as they did all the time, for the day and a ship to take them off.

Some account must now be attempted of the journey of the fleet of boats to the *Carpathia*, but it must necessarily be very brief. Experiences differed considerably: some had no encounters at all with icebergs, no lack of men to row, discovered lights and food and water, were picked up after only a few hours' exposure, and suffered very little discomfort; others seemed to see icebergs round them all night long and to be always rowing round them; others had so few men aboard – in some cases only two or three – that ladies had to row and in one case to steer, found no lights, food or water, and were adrift many hours, in some cases nearly eight.

The first boat to be picked up by the *Carpathia* was one in the charge of Mr Boxhall. There was only one other man rowing and ladies worked at the oars. A green light burning in this boat all night was the greatest comfort to the rest of us who had nothing to steer by: although it meant little in the way of safety in itself, it was a point to which we could look. The green light was the first intimation Captain Rostron had of our position, and he steered for it and picked up its passengers first.

Mr Pitman was sent by First Officer Murdoch in charge of boat 5, with 40 passengers and five of the crew. It would have held more, but no women could be found at the time it was lowered. Mr Pitman says that after leaving the ship he felt confident she would float and they would all return. A passenger in this boat relates that men could not be induced to embark when she went down, and made appointments for the next morning with him. Tied to boat 5 was boat 7, one of those that contained few people: a few were transferred from No. 5, but it would have held many more.

Fifth Officer Lowe was in charge of boat 14, with 55 women and children, and some of the crew. So full was the boat that as she went down Mr Lowe had to fire his revolver along the ship's side to prevent any more climbing in and causing her to buckle. This boat, like boat 13, was difficult to release from the lowering tackle, and had to be cut away after reaching the sea. Mr Lowe took in charge four other boats, tied them together with lines, found some of them not full, and transferred all his passengers to these, distributing them in the darkness as well as he could. Then returning to the place where the *Titanic* had sunk, he picked up some of those swimming in the water and went back to the four boats. On the way to the *Carpathia* he encountered one of the collapsible boats, and took aboard all those in her, as she seemed to be sinking.

Boat 12 was one of the four tied together, and the seaman in charge testified that he tried to row to the drowning, but with 40 women and children and only one other man to row, it was not possible to pull such a heavy boat to the scene of the wreck.

Boat 2 was a small ship's boat and had four or five passengers and seven of the crew. [Beesley is confusing lifeboat 2 with lifeboat 1 here]

Boat 4 was one of the last to leave on the port side, and by this time there was such a list that deckchairs had to bridge the gap between the boat and the deck. When lowered, it remained for some time still attached to the ropes, and as the *Titanic* was rapidly sinking it seemed she would be pulled under. The boat was full of women, who besought the sailors to leave the ship, but in obedience to orders from the captain to stand by the cargo port, they remained near; so near, in fact, that they heard china falling and smashing as the ship went down by the head, and were nearly hit by wreckage thrown overboard by some of the officers and crew and intended to serve as rafts. They got clear finally, and were only a short distance away when the ship sank, so that they were able to pull some men aboard as they came to the surface.

This boat had an unpleasant experience in the night with icebergs; many were seen and avoided with difficulty.

Quartermaster Hichens was in charge of boat 6, and in the absence of sailors Major Peuchen was sent to help to man her. They were told to make for the light of the steamer seen on the port side, and followed it until it disappeared. There were 40 women and children here.

Boat 8 had only one seaman, and as Captain Smith had enforced the rule of 'Women and children only', ladies had to row. Later in the night, when little progress had been made, the seaman took an oar and put a lady in charge of the tiller. This boat again was in the midst of icebergs.

Of the four collapsible boats – although collapsible is not really the correct term, for only a small portion collapses, the canvas edge; 'surf boats' is really their name – one was launched at the last moment by being pushed over as the sea rose to the edge of the deck, and was never righted. This is the one 20 men climbed on [lifeboat B]. Another was caught up by Mr Lowe and the passengers transferred, with the exception of three men who had perished from the effects of immersion [lifeboat A]. The boat was allowed to drift away and was found more than a month later by the *Celtic* in just the same condition. It is interesting to note how long this boat had remained afloat after she was supposed to be no longer seaworthy. A curious coincidence arose from the fact that one of my brothers happened to be travelling on the *Celtic*, and looking over the side, saw adrift on the sea a boat belonging to the *Titanic* in which I had been wrecked.

The two other collapsible boats came to the *Carpathia* carrying full loads of passengers: in one, the forward starboard boat and one of the last to leave, was Mr Ismay [lifeboat C]. Here four Chinamen were concealed under the feet of the passengers. How they got there no one knew – or indeed how they happened to be on the *Titanic*, for by the immigration laws of the United States they are not allowed to enter her ports.

It must be said, in conclusion, that there is the greatest cause for gratitude that all the boats launched carried their passengers safely to the rescue ship. It would not be right to accept this fact without calling attention to it: it would be easy to enumerate many things which might have been present as elements of danger.

But at the same time, one question recurs constantly to thought, and seems to call instantly for some reply.

Was it not possible during the three and a half hours that elapsed between the collision and the foundering to construct some kind of raft, sufficiently substantial to keep some of the passengers afloat?

The captain certainly knew such a raft would be urgently needed: it would seem to have been possible to tear up the decks and lash the planks to tables, wardrobes, deckchairs, etc.

But the only men who could really undertake such work – the sailors – were far too few even to lower and man the boats: not one of them could be spared for making rafts.

Again, perhaps the very tools with which such work would be carried out were in those parts of the hold which were from the first flooded with water. Perhaps these are the answers to a question which must have been asked hundreds of times.

Chapter 7 The *Carpathia*'s Return to New York

The journey of the *Carpathia* from the time she caught the 'CQD' from the *Titanic* at about 12.30 a.m. on Monday morning and turned swiftly about to her rescue, until she arrived at New York on the following Thursday at 8.30 p.m. was one that demanded of the captain, officers and crew of the vessel the most exact knowledge of navigation, the utmost vigilance in every department both before and after the rescue, and a capacity for organisation that must sometimes have been taxed to the breaking point.

The extent to which all these qualities were found present and the manner in which they were exercised stands to the everlasting credit of the Cunard Line and those of its servants who were in charge of the *Carpathia*. Captain Rostron's part in all this is a great one, and wrapped up though his action is in a modesty that is conspicuous in its nobility, it stands out even in his own account as a piece of work well and courageously done.

As soon as the *Titanic* called for help and gave her position, the *Carpathia* was turned and headed north: all hands were called on duty, a new watch of stokers was put on, and the highest speed of which she was capable was demanded of the engineers, with the result that the distance of 58 miles between the two ships was covered in three and a half hours, a speed well beyond her normal capacity. The three doctors on board each took charge of a saloon, in readiness to render help to any who needed their services, the stewards and catering staff were hard at work preparing hot drinks and meals, and the purser's staff ready with blankets and berths for the shipwrecked passengers as soon as they got on board. On deck the sailors got ready lifeboats, swung them out on the davits, and stood by, prepared to lower away their crews if necessary; fixed rope ladders, cradle-chairs, nooses, and bags for the children at the hatches, to haul the rescued up the side. On the bridge was the captain with his officers, peering into the darkness eagerly to catch the first signs of the crippled *Titanic*, hoping, in spite of her last despairing message of 'Sinking by the head', to find her still afloat when her position was reached. A double watch of lookout men was set, for there were other things as well as the *Titanic* to look for that night, and soon they found them. As Captain Rostron said in his evidence, they saw icebergs on either side of them between 2.45 and 4 a.m., passing 20 large ones, 100 to 200 feet high [*c.* 30–60 metres], and many smaller ones, and 'frequently had to manoeuvre the ship to avoid them'. It was a time when every faculty was called upon for the highest use of which it was capable. With the knowledge before them that the enormous *Titanic*, the supposedly unsinkable ship, had struck ice and was sinking rapidly; with the lookout constantly calling to the bridge, as he must have done, 'Icebergs on the starboard', 'Icebergs on the port', it required courage and judgement beyond the ordinary to drive the ship ahead through that lane of icebergs and 'manoeuvre round them'. As he himself said, he 'took the risk of full speed in his desire to save life, and probably some people might blame him for taking such a risk'. But the Senate Committee assured him that they, at any rate, would not, and we of the lifeboats have certainly no desire to do so.

The ship was finally stopped at 4 a.m., with an iceberg reported dead ahead (the same no doubt we had to row around in boat 13 as we approached the *Carpathia*), and about the same time the first lifeboat was sighted. Again she had to be manoeuvred round the iceberg to pick up the boat, which was the one in charge of Mr Boxhall. From him the captain learned that the *Titanic* had gone down, and that he was too late to save anyone but those in lifeboats, which he could now see drawing up from every part of the horizon. Meanwhile, the passengers of the *Carpathia*, some of them aroused by the unusual vibration of the screw, some by sailors tramping overhead as they swung away the lifeboats and got ropes and lowering tackle ready, were beginning to come on deck just as day broke; and here an extraordinary sight met their eyes. As far as the eye could reach to the north and west lay an unbroken stretch of field ice, with icebergs still attached to the floe and rearing aloft their mass as a hill might suddenly rise from a level plain. Ahead and to the south and east huge floating monsters were showing up through the waning darkness, their number added to moment by moment as the dawn broke and flushed the horizon pink. It is remarkable how 'busy' all those icebergs made the sea look: to have gone to bed with nothing but sea and sky and to come on deck to find so many objects in sight made quite a change in the character of the sea: it looked quite crowded; and a lifeboat alongside and people clambering aboard, mostly women, in nightdresses and dressing gowns, in cloaks and shawls, in anything but ordinary clothes! Out ahead and on all sides little torches glittered faintly for a few moments and then guttered out – and shouts and cheers floated across the quiet sea. It would be difficult to imagine a more unexpected sight than this that lay before the *Carpathia's* passengers as they lined the sides that morning in the early dawn.

No novelist would dare to picture such an array of beautiful climatic conditions – the rosy dawn, the morning star, the moon on the horizon, the sea stretching in level beauty to the skyline – and on this sea to place an icefield like the Arctic regions and icebergs in numbers everywhere – white and turning pink and deadly cold – and near them, rowing round the icebergs to avoid them, little boats coming suddenly out of mid-ocean, with passengers rescued from the most wonderful ship the world has known. No artist would have conceived such a picture: it would have seemed so highly dramatic as to border on the impossible, and would not have been attempted. Such a combination of events would pass the limit permitted the imagination of both author and artist.

The passengers crowded the rails and looked down at us as we rowed up in the early morning; stood quietly aside while the crew at the gangways below took us aboard, and watched us as if the ship had been in dock and we had rowed up to join her in a somewhat unusual way. Some of them have related that we were very quiet as we came aboard: it is quite true, we were; but so were they. There was very little excitement on either side: just the quiet demeanour of people who are in the presence of something too big as yet to lie within their mental grasp, and which they cannot yet discuss. And so they asked us politely to have hot coffee, which we did, and food, which we generally declined – we were not hungry – and they said very little at first about the lost *Titanic* and our adventures in the night.

Much that is exaggerated and false has been written about the mental condition of passengers as they came aboard: we have been described as being too dazed to understand what was happening, as being too overwhelmed to speak, and as looking before us with 'set, staring gaze', 'dazed with the shadow of the dread event'. That is, no doubt, what most people would expect in the circumstances, but I know it does not give a faithful record of how we did arrive: in fact it is simply not true. As remarked before, the one thing that matters in describing an event of this kind is the exact truth, as near as the fallible human mind can state it; and my own impression of our mental condition is that of supreme gratitude and relief at treading the firm decks of a ship again. I am aware that experiences differed considerably according to the boats occupied; that those who were uncertain of the fate of their relatives and friends had much to make them anxious and troubled; and that it is not possible to look into another person's consciousness and say what is written there; but dealing with mental conditions as far as they are delineated by facial and bodily expressions, I think joy, relief, gratitude were the dominant emotions written on the faces of those who climbed the rope ladders and were hauled up in cradles.

It must not be forgotten that no one in any one boat knew who were saved in other boats: few knew even how many boats there were and how many passengers could be saved. It was at the time probable that friends would follow them to the *Carpathia*, or be found on other steamers, or even on the pier at which we landed. The hysterical scenes that have been described are imaginative; true, one woman did fill the saloon with hysterical cries immediately after coming aboard, but she could not have known for a certainty that any of her friends were lost: probably the sense of relief after some hours of journeying about the sea was too much for her for a time.

One of the first things we did was to crowd round a steward with a bundle of telegraph forms. He was the bearer of the welcome news that passengers might send Marconigrams to their relatives free of charge, and soon he bore away the first sheaf of hastily scribbled messages to the operator; by the time the last boatload was aboard, the pile must have risen high in the Marconi cabin. We learned afterwards that many of these never reached their destination; and this is not a matter for surprise. There was only one operator – Cottam – on board, and although he was assisted to some extent later, when Bride from the *Titanic* had recovered from his injuries sufficiently to work the apparatus, he had so much to do that he fell asleep over this work on Tuesday night after three days' continuous duty without rest. But we did not know the messages were held back, and imagined our friends were aware of our safety; then, too, a roll call of the rescued was held in the *Carpathia*'s saloon on the Monday, and this was Marconied to land in advance of all messages. It seemed certain, then, that friends at home would have all anxiety removed, but there were mistakes in the official list first telegraphed. The experience of my own friends illustrates this: the Marconigram I wrote never got through to England; nor was my name ever mentioned in any list of the saved (even a week after landing in New York, I saw it in a black-edged 'final' list of the missing), and it seemed certain that I had never reached the *Carpathia*; so much so that, as I write, there are before me obituary notices from the English papers giving a short sketch of my life in England. After landing in New York and realising from the lists of the saved which a reporter showed me that my friends had no news since the *Titanic* sank on Monday morning until that night (Thursday 9 p.m.), I cabled to England at once (as I had but two shillings rescued from the *Titanic*, the White Star Line paid for the cables), but the messages were not delivered until 8.20 a.m. next morning. At 9 a.m. my friends read in the papers a short account of the disaster which I had supplied to the press, so that they knew of my safety and experiences in the wreck almost at the same time. I am grateful to remember that many of my friends in London refused to count me among the missing during the three days when I was so reported.

There is another side to this record of how the news came through, and a sad one, indeed. Again I wish it were not necessary to tell such things, but since they all bear on the equipment of the transatlantic lines – powerful Marconi apparatus, relays of operators, etc. – it is best they should be told. The name of an American gentleman – the same who sat near me in the library on Sunday afternoon and whom I identified later from a photograph – was consistently reported in the lists as saved and aboard the *Carpathia*: his son journeyed to New York to meet him, rejoicing at his deliverance, and never found him there. When I met his family some days later and was able to give them some details of his life aboard ship, it seemed almost cruel to tell them of the opposite experience that had befallen my friends at home.

Returning to the journey of the *Carpathia* – the last boatload of passengers was taken aboard at 8.30 a.m., the lifeboats were hauled on deck while the collapsibles were abandoned, and the *Carpathia* proceeded to steam round the scene of the wreck in the hope of picking up anyone floating on wreckage. Before doing so the captain arranged in the saloon a service over the spot where the *Titanic* sank, as nearly as could be calculated – a service, as he said, of respect to those who were lost and of gratitude for those who were saved.

She cruised round and round the scene, but found nothing to indicate there was any hope of picking up more passengers; and as the *Californian* had now arrived, followed shortly afterwards by the *Birma*, a Russian tramp steamer, Captain Rostron decided to leave any further search to them and to make all speed with the rescued to land. As we moved round, there was surprisingly little wreckage to be seen: wooden deckchairs and small pieces of other wood, but nothing of any size. But covering the sea in huge patches was a mass of reddish-yellow 'seaweed', as we called it for want of a name. It was said to be cork, but I never heard definitely its correct description.

The problem of where to land us had next to be decided. The *Carpathia* was bound for Gibraltar, and the captain might continue his journey there, landing us at the Azores on the way; but he would require more linen and provisions; the passengers were mostly women and children, ill-clad, dishevelled, and in need of many attentions he could not give them. Then, too, he would soon be out of the range of wireless communication, with the weak apparatus his ship had, and he soon decided against that course. Halifax was the nearest in point of distance, but this meant steaming north through the ice, and he thought his passengers did not want to see more ice. He headed back therefore to New York, which he had left the previous Thursday, working all afternoon along the edge of the icefield which stretched away north as far as the unaided eye could reach. I have wondered since if we could possibly have landed our passengers on this ice-floe from the lifeboats and gone back to pick up those swimming, had we known it was there; I should think it quite feasible to have done so. It was certainly an extraordinary sight to stand on deck and see the sea covered with solid ice, white and dazzling in the sun and dotted here and there with icebergs. We ran close up, only two or three hundred yards [*c.* 182–274 metres] away, and steamed parallel to the floe, until it ended towards night and we saw to our infinite satisfaction the last of the icebergs and the field fading away astern. Many of the rescued have no wish ever to see an iceberg again. We learnt afterwards the field was nearly 70 miles long and 12 miles wide, and had lain between us and the *Birma* on her way to the rescue. Mr Boxhall testified that he had crossed the Grand Banks many times, but had never seen field ice before. The testimony of the captains and officers of other steamers in the neighbourhood is of the same kind: they had 'never seen so many icebergs this time of the year', or 'never seen such dangerous ice-floes and threatening bergs'. Undoubtedly the *Titanic* was faced that night with unusual and unexpected conditions of ice: the captain knew not the extent of these conditions, but he knew somewhat of their existence. Alas, that he heeded not their warning!

During the day, the bodies of eight of the crew were committed to the deep: four of them had been taken out of the boats dead and four died during the day. The engines were stopped and all passengers on deck bared their heads while a short service was read; when it was over the ship steamed on again to carry the living back to land.

The passengers on the *Carpathia* were by now hard at work finding clothing for the survivors: the barber's shop was raided for ties, collars, hair-pins, combs, etc., of which it happened there was a large stock in hand; one good Samaritan went round the ship with a box of toothbrushes offering them indiscriminately to all. In some cases, clothing could not be found for the ladies and they spent the rest of the time on board in their dressing gowns and cloaks in which they came away from the *Titanic*. They even slept in them, for, in the absence of berths, women had to sleep on the floor of the saloons and in the library each night on straw *paillasses*, and here it was not possible to undress properly. The men were given the smoking room floor and a supply of blankets, but the room was small, and some elected to sleep out on deck. I found a pile of towels on the bathroom floor ready for next morning's baths, and made up a very comfortable bed on these. Later I was waked in the middle of the night by a man offering me a berth in his four-berth cabin: another occupant was unable to leave his berth for physical reasons, and so the cabin could not be given up to ladies.

On Tuesday the survivors met in the saloon and formed a committee among themselves to collect subscriptions for a general fund, out of which it was resolved by vote to provide as far as possible for the destitute among the steerage passengers, to present a loving cup to Captain Rostron and medals to the officers and crew of the *Carpathia*, and to divide any surplus among the crew of the *Titanic*. The work of this committee is not yet (1 June) at an end, but all the resolutions except the last one have been acted upon, and that is now receiving the attention of the committee. The presentations to the captain and crew were made the day the *Carpathia* returned to New York from her Mediterranean trip, and it is a pleasure to all the survivors to know that the United States Senate has recognised the service rendered to humanity by the *Carpathia* and has voted Captain Rostron a gold medal commemorative of the rescue. On the afternoon of

Tuesday, I visited the steerage in company with a fellow passenger, to take down the names of all who were saved. We grouped them into nationalities – English, Irish, and Swedish mostly – and learnt from them their names and homes, the amount of money they possessed, and whether they had friends in America. The Irish girls almost universally had no money rescued from the wreck, and were going to friends in New York or places near, while the Swedish passengers, among whom were a considerable number of men, had saved the greater part of their money and in addition had railway tickets through to their destinations inland. The saving of their money marked a curious racial difference, for which I can offer no explanation: no doubt the Irish girls never had very much but they must have had the necessary amount fixed by the immigration laws. There were some pitiful cases of women with children and the husband lost; some with one or two children saved and the others lost; in one case, a whole family was missing, and only a friend left to tell of them. Among the Irish group was one girl of really remarkable beauty, black hair and deep violet eyes with long lashes, and perfectly shaped features, and quite young, not more than 18 or 20; I think she lost no relatives on the *Titanic*.

The following letter to the London *Times* is reproduced here to show something of what our feeling was on board the *Carpathia* towards the loss of the *Titanic*. It was written soon after we had the definite information on the Wednesday that ice warnings had been sent to the *Titanic*, and when we all felt that something must be done to awaken public opinion to safeguard ocean travel in the future. We were not aware, of course, how much the outside world knew, and it seemed well to do something to inform the English public of what had happened at as early an opportunity as possible. I have not had occasion to change any of the opinions expressed in this letter.

Sir

As one of few surviving Englishmen from the steamship *Titanic*, which sank in mid-Atlantic on Monday morning last, I am asking you to lay before your readers a few facts concerning the disaster, in the hope that something may be done in the near future to ensure the safety of that portion of the travelling public who use the Atlantic highway for business or pleasure.

I wish to dissociate myself entirely from any report that would seek to fix the responsibility on any person or persons or body of people, and by simply calling attention to matters of fact the authenticity of which is, I think, beyond question and can be established in any Court of Inquiry, to allow your readers to draw their own conclusions as to the responsibility for the collision.

First, that it was known to those in charge of the *Titanic* that we were in the iceberg region; that the atmospheric and temperature conditions suggested the near presence of icebergs; that a wireless message was received from a ship ahead of us warning us that they had been seen in the locality of which latitude and longitude were given.

Second, that at the time of the collision the *Titanic* was running at a high rate of speed.

Third, that the accommodation for saving passengers and crew was totally inadequate, being sufficient only for a total of about 950. This gave, with the highest possible complement of 3,400, a less than one in three chance of being saved in the case of accident.

Fourth, that the number landed in the *Carpathia*, approximately 700, is a high percentage of the possible 950, and bears excellent testimony to the courage, resource, and devotion to duty of the officers and crew of the vessel; many instances of their nobility and personal self-sacrifice are within our possession, and we know that they did all they could do with the means at their disposal.

Fifth, that the practice of running mail and passenger vessels through fog and iceberg regions at a high speed is a common one; they are timed to run almost as an express train is run, and they cannot, therefore, slow down more than a few knots in time of possible danger.

I have neither knowledge nor experience to say what remedies I consider should be applied; but, perhaps, the following suggestions may serve as a help:

First, that no vessel should be allowed to leave a British port without sufficient boat and other accommodation to allow each passenger and member of the crew a seat; and that at the time of booking this fact should be pointed out to a passenger, and the number of the seat in the particular boat allotted to him then.

Second, that as soon as is practicable after sailing each passenger should go through boat drill in company with the crew assigned to his boat.

Third, that each passenger boat engaged in the transatlantic service should be instructed to slow down to a few knots when in the iceberg region, and should be fitted with an efficient searchlight.

Yours faithfully,

Lawrence Beesley

It seemed well, too, while on the *Carpathia* to prepare as accurate an account as possible of the disaster and to have this ready for the press, in order to calm public opinion and to forestall the incorrect and hysterical accounts which some American reporters are in the habit of preparing on occasions of this kind. The first impression is often the most permanent, and in a disaster of this magnitude, where exact and accurate information is so necessary, preparation of a report was essential. It was written in odd corners of the deck and saloon of the *Carpathia*, and fell, it seemed very happily, into the hands of the one reporter who could best deal with it, the Associated Press. I understand it was the first report that came through and had a good deal of the effect intended.

The *Carpathia* returned to New York in almost every kind of climatic conditions: icebergs, icefields and bitter cold to commence with; brilliant warm sun, thunder and lightning in the middle of one night (and so closely did the peal follow the flash that women in the saloon leaped up in alarm saying rockets were being sent up again); cold winds most of the time; fogs every morning and during a good part of one day, with the foghorn blowing constantly; rain; choppy sea with the spray blowing overboard and coming in through the saloon windows; we said we had almost everything but hot weather and stormy seas. So that when we were told that Nantucket Lightship had been sighted on Thursday morning from the bridge, a great sigh of relief went round to think New York and land would be reached before next morning.

There is no doubt that a good many felt the waiting period of those four days very trying: the ship crowded far beyond its limits of comfort, the want of necessities of clothing and toilet, and above all the anticipation of meeting with relatives on the pier, with, in many cases, the knowledge that other friends were left behind and would not return home again. A few looked forward to meeting on the pier their friends to whom they had said au revoir on the *Titanic*'s deck, brought there by a faster boat, they said, or at any rate to hear that they were following behind us in another boat: a very few, indeed, for the thought of the icy water and the many hours' immersion seemed to weigh against such a possibility; but we encouraged them to hope the *Californian* and the *Birma* had picked some up; stranger things have happened, and we had all been through strange experiences. But in the midst of this rather tense feeling, one fact stands out as remarkable – no one was ill. Captain Rostron testified that on Tuesday the doctor reported a clean bill of health, except for frostbites and shaken nerves. There were none of the illnesses supposed to follow from exposure for hours in the cold night – and, it must be remembered, a considerable number swam about for some time when the *Titanic* sank, and then either sat for hours in their wet things or lay flat on an upturned boat with the sea water washing partly over them until they were taken off in a lifeboat; no scenes of women weeping and brooding over their losses hour by hour until they were driven mad with grief – yet all this has been reported to the press by people on board the *Carpathia*. These women met their sorrow with the sublimest courage, came on deck and talked with their fellow men and women face to face, and in the midst of their loss did not forget to rejoice with those who had joined their friends on the *Carpathia*'s deck or come with them in a boat. There was no need for those ashore to call the *Carpathia* a 'death-ship', or to send coroners and coffins to the pier to meet her: her passengers were generally in good health and they did not pretend they were not.

Presently land came in sight, and very good it was to see it again: it was eight days since we left Southampton, but the time seemed to have 'stretched out to the crack of doom', and to have become eight weeks instead. So many dramatic incidents had been crowded into the last few days that the first four peaceful, uneventful days, marked by nothing that seared the memory, had faded almost out of recollection. It needed an effort to return to Southampton, Cherbourg and Queenstown, as though returning to some event of last year. I think we all realised that time may be measured more by events than by seconds and minutes: what the astronomer would call '2.20 a.m. 15 April 1912', the survivors called 'the sinking of the *Titanic*'; the 'hours' that followed were designated 'being adrift in an open sea', and '4.30 a.m.' was 'being rescued by the *Carpathia*'. The clock was a mental one, and the hours, minutes and seconds marked deeply on its face were emotions, strong and silent.

Surrounded by tugs of every kind, from which (as well as from every available building near the river) magnesium bombs were shot off by photographers, while reporters shouted for news of the disaster and photographs of passengers, the *Carpathia* drew slowly to her station at the Cunard pier, the gangways were pushed across, and we set foot at last on American soil, very thankful, grateful people.

The mental and physical condition of the rescued as they came ashore has, here again, been greatly exaggerated – one description says we were 'half-fainting, half-hysterical, bordering on hallucination, only now beginning to realise the horror'. It is unfortunate such pictures should be presented to the world. There were some painful scenes of meeting between relatives of those who were lost, but once again women showed their self-control and went through the ordeal in most cases with extraordinary calm. It is well to record that the same account added: 'A few, strangely enough, are calm and lucid'; if for 'few' we read 'a large majority', it will be much nearer the true description of the landing on the Cunard pier in New York. There seems to be no adequate reason why a report of such a scene should depict mainly the sorrow and grief, should seek for every detail to satisfy the horrible and the morbid in the human mind. The first questions the excited crowds of reporters asked as they crowded round were whether it was true that officers shot passengers, and then themselves; whether passengers shot each other; whether any scenes of horror had been noticed, and what they were.

It would have been well to have noticed the wonderful state of health of most of the rescued, their gratitude for their deliverance, the thousand and one things that gave cause for rejoicing. In the midst of so much description of the hysterical side of the scene, place should be found for the normal – and I venture to think the normal was the dominant feature in the landing that night. In the last chapter I shall try to record the persistence of the normal all through the disaster. Nothing has been a greater surprise than to find people that do not act in conditions of danger and grief as they would be generally supposed to act – and, I must add, as they are generally described as acting.

And so, with her work of rescue well done, the good ship *Carpathia* returned to New York. Everyone who came in her, everyone on the dock, and everyone who heard of her journey will agree with Captain Rostron when he says, 'I thank God that I was within wireless hailing distance, and that I got there in time to pick up the survivors of the wreck.'

Chapter 9 Some Impressions

No one can pass through an event like the wreck of the *Titanic* without recording mentally many impressions, deep and vivid, of what has been seen and felt. In so far as such impressions are of benefit to mankind they should not be allowed to pass unnoticed, and this chapter is an attempt to picture how people thought and felt from the time they first heard of the disaster to the landing in New York, when there was opportunity to judge of events somewhat from a distance. While it is to some extent a personal record, the mental impressions of other survivors have been compared and found to be in many cases closely in agreement. Naturally it is very imperfect, and pretends to be no more than a sketch of the way people act under the influence of strong emotions produced by imminent danger.

In the first place, the principal fact that stands out is the almost entire absence of any expressions of fear or alarm on the part of passengers, and the conformity to the normal on the part of almost everyone. I think it is no exaggeration to say that those who read of the disaster quietly at home, and pictured to themselves the scene as the *Titanic* was sinking, had more of the sense of horror than those who stood on the deck and watched her go down inch by inch. The fact is that the sense of fear came to the passengers very slowly – a result of the absence of any signs of danger and the peaceful night – and as it became evident gradually that there was serious damage to the ship, the fear that came with the knowledge was largely destroyed as it came. There was no sudden overwhelming sense of danger that passed through thought so quickly that it was difficult to catch up and grapple with it – no need for the warning to 'be not afraid of sudden fear', such as might have been present had we collided head on with a crash and a shock that flung everyone out of his bunk to the floor. Everyone had time to give each condition of danger attention as it came along, and the result of their judgement was as if they had said, 'Well, here is this thing to be faced, and we must see it through as quietly as we can.' Quietness and self-control were undoubtedly the two qualities most expressed. There were times when danger loomed more nearly and there was temporarily some excitement – for example when the first rocket went up – but after the first realisation of what it meant, the crowd took hold of the situation and soon gained the same quiet control that was evident at first. As the sense of fear ebbed and flowed, it was so obviously a thing within one's own power to control, that, quite unconsciously realising the absolute necessity of keeping cool, everyone for his own safety put away the thought of danger as far as was possible. Then, too, the curious sense of the whole thing being a dream was very prominent: that all were looking on at the scene from a nearby vantage point in a position of perfect safety, and that those who walked the decks or tied one another's lifebelts on were the actors in a scene of which we were but spectators: that the dream would end soon and we should wake up to find the scene had vanished. Many people have had a similar experience in times of danger, but it was very noticeable standing on the *Titanic*'s deck. I remember observing it particularly while tying on a lifebelt for a man on the deck. It is fortunate that it should be so: to be able to survey such a scene dispassionately is a wonderful aid in the destruction of the fears that go with it. One thing that helped considerably to establish this orderly condition of affairs was the quietness of the surroundings. It may seem weariness to refer again to this, but I am convinced it had much to do with keeping everyone calm. The ship was motionless; there was not a breath of wind; the sky was clear; the sea like a mill pond – the general 'atmosphere' was peaceful, and all on board responded unconsciously to it. But what controlled the situation principally was the quality of obedience and respect for authority which is a dominant characteristic of the Teutonic race. Passengers did as they were told by the officers in charge: women went to the decks below; men remained where they were told and waited in silence for the next order, knowing instinctively that this was the only way to bring about the best result for all on board. The officers, in their turn, carried out the work assigned to them by their superior officers as quickly and orderly as circumstances permitted, the senior ones being in control of the manning, filling and lowering of the lifeboats, while the junior officers were lowered in individual boats to take command of the fleet adrift on the sea. Similarly, the engineers below, the band, the gymnasium instructor, were all performing their tasks as they came along: orderly, quietly, without question or stopping to consider what was their chance of safety. This correlation on the part of passengers, officers and crew was simply obedience to duty, and it was innate rather than the product of reasoned judgement.

I hope it will not seem to detract in any way from the heroism of those who faced the last plunge of the *Titanic* so courageously when all the boats had gone – if it does, it is the difficulty of expressing an idea in adequate words – to say that their quiet heroism was largely unconscious, temperamental, not a definite choice between two ways of acting. All that was visible on deck before the boats left tended to this conclusion and the testimony of those who went down with the ship and were afterwards rescued is of the same kind.

Certainly it seems to express much more general nobility of character in a race of people – consisting of different nationalities – to find heroism an unconscious quality of the race than to have it arising as an effort of will, to have to bring it out consciously.

It is unfortunate that some sections of the press should seek to chronicle mainly the individual acts of heroism: the collective behaviour of a crowd is of so much more importance to the world and so much more a test – if a test be wanted – of how a race of people behaves. The attempt to record the acts of individuals leads apparently to such false reports as that of Major Butt holding at bay with a revolver a crowd of passengers and shooting them down as they tried to rush the boats, or of Captain Smith shouting, 'Be British,' through a megaphone, and subsequently committing suicide along with First Officer Murdoch. It is only a morbid sense of things that would describe such incidents as heroic. Everyone knows that Major Butt was a brave man, but his record of heroism would not be enhanced if he, a trained army officer, were compelled under orders from the captain to shoot down unarmed passengers. It might in other conditions have been necessary, but it would not be heroic. Similarly there could be nothing heroic in Captain Smith or Murdoch putting an end to their lives. It is conceivable men might be so overwhelmed by the sense of disaster that they knew not how they were acting; but to be really heroic would have been to stop with the ship – as of course they did – with the hope of being picked up along with passengers and crew and returning to face an inquiry and to give evidence that would be of supreme value to the whole world for the prevention of similar disasters. It was not possible; but if heroism consists in doing the greatest good to the greatest number, it would have been heroic for both officers to *expect* to be saved. We do not know what they thought, but I, for one, like to imagine that they did so. Second Officer Lightoller worked steadily at the boats until the last possible moment, went down with the ship, was saved in what seemed a miraculous manner, and returned to give valuable evidence before the commissions of two countries.

The second thing that stands out prominently in the emotions produced by the disaster is that in moments of urgent need men and women turn for help to something entirely outside themselves. I remember reading some years ago a story of an atheist who was the guest at dinner of a regimental mess in India. The colonel listened to his remarks on atheism in silence, and invited him for a drive the following morning. He took his guest up a rough mountain road in a light carriage drawn by two ponies, and when some distance from the plain below, turned the carriage round and allowed the ponies to run away – as it seemed – downhill. In the terror of approaching disaster, the atheist was lifted out of his reasoned convictions and prayed aloud for help, when the colonel reined in his ponies, and with the remark that the whole drive had been planned with the intention of proving to his guest that there was a power outside his own reason, descended quietly to level ground.

The story may or may not be true, and in any case is not introduced as an attack on atheism, but it illustrates in a striking way the frailty of dependence on a man's own power and resource in imminent danger. To those men standing on the top deck with the boats all lowered, and still more so when the boats had all left, there came the realisation that human resources were exhausted and human avenues of escape closed. With it came the appeal to whatever consciousness each had of a power that had created the universe. After all, some power had made the brilliant stars above, countless millions of miles away, moving in definite order, formed on a definite plan and obeying a definite law: had made each one of the passengers with ability to think and act; with the best proof, after all, of being created – the knowledge of their own existence; and now, if at any time, was the time to appeal to that power. When the boats had left and it was seen the ship was going down rapidly, men stood in groups on the deck engaged in prayer, and later, as some of them lay on the overturned collapsible boat, they repeated together over and over again the Lord's Prayer – irrespective of religious beliefs, some, perhaps, without religious beliefs, united in a common appeal for deliverance from their surroundings. And this was not because it was a habit, because they had learned this prayer 'at their mother's knee': men do not do such things through habit. It must have been because each one saw removed the thousand and one ways in which he had relied on human, material things to help him – including even dependence on the overturned boat with its bubble of air inside, which any moment a rising swell might remove as it tilted the boat too far sideways, and sink the boat below the surface – saw laid bare his utter dependence on something that had made him and given him power to think – whether he named it God or Divine Power or First Cause or Creator, or named it not at all but recognised it unconsciously – saw these things and expressed them in the form of words he was best acquainted with in common with his fellow men. He did so, not through a sense of duty to his particular religion, not because he had learned the words, but because he recognised that it was the most practical thing to do – the thing best fitted to help him. Men do practical things in times like that: they would not waste a moment on mere words if those words were not an expression of the most intensely real conviction of which they were capable. Again, like the feeling of heroism, this appeal is innate and intuitive, and it certainly has its foundation on a knowledge – largely concealed, no doubt – of immortality. I think this must be obvious: there could be no other explanation of such a general sinking of all the emotions of the human mind expressed in a thousand different ways by a thousand different people in favour of this single appeal.

The behaviour of people during the hours in the lifeboats, the landing on the *Carpathia*, the life there and the landing in New York, can all be summarised by saying that people did not act at all as they were expected to act – or rather as most people expected they would act, and in some cases have erroneously said they did act. Events were there to be faced, and not to crush people down. Situations arose which demanded courage, resource, and in the cases of those who had lost friends most dear to them, enormous self-control; but very wonderfully they responded. There was the same quiet demeanour and poise, the same inborn dominion over circumstances, the same conformity to a normal standard which characterised the crowd of passengers on the deck of the *Titanic* – and for the same reasons.

The first two or three days ashore were undoubtedly rather trying to some of the survivors. It seemed as if coming into the world again – the four days shut off from any news seemed a long time – and finding what a shock the disaster had produced, the flags half-mast, the staring headlines, the sense of gloom noticeable everywhere, made things worse than they had been on the *Carpathia*. The difference in 'atmosphere' was very marked, and people gave way to some extent under it and felt the reaction. Gratitude for their deliverance and a desire to 'make the best of things' must have helped soon, however, to restore them to normal conditions. It is not at all surprising that some survivors felt quieter on the *Carpathia* with its lack of news from the outside world, if the following extract from a leading New York evening paper was some of the material of which the 'atmosphere' on shore was composed:

> Stunned by the terrific impact, the dazed passengers rushed from their staterooms into the main saloon amid the crash of splintering steel, rending of plates and shattering of girders, while the boom of falling pinnacles of ice upon the broken deck of the great vessel added to the horror … In a wild ungovernable mob they poured out of the saloons to witness one of the most appalling scenes possible to conceive … For a hundred feet the bow was a shapeless mass of bent, broken and splintered steel and iron.

And so on, horror piled on horror, and not a word of it true, or remotely approaching the truth.

This paper was selling in the streets of New York while the *Carpathia* was coming into dock, while relatives of those on board were at the docks to meet them and anxiously buying any paper that might contain news. No one on the *Carpathia* could have supplied such information; there was no one else in the world at that moment who knew any details of the *Titanic* disaster, and the only possible conclusion is that the whole thing was a deliberate fabrication to sell the paper.

This is a repetition of the same defect in human nature noticed in the provision of safety appliances on board ship – the lack of consideration for the other man. The remedy is the same – the law: it should be a criminal offence for anyone to disseminate deliberate falsehoods that cause fear and grief. The moral responsibility of the press is very great, and its duty of supplying the public with only clean, correct news is correspondingly heavy. If the general public is not yet prepared to go so far as to stop the publication of such news by refusing to buy those papers that publish it, then the law should be enlarged to include such cases. Libel is an offence, and this is very much worse than any libel could ever be.

It is only right to add that the majority of the New York papers were careful only to report such news as had been obtained legitimately from survivors or from *Carpathia* passengers. It was sometimes exaggerated and sometimes not true at all, but from the point of reporting what was heard, most of it was quite correct.

One more thing must be referred to – the prevalence of superstitious beliefs concerning the *Titanic*. I suppose no ship ever left port with so much miserable nonsense showered on her. In the first place, there is no doubt many people refused to sail on her because it was her maiden voyage, and this apparently is a common superstition: even the clerk of the White Star Office where I purchased my ticket admitted it was a reason that prevented people from sailing. A number of people have written to the press to say they had thought of sailing on her, or had decided to sail on her, but because of 'omens' cancelled the passage.

Many referred to the sister ship, the *Olympic*, pointed to the 'ill luck' that they say has dogged her – her collision with the *Hawke*, and a second mishap necessitating repairs and a wait in harbour, where passengers deserted her; they prophesied even greater disaster for the *Titanic*, saying they would not dream of travelling on the boat. Even some aboard were very nervous, in an undefined way. One lady said she had never wished to take this boat, but her friends had insisted and bought her ticket and she had not had a happy moment since. A friend told me of the voyage of the *Olympic* from Southampton after the wait in harbour, and said there was a sense of gloom pervading the whole ship: the stewards and stewardesses even going so far as to say it was a '*death-ship*'. This crew, by the way, was largely transferred to the *Titanic*.

The incident with the *New York* at Southampton, the appearance of the stoker at Queenstown in the funnel, combine with all this to make a mass of nonsense in which apparently sensible people believe, or which at any rate they discuss. Correspondence is published with an official of the White Star Line from someone imploring them not to name the new ship 'Gigantic', because it seems like 'tempting fate' when the *Titanic* has been sunk. It would seem almost as if we were back in the middle ages when witches were burned because they kept black cats. There seems no more reason why a black stoker should be an ill omen for the *Titanic* than a black cat should be for an old woman.

The only reason for referring to these foolish details is that a surprisingly large number of people think there may be 'something in it'. The effect is this: that if a ship's company and a number of passengers get imbued with that undefined dread of the unknown – the relics no doubt of the savage's fear of what he does not understand – it has an unpleasant effect on the harmonious working of the ship: the officers and crew feel the depressing influence, and it may even spread so far as to prevent them being as alert and keen as they otherwise would; may even result in some duty not being as well done as usual. Just as the unconscious demand for speed and haste to get across the Atlantic may have tempted captains to take a risk they might otherwise not have done, so these gloomy forebodings may have more effect sometimes than we imagine. Only a little thing is required sometimes to weigh down the balance for and against a certain course of action.

At the end of this chapter of mental impressions it must be recorded that one impression remains constant with us all today – that of the deepest gratitude that we came safely through the wreck of the *Titanic*; and its corollary – that our legacy from the wreck, our debt to those who were lost with her, is to see, as far as in us lies, that such things are impossible ever again. Meanwhile we can say of them, as Shelley, himself the victim of a similar disaster, says of his friend Keats in 'Adonais':

> Peace, peace! he is not dead, he doth not sleep,
> He hath awakened from the dream of life …
> He lives, he wakes – 'Tis Death is dead, not he;
> Mourn not for Adonais.

33

Washington Dodge, First Class Passenger

This is the text of an address given in May 1912 to the Commonwealth Club in San Francisco. Dodge and his family survived the *Titanic* voyage but in 1919, following a period of mental ill health, committed suicide. Dr Washington Dodge was a prominent politician in San Francisco.

Mr President and Fellow Members

A few days since I was approached by the chairman of the Committee on Program, Dr Giannini, who requested me to make a few remarks to the Club on the subject of the wreck of the *Titanic*. To this request I demurred. The doctor, however, was quite insistent and stated that, owing to the widespread interest in this catastrophe, and owing to the many conflicting reports of the same which had been published, he hoped I would grant his request. I knew what the doctor stated to be true, for on my return to San Francisco I had seen numerous interviews, both with myself and my wife, which purported interviews had been wired from New York and published in our local papers. My wife had never given an interview, and had made none of the statements attributed to her. With one exception, all of the interviews attributed to me were wholly unfounded. On reconsideration, I decided to comply with the doctor's request. Having little time to give to the preparation of these remarks, and desiring in the short space of time allotted to me to cover the matter as fully as possible, I decided this could best be done by me, with the assistance of my stenographer. This is my reason for reading this narrative.

In the past 10 days following the first uncertain and contradictory reports in the press of the disaster, the actual occurrences connected with the same have been positively established. The full evidence given under oath before the congressional committee has been published in several of the New York papers, as well as in several weekly publications. I presume that most of those present have had an opportunity to read some such authentic report, and for that reason I have, in compliance with Dr Giannini's request, based my narrative of events largely on my personal experiences and observations.

I will first state briefly the facts of the wreck. On 10 April the White Star liner *Titanic* started from Southampton on her maiden trip across the Atlantic. She was the largest vessel afloat – a little less than 900 feet [*c.* 274 metres], or over one sixth of a mile in length – and was heralded by her builders and owners as an unsinkable ship, having, in addition to a double bottom, 15 watertight compartments. She carried 2,340 persons. Five days later she was at the bottom of the ocean and through her loss over two thirds of those on board, or 1,635 people, had perished.

The voyage, up to the time of the disaster, had been a perfect one. The weather was fine and the sea calm. At all times one might walk the decks, with the same security as if walking down Market Street, so little motion was there to the vessel. It was hard to realise, when dining in the spacious dining saloon, that one was not in some large and sumptuous hotel.

The Sunday evening of the night of the disaster was a clear cold night. The temperature had fallen rapidly after sundown until it had reached 31 degrees. This was undoubtedly due to our close proximity to the immense icefield, and to the numerous icebergs, which were revealed the next morning. The temperature of the water had been taken every two hours throughout the day and evening, but had failed to show our close proximity to the icefield. The great vessel was ploughing ahead at a speed of approximately 21½ knots an hour. The ship's officers had been warned by wireless of their proximity to icebergs, and the orders had been given to the lookout in the crow's nest to keep a sharp watch for small icebergs.

According to the evidence given at the congressional investigation, Chief Officer Murdoch relieved Second Officer Lightoller on the bridge at 10 o'clock. The men discussed the icebergs, which the ship was known to be approaching, and decided that they would probably encounter them within about an hour.

At about 20 minutes to 12, the lookout in the crow's nest rang a signal on the bridge of three bells, meaning 'danger ahead'. A few seconds thereafter he telephoned to the bridge, 'Large iceberg right ahead.' An order was given to the man at the wheel to throw the vessel to port. This was done and the engines reversed, but in an instant later the ship had been struck beneath the waterline by the iceberg. The lever was then thrown, which from the bridge, closes all the watertight compartments in 30 seconds.

These facts were related to me on the *Carpathia* by Quartermaster Hichens, who was at the wheel on the *Titanic*. It was he who received the signals from the crow's nest, and he to whom the order was given by the chief officer to throw the vessel to port.

The shock to the steamer was so slight, that many of the passengers, who had already retired, were not awakened thereby. My wife and I, however, were both awakened by the shock to the vessel. Listening for a moment, I became aware of the fact that the engines had been stopped, and shortly afterwards hearing hurried footsteps on the boat decks which was directly over our stateroom, I concluded that I would go out and inquire what had occurred. Partially dressing I slipped out of our room into the forward companionway, there to find possibly half a dozen men, all speculating as to what had happened. While we stood there an officer passed by somewhat hurriedly, and I asked him what was the trouble; he replied that he thought something had gone wrong with the propeller, but that it was nothing serious.

Leaving the few passengers that I had observed, still laughing and chatting, I returned to my stateroom. My wife being somewhat uneasy desired to arise and dress. I assured her that nothing had occurred which would harm the ship, and persuaded her to remain in bed. I informed my wife what the officer had told me; that something had gone wrong with the propeller. We both agreed, however, judging from the nature of the shock, that something had struck the vessel on its side. This, however, owing to the slight jar to the vessel, and to our knowledge of her immense size, and unsinkable construction, did not alarm us. I decided, nevertheless, to again go out and investigate further.

This time I went from the companionway out on to the promenade deck, where I found a group of possibly six or eight men, who were gaily conversing about the incident.

I heard one man say that the impact was due to ice. Upon one of his listeners questioning the authority of this, he replied, 'Go up forward and look down on the poop deck, and you can see for yourself.' I at once walked forward to the end of the promenade deck, and looking down could see, just within the starboard rail, small fragments of broken ice, amounting possibly to several cartloads. As I stood there an incident occurred which made me take a more serious view of the situation, than I otherwise would.

Two stokers, who had slipped up on to the promenade deck unobserved, said to me, 'Do you think there is any danger, sir?' I replied, 'If there is any danger it would be due to the vessel having sprung a leak, and you ought to know more about it than I.' They replied, in what appeared to me, to be an alarmed tone, 'Well, sir, the water was pouring into the stoke 'old when we came up, sir.' At this time I observed quite a number of steerage passengers, who were amusing themselves by walking over the ice, and kicking it about the deck. No ice or iceberg was to be seen in the ocean.

Not observing any sign of apprehension on the part of anyone, nor seeing any unusual number of persons on any part of the ship, I again returned to my cabin and told my wife what I had seen and heard.

As the vessel was still stationary, I again stepped out into the companionway, and observing our steward standing in the centre of the same, I asked him if he had heard anything. He replied that the order had just come down for all passengers to put on life preservers. Asking him if he really meant it, and being convinced from his manner and answer that the command had actually been given, I at once sprang to my stateroom door, which was but a few steps from where I was standing, and hurriedly told my wife to throw on something warm and come with me. While she partly dressed herself and our child, I pulled down the three life preservers which were in the stateroom, and threw them over my arm. We then quickly made our way to the boat deck. In order to reach this we had to ascend only one short flight of stairs, and passing on to the boat deck on the starboard side, we were at once next to the forward lifeboats. I learned afterwards that the order was given by the officers for the women and children to go to the port side of the vessel. It was on this side that the captain had taken charge of the launching of the lifeboats. At the time that we reached the boat deck, the first boat on the starboard side, No. 1, was hanging over the side of the vessel from the davits, and a few persons, men and women, were seated therein. The officer in charge was calling for women and children to fill the boat, but seemed to have difficulty in finding those who were willing to enter. I myself hesitated to place my wife and child in this boat, being unable to decide whether it would be safer to keep them on the steamer, or to entrust them to this frail boat which was the first to be launched, and which hung over 80 feet [*c.* 24 metres] above the water. In the meantime I busied myself with strapping on their life preservers, and heard the officer give the command to 'lower away'. This boat was launched with but 26 persons in it, although its capacity was over 50, and about one third were male passengers.

As I observed this boat lowered without accident, I placed my wife and child in the next boat, No. 3 – boats on the starboard side having the odd numbers. This boat was ordered lowered when it contained less than 35 persons. In neither case were additional women to be found. Each of these boats contained at least 10 male passengers. As I saw this boat lowered, containing my wife and child, I was overwhelmed with doubts as to whether or not I was exposing them to greater danger than if they had remained on board the ship.

During the ensuing half or three quarters of an hour, I watched the boats on the starboard side, as they were successively filled and lowered away. At no time during this period was there any panic or evidence of fears or unusual alarm. I saw no women nor children weep, nor were there any evidences of hysteria observed by me.

Many expressed their determination to take their chances with the steamer rather than embark in the lifeboats. This unusual circumstance may be accounted for by the fact that the officers had insisted that, under the worst conditions possible, the *Titanic* could not sink in less than eight or 10 hours, and that a number of steamers had been communicated with by wireless, and would be standing by to offer relief within an hour or two.

I watched all boats on the starboard side comprising the odd numbers from 1 to 13, as they were launched. Not a boat was launched which would not have held from 10 to 25 more persons. Never were there enough women or children present to fill any boat before it was launched. In all cases, as soon as those who responded to the officers' call were in the boats, the order was given to 'lower away'.

At no time were there many people on the starboard side that night. Why was that? The most reasonable explanation that I can give is that the captain was in charge of the launching of the boats on port side. Now, in times of danger the captain always draws a crowd. The more notable men on board, who were known by sight to the other passengers, knew Captain Smith personally and remained near him. These men attracted others. In this way the crowd grew on the port side, while at no time was there anything like a crowd on the starboard side. Again, the orders for women and children to go to the port side greatly increased the number there.

Now this condition may explain many things. It may explain why the boats were launched from the starboard side so much more quickly and successfully, and why when the last boats on this side were reached, numbers 13 and 15, there were practically no women around, and not many men. When the order to launch the boats was given, Captain Smith took command of the port side and never left there. Chief Officer Murdoch took command on the starboard side.

What the conditions were on the port side of the vessel I had no means of observing. We were in semi-darkness on the boat deck, and owing to the immense length and breadth of the vessel, and the fact that between the port and starboard side of the boat deck there were officers' cabins, staterooms for passengers, a gymnasium, and innumerable immense ventilators, it would have been impossible, even in daylight, to have obtained a view of but a limited portion of this boat deck. We only knew what was going on about us within a radius of possibly 40 feet [*c.* 12 metres].

Lifeboats 13 and 15 were swung from the davits at about the same moment. I heard the officer in charge of No. 13 say, 'We'll lower this boat to deck A.' Observing a group of possibly 50 or 60 about lifeboat 15, a small proportion of which number were women, I descended by means of a stairway close at hand to the deck below, deck A. Here, as the boat [lifeboat 13] was lowered even with the deck, the women, about eight in number, were assisted by several of us over the rail of the steamer into the boat. The officer in charge then held the boat, and called repeatedly for more women. None appearing, and there being none visible on the deck, which was then brightly illuminated, the men were told to tumble in. Along with those present I entered the boat.

As there seems to be in the minds of a few of the people in this community a question as to why any of the 80 men saved from the first class passengers should have been, when later events disclosed the fact that there were women remaining on board, I would like to quote here from an article of the *New York Times* of recent date, by Mr Lawrence Beesley, a very intelligent man, and a close observer evidently, who also wrote a review of the disaster for the London *Times*. On reading this article I ascertained that Mr Beesley had left the steamer in the same boat that I had. His words on the subject were as follows:

> I will finish with a few purely personal remarks. My only excuse for putting them on record is that to me they are absolutely true. I do not make them with any intention of asking a single person to believe in them, or to agree with me in what I say, but, having been face to face with the possibility of death, and having seen its shadow rather near, I may perhaps not be trespassing on the columns of the *Times* in saying how I consider I was saved.
>
> I left in lifeboat 13, when a call for ladies had been made three times and not answered, and no ladies were visible, and was then invited to enter the boat. I had stood quietly on the deck watching boats being launched, until the moment arrived when I was able to get a seat in a boat without depriving anyone of room. I was asked to go by one of the crew, and when the boat was lowered, the deck was left quite clear.

This statement of facts by Mr Beesley coincides exactly with my observations. Mr Ismay, who left in the next boat, No. 15, which was being launched about the same time, testified, under oath, before the Congressional Committee, to exactly the same conditions.

Curiously enough another newspaper record of the experiences of a survivor who escaped in my boat came into my possession a few days since. This paper was handed to me by Mr Madison Kirby, of this city, with the remark that he had just received it from his old home in Illinois, and he thought the account referred to might interest me. To my surprise I again found that the narrative was given by an occupant of lifeboat 13. This article appeared in the *Roseville Times-Citizen*, printed under date of 26 April in Roseville, Illinois. The article, which is rather lengthy, gives a detailed account written by the Revd A. F. Caldwell of the escape of himself, wife, and little son from the *Titanic*. Mr Caldwell, it appears, gave this interview on arriving at his home in Roseville. He describes in this article the incidents connected with the filling and launching of boat No. 13, and the narrow escape of the boat from being swamped, which I will relate presently.

He relates that after being awakened by the shock he dressed and went out on the deck, and was told by an officer that the vessel had struck an iceberg, but he, not being conscious of the real peril and seeing so few scenes of serious danger, returned to bed. When awakened later by the shouting of orders for all to go on the deck, he and his family dressed fully and went to A deck. He then proceeds: 'As we joined the group gathered there, lifeboat No. 13 was about to be lowered and Mrs Caldwell was put into it. She was the last woman left in the group, and I was about to lower the baby down to her when she said, "Can't my husband come too?" There being ample room, I was put into the boat and other men followed and the work of lowering away began.'

Mr Caldwell also states in his account that just before he left the steamer, the passengers were repeatedly assured that there was no danger; that the *Olympic* was near and would take off the passengers and crew. He believed, when he embarked in the lifeboat, that it could be more prudent to stay on the steamer. In common with others he felt that the *Titanic* was so big, and so strongly constructed, that her sinking was unbelievable, and he remarks that it was this belief that resigned so many to stay on board, as they thought that no matter how seriously she was injured she would certainly keep afloat for hours, and perhaps days.

At the Congressional investigation Fifth Officer Lowe testified as follows:

Q. Did you have any difficulty in filling No. 3?

A. Yes, sir; I had difficulty all along. I could not get enough people.

Q. Did any women attempt to get in either of these boats, No. 3 or 5, and did not succeed in getting in?

A. No, sir.

Q. Did any men so attempt and fail to get in?

A. No, not one.

Q. What did you do about it yourself; did you arbitrarily select from the deck?

A. You say 'select'. There was no such thing as selecting. It was simply the first woman, either first class, second class, third class, or sixty-seventh class; it was all the same – women and children were first.

Q. Do you mean that there was a procession of women?

A. The first woman was first into the boat; the second woman was second into the boat, no matter whether she was a first class passenger or another class.

Q. Now as they came along, you would pass them one at a time into the lifeboat? What order did you have 'to pass women and children'?

A. I simply shouted, 'Women and children first; men stand back.'

Q. How did it happen that you did not put more people into lifeboat No. 3 than 45?

A. There did not seem to be any people there.

Q. You did not find anybody that wanted to go?

A. Those that were there did not seem to want to go. I hallowed out: 'Who's next for the boat?' And there was no response.

In view of these conditions the query arises, why were any women lost? The list of survivors shows that of the first class women passengers only 15 were lost. Of these, nine were ladies' maids travelling with their ladies. What follows may account for so many of these latter being lost. It was related to me by a woman in my lifeboat that just before she came on deck, and got into the boat, she saw the purser's office surrounded by a crowd demanding their valuables, which the purser and his assistant were endeavouring to hand out as quickly as possible. In this crowd were many women. I believe further that there were some women, on some of the lower decks, who were not awakened at all. One of the crew of the *Titanic*, the head baker, testified at the official investigation in London that some women had to be carried from the lower decks up to the lifeboats. That many refused to get into the boats under any consideration. In this connection your attention is drawn to the fact that the *Titanic* had 12 steel decks, and that passengers had rooms on decks which were seven and eight decks below the boat deck.

The boat in which I embarked was rapidly lowered, and as it approached the water I observed, as I looked over the edge of the boat, that the bow, near which I was seated, was being lowered directly into an enormous stream of water, three or four feet [*c.* one metre] in diameter, which was being thrown with great force from the side of the vessel. This was the water thrown out by the condenser pumps. Had our boat been lowered into the same it would have been swamped in an instant. The loud cries which were raised by the occupants of the boat caused those who were 60 or 70 feet [*c.* 18–21 metres] above us to cease lowering our boat. Securing an oar with considerable difficulty, as the oars had been firmly lashed together by means of heavy tarred twines and as in addition they were on the seat running parallel with the side of the lifeboat, with no less than eight or 10 occupants of the boat sitting on them, none of whom showed any tendency to disturb themselves – we pushed the bow of the lifeboat, by means of the oar, a sufficient distance away from the side of the *Titanic* to clear this great stream of water which was gushing forth. We were then safely lowered to the water. During the few moments occupied by these occurrences I felt for the only time a sense of impending danger.

We were directed to pull our lifeboat from the steamer, and to follow a light which was carried in one of the other lifeboats, which had been launched prior to ours. Our lifeboat was found to contain no lantern, as the regulations require; nor was there a single sailor, or officer in the boat. Those who undertook to handle the oars were poor oarsmen, almost without exception, and our progress was extremely slow. Together with two or three other lifeboats which were in the vicinity, we endeavoured to overtake the lifeboat which carried the light, in order that we might not drift away and possibly become lost. This light appeared to be a quarter of a mile distant, but in spite of our best endeavours, we were never enabled to approach any nearer to it, although we must have rowed at least a mile.

When I left the steamer, which, as near as I can fix the time, must have been from an hour to an hour and a half after the collision, I was not conscious that the *Titanic* showed any list or displacement whatever.

After we had been afloat possibly half an hour I observed, on looking at the steamer, that the line of lights from the portholes showed that the vessel had settled forward into the water, but to no great extent. This was a matter of considerable surprise to me at the moment. Watching the vessel closely, it was seen from time to time that this submergence forward was increasing. No one in our boat, however, had any idea that the ship was in any danger of sinking. In spite of the intense cold, a cheerful atmosphere pervaded those present and they indulged, from time to time, in jesting and even singing, 'Pull for the shore, sailor.'

The gradual submersion of the vessel forward increased, and in about an hour was suddenly followed by the extinguishment of all the lights, which had been burning brightly, illuminating every deck and gleaming forth from innumerable portholes. We saw the vessel then clearly outlined as a great dark shadow on the water, probably at a distance of about a mile. It was remarked by several that, if the vessel should sink, fortunately there had been plenty of time for everyone aboard to get off. I had the same feeling, believing that if events subsequent to our departure had shown that the ship was liable to sink, all those on board would have had an opportunity to leave her.

Suddenly, while I was looking at the dark outline of the steamer, I saw her stern rise high from the water, and then the vessel was seen to completely disappear from sight with startling rapidity. A series of loud explosions, three or four in number, were then heard, due, as we all believed, to bursting boilers.

Any impression which I had had that there were no survivors aboard was speedily removed from my mind by the faint, yet distinct, cries which were wafted across the waters. Some there were in our boat who insisted that these cries came from occupants of the different lifeboats, which were nearer the scene of the wreck than we were, as they called one to another. To my ear, however, they had but one meaning, and the awful fact was borne in upon me that many lives were perishing in those icy waters.

With the disappearance of the steamer, a great sense of loneliness and depression seemed to take possession of those in our boat. Few words were then spoken. I heard the remark: 'This is no joke; we may knock about here days before we are picked up, if at all.' And the hours between this and daylight were spent in ceaselessly scanning the ocean for some sign of a steamer's light. It was recalled how we had been told that four or five steamers would be standing by within an hour or two, and every pair of eyes were strained to the utmost to discover the first sign of approaching help.

Out of the 16 lifeboats there were probably four or five that carried lanterns. The occupants of the other boats were, from time to time, apparently burning a piece of paper, as were we in our boat. These facts led several in our boat to assert many times that they saw a new light, which certainly must be a steamer's light. With each disappointment, added gloom seemed to settle upon our little company, as they began to realise the seriousness of our situation.

About this time, quite a breeze began to spring up, and the ocean became more rough. It was apparent that we were drifting with the wind, being only partially able to keep the bow of the boat headed into the winds.

Shortly before dawn, one of the occupants announced that he was sure that he saw a new light on the horizon. No one, however, placed any credence in his statement, although all could see dimly a light, which appeared to be similar to those that we had seen repeatedly in the different lifeboats. It was not many minutes, nevertheless, before the same person declared that he could now see two lights, where formerly there was but one. Personally, I was unable to distinguish but one light. Five minutes later, however, two lights were plainly discerned, one above the other, appearing to be close together. The conviction grew that help was approaching. This was made a certainty a very few moments later, when the lights of a large steamer could be plainly discerned. The steamer was bearing directly down upon our lifeboat, when suddenly she was seen to change her course, and steam off in the direction of a lifeboat which had been, from time to time, displaying coloured lights.

Just about this time, day began to dawn, and we could see the steamer come to rest, where we knew this lifeboat to be located. At this time, the man who was pulling the oar next to the one which I handled turned to me and said, 'Doctor, are your wife and baby safe?' I told him that I had placed them in one of the first boats to be launched. Recognising the speaker as our table steward, I said to him, 'I had no idea that you were here.' To which he replied, 'Why, I was right behind you as we left the steamer, and called to you to get in.'

We now began to pull towards the vessel, but although it was not more than two miles distant, we did not reach her until long after sunrise, notwithstanding that the wind was directly astern of us. We could now see numerous other lifeboats coming from all points and rowing towards the *Carpathia*, for such our rescuing steamer proved to be. We could also see numerous icebergs, and an icefield to the north of us, which proved to be over 50 miles long.

When our boat reached the ship's side we passed in front of her bow, to reach the port side, where we would have the shelter from the wind, and a smoother sea to disembark. An officer of the *Carpathia* called to us to come up on the starboard side. The vessel was then unloading lifeboats on each side. Those of us who were rowing endeavoured for five minutes to pull back across the bow of the ship, but so ineffective were our efforts that we were unable against the wind to make any progress. We finally had to disembark on the port side.

As the *Carpathia* had taken aboard the occupants of four or five lifeboats before ours arrived, I was naturally consumed with anxiety to ascertain whether my wife and child were aboard. After a short search I found them in the dining room, where the women and children were being tenderly cared for, and being revived by the administration of warm drinks and the application of warm wraps.

The *Carpathia* lay to, for several hours, while the occupants of the various lifeboats were being taken aboard as they rowed up, one by one. Several of those who were passengers on the *Carpathia* busied themselves by taking photographs of the lifeboats, as they drew alongside of the steamer. These photographs have been reproduced in many of the newspapers and magazines of the country, and show many of the lifeboats to have been but half filled. None of them were properly manned, there being few seamen in any of them.

There were taken aboard the *Carpathia* 705 persons. A number of the lifeboats contained the bodies of men who had been rescued from the icy waters but who had died before the boats reached the *Carpathia* from the cold and exposure incident to their immersion. Several men were brought aboard in a condition of collapse, these being some of those who had jumped from the steamer as she sank, and who had been immersed in the water for from two to three hours. I helped to resuscitate several of these men, and on the following days, before the *Carpathia* reached New York, learned from them the conditions which prevailed aboard the *Titanic* after my departure, and the events which immediately preceded her sinking. This information thus obtained at first hand I will set forth later.

Scarcely had I set foot on the *Carpathia* when I was greeted by Mr Wallace Bradford, of the firm of Hulse-Bradford Company of this city, who was a passenger on the *Carpathia* bound for Triest. He insisted upon putting his stateroom at the disposal of my wife and child, which offer I gladly accepted.

The *Carpathia*, being comfortably well filled by her own passengers, was extremely overcrowded by our 700 additional persons. All, however, were comfortably cared for.

The male passengers aboard, and in many instances the ladies, surrendered their cabins to women and children of the *Titanic*. So ably and tenderly were the survivors cared for by the captain and crew of the *Carpathia* that the former subscribed to a purse of several thousand dollars to be given to the officers and crew, and to purchase a loving cup suitably inscribed for the captain.

In the preceding remarks I have set forth the facts connected with the loss of the *Titanic* as observed by myself. My knowledge of subsequent events, as stated, is derived from extended conversation held with several of the men who swam off the *Titanic* as she sank. By observing and noting the points in their narratives in which there was no conflict, I was enabled to form, I think, a fairly accurate opinion of the events connected with and preceding the sinking of the ship.

The lifeboats on the starboard side were all launched a considerable length of time, possibly three quarters of an hour, before those on the port side were launched. There had been some trouble in launching the boats on the port side. The fact that orders had been given for the women and children to assemble on the port side, where the captain was, caused a greater congestion on this side of the vessel. The boats, however, on that side were all successfully launched and no panic, or great fear, was manifested among the passengers. Shortly after the launching of the last lifeboat, however, when there was still left four collapsible boats unlaunched, the male steerage passengers swarmed upon the boat deck. Many of these carried drawn daggers and knives in their hands, and others were armed with clubs of wood. They began to fight their way desperately to the collapsible boats, and try to gain possession of the same.

About this time the steamer suddenly settled to a very much greater degree forward, so that the waters at the forward end of the boat deck approached to within 8 or 10 feet [*c.* 2.5–3 metres] of the same. With these conditions prevailing, panic ensued. Those fighting their way to the lifeboats attempted to jump into the same, and several were shot down by officers.

Only one collapsible boat was successfully launched, another was hanging from the davits ready to be launched, and a third was hastily pushed over the side of the steamer into the waters below, but unfortunately fell upside down and drifted from the ship. A number of the men then jumped from the steamer and swam to this overturned collapsible boat, which, by the way, was a flat-bottomed boat. They managed to climb upon the same, using it as a raft.

At this time, one of the survivors, who related the incident to me, was endeavouring to cut the ropes that bound the remaining collapsible boat to the deck. He had about half of these severed when the bow of the *Titanic* was suddenly submerged, and the rush of waters tore the remaining fastenings loose. He, being flung into the water, saved himself by clinging to the boat. At this instant, many of those who were on the forward end of the boat deck were either washed off or jumped into the water clinging to wreckage.

Captain Smith, so I was told by an eyewitness, called out, 'Now it's every man for himself,' and sprang into the water. Three of those who were at this time in the water told me the same story of the succeeding events.

They stated that as the *Titanic*'s bow sank deeper and deeper into the water, they heard a series of two or three reports following each other at intervals, apparently from the hold of the vessel toward the bow. These reports, they stated, resembled those of a gun. Following the last and the loudest report, they stated that an immense volume of water rushed upward within the vessel, above the level of the ocean, bursting the windows and doors outward. These reports, they went on to state, were, in their opinion, caused by the successive giving away of the submerged bulkheads, constituting the watertight compartments forward. With the last report, connected with the upward rush of the water within the steamer, the bow of the vessel disappeared beneath the level of the sea, and her whole stern was lifted high into the air. As one who was then in the ocean expressed it, 'It looked like a great mountain hanging directly over my head, which I expected would instantly fall back upon me.' Following this the vessel was seen to buckle close to the waterline, and immediately she took her final plunge into the ocean depths. All of these latter events transpired in the space of a very few moments.

My idea is that when the stern of the ship was lifted high out of the water by the bursting of the watertight compartments, in the forward end of the vessel, that the vast freight of the machinery caused the framework and the plates of the ship to give way, thus allowing the great inrush of waters to complete her destruction.

From the preceding narrative it is seen that those who escaped in the lifeboats, had little or no knowledge of the terrible events which transpired with the sinking of the ship. As near as I can fix the lapse of time, an hour or an hour and a quarter elapsed after the lifeboat, in which I left the vessel, was launched, up to the time of the sinking of the steamer.

The tales told me, however, by these men who were on board the vessel, or in the water, as she sunk, are almost too harrowing for repetition. These men, for hours after their arrival on the *Carpathia* would burst forth in tears, lamenting the terrible scenes through which they passed.

With some of these men, there clambered on to the bottom of the collapsible boat other survivors, until it held in the neighbourhood of 40 persons. So many, however, climbed upon the same, that it was constantly submerged from six inches to three feet [*c.* 15 cm – 1 metre], and there they stood shoulder to shoulder, endeavouring to balance and prevent the raft from overturning. Numbers died on this raft, chilled by the icy waters to the point where they succumbed, when their bodies were cast into the sea by the survivors. Several times the raft was capsized, and always some would be lost in their attempt to clamber back upon it. When the survivors were taken off the raft, but 16 remained of the original 40. (The preceding was all given me in detail by several who were on the raft.)

Following the collision the band, which had earlier in the evening given the usual Sunday evening concert, continued to play. They played ragtime and other lively music. But a few moments before the steamer sank, when the danger was apparent to all, they were playing 'Lead Kindly Light'. There were five musicians, all of whom were lost.

When all of the survivors were gathered aboard the *Carpathia*, word was circulated requesting that all first class and second class passengers give their names to the purser, in order that a list of the rescued might be sent ashore by means of the Marconi wireless. The purser had a book in which the survivors wrote their names. I wrote in this book distinctly the name of myself, with that of my wife and that of my little son. Unfortunately, somewhere in the repetition of this list, after it had left the *Carpathia*, by the vessel relaying the same, or the operator ashore, the error was made of reporting my name as Mr Washington, the Dodge being omitted. The fact that my name was correctly sent off the day of the disaster, by the Marconi operator of the *Carpathia*, is proven by what, to me, is a most interesting incident.

I received, only three days since, a letter written on board the steamship *Olympic*, which was the sister ship to the *Titanic*, and which at the time of the disaster was on her way to England from New York. This letter is as follows:

> On Board RMS *Olympic*, at sea, 15 April, Dr Washington Dodge.
>
> Dear Sir: I want to congratulate you, Mrs Dodge, and your little child, on your escape from the awful disaster. We, on the sister ship, have been rushing to your aid all day, but alas, to no effect. We have positively no news of the disaster, except a partial list of survivors, among whom I was very happy to see your names.
>
> Hoping that your family suffers no ill effects, I remain,
>
> Yours very truly,
>
> B. M. JOSEPH,
>
> With Raphael, Weill & Co.

Mr Joseph, a buyer for the White Houses, was on his annual trip to Europe, and on reaching Southampton mailed this letter which, as stated, only reached me a few days since. Had this error not been made my relatives, and friends, would have been spared the two days of suspense which I learned of after reaching New York. The *Olympic*, on which Mr Joseph was a passenger, received our first wireless call for help. Later in the day she received a wireless from the *Carpathia* informing her of the *Titanic*'s loss and giving a list of those rescued.

A question frequently asked me has been whether, following the collision, the passengers believed that they were in any immediate danger. I think that what I have narrated shows that up to the time following the launching of the last lifeboat, little apprehension existed in the minds of most of the passengers. This, to some, may seem almost incredible. When one rejects, however, that the *Titanic* was considered by all, in itself, a lifeboat, and an unsinkable vessel, and that no one had any idea of the terrible injury to the ship caused by a shock so slight as that given by the impact with the iceberg, when she was seen to be afloat with apparently no displacement, on a calm sea, with no ice in sight, it can readily be conceived that the idea of the vessel sinking did not impress itself on the minds of the passengers.

When, to these facts, there was added the assurance of the officers that, under no conditions, could the ship sink in less than eight or 10 hours, and that within an hour or two, not one, but three or four, steamers would be alongside – they having been signalled by wireless – it can readily be seen how this confidence grew.

Perhaps a few incidents which came to my knowledge will serve to illustrate these facts more forcibly. Mr Carter and Mr Widener were two prominent Philadelphians aboard the steamer. Mr Carter was saved. Mr Widener was lost. Mr Carter related the following circumstances: 'We had been together on the port side of the steamer, and had seen a number of boats launched. I said to my friend: "Harry, let's go around on the starboard side, as we might have a chance to get aboard a boat there." He replied, "You go ahead, old man, if you want to, I am going to take my chance with the steamer."' Mr Carter related that he then went to the starboard side, and there entered the last boat on that side which was then being launched. This was boat 15 in which Mr Ismay embarked, and which boat I saw launched.

Another incident. Myself and my wife were acquainted with a couple residing in Los Angeles, who were passengers on the *Titanic*. On the *Carpathia*, the morning after the disaster, we found the wife, but the husband was missing. The wife related the following: at the time of the collision her husband was on the upper deck (deck A) in the card room, engaged with some friends in a game of cards. She was on one of the lower decks (C deck, I think) preparing to retire, being partially disrobed. Being conscious of the jar, and noticing that the engines had stopped, she put on her clothing, and went up two decks above to her husband in the card room. He assured her that there was nothing to be alarmed at, that he had been so told by one of the officers, and told her to return to her stateroom, where he would join her presently. This she did; he continuing in the game of cards. As she reached her stateroom door, she saw a man with a life preserver on, hurrying along the corridor. She laughed at him, and said, 'Well, you must be a pretty nervous man.' He then told her that the order had been given for all passengers to put on life preservers. She again went up to A deck and informed her husband of what she had been told. They then went down to their stateroom, put on warmer underclothing, and dressed in the warmest clothing that they had. After this they proceeded to the boat deck, where they were joined by another couple they knew, and there watched the boats being launched. The ladies refused to enter the lifeboats, stating that they would wait and go with their husbands later. Eventually, after several of the boats were launched, the officers insisted that they get into a boat, their husbands adding their request, and assisting them into the boat. After this neither of them ever saw or heard anything of her husband. But as this lady in narrating the circumstances stated, 'Neither of us thought that there was any danger of our not meeting again. My husband handed me some money saying, "We may be separated, and you might need this." But he did not kiss me goodbye, nor did he even say goodbye. I know he had no more idea of the possibility of his being lost than had I.'

Those who swam from the sinking steamer at the last moment had no idea that the vessel was in danger of sinking, until her body suddenly sank deeper in the waters a few moments before she sank. As they stated, had they believed the vessel was in any danger of sinking they would have had sufficient time, following the launching of the lifeboats, to have prepared temporary life rafts sufficient, in that calm sea, to have saved the lives of hundreds.

There were on the decks, stacked against the cabins, over 800 folding steamer chairs made of heavy oak frames. A few of these lashed together would have formed an emergency raft capable of sustaining one or more persons indefinitely. Hundreds of heavy wooden doors, and dining room tables and other material were easily available for the same purpose.

These survivors stated, however, that until the sudden downward dip of the vessel forward, coincident with the rush on to the boat deck of the steerage passengers, they did not apprehend that there was any danger of the vessel sinking for hours or days, if at all. I quote again from the very able review published in the London papers, and in the *New York Times*, by Mr Lawrence Beesley, a passenger to whom reference has already been made: 'When the *Titanic* struck everyone said, "We are all right, this boat cannot sink. We will only have to wait around until another ship comes along to take us off." This,' he states, 'no doubt stopped the panic, and prevented those rushes after boats which probably would have occurred had this theory not been so widely and firmly held.'

There are a few matters relating to this disaster which have caused widespread criticism and discussion, which I will briefly touch upon. I am aware, however, that there are probably many present who are far better qualified than I to express an opinion on these matters.

The criticism has been made that gross carelessness was displayed in driving the steamship at such a rate of speed after warnings of icebergs ahead had been given. The charge is also made that the steamer was equipped with lifeboats sufficient to carry less than one third of those aboard. Also, that not enough seamen to launch properly and man the lifeboats were at hand, and that the steamer was not provided with a searchlight.

There can be no question of the fact that the steamer was running at an unwarranted rate of speed after it had received the warning it had. Neither can there be any question of the fact that the lifeboats were not sufficient to carry all of those aboard. The number of seamen was positively insufficient. Owing to this great insufficiency, there being but 16 seamen to launch and man 20 lifeboats, the lifeboats appeared to be filled and lowered consecutively, rather than simultaneously.

The seriousness of this point is apparent when we consider that when the ship sank, nearly three hours after she struck, there still remained three collapsible boats, each capable of holding 30 or more persons, unlaunched. As to the searchlight, it is not disputed that the steamer was without one.

In answer to these criticisms the only excuse that can be offered is the following. Many steamship companies undoubtedly endeavour to meet the requirements of the public for rapid transit. The fast liners that advertise to leave New York on Mondays and take dinner in London on Saturday seldom fail to arrive on schedule time. As the craze on the part of the public for speed, and the incident saving of time is manifested on the water, so we see the same evidenced on shore by the 'cannon-ball express', and '20th century limited' trains. Sleet, snow, and even fog are often disregarded in the ruining of these trains and boats, no matter how great the menace, if only the time schedule can be lived up to. As was done by the captain of the *Titanic*, so many captains for years past have done, that is, to run at full speed through the iceberg region. While this is not done by every captain, yet it is not an uncommon occurrence for captains of fast passenger-mail steamers to do so. Considering the vastness of the ocean, and the small size of an iceberg, the chance of striking one are about as remote as the finding of the proverbial needle in a haystack. These chances of disaster have been taken thousands of times previous to the disaster of the *Titanic*, but unfortunately here the chance was taken once too often. The *Titanic* encountered the only thing in the ocean which was capable, in my opinion, of sinking her. There is, to my mind, no excuse for such a catastrophe, but it is difficult to free the travelling public from all responsibility for such disasters.

As to the insufficiency of lifeboats, taking into consideration the unsinkable qualities of the *Titanic*, and the fact, as Captain Rostron of the *Carpathia* stated it, 'She was herself a lifeboat,' she was probably better equipped than are the majority of passenger steamers today.

Very similar conditions prevail on other steamers regarding the insufficiency of seamen. The crews are made up principally of engineers, oilers, stokers, and stewards. When a catastrophe such as this occurs, the lack of seamen to man the lifeboats is a serious matter. Had the sea not been unusually calm, not one fourth of those saved would have been rescued.

The absence of a searchlight seems inexcusable. The fact that passenger steamers at this time of the year, when icebergs are a menace, take the northern route, rather than a more southern and safer route, simply because this northern route is shorter, and entails less expense and time in making the trip, seems positively unwarranted.

In conclusion, I will state that I hope this narrative has given you a clearer understanding of the events connected with this great disaster. There is no doubt that the catastrophe will result in the adoption of rules, regarding the equipment of oceangoing steamers, and their navigation, which will make the repetition of such a disaster less liable.

34

Mary Hewlett, Second Class Passenger

Mary Hewlett was a 56-year-old Englishwoman who had been resident in Lucknow, India, prior to boarding the *Titanic* at Southampton.

Evanston Daily News, 25 April 1912 It was evidently but a moment after the collision that I was awakened by hearing a noise in the hallway. There were a great many young people on my deck and they were in the habit of making much noise, laughing and joking throughout the night. When I was awakened I listened and the noise I heard did not sound like that of previous evenings. I noticed the engines had stopped. Getting out of bed I opened my door. There was the steward dressed in full uniform. I asked what was the cause of the commotion and he assured me that nothing was wrong. I then asked him if I had better get dressed and go to the deck. He told me that perhaps I had. I put on a few clothes and then my heavy fur coat and started. On my way I noticed most of the passengers strapping lifebelts on themselves. I asked for one. I was told that they were being distributed in the dining room. I went there but found no one. On returning I met a man with two lifebelts and asked him for one. He gave me one and I strapped it on myself. I then started for the deck. I was directed to a small and narrow iron ladder. They told me it was the only way to the main deck. Just as I was climbing the ladder a throng of steerage passengers fought their way up and started clambering for the stairs. When I reached the deck the men forced me into the lifeboat waiting to be lowered. It was boat No. 13 and next to the last lifeboat to leave the doomed vessel. When I got into the lifeboat it was very nearly filled and there were more men than women. Fifty were saved and there were not more than 10 women in that number. The majority of the passengers in the boat I was in were steerage people. There were men with their wives in this boat while many first class men were separated from their wives. I cannot understand this. The boat was lowered and we were alone on the calm sea. It seemed much longer than it really was before we saw the *Carpathia* and were picked up by that boat. The treatment we were given on the *Carpathia* could not have been better, everything possible being done for us. Sleeping quarters were given to as many as possible and the rest were taken care of in the best possible manner. The library steward on the *Carpathia* was a kind man. He did everything he could to ensure our comfort and I never will forget the work he did. When the *Carpathia* landed in New York I was met by friends and taken to the Astor house where I remained until my son arrived in New York to take me to his home in South Dakota. A great fault with the *Titanic* was that there were not enough sufficiently experienced seamen on the boat. The majority of the crew was recruited from the streets in Southampton.

35

Frederick Barrett, Leading Fireman

Frederick Barrett was a very lucky man. Feeding the ship's boilers deep within the *Titanic*, he was on duty when the iceberg tore her side, and water started gushing in. Here Barrett vividly describes how he managed to escape before the automatic watertight doors were closed. Frederick Barrett was back at sea within a matter of weeks, working on *Titanic*'s sister ship *Olympic*.

US Senate Inquiry (inquiry question is followed immediately by witness's answer) What is your name? Frederick Barrett.

Place of residence? Southampton.

You were a fireman on the *Titanic*? I was leading fireman.

Were you on duty on the night of the accident? Yes.

Where? In 6 section [see illustration 57 for location of No. 6 boiler room].

Were you there when the accident occurred? Yes. I was standing talking to the second engineer. The bell rang, the red light showed. We sang out shut the doors [ash doors to the furnaces] and there was a crash just as we sung out. The water came through the ship's side. The engineer and I jumped to the next section. The next section to the forward section is No. 5 [see illustration 57 for location of No. 5 boiler room].

Where did the water come through? About two feet [*c.* 60 cm] above the floor plates, starboard side.

How much water? A large volume of water came through.

How big was this hole in the side? About two feet above the floor plates.

You think it was a large tear? Yes; I do.

All along the side of No. 6? Yes.

How far along? Past the bulkhead between sections 5 and 6, and it was a hole two feet into the coal bunkers. She was torn through No. 6 and also through two feet abaft the bulkhead in the bunker at the forward head of No. 5 section. We got through before the doors broke, the doors dropped instantly automatically from the bridge. I went back to No. 6 fireroom and there was eight feet [c. two and a half metres] of water in there. I went to No. 5 fireroom when the lights went out. I was sent to find lamps, as the lights were out, and when we got the lamps we looked at the boilers and there was no water in them. I ran to the engineer and he told me to get some firemen down to draw the fires. I got 15 men down below.

Did you not have fires in No. 6? Yes, the fires were lit when the water came.

I would like to know how many boilers were going that night? There were five boilers not lit.

How many were there going? There was 24 boilers lit and five without. Fires were lighted in three boilers for the first time Sunday, but I don't know whether they were connected up or not.

This tear went a couple of feet past the bulkhead in No. 5. How were you able to keep the water from reaching? It never came above the plates, until all at once I saw a wave of green foam come tearing through between the boilers and I jumped for the escape ladder.

Was there any indication of any explosion of a boiler? There was a knocking noise, but no explosion, only when the ship was sinking a volume of smoke came up.

Can you tell us how long you have been on the *Titanic*? I only joined it at Southampton.

How did you escape? I got in lifeboat 13.

Was it a collapsible boat? I cannot tell.

You were in charge of No. 13 for about an hour – how many were in that boat? 65 or 70.

How many sailors? I cannot tell.

What officer was in charge? No officer in it. Because I had no clothes I felt myself giving out and gave it to somebody else. I do not know who it was.

Was there any objection to your getting in the boat? No, sir.

Where was it loaded? At A deck. It was lowered to A deck. They were very full up when we got in.

Was there an officer there at the time? No, sir.

You got in and took charge of the boat and remained in charge until you got chilled? Yes.

Then who took it over? I could not say who it was.

Was there any large number of people in A deck at the time you got up there? There was not, sir.

How did you reach A deck? I came up along the hatchway.

Did you meet any third class passengers? No, sir.

Were they held off in any way? No, sir.

They had the same privilege to go up on A deck? They had as much privilege as anybody else.

36

Daniel Buckley, Third Class Passenger

Daniel Buckley was one of the very few third class passengers called to give evidence to the US inquiry. Most of those travelling third class were planning to start a new life in the US. In an event later portrayed in the *Titanic* film, Buckley describes a gate locked to keep 'steerage' passengers below. But interestingly Buckley (who was 21) also insists that steerage passengers 'had as good a change as first and second class' passengers to get in lifeboats. Daniel is mistaken in referring to Mrs Astor, who left in lifeboat 4.

US Senate Inquiry (inquiry question is followed immediately by witness's answer) Where did you get aboard the *Titanic*? At Queenstown.

Had you been living in Ireland? Yes; I lived in King Williamstown, Town Court.

How did you happen to come over to America? *Witness answers:* I wanted to come over here to make some money. I came in the *Titanic* because she was a new steamer. This night of the wreck I was sleeping in my room on the *Titanic*, in the steerage. There were three other boys from the same place sleeping in the same room with me. I heard some terrible noise and I jumped out on the floor, and the first thing I knew my feet were getting wet; the water was just coming in slightly. I told the other fellows to get up, that there was something wrong and that the water was coming in. They only laughed at me. One of them says, 'Get back into bed. You are not in Ireland now.' I got on my clothes as quick as I could, and the three other fellows got out. The room was very small, so I got out to give them room to dress themselves. Two sailors came along, and they were shouting, 'All up on deck! Unless you want to get drowned.' When I heard this, I went for the deck as quick as I could. When I got up on the deck I saw everyone having those lifebelts on only myself; so I got sorry, and said I would go back again where I was sleeping and get one of those life preservers, because there was one there for each person.

I went back again, and just as I was going down the last flight of stairs the water was up four steps, and dashing up. I did not go back into the room, because I could not. When I went back toward the room the water was coming up three steps up the stairs, or four steps; so I did not go any farther. I got back on the deck again, and just as I got back there, I was looking around to see if I could get any of those lifebelts, and I met a first class passenger, and he had two. He gave me one, and fixed it on me. Then the lifeboats were preparing. There were five lifeboats sent out. I was in the sixth. I was holding the ropes all the time, helping to let down the five lifeboats that went down first, as well as I could. When the sixth lifeboat was prepared, there was a big crowd of men standing on the deck. And they all jumped in. So I said I would take my chance with them.

Who were they? *Witness answers:* Passengers and sailors and firemen mixed. There were no ladies there at the same time. When they jumped, I said I would go too. I went into the boat. Then two officers came along and said all of the men could come out. And they brought a lot of steerage passengers with them; and they were mixed, every way, ladies and gentlemen. And they said all the men could get out and let the ladies in. But six men were left in the boat. I think they were firemen and sailors. I was crying. There was a woman in the boat, and she had thrown her shawl over me, and she told me to stay in there. I believe she was Mrs Astor. Then they did not see me, and the boat was lowered down into the water, and we rowed away out from the steamer. The men that were in the boat at first fought, and would not get out, but the officers drew their revolvers, and fired shots over our heads, and then the men got out. When the boat was ready, we were lowered down into the water and rowed away out from the steamer. We were only about 15 minutes out when she sank.

What else happened? *Witness answers:* One of the firemen that was working on the *Titanic* told me, when I got on board the *Carpathia* and he was speaking to me, that he did not think it was any iceberg; that it was only that they wanted to make a record, and they ran too much steam and the boilers bursted. That is what he said. We sighted the lights of the big steamer, the *Carpathia*. All the women got into a terrible commotion and jumped around. They were hallooing and the sailors were trying to keep them sitting down, and they would not do it. They were standing up all the time. When we got into the *Carpathia* we were treated very good. We got all kinds of refreshments.

Did you feel a shock from the collision when the ship struck? Yes; I did.

And did that wake you up? It did. I did not feel any shock in the steamer; only just heard a noise. I heard a kind of a grating noise.

Did you get right out of bed? Yes; I did.

When you got out, you got into the water? There was water in your compartment in the steerage? Yes; water was there slightly. There was not very much.

How much? The floor was only just getting wet. It was only coming in under the door very slightly.

You had two or three boys with you? Yes; three boys that came from the same place in Ireland.

What became of those other three boys? I cannot say. I did not see them any more after leaving the room where I parted from them.

They were lost? Yes; they were lost.

Was there any effort made on the part of the officers or crew to hold the steerage passengers in the steerage? I do not think so.

Were you permitted to go on up to the top deck without any interference? Yes, sir. They tried to keep us down at first on our steerage deck. They did not want us to go up to the first class place at all.

Who tried to do that? I cannot say who they were. I think they were sailors.

What happened then? Did the steerage passengers try to get out? *Witness answers:* Yes; they did. There was one steerage passenger there, and he was getting up the steps, and just as he was going in a little gate a fellow came along and chucked him down; threw him down into the steerage place. This fellow got excited, and he ran after him, and he could not find him. He got up over the little gate. He did not find him.

What gate do you mean? A little gate just at the top of the stairs going up into the first class deck.

There was a gate between the steerage and the first class deck? Yes. The first class deck was higher up than the steerage deck, and there were some steps leading up to it; 9 or 10 steps, and a gate just at the top of the steps.

Was the gate locked? It was not locked at the time we made the attempt to get up there, but the sailor, or whoever he was, locked it. So that this fellow that went up after him broke the lock on it, and he went after the fellow that threw him down. He said if he could get hold of him he would throw him into the ocean.

Did these passengers in the steerage have any opportunity at all of getting out? Yes; they had.

What opportunity did they have? I think they had as much chance as the first and second class passengers.

After this gate was broken? Yes; because they were all mixed. All the steerage passengers went up on the first class deck at this time, when the gate was broken. They all got up there. They could not keep them down.

How much water was there in the steerage when you got out of the steerage? There was only just a little bit. Just like you would throw a bucket of water on the floor; just very little, like that.

But it was coming in, was it? Yes; it was only just commencing to come in. When I went down the second time, to get one of the life preservers, there was a terrible lot of water there, in a very short time.

How much? It was just about three steps up the stairs, on the last flight of stairs that I got down.

Did you find any people down in the steerage when you went back the second time? There were a number, but I cannot say how many. All the boys and girls were coming up against me. They were all going for the deck.

Were they excited? Yes; they were. The girls were very excited, and they were crying; and all the boys were trying to console them and saying that it was nothing serious.

Were you crying at the time? Not at this time. There was a girl from my place, and just when she got down into the lifeboat she thought that the boat was sinking into the water. Her name was Bridget Bradley. She climbed one of the ropes as far as she could and tried to get back into the *Titanic* again, as she thought she would be safer in it than in the lifeboat. She was just getting up when one of the sailors went out to her and pulled her down again.

How many people were there in the steerage when you got out of bed? I cannot say.

Could you see many people around? Yes, sir; there was a great crowd of people. They were all terribly excited. They were all going for the decks as quick as they could. The people had no difficulty in stepping into the lifeboat. It was close to the ship.

I want to ask you whether, from what you saw that night, you feel that the steerage passengers had an equal opportunity with other passengers and the crew in getting into the lifeboats? Yes; I think they had as good a chance as the first and second class passengers.

You think they did have? Yes. But at the start they tried to keep them down on their own deck.

But they broke down this gate to which you have referred? Yes, sir.

And then they went on up as others did, mingling all together? Yes; they were all mixed up together.

Have you told all you know, of your own knowledge, about that? Yes.

Were you where you could see the ship when she went down? I saw the lights just going out as she went down. It made a terrible noise, like thunder.

I wish you would tell the committee in what part of the ship this steerage was located. *Witness answers:* Down, I think, in the lower part of the steamer, in the after part of the ship; at the back.

LIFEBOAT 15
Starboard Side, Launched 1.40 a.m.

Lifeboat 15 was launched very soon after number 13 and was the last standard lifeboat to be launched from the starboard side. Steward John Hart remembers 25 of his passengers being put in this lifeboat before it was lowered down to A deck where it picked up another 10 passengers. This is contradicted by the testimony of George Cavell, who thought passengers were picked up at three points. Given this contradictory testimony we can understand how difficult a task it was for the inquiry team to establish exactly what happened that night. Fireman Frank Dymond (sometimes spelt Diamond) was put in charge of this boat. Male crew: 13; male passengers: four; women and children: 53; total for lifeboat: 70 (British Board of Inquiry).

37

John Hart, Third Class Steward

Steward John Hart's testimony is interesting as he led two groups of third class passengers up to the boat deck. Without Hart's diligence many of these passengers would not have escaped. The *Titanic* was a huge ship and it is unlikely that these passengers would have been able to make their way up in time to secure an increasingly scarce lifeboat place. Hart was about to go and fetch another group of passengers when First Officer Murdoch told him to climb in. At various points members of the inquiry team cross-examine Hart's recollections and the atmosphere becomes increasingly tense.

British Board of Trade Inquiry (inquiry question is followed immediately by witness's answer) At the time when the collision occurred were you off duty and in your bunk? Yes.

What deck is your room on? The glory hole below E deck, below the main working alleyway.

Do you mean that it is on E deck, or below E deck? Below E deck.

Is it a room in which a number of third class stewards are together? Yes.

I see a room on the plan that is marked '42 third class stewards' would that be it? We have two rooms for third class stewards. They are both on the same level, but one is beside the third class dining room.

And the other one? The other is further along - more amidships.

I see, which was yours? Just beside the third class dining room.

It is marked '38 third class stewards', on deck F, I think? I think it is.

Close to the bakers? Yes.

There is a room for six bakers next door? Yes.

Very well, that is your room. Were you awakened by the collision? No.

Did somebody else come and wake you up? Yes, somebody came along and woke me.

You heard there had been an accident? Yes, they said there had been an accident.

I think at first you did not think it was serious, and did not take much notice of it? Yes, and went to sleep.

Who was it who came afterwards and gave instructions? The chief third class steward, Mr Kieran.

What were the orders to pass along? He passed several orders. To me he said, 'Go along to your rooms and get your people about.'

Would your rooms be the third class passengers' rooms? Yes.

Which part of the third class accommodation is it that you were responsible for? Section K and part of M, the adjoining section, on E deck.

That is part of the after third class accommodation? Yes.

K and M? Yes.

Do not they lie between two watertight bulkheads? Yes, there are two watertight bulkheads at the after part of the beginning of the third class.

I thought K lay between two, and M between two others, and so on? Yes, that is quite correct, K lies between two.

I thought we noticed when we went to see the ship that they used the letters of the alphabet to indicate the different compartments right along? That is it.

Anyhow, your third class passengers were in the K section and in the M section? Part of M, yes.

Are the third class passengers accommodated in different parts of the ship according as they are single men or married couples, and so on? Yes.

And what is it you had in your section? I had part single women and part married.

Married couples, I suppose? Yes.

How many third class passengers had you in your sections altogether? Somewhere about 58.

That would be including children? All told.

And of those 58, how many would be in the married couples' part? How many married couples, do you mean?

Yes, or put it the other way, you have a certain number of married men with their wives and families and a certain number of single women. Just divide it up? At the same time we had some married women travelling with their children.

Take your 58? I had about nine married couples with children.

I understand you had no single men? No, no single men.

That would mean that you had got nine men? Nine husbands travelling with their wives.

Nine husbands altogether? Yes.

And the rest would be either ladies travelling alone, or wives or children? Yes.

All the others were women or children? Yes.

When you got those instructions just tell us what you did? The chief third class steward was there, and he said 'Get your people roused up and get lifebelts placed upon them. See that they have lifebelts on them.' I did so.

I suppose most of those people would have retired for the night? The majority had retired.

Did you knock them all up? Yes.

Can you tell us so far as your third class passengers are concerned, did you go to each third class compartment and rouse up your people? I went to each third class room and roused them.

Were most of them up or were they asleep? The majority were up. They had been aroused before I got there.

They are not single cabins, these third class compartments, are they? Not single berths? They consisted of four berth-rooms and two berth-rooms, and two six berth-rooms.

And what did you do about the lifebelts? I saw the lifebelts placed on them that were willing to have them put on them.

Some would not put them on? Some refused to put them on.

Did they say why? Yes, they said they saw no occasion for putting them on, they did not believe the ship was hurt in any way.

Up to this time were any instructions given for your people to go to any other part of the ship? Not to my knowledge.

Just tell us next what the next instructions were, or the next thing that you did. I will put the question in another way. You have told us that the instructions you got from Mr Kieran, that you were to rouse up your people and get lifebelts on them. Did he say anything about future instructions that would be given? He said there would be further instructions, that I was to stand by my own people.

So you were expecting further orders? Yes.

Now you can tell us what happened. What further orders were given? He said, 'Have you placed lifebelts on those who are willing to have them?' I said, 'Yes.' After that there was a large number of men coming from the forward part of the ship with their baggage, those that were berthed up forward - single men.

Third class? Yes. When I saw that my own people had the required number of lifebelts, or those who were willing to have them, I placed the remainder of the lifebelts in one of the alleyways beside which these people would have to pass in case any came through without lifebelts from the forward part of the boat.

This is also on deck E? Yes.

You told us these third class passengers who were berthed forward came down to the aft? Yes.

That would be down that alleyway? Yes, down to the after part of the ship.

And whether a third class passenger is berthed forward or berthed aft, is the third class dining room aft? The third class dining room runs from almost amidships to aft.

What I mean is the third class passengers who are berthed forward would know their way aft, because they had been accustomed to go to the dining room? Yes.

These men coming from the forward part of the ship would come along the alleyway and then go down a companion ladder and get to the dining saloon? Yes.

On the deck below? Yes.

Where was it you saw them? I saw them where I was placed in my part of the ship, where my people were.

That is K and M? Yes, on the main alleyway.

I think the next thing you will be able to tell us will be the further instructions as to where these people were to go? I waited about there with my own people trying to show them that the vessel was not hurt to any extent to my own knowledge, and waited for the chief third class steward, or some other officer, or somebody in authority to come down and give further orders. Mr Kieran came back. He had been to sections S, and Q, and R to see that those people also were provided with lifebelts.

S, and Q and R are all in the extreme after part of the ship, are not they? That is correct.

S is on deck G, R is on deck F, and Q is on deck E, all in the extreme after part of the ship? Yes.

He had been there to your knowledge? Yes, he had also his assistant with him, one by name, Sedginary.

The chief steward and his assistant, Sedginary, went right aft, did they? Yes.

To S, R and Q? Q, S and R.

Would those two people you have spoken of, Mr Kieran and Mr Sedginary, have any responsibility except for third class passengers? No, I think not. That is their own department of the ship.

What about the assistant, you say his assistant was with him? Yes.

In these compartments, do you mean? Going around he went round with him.

Did Kieran survive? No.

He was drowned? Yes.

And the other man? The assistant also, he was drowned.

You would have colleagues, other of the third class stewards, of course. Do you know whether they were doing what you were doing? All the men that had rooms were.

All the third class stewards who had got rooms? The third class stewards do not all have rooms. The third class stewards that had rooms went round to their respective sections and were doing the same as I was doing.

You mean those who had charge of rooms? Yes.

You mean to say they roused the passengers and tried to get them to put on lifebelts? Yes.

How many third class stewards would there be who would have charge of rooms in the after end of the ship? Eight.

As far as you know they were each engaged in doing this? Yes.

Now just tell us about the next thing? I was standing by waiting for further instructions. After some little while the word came down, 'Pass your women up on the boat deck.' This was done.

That means the third class? Yes, the third class.

Anything about children? Yes. 'Pass the women and children.'

'Pass the women and children up to the boat deck'? Yes, those that were willing to go to the boat deck were shown the way. Some were not willing to go to the boat deck, and stayed behind. Some of them went to the boat deck, and found it rather cold, and saw the boats being lowered away, and thought themselves more secure on the ship, and consequently returned to their cabin.

You say they thought themselves more secure on the ship? Did you hear any of them say so? Yes, I heard two or three say they preferred to remain on the ship than be tossed about on the water like a cockle shell.

Can you in any way help us to fix the time, or about the time, when the order was given to pass the third class women and children up to the boat deck? Could you tell us how long it was after you were first roused, or how long it was before the ship went down? Well, as near as I can. The vessel struck, I believe, at 11.40 p.m. That would be 20 minutes to 12. It must have been three parts of an hour before the word was passed down to me to pass the women and children up to the boat deck.

This would be about 12.30 a.m? Yes, my lord, as near as can be.

You say the word was passed down and you heard it? Yes.

And you had your other colleagues there, other third class stewards. Was the word passed along? Yes, we were in a bunch. The whole sections are in a bunch. The word was passed right round, 'Women and children to the boat deck,' at somewhere about 12.30 a.m.

When you heard it you would repeat it? The word was passed along, it was said loud enough for anybody to hear.

In order that your third class women and children should get from those quarters up to the boat deck, they would have to mount a number of decks and go up a number of stairs? I did not take them that way.

How did you take them? I took them along to the next deck, the C deck, the first saloon deck.

You are making it very clear. There is a third class stairway going up? Yes.

Did you take them by the third class stairway up to C deck? I took them up into the after well deck, that would be the third class deck up one companion to C deck.

Do you see the plan (pointing on the plan)? There is no occasion. I know the ship.

It is to help us, not you. You say there are a series of stairways indicated. It is the third class stairway going up, is it not? Yes.

The regular way by which third class passengers would go up if they were going to get to? The after well deck.

And is that the way you took them up? Yes.

As far as the C deck? Yes.

It is marked on the plan? It is up one companion.

It is marked on the plan, 'Third class Entrance,' I think? I do not know how the plan is marked.

Is it a wide stairway with rails dividing the stairs into sections? Yes, it is very wide.

So that 20 or 30 people could walk up abreast? Well, hardly that.

Well, 15 people? I should imagine six aside could go up easily.

That would bring them up then, as I follow you, to the C deck, to the after well deck, and how would you get them from there to the boat deck? I took them along to the first class main companion from there.

You did yourself? Yes.

You led them, you guided them? I went ahead of them.

That would mean on C deck going forward. Would it mean passing the second class library, and all that? Yes. The beginning of that deck is the second class, and further along, the saloon.

And goes still forward until he comes to the first class stairs, which is next to what is marked 'Barber's shop,' a big stairway. Then did you guide them up that first class stairway to the boat deck? *Witness answers:* Right to the boat deck.

At that time, when you took up your people by that route, was there any barrier that had to be opened, or was it open to pass? There were barriers that at ordinary times are closed, but they were open.

They were open when you got there? Yes.

How many people of your lot did you take up the first time you went up this course to the boat deck? Somewhere about 30.

All women and children of the third class? Yes, on that occasion, on the first occasion.

And having got them to the boat deck, do you remember whereabouts on the boat deck you took them to? Yes. I took them to boat No. 8, which was at that time being lowered.

That is the fourth boat on the port side? Yes.

Practically opposite the second funnel, or a little more forward than the second funnel? Yes.

Did you leave them there? I left them there and went back again.

And when you went back what happened then? But on the way of my getting back other passengers were coming along, third class passengers. They were also being shown the way to the boats. Amongst them were females – the husbands and fathers were with them.

Who was showing them the way? One by the name of Cox.

Is he a steward? Yes.

One of your colleagues? One of the third class stewards.

Was Cox saved, do you know? No.

Did they follow the same route to go to the boat deck? Well, by the way he was taking them they must have done.

You returned to your people? I returned to my own part of the ship.

Did you bring up any more? Yes, about 25. I had some little trouble in getting back owing to the males wanting to get to the boat deck.

The men? Yes. After the word was passed round for women and children, I was delayed a little time in getting a little band together that were willing to go to the boats.

A band of women and children? Yes.

How many did you gather? Somewhere about 25.

Were those all people from the rooms you were responsible for? No, also from other sections.

Were they all third class passengers? Yes.

Did you guide them by the same route? Yes.

Where did you take them to? I took them to the only boat that was left then, boat No. 15.

This is an important thing. You say the only boat that was left? That I could see.

Do you mean the only boat that was left on either side of the ship? I came along the starboard side of the vessel and on that side of the vessel that was the only remaining boat.

That is the aftermost boat on the starboard side? Yes, the last boat on the starboard side.

That is the boat we have had some evidence about this morning. Can you tell me whether at that time there were any boats on the port side? I cannot say, I did not go. The last boat I saw on the port side launched was when I took my first lot of passengers to boat No. 8.

At that time when you took your lot of passengers to boat No. 8 on the port side were there any other boats left on the port side? It is like this. From boat No. 8 I believe there is a big square right amidships. I did not look further.

You mean there is a big empty space? Yes.

Of course boat No. 8 is one of the forward lot of boats? Yes.

You would come up by the main companion way, and coming up by the main companion way would come up almost opposite boat No. 8? Yes.

And so you went straight to it? Yes.

You really cannot tell us whether at that time the after boats on the port side were still there or not? I cannot tell you.

And when you came up the second time you say you went to the starboard side? I came up on the starboard side. It was on the starboard side that I came up. I went across in the first place to the port, because at that time they were lowering away the port boats.

You mean the first time you came on the boat deck? Yes, and on my return to the deck the second time, I could see that there were no boats being lowered away from the port.

You could? Yes, from the open space which is right opposite. I then took them to the starboard side. There was on that side one remaining boat, No. 15.

I see that in order to get from the first class companion up which you came to boat No. 15, you would come out on the boat deck, if you look at the model, just in front of the second funnel, and you would have to walk right back to the aftermost boat, which we see there. That is right, is it not? Yes.

And you could see, of course, that there were no boats left until you got to No. 15? On the starboard side there were no boats left except that one.

When you got with these people to No. 15 was there room for them in it? Yes, they were placed in it.

Now this is on the boat deck? Yes.

Not on A deck? No.

Do you mean that these people were put into it from the boat deck? From the boat deck. The boat was lowered right flush with the rail on the boat deck.

From the davits? From the davits to the level of the rail to enable the people to get in easier.

I had better tell you why, because it helps us all. We have had other evidence, you see, and it is not very clear from the other evidence where the people got in? *Witness answers:* Am I clear?

You are clear. Are you quite clear in your own mind that they got in from the boat deck? Yes.

25? *Witness answers:* There were more than 25, but I took up 25.

Your 25 got into No. 15 boat from the boat deck? Yes.

I daresay you can tell us a bit further about it. When you got to boat 15 with these 25 people, were there any people in boat No. 15 already? Yes.

About how many, or who? Well, I can give you a rough estimate.

Yes, of course? The last 25 were passed in from the boat deck.

Your 25? Yes.

Were they mixed, women and children, or were they women? There were three children with them, my lord.

22 women and three children? The boat was then lowered to A deck. We there took in about five women, three children, and one man. He had a baby in his arms.

Five women, three children, and a man with a baby from A deck? Yes. The boat was then lowered away.

Into the water? Yes.

You were in her, as I understand? Yes.

Did you get in her from the boat deck? Yes.

At the time when your second contingent got in? After, yes.

How many people do you think were in boat No. 15 after she got into the water, and when she was saved? I would not like to vouch for its accuracy, but I can give you an estimate.

What is your estimate? I should say somewhere about 70 after we left A deck.

Another witness has told us he thinks 68? Well, it is a rough estimate, it is pretty near it.

Now let us see if you can help us as to how many members of the crew there were in boat No. 15. There is yourself, of course? Yes.

Can you tell us how many other members of the crew there were in boat No. 15? I should say about 13 or 14 all told of the crew.

There is a man named Cavell, a little short man, who is a trimmer? Yes.

Do you know him? Yes.

He was in the boat? Yes.

Do you know a bathroom steward named Rule? Yes, I know him.

He was in the boat? I saw him get out of the boat.

That will prove it. Then a man named Diamond we have heard of. He was a fireman? Yes.

Was he in the boat? Yes.

Who was in charge of her? This Diamond - at least, he had all the say, and so I take it he was in charge.

There is only one other name I have heard, that is Lewis. Was there a man named Lewis, said to be a third class steward? I no doubt know them by sight, but we had nearly 60 third class stewards, and it is rather difficult to know their names.

Then we have heard something about somebody called Jack Stewart. Is that somebody else? Well, I know the name, but I would not like to vouch for him being in the boat, as I did not see him.

I want to be sure we do justice to you. You got your second contingent, 20 or 25, into the boat. They got in before you did? Yes.

Now, were any directions given about your getting into the boat? Yes, I was ordered to get into the boat.

Please, tell us about it? After I saw my people in, the officer who had charge of the lowering away of that boat.

That was Mr Murdoch, was it not? Yes, Mr Murdoch. It was rather dark on the deck. He said, 'What are you?' I said, 'One of the crew. I have just brought these people up.' He said, 'Go ahead, get into the boat with them.'

And that is how you came to get in? Yes.

Let us take your estimate - 13 or 14 of the crew out of some 70? Yes.

That will leave us something like 55 others? Yes, or 57.

You have told us of that 55 or 56, some 25 were your contingent, your women and children that you brought up? Yes.

That is 25 out of the 55. That leaves about another 30? Yes.

And you have told us that, besides, there were taken in from the A deck five women, three children, and a man with a baby? Yes.

That knocks off 10 more? Yes.

That leaves 15 more people. Now, can you give us any idea whether those 15 remaining people were men, women, or children, or what? Yes.

Will you tell us? There were about three male passengers and the rest were women.

Do the three that you talk about include the man who came on board with a baby in his arms? No.

Then there were four men? There were four men.

Four men and 13 or 14 of the crew? Yes.

Then out of the whole boatload of 70 there were about 18 men? Yes.

And it follows that if that is right there would be about 50 women and children? Yes.

Your people that you were responsible for were third class people? Yes.

Can you tell us about the people that were taken in from the A deck, the five women and three children and the man with the baby. Do you know at all what class they belonged to? Yes.

What were they? They were also third class.

And those people who were on the boat before your contingent got into it, what class did they belong to as far as you know? I should imagine they were either first class or second.

Then it comes to this, that as far as you can tell us, it was either first or second class people who were in that boat before you got there. Then your people got in and some more people got in from A deck, and those people you think were third class people? Yes.

When you left the third class part of the ship the second time, the last time, were there any more third class passengers down there? Yes, there were some that would not come to the deck.

They would not come? They would not leave their apartments.

Of course by that time you at any rate had realised that this was a very serious accident? Yes, but they would not be convinced.

Did you do your best to convince them? Everybody did their best.

Did you hear other people trying to persuade them? Yes.

On this second journey of yours, the last journey, did you see other stewards or not engaged in getting people? Yes, I met several on the deck directing them the way to the boat deck. There was one man at the foot of the companion leading from the sleeping accommodation to the after well deck, there was one man at the end of the companion leading from the well deck to the E deck, and there were others along the saloon and second cabin deck showing them the way to the boat deck. So that there was no difficulty for anybody who wanted to get to the boats to find their way there.

There is a third class interpreter, is there not? Yes.

Did you see him about? Yes.

Some of your third class passengers are foreigners? Yes.

What was he doing? He was trying to keep some of the foreigners quiet.

We have been told that there is an emergency door that can be opened and will let people from the third class into the alleyway, so that they could use the second class companion? Yes.

You did not go by that route, I know? No.

Did you see whether or not that door was open? Yes, I could see the door was open.

Could you see whether it was being used as a means of getting from the third to the second? The people that were coming from the forward part of the ship were making right for the after well deck of the third class, and one was following in the others' train.

And would they pass through that door? No, they would have to pass that door but not through it.

What I wanted you to tell me was, whether that door which you say was open in order that people could get through, was used at all? I cannot tell you that. I saw nobody use it.

When this boat No. 15 left the boat deck with your 25 women and children in it and then you following in as Mr Murdoch told you, were there any other women and children on the boat deck there? Yes, there were some first cabin passengers.

Women? Women with their husbands, I take it.

This was the last boat to leave, at any rate, on the starboard side? Yes.

Were there men there? Yes.

A number of them? A number of them.

What was the discipline? What was the order then? Absolute quietness.

On the boat deck? Yes.

And when this last boat No. 15 got to the A deck and took in these five women and three children and the man, were there any other people on the A deck? Yes, there were some men.

Men? Yes.

Do you mean that there were only men left on the A deck? Yes.

When the boat got to the A deck did you hear any orders given or any cry raised to see whether there were women and children? Yes, there had been repeated cries before that boat was lowered, for the women and children.

And were they looked for when it reached the A deck? Well, there were stewards all round the ship. I take it that there were.

I understand you to say that so far as you know there were no other women and children on the A deck? No. I saw none.

As a matter of fact, was there any room in your boat when it left A deck, or was it full? *Witness answers:* Had there been any more women or children I take it they would have made room. Had there been any more I have no doubt a place would have been found for them, even if they had to lie on others.

Lord Mersey has just pointed out that you told us, on the boat deck where the boat left there were some women and their husbands. How was it they did not get into the boats? Because the cry was for the women and children, and the boat at that time was practically full of women and children, and these women would not leave their husbands.

That is what I wanted, that was the impression you got, was it? Yes.

Did you hear any of them say so on the boat deck? Yes.

You have told us that you were one of a number of some 60 third class stewards? Yes.

Can you tell me how many third class stewards were saved? Yes, I believe 11 or 12.

Out of 60? Yes.

And you have told me that you had about 55 or 60 people to look after in the third class cabins that were your duty? Yes.

Can you tell me of those how many were saved? I would not vouch for those that got away in other boats outside of the one that I was in myself.

Do you know how many of your own lot of people you were able to save? I would not like to say 'able to save,' but I saw in the same boat as myself those that I took to the boat - in the boat I got away in, No. 15.

And the others? They were not all mine.

They did not all come out of your section of the after part, some belonged to other stewards? Yes, other sections.

I thought you might have been able to see them afterwards on the *Carpathia*? Yes, I saw a lot of them.

I thought that you could tell us probably how many people that were under your charge were saved? I see what you mean. I should like to give you some idea. I saw about 20.

Whom you recognise as being in the cabins you had? Whom I recognised as being in my rooms.

That is 20 out of 58? Yes.

The others came from other sections. I am told I may have made a mistake, and we ought to get it right. It is the first class companion up which you came. I said it was the one near the barber's shop. Is that right or not? *Witness answers:* To tell you the truth, I did not know where the barber's shop was.

Is it the main companion? The main companion.

The big one? Yes.

And, putting it another way, it would bring him up between the first and second funnels of the ship. That is the one, Mr Hart, is it not? Yes.

At first, I take it, you were trying to assure the passengers under your charge that they were in safety? Yes.

When you realised that the position was very serious, what did you say to those people? I told the people to lose no time in getting to the boat deck.

Did you tell them the ship was sinking? No, I did not know the ship was sinking.

Even amongst the 49 women and children for whom you were responsible, did some of those go back to their quarters? Yes.

And refused to go? Yes.

When those people refused to go, did you again go back to them and tell them that those in charge knew that the ship was in a very dangerous condition? Yes. They were informed the second time I went back.

You made it perfectly clear to them? Everything was clear.

At the time you were leaving in No. 15 boat, were there rockets being sent up? Yes. Rockets had been fired some time previous to that.

You saw that yourself? I saw the rockets fired, yes.

You have told us that when you got the order to muster the women and children it was about half-past 12, you think? Somewhere about that.

Now I want you to give us your best estimate of the time when you left the ship – when the boat was lowered from the ship? When boat No. 15 was lowered?

Yes, it was the last boat, was it not? Yes.

What is your idea about the time then? I should say about a quarter after one.

You had been going between half-past 12 and a quarter-past one two or three times backwards and forwards from the deck to your quarters at K that you had charge of? Yes.

To do that you passed 'engine room casing'? I could not tell you anything about the engine room casing.

You pass along E deck, do you not? No, I did not go along E deck.

What deck were you on? I was on E deck, but I went right aft.

You never went as far as the engine room? No.

Was the electric light going all the time? Yes.

But what the engines were doing you do not know? No, the light was burning brightly.

But what the main engines were doing, you did not know? I cannot vouch for what they were doing.

Did you ever see any of the engineers on the boat deck? No. I would not know them, perhaps, if I saw them.

You would not know them at all? No.

How many officers did you see on the boat deck? You saw Mr Murdoch? *Witness answers:* I saw Mr Murdoch on two occasions, the only two occasions on which I went to the boat deck.

You never were on any deck below E deck at that time? Yes, the third class dining room is below E deck. Our own quarters are below it.

The watertight bulkheads are there and extend up to E deck, I understand? Yes.

They extend up as high as E deck. When you passed along to go to the third class dining saloon, was the watertight bulkhead in the way there, open or shut? Open.

It is F deck you are talking about? It is the deck below E deck.

It is F you are speaking of? Yes, that is where the dining room is situated, and where I was sleeping.

You were there in your berth at the time of the collision? Yes.

You went up from there to E deck? Yes.

Pretty soon? Yes, pretty soon, when I realised the ship's condition.

When you went along to get up you passed the position where the watertight bulkheads were? Yes.

Were they open or shut? Open.

Did you go down on to that deck again at any time? No.

You cannot tell us at all whether those watertight bulkheads were open or shut? No, I cannot tell you.

How long after the collision was it that you went up? Five minutes, 10 minutes, or only a few minutes? *Witness answers:* Well, after the collision, on being aroused first by a man coming from forward, a steward, he said there had been an accident, and I closed my eyes and went to sleep again. I did not believe it.

How long for, do you suppose? Oh, I should imagine somewhere about 15 or 20 minutes.

And when you left 15 or 20 minutes or longer than that, after the contact with the berg, the watertight bulkheads were open? Yes.

Did I rightly understand you to say that very shortly after the impact Kieran told you to go down to your people and rouse them up? Yes.

Did I rightly understand you also to say that you went round the whole of the two sections allotted to you? Yes.

Did you go to each of these cabins and arouse the occupants of each compartment? Yes, those that were not already aroused.

Those that were not already up or had not gone to bed. Now, I should like to know what are the means employed to prevent the third class passengers during the voyage from straying into the first and second class decks and quarters of the ship. First, are there collapsible gates? Yes, gates that can be removed. Dividing the third class deck there is a companion, dividing the second class deck and the first class deck there is a barrier.

Are those kept fastened during the course of a voyage - the barrier and the companion? No.

Are they open? Well, the barrier that lifts over and the gate that fixes in, you can just take it out with your hand. It is never locked.

Do I understand you to say that those gates are not locked at any time and the barrier is not fastened? Not to my knowledge.

So that at any time a third class passenger, by pushing the gate or by raising the barrier, can go to the second class deck or to the first class deck. Is that right? That is correct. That is, of course, if there is nobody there on watch. There usually is a quartermaster standing by there or a seaman.

Have you ever seen those gates locked? No, I was not long enough on the ship to see them locked.

I mean, any other ship. What ship were you on before you came on to this ship? I have been in the whole four of the American Line boats.

On any of the previous boats have you seen those barriers or gates locked to prevent the third class passengers straying on to the first or second class decks? You see, the ships are built differently. The American Line boats are built entirely differently from the *Titanic*.

I want to make it quite clear. Is it the usual practice on transatlantic passenger steamers to keep the gates locked and the barriers fixed so that they cannot be opened by third class passengers? I do not know of it.

Have you seen it? I have not seen it.

How many days had you been on the *Titanic* before the accident took place? What day did you join? The ship left on the 10th, on the Wednesday. I joined the ship on the Friday before the Wednesday.

You had been on board a number of days then, and during the time that you had been on board had you looked whether or not those gates were locked or the barriers fixed? No.

You had not looked? No.

Do I rightly understand you to say that you do not know whether they were locked or not? Is that the effect of your evidence? No. I fail to understand you.

You did not look whether the gates were locked or the barrier closed from the time you went on to the *Titanic* until the time of the accident. Is that so? I do not see how they could be locked. I do not think so at all.

Did you look to see whether the gates were locked or the barriers permanently fixed down? *Witness answers:* Prior to the accident?

Yes: *Witness answers:* No.

Therefore you do not know whether they were or were not? Previous to the accident I cannot answer.

Therefore at the time of the collision you do not know? No. I say previous to the accident.

They were all down, as I understand, when you were bringing the passengers away? Yes, my lord.

All three were opened? Yes, my lord.

Did you see anybody open these gates or raise these barriers? No, I did not see anybody open them, but I had to pass through them, and I saw them open.

You do not know who opened them? No.

You saw them open? Yes.

That was when you were taking up the first batch of third class passengers? Yes.

Do I gather rightly from you that it was a considerable time after the third class steward had told you to rouse up your people that you went about reassuring these people and telling them that the vessel was not hurt? No, right from the very first we were trying to convince the people that she was not hurt.

Did I understand you rightly when you said that 'A large number of men were coming from forward, from the front part of the ship. I went about among my people trying to show them that the vessel was not hurt'? *Witness answers:* Trying to 'assure' them – not to 'show' them.

I accept your correction – 'trying to assure them that the vessel was not hurt' – is that what you said? That is so.

Why did you on your own authority, after you had been told by the first class steward? *Witness answers:* By who?

By your chief third class steward to go down and rouse these people. Why did you upon your own authority go round and tell them that the vessel was not hurt? It was not on my own authority at all.

Who told you to do that? The third class steward told me to get my people about as quietly as possible.

Why did he tell you to get them up? I cannot answer why he did. I take it, on account of the collision. He must have had word that there had been an accident.

And, knowing from him that there must have been an accident, and that he considered the accident was of such a character that these people should be roused, you went round among them, and tried to assure them that the vessel was not hurt? In the first place.

Why did you do that? Because it was my instructions to.

Why? To keep them quiet. It is quite obvious.

I put it to you that it was as a result of these assurances of yours that the people refused to go up on deck? *Witness answers:* You put it to me as such?

I put it to you that as a result of these assurances given to the people they refused to leave their berths? *Witness answers:* I do not take it as such.

Was it so? It was not so. If you will pay a little attention you will find that some people were taken to the boat deck.

Please do not be impertinent. *Witness answers:* I do not wish to be impertinent.

I suggest to you that it was as a result of these assurances given by you that they were declining to leave their berths? You take it as such.

I ask you, is that so? I do not know.

How many women refused to leave their berths? Several.

Could you give us any estimate? I might if I think.

Were there half-a-dozen out of the 58? I take it there was.

You do not know? I could not vouch for the number.

Was it a small number compared with the number who came up with you? Oh, yes.

A very small number? Yes.

So that I am right in assuming that all except a small number responded to your warnings? That I can account for myself in my own part of the ship.

That it was only a small number who refused to leave? It was only a small number who refused to leave.

You have told us, I think, that there were 60 third class stewards? Yes.

How many of those 60 were in the after part of the ship? None.

Can you tell us how many were in the after, and how many were in the forward part? No.

You have no means of telling? I could not tell you.

Could you give us any estimate of the number of women and children who were in the after part of the ship – third class men, women and children? No.

Who will be able to tell me that? No doubt the White Star Line can tell you. The single men were all berthed in the fore part of the ship.

You can give us no estimate of the numbers of the third class passengers who were in the after portion? No.

And therefore you cannot tell me how many stewards were allotted to look after the third class passengers? In the after part of the ship, I can.

That is what I am asking you? Eight.

Eight stewards to look after all the third class passengers in that portion? That is for the sleeping accommodation.

It is a considerable distance, is it not, from the aft part of the ship to the boat deck? Yes.

You have told us that you saw a number of stewards placed at various portions to direct the third class passengers how they were to go? Yes.

About how many stewards were so placed? I passed about five or six on the starboard side.

Who else besides you, then, were bringing the people from their berths – rousing them and bringing them up to the boat deck? How many others? *Witness answers:* Almost eight. A portion of the third class stewards were room stewards, of whom I am the only survivor.

I understood that there were only eight third class stewards in the aft portion altogether? To look after them.

Who were stationed at various places to direct the third class passengers the way they were to go? Not of that eight.

There were five? Five others.

What class stewards were they? I could not tell you. Stewards were placed all round the ship.

Do you know who placed them there? I cannot tell you.

Do you know the stewards by sight who were placed to direct the third class passengers? No.

But you say they were not third class stewards? They were not third class stewards.

Did you see the emergency door open? I saw it open.

Do you know at what time it was opened? Yes, I can tell you. It was open at half-past 12.

Would it be right if anyone said that a number of sailors were keeping back the third class passengers from reaching the boat deck? *Witness answers:* Would it be right to do so?

Would it be right if anyone said so? I do not say that it would be right.

I asked you would it be right if anyone said so? I would not like to say it would be right.

Would it be true? I should not think so.

Did you see anyone keeping the third class passengers back, so as to prevent them getting to the boat deck? No, my lord.

You told us about a rush of men from the front part of the ship coming aft? Yes.

They were coming towards the third class quarters? Yes.

They were third class passengers? They were.

Why do you think they were coming aft? Because I saw them coming aft.

I quite realise that you saw them. But what was it caused them, do you think, to do that? Was it because they could not escape to the boat deck by the companion ladder leading to the front part of the ship? I do not believe so.

Did you ask them why they were coming aft? No, Sir, there was no occasion to ask.

Did you form any opinion at the time? I knew why they were coming aft.

That is what I want to know. Why did they come aft? Because the forward section had already taken water.

And that was the only way they could escape? Not necessarily, no. They could escape from the fore part of the ship.

Up the companion ladder would have been the nearest way for them, would not it? Yes.

But they did not do that, they chose the other way? *Witness answers:* They chose the other way?

That is rather curious, is it not? No, it is not curious at all.

Is it not? No.

That is to say, they go the whole length of the ship and come up from the well deck at the back, rather than go up the companion ladder leading from the fore deck to the boat deck? Perhaps the people did not stop to think where they were going to.

If there had been anybody to show them, they would not have had occasion to think? That may be so.

According to you - and, of course, I am not disputing the accuracy of your figures at all - you took practically the whole of your section, the greater number of them, up. You took two batches? Yes, but they were not all men.

All your own went up except the few who refused to go? All of mine went up except a few.

Except the few who you say refused to go? Yes. All went to the boat deck.

Except the few who refused to go? Yes.

With regard to the ones who went up and went back again when they found, I think you said, it was rather cold on the boat deck, did they belong to the first or second lot that you took up? *Witness answers:* How do you mean? Please say that again.

You said a number went to the boat deck and returned to their berths? They belonged to the first lot, because the second lot I saw placed in boat No. 15.

The whole of them? Yes.

How many of the first lot returned to their berths? I cannot tell you that.

You cannot give any estimate? No. I know I saw them to the boat deck.

According to you, all the women and children, from the aft part of the boat who were taken up and who wanted to escape could have done so? I do not doubt that for a moment.

Can you explain how it was, that being so, that 55 percent of the women of the third class were drowned? I cannot account for it. No, sir.

38

George Cavell, Trimmer

Trimmers ensured a constant supply of coal was delivered through to the stokers and Cavell was in a coal bunker at initial impact. This was some of the most physically demanding and low paid work on the ship. Although only seven of the 83 firemen survived this is a better survival rate than other occupations. Not one of the *Titanic's* 25 engineers or 10 electricians survived. They were operating the pumps and generators until the last possible moments giving the ship valuable extra minutes afloat and doubtless saving many lives. Note that Cavell thinks lifeboat 15 took on board passengers from two decks in addition to off the boat deck. This contrasts with Harts previous recollection.

British Board of Trade Inquiry (inquiry question is followed immediately by witness's answer) Tell us what happened? I felt a shock, Sir, and with that all the coal round me fell around me. I had a job to get out myself.

You felt a shock and the coal fell in the bunker. Did the shock knock you over? It did not have time to knock me over. The coal surrounded me before I knew where I was.

You were carried down with the coal? Yes.

And you got out? Yes.

You got out into the stokehold there, I suppose? Yes. After that I came up right up to the bunker door, and then came into the stokehold.

Is that higher up, at a higher level? Yes.

And you climbed out of that, did you? Yes.

And you got into the stokehold? I came down the ladder and came into the stokehold.

On to the plate? Yes.

When you got there did you find that the signal for 'stop' had appeared on a red disc? Yes.

Who was in charge – who would be the leading hand? A leading fireman.

In charge of No. 4? Yes.

Did you hear him give any orders, or had they been given already? I never saw him, Sir.

Did you notice – had the dampers been put in by the time you got down? No.

Now tell us what happened or what you did? After I came into the stokehold the lights in the stokehold went out.

In No. 4? Yes.

Did you notice whether the watertight doors fore and aft of your stokehold had been closed? I heard the bell go and I knew in a minute what it was for.

When the lights went out what happened? I went on deck to see what it was, and I saw people running along wet through with lifebelts in their hands. My mate said we had struck an iceberg.

How far up did you go; what deck did you go up to? The alleyway.

Was it along the alleyway that you saw the people going? Yes.

Were they passengers? Yes.

And they had lifebelts on? They had lifebelts in their hands.

This alleyway that you came up to, I think, is on E deck. Is it the working alleyway on the port side or is it the one on the starboard side? On the port side.

And to get up to it from No. 4 there was a stairway that went over the boilers and came out in the alleyway? You have to go across the boilers and up an escape ladder.

Is there a different escape ladder from each section? Yes.

Did you get into the alleyway immediately above No. 4? Yes.

When you got up into the alleyway and you saw these passengers, was there any light in the alleyway? Yes.

You said you saw people going along with lifebelts wet through, can you remember which way they were going? They were going towards after-way.

Coming from the forward end? Yes.

Could you tell what class passengers they were? I should think they were the third class passengers.

You went up, I understand, to get some lamps. Did you get them? Yes.

Did you go back to your stokehold? Yes.

With the lamps? Yes.

What about the lights in the stokehold? They were on by the time I got back.

The lights only went out for a few minutes? Yes.

There is a thing I have not asked you that I ought to have asked you before. Up to the time that you left No. 4 and went up to the alleyway, had you seen water in No. 4? No.

Not coming through the floor, or the sides, or anywhere? No.

When you came back to No. 4, and you found the lights were on again, did you see any water in No. 4? No.

When you got back to No. 4, do you remember hearing an order being given? Yes.

What was it? Draw fires.

Is that any part of a trimmer's work as a rule? In an emergency.

And did you lend a hand to draw the fires in No. 4? Yes.

And were they drawn? Partly drawn.

What would there be – 30 furnaces? Yes.

Were the firemen there helping to draw, too? Yes.

You say they were only partly drawn? Yes.

What happened then? The water started coming up over her stokehold plates.

In No. 4? Yes.

Did that happen gradually or did it happen suddenly? It came gradually.

The water did it seem to come up from below? Yes.

As far as you saw in No. 4, did any water come in from the side of the ship? Not so far as I saw.

When the water came up through the plates what was done then? We stopped as long as we could. And then I thought to myself it was time I went for the escape ladder.

They were still drawing the fires, these men, were they? Yes.

How much water were they standing in before they left? About a foot.

Working up to their knees? Yes.

Scraping the cinders out? Yes.

When you were in No. 4, as you have described, did you see anything of the engineers coming in through the emergency door behind? No.

You know what I am referring to, Cavell, do not you? Yes.

There was a watertight door behind and a watertight door before you? Yes.

As far as you knew, and as far as you observed, was the watertight door which was abaft of you raised at all? No, Sir.

There would be a lot of steam, would not there? There would.

And were all the men there working as fast as they could? Yes.

This watertight door is in a sort of tunnel, is it not? Yes.

You say you worked as long as you could, and then you came up the emergency ladder? Yes.

When you got into the alleyway where did you go? I went along on to the boat deck.

Whereabouts on the boat deck did you go? Right aft.

Did you see whether the boats had been lowered, or whether they were still there on the boat deck? There was only two boats left, and one they were lowering.

Two boats left, one had not yet been lowered, and one was being lowered? Yes.

Did you look at both sides, the port side and the starboard side? No.

Which side did you look at? The starboard side.

When you say there were only two boats left you mean there were two boats left on the starboard side? Yes.

Do you know one way or the other whether there were any left on the port side? I could not say.

The two boats you refer to were the two right aft? Right aft.

Which was the one which was being lowered? The second one from the end.

The last but one? Yes.

Were there people on the deck? They were all in the boat, barring five firemen.

Was not there anybody left on the boat deck? Only the men that lowered the boat.

No women left? I never saw any.

And the men who were lowering the boats, were they members of the crew? Yes.

Did you see any officer? Yes.

Who was he? I do not know his name.

What did you do? I stopped alongside No. 15 boat.

What happened to you after that? The officer ordered five of us into it.

And the boat was lowered? Yes.

Did it get down to the water safely? We lowered it just aft the boat deck to the first class. We called out there for women. We got a few there till we got no more, and then we lowered down to the third class, and we took more till we could get no more.

First of all, you lowered from the boat deck to what you call the first class? Yes.

Is that what one sees there, the open deck just below the boat deck? Yes.

When you got there, you say you called out for more women? Women and children.

You mean called out from the boat? Yes.

And were there people there? Only a very few came, Sir.

And when they did come, was there room for them in the boat? Plenty.

About how many? About five we got off the first class.

That is from the first class deck – A deck? Yes.

Were there any men on that deck? I never see any, Sir.

You mean that you took into your boat everybody who came on deck A? Barring what the officer may have stopped alongside the davits.

The davits would be on the boat deck? Yes.

Then you were lowered a bit further, were you? Yes.

What do you mean by saying you were lowered to the third class? To the lower deck – here [witness pointing on the model on display at the inquiry, it is not recorded which actual deck was indicated].

As it is in this model here it looks as though those decks were shut in with windows and casing. Was that so? No.

Do you remember whether when you got to this lower deck there were windows that had to be opened, or whether it was clear? No.

Which was it? All clear.

Then you called for more people there, did you? Yes.

And how many people came there? Crowds of them.

Did more come than you could take in? No.

How many do you think you took in from the lower deck? We took in about 60, Sir.

That is in addition to the five that you had taken from the boat deck, from the upper deck A? Yes.

Perhaps you can tell us this - when you were ordered in at the boat deck you and five others, was there nobody in the boat already? No.

Then it was lowered to the A deck and you took in about how many? Five.

That would make 10? Yes.

And then you are lowered to the lower deck, and you take in you think about 60? Yes.

That would make about 70? Yes.

Do you say that you took in everybody who came at that time at the lower deck? Yes.

You left nobody behind? No, Sir.

Can you tell me about these 60 - first of all were they men or women? All women and children.

Were there no men about? Yes, Sir.

You did not take them in? No, Sir.

Were they on this same lower deck? Yes.

How was that, were they standing back? Yes.

Did you see anybody there keeping order? No.

Were the men passengers, or stewards, or crew, or what? They seemed to be third class passengers.

When you say they were third class passengers what makes you think so? I generally know the difference between a third class passenger and a second.

At this rate, you did not take any second class passengers into your boat? Not to my knowledge, Sir.

Of course, the deck he is speaking of is, undoubtedly, a second class deck. That was your impression, was it? Yes.

These women that you think came from the third class, were some of them foreigners? They were Irish girls.

Then, your boat, I suppose, was as full as it would hold, was it? Yes.

Who took charge of it? One of the firemen, Diamond.

Then there was you, and were there only three others of the crew? Three more.

You pulled away from the ship a bit? Yes.

Any sailormen at all? No sailormen.

Was there anyone in that boat, No. 15, who knew about managing a boat? Five of we crew did.

Had you sufficient of a crew to row safely? We done our best, which we did, we managed her.

LIFEBOAT 2,
Port Side, Launched 1.45 a.m.

Lifeboat 2 was one of the smaller 'emergency' lifeboats with a capacity of 40. It left just two thirds full despite there being only half an hour left till *Titanic* finally sank. Fourth Officer Joseph Boxhall was in charge of this lifeboat. Boxhall had been in charge of trying to contact nearby ships by sending up emergency flares and using a Morse lamp. Lifeboat 2 is sometimes referred to as the 'signal' boat as it kept a green light burning all night. This was the first boat to be picked up by the *Carpathia* at just after 4.00 a.m. Male crew: four; male passengers: one; women and children: 21; total for lifeboat: 26 (British Board of Inquiry).

39

Mahala Douglas, First Class Passenger

Mahala Douglas was travelling with her husband Walter and her maid, Berthe Leroy. Whilst Walter did not survive, Berthe also managed to board lifeboat 2, and continued to work for Douglas for another 33 years, until Douglas' death in 1945. The 'trouble at Southampton' that Douglas refers to was *Titanic*'s near collision with the *New York* when leaving port. The description of an encounter with Bruce Ismay served to further fuel Major Peuchen's public allegation that Ismay ordered *Titanic* to speed up when ice warnings were received.

Affidavit given to the US Senate Inquiry We left Cherbourg late on account of trouble at Southampton, but once off, everything seemed to go perfectly. The boat was so luxurious, so steady, so immense, and such a marvel of mechanism that one could not believe he was on a boat – and there the danger lay. We had smooth seas, clear, starlit nights, fresh favoring winds; nothing to mar our pleasure.

On Saturday, as Mr Douglas and I were walking forward, we saw a seaman taking the temperature of the water. The deck seemed so high above the sea I was interested to know if the tiny pail could reach it. There was quite a breeze, and although the pail was weighted, it did not. This I watched from the open window of the covered deck. Drawing up the pail the seaman filled it with water from the stand pipe, placed the thermometer in it, and went with it to the officer in charge.

On Sunday we had a delightful day, everyone in the best of spirits. The time the boat was making was considered very good, and all were interested in getting into New York early. We dined in the restaurant, going in about eight o'clock. As far as I have been able to learn, not a man in that room from the head steward down, including Mr Gatti, in charge, the musicians who played in the corridor outside, and all the guests were lost except Sir Cosmo Gordon-Duff, Mr Carter and Mr Ismay. All stories of excessive gaiety are, to my mind, absolutely unfounded. We did not leave the tables until most of the others had left, including Mr Ismay, Mr and Mrs Widener, and their guests, and the evening was passed very quietly.

As we went to our stateroom, C-86, we both remarked that the boat was going faster than she ever had. The vibration as one passed the stairway in the center was very noticeable. The shock of the collision was not great to us. The engines stopped, then went on for a few moments, then stopped again. We waited some little time, Mr Douglas reassuring me that there was no danger before going out of the cabin. But later Mr Douglas went out to see what had happened, and I put on my heavy boots and fur coat to go up on deck later. I waited in the corridor to see or hear what I could. We received no orders, no one knocked at our door. We saw no officers nor stewards, no one to give an order or answer our questions. As I waited for Mr Douglas to return I went back to speak to my maid, who was in the same cabin as Mrs Carter's maid. Now people commenced to appear with life preservers, and I heard from someone that the order had been given to put them on. I took three from our cabin, gave one to the maid, telling her to get off in the small boat when her turn came. Mr Douglas met me as I was going up to find him and asked, jestingly, what I was doing with those life preservers. He did not think even then that the accident was serious. We both put them on, however, and went up on the boat deck. Mr Douglas told me if I waited we might both go together, and we stood there waiting. We heard that the boat was in communication with three other boats by wireless. We watched the distress rockets sent off – they rose high in the air and burst.

No one seemed excited. Finally, as we stood by a collapsible boat lying on the deck and an emergency boat [lifeboat 2] swinging from the davits was being filled, it was decided I should go. Mr Boxhall was trying to get the boat off, and called to the Captain on the bridge, 'There's a boat coming up over there.' The Captain said 'I want a megaphone'. Just before we got into the boat the Captain called, 'How many of the crew are in that boat? Get out of there, every man of you' and I can see a solid row of men, from bow to stern, crawl over on to the deck. We women then got in. I asked Mr Douglas to come with me, but he replied, 'No, I must be a gentleman,' turning away. I said, 'Try and get off with Mr Moore and Major Butt. They will surely make it.'

Major Butt and Clarence Moore were standing together near us, also Mr Meyer, and I remember seeing Mr Ryerson's face in the crowd. There were many people about. I got into the boat and sat under the seats on the bottom, just under the tiller. Mr Boxhall had difficulty about getting the boat loose and called for a knife. We finally were launched.

Mrs Appleton and a man from the steerage faced me. Mrs Appleton's sister was back to me, and on the seat with her, the officer. Mr Boxhall tried to have us count in order to find the number in the boat but he did not succeed in getting any higher than 10, as so many did not speak English - I think there were 18 or 20. There was one other member of the crew. The rowing was very difficult, for no one knew how. I tried to steer, under Mr Boxhall's orders, and he put the lantern - an old one, with very little light in it - on a pole which I held up for some time. Mr Boxhall got away from the ship and we stopped for a time. Several times we stopped rowing to listen for the lapping of the water against the icebergs. In an incredibly short space of time, it seemed to me, the boat sank. I heard an explosion. I watched the boat go down, and the last picture to my mind is the immense mass of black against the starlit sky, and then nothingness.

Mrs Appleton and some of the other women had been rowing and did row all of the time. Mr Boxhall had charge of the signal lights on the *Titanic*, had put in the emergency boat a tin of green lights, like rockets. These he commenced to send off at intervals, and very quickly we saw the lights of the *Carpathia*, the Captain of which stated he saw our green lights 10 miles away, and, of course, steered directly to us, so we were the first boat to arrive at the *Carpathia*.

When we pulled alongside Mr Boxhall called out, 'shut down your engines and take us aboard. I have only one sailor.' At this point I called out, 'The *Titanic* has gone down with everyone on board,' and Mr Boxhall told me to 'shut up.' This is not told in criticism. I think he was perfectly right. We climbed a rope ladder to the upper deck of the *Carpathia*. I at once asked the Chief Steward, who met us, to take the news to the Captain. He said the officer was already with him.

The history of our wonderful treatment on the *Carpathia* is known to the world. It has been underestimated. We reached the *Carpathia* at 4.10 a.m., and I believe by 10 o'clock all of the boats had been accounted for. We sailed away, leaving the *Californian* to cruise about the scene. We circled the point where the *Titanic* had gone down, and I saw nothing except quantities of cork, loose cork floating in the current, like a stream, nothing else. In the afternoon I sent a brief Marconigram with the news that Mr Douglas was among the missing. I went myself to the purser several times every day, and others also made inquiries for me in regard to it, but it was not sent.

We heard many stories of the rescue from many sources. These I tried to keep in my mind clearly, as they seemed important. Among them I will quote Mrs Ryerson, of Philadelphia. This story was told in the presence of Mrs Meyers of New York, and others. Emily Ryerson:

'Sunday afternoon Mr Ismay, whom I know very slightly, passed me on the deck. He showed me, in his brusque manner, a Marconigram, saying, 'We have just had news that we are in the icebergs.'

'Of course, you will slow down,' I said. 'Oh, no' he replied, 'we will put on more boilers and get out of it.'

An Englishwoman, who was going to her sons in Dakota, told me:

'I was in a boat with five women and 50 men - they had been picked up from the London unemployed to fill out the crew. They would not row, told frightful stories to alarm the women, and when the *Carpathia* was sighted, said; 'We are jolly lucky. No work tonight; nothing to do but smoke and yarn. Back in London next week with the unemployed.'

Major Peuchen came to me just before landing in New York with Mr Beattie, of the London *Times*. They asked me to repeat some things I had said, which I did. They took my address. Major Peuchen said:

'I have just been called up (I took this to mean before the officers of the *Titanic*) and asked what I meant by getting testimony and stirring up the passengers. I replied, you have not answered my questions. I will not answer yours.'

All the women told of insufficient seamen to man the boats, all women rowed, some had to bail water from their boats. Mrs Smith was told to watch a cork in her boat, and if it came out to put her finger in place of it.

When we arrived in New York the crew of the *Titanic* was ordered to get off in the lifeboats before we could dock.

I sat in a deck chair and listened and looked. The unseamanlike way of going at their simple tasks without excitement showed me more plainly than anything I had seen or heard the inefficiency of the crew, and accounted, in some measure, for the number of the crew saved and the unfilled lifeboats. A passenger on the *Carpathia* also spoke to me of this.

Mr Lightoller and Mr Boxhall were extremely courteous and kind on board the *Carpathia*. I think them both capable seamen and gentlemen.

40

Joseph Boxhall, Fourth Officer

Joseph Boxhall was off duty at the point of collision but quickly made his way up to the bridge after hearing the lookout bell ring. Boxhall was then sent to find the ship's carpenter Thomas Andrews and to ascertain the level of damage. Boxhall then reports seeing a 'steamer' in the distance and tried in vain to contact the ship by both distress flare and Morse lamp. When aboard lifeboat 2 Boxhall launched flares to guide the *Carpathia* towards them. Boxhall lived to be 83 and before his death asked that his ashes were scattered in the spot where the *Titanic* went down.

British Board of Trade Inquiry (inquiry question is followed immediately by witness's answer) Did you hear an order given by the First Officer? I heard the First Officer give the order, 'Hard-a-starboard,' and I heard the engine room telegraph bells ringing.

Was that before you felt the shock, or afterwards? Just a moment before.

Did you go on to the bridge immediately after the impact? I was almost on the bridge when she struck.

Did you notice what the telegraphs indicated with regard to the engines? 'Full speed astern,' both.

Was that immediately after the impact? Yes.

Did you see anything done with regard to the watertight doors? I saw Mr Murdoch closing them then, pulling the lever.

And did the Captain then come out on to the bridge? The Captain was alongside of me when I turned round.

Did you hear him say something to the First Officer? Yes, he asked him what we had struck.

What conversation took place between them? The First Officer said, 'An iceberg, Sir. I hard-a-starboarded and reversed the engines, and I was going to hard-a-port round it but she was too close. I could not do any more. I have closed the watertight doors.' The Commander asked him if he had rung the warning bell, and he said 'Yes.'

Did the Captain and the First Officer go to the starboard side of the bridge to see if they could see the iceberg? Yes.

Did you see it yourself? I was not too sure of seeing it. I had just come out of the light, and my eyes were not accustomed to the darkness.

What did you do next, did you leave the deck? Yes, I went down forward, down into the third class accommodation, right forward on to the lowest deck of all with passenger accommodation, and walked along these looking for damage.

That would be F deck, would it not? Yes, F deck. I walked along there for a little distance just about where I thought she had struck.

Did you find any signs of damage? No, I did not. It was the lowest deck I could get to without going into the cargo space.

How did you get down to the lowest of these decks which you went to? Through a staircase under the port side of the forecastle head which takes me down into D deck, and then walked along aft along D deck to just underneath the bridge, and down the staircase there on the port side, and then I am down on E deck near E deck doors, the working alleyway, and then you cross over to the starboard side of E deck and go down another accommodation staircase on to F deck. I am not sure whether I went lower. Anyhow, I went as low as I could possibly get.

Did you then go up again through the other decks as far as C deck? I came up the same way as I went down.

Without noticing any damage? I did not see any damage whatever.

When you got to C deck did you see some ice there on the deck? Yes, I took a piece of ice out of a man's hand, a small piece about as large as a small basin, I suppose, very small. He was going down again to the passenger accommodation, and I took it from him and walked across the deck to see where he got it. I found just a little ice in the well deck covering a space of about three or four feet from the bulwarks right along the well deck, small stuff.

Did you then go and report to the Captain? I went on to the bridge and reported to the Captain and First Officer that I had seen no damage whatever.

Did the Captain then tell you to find the carpenter? Yes, I think we stayed on the bridge just for a moment or two, probably a couple of minutes, and then he told me to find the carpenter and tell him to sound the ship forward.

Did you find the carpenter? I met the carpenter. I think it would be on the ladder leading from the bridge down to A deck, and he wanted to know where the Captain was. I told him he was on the bridge.

Did the carpenter tell you anything about there being water? Yes, he did. He said the ship was making water fast, and he passed it on to the bridge.

What did you do? I continued with the intention of finding out where the water was coming in, and I met one of the mail clerks, a man of the name of Smith.

Did he say something? He also asked for the Captain, and said the mail hold was filling. I told him where he could find the Captain and I went down to the mail room. I went down the same way as I did when I visited the third class accommodation previously. I went down as far as E deck and went to the starboard alleyway on E deck and the watertight door stopped me getting through.

The watertight door on E deck was closed? Yes. Then I crossed over and went into the working alleyway and so into the mail room.

What did you find in the mail room? I went down in the mail room and found the water was within a couple of feet of G deck, the deck I was standing on.

The mail room is between the Orlop deck and G deck? Yes, that is the mail hold.

Was the water rising or stationary? It was rising rapidly up the ladder and I could hear it rushing in.

Did you go back and report that to the Captain on the bridge? I stayed there just for a minute or two and had a look. I saw mail bags floating around on deck. I saw it was no use trying to get them out so I went back again to the bridge. I met the Second Steward, Mr Dodd, on my way to the bridge – as a matter of fact in the saloon companion way – and he asked me about sending men down below for those mails. I said 'You had better wait till I go to the bridge and find what we can do.' I went to the bridge and reported to the Captain.

We have been told that at some time you called the other officers. Both Mr Lightoller and Mr Pitman said you called them? I did. That was after I reported to the Captain about the mail room.

Could you form any opinion as to how long that was after the impact? No, but as near as I could judge. I have tried to place the time for it, and the nearest I can get to it is approximately 20 minutes to half-an-hour.

I think those are the times which are given by Mr Pitman and Mr Lightoller. After calling those officers did you go on to the bridge again? Yes, I think I went towards the bridge, I am not sure whether it was then that I heard the order given to clear the boats or unlace the covers. I might have been on the bridge for a few minutes and then heard this order given.

Had you a boat station of your own, did you know what it was? I did not know what it was.

We have been told it is customary for the third and fourth officers to be assigned to the emergency boats? Yes, it is for emergency purposes.

The Third Officer was assigned to No. 1. Were you assigned to No. 2? For emergency purposes I was assigned to No. 1 as a matter of fact, the starboard boat.

When the order was given to clear the boats what did you do, did you go to any particular boat? No, I went right along the line of boats and I saw the men starting, the watch on deck, our watch.

Which side of the ship? The port side, I went along the port side, and afterwards I was down the starboard side as well but for how long I cannot remember. I was unlacing covers on the port side myself and I saw a lot of men come along – the watch I presume. They started to screw some out on the after part of the port side. I was just going along there and seeing all the men were well established with their work, well under way with it, and I heard someone report a light, a light ahead. I went on the bridge and had a look to see what the light was.

Someone reported a light ahead? Yes. I do not know who reported it. There were quite a lot of men on the bridge at the time.

Did you see the light? Yes, I saw a light.

What sort of light was it? It was two masthead lights of a steamer. But before I saw this light I went to the chart room and worked out the ship's position.

Is that the position we have been given already - 41 deg. 46 min. N., 50 deg. 14 min. W? That is right, but after seeing the men continuing with their work I saw all the officers were out, and I went into the chart room to work out its position.

Was it after that you saw this light? It was after that, yes, because I must have been to the Marconi office with the position after I saw the light.

You took it to the Marconi office in order that it might be sent by the Wireless Operator? I submitted the position to the Captain first, and he told me to take it to the Marconi room.

And then you saw this light which you say looked like a masthead light? Yes, it was two masthead lights of a steamer.

Could you see it distinctly with the naked eye? No, I could see the light with the naked eye, but I could not define what it was, but by the aid of a pair of glasses I found it was the two masthead lights of a vessel, probably about half a point on the port bow, and in the position she would be showing her red if it were visible, but she was too far off then.

Could you see how far off she was? No, I could not see, but I had sent in the meantime for some rockets, and told the Captain I had sent for some rockets, and told him I would send them off, and told him when I saw this light. He said, 'Yes, carry on with it.' I was sending rockets off and watching this steamer. Between the time of sending the rockets off and watching the steamer approach us I was making myself generally useful round the port side of the deck.

How many rockets did you send up about? I could not say, between half a dozen and a dozen, I should say, as near as I could tell.

What sort of rockets were they? The socket distress signal.

Can you describe what the effect of those rockets is in the sky, what do they do? You see a luminous tail behind them and then they explode in the air and burst into stars.

Did you send them up at intervals one at a time? One at a time, yes.

At about what kind of intervals? Well, probably five minutes. I did not take any times.

Did you watch the lights of this steamer while you were sending the rockets up? Yes.

Did they seem to be stationary? I was paying most of my attention to this steamer then, and she was approaching us, and then I saw her sidelights. I saw her green light and the red. She was end-on to us. Later I saw her red light. This is all with the aid of a pair of glasses up to now. Afterwards I saw the ship's red light with my naked eye, and the two masthead lights. The only description of the ship that I could give is that she was, or I judged her to be, a four-masted steamer.

Why did you judge that? By the position of her masthead lights. They were close together.

Did the ship make any sort of answer, as far as you could see, to your rockets? I did not see it. Some people say she did, and others say she did not. There were a lot of men on the bridge. I had a quartermaster with me, and the Captain was standing by, at different times, watching this steamer.

Do you mean you heard someone say she was answering your signals? Yes, I did, and then she got close enough, and I Morsed to her – used our Morse lamp.

When people said to you that your signals were being answered, did they say how they were being answered? I think I heard somebody say that she showed a light.

Do you mean that she would be using a Morse lamp? Quite probably.

Then you thought she was near enough to Morse her from the *Titanic*? Yes, I do think so.

What distance did you suppose her to be away? I judged her to be between five and six miles when I Morsed to her, and then she turned round – she was turning very, very slowly – until at last I only saw her stern light, and that was just before I went away in the boat.

Did she make any sort of answer to your Morse signals? I did not see any answer whatever.

Did anyone else, so far as you know, see an answer? Some people say they saw lights, but I did not.

Did they think they saw them Morsing in answer to your Morse signals? Did anyone say that? They did not say she Morsed, but they said she showed a light. Then I got the quartermaster who was with me to call her up with our lamps, so that I could use the glasses to see if I could see signs of any answer, but I could not see any.

You could not see any with the glasses? No, and Captain Smith also looked, and he could not see any answer.

He also looked at her through the glasses? Yes.

After a time you saw what you took to be the stern light of a ship? It was the stern light of the ship.

Did you infer from that that the ship was turned round, and was going in the opposite direction? Yes.

When you first saw her, I understand you to say she was approaching you? She was approaching us, yes.

For about how long did you signal before it seemed to you that she turned round? I cannot say. I cannot judge any of the times at all.

Do you know at all whether the *Titanic* was swinging at this time? No, I do not see how it was possible for the *Titanic* to be swinging after the engines were stopped. I forget when it was I noticed the engines were stopped, but I did notice it; and there was absolutely nothing to cause the *Titanic* to swing.

After sending up those signals for some time did you turn your attention to the boats? I was sending the rockets up right to the very last minute when I was sent away in the boat.

When you say right up to the last minute, can you give me any idea of what you mean by that? Yes, right up to the time I was sent away in the boat.

How long before the vessel sank were you sent away in the boat? I cannot give the time, but I have approximated it nearly half-an-hour, as near as I could tell.

What boat was it you were sent away in? In the emergency boat No. 2.

It would be about a quarter to 2. Who was superintending the filling of that boat? Mr Wilde, or, I presume, Mr Wilde was superintending the filling. The order was given to lower away when I was told to go in it and the boat was full. They had started the tackles when I got in.

Did you notice what other boats there were on the port side at the time? There was only one boat hanging there in the davits, No. 4.

That was the boat next to yours? Yes.

Can you say how many people were in that boat No. 2? I endeavoured to count them, but I did not succeed very well. I judge between 25 and 30 were in her.

Were they mostly women, or were they mixed men and women? The majority were women. I know there were three crew, one male passenger, and myself.

And you think the rest were women? They were. There were several children in the boat.

Did you notice when the people were being put in that boat No. 2 whether there were many passengers on deck at the time, round about? I did not notice the passengers being put into the boat. I was not taking any notice of the boat at all, until I was sent to her.

Did you notice whether there were passengers on the deck at the time the boat was lowered? Yes, there were passengers round the deck, but I noticed as I was being lowered that they were filling No. 4 boat.

Were there any women about? I did not see any women.

I do not know whether you can say with regard to the starboard boats at all whether there were any starboard boats on the *Titanic* at this time, or whether they had all gone? No, I cannot say. I know the starboard emergency boat had gone some time, and that they were working on the collapsible boats when I went, because I fired the distress signals from the socket in the rail just close to the bows of the emergency boat on the starboard side. Every time I fired a signal I had to clear everybody away from the vicinity of this socket, and then I remember the last one or two distress signals I sent off the boat had gone, and they were then working on the collapsible boat which was on the deck.

Had you any lamp in your boat No. 2? Yes.

Had you put that in yourself or did you find it there? There is always a lamp in the emergency boats.

Lamps are always kept there? They are lighted every night at six o'clock.

Do you mean they are not kept in the other boats usually? They were not kept in the other boats, no.

Did you see any put in the other boats? Yes.

Was that by your orders? Well, it was through my speaking to the Chief Officer about it. I mentioned to him that there were no lamps. That was earlier on, when they started to clear the boats. I mentioned to him the fact that there were no lamps in any of the boats, or compasses, and he told me to get hold of the lamp trimmer.

When did you notice this? Oh, shortly after the orders were given to clear the boats.

You said 'in any of the boats.' Did you examine all the boats? *Witness answers:* Did I examine the boats after the accident?

Yes? *Witness answers:* No, I did not.

Then you cannot speak from your knowledge? I examined the boats on purpose. The lamps were in the lamp room then.

The lamps are in the lamp room. The compasses are apparently kept in some locker. That is right, is it? Yes.

Did you have the lamps taken up? Yes. The Chief Officer told me to find the lamp trimmer. I did find him after a little trouble. I really forget where I found him. He was on the boat deck working amongst the men. I told him to take a couple of men down with him and fetch the lamps, and he was afterwards seen to bring the lamps along the deck and put them in the boats.

Do you know how many lamps were put into how many boats? No, I do not know.

In your boat did you also put in some green lights? Yes, there were some green lights lying in the wheelhouse. I told the quartermaster or someone who was around there to put them in the boat.

Was any order given to you when you were lowered with regard to what you should do when you got into the water? No, I do not remember any.

What did you do when you got into the water? I pulled a little way from the ship, probably 100 feet away from the ship, and remained there for a while.

How long did you remain there, did you remain there until the ship sank? Oh, no, I did not. I did not remain there very long. I got the crew squared up and the oars out properly and the boat squared when I heard somebody singing out from the ship, I do not know who it was, with a megaphone, for some of the boats to come back again, and to the best of my recollection they said 'Come round the starboard side,' so I pulled round the starboard side to the stern and had a little difficulty in getting round there.

Why was that, because you had not enough people to row? I had not enough people. My boat was rather deep. I had only one man who seemed to understand boat orders. I was pulling the stroke oar and trying to steer the boat at the same time myself.

There was only one seaman in your boat? That is all.

Do you know whether there was a man named Osman? Yes, Osman or Osram [Frank Osman, see following chapter 41], or something like that.

Who else rowed besides you and the seaman? You were rowing and steering at the same time? *Witness answers:* Everybody was rowing with the exception of a male passenger. He did not seem to do much.

You have told us there were two stewards or a steward and a sculleryman. They were both rowing? Oh, yes, they were rowing.

With some difficulty you rowed round to the starboard side of the ship? Yes, round the stern.

What did you do when you got round to the starboard side? Well, I stayed round on the starboard side, probably about 200 feet [*c.* 60 metres] away from the ship. I found there was a little suction and I decided that it was very unwise to have gone back to the ship so I pulled away.

Why was there suction at this time? The ship settling down badly, I suppose.

Was it settling down rapidly. Could you see it settling down at this time? Yes, I could see her settling down. I was watching the lines of lights.

She was settling down by the head? She was settling down by the head, my lord.

Where were you at this time? Just a little, probably 200 feet, on the starboard beam of the ship, or probably a little abaft the starboard beam of the ship.

Would there be any suction there? Well, I felt it. I saw it by the work we had pulling it round the ship's stern, seeing she was only a small boat, I judged there was quite a lot of suction.

Did you remain in that position, about 200 feet away from the ship, until she sank? No, I did not. I turned the boat away and pulled in a north-easterly direction.

You mean, you pulled further away from the ship? Yes.

How far were you from the ship when she did sink? Approximately, half-a-mile [*c.* 800 meters].

That means that you could not see what happened? No, I could not.

After she sank, did you hear cries? Yes, I heard cries. I did not know when the lights went out that the ship had sunk. I saw the lights go out, but I did not know whether she had sunk or not, and then I heard the cries. I was showing green lights in the boat then, to try and get the other boats together, trying to keep us all together.

Were there other boats round about near yours? I could not see any boats, not when I had got so far away as that. Some of them had gone in a more northerly direction than I had gone.

Did you go back at all towards the ship, when you heard those cries? No, I did not.

Was any suggestion made of going back? There was a suggestion made. I spoke about going back to the sailor man that was in the boat – that was whilst I was pulling round the stern – about going back to the ship, and then I decided that it was very unwise to have attempted it. So we pulled away, and then we did not pull back at all.

What did you intend to go back to the ship for? I intended to go back to try and obey orders that I heard given through the megaphone.

Was that to stand by the gangway door or what? I do not know whether it was to stand by the gangway door. I do not remember any gangway doors being open.

What were the orders? Just simply to come round to the starboard side.

Why was it dangerous to try to do that, was it the suction? The suction and the chance of the boat, by not being properly manned, being rushed and losing everybody in the boat. I did not think it was possible to get any more than three people in the boat.

Three more people? Yes, I thought I could get about three more in, and that is all. I gave the men orders I intended to put the boat bow-on to the ship, and I gave orders to back water as soon as I told them.

So you did not go back? No.

Did not you see anyone in the water at all? No, there was no one in the water at all.

Did you see people in the water later? No, I did not see anyone in the water at all.

Did you meet with any of the other boats later on? I did not see any boat near us, although I was showing these green lights occasionally, with the intention of getting all the boats together. There was not a boat anywhere near us. I did not see any. I was the first boat picked up on board the *Carpathia*.

You were the first picked up? Yes. He saw our green lights and steamed down for them.

Did you watch all the other boats being picked up after you got on board the *Carpathia*? I was down in the other boats. I suppose a good half-an-hour had elapsed before any of the other boats were there.

Can you tell us how many boats were picked up by the *Carpathia*? No, I did not count them. They counted them, but all our boats were picked up with the exception of the one collapsible boat, where the crew were taken out of her in a sinking condition.

One collapsible boat and two lifeboats, did you say? Yes.

When I say picked up I do not mean taken on board. We know 13 were taken on board, but I mean how many were accounted for? I really forget now how many were accounted for. I remember we turned some of them adrift.

Did you see any ice when the day broke? Yes, I saw quite a lot of ice at daybreak.

Large bergs, did you see? The first ice I saw, I saw it probably about half-a-mile on the port bow of the *Carpathia* just as I was approaching it, when I got about two ships' lengths away from her. Day was breaking then.

After the collision I understand that you and some other officers went on the bridge to look at the iceberg. Is that so? That is so. Yes.

And you saw the iceberg? Well, I was not quite sure of seeing it.

What length of time was this after the collision? Only a couple of minutes afterwards.

What distance from you did the iceberg appear to be then? I do not think it would be a couple of minutes afterwards. It appeared to me, what I fancy I saw, about a ship's length away from the ship's bridge.

Now, you were examined in America in regard to the appearance which the iceberg presented at that distance? Yes.

Would you give your impression of it to my lord? Yes, I said I fancied I saw a black mass, a low-lying black mass on the quarter.

Was it difficult to discern what the object was even at that short distance, a ship's length? That is only an approximate distance you understand, it might have been more.

It might have been three ship's lengths? It might have been three ship's lengths.

Would that be the outside, three ship's lengths? No, I am not sure. You must understand I had just come out of the light into the darkness and my eyes were not accustomed to it.

I also recollect that we have been told in the evidence that after the collision you went astern? The engines were going full speed astern for quite a little time.

Did you go forward after that? Not that I know of.

So that from the place where the collision occurred you had not moved much up to the time you went on the bridge to look for this iceberg? No, I do not think the ship could have gone so very far.

So that you were within a few ships' lengths of her probably? Yes.

Is it your evidence that even at that distance it was very difficult to make out that this was an iceberg – to make out what it was? To make out what it was, yes.

Was that on account of the weather conditions or the condition of the atmosphere? I think it was due to the conditions that were then prevailing at the time, a calm oily sea.

It appears to me to be more due to the fact that he had come out of the light room. Besides you who else were on the bridge? Mr Murdoch and Captain Smith.

They had not been in the lighted chart room up to that time? Not that I know of. Mr Murdoch and Captain Smith were on the bridge as far as I know when I went there.

Was Mr Murdoch standing with you while you were observing the iceberg? Yes, he pointed at it – like that.

How long were you watching it? That I cannot say. It was not very long because I went down below into the passengers' accommodation.

A couple of minutes? I am not going to stick to minutes. I do not know what it was.

Before you took your eyes off this iceberg had you been there a sufficient length of time to accustom your eyes to the difference in light from the chart room to the bridge? No, I do not say so.

Just tell me about a few matters, if you can. When you came from where you had been making those observations, you heard the order 'Hard-a-starboard,' and you felt the shock of the collision? Yes, there was not much of a shock to feel.

But you felt the collision? Yes.

And you knew the engines were reversed, full speed astern? I heard the bells ring, but I did not know what the movement was until I got to the bridge.

And then you knew that the collision bulkheads were closed because you heard the bell ring? No, I did not hear the bell ring. I saw Mr Murdoch pulling the lever.

I thought you told my Lord that you heard the warning bell ring? No.

You heard the Captain ask? I heard the Captain ask.

Whether the warning bell had been rung? Yes.

You had already got that knowledge. Now you left the bridge to go down below to see what damage was done? To see if I could find any damage.

When you left do you know if the engines were still reversing or had they stopped? I cannot say.

Perhaps you can tell us in this way. Was steam blowing off then? No, I cannot tell you that either.

When you came back was steam blowing off? Yes, it was when I came back.

How long were you away, do you think? I could not say.

A quarter of an hour or 20 minutes? Oh, no.

Less? You can give us an idea, 10 minutes? *Witness answers:* I do not think I should be 10 minutes.

Something less than 10 minutes, five minutes? Somewhere between five and 10 minutes.

Now, having come back, then you were on the bridge obeying orders and letting off rockets? I went down to the mail room after that.

Yes, you went down again? Yes.

How long before you went down to the mail room again, 5 or 10 minutes? Almost immediately.

And then you came up again on to the bridge? Yes.

Not having been away very long, I suppose? No, I had not been down in the mail room very long. I spent a little more time there than when I went down the first time.

And then you came up and reported to the Commander? Yes.

What did he say? He walked away and left me. He went off the bridge, as far as I remember.

He did not say anything to you that was fixed in your memory? No.

Now do you know if anything was done in regard to the collision bulkheads after that? No, the last movement that I saw was the First Officer closing them.

And you know nothing more about them after that? Nothing further.

Now I want to ask you one or two other matters. Certain orders were given with regard to getting up women and children, and so forth, between that time and the sinking of the vessel? Yes.

Did you know those orders were being given? I cannot say that I heard them. I never heard an order for any boat to be lowered, or even for women to be put in. The only order I heard was clearing the boats, and then I was employed the greater part of my time with these rockets on the bridge. I know very little about it.

Except the order for clearing the boats, which came very early in the proceedings? Yes. I knew one of the boats had gone away, because I happened to be putting the firing lanyard inside the well-house after sending off a rocket, and the telephone bell rang. Somebody telephoned to say that one of the starboard boats had left the ship, and I was rather surprised.

At their doing it so quickly? No, I was rather surprised. I did not know the order had been given even to fill the boats. I reported it to the Commander.

You had only heard the order, 'Clear away,' and the next thing was a telephone message that the starboard boat had left the ship? Yes, the starboard after boat.

Do you know anything about any other general order that was given except the order, 'Clear away'? No.

Some evidence has been given by one witness – I think it was the baker – that at some stage an order was given that all hands were to look after themselves. Did you ever hear that order? No, I did not.

I do not think you heard any general order after the one you heard for clearing the boats? No.

It was directed to finding out whether the engineers were doing their duty at the time of the sinking or not. Did you see any of the engineers on deck at all when you were attending to your boat? No.

Not one? No.

Did you hear the Captain say anything to anybody about the ship being doomed?

The Captain did remark something to me in the earlier part of the evening after the order had been given to clear the boats. I encountered him when reporting something to him, or something, and he was inquiring about the men going on with the work, and I said, 'Yes, they are carrying on all right.' I said, 'Is it really serious?' He said, 'Mr Andrews tells me he gives her from an hour to an hour-and-a-half.' That must have been some little time afterwards. Evidently Mr Andrews had been down.

Can you tell us how long it was after the collision that the Captain said that? No, I have not the slightest idea.

Did you say as a matter of fact in America that it was about 20 minutes after the collision? No, I do not think so.

In addition to the difficulties you had to contend with which you have spoken of, the lack of proper crew and the suction, had you also a number of foreigners in your boat? Yes, there was a foreign family.

Had you a number of foreigners in your boat? Yes, there was a foreign family I knew of, that were close to the after part of the boat, where I was standing.

Were they a foreign family that could understand English? No, they did not seem to be able to speak English or understand English.

Did you find there were people totally incapable of understanding any orders you might give to them? They were.

And if you had had to manoeuvre the boat to get more people in, it would have added to your difficulties? Yes, I think so.

41

Frank Osman, Able Seaman

38 at the time of the inquiry, Frank Osman had been in the navy for 11 years prior to joining the White Star Line. His description of seeing a mass of 'steerage passengers' climbing up the *Titanic* as she went down echoes that of other survivor accounts.

US Senate Inquiry (inquiry question is followed immediately by witness's answer) Where were you when the collision occurred? Outside the seamen's dining room.

Tell us what happened. *Witness answers:* I was waiting for one bell, which they strike, one bell just before the quarter of the hour, before the four hours, when you get a call to relieve; and I heard three bells strike, and I thought there was a ship ahead. Just after that I heard the collision, and I went out in the foresquare, that is, the fore well deck, just against the seamen's mess room. Looking in the fore well square I saw ice was there. I went down below and stepped down there, and seen the ship was getting a bit of a list. Then they passed the order that all the seamen had to go up and clear away all the boats. All of us went up and cleared away the boats. After that we loaded all the boats there were, and I went away in No. 2 boat, the fourth from the last to leave the ship.

Who had command of that boat? The Fourth Officer, Mr Boxhall.

Did he direct the loading of the boat? No, sir the Chief Officer, Mr Murdoch.

How many were in that boat? First the seamen and then the passengers. *Witness answers:* There was one able seaman, sir, a cook, and a steward, and an officer. That was all the men there was in the boat out of the crew. There was one man, a third class passenger, and the remainder were women and children.

You were the able seaman? Yes, sir.

How many women were in the boat? I could not say exactly how many there were, but there were between 25 and 30, all told.

Including the seamen? Including the crew. This was one of the emergency boats.

Did you have any trouble in lowering the boat? No, sir. The boat went down very easy, very steady indeed.

Was it full? Yes sir, full right up.

Did you get along comfortably or was there suffering? There was only one lady there, a first class passenger – I did not know her name – who was worrying. That was the only thing that was said.

In what order were you taken on to the *Carpathia*? I was the first boat back, sir. After I got in the boat the officer found a bunch of rockets, which was put in the boat by mistake for a box of biscuits. Having them in the boat, the officer fired some off, and the *Carpathia* came to us first and picked us up a half an hour before anybody else.

Did you steer for a light? No sir, we saw a light but the other boats were making for it and the officer was not sure whether it was a light or whether it was not, and as he had the rockets they could repeat the signals.

Did you see that light? Yes sir.

What did you think it was? I thought it was a sailing vessel from the banks.

When did you last have a sight of that light? About an hour afterwards.

What do you think about it? Did it sail away? *Witness answers:* Yes sir she sailed right away.

What was it, a stern light? No sir, a masthead light.

Does a sailing ship have a white light on her masthead? Yes sir.

Just what happened when you were on the boat? Did you see this iceberg? *Witness answers:* Not until the morning.

Are you sure it was the one? Yes sir you could see it was the one.

How high was it? At a rough estimate it was 100 feet out of the water.

What shape was it? It was round, and then had one big point sticking up on one side of it.

What was its colour? It was apparently dark, like dirty ice.

How far away from it were you when you saw it? About 100 yards.

How did you know that was the one you struck? We could see it was the biggest berg there, and the other ones would not have done so much damage, I think.

Was there any mark on the side, as if it had collided with something? It looked as if there was a piece broken off after she struck, and the ice fell on board. I went and picked up a piece of ice and took it down below in my sleeping room.

There was some little time that you were down below, was there not? Yes, sir a matter of 10 minutes.

I do not see, quite, how you account for all the time after the collision before you took to the boat. *Witness answers:* It is only just like walking out of the door.

About what time was this boat lowered in which you went away? I could not say exactly the time.

About how long after the collision? About an hour, I suppose – an hour-and-a-half.

You say the boat listed. Did it list to the port or the starboard? To the starboard.

How much? A gradual list, it was, four or five degrees.

Was there any panic? No, there was no panic at all. I was helping women and children in the boat and the crew was lowering boats.

When you were down on that lower deck, did you see persons moving about there? No, there was nobody there at all, because Mr Murdoch was singing out, 'Is there any more women and children here to put in my boat?'

I mean, before you went up to man the boat, were there any people moving about where you were, down on the lower deck? Oh, no, sir there was nobody there.

Where are the seamen's quarters? Up here, underneath the forecastle head.

They are on the upper deck, underneath the forecastle head? That is it sir.

How many seaman are there? 44, altogether.

You did not have all the boat's crew there, then; there are more than 44 in the crew, are there not? You mean by that able seamen, do you not? *Witness answers:* Yes sir.

You do not mean quartermasters, and such as that? No. I do not count quartermasters with the seamen.

Do you count lookout men with the able seamen? Yes. They all live in the same place. But the quartermaster is in a different place, on the other side.

You do not mean that those were all of the crew, even excluding the quartermasters, do you? That is all there is in the crew, sir.

Just count those again? There was 25 altogether in both watches, 13 in one watch and 12 in the other; then there was two deckmen, the cook of the forecastle, two window cleaners, six lookout men, and two masters-at-arms counted with the seamen.

You are just counting the men in your mess? Yes sir.

How many quartermasters? Six quartermasters. One boatswain, boatswain's mate, carpenter, and joiner.

How far were you away from the boat when she sank? 60 to 100 yards.

Was there much suction? There was no suction whatever. When we were in the boat we shoved off from the ship, and I said to the officer, 'See if you can get alongside to see if you can get any more hands, to see if you can squeeze any more hands in.' So the women then started to getting nervous after I said that, and the officer said 'All right.' The women disagreed to that. We pulled around to the starboard side of the ship and found we could not get to the starboard side because it was listing too far. We pulled astern that way again, and after we got astern we lay on our oars and saw the ship go down. After she got to a certain angle she exploded, broke in halves, and it seemed to me as if all the engines and everything that was in the after part slid out into the forward part, and the after part came up right again, and as soon as it came up right down it went again.

What do you think those explosions were? The boilers bursting.

What makes you think that? The cold water coming under the red-hot boilers caused the explosions.

You reasoned that out? Yes, but you could see the explosions by the smoke coming right up the funnels.

Did you see any steam and smoke coming? Yes.

Did you see any sparks? It was all black, looked like as if it was lumps of coal, and all that.

Coming up through the funnels? Through the funnels.

That is, there was a great amount of black smoke coming up through the funnels just after this explosion? Just after the explosion.

Why did you not go back to the place where the boat had sunk after she had gone down? The women were all nervous and we pulled around as far as we could get to her, so that the women would not see, and it would not cause a panic, and we got as close as we would dare to by the women. We could not have taken any more hands into the boat, it was impossible. We might have got one in. That is about all. The steerage passengers were all down below, and after she got a certain distance it seemed to me all the passengers climbed up her.

Steerage passengers, too? All the passengers there were.

That were left on board? Yes.

Did you see any of them climb up there? It looked blacker. She was white around there (indicating), and it looked like a big crowd of people.

Then you think the passengers, first, second, and third class, went up on the top deck? On the top deck yes.

Was there any panic amongst these steerage passengers when they started manning the boats? No. I saw several people come up from there, and go straight up on the boat deck. That is one thing I saw and the men stood back while the women and children got in the boat.

Steerage passengers, as well as others? One steerage passenger, a man, and his wife and two children, were in my boat, all belonged to the one family.

You took the man? Yes, that was the only man passenger we had in the boat.

What do you think? Do you think they believed the ship would float? *Witness answers:* I thought so, myself. I thought it was going down a certain depth, and would float after that.

Did you hear any conversation around among the passengers as to whether she would sink or not? No. I never heard anything amongst the passengers as to whether she would sink. The only thing I heard was one passenger was saying he was not going in the boat, and stand by the ship.

You heard one passenger say that? Yes.

Would you rather have gotten into the boat, or stayed on the ship? I was put into the boat.

Which would you rather have done? You see it was rather dangerous to stop aboard.

The *Titanic* was dangerous? Yes.

So in your judgment it was safer to have gone in the boat than to have stayed on the *Titanic*? Oh, yes, sir.

That was when you left? Yes sir.

What did you think when the first boat was launched? I did not think she was going down then.

LIFEBOAT 10
Port Side, Launched 1.50 a.m.

By now some second and third class passengers were beginning to reach the boat deck and lifeboat 10 was more than half filled by second class women and children. The sense of urgency is developing fast with women reportedly being thrown into the lifeboats and lifeboats being filled to a much greater degree. Within this boat was Milvina Dean, a two-month-old baby travelling third class. Until her death in 2009 Milvina was the last living survivor of the *Titanic* disaster. Male crew: five; male passengers: 0; women and children: 50; total for lifeboat: 55 (British Board of Inquiry).

42
Edward Buley, Able Seaman

Ex-Royal Navy serviceman Edward Buley was put in charge of lifeboat 10 by First Officer Murdoch (not the 'chief officer' as Buley describes him). Edward Buley switched from lifeboat 10 into lifeboat 14 when Fifth Officer Lowe gathered together seamen to return to the scene in an attempt to pick up survivors.

US Senate Inquiry (inquiry question is followed immediately by witness's answer) What was your first notice of the collision? The slight jar. It seemed as though something was rubbing alongside of her, at the time. I had on my overcoat and went up on deck, and they said she had struck an iceberg.

Who said that? I think it was a couple of firemen. They came down. One of our chaps went and got a handful of ice and took it down below. They turned in again. The next order from the Chief Officer, Murdoch, was to tell the seamen to get together and uncover the boats and turn them out as quietly as though nothing had happened. They turned them out in about 20 minutes.

How do you mean? Uncovered and turned them out. They are on deck, and the davits are turned inboard. You have to unscrew these davits and swing the boat out over the ship's side. The next order was to lower them down to a line with the gunwale of the boat deck, and then fill the boats with women and children. We turned them up and filled them with women and children.

Where were you stationed? I was over on the starboard side at first, sir.

Did you lower the boats? I helped lower all the starboard boats.

That is, to lower them as far as the boat deck, to get the gunwales in line? Yes sir.

That is the deck on which the boats were? Yes sir.

Not to any lower deck? No, sir not to the lower deck. We lowered all the starboard boats, and went over and done the same to the port boats. There was No. 10 boat, and there was no one there, and the Chief Officer asked what I was, and I told him, and he said, 'Jump in and see if you can find another seaman to give you a hand.' I found Evans, and we both got in the boat, and Chief Officer Murdoch and Baker also was there. I think we were the last lifeboat to be lowered. We got away from the ship.

How many people were in that boat? From 60 to 70.

Mostly women? Women and children.

How many men? There were the steward and one fireman.

And yourself? And myself and Evans, the able seaman.

The other passengers were women? That is all there was. All the others were ladies and children.

Were any ladies on the deck when you left? No, sir. Ours was the last boat up there, and they went around and called to see if there were any, and they threw them in the boat at the finish, because they didn't like the idea of coming in.

Pushed them in, you mean? Threw them in. One young lady slipped, and they caught her by the foot on the deck below, and she came up then and jumped in. We got away from the ship, and about an hour afterwards Officer Lowe came alongside, and he had his boat filled up, and he distributed them among the other boats, and he said to all the seamen in the boat to jump in his boat until he went back among the wreckage to see if there were any people that had lived.

Did you go in the last boat? Yes sir.

Who had charge of the boat you were in? I was in charge of that.

But when you left that? I left that, and I believe he put some more stewards in the boat to look after the women. All the boats were tied together.

You were then with Lowe in his boat and went back to where the *Titanic* sank? Yes, sir and picked up the remaining live bodies.

How many did you get? There were not very many there. We got four of them. All the others were dead.

Were there many dead? Yes, sir there were a good few dead, sir. Of course you could not discern them exactly on account of the wreckage, but we turned over several of them to see if they were alive. It looked as though none of them were drowned. They looked as though they were frozen. The lifebelts they had on were out of the water, and their heads were laid back, with their faces on the water, several of them.

They were head and shoulders out of the water? Yes sir.

With the head thrown back? Yes sir.

And the face out of the water? Yes sir.

They were not, apparently, drowned? It looked as though they were frozen altogether, sir. In the morning, after we picked up all that was alive, there was a collapsible boat we saw with a lot of people, and she was swamped, and they were up to their knees in water. We set sail and went over to them, and in a brief time picked up another one.

Another boat? Another boat filled with women and children, with no one to pull the oars, and we took her in tow. We went over to this one and saved all of them. There was one woman in that boat. After that we seen the *Carpathia* coming up, and we made sail and went over to her. I think we were about the seventh or eighth boat alongside. During the time I think there was two died that we had saved, two men.

How far were you from the *Titanic* when she went down? About 250 yards.

Could you see people on the decks before she went down? No. All the lights were out.

Could you hear the people? Yes, you could hear them.

Calling? Yes sir.

Before she went down? Yes sir and we laid to, not because we could give any assistance, but because the boat I was in was full up, and we had no one to pull the oars. There was three only to pull the oars, and one could not pull at all. He was a fireman. That left but two people to pull the oars, so I directed the steward to take the coxswain's watch.

Before she went down, you could hear people calling for help? Yes sir.

Was there very much of that? Yes sir, it was terrible cries.

Most of the witnesses have said they could hear no cries for help until after the ship went down. *Witness answers:* This was after the ship went down when we heard them.

I have been asking you about hearing cries before the ship went down. *Witness answers:* No sir. There was no signs of anything before that at all.

Before the ship went down you did not hear any cries for help? No cries whatever, sir. Her port bow light was under water when we were lowered.

How long after you were lowered and put in the water was it before she went down? I should say about 25 minutes to half an hour.

Was yours the last boat? Mine was the last lifeboat, No. 10.

Were the collapsibles lowered after that? The collapsibles were washed off the deck, I believe, sir. The one we picked up that was swamped, I think they dropped her and broke her back, and that is why they could not open her.

Were there people in that collapsible? She was full up, sir. That is the one we rescued the first thing in the morning.

How soon after the *Titanic* went down was it before you got back there with Lowe to help rescue people? From an hour to an hour-and-a-half.

And your idea is that the people were frozen. *Witness answers:* Yes, frozen.

Frozen in the meantime? If the water had been warm, I imagine none of them would have been drowned, sir.

Then you got some people out of the water, and some of those died after you rescued them, did they? Yes sir.

Were they injured in any way? No sir. I think it was exposure and shock.

On account of the cold? Yes sir. We had no stimulants in the boat to revive them, at all.

They seemed to be very cold when you got them out of the water? Yes sir, and helpless.

Numb? Yes sir. There were several in the broken boat that could not walk. Their legs and feet were all cramped. They had to stand up in the water in that boat.

Do you know of any banquets or drinking on board the ship that night? No sir.

So far as you know, the crew were sober. *Witness answers:* The crew were all asleep, sir.

Did you see any of the crew arousing people or giving the alarm? That was the steward's work, sir. We had nothing to do with that.

The question is whether you observed it, in any way? No sir. We were away from the saloons altogether. We were in the forecastle head.

Do you know when the water began to come into the ship? Yes sir. A little after she struck. You could hear it.

Immediately? You could hear it immediately. Down where we were, there was a hatchway, right down below, and there was a tarpaulin across it, with an iron batten. You could hear the water rushing in, and the pressure of air underneath it was such that you could see this bending. In the finish I was told it blew off.

What part of the ship would you call that? The forecastle head.

How far was that from the bow? About 20 yards, I should think.

That condition could not have obtained unless the steel plates had been torn off from the side of the ship? From the bottom of the ship. It was well underneath the waterline.

And the plates must have been ripped off by the iceberg? Yes sir.

There was no way of closing that up so as to prevent water coming in? It was already closed up. The carpenter went down and tested the wells, and found she was making water, and the order was given to turn the boats out as well as possible, and then to get the lifebelts on.

Could not that ship take a great deal of water and still float? She ought to be able to do it, sir.

There was no way of filling one compartment completely, and still not affecting the other part of it? No. I should think if that had been a small hole, say about 12 by 12 feet square, in a collision, or anything like that, it would have been all right, but I do not think they carried collision mats.

What is a collision mat? It is a mat to shove over the hole to keep the water from rushing in.

You think she did not carry collision mats? I do not believe she did. I never saw one.

Did you ever see collision mats used on merchant ships? I had never been on a merchant ship before. I have seen them frequently used in the navy.

You think if she had had collision mats, she might have been saved? That would not have done much good with her, because I believe she was ripped up right along.

For what distance? I should say half way along, according to where the water was. I should say the bottom was really ripped open altogether.

The steel bottom? Yes sir.

So no amount of mats would have done any good? It would not have done any good in that case. Should the ship have had a collision or anything like that, it would have done some good.

You did not see the iceberg? No sir. I never saw any ice until morning. We thought it was a full-rigged ship. We were right in amongst the wreckage, and we thought it was a sailing ship, until the light came on and we saw it was an iceberg.

Did you get very far away from where the *Titanic* went down before the *Carpathia* was in sight? No sir. When the *Carpathia* came and hove to, we were still amongst the wreckage looking for bodies.

By that time there were none of those afloat who were alive, so far as you could see? No sir there were no more alive, then.

The lifebelts were all in good condition, were they? Yes, all new lifebelts. When you once put them on, there is no fear of them pulling off again in the water.

Do you think there was a sufficient number of lifebelts for all the passengers? Yes sir, more than sufficient. Of course the seamen did not have a chance to get them – did not have time to get them.

The seamen? Yes sir.

Did the passengers have time, after the alarm was given, to get the belts? They had the belts on a good hour before she went down.

You think all the passengers were notified and were able to get out of their cabins? I should say so. They were all on the boat deck.

What became of them? You got all that were in sight when you loaded the last boat? *Witness answers:* We loaded all the women we could see, and the Chief Officer rushed around trying to find more, and there was none, and our boat was lowered away.

What became of the passengers on the boat? They were taken aboard the *Carpathia.*

I mean all the passengers on the *Titanic*? I could not say sir.

You did not see them around the deck when you were leaving? When we left they were still working, getting rafts ready, and throwing chairs over the side.

Getting rafts ready? Yes sir.

How many rafts were there? That is, what they call rafts. They did not have time to make any rafts.

Who was doing that? The stewards and the firemen.

Were there any passengers jumping overboard? I never seen anyone jump overboard sir.

Did you see any passengers on the deck when you left? Only men sir.

Were there many of those? Yes, sir there were plenty of them sir. If she had had sufficient boats I think everyone would have been saved.

Were these men that you saw on deck desiring or wanting to get into the boats? No sir.

Or did they seem to think the ship was going to float? I think that is what the majority thought, that the ship would float. They thought she would go down a certain distance and stop there.

Did you hear any of them say that? Yes, several of them. They said they were only getting the boats out for exercise and in case of accident.

Right: **63.** Located on A deck aft of the first class smoking room, just off the Café Parisien near the stern, the Veranda Café (also known as the Palm Room or Palm Court). Like the Café Parisien, there was real ivy growing up the walls. Also, there were real palm trees. There were actually two identical verandas on either side of the ship. Archibald Gracie: 'That night after dinner, with my table companions, Messrs James Clinch Smith and Edward A. Kent, according to usual custom, we adjourned to the palm room, with many others, for the usual coffee at individual tables where we listened to the always delightful music of the *Titanic*'s band... From the palm room, the men of my coterie would always go to the smoking room.'

Below right: **64** First class reading room of the *Titanic*. On the promenade deck, as a counterpoint to the men's smoking room, this stylish area was primarily intended for the first class female passengers. After dinner the women could gravitate to this cozy space for coffee and conversation.

Above: 65. Rear starboard boat deck and the second class promenade area. The lifeboats shown are 15 (nearest), 13, 11 and 9. In the distance can just be seen lifeboats 7, 5 and 3. Lawrence Beesley (lifeboat 13): 'I was now on the starboard side of the top boat deck; the time about 12.20 a.m. We watched the crew at work on the lifeboats, numbers 9, 11, 13, 15, some inside arranging the oars, some coiling ropes on the deck, the ropes which ran through the pulleys to lower to the sea, others with cranks fitted to the rocking arms of the davits. As we watched, the cranks were turned, the davits swung outwards until the boats hung clear of the edge of the deck. Just then an officer came along from the first class deck and shouted above the noise of escaping steam, "All women and children get down to deck below and all men stand back from the boats." The men fell back and the women retired below to get into the boats from the next deck. Two women refused at first to leave their husbands, but partly by persuasion and partly by force they were separated from them and sent down to the next deck.'

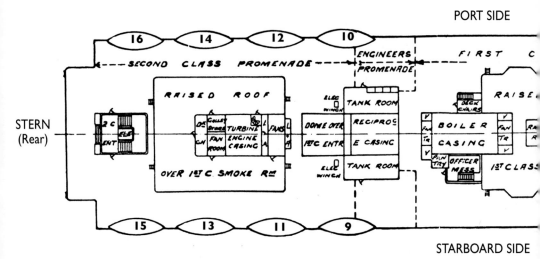

67. Forward starboard boat deck. The *Titanic* Good Friday, 5 April 1912, the liner was thrown open to the public for the day in Southampton. This was the only occasion the ship was dressed overall in flags. The lifeboats shown are 3 (nearest), 5 and 7. In the distance can be seen lifeboats 9, 11, 13 and 15. The exit onto the boat deck from the gym and grand staircase is opposite lifeboat 7. Elizabeth Shutes, lifeboat 3 remembered: '... the awful goodbyes, the quiet look of hope in the brave men's eyes as the wives were put into the lifeboats. Nothing escaped one at this fearful moment. We left from the boat deck, 75 feet above the water. Mr Case and Mr Roebling, brave American men, saw us to the lifeboat, made no effort to save themselves, but stepped back on deck.'

Below: 66. Plan of the boat deck of the *Titanic* showing the position of all 20 lifeboats, 1 to 16 and collapsibles A, B, C & D.

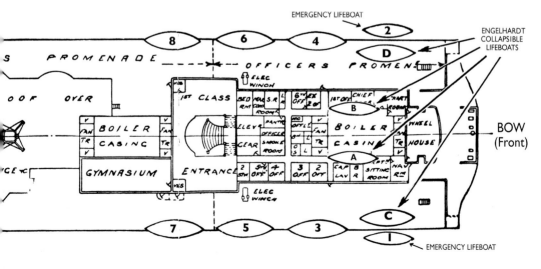

Above: **68**. Promenade deck (A) which ran nearly the whole length of the ship. John Astor helped his wife Madeleine to climb through the windows of the enclosed promenade into lifeboat 4 along a steamer chair. Many female passengers were loaded into lifeboats from this deck.

Left: **69**. Port side towards the stern of the ship showing position of lifeboat 16. Stewardess Mary Sloan (lifeboat 16): 'I was still standing when I saw Captain Smith getting excited, passengers would not have noticed, I did. I knew then we were soon going, the distress signals then were going every second, so I thought if anyone asked me again to go I should do so, there was a big crush from behind me, at last they realised their danger, so I was pushed into the boat. I believe it was one of the last boats to leave. We had scarcely got clear when she began sinking rapidly.'

70. This photograph from the *Olympic* reveals how the first class smoking room (A deck behind the fourth funnel) on the *Titanic* would have looked. Hugh Woolner (lifeboat D) describes the collison: 'We felt it under the smoking room. We felt a sort of stopping, a sort of, not exactly shock, but a sort of slowing down; and then we sort of felt a rip that gave a sort of a slight twist to the whole room. Everybody, so far as I could see, stood up and a number of men walked out rapidly through the swinging doors on the port side.'

71. First class dining room (or dining saloon). Positioned on D deck between funnels 3 and 4, it could seat over 500 pasengers and was the largest room aboard *Titanic*. Washington Dodge, first class passenger, lifeboat 13: 'So little motion was there to the vessel it was hard to realise, when dining in the spacious dining saloon, that one was not in some large and sumptuous hotel.' Among the passengers that dined there on the last night were Benjamin Guggenheim, Isidor and Ida Straus, and Molly Brown.

Above & Below: 72 & 73. Forward first class grand stairway immortalised in the *Titanic* film. The top landing led out directly onto the boat deck. Ella White: 'Captain Smith came down the stairway and ordered us all to put on our life preservers, which we did.' Ella escaped shortly after on the fourth lifeboat to leave, lifeboat 8, immediately outside the exit of the grand staircase on the boat deck. Elizabeth Shutes, lifeboat 3: 'How different are these staircases now! No laughing throng, but on either side stand quietly, bravely, the stewards, all equipped with the white, ghostly life preservers.'

Opposite: 74. A cross section through the *Titanic* showing the forward first class grand staircase, the wireless room, first class gym, first class reception room, turkish bath and boilers.

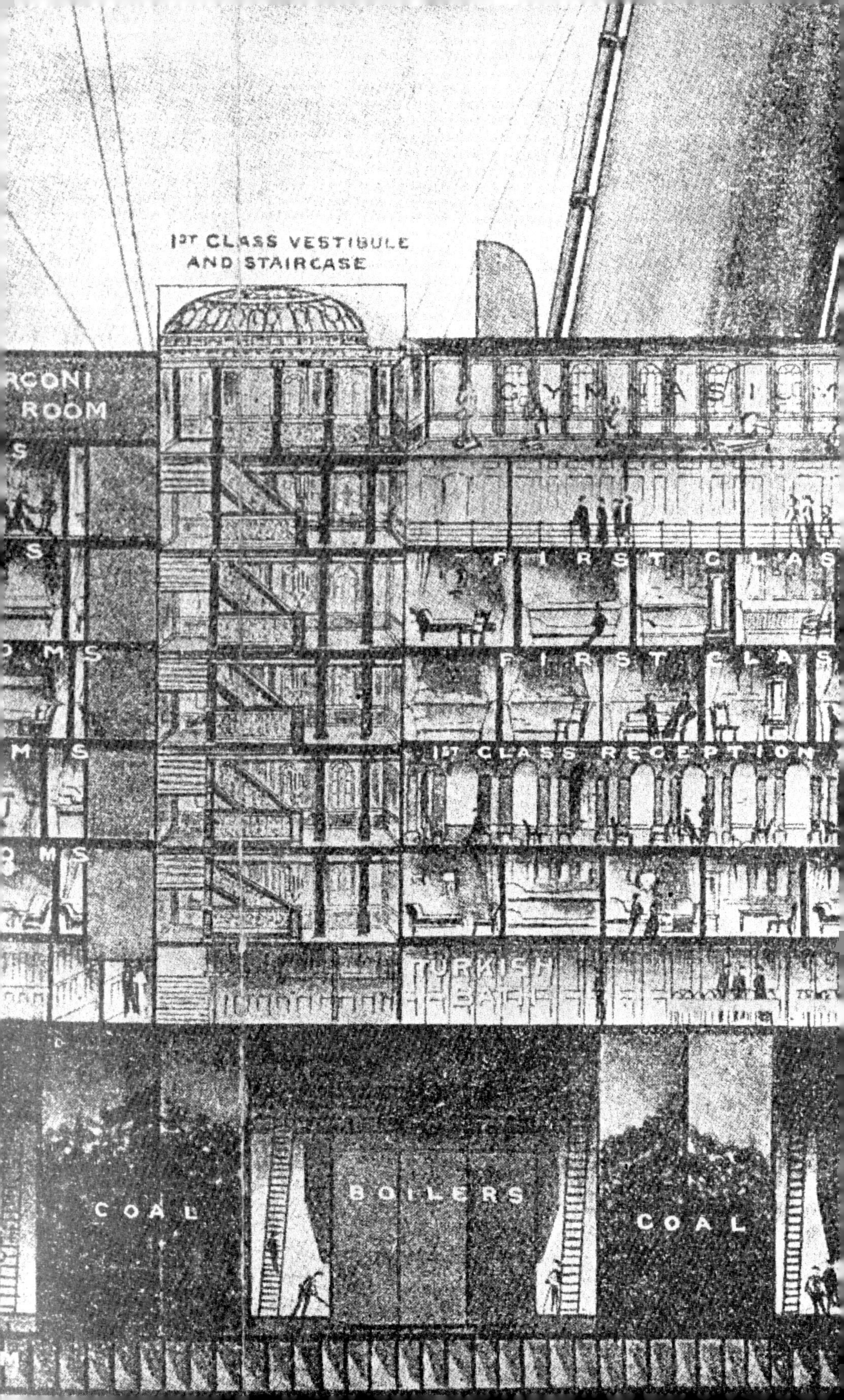

1ST CLASS VESTIBULE
AND STAIRCASE

RCONI
ROOM

GYMNASIUM

FIRST CLAS

FIRST CLAS

1ST CLASS RECEPTION

TURKISH BATH

COAL   BOILERS   COAL

75. Reception room. This was located on D deck between the first class grand staircase and the first class dining room. This is where first class passengers would gather for aperitifs prior to taking their seats in the adjacent dining room.

76. Lounge room. Martha Stephenson (lifeboat 4): 'About nine-thirty we went up to the lounge, a most beautiful room with open fire. I, having finished all my books, got the library steward to lend me Sir Ernest Shackleton's book of the South Pole and I spent half an hour looking at pictures of icebergs and ice fields, little realising that I should ever see similar ones.'

Right: 77. Captain Smith on the starboard side of the bridge. Jack Lawrence, Ship News Reporter, *New York Times*: 'Some of his contemporaries thought that Captain Smith was old fashioned. He certainly looked old fashioned with his rolling gait, his puckered eyes and his white beard.'

Below: 78. Crow's nest where at 11.40 p.m. lookouts Frederick Fleet (lifeboat 6) and Reginald Lee (lifeboat 13) spotted a large iceberg directly ahead of the ship. Sounding the ship's bell three times, Fleet telephoned Sixth Officer James Moody on the bridge exclaiming, 'Iceberg, right ahead!' The deck at the bow was known as the forecastle. The lower deck to the bottom of the photo is the fore well deck.

THE MAJESTIC HYMN PLAYED BY THE TITANIC BAND AS THE VESSEL SANK

AUTUMN 8.7.8.7. D.   Louis von Esch, c. 1810.

God of mercy and compassion, Look with pity on my pain;

Hear a mournful, broken spirit Prostrate at Thy feet complain;

Many are my foes and mighty; Strength to conquer I have none;

Nothing can uphold my goings But Thy blessed Self alone. AMEN

Saviour, look on Thy beloved,
  Triumph over all my foes;
Turn to heavenly joy my mourning,
  Turn to gladness all my woes;
Live or die, or work or suffer,
  Let my weary soul abide,
In all changes whatsoever,
  Sure and steadfast by Thy side.

When temptations fierce assault me,
  When my enemies I find,
Sin and guilt, and death and Satan,
  All against my soul combined,
Hold me up in mighty waters,
  Keep my eyes on things above—
Righteousness, divine atonement,
  Peace and everlasting love.

Above: 79. Cartoon from a 1912 newspaper about the *Titanic* disaster showing the despair of wives being physically parted by the crew and put aboard the lifeboats. Olaus Abelseth, third class passenger (lifeboat A): 'I saw there was an old couple standing there on the deck, and I heard this man say to the lady, "Go into the lifeboat and get saved." He put his hand on her shoulder and I think he said: "Please get into the lifeboat and get saved." She replied: "No; let me stay with you." I could not say who it was, but I saw that he was an old man. I did not pay much attention to him, because I did not know him.' Some women were man-handled by crew to force them to enter the lifeboats. Constance Willard (lifeboat 8): 'Women were being placed in the boats, and two men took hold of me and almost pushed me into a boat. I did not appreciate the danger and I struggled until they released me. "Do not waste time; let her go if she will not get in," an officer said.'

Left: 80. *Titanic* author Logan Marshall's offering for the hymn played as the ship went down, not *Nearer My God to Thee*, but *Autumn* as suggested by Harold Bride (lifeboat B).

Right: 81. A scene depicted in a cartoon from a 1912 newspaper showing children being lowered into the lifeboats.

Below right: 82. Sketch of the lifeboats being lowered based on descriptions from eyewitnesses. Elizabeth Shutes (lifeboat 3): 'Our lifeboat, with 36 in it, began lowering to the sea. This was done amid the greatest confusion. Rough seamen all giving different orders. No officer aboard. As only one side of the ropes worked, the lifeboat at one time was in such a position that it seemed we must capsize in midair. At last the ropes worked together, and we drew nearer and nearer the black, oily water. The first touch of our lifeboat on that black sea came to me as a last goodbye to life, and so we put off – a tiny boat on a great sea rowed away from what had been a safe home for five days.'

Left: 83. The lowering of the lifeboats. Charlotte Collyer, lifeboat 14: 'There came the terrible cry: "Lower the boats. Women and children first! Women and children first!" They struck utter terror into my heart, and now they will ring in my ears until I die. They meant my own safety; but they also meant the greatest loss I have ever suffered – the life of my husband.' *Below*: 84. Survivors look on in horror as the *Titanic* sinks and passengers fling themselves off the stern of the massive ship. Harold Lowe, Fifth Officer, and in command of lifeboat 14, was asked at the British inquiry into the sinking why he didn't immediately return to the wreckage after the *Titanic* had sunk: 'Because it would have been suicide to go back there until the people had thinned out.' *Opposite*: 85. View from the lifeboats of the *Titanic*. Catherine Crosby (lifeboat 7): 'I heard the terrible cries of the people that were on board when the boat went down, and heard repeated explosions, as though the boilers had exploded.'

SETTLES TO FORWARD STACK
BREAKS BETWEEN STACKS

—1.40 A

Above: 86. Monday 15 April 1912, '1.40 a.m. *Titanic* settles to forward stack, breaks between stacks'.
August Weikman (lifeboat A): 'I was proceeding to launch the next boat when the ship suddenly sank
at the bow and there was a rush of water that washed me overboard... that was the last moment it
was possible to launch any more boats, because the ship was at an angle that it was impossible for
anybody to remain on deck... [I] started to swim for some dark object in the water. This was about
1.50 a.m. toward the stern... my watch was stopped at that time by the water.'
Below: 87. Cartoon from a 1912 newspaper about the *Titanic* disaster.

—*Detroit News*

EVERYTHING FOR ENJOYING LIFE, BUT NOT MUCH TO SAVE IT

Right: 88. Cartoon from a 1912 newspaper about the *Titanic* disaster showing the horrific predicament of passengers on the boat deck as *Titanic*'s bow slipped beneath the waves. *Below right*: 89. After deck *Olympic* 1911. View towards the decks at the stern of the ship. Helen Bishop (lifeboat 7) describes the last moments of the *Titanic*: 'When the forward part of the ship dropped suddenly at a faster rate so that the upward slope became marked, there was a sudden rush of passengers on all decks toward the stern. It was like a wave. We could see the great black mass of people in the steerage sweeping to the rear part of the boat... Then it began to slide gently downwards. Its speed increased as it went down head first, so that the stern shot down with a rush. The lights continued to burn till it sank. We could see the people packed densely in the stern till it was gone.'

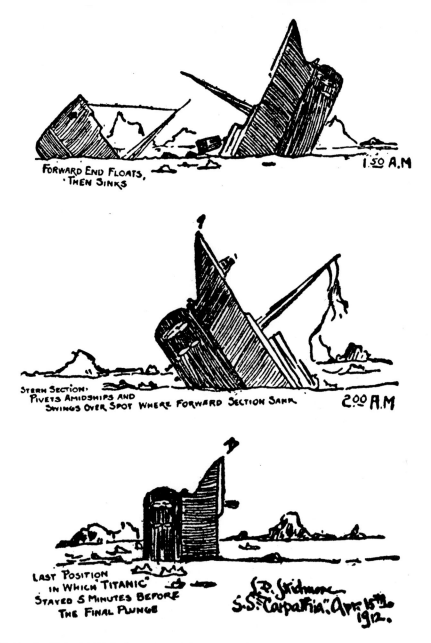

FORWARD END FLOATS,
·THEN SINKS

1.50 A.M

STERN SECTION·
PIVETS AMIDSHIPS AND
SWINGS OVER SPOT WHERE FORWARD SECTION SANK

2.00 A.M

LAST POSITION
IN WHICH "TITANIC"
STAYED 5 MINUTES BEFORE
THE FINAL PLUNGE

P. Skidmore
S.S. "Carpathia". Apr 15th 1912.

Top: 90. Monday 15 April 1912, '1.50 a.m. *Titanic*'s forward end floats then sinks'. Archibald Gracie (lifeboat B): 'The force of the wave that struck Clinch Smith and the others undoubtedly knocked most of them there unconscious against the walls of the officers' quarters and other appurtenances of the ship on the boat deck. As the ship keeled over forward, I believe that their bodies were caught in the angles of this deck, or entangled in the ropes, and in these other appurtenances thereon, and sank with the ship.' Charles Lightoller, Second Officer, lifeboat B: 'Striking the water was like a thousand knives being driven into one's body, and, for a few moments, I completely lost grip of myself.' *Centre*: 91. Monday 15 April 1912, '2.00 a.m. Stern section of *Titanic* pivots and swings over spot where forward section sank'. *Above*: 92. Monday 15 April 1912, *c.* 2.15 a.m. 'final position in which *Titanic* stayed for several minutes before the final plunge'. Helen Bishop (lifeboat 7): 'Suddenly the ship seemed to shoot up out of the water and stand there perpendicularly. It seemed to us that it stood upright in the water for four full minutes. Then it began to slide gently downwards. Its speed increased as it went down head first, so that the stern shot down with a rush. We could see the people packed densely in the stern till it was gone. As the ship sank we could hear the screaming a mile away. Gradually it became fainter and fainter and died away.'

Right: 93. A *Titanic* lifeboat rowing amongst the icebergs. The 'unsinkable' Molly Brown (lifeboat 6) described what she saw from the lifeboat as the sun rose on the morning of 15 April: 'On every side was ice. Ice 10 feet high was everywhere, and to the right and left and back and front, were icebergs. This sea of ice was 40 miles wide, they told me. Imagine some artist able to picture what we saw from that boat at dawn in that field of ice, with the red sun playing on those giant icebergs.'

Below: 94. The recovered *Titanic* lifeboats on board the *Carpathia*. Catherine Crosby (lifeboat 7): 'We had to row quite a long time and quite a distance before we were taken on board the *Carpathia*; I was suffering from the cold while I was drifting around, and one of the officers put a sail around me and over my head to keep me warm.'

Below right: 95. 1912 illustration of lifeboats among the ice field with the *Carpathia* in the distance. Ella White (lifeboat 8): 'The men in our boat were anything but seamen, with the exception of one man. The women all rowed, every one of them. The men could not row. They did not know the first thing about it. Miss Swift from Brooklyn rowed every mile, from the steamer to the *Carpathia*. Miss Young rowed every minute also, except when she was throwing up, which she did six or seven times. Countess Rothes stood at the tiller. Where would we have been if it had not been for our women, with such men as that put in charge of the boat?'

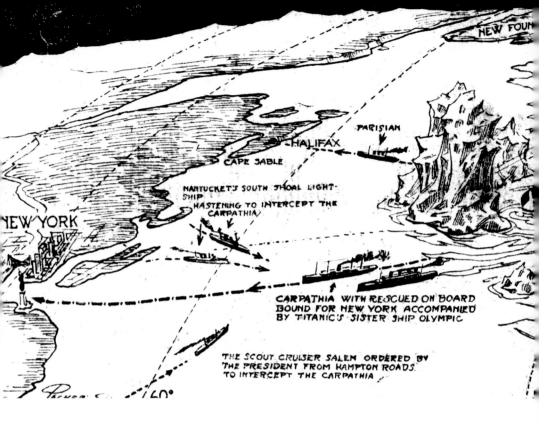

NEW FOUN

PARISIAN

HALIFAX

CAPE SABLE

NANTUCKET'S SOUTH SHOAL LIGHT-
SHIP
HASTENING TO INTERCEPT THE
CARPATHIA

NEW YORK

CARPATHIA WITH RESCUED ON BOARD
BOUND FOR NEW YORK ACCOMPANIED
BY TITANIC'S SISTER SHIP OLYMPIC

THE SCOUT CRUISER SALEM ORDERED BY
THE PRESIDENT FROM HAMPTON ROADS.
TO INTERCEPT THE CARPATHIA

Above: 96. A contemporary newspaper depiction of the location of the sinking of the *Titanic* and positions of other ships in the area.

Left: 97. Captain Arthur Rostron who rushed his ship *Carpathia* to rescue *Titanic*'s survivors and bring them to New York.

VIRGINIA REJUMES YOYAGE
TO LIVERPOOL

CAPE
RACE

110°

Right: 98. Photograph of the *Carpathia* with the recovered *Titanic* lifeboats.

Below right: 99. Sketch of the iceberg believed to have sunk the *Titanic* by Colin Campbell Cooper. A renowned artist, he and his wife were aboard the *Carpathia* during its rescue mission. He assisted in the rescue, and created several paintings which document the events. The consensus that emerges from the survivor accounts is that the iceberg was 100 feet high (above the water).

Colin Campbell Cooper

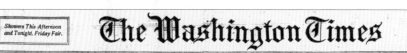

Top: 100. The front page of *The World*, Tuesday 16 April 1912, describing the sinking to a hungry audience. Note the exaggerated claim for the number of women and children saved.
Centre: 101. *New York Tribune*, Tuesday 16 April 1912.
Above: 102. *Washington Times*, Thursday 18 April 1912. Note the sensationalised headline, no lifeboats was sucked under by the sinking liner.

Top: 103. Getting *Titanic* news. White Star Office, April 1912.

Above: 104. A photograph of Mrs Florette Guggenheim leaving the White Star offices in New York after trying to get news of her husband. Mr Guggenheim was accompanied aboard *Titanic* by his mistress, a French singer named Madame Léontine Aubart. On the night of the disaster he put his mistress aboard lifeboat 9. He was last seen, with his valet, seated in deckchairs in the grand staircase sipping brandy and smoking cigars.

Right: 105. Crowds wait in New York for news of those who have been saved and who have been lost on the *Titanic*. Firm news took several days to come through.

106. Cartoon from a 1912 newspaper about the *Titanic* disaster showing the misery of family discovering that loved ones have perished on board *Titanic*. Hundreds flocked to the White Star Line offices in London, Southampton and New York seeking news.

107. Seeking information about lost relatives and friends at the office of the steamship company in New York.

108. Interior of the Cunard Line pier all cleared out ready to receive the survivors of the *Titanic* on arrival of the *Carpathia*, where they were met by relatives, doctors and nurses.

109. Cartoon from a 1912 newspaper about the *Titanic* disaster showing the family of passengers on board the *Titanic* waiting at New York for the survivors to disembark from *Carpathia*. Jack Lawrence, Ship News Reporter, *New York Times*: 'The first *Titanic* survivor to come down the gangplank was a woman, a sailor's oilskin thrown over her shoulders. At the foot of the gangplank a man faced her with outstretched arms. She collapsed in those arms and he carried her away, a Red Cross nurse trotting after him.'

110. Arrival of the *Carpathia* into New York on Thursday 18 April 1912. *Carpathia* dropped off the empty *Titanic* lifeboats at Pier 59, as property of the White Star Line, before unloading the survivors at Pier 54 where thousands of friends and relatives of the survivors were waiting.

111. Harold Bride (lifeboat B), surviving wireless operator of the *Titanic*, with feet bandaged, being carried up ramp of ship. He was washed off the deck of the *Titanic* just as it sank but managed to attach himself to the upturned hull of collapsible lifeboat B: 'There were men all around me – hundreds of them. The sea was dotted with them, all depending on their lifebelts.'

Right: 112. Stuart Collett (second class passenger, lifeboat 9) survivor of the *Titanic* on board *Carpathia* on arrival in New York. *Below*: 113. Crowd awaiting *Titanic* survivors April 1912.

THE CALL LEADS IN
POLITICAL
THEATRICAL
REAL ESTATE
SPORTING
COMMERCIAL
SOCIETY
FINANCIAL

NEWS

THE ⊕ CALL

VOLUME CXL—NO. 141.   SAN FRANCISCO, FRIDAY, APRIL 19, 1912.   **   PRICE FIVE CENTS.

WRECK SURVIVORS TELL TALES OF HORROR

Grief Ship Reaches Port With Those Rescued From Titanic

New-York ⸺ Tribune.

VOL. LXXII...N° 23,896.   To-day, cloudy, To-morrow, fair; west winds.   NEW-YORK, FRIDAY, APRIL 19, 1912.—SIXTEEN PAGES.   **   PRICE ONE CENT In City of New York, Jersey City and Hoboken, ELSEWHERE TWO CENTS.

HIT BERG AT 21-KNOT SPEED

CARPATHIA'S STORY OF TITANIC'S LOSS, WITH THRILLING DETAILS OF RESCUE

The Washington Times

Increasing Cloudiness and Showers.   Sunday Evening EDITION

NUMBER 7426.   Yesterday's Circulation, 63,753.   WASHINGTON, SUNDAY EVENING, APRIL 21, 1912.   Twenty Pages.   PRICE ONE CENT.

BODIES OF VICTIMS OF THE TITANIC DISASTER SIGHTED NEAR SCENE OF THE WRECK YESTERDAY

SALOON, CABIN, AND STEERAGE ALIENS MUST BE COMPLETELY MANIFESTED.

LIST OR MANIFEST OF ALIEN PASSENGERS FOR THE UNITED

Required by the regulations of the Secretary of Commerce and Labor of the United States, under Act of Congress approved February 20, 1907, to be delivered

S. S. _____ sailing from _____ , 190_

Opposite Top: 114. *The Call*, Friday 19 April 1912. Survivor testimony was the stock and trade of most of the new stories relating to the sinking.

Opposite Centre: 115. *New York Tribune*, Friday 19 April 1912, the day after the *Carpathia* had arrived in New York with survivors.

Opposite below: 116. *The Washington Times*, Sunday 21 April 1912. The *Mackey-Bennet*, a ship charted by the White Star Line to recover bodies from the scene, had arrived at the scene of the sinking on 20 April. Over 300 bodies were eventually recovered.

Opposite bottom: 117. The *Titanic's* 13 surviving lifeboats in New York. Their nameplates and White Star flags were removed and the lifeboats disappeared.

Above: 118. Partial list of survivors of the *Titanic* who were taken aboard the *Carpathia*. This page includes the names of John Thayer junior, Emily Ryerson, Martha Stephenson, Eleanor Widener, Elizabeth Shutes and Mary Marvin.

Above left: 119. Noted first class passenger Isidor Straus. His wife Ida reportedly would not leave Isidor, refusing to get in a lifeboat without him. The officer filling up the boat told Isidor that he could get into the boat with his wife, but he refused to do so ahead of younger men but instead sent his wife's maid, Ellen Bird, into the boat (lifeboat 8). Ida reportedly said: 'I will not be separated from my husband. As we have lived, so will we die together.' Isidor and Ida were last seen on deck sitting in deckchairs holding hands when a huge wave washed them into the sea. The couple are portrayed in the 1958 film *A Night to Remember*, in scenes that are faithful to the accounts just cited. In the 1997 film *Titanic*, the Strauses are briefly depicted comforting each other as their stateroom floods with water. *Above right*: 120. Noted first class passenger William T. Stead, a well-known author, went down with the ship sitting in the first class smoking room quietly reading a book.

Above left: 121. Charles Hays, a first class passenger, who drowned. An hour before the collision, Hays relaxed with Archibald Gracie in the first class smoking room. Hays never believed the ship would sink quickly and as he put both his wife, Clara Hays, and daughter, Orian Davidson, into lifeboat 3 he assured them *Titanic* would 'Stay afloat for at least ten hours'. His son-in-law, Thornton Davidson, also died in the sinking. *Above right*: 122. The millionaire John Astor who went down with the *Titanic* but not before putting his pregnant wife, Madeleine Astor, in lifeboat 4.

Above left: 123. James Clinch Smith, friend of Archibald Gracie who went down with the *Titanic*. It was Clinch who told Gracie of the collision and collected some of the iceberg fragments. Gracie: 'He opened his hand and showed me some ice, flat like my watch, coolly suggesting that I might take it home for a souvenir.'
Above right: 124. John B. Thayer who went down with *Titanic*. He was Jack Thayer's father, who was one of the few survivors to have survived exposure in the Atlantic before scrambling aboard lifeboat B.

Above left: 125. George Widener, husband of Eleanor Widener (lifeboat 4), who was lost in the sinking with his son. Archibald Gracie's account states that George had bravely assisted Second Officer Charles Lightoller in the loading of the last lifeboat, D, launched at about 2.05 a.m. and was last seen making his way to the stern of the *Titanic*. *Above right*: 126. Another noted *Titanic* victim, first class passenger Archibald Butt, military aid to two US presidents. He was seen on the bridge five minutes before the last boat left the ship. The reports of him beating back a crowd rushing a lifeboat with an iron bar or a pistol are believed to be media exaggerations.

Left: 127. Unidentified family who survived the *Titanic* disaster.

Above: 128. Trevor Allison, 11 months, with his nursemaid Alice Cleaver. Both escaped on lifeboat 11. Trevor was the sole survivor of his wealthy Canadian family. His mother, father and sister all drowned.

Below: 129. Frederick Dent Ray (lifeboat 13), one of the saloon stewards in the main dining saloon, five decks down.

above left: 130. Frederick Fleet (lifeboat 6), Lookout on the *Titanic* who spotted the iceberg. He described the moment the *Titanic* struck the iceberg at 11.40 p.m.: 'We struck the iceberg on the starboard bow, just before the foremast. There was scarcely any jar, and I thought and said we had had a narrow escape.' The experience of first impact was very different for fireman Frederick Barratt in boiler room 6 on the lowest deck of the ship: 'There was a crash... I saw a wave of green foam come tearing through between the boilers and I jumped for the escape ladder.'

above right: 131. John Thompson, Fireman (left) lifeboat A. Thomas Whiteley, Saloon Steward (right), lifeboat B: 'In some way I got overboard myself and found something to hold on to – an oak dresser about the size of this hospital bed. I wasn't more than 60 feet from the *Titanic* when she went down. I was aft and could see her big stern rise up in the air as she went down bow first. I saw all the machinery drop out of her. I was in the water about half an hour and could hear the cries of thousands of people, it seemed. Then I drifted near a boat wrong side up. About 30 men were clinging to it. They refused to let me get on. Someone tried to hit me with an oar, but I scrambled on to her.'

below: 132. P. A. S. Franklin, White Star Line Vice President. When the New York office of the White Star Line was informed that *Titanic* was in trouble, he announced, 'We place absolute confidence in the *Titanic*. We believe the boat is unsinkable.' By the time Franklin spoke those words *Titanic* was at the bottom of the ocean.

THE ICEBERG

" My conscience is clear" Ismay.

Above left: 133. Senate Investigating Committee questioning Harold Cottam at the Waldorf Astoria, 29 May 1912. Harold Cottam was the Wireless Operator on the *Carpathia* on the night the *Titanic* struck an iceberg. It was he who alerted Captain Rostron, who immediately turned the ship round and put on all possible speed.

Above right: 134. Contemporary newspaper cartoon attacking Bruce Ismay, Managing Director of the White Star Line. His survival on lifeboat C when so many women and children failed to make it into the lifeboats caused a major controversy.

Below: 135. Bruce Ismay being questioned by the Senate Investigating Committee. When asked by the US Senate Inquiry why he got in the lifeboat he replied simply: 'Because there was room in the boat. She was being lowered away. I felt the ship was going down, and I got into the boat.'

After you left her, her bow continued to go under? Settled down yes, sir. She went down as far as the after funnel, and then there was a little roar, as though the engines had rushed forward, and she snapped in two, and the bow part went down and the after part came up and staid up five minutes before it went down.

Was that perpendicular? It was horizontal at first, and then went down.

What do you mean by saying she snapped in two? She parted in two.

How do you know that? Because we could see the after part afloat, and there was no fore part to it. I think she must have parted where the bunkers were. She parted at the last, because the after part of her settled out of the water horizontally after the other part went down. First of all you could see her propellers and everything. Her rudder was clear out of the water. You could hear the rush of the machinery, and she parted in two, and the after part settled down again, and we thought the after part would float altogether.

The after part kind of righted up horizontally? She uprighted herself for about five minutes, and then tipped over and disappeared.

Did it go on the side? No sir, went down head foremost.

That makes you believe the boat went in two? Yes sir. You could see she went in two, because we were quite near to her and could see her quite plainly.

You were near and could see her quite plainly? Yes sir.

Did you see any people on her? I never saw a soul.

You must have been too far away to see that? It was dark.

Were there lights on that half part? The lights were all out. The lights went out gradually before she disappeared.

Notwithstanding the darkness you could see the outline of the ship? Yes sir, we could see the outline of the ship.

You could see the funnel? Quite plainly.

Were there any cinders or sparks or anything of that sort from the funnel? No sir. We were lying to there. The people in the boat were very frightened that there would be some suction. If there had been any suction we should have been lost. We were close to her. We couldn't get away fast enough. There was nobody to pull away.

How far were you when she went down? We were about 200 yards.

Do you know the names of the men in the boat with you? I only know one, sir. That is Evans, Able Seaman.

Is he here? Yes sir. He is coming up tonight at eight o'clock.

Who was in charge of your boat? I was, sir.

You opinion is, if they had had enough lifeboats here, these people could all have been saved? Yes sir they could all have been saved. There was a ship of some description there when she struck, and she passed right by us. We thought she was coming to us and if she had come to us, everyone could have boarded her. You could see she was a steamer. She had her steamer lights burning. She was off our port bow when we struck, and we all started for the same light, and that is what kept the boats together.

But you never heard of that ship any more? No, we could not see anything of her in the morning when it was daylight. She was stationary all night. I am very positive for about three hours she was stationary, and then she made tracks.

How far away was she? I should judge she was about three miles.

Why could not she see your skyrockets? She could not help seeing them. She was close enough to see our lights and to see the ship itself, and also the rockets. She was bound to see them.

You are quite certain that it was a ship? Yes sir, it was a ship.

How many lights did you see? I saw two masthead lights.

No stern lights? You could not see the stern lights. You could not see her bow lights. We were in the boat at the time.

Did you see that ship before you were in the water? Yes sir. I saw it from the ship. That is what we told the passengers. We said, 'There is a steamer coming to our assistance.' That is what kept them quiet, I think.

Did she come toward you bow on? Yes sir, bow on toward us and then she stopped, and the lights seemed to go right by us.

If she had gone by you, she would have been to your stern? She was stationary there for about three hours, I think, off our port, there, and when we were in the boat we all made for her, and she went by us. The northern lights are just like a searchlight, but she disappeared. That was astern of where the ship went down.

She gave no signal? No signal whatever. I could not say whether she gave a signal from the bridge or not. You could not see from where we were, though.

Do you suppose she was fastened in the ice? I could not say she was.

She must have known the *Titanic* was in distress? She must have known it. They could have seen the rockets and must have known there was some distress on.

The *Titanic* had sirens? Yes she had sirens, but she never blew them. They fired rockets.

They did not blow the siren or whistle? No sir.

But the steam was escaping and making quite a noise? Yes sir, you could not hear yourself speak then. That had quieted down. The firemen went down and drew nearly all the fires.

When she went down, she had no fire in her of any consequence? She might have had fire, but very little.

When did you first see that boat on the bow? How long was it before you launched? *Witness answers:* When we started turning the boats out. That was about 10 minutes after she struck.

Did that boat seem to be getting farther away from you? No it seemed to be coming nearer.

You are possessed of pretty good eyes? I can see a distance of 21 miles, sir.

This was a clear night and no fog? A clear night and no fog.

A smooth sea? Yes sir.

You are quite positive there was no illusion about that boat ahead? It must have been a boat, sir. It was too low down in the sea for a star. Then we were quite convinced afterwards, because we saw it go right by us when we were in the lifeboats. We thought she was coming toward us to pick us up.

When did you last see the Captain that night? I never saw him at all, sir.

43

Mary Marvin, First Class Passenger

Mary and Daniel Marvin were married five weeks before boarding the *Titanic* in Southampton. Daniel did not survive. Mary must have been pregnant on board as she later gave birth to a baby girl. There were no fishing boats around the *Titanic*, Mary probably mistook the other lifeboats for fishing vessels.

New York Times, 19 April 1912 Mrs D. W. Martin, who was on a honeymoon trip with her husband, was prostrated when she reached the pier as her husband was lost.

'My God, don't ask me too much, tell me have you any news from Dan? He grabbed me in his arms and knocked down men to get me in the boat. As I was put in the boat he cried, "It's all right little girl! You go and I'll stay a little while. I'll put on a life preserver and jump off and follow you." The boat started off and he threw a kiss at me.

'We were in our stateroom when the shock came, and when we reached the deck we were in darkness.

'While on the deck I heard at least 10 revolver shots. See these powder marks.

'There were fishing boats about the boat and I think others must have been saved. Dan and I saw them before we went to our room. The men whom I saw were brave, for they pushed aside others when the cowards made for the boats before the women.

'I am not at all sure, but when we pulled away from the *Titanic* I think I saw Major Butt, whom I knew slightly standing near where they were loading the boats, with an iron bar or stick in his hand beating back the frenzied crowd who were attempting to overcrowd the lifeboats.

At this point Mrs Marvin was interrupted by her mother who burst into tears. 'Why didn't you send a message to us that you were safe?'

'Why I did mother, from the *Carpathia* just as soon as I could'. 'I never got it' sobbed the mother, and the two women threw their arms around each other and sobbed.

After she had regained her composure Mrs Marvin, talking to her mother and said: 'I don't know why it was, but for some reason on board the *Carpathia* they wouldn't take any message telling anything about the wreck. We were told we could send short messages without names, that was all.'

Then, as if recollecting something that had slipped her mind in the joy of being ashore she told me one of the most beautiful stories related on the dock. Just as she got into a seat on the lifeboat, she said a little French girl, about five, was shoved into her arms by someone she did not see.

Mrs Marvin carried the baby during the five hours she was in the lifeboat and then cared for her little unknown charge while on the *Carpathia*. On docking last night she turned over the brown eyed waif to Mrs Irwin, Chairman of the Woman's Relief Committee. Mrs Marvin is but 18 years old, and was married only five weeks ago.

44

Gretchen Longley & Kornelia Andrews, First Class Passengers

Gretchen Longley was travelling with her two aunts, Kornelia (not Corinne as below) Andrews and Anna Hogeboom (not Hogeboon as below). The party had been in France and had boarded the *Titanic* at Cherbourg.

New York Times, 19 April 1912 'I was in my stateroom when the *Titanic* struck the iceberg. After the shock I went out into the corridor twice. Each time things were so quiet that I thought there was no reason for alarm. My aunt, Mrs Corinne Andrews, however was nervous. She insisted that something had happened. As a result of her persistence that things were wrong we went up on deck.

'When we got above we found a number of people gathering, and heard the order to lower the boats given. Before we left another iceberg came along and scraped the sides, forcing ice through the portholes. We left the ship in the second boat with Mrs J. C. Hogeboon.

'I think that there were people on board the ship when she sunk who died without knowing that she had struck and who did not realize anything was wrong until the water rushed into their staterooms.

'The men behaved splendidly. We were undressed in the bitter cold. The men in the lifeboat gave us their garments to protect us.

Her aunt, Mrs Andrews said: 'In the first boat many husbands got away with their wives. The reason for this was that at that time there were not enough women on the deck to fill the boats. The officers knew the desperate need of the situation and the urgency off getting the boats off quickly, so they filled the boats with those on the deck and got them away.'

Of the husbands who remained behind after putting their wives in the lifeboats only three were reunited.

'We were a mile away from the *Titanic* when there was a great explosion. It appeared to me as if the boilers had blown up and the *Titanic* had been lifted up amidships and broken in half. This is the way it appeared to me.

'The boat ahead of us picked up 17 persons from the water. The cold was so severe that two of them died. One of these was a woman. A man who was picked up out of the water went mad.

'The men in the lifeboats took off their coats and gave them to the women, who were for the most part, scantily clothed. Fortunately some of those rescued had brought blankets with them from their staterooms when they came up on deck.

'The most pathetic thing I heard was that on one of the boats, a collapsible lifeboat, holding 16 to 20 persons, the party were up to their knees in water for six hours so that one man had his legs frozen and eight died.

The eight were thrown overboard to lighten the boat and to keep it from being swamped.

'My impression is that the *Titanic* struck an obstruction at 11.40 p.m. and sank after two hours. There was ice all around us. I can never begin to tell of the feeling which came over us when we saw the *Carpathia* approaching in the gray of the early morning. It was about eight o'clock I think.

'There was no panic aboard the *Titanic* that I know about. When I was on the deck the officers I saw were busy getting the boats over the sides and directing the passengers. The men had apparently gone to their quarters at the first call of danger. The Captain remained on the bridge. On the *Carpathia* the officers did all they could for those they rescued.

LIFEBOAT 4
Port Side, Launched 1.50 a.m.

By the time lifeboat 4 was launched it only had to be lowered 15 or 20 feet before it reached the water. This boat contained the wives of some of the most eminent first class passengers, Mrs Astor, whose husband multimillionaire John Jacob Astor was refused permission to board by Second Officer Lightoller, Mrs Thayer, and Mrs Widner. Their husbands stayed on board, following Mrs Thayer's expressed sentiments that they would 'better die than live dishonoured'. This boat picked up several men from the water, a couple of whom were alleged to be drunk. As the night wore on the lifeboat began to take on water, with survivors reporting a 'foot' of water in the bottom. Male crew: four; male passengers: 0; women and children: 36; total for lifeboat: 40 (British Board of Inquiry).

45
Martha Stephenson & Elizabeth Eustis, First Class Passengers

Martha Stephenson boarded at Cherbourg with her sister Elizabeth Eustis (who also survived). They wrote down their experiences shortly after the sinking in a pamphlet they titled *The Titanic: Our Story*. Archibald Gracie used an extract from this in his account of lifeboat 4. The entire account is reproduced below.

Sunday morning, 14 April 1912, was a beautiful clear day, high wind and cold. Elizabeth and I wrote letters before the service, remarking at the service that they did not sing the hymn *For Those in Peril on the Sea*. Then read the chart and noticed we had made a run of 547 miles. After lunch we spoke to Penrose, our room steward, about the run and he said it was nothing to what we would do on Monday, when they expected to do 580.

We spent our afternoon reading, had tea on deck, then went to see the restaurant before going down. McElroy, the Purser, was walking on the boat deck when we took our last walk before dinner. We had a delicious dinner with souvenir menus, our steward bringing us many views of the ship. We spent our evening in the reception room listening to a fine musical program, with many whom we knew sitting about us. About 9.30 p.m. we went up to the lounge, a most beautiful room with an open fire. I, having finished all my books, got the library steward to lend me Sir Ernest Shackleton's book of the South Pole and I spent half-an-hour looking at pictures of icebergs and icefields, little realizing that I should ever see similar ones. At 10 o'clock we started down to bed and on our deck D found Mr and Mrs Thayer, with whom we sat until quarter of eleven talking of our wonderful trip. We then said goodnight and turned in. I remarked to Elizabeth that we had but two more nights, and neither of us had had one bit of discomfort from seasickness.

I was sound asleep when at quarter before twelve I was awakened by a terrible jar with ripping and cutting noise which lasted a few moments. We both were much frightened, sitting up in our beds and turning on the electricity. Our door was on the hook and we soon heard voices in the hall so that Elizabeth put on her wrapper, slippers and cap and ran out. I was bitterly cold, and, shivering from fright and cold, sat undecided as to what to do. Our steward came down to close the porthole and I asked him if the order had been given to close all the ports, but he said 'No, it's only cold, go to bed. It's nothing at all.' Before Elizabeth returned I decided to get dressed as I had seen a gentleman in one of the rooms opposite pull his shoes in from the passageway. When she came in she told of many people outside half-dressed, one woman having a thin white pigtail down her back and a feather hat, also that some man had locked himself in his room and was unable to open his door. He was much worried, calling for help, and young Williams put his shoulder to the panels and broke it in. The steward was most indignant and threatened to have him arrested for defacing the beautiful ship.

I had my shoes nearly buttoned, and Elizabeth said 'Why, Martha, are you dressing?' and I said I should feel much safer with my clothes on and could go to bed later if all was right. She then decided to dress also. We did not hurry, and dressed fully as if for breakfast, putting on our burglar pockets containing our letters of credit and money. I determined also to do my hair and put on a lined waist and old winter suit as it was so cold. While Elizabeth was doing her hair the ship suddenly settled, frightening me very much, and I urged her not to take pains but to hurry.

Just as I was wholly dressed and she hooking her waist Mr Thayer appeared at our door, which we had opened, and said he was very glad that we had dressed. He thought there was no danger, but we had struck ice and there was much on deck and he urged us to come up and see it, saying we would find him and Mrs Thayer on the deck. I put on my fur coat over everything and Elizabeth said she thought she would wear her watch, which reminded me that mine was hanging by the bureau and I quickly put it on. I took my glasses and small change purse, also a clean handkerchief and was dressed as if for breakfast. We then left our room, leaving the electric lights on, also the electric heater so it would be warm on our return. We closed the door and started down the long passageway and up the stairs.

On the next deck we met the Thayer family, who seemed to be waiting for us, and started up to go on the deck when a steward called 'All back to staterooms for life preservers.' We turned around and I cannot remember that we ran, but we walked quickly to our rooms and Elizabeth climbed up, pulling down two life preservers from off the top of her closet. We said then we felt it must be serious if they had ordered the lifebelts, and we were much frightened though very quiet. We again went up the stairs, with our life preservers in our hands and once more joined the Thayer family. We quietly read the notices of 'inside front' and 'inside back' and put them on over our heads, Elizabeth tying mine and I tying hers. We put ours on over our heavy coats. After our life preservers were on, Mrs Thayer suggested getting Jack's coat, and Elizabeth and I followed to the steward's room, and when Mrs Thayer took the coat we each took our steamer rugs, not knowing why, but simply that we were there.

My mind is a blank as to a trip we took to the boat deck, when I distinctly remember being beside the gymnasium on starboard side and seeing Mr Ismay come out, noting the fact that he had dressed hurriedly, as his pajamas were below his trousers. After getting our rugs we were in the companionway of A deck when order came for women and children to boat deck and men to starboard side.

Elizabeth and I took each other's hands, not to be separated in the crowd, and all went on deck, we following close to Mrs Thayer and her maid and going up narrow iron stairs to the forward boat deck which, on the *Titanic*, was the captain's bridge.

At the top of the stairs we found Captain Smith looking much worried, and anxiously waiting to get down after we got up. The ship listed heavily to port just then. As we leaned against the walls of the officers' quarters rockets were being fired over our heads, which was most alarming, as we fully realized if the *Titanic* had used her wireless and was sending rockets it must be serious. Shortly after that the order came from the head dining saloon steward to go down to the A deck, when Mrs Thayer remarked, 'Tell us where to go and we will follow. You ordered us up here and now you are taking us back,' and he said 'Follow me.'

On reaching the A deck we could see, for the decks were lighted by electricity, that a boat was lowered parallel to the windows, those were opened, and a steamer chair put under the rail for us to step on. The ship had listed badly by that time and the boat hung far out from the side so that some of the men said, 'No woman could step across that space.' A call was made for a ladder on one of the lower decks, but before it ever got there we were all in the boat. Whether they had drawn the boat over with boathooks nearer the side I do not know, but the space we easily jumped with the help of two men in the boat. The only gentleman I remember seeing at all was Colonel Astor, who was stepping through the window just in front of me when the crew said, 'Step back sir, no men in this boat.' He remarked that he wanted to take care of his wife, but on being told again that no men could go, he called 'Goodbye' and said he would follow in another boat, asking the number of our boat, which they said was 'No. 4.' In going through the window I was obliged to throw back the steamer rug, for, with my fur coat and huge cork life preserver, I was very clumsy. Later we found the stewards or crew had thrown the steamer rugs into the boat, and they did good service, Elizabeth's around a thinly clad baby, and mine for a poor member of the crew pulled in from the sea.

Our boat I think took off every woman on the deck at that time and was the last on the port side to be lowered. Only one man went down with us. The boat was lowered slowly, first at the bow, then at the stern, and very carefully. When near the water the man gave the order to 'Let her go,' but we all called 'Not yet, it's a long way to the water.' On reaching the water they called from the deck to know who was in command, and a man answered 'The quartermaster.' They then said 'Who else?' and he said 'I am alone.' Then they said 'We will send you two more men,' and shortly a boatswain and common sailor came down over the davit ropes into the boat. When we reached the sea we found the ship badly listed, her nose well in so that there was water to the D deck, which we could plainly see as the boat was lighted and the ports on D deck were square instead of round. No lights could be found in our boat and the men had great difficulty in casting off the blocks as they did not know how they worked. My fear here was great, as she seemed to be going faster and faster and I dreaded lest we be drawn in before we could cast off.

When we finally were ready to move on the order was called from the deck to go to the stern hatch and take off some men. There was no hatch open and we could see no men, but our crew obeyed orders, much to our alarm, for they were throwing wreckage over and we could hear a cracking noise resembling china breaking, which we learned later was the cracking of the boiler plates. We implored the men to pull away from the ship, but they refused, and we pulled three men into the boat who had dropped off the ship and were swimming toward us. One man was drunk and had a bottle of brandy in his pocket which the quartermaster promptly threw overboard and the drunk was thrown into the bottom of the boat and a blanket thrown over him.

After getting in, these three men told how fast she was going down and we all implored them to pull for our lives to get out from the suction when she should go down. The lights on the ship burned till just before she went. When the call came that she was going I covered my face and then heard someone call, 'She's broken.' After what seemed a long time I turned my head only to see the stern almost perpendicular in the air so that the full outline of the blades of the propeller showed above the water. She then gave her final plunge and the air was filled with cries. We rowed back and pulled in five more men from the sea. Their suffering from the icy water was intense and two men who had been pulled into the stern afterwards died, but we kept their bodies with us until we reached the *Carpathia*, when they were taken aboard and Monday afternoon given a decent burial with three others.

After rescuing our men we found several lifeboats near us and an order was given to tie together, which we obeyed. It did not seem as if we were together long when one boat said they could rescue more if they could get rid of some of the women and children aboard, and those were put into our boat. Soon after cries of 'ship ahoy' and a long low moan came to us and an officer in command of one of the boats ordered us to follow him. We felt we were already too crowded to go, but the other three boats refused to stir, and our men, with quartermaster and boatswain in command, followed the officer and we pulled over to what proved to be an overturned boat crowded with men. We had to approach it very cautiously, fearing our wash would sweep them off. We could take only a few and they had to come very cautiously. The other boat took most of the men and we then rowed away, the cries soon ceasing.

The sea was smooth and the night brilliant with more stars than I had ever seen. We could see the outline of several icebergs and scanned the horizon hoping to see the light of some vessel. Occasionally a green light showed, which proved to be on the emergency boat, and our men all recognized it as such. We all prayed for dawn, and there was no conversation, everyone being so awed by the disaster and bitterly cold. We found ourselves in the boat with Mrs Arthur Ryerson, her boy, two daughters, governess and maid, Mrs Thayer and maid, Mrs Widener and maid, Mrs Astor, her trained nurse and maid, Mrs Carter, her two children and maid, Mrs Cumings, and Mrs Clark of Los Angeles, with many from second and third cabin besides the eight men whom we had pulled in from the sea. By a strange coincidence Mrs Cumings discovered that the man whom she pulled in was her own bedroom steward. By this time our women, Mrs Thayer and Mrs Cumings, were helping two of the half-drowned sailors pull on the oars, as the boat was tremendously heavy.

With the dawn came the wind and before long quite a sea was running. Just before daylight on the horizon we saw what we felt sure must be the lights of a ship. The quartermaster was a long time in admitting that we were right, urging that it was the moon, but we insisted and they then said it might be the *Carpathia* as they had been told before leaving the *Titanic* that she was coming to us. For a long time after daylight we were in great wreckage from the *Titanic*, principally steamer chairs and a few white pilasters. Before leaving the *Titanic* they had been breaking off planks and throwing seats from the upper deck which we realized were thrown over for people to float on. We felt we could never reach the *Carpathia* when we found she had stopped, and afterwards when we asked why she didn't come closer we were told that some of the early boats which put off from the starboard side reached her a little after four, while it was after six when we drew under the side of the open hatch.

It had been a long trying row in the heavy sea and impossible to keep bow on to reach the ship. We stood in great danger of being swamped many times and Captain Rostron, who watched us come up, said he doubted if we could have lived an hour longer in that high sea. Our boat had considerable water in the centre, due to the leakage and also the water brought in by the eight men from their clothing. They had bailed her constantly in order to relieve the weight. Two of the women near us were seasick, but the babies with us slept most of the night in their mothers' arms. The boatswain's chair was slung down the side and there were also rope ladders. Only few, however, of the men were able to go up the ladders. Mail bags were dropped down in which the babies and little children were placed and hoisted up. We were told to throw off our life preservers and then placed in a boatswain's chair and hoisted to the open hatch where ready arms pulled us in. Warm blankets waited those in need and brandy offered to everybody. We were shown at once to the saloon, where hot coffee and sandwiches were being served. We asked anxiously for the men and nothing had been heard of any of them excepting Mr Carter, who was already on the *Carpathia* with Mr Ismay, they having gone off together in a lifeboat. Watching the other boats come in we found Jack Thayer who, it seems, was on the overturned boat, but got into the other boat and not ours. He had lost his father after the women left and could not find him. He picked up young Long of Springfield and with him decided to jump as the ship went down. After being sucked under twice he swam for the overturned boat, was pushed back into the water three times, finally finding a place and sitting there till rescued. He never saw young Long after they slid over the side.

The *Carpathia* was small and so crowded. We fortunately found friends on the ship who took us to their stateroom, letting us do our hair and wash our faces and hands. At about nine o'clock or later we had a regular breakfast. From the deck of the *Carpathia* we scanned the sea and such fields of ice only Shackleton's book the night before had shown me. The entire horizon for the complete circle had bergs stationed like sentinels.

The *California* came up to us at about eight o'clock and stood so close that the wireless could not be used, but for nearly an hour they wigwagged and used the semaphore and finally the *Carpathia*'s captain steamed away with the feeling that all boats were accounted for and the *California* had promised to stand by with the hope of rescuing any people then living. But we felt sure that Captain Rostron believed that he had everybody.

No one will ever know the kindness and consideration shown us by passengers and crew of the *Carpathia*. Stewards and stewardesses worked without sleep and were indefatigable trying to give help and comfort to the rescued. Passengers gave up staterooms and everybody took someone in where they had a vacant berth or sofa. The barber shop was soon sold out. Elizabeth secured a small comb, toothpaste, nail file, sponges and wash cloths, also a buttonhook. The purser was able to give us a small inside room with four berths that had only been used as a dressing room for many years. However, we slept there very comfortably and took Mrs Cumings and Mrs Astor's maid for the other two berths. We lived on deck as there was no place on the ship to sit.

Two days the sun shone, then came fearful weather with fog and thunder storm so that at times it seemed as if the Lord had intended us all to go. Captain Rostron was more than thoughtful, knowing how our nerves had already been under great strain. The fog horn was blown only when absolutely necessary and as soon as it lightened the least bit it was promptly stopped.

Our meals were remarkable. Of course, the saloon was set up always twice and sometimes three times for people to go, and while we had no appetites still the menu was the same as on all ocean steamers. Broth and tea were served on deck every day. The few of the rescued stewards from the *Titanic* gladly worked in the dining room. The stewardesses, however, were not asked to help. We found our woman, Mrs Pritchard, was saved, but Penrose, our steward, I never saw after he told me to go back to bed, that it was nothing, and I am confident that his belief after 30 years at sea, that nothing could sink the *Titanic*, made him stick close to the decks.

When we reached the Ambrose Channel Lightship the pilot boat was bearing down on us. Also two tugs bearing large signs of *New York Tribune* and *New York World*. Then began such a scene as I never hope to witness. In the small pilot boat with the pilot in some way a reporter had secreted himself and when the boat came alongside the rope ladder this man fought with the sailors to get aboard. It was most exciting as Captain Rostron stood on the bridge with the megaphone ordering the men not to allow anyone but the pilot to come aboard and the two sailors who were trying hard to keep their small rowing boat from being crushed against our side had at the same time to overcome this reporter and throw him back into the bottom of the boat. The tugs then began their rush. One of them struck us such a blow on the side that she jarred the whole ship and frightened us badly. The men on board the tugs were screaming through megaphones, asking names and asking for stories, offering large prices for any story that would be written and passed over to them. The Captain, with the pilot on the bridge, soon got under way again and fortunately we left those tugs far behind.

Our stop at quarantine was very short. Dinner was served, but no one had any appetite. When we got up the North River small boats were as thick as bees. At the foot of the Cunard pier we stopped and a large lighter came alongside from the White Star Company to take off the 14 lifeboats which Captain Rostron had taken aboard in case of accident to the *Carpathia*. While standing, a small newspaper tug which was under us caused us some amusement. A sudden rush of water frightened us, but on inquiry we discovered Captain Rostron had turned the hose on her and she was scurrying off at full speed and I trust the men were well soaked. We were soon off at the pier and among the earliest to leave the ship, as we had been on the deck all the way up and the gangplank was put on right beside us so we only had a few steps to walk.

The family were all close to us and we quickly got away, all going first to the Pennsylvania station, where I left with George, Helen, Ned, Jim Boyd and Dr Christie. Elizabeth went with Tracy, Martha, Arthur, Mary and Angie to the Belmont, where they spent the night, going to Boston the next day. A special train was run to Philadelphia and we left at North Philadelphia, where Joseph met us with the motor and we got to Haverford a little after three in the morning.

46

Emily Ryerson, First Class Passenger

The Ryerson family embarked at Cherbourg. The family consisted of Emily and Arthur Ryerson and their three children; two girls and one boy. Whilst Emily and the children survived, Arthur was not so lucky and his body was never recovered. Their son aged 13 was only just allowed to board by Second Officer Lightoller, who was rigidly sticking to a policy of 'women and children' only.

US Senate Inquiry Extract from Affidavit I was a passenger on the steamship on *Titanic* 14 April 1912. At the time of collision I was awake and heard the engines stop, but felt no jar. My husband was asleep, so I rang and asked the steward, Bishop, what was the matter. He said, 'There is talk of an iceberg, ma'am, and they have stopped, not to run into it.' I told him to keep me informed if there were any orders. It was bitterly cold, so I put on a warm wrapper and looked out the window (we were in the large cabins on the B deck, very far aft) and saw the stars shining and a calm sea, but heard no noise. It was 12 o'clock. After about 10 minutes I went out in the corridor, and saw far off people hurrying on deck. A passenger ran by and called out, 'Put on your lifebelts and come up on the boat deck'.

I said, 'Where did you get those orders?' He said, 'From the captain.' I went back then and told Miss Bowen and my daughter, who were in the next room, to dress immediately, roused my husband and the two younger children, who were in a room on the other side, and then remembered my maid, who had a room near us. Her door was locked and I had some difficulty in waking her. By this time my husband was fully dressed, and we could hear the noise of feet tramping on the deck overhead. He was quite calm and cheerful and helped me put the lifebelts on the children and on my maid. I was paralysed with fear of not all getting on deck together in time, as there were seven of us. I would not let my younger daughter dress, but she only put on a fur coat, as I did over her nightgown. My husband cautioned us all to keep together, and we went up to A deck, where we found quite a group of people we knew. Everyone had on a lifebelt, and they all were very quiet and self-possessed.

We stood about there for quite a long time, fully half an hour, I should say. I know my maid ran down to the cabin and got some of my clothes. Then we were ordered to the boat deck. I only remember the second steward at the head of the stairs, who told us where to go. My chief thought and that of everyone else was, I know, not to make a fuss and to do as we were told. My husband joked with some of the women he knew, and I heard him say, 'Don't you hear the band playing?' I begged him to let me stay with him, but he said, 'You must obey orders. When they say, 'Women and children to the boats' you must go when your turn comes. I'll stay with John Thayer. We will be all right. You take a boat going to New York.' This referred to the belief that there was a circle of ships around waiting. The *Olympic*, the *Baltic*, were some of the names I heard.

All this time we could hear the rockets going up, signals of distress. Again, we were ordered down to A deck, which was partly enclosed. We saw people getting into boats, but waited our turn. There was a rough sort of steps constructed to get up to the window. My boy, Jack was with me. An officer at the window said, 'That boy can't go.' My husband stepped forward and said, 'Of course, that boy goes with his mother, he is only 13.' So they let him pass. They also said, 'No more boys.' I turned and kissed my husband, and as we left he and the other men I knew – Mr Thayer, Mr Widener, and others – were all standing there together very quietly. The decks were lighted, and as you went through the window it was as if you stepped out into the dark. We were flung into the boats. There were two men – an officer inside and a sailor outside – to help us. I fell on top of the women who were already in the boat, and scrambled to the bow with my eldest daughter. Miss Bowen and my boy were in the stern and my second daughter was in the middle of the boat with my maid. Mrs Thayer, Mrs Widener, Mrs Astor and Miss Eustis were the only others I knew in our boat.

Presently an officer called out from the upper deck, 'How many women are there in that boat? Someone answered, '24.' 'That's enough; lower away.' The ropes seemed to stick at one end and the boat tipped, someone called for a knife, but it was not needed until we got into the water, as it was but a short distance, and I then realized for the first time how far the ship had sunk. The deck we left was only about 20 feet from the sea. I could see all the portholes open and water washing in, and the decks still lighted. Then they called out, 'How many seamen have you,' and they answered one. 'That is not enough,' said the officer, 'I will send you another,' and he sent a sailor down the rope. In a few minutes after several other men not sailors came down the ropes over the davits and dropped into our boat.

The order was given to pull away, then they rowed off – the sailors, the women, anyone – but made little progress. There was a confusion of orders. We rowed toward the stern, someone shouted something about a gangway, and no one seemed to know what to do. Barrels and chairs were being thrown overboard. Then suddenly, when we still seemed very near, we saw the ship was sinking rapidly. I was in the bow of the boat with my daughter and turned to see the great ship take a plunge toward the bow, the two forward funnels seemed to lean and then she seemed to break in half as if cut with a knife, and as the bow went under the lights went out. The stern stood up for several minutes, black against the stars, and then that, too, plunged down, and there was no sound for what seemed like hours, and then began the cries for help of people drowning all around us, which seemed to go on forever. Someone called out 'Pull for your lives, or you'll be sucked under' and everyone that could, rowed like mad. I could see my younger daughter and Mrs Thayer and Mrs Astor rowing, but there seemed to be no suction. Then we turned to pick up some of those in the water. Some of the women protested, but others persisted, and we dragged in six or seven men. The men we rescued were principally stokers, stewards, sailors, etc., and were so chilled and frozen already they could hardly move. Two of them died in the stern later and many were raving and moaning and delirious most of the time. We had no lights or compass. There were several babies in the boat, but there was no milk or water. I believe these were all stowed away somewhere, but no one knew where, and as the bottom of the boat was full of water and the boat full of people it was very difficult to find anything.

After the *Titanic* sank we saw no lights, and no one seemed to know what direction to take. Lowe, the officer in charge of the boat, had called out earlier for all to tie together, so we now heard his whistle, and as soon as we could make out the other boats in the dark, five of us were tied together, and we drifted about without rowing, as the sea was calm, waiting for the dawn. It was very cold, and soon a breeze sprang up, and it was hard to keep our heavy boat bow on. But as the cries died down we could see dimly what seemed to be a raft with about 20 men standing on it, back to back. It was the overturned boat, and as the sailors on our boat said we could still carry eight or 10 more people, we called for another boat to volunteer and go to rescue them. So we two cut loose and between us got all the men off. They were nearly gone and could not have held out much longer. Then, when the sun rose we saw the *Carpathia* standing up about five miles away, and for the first time saw the icebergs all around us. The *Carpathia* steamed toward us until it was full daylight, then she stopped and began picking up boats, and we got on board about eight o'clock. Very soon after we got on board they took a complete list of the names of all survivors. The kindness and the efficiency of all the arrangements on the *Carpathia* for our comfort can never be too highly praised.

47

Gertrude Hippach, First Class Passenger

From Chicago and aged just 17, Gertrude Hippach was travelling with her mother Ida Hippach, who also survived the disaster.

Quoted in Marshall Everett's book The Wreck & Sinking of the Titanic, 1912 Yes it was terrible. But it already seems like a dream to me the *Titanic* was so huge that it is hard to give an idea of it. It was over 800 feet, two blocks long, and wide in proportion. The staterooms were like rooms in a hotel. We had a regular bed and a handsome dressing table and chairs, and there was the lavatory with hot and cold water and there were electric lights and an electric fan, and an electric curling iron and of course push buttons – everything you could think of. One of our friends, when her husband asked her if she could think of anything to add to the equipment laughed and said, 'Well, we might have butter spreaders, I can't think of anything else.'

'Yet, there was no searchlight,' suggested a friend. Miss Hippach's face was grave as she echoed in a low tone, 'No searchlight!'

We had been to the concert in the evening till half past 10. There was lovely music. The orchestra gave three fine programs everyday before luncheon, in the afternoon and after dinner every evening. They were all real musicians and were appreciated by the people on board, who were the finest lot of people I ever crossed with – people of leisure and good breeding, all of them.

Well, we were asleep when the crash came. It was on our side and we awoke instantly and sat up in bed. Then the big boat shivered from the shock and then there was a long scraping, grating kind of noise and bumping, and then it was still.

We ran out and found everybody out in the corridor, asking what was the matter. A steward came along and said it was nothing, we had only grazed an iceberg. He advised us to go back to bed. We went back. But mother said, 'I've never seen an iceberg, and I'm going to put on some clothes and go on deck.' I tried to persuade her to go back to bed, but she was determined. I didn't want to be left alone, so I dressed, too. I was so sleepy it took me a long time to get dressed; but we both put on real warm clothes.

If it had not been for Mr Astor I believe we would have been among the lost. The last lifeboat was being lowered when Mr Astor saw us. He ordered the boat raised so that my mother could get into it. 'Don't lower that boat until this women gets in.' said Mr Astor. We were compelled to climb through a porthole in order to reach the boat, but mother would not get into it unless I joined her. Mr Astor again showed chivalry by pleading with the officers to permit me to get into the lifeboat, and they did.

Mr Astor was the calmest man during the exciting moments on the *Titanic* I ever saw. He smiled as he engineered the work of putting the women and children aboard the lifeboats. 'Don't worry, the *Titanic* will not sink, and we will all be saved,' said Mr Astor, as he aided the frightened passengers into the boats.

Well, we got into the lifeboat, though it didn't seem necessary, and it was so cold and so far down to the sea. But everybody was getting in. Ours was the last boat. Mrs J. B. Thayer was in it. She rowed all night, hardly resting at all. She was so brave, although she must have known that her son and her husband – you know, she was the one who said her husband had 'better die than live dishonoured,'

And Mrs Astor, too, was in our boat. We already knew her, that is we knew who she was. She was crying and her face was bleeding from a cut. One of the oars struck her somehow. There was a little bride in our boat with her husband. She clung to him and cried that she would not go and leave him, so the officers finally pushed them both in together. There were about 35 in all in our boat, mainly from the steerage.

In describing the lifeboat Miss Hippach indicated its length roughly as about 30 feet and explained that the air compartments were up just under the gunwale all around. She said that it was about five feet deep, with seats against the sides.

We had gone back for our lifebelts before we got in, as the officers told us to do. I got mine on wrong side before and the officer changed it. That was the reason, perhaps, why some people couldn't sit down with them on. And we went back still another time and got some heavy steamer rugs, two of them, as the officers said it was going to be very cold on the water and we might have to stay our several hours. Even then we didn't expect the *Titanic* to go down, you see. The rugs were more than we needed, and we gave them to a poor woman who had on only a nightgown and a waterproof coat and her baby was in a nightgown only. That poor little baby! It slept through everything!

After we had pushed away a little we looked at the steamer and I said to mother, 'It surely is sinking. See the water is up to those portholes!' And very soon it went under. To the last those poor musicians stood there, playing *Nearer, My God to Thee.*

The girl's voice trembled and stopped.

We had only one or two in the boat who knew anything about rowing and they kept turning it this way and that and again and again it seemed as if we might be capsized. But we did get away from the *Titanic* a little distance before it went down.

We picked up eight men from the water, all third class passengers, I think. The water was very still and the sky – so many stars! Nothing but the sea and the sky. You can't think how it felt out there alone by ourselves in the Atlantic. And there were so many shooting stars. I never saw so many in all my life. You know they say when you see a shooting star someone is dying. We thought of that, for there were so many dying, not far from us.

It was so long, such a long, long night. At last there was a little faint light. The first thing we saw we thought was one of the *Titanic's* funnels sticking out of the water. But it wasn't. It was the raft, the collapsible boat that didn't open, with 12 men on it, standing close together. They came up to us and demanded that we take them. But we thought they ought to say who they were, we were already pretty full and the water was getting rough. But they said they would jump in anyhow, so we let them come aboard, as we knew that jumping would surely capsize us. They were all stewards and waiters, men of the service of the *Titanic.* After we took them in it got still rougher, so that we sometimes shipped water. In fact, there was nearly a foot of water in the bottom of the boat and we hadn't as much as a cup to ship it out with. Meanwhile the waves were rising and if we hadn't been picked up when we were, another half hour would surely have been the end of us.

How did you find things on the Carpathia? was asked.

Just lovely. Nobody could have been kinder that they were. They kept their own people waiting and just took care of us. There was a warm blanket ready for each one and they had hot punch ready for us, or hot coffee and food.

We couldn't sleep till night. We had to be crowded in somewhat. The passengers of the *Carpathia* gave up their rooms or shared them. We were with two old ladies who were very nice. But the first night we gave up our chance to two little brides who were very, very ill. They were from the *Titanic*. We slept on sofas in the dining saloon. The next night we had mattresses on the floor of the stateroom with the little brides and the old ladies slept somewhere else. The third night we slept in a regular bed.

Asked about the officers and servants of the ill-fated vessel Miss Hippach said:

They said cheerful things right through. You know they are under orders never to alarm the passengers, no matter what happens. So the stewardess spoke soothingly, and assured us it was only a little accident, that we should all be coming back on board again in the morning, probably. But they knew, they knew they were lying.

48

Marian Thayer, First Class Passenger

Marian Thayer was travelling with her husband John, vice president of the Pennsylvanian railroad, and Jack, their 17-year-old son. Neither father nor son were allowed to board the lifeboat with Marian. Jack Thayer later jumped into the water and managed to climb on to the overturned lifeboat collapsible B.

Mrs Thayer's affidavit from Archibald Gracie's book The Truth About the Titanic The after part of the ship then reared in the air, with the stern upwards, until it assumed an almost vertical position. It seemed to remain stationary in this position for many seconds (perhaps 20), then suddenly dove straight down out of sight. It was 2.20 a.m. when the *Titanic* disappeared, according to a wrist watch worn by one of the passengers in my boat.

We pulled back to where the vessel had sunk and on our way picked up six men who were swimming – two of whom were drunk and gave us much trouble all the time. The six men we picked up were hauled into the boat by the women. Two of these men died in the boat.

The boat we were in started to take in water. I do not know how. We had to bail. I was standing in ice cold water up to the top of my boots all the time, and rowing continuously for nearly five hours. We took off about 15 more people who were standing on a capsized boat. In all, our boat had by that time 65 or 66 people. There was no room to sit down in our boat, so we all stood, except some sitting along the side.

I think the steerage passengers had as good a chance as any of the rest to be saved.

The boat I was in was picked up by the *Carpathia* at 7 a.m. on Monday, we having rowed three miles to her, as we could not wait for her to come up on account of our boat taking in so much water that we would not have stayed afloat much longer.

I never saw greater courage or efficiency than was displayed by the officers of the ship. They were calm, polite and perfectly splendid. They also worked hard. The bedroom stewards also behaved extremely well.

LIFEBOAT C
Starboard Side, Launched 2.00 a.m.

Lifeboat C was stowed next to emergency lifeboat I and once lifeboat I had been launched, collapsible C was slotted into the davits. These collapsible lifeboats had wooden bottoms, canvas sides which needed to be manually raised and a capacity of about 47 people. The British Board of Inquiry recorded 71 people in this boat, which is close to the testimony of Alfred Pearcey. Archibald Gracie (possibly using the figure Quartermaster George Rowe gives in his testimony) suggests that this lifeboat contained 39 people, while Bruce Ismay, it's most controversial passenger, suggested there were 45 on board. The true figure will never be known, but it is likely to be nearer 40 than 71. Quartermaster Rowe was put in charge by Captain Smith and Chief Officer Wilde. At the last minute Bruce Ismay, chairman of the White Star Line climbed into this lifeboat. Several eyewitnesses report that an officer (probably First Officer Murdoch) had to fire his gun to maintain order when loading this lifeboat.

49
Albert Pearcey, Third Class Steward

Like Steward John Hart, Albert Pearcey relates how he directed third class passengers through first class quarters up to the boat deck. Pearcey also describes how First Officer Murdoch ordered him into a boat with two babies in his arms. He had worked for the White Star Line for five years and had transferred from *Olympic* to *Titanic*. Like many on board ship, Peacey couldn't always accurately identify locations where he had been, such was the complexity of the system of decks and companionways on board *Titanic*.
British Board of Trade Inquiry (inquiry question is followed immediately by witness's answer) Were you off duty when this collision occurred on that Sunday night? Yes.

Were you standing with others outside the pantry? Yes.

Is that on E deck? Yes, I think it is E deck. I am not quite sure.

Do you remember where it was? Just outside the pantry door in the main alleyways. Just under the main alleyway of E deck.

He said E deck, but I am not sure that he is right. *Witness answers:* I am not sure I am right. I know it is just outside the pantry.

I am going to put a question that will clear that up. Was it on the same deck as the third class stewards had their quarters? Yes.

On the same deck as the third class dining saloon? Yes.

Then it is F deck.

On the port side? *Witness answers:* On the starboard side it is close to the dining saloon.

So it is, I think, on the other. Both on the port and starboard side it is just abaft of the third class dining saloon. The boiler casing is marked in between. *Witness does not respond.*

Did you feel the collision? Not at all.

What was it that first indicated to you that there had been a collision with the iceberg? There was just a small motion, but nothing to speak of.

What happened immediately after this motion? The order was 'All watertight doors to be closed.'

Are you referring to the watertight doors of this F deck? Yes.

Were they closed? Yes.

Did you help to close them? Yes.

Did several other men help with you? Yes.

Where did you close them? I closed them on towards aft. I closed the pantry doors of my pantry on the starboard and port sides.

You said you were a third class pantryman. What was your duty? Had you any duty in connection with the passengers? *Witness answers:* No, not at all.

Who was the chief third class steward? Mr Kieran.

Did he give any orders that you heard? The order that I heard was, 'Assist all passengers on to boat deck.'

That meant, I suppose, 'Assist all passengers'? *Witness answers:* Assist third class passengers. When Mr Kieran gave that he would mean to say the third class passengers.

Tell us what you did? I put the lifebelts over their heads, and I tied the strings round them.

Then when you had done that, where did you go? I passed all the passengers I could see forward to the boat deck.

How did you pass them forward to the boat deck? Through the emergency door.

Where was that emergency door to which you are referring? The one right forward.

Where does it lead through? Right through the saloon companion.

What saloon? The first class.

Right through the first class saloon companion? Yes.

That would be on the next deck, would it not, on the upper deck? Yes.

Deck E? Yes.

Would that be leading into the alleyway? Yes.

As the people came along there you passed them through this door, did you? Yes.

Where did the people come from? They came from forward.

Were they men or women? All men, Sir.

You passed them up to that door, did you give them any directions? Yes, passed the directions right up. There were stewards besides me.

Right up the whole way? Right through the saloon to the companion, right through that door right up the saloon companion leading to the top deck.

To the boat deck? Yes.

Were there stewards posted at stations all along the way? Yes.

Did you go down to the passengers quarters at all? No, not at all.

It was not part of your duty? It was not part of my duty at all.

You were carrying out what you were told by the steward to assist them up to the boat deck? Yes.

Did a great number of passengers come along that alleyway? Yes.

Did you remain there until there were no more coming along the alleyway? As far as I could see.

You remained there until you could see no more passengers coming along the alleyway, is that right? Yes.

What did you do then? I went to the boat deck myself.

What was the time then? It was nearly half-past one.

You had nothing to do with the passengers who came from the after part of the ship? No.

When you found there were no more passengers coming along, you went up to the boat deck yourself? Yes, I went up to the boat deck myself.

Did the other stewards go with you? Yes.

And those who had been stationed there and who had been assisting in the directions? Yes.

When you got to the boat deck will you tell us what you saw? I saw two babies on the deck. I picked them up in my arms and took them to the boat.

Do you know what boat it was you took them to? A collapsible boat.

Was there any officer there? Yes.

Who? The chief, Mr Murdoch.

Do you remember whether the collapsible was on the starboard or the port side? On the starboard side.

Did Mr Murdoch give you any order? Yes.

What was it? He told me to get inside with the babies and take charge of them.

Were you attached to any boat, had you a station on any boat? Yes.

What was it? No. 3 on the starboard side.

That was the second boat, the first lifeboat after the emergency? Yes.

Did you notice what had happened with regard to any of the other boats on the starboard side when you were ordered into the collapsible? Not at all.

When you came on the boat deck you did not see? No.

Did you notice whether No. 3 boat, your own boat, was there or not? Yes, it was gone.

Where was the collapsible when you were told to get into it? By the side of No. 3 on the starboard side.

On the starboard side? Yes, on the starboard side close to number 3. That was the boat I was stationed in.

Close by where number 3 would have been if it had been in its ordinary place? Yes.

Had it been moved or was it where you usually saw it? It was where I always saw it.

Did you notice whether the emergency boat had gone or not? No.

Were there people in the collapsible boat? Yes.

Were they women or men? All women, Sir.

And children? Children and women.

And some of the crew? Five of the crew with the quartermaster.

Did that include yourself? There were three firemen, myself, and a quartermaster.

Do you remember how many you were in the boat? Just about 66.

Does that include the crew? That is without counting the crew.

That means 71 in all, does it? Yes.

Do you remember how the collapsible was launched at all into the water? No. It is launched, of course. It is put down the side.

It is put over the side? It was swung out.

By the davits? Yes.

Were there any women or children on the deck in the neighbourhood of the boat when you left? I did not notice. I never noticed at all.

I want to quite understand what you mean when you say you never noticed. Do you mean that you did not see any, or you do not know whether any were there? *Witness answers:* I did not see any women there at all.

Your boat was launched over the side by means of the falls? What happened to it, do you remember? What happened when you first got to the water? Did it float all right? *Witness answers:* Yes.

Were the sides up - the canvas bulwarks? Yes.

Was it dry when you got into the water? Yes.

Who was in charge? The quartermaster.

Do you remember his name? No, I do not.

Tell us what happened to it. I want you to tell us all you can. You got into the boat, there was the quartermaster in charge. I suppose some of you started rowing? Yes. I handed the babies over to the passengers, and I took the oars.

Did any of the passengers help you to row, or was it all done by you, the crew? Done by the crew.

How far did you row? Did you row right away from the ship? *Witness answers:* Yes. We rowed away from the ship. We rowed her a distance out.

You could not tell us how far? No.

Did you notice when you rowed away whether the ship had any list? Yes, the ship had a list on her port side.

Did you notice whether she was down by the head? No, I did not notice.

Did you notice whether she appeared to be going deeper into the water forward - did you notice that? No.

Did you see the vessel go down? Yes.

Can you give us any idea of how long it was after you had started rowing away from the *Titanic* before she sank? No, I cannot. It was 20 minutes to two when we came away from her.

That will help us. It was 20 minutes to two, you remember, when you started rowing away from the ship's side – is that right? Yes.

Not when you came up on deck, but when you started rowing away? Yes, when we got away. It was just in time.

How do you remember it was 20 minutes to two? Because I looked at the time.

That is what I wanted to know. Where did you look at the time? One of the passengers had the time.

Explain to the court what you saw when the vessel sank? Of course, when she sank she went down. She went down this way (showing) I could not exactly say. I am only rough myself, and I cannot describe it.

Let us see if we can help you. Did she appear to be plunging down by the head or the stern? She was plunging forward.

Did you see her stern out of the water at all? Yes sir.

Was the stern upstanding? Yes.

Could you tell that her keel was visible? Yes, the keel was visible.

Then, when you saw that, what did you next see happen to the stern? She went down, you see. It upset me, and I could not exactly say.

Did you remain in this collapsible boat until you were picked up by the *Carpathia*? Yes.

And all your passengers? Yes.

When this collapsible boat was lowered was the water practically up to the deck? Not on that side, not on our side. That was the starboard side.

50

Mariana Assaf, Third Class Passenger

Mariana Assaf was a 45-year-old Syrian woman who had emigrated to Canada several years earlier. Following the sinking she spent some time in hospital before finally arriving in Ottawa on 23 April. Her story was published in the *Ottawa Citizen* 24 April 1912 and repeated in the *Quebec Chronicle* of the same day where she reiterated that steerage passengers were assured that there was no danger.

I was with others of my relations and friends for many of us Syrians on board were known to me and we had all gone to bed when the ship struck. Although it did not seem to be much at first and we did not feel very much except a jar, some of us wanted to go on deck to see what happened.

We were told that everything was all right, and we did not think there was a danger. But the ship did not go on, then some of us began to think they were not telling us the truth and that we might be sinking. I think somebody must have said the boat was going to go down for suddenly there was great confusion and everybody tried to rush the deck.

There were many in third class who tried to rush the boats and at those some of the officers fired revolvers and some of them were shot dead. The rest were driven back. They were not given a chance to escape. As for me, when I thought the ship might sink, I forgot everything and rushed away from third class and up to the deck where the first class passengers are. I could not think of anything. I never saw any of my relations so I do not know what became of them. The last I saw of them was when we were all in the third class.

When I ran up to first class, I saw that the ship must be going to sink and I lost my head. But a man, I think he was one of the sailors, when he saw that I was there, he pushed me into one of the boats where there were already many women and a few men. The boat was lowered into the water and then the men rowed it away for they were afraid that when a big ship went down it would take them with it. Some said the band was playing, but I did not hear it. I was so out of my mind. It was an hour-and-a-half after the boat struck before I was put into a small boat.

Then *Titanic* sank and we drifted about all night. It was terribly cold, and I could never forget my relations and my friends whom I would never see again. When I thought of them I felt that I was going to go crazy. Six hours after we left *Titanic* somebody said 'there's a steamer,' we were saved and we were taken aboard *Carpathia*. When we got on board the *Carpathia* everyone was very kind and gave me clothes to wear. But I don't remember very much, I could hardly think.

51
Abraham Hyman, Third Class Passenger

Abraham Hyman was from Manchester and was going to America to join his brother in New Jersey. As with many survivors there is some confusion over which lifeboat he got off the *Titanic* on and it is possible that Hyman got away in lifeboat 13, not lifeboat C.

New York Herald, 19 April 1912 My stateroom was in the third class cabin, well forward, and about two decks down from the top deck. Sunday night I sat chatting with several other passengers and went to bed a few minutes after 10 o'clock. It must have been about half past eleven when I was awakened by a terrible shock. There was only one – just a bang and a rip – lasting a couple of seconds. Then everything was quiet. I didn't know what had happened, but never dreamed it could be anything serious, so I lay in my bunk for 20 minutes listening. I could hear doors banging and passengers running to and fro asking what was the matter. Someone said everything was all right, but some were afraid.

Then I got up and dressed and went out into the passage. A steward standing there told me roughly to go to the back of the ship, and I walked along the passage which ran the whole length of the vessel. On the way I passed a group of engineers and stokers, laughing, chatting and smoking cigarettes. I reached the after third class cabin, then climbed up to the top deck, where I stood fully 20 minutes. I knew the ship had hit something, but I didn't think it could be anything serious – I don't believe anybody on board suspected anything serious.

All around me were passengers putting on lifebelts. Some of the women were a little frightened, but most were calm, and I thought the lifebelts were just an extra precaution. I looked for one but couldn't find one. There were several back in my room, but I never thought to bring one along. I saw several people climbing up the stairs which led to a sort of house on the deck just in front of me, and I thought I would see what was the matter up there. I asked several officers if there was any danger, and they said 'No, no just keep calm.'

I climbed up the stairs, and there were a lot of men and women standing about a lifeboat. The women were being helped in, but the men didn't seem to want to get in. Then I noticed that it was the next to the last boat in that part of the ship. The others were all lowered, and I got a little uneasy. I climbed up on to the rail, and watching for my chance, slipped into the boat just before they began to lower away. Most of the men thought they would be safer back on the boat, and some of them smiled at us as we went down.

When we were nearly to the water we passed a big hole in the side of the boat. This was about three quarters of the way back toward the stern and the pumps were throwing a great stream of water out through it. It threatened to swamp our boat, and we got scared there were about 10 men in the boat and we each took an oar and pushed the boat away from the side of the ship. That's all that saved us.

When we settled into the water we pulled away like mad, because we didn't know whether the *Titanic* would sink or not and were afraid of the suction. When we were about 50 yards away I noticed that the portholes forward were lower than those aft, and then got my first impression that the ship was sinking. When we had pulled further away I saw the iceberg. It was black and was about 50 yards astern of the *Titanic*.

We pulled away about half a mile and then rested and watched. One by one I saw the forward portholes go out, just like some one was walking back through the ship and turning out the electric lights. Then we heard a small explosion and a terrible cry. The cry was blood curdling and never stopped until the *Titanic* went down, when it seemed to be sort of choked off. The cry is ringing in my ears now and always will. We sat there silent, we were terror stricken. In less than 10 minutes there came a terrible explosion, and I could see men, women and pieces of the ship blown into the air from the after deck. Later I saw bodies partly blown to pieces floating around, and I am sure more than a hundred persons were blown off into the sea by that explosion. I met one man on the *Carpathia* who was blown off, but caught a piece of a table and floated.

At the second explosion the lights went out, all at once. Even the lights on the masthead went out. And everything was dark for a few moments. A terrible hissing of steam began and the awful cry went on. I tried to close my ears, but there was some mysterious attraction and I had to hear that cry.

When my eyes got used to the dark I could make out the *Titanic*, still with the front part down in the water. That was about half-past-one, I guess. The hissing and screaming kept up, and finally the ship seemed to right itself, then suddenly the front end plunged down and she sank like a stone. The cry was choked off, and the hissing of steam stopped, but the sudden silence was almost more terrifying than the screams. We didn't feel the suction, except for a big wave that rocked our boat about two minutes after.

The women were crying, but the men in our boat were still. We rowed about for a while to try and find the other boats and finally came upon four more. We also found a lot of men floating around on tables and chairs but had no room to pick up any of them. One man had tied three deck chairs together and was floating all night.

It was terribly cold. Some of the men in our boat took off their coats and threw them around the women, who were almost frozen. The wind began to blow sharply, and the boat started rocking a little, but the sea was never dangerous. In about two hours we saw a glint of light off to the west. We watched it for an hour, and then we could see that there were two lights and it must be a ship, so we rowed toward it. The exercise kept us men warm, but the women, most of them first cabin passengers, were nearly frozen to death. As soon as it got light we could see that the ship was the *Carpathia*, and we reached it in another hour. We had to be lifted aboard, as some of the women were unconscious. They gave us coffee and brandy and we felt better.

There were boats coming towards the *Carpathia* from all sides. In some were men and women badly mangled. They had to be lifted aboard on stretchers, and if it hadn't been so calm they could never have gotten aboard at all.

The *Carpathia* stood by for about four hours, then another ship came up. I don't know the name of it. They signalled to each other, then began to take a big circle, one on each side. The circle was about 20 miles across and in the middle was a big ice floe, fully 10 miles wide, but I don't think it was the one the *Titanic* struck. We picked up altogether 16 boats, besides those we found three empty ones, and one had been capsized, with a man floating on top.

The *Carpathia* then came back to where the *Titanic* sank. You could tell the place by the corks, boxes, bottles, chairs and things floating around on the water, and now and then a big cloud of bubbles would come up. Then we turned around and made for New York.

52

George Rowe, Quartermaster

32-year-old George Rowe assisted Fourth Officer Boxhall to launch distress flares before taking charge of lifeboat C. Rowe describes the escape of Bruce Ismay, which was one of the most controversial events of the night. As chairman of the White Star Line Ismay was ultimately responsible for the design of *Titanic* and therefore its inadequate lifeboat provision. There were many who thought he should have gone down with the ship. Rowe's station was on the poop deck, the raised deck at the rear of *Titanic*, infamous for the dying scenes of the film *Titanic* and the last part of the ship to be submerged. Earlier in the voyage *Titanic*'s third class passengers would have used this space to rest on benches or to promenade.

US Senate Inquiry (inquiry question is followed immediately by witness's answer) Where were you the night of the collision? I felt a slight jar and looked at my watch. It was a fine night, and it was then 20 minutes to 12. I looked toward the starboard side of the ship and saw a mass of ice. I then remained on the after bridge to await orders through the telephone. No orders came down, and I remained until 25 minutes after 12, when I saw a boat on the starboard beam.

What was the number of the boat? I could not tell the number. I telephoned to the fore bridge to know if they knew there was a boat lowered. They replied, asking me if I was the third officer. I replied, 'No. I am the quartermaster.' They told me to bring over detonators, which are used in firing distress signals.

What next happened? I took them to the fore bridge and turned them over to the Fourth Officer. I assisted the officer to fire them, and was firing the distress signals until about five and 20 minutes after 1. At that time they were getting out the starboard collapsible boats. The Chief Officer, Wilde, wanted a sailor. I asked Captain Smith if I should fire any more, and he said 'No, get into that boat.' I went to the boat. Women and children were being passed in. I assisted six, three women and three children. The order was then given to lower the boat. The Chief Officer wanted to know if there were more women and children. There were none in the vicinity. Two gentlemen passengers got in, the boat was then lowered. When we reached the water we steered for a light in sight, roughly five miles. We pulled through the night, but seemed to get no nearer to the lights. So we altered our course back to a boat that was carrying a green light. During that time daylight broke and the *Carpathia* was in sight.

There was nothing special about your getting on the *Carpathia*? No sir. In the meantime I found that one of the two gentlemen was Mr Ismay. I don't know who the other was. 39 in the boat, all told.

How many of those were crew or sailors? Myself was the only sailor, three firemen, and one steward.

You had no trouble in managing the boat? Not a bit.

The passengers, aside from you sailors, were all women and children? Except Mr Ismay and another gentleman. When daylight broke, we found four men, Chinamen, I think they were, or Filipinos.

Were those additional to the 39? Yes sir.

When day broke, you found four Chinamen or Filipinos under the seats? Not under the seats then, sir. They came up between the seats. Ours was about the ninth boat which was unloaded upon the *Carpathia*. The night was very cold, but those who were in the boat were very well wrapped up and did not suffer.

Now, tell us the circumstances under which Mr Ismay and that other gentleman got in the boat. *Witness answers:* When Chief Officer Wilde asked if there was any more women and children there was no reply. So Mr Ismay came aboard the boat.

You could see around there on the deck, could you not? I could see the fireman and steward that completed the boat's crew, but as regards any females I could not see any.

Was it light enough so that you could see anyone near by? Yes sir.

If I understand, there were firemen and stokers around in that neighbourhood? Yes sir.

But no women and children? No women or children, sir.

And, so far as you could see, no other passengers except Mr Ismay and this other gentleman? Yes.

Did you know Mr Ismay at the time? I did know him, sir, because I had seen the gentleman before.

In going along on the water, did he give any directions? I was in charge of the boat.

Did you see any ice when on the watch? No sir, only when we struck, when we passed it on the starboard side.

About how high was that iceberg? Roughly, 100 feet, sir.

Was there anything distinctive about the colour of that iceberg? No a bit sir. Just like ordinary ice.

You saw it as it was brushing by? Yes sir. It was very close to the ship, almost touching it.

Did you see Mr Ismay and Mr Carter get in the boat? I saw the gentlemen get in yes sir.

Did you hear anyone ask them to get in? No sir.

How were you occupied at the time they got in? I was occupied in attending the after fall sir.

Were you watching Chief Officer Wilde? Yes sir.

Did you see him speak to them? No sir.

If he had spoken to them would you have known it? I think so, because they got in the after part of the boat.

And you were in the after part of the boat? I was in the after part yes.

Did you hear any order to abandon the ship, or anything like that? No sir.

Did you hear any general alarm? No sir.

Did you hear the sirens? No sirens, sir but there was an awful noise made by the escape of steam.

Was that noise below or up at the escape pipe? At the exhaust pipe.

Were there any detonators or other signals kept aft? The detonators, such as the distress signal rockets, green lights, and blue lights.

Were there any kept forward? Yes, on the fore bridge. There was a private locker aft.

Were you at any time on any other deck aside from the top or bridge deck? No sir, not after eight o'clock.

Was there any panic that you saw? Not a bit.

Might not a number of persons have been on the lower decks? Yes sir, undoubtedly.

Did you hear any sign or hear any indication of an alarm to call the passengers? No sir.

Just where were you when you saw the iceberg? On the poop sir, underneath the after bridge.

You were located practically right on the stern of the boat. *Witness answers:* Right on the stern, sir. The poop.

And the iceberg, when the boat rubbed against it, was right near, was it? Yes sir.

How far, would you say? It was so near that I thought it was going to strike the bridge.

Did it strike the bridge? No sir, never.

Only 10 or 20 feet away? Not that far sir.

Did you notice the iceberg when the boat got clear of it? No sir. I went on the bridge then, to stand by the telephone.

Could you hear the ice scraping along on the boat where you were? No sir.

So you do not know whether it was rubbing against the hull there or not? No sir.

What is your best judgment about that? I do not think it was.

How near were you to the starboard side of the boat when you first noticed it rubbing? About eight or 10 feet. I went to the side.

Did you go immediately to the side? Yes sir.

What were your duties as quartermaster aft? My duties were to attend the log and night signals by night, logging ensign by day, and to look out for any accidents, a man overboard or something like that.

How soon after she struck was it before she started to tilt or go down by the head? She did not list, did she? *Witness answers:* No sir, not at that time, I don't think.

Did she at any time list over to starboard or port? She did not list, so far as I know, until the time when my boat was lowered. Then she listed to port. She listed about five or six degrees.

What side was your boat on? The starboard side, sir. All the time my boat was being lowered the rubbing strake kept on catching on the rivets down the ship's side, and it was as much as we could do to keep her off.

Was the *Titanic* down by the head? Yes sir. When we left the ship the fore well deck was awash, that is when we pushed off from the ship. It was 1.25 a.m. when I left the bridge to get into the boat. When the boat was in the water the well deck was submerged. It took us a good five minutes to lower the boat on account of this rubbing going down.

She must have sunk soon after you left? 20 minutes, I believe.

Did any boats get away after yours? One boat got away after mine, on the port side [one further lifeboat – D – was *launched* from the port side after lifeboat C. Lifeboats A and B *floated* off and weren't launched as such].

How long did the rubbing or grinding against the ice last? I never heard anything except the first contact. The first jar was all I knew about it. I never heard any rubbing at all.

Did you hear any revolver shots? No sir.

Did you see the light of a boat, or anything of that kind? I saw the light, that was the light we were pulling for when we left the ship.

What do you conclude that light was? A sailing ship.

What sort of light was it? A white light.

And was she the sailing ship going away from you? Toward daylight the wind sprung up and she sort of hauled off from us.

Did you see her? No sir.

The light you saw was a white light? Yes sir.

What did you judge it to be, a stern light? I judged it to be a stern light yes sir.

What was its bearing with regard to the *Titanic*, forward or aft? Right forward, sir.

Dead ahead? Not dead ahead, but just a little on the port bow.

When did you first see her? When I was on the bridge firing the rockets. I saw it myself, and I worked the Morse lamp at the port side of the ship to draw her attention.

Was there any steam coming up through any of the hatches or ventilators? No sir. The only steam I saw was coming out of exhaust pipes.

How far from the ship were you when she went down? About three-quarters of a mile, sir.

Did you see her go down? I saw her stern disappear at the finish, sir.

British Board of Trade Inquiry (inquiry question is followed immediately by witness's answer) When the boat got down to the water, how many people were in it? 39.

How was that number made up. Were there two gentlemen? Yes.

And how many crew? Myself, three firemen and one steward.

And the rest of the people were what? What I thought were women and children.

Did they prove to be women and children? No, not at daybreak.

Why? Tell me about that? I found four Chinamen aboard.

How they got in you do not know, I suppose? No.

Were they all women and children, with the exception of three Chinamen? Four Chinamen and Mr Ismay and Mr Carter.

How many women would that be? I cannot say how many women, because there were children there as well, 28 I think.

Mr Pearcey, who was a third class pantry steward, gave evidence about this boat. He took the view that there were '66 passengers and five of the crew, 71'. You do not think there were as many? *Witness answers:* I am certain.

That boat remained in the water and none of the passengers were taken out, and all of them were put out of the collapsible into the *Carpathia*? Yes.

This collapsible boat you got into, was it the last boat put off from the starboard side? Yes.

When you put off, was the vessel awash in the fore well deck? Yes.

The fore well deck was under water? Yes, the forecastle head was not submerged.

53

Bruce Ismay, First Class Passenger

Ismay became the chairman of the White Star Line in 1899 upon the death of his father. He commissioned *Titanic* and was ultimately accountable for its design and, crucially, its lack of adequate lifeboat provision. Ismay had chosen to accompany *Titanic* on its maiden voyage.

Ismay was the first witness called to the US inquiry and his appearance was eagerly anticipated. Questions had already been raised in the press both about the White Star's negligence, and the personal conduct of its most senior representative. In addition several passengers alleged that Ismay had encouraged Captain Smith to go faster, ignoring the ice warnings that had been received.

Having had the good fortune to survive, Ismay's actions that night received the highest level of scrutiny, with many thinking that, like Captain Smith, Ismay should have gone down with his ship. The media branded Ismay a coward and he was widely vilified. Ismay resigned as chairman just over a year later.

US Senate Inquiry (inquiry question is followed immediately by witness's answer) Will you describe what you did after the impact or collision? I presume the impact awakened me. I lay in bed for a moment or two afterwards, not realizing, probably, what had happened. Eventually I got up and walked along the passageway and met one of the stewards, and said, 'What has happened?' He said, 'I do not know, sir.' I then went back into my room, put my coat on, and went up on the bridge, where I found Captain Smith. I asked him what had happened, and he said, 'We have struck ice.' I said, 'Do you think the ship is seriously damaged?' He said, 'I am afraid she is.' I then went down below, I think it was, where I met Mr Bell, the Chief Engineer, who was in the main companionway. I asked if he thought the ship was seriously damaged, and he said he thought she was, but was quite satisfied the pumps would keep her afloat. I think I went back on to the bridge. I heard the order given to get the boats out. I walked along to the starboard side of the ship, where I met one of the officers. I told him to get the boats out. I assisted, as best I could, getting the boats out and putting the women and children into the boats. I stood upon that deck practically until I left the ship in the starboard collapsible boat, which is the last boat to leave the ship, so far as I know. More than that I do not know.

Were you outside on the deck, or on any deck, when the order was given to lower the lifeboats? I heard Captain Smith give the order when I was on the bridge.

Will you tell us what he said. *Witness answers:* I know I heard him give the order to lower the boats. I think that is all he said. I think he simply turned around and gave the order.

Was there anything else said, as to how they should be manned or occupied? No, sir not that I heard. As soon as I heard him give the order to lower the boats, I left the bridge.

Did you see any of the boats lowered? Yes sir.

How many? Certainly three.

Will you tell us, if you can, how they were lowered? They were swung out, people were put into the boats from the deck, and then they were simply lowered away down to the water.

Were you on the bridge at any time? I was never on the bridge until after the accident.

How long after the accident? I should think it might have been 10 minutes.

Was the Captain there at that time? The Captain was there yes.

Was that the only time you saw the Captain on the bridge? I saw him afterwards, when I went up the second time to the bridge.

How long after? I should think it might be 35 minutes. It is very difficult to place the time.

After the impact? Yes sir.

What, if anything, did he say to you about the collision? The only conversation I had with Captain Smith was when I went up on the bridge. I asked him what had happened, and he said we had struck ice.

When you were on the bridge with the Captain, after the accident, did he say anything to you about her condition at that time? No sir. When I went up to ask him what had happened, he told me we had struck an iceberg, and I asked him whether he thought the matter was serious, and he said he thought it was.

That was the first intimation you had? That was the first intimation I had.

Did you hear any order given to call the passengers? I did not, sir.

Or any other alarm? No, sir.

Did the Chief Engineer of the *Titanic* state to you the extent of the damage? He said that he thought the damage was serious that he hoped the pumps would be able to control the water.

How long was that after the impact? I should think it would be perhaps a half-an-hour afterwards, 35 or 40 minutes.

I think in my prior examination in New York you said you entered the lifeboat from the A deck? From the boat deck, sir.

And that at the time there were no other persons around, no women, particularly? Absolutely none that I saw, sir.

Was that the last lifeboat or the last collapsible boat to leave? It was the last collapsible boat that left the starboard side of the ship.

Was it filled to its capacity? No it was not.

Do you know how many people were in it? I should think there were about 40 women in it, and some children. There was a child in arms. I think they were all third class passengers, so far as I could see.

And this boat was from the starboard side of the boat deck, or top deck, near the bridge? Yes, sir.

Who, if anyone, told you to enter that lifeboat? No one sir.

Why did you enter it? Because there was room in the boat. She was being lowered away. I felt the ship was going down, and I got into the boat.

British Board of Trade Inquiry (inquiry question is followed immediately by witness's answer) When you got into the boat you thought that the *Titanic* was sinking? I did.

Did you know that there were some hundreds of people on that ship? Yes.

Who must go down with her? Yes I did.

Has it occurred to you that, except perhaps apart from the Captain, you, as the responsible Managing Director, deciding the number of boats, owed your life to every other person on that ship? It has not.

According to your statement you got into this boat last of all? I did.

So that if a witness says that you, in fact, got into the boat earlier and helped the women and children in, that would not be true? It would not.

Now, it has been given in evidence here that you took an actual part in giving directions for the women and children to be placed in the boats. Is that true? I did, and I helped as far as I could.

If you had taken this active part in the direction up to a certain point, why did you not continue and send to other decks to see if there were passengers available for this last boat? I was standing by the boat. I helped everybody into the boat who was there, and, as the boat was being lowered away, I got in.

That does not answer the question. You had been taking a responsible part, according to the evidence and according to your own admission, in directing the filling of the boats? No, I had not. I had been helping to put the women and children into the boats as they came forward.

I am afraid we are a little at cross purposes. Is it not the fact that you were calling out 'Women and children first,' and helping them in? Yes it is.

Is it not the fact that you were giving directions as to women and children getting in? *Witness answers:* I was helping the women and children in.

Please answer my question. Is it not the fact that you were giving directions in helping them? *Witness answers:* I was calling for the women and children to come in.

What I am putting to you is this, that if you could take an active part at that stage, why did you not continue the active part and give instruction, or go yourself to other decks, or round the other side of that deck, to see if there were other people who might find a place in your boat? *Witness answers:* I presumed that there were people down below who were sending the people up.

But you knew there were hundreds who had not come up. That is your answer, that you presumed that there were people down below sending them up? Yes.

And does it follow from that that you presumed that everybody was coming up who wanted to come up? I knew that everybody could not be up.

Then I do not quite see the point of the answer? Everybody that was on the deck got into that boat.

I want to get it from this witness, inasmuch as he took upon himself to give certain directions at a certain time, why he did not discharge the responsibility even after that, having regard to other persons or passengers? There were no more passengers to get into that boat. The boat was actually being lowered away.

You helped the women and children in, but not from inside the boat? That is so.

And you did not go into it until the last moment, as you have told us? Not till she was leaving, at the last moment.

US Senate Inquiry (inquiry question is followed immediately by witness's answer) Did you see the ship after you left her in the collapsible boat? I saw her once.

What was her position then? She was very much down by the head. Her starboard light was just about level with the water.

How far did you have to lower the collapsible boat from the boat deck to the water? It was very difficult to judge, because we had considerable difficulty in getting our boat down at all.

You did not have enough men? The ship had quite a list to port. Consequently this canvas boat, this collapsible boat, was getting hung up on the outside of the ship, and she had to rub right along her, and we had to try to shove her out, and we had to get the women to help to shove to get her clear of the ship. The ship had listed over that way.

Did you have enough help from the crew of the *Titanic*? Oh yes, they lowered the boat away.

How many men were in the boat? Three to four. We found four Chinamen stowed away under the thwarts after we got away. I think they were Filipinos, perhaps. There were four of them.

Were those oarsmen? I believe one was a cook, another was the butcher, and another was the quartermaster.

Did you handle the oars? Yes sir. I was rowing from the time we got into the boat until we got out, practically.

Mr Ismay, what can you say about the sinking and disappearance of the ship? Can you describe the manner in which she went down? *Witness answers:* I did not see her go down.

How far were you from the ship? I do not know how far we were away. I was sitting with my back to the ship. I was rowing all the time I was in the boat. We were pulling away.

You were rowing? Yes. I did not wish to see her go down.

You did not care to see her go down? No. I am glad I did not.

When did you last see her? I really could not say. It might have been 10 minutes after we left her. It is impossible for me to give any judgment of the time. I could not do it.

Was there much apparent confusion on board when you saw her last?

I did not look to see sir. My back was turned to her. I looked around once only, to see her red light, her green light rather.

Did you yourself see any icebergs at daybreak the following morning? I should think I saw four or five icebergs when day broke on Monday morning.

How near the scene of the *Titanic* disaster? I could not tell where she went down. We were some distance away from it.

Not desiring to be impertinent at all, but in order that I may not be charged with omitting to do my duty, I would like to know where you went after you boarded the *Carpathia*, and how you happened to go there? *Witness answers:* I understand that my behavior on board the *Titanic*, and subsequently on board the *Carpathia*, has been very severely criticized. I want to court the fullest inquiry, and I place myself unreservedly in the hands of yourself and any of your colleagues, to ask me any questions in regard to my conduct; so please do not hesitate to do so, and I will answer them to the best of my ability. So far as the *Carpathia* is concerned, sir, when I got on board the ship I stood up with my back against the bulkhead, and somebody came up to me and said, 'Will you not go into the saloon and get some soup, or something to drink?' 'No,' I said, 'I really do not want anything at all.' He said, 'Do go and get something.' I said, 'No. If you will leave me alone I will be very much happier here.' I said, 'If you will get me in some room where I can be quiet, I wish you would.' He said, 'Please go in the saloon and get something hot.' I said, 'I would rather not.' Then he took me and put me into a room. I did not know whose the room was, at all. This man proved to be the doctor of the *Carpathia*. I was in that room until I left the ship. I was never outside the door of that room. During the whole of the time I was in this room, I never had anything of a solid nature, at all. I lived on soup. I did not want very much of anything. The room was constantly being entered by people asking for the doctor. The doctor did not sleep in the room the first night. The doctor slept in the room the other nights that I was on board that ship. Mr Jack Thayer was brought into the room the morning we got on board the *Carpathia*. He stayed in the room for some little time, and the doctor came in after he had been in, I should think, about a quarter of an hour. The doctor did not have a suite of rooms on the ship. He simply had this one small room, which he himself occupied and dressed in every night and morning.

Was the knowledge of the sinking of the *Titanic* that was in your possession communicated by you to your company in Liverpool or to your offices in New York on the journey from the place of the collision to New York? *Witness answers:* Yes sir. I sent the message on Monday morning, very shortly after I got on board the *Carpathia*. The Captain came down to me and said, 'Don't you think sir you had better send a message to New York, telling them about this accident?' I said, 'Yes. I wrote it out on a slip of paper, and I turned to the commander of the *Carpathia* and I said, 'Captain, do you think that is all I can tell them?' He said, 'Yes.' Then he took it away from the room. I have a copy here, sir of every Marconi message which I sent away from the *Carpathia*. I had no communication with any other ship, and there is a record of every message which I received.

Please read them. *Witness answers:* The first message I sent was on 15 April, which was on Monday morning.

At what hour? I have not got the hour sir, but I should think it was about eight o'clock.

You say that shortly after you boarded the *Carpathia* you sent this message? Yes, sir.

You boarded the *Carpathia* about sunrise? I think that I boarded the ship *Carpathia* at a quarter to six or a quarter past six.

Ship's time? Yes. I happened to see a clock somewhere on the ship when I got on her. This is the message I sent, which was received by Mr Franklin on the 17 April 1912. I would like to draw your attention to the fact that I sent the message on the 15 April, and it did not reach Mr Franklin until 17 April.

How are you able to say that, Mr Ismay? Mr Franklin has told me so.

It will not take long, and I think I would like to have you read them, inasmuch as they came from you. *Witness answers:* Yes sir, I will do so. This is a message I sent on 15 April: 'Deeply regret advise you *Titanic* sank this morning after collision iceberg, resulting serious loss life. Full particulars later. Bruce Ismay.' The next one I sent, but I do not know the date of it, but presumably it was received by Mr Franklin on the 17 April at 9 a.m. I wired: 'Very important you should hold *Cedric* daylight Friday for *Titanic's* crew. Answer. YAMSI.' [YAMSI is simply Ismay spelt backwards] This is a message sent by Mr Franklin to me on 17 April 1912 at 3.30 p.m.: 'So thankful you are saved, but grieving with you over terrible calamity. Shall sail Saturday to return with you. Florence.' That was from my wife, and was forwarded to me by Mr Franklin, who said: 'Accept my deepest sympathy horrible catastrophe. Will meet you aboard *Carpathia* after docking. Is Widener aboard? Franklin.' This is a message I sent. I have not the date of it, but it was received by Mr Franklin on 17 April 1912 at 5.20 p.m.: 'Most desirable *Titanic* crew aboard *Carpathia* should be returned home earliest moment possible. Suggest you hold *Cedric*, sailing her daylight Friday, unless you see any reason contrary. Propose returning in her myself. Please send outfit of clothes, including shoes, for me to *Cedric*. Have nothing of my own. Please reply. YAMSI.' This is a message I received from Mr Franklin, which was dispatched by wire on the 17 April 1912 at 8 p.m.: 'Have arranged forward crew *Lapland* sailing Saturday, calling Plymouth. We all consider most unwise delay *Cedric* considering all circumstances. FRANKLIN'. I sent a message which was received by Mr Franklin on the 18 April, at 5.35 a.m., as follows: 'Send responsible ship officer and 14 White Star sailors in two tugboats to take charge of 13 *Titanic* boats, at quarantine. YAMSI.' That message I sent at the request of the Captain of the *Carpathia*, who told him it would be impossible to dock the ship with these lifeboats on deck. He was all hampered up, and would not be able to handle his ropes and what not. I drew up that message and showed it to the Captain and asked if that would answer the purpose, and he said 'Yes,' and I gave it to him, and he sent it, I presume. I telegraphed Mr Franklin, or Marconied him, and he received it on the 18 April 1912, at 5.35 a.m.: 'Please join *Carpathia* at quarantine if possible.' I sent a further message, which Mr Franklin received on 18 April 1912, at 8 a.m., as follows: 'Very important you should hold *Cedric* daylight Friday for *Titanic* crew. Reply. YAMSI.' I sent a further message, which was received by Mr Franklin on 18 April 1912, at 8.23 a.m.: 'Think most unwise keep *Titanic* crew until Saturday. Strongly urge detain *Cedric* sailing her midnight, if desirable.' I sent another message, which was received by Mr Franklin on 18 April 1912, at 8.44 a.m.: 'Unless you have good and sufficient reason for not holding *Cedric*, please arrange do so. Most undesirable have crew New York so long.' This is a message which Mr Franklin dispatched to me on the 18 April 1912, at 4.45 p.m., and which I received when the *Carpathia* got alongside the dock in New York, which was handed to me in the room: 'Concise Marconigram account of actual accident greatly needed for enlightenment public and ourselves. This most important. FRANKLIN.' I received it, I presume, about nine o'clock that night, when we were alongside the dock. Then I sent this message to Mr Franklin, which he received on 18 April 1912, at 5.38 p.m.: 'Widener not aboard. Hope see you quarantine. Please cable wife am returning *Cedric*. YAMSI.' That is a copy of every message I sent and every message I received and I had absolutely no communication with any other ship or any shore station, or with anyone.

Judging from the messages, it was your intention to return the night you landed, if possible, to Liverpool? Yes sir. At that time, you understand, I had not the slightest idea there was going to be any investigation of this sort.

LIFEBOAT D
Port Side, Launched 2.05 a.m.

This lifeboat was launched by Second Officer Charles Lightoller and Chief Officer Henry Wilde, who put Quartermaster Arthur Bright in charge. By now the atmosphere on deck had become so desperate that Lightoller had to order that the crew lock arms around lifeboat D, to ensure that only women and children were able to board. The waterline was now at the bottom of the bridge rail.

Two French brothers Michel and Edmond Navratil aged just three and two years respectively were put into this lifeboat by their father. Their father didn't survive. Their mother recognised them from press reports about the *Titanic* 'orphans' and was reunited with them a month later. It emerged that their father was estranged from their mother and had taken them without her permission to live in America.

After the launch of lifeboat D the only boats left were the two collapsible lifeboats stowed on top of the officers' quarters.

Again, there are varying accounts of the numbers in this lifeboat, which had a maximum capacity of 47. Some people (including testimony from both John Hardy and Hugh Woolner below) refer only to the numbers of women and children loaded and there is also the additional confusion caused by Fifth Officer Lowe's transfer of additional passengers over to this lifeboat during the night. All accounts indicate, however, that, despite this lifeboat being launched so late into the night, she was still not full. Lightoller recalled: 'In the case of the last boat I got out... I had the utmost difficulty in finding women... I called for women and could not get any... This was on the boat deck where all the women were supposed to be' (US Senate Inquiry). The answer must be that many third class women were unable to reach the boat deck. Continuing the pattern of the night, when there were no more women available, Lightoller ordered the boat to be launched with empty seats, while men simply watched. The British inquiry recorded a total figure (below) at 44, but this is the number that were taken on board *Carpathia*, i.e. after the transfer of additional survivors during the night. Lowe, in lifeboat 14, towed lifeboat D under sail in to the *Carpathia*.

Male crew: two; male passengers: two; women and children: 40; total for lifeboat: 44 (British Board of Inquiry).

54

John Hardy, Chief Second Class Steward

John Hardy lived in Southampton with his wife and two children and was 36 at the time of the US Inquiry. Hardy had worked for the White Star Line for 12 years and had been the chief second class steward for seven.

US Senate Inquiry (inquiry question is followed immediately by witness's answer)
Witness: We launched this boat filled with passengers. Mr Lightoller and myself loaded it. I went away in it with the quartermaster (Bright) and two firemen. There were Syrians in the bottom of the boat, third class passengers, chattering the whole night in their strange language. There were, about 25 women and children. We lowered away and got to the water. The ship then had a heavy list to port. We got clear of the ship and rowed out some distance from her. Mr Lowe told us to tie up with other boats, that we would be better seen and could keep better together. He, having a full complement of passengers in his boat, transferred about 10 to ours, making 35 in our boat.

When we left the ship, where we were lowered, there were no women and children there in sight at all. There was nobody to lower the boat. No men passengers when we were ready to lower it. They had gone, where, I could not say. We were not more than 40 feet from the water when we were lowered. We picked up the husband (Frederick Hoyt) of a wife that we had loaded in the boat. The gentleman took to the water and climbed in the boat after we had lowered it. He sat there wringing wet alongside me, helping to row.

I had great respect and great regret for First Officer Murdoch. I was walking along the deck forward with him and he said: 'I believe she is gone, Hardy.' This was a good half hour before my boat was lowered.

Where were all these passengers, these 1,600 people? *Witness answers:* They must have been between decks or on the deck below or on the other side of the ship. I cannot conceive where they were.

55

Frederick & Anne Hoyt, First Class Passengers

Frederick Hoyt's story of survival is interesting not only because he was one of the few survivors to have survived having leapt from *Titanic* into the icy waters of the Atlantic, but also for his comments about his conversation with Captain Smith, as the two were well acquainted. Hoyt was also a naval architect and yachtsman and had a keener understanding of ships and the sea than most passengers. The first extract is from Jack Lawrence's 1940 book *When the Ships Came In*. It plays a little fast and loose with some rather crucial facts but is revealing nevertheless when we consider that Lawrence was a very well-placed New York 'ship news' journalist. The second is from a letter Frederick sent to Archibald Gracie to aid the latter's research for his book, *The Truth About the Titanic* (which forms the basis of Gracie's survivor testimony reproduced later in this book).

Account of Frederick and Anne Hoyt's escape as told by Jack Lawrence In their cabin on B deck on the starboard side were Mr and Mrs Frederick M. Hoyt of Larchmont, N.Y. Mr Hoyt, a yachtsman and one of America's cleverest racing skippers, was also a naval architect on whose boards the lines of many famous vessels had been drawn. With Mrs Hoyt he had originally booked his homeward passage on the *Olympic*, but when he heard that Captain Smith was to command the new *Titanic* he changed his plans. He had crossed with Captain Smith many times and they were old friends. On several occasions the *Titanic's* skipper had been Mr Hoyt's guest at the New York Yacht Club on 44 Street and also at his home in Larchmont and at the Larchmont Yacht Club.

Mrs Hoyt was in bed and her husband was in his pajamas and bathrobe reading a book when in felt the ship rock slightly and heard a far-off grating sound that seemed to start somewhere under the starboard bow and run along the ship's side. To the sensitive ear of the naval architect and sailor that sound had a sinister significance. He was familiar with the waters through which *Titanic* was passing. That sound fastened his mind on only one thing. Ice. He was probably the first man of all the *Titanic* company to realize that the ship was in trouble – deep, mortal trouble.

Putting aside his book, Mr Hoyt dressed hurriedly. He put on the warmest clothes he could find. Then he awakened Mrs Hoyt and said: 'I think this ship is in trouble. I'm going up to the bridge to see Captain Smith. You must get dressed quickly. Put on the warmest clothes you can own. Gather up your jewels and money – but nothing else. Then wait here until I come back. Don't leave this cabin.'

Hoyt didn't encounter a soul as he hurried down the long rubber-paved corridor and stepped out on deck. He was probably the only passenger on the entire ship who suspected that anything was wrong. As he reached the deck an officer and several sailors passed him running aft. By the starboard companionway he made his way toward the bridge. He noticed that the *Titanic* was rapidly losing headway and he thought he could detect a slight starboard list. She also seemed to be slightly down by the head.

On the bridge the first man he met was Captain Smith. The latter wasted no words.

'I think we're in a bad way,' he said frankly. 'Fouled an iceberg. I have ordered all passengers in to the boats. No. 2 boat on the starboard side will be leaving in five minutes. Get yourself and Mrs Hoyt into that boat immediately.'

That was all he said and all that Frederick Hoyt needed to hear.

Returning to his cabin he found Mrs Hoyt already dressed, a small leather jewel case in her hand. Hoyt stopped only long enough to fill a pint flask with brandy. This he gave to his wife and guided her to the lifeboat designated by Captain Smith [in fact she got into lifeboat D on the port side].

At boat 2 [in fact lifeboat D], Hoyt had been giving two ship's officers a hand in helping women and children over the side. Several times, also, he had turned to help in beating back men who had rushed the boat. When the order came at last to lower away there was still plenty of room in the boat but no more passengers could be induced to enter it.

'You'd better get in Mr Hoyt, plenty of room in there for you,' an officer said.

Hoyt shook his head.

'No,' he said, 'I'll give you a hand with some of those other boats you'll probably need it.'

'Stand by to lower!' the officer shouted.

The davits groaned and creaked as the boat was pushed over the side. The blocks whined as new rope passed through them and the boat lowered slowly into the sea.

Mrs Hoyt had been the last woman to enter that boat. It is probable that she was the last woman to leave the *Titanic's* deck.

Frederick Hoyt stood there at the rail watching the big double-ended craft as it rose and fell in the long groundswell. He looked aft along the *Titanic's* deck and saw that all the other boats were either free of the ship or being lowered. The last boat had gone. Down below him he saw the boats idling nearby, many with empty seats, their crews hanging motionless on their oars and gazing up at the stricken vessel as though fascinated.

By this time the *Titanic's* bow – that once proud stem – was far down in the water. Soon her forward well deck would be awash. Her great stern was rising steadily out of the sea. In a little while the stars would be able to read her name and her home port in gold letters on her counter – T I T A N I C Liverpool.

Hoyt looked about him. Officers and passengers had disappeared from that part of the boat deck. There had been a rush for the boats on the port side [Hoyt was in fact on the port side]. He was alone. Down below him the lifeboat with his wife in it was still lying there – perhaps, like the others, because it had no place in particular to go. It still had many empty seats. One face in that boat was turned toward him. One woman there was living through an agony far worse than any drowning could possibly be.

Hoyt removed his overcoat. He felt in the pockets for the brandy flask and then remembered he had given it to his wife.

Climbing over the rail he stood poised for a moment and looked down on a sea that was studded with the reflection of a thousand stars. He remembered the thermometer on the *Titanic's* bridge. It had read 30 degrees. The water would be a lot colder than that in this latitude – too cold for a man to live in it for very long. But a man wouldn't live very long on the *Titanic's* deck, either.

Hoyt waved to his wife and then dropped feet first into the sea.

The shock of the icy water was almost paralysing, but he struggled desperately to hold his breath until he came to the surface. If the water was cold it was also marvelously buoyant and he came up almost as fast as he had gone down. He was a good swimmer. He shook the water out of his eyes. Close at hand was one of the *Titanic's* lifeboats. A woman in it waved a handkerchief. A few swift strokes brought him close enough to grasp the gunwale. In another moment he was hauled aboard and his wife's arms were about him as she pressed the brandy flask to his lips.

Hoyt's life was saved, but that plunge from the *Titanic's* deck perforated both eardrums and left him partly deaf.

Many other passengers, hauled from the icy water as Hoyt was, failed to survive the experience. In one boat alone eight men died after being dragged from the sea. With their lifeboats still about them the bodies were toppled back into the sea to make room for other survivors. Drifting about on the starlit surface they remained erect and only their drooping heads indicated that they no longer needed help.

Letter from Frederick Hoyt to Archibald Gracie I knew Captain Smith for over 15 years. Our conversation that night amounted to little or nothing. I simply sympathized with him on the accident, but at that time, as I then never expected to be saved, I did not want to bother him with questions, as I knew he had all he wanted to think of. He did suggest that I go down to A deck and see if there were not a boat alongside. This I did, and to my surprise saw the boat D still hanging on the davits (there having been some delay in lowering her), and it occurred to me that if I swam out and waited for her to shove off they would pick me up, which was what happened.

56

Hugh Woolner, First Class Passenger

A Cambridge University graduate and son of the sculptor Thomas Woolner, Hugh Woolner was returning to the US having attended his mother's funeral in England. Woolner's testimony claims that he and friend Hokan Steffanson jumped into lifeboat D as it was being lowered past A deck.

US Senate Inquiry (inquiry question is followed immediately by witness's answer) Did you have any friends aboard ship? One lady was recommended to my care by letters from friends in England. She joined the ship at Cherbourg, but I had not known her before.

Was she a survivor? Yes sir, Mrs Candee.

Tell us in your own way whether you paid any special attention to the movements of the ship, to the weather, to the equipment, and any circumstance that may tend to throw light upon this calamity up to the time of the collision? I took the ordinary passenger's interest in the number of miles we did each day. Beyond that I did not take any note of the speed of the ship.

What were your observations? I noticed that, so far as my memory serves me, the number of miles increased per day as we went on. If I remember right, one day it was 314, and the next day was 356, and that was the last number I remember, I think that was the last number that was put up on the ship's chart, or whatever it is called.

Did you have occasion to see the Captain occasionally? Did you see him the night of the accident? Not until I came up on to the boat deck, and he was there on the port side.

Where was he? He was between the two lifeboats that were farthest astern on the port side, giving orders.

The two that were farthest astern? Yes sir.

How long was this after the collision? I did not look at my watch, but I should think it was half an hour.

Did you hear him say anything or did you say anything to him? Yes I did. I made one remark to him. He said: 'I want all the passengers to go down on A deck, because I intend they shall go into the boats from A deck.' I remembered noticing as I came up that all those glass windows were raised to the very top; and I went up to the captain and saluted him and said: 'Haven't you forgotten, sir, that all those glass windows are closed?' He said: 'By God, you are right. Call those people back.' Very few people had moved, but the few that had gone down the companionway came up again, and everything went on all right.

Were the boats lowered to A deck and filled from A deck? No, from the boat deck.

Then the order must have been countermanded? Immediately.

If you can, I would like to have you tell the committee where you were on Sunday preceding that accident? I was in the smoking room at the time of the shock.

Who was in there with you, if anyone, that you now know or could name? Mr Steffanson, a Swedish gentleman, whose acquaintance I made on board, who sat at my table.

Anyone else? Yes, a Mr Kennett.

Anyone else? I think, but I am not quite certain, a Mr Smith. He had been with us quite a short time before.

When did you first know of the impact? We felt it under the smoking room. We felt a sort of stopping, a sort of, not exactly shock, but a sort of slowing down, and then we sort of felt a rip that gave a sort of a slight twist to the whole room. Everybody, so far as I could see, stood up and a number of men walked out rapidly through the swinging doors on the port side, and ran along to the rail that was behind the mast – I think there was a mast standing out there – and the rail just beyond.

What did you do? I stood hearing what the conjectures were. People were guessing what it might be, and one man called out, 'An iceberg has passed astern,' but who it was I do not know. I never have seen the man since.

What did you do then? I then went to look for Mrs Candee, because she was the lady in whom I was most interested and I met her outside her stateroom.

What took place? Just detail what you did? I said: 'Some accident has happened, but I do not think it is anything serious. Let us go for a walk.' We walked the after deck for I should think for 10 minutes or more. As we passed one of the entrances to the corridor, I saw people coming up with lifebelts, so I went inside and asked the steward: 'Is this orders?'

That is, you asked him if the lifebelts were ordered? Yes. I shouted to someone going by.

An employee with a lifebelt on? No, standing at the entrance and he said, 'Orders.' I went back to Mrs Candee and took her to her stateroom, and we got her lifebelt down from the top of the wardrobe, and tied hers on to her, and then she chose one or two things out of her baggage, little things she could put into her pocket, or something of that sort, and I said, 'We will now go up on deck and see what has really happened.'

Did you yourself put a lifebelt on? Yes sir. I missed that. I went back to my cabin and brought out and put one on myself, and I took the other one – there were two in the room – with me. I met some one in the passage who said, 'Do you want that?' and I said 'No,' and gave it to him.

What did you do then? I then took Mrs Candee up on to the boat deck, and there we saw preparations for lowering the boats going on. My great desire was to get her into the first boat, which I did, and we brought up a rug, which we threw in with her, and we waited to see that boat filled. It was not filled but a great many people got into it, and finally it was quietly and orderly lowered away.

What boat was that? That was the stern most boat on the port side [lifeboat 6].

Were any officers standing near it? The Captain was close by at that time.

Did he assist in loading it? Yes. He sort of ordered the people in. He said 'Come along, madam,' and that sort of thing.

Was there any difficulty in getting them to enter the lifeboat? Yes. There was a certain amount of reluctance on the part of the women to go in, and then some officer said, 'It is a matter of precaution,' and then they came forward rather more freely.

After you had put her in the boat, what did you do? I looked around to see what else I could do.

Did you find anything to do? I did what a man could. It was a very distressing scene, the men parting from their wives.

Did you assist in loading the boats? Yes sir.

How many boats? I think nearly all, except one on the port side, and Mr Steffanson stayed by me all the time, also.

This Swedish acquaintance you formed stayed by you? Yes sir.

What, if any, order was given by officers, or what did you hear regarding the filling of the lifeboats? I do not think I remember any orders. I do not think any orders were necessary.

You mean that the men stood back and passed the women and children forward? Yes.

There was no crowding? None.

No jostling? None.

Were these boats on the port side all filled in your presence? Not all. I think we missed one, because I said to Steffanson: 'Let us go down on the deck below and see if we can find any people waiting about there.' So we went down on to A deck and we found three women who did not seem to know their way, and we brought them up.

Who were they? I should think, second or third class passengers, but I did not examine them very carefully. You see, it was not very light.

You took them up to the boat deck? Yes, and they got on all right.

Did you see officers at these boats besides the Captain? Yes, the First Officer Mr Murdoch was very active.

From your own observation are you enabled to say that, so far as you know, the women and children all got aboard these lifeboats? So far as I could see, with the exception of Mrs Straus.

Did you see her get into the boat? She would not get in. I tried to get her to do so and she refused altogether to leave Mr Straus. The second time we went up to Mr Straus, and I said to him: 'I am sure nobody would object to an old gentleman like you getting in. There seems to be room in this boat.' He said: 'I will not go before the other men.'

What happened then? Then they eventually lowered all the wooden lifeboats on the port side, and then they got out a collapsible and hitched her on to the most forward davits and they filled that up, mostly with steerage women and children, and one seaman, and a steward, and I think one other man – but I am not quite certain about that – and when that boat seemed to be quite full, and was ready to be swung over the side, and was to be lowered away, I said to Steffanson: 'There is nothing more for us to do here.' Oh no, something else happened while that boat was being loaded. There was a sort of scramble on the starboard side, and I looked around and I saw two flashes of a pistol in the air.

Two flashes of a pistol? Yes.

Pistol shots? Yes, but they were up in the air, at that sort of an angle (indicating). I heard Mr Murdoch shouting out, 'Get out of this, clear out of this,' and that sort of thing, to a lot of men who were swarming into a boat on that side.

Swarming into the boat? Yes.

Was that into this collapsible boat? It was a collapsible sir.

That was the first collapsible that was lowered on the port side? On the starboard side. That was the other side.

You were then on the starboard side? Yes. We went across there because we heard a certain kind of shouting going on, and just as we got around the corner I saw these two flashes of the pistol, and Steffanson and I went up to help to clear that boat of the men who were climbing in, because there was a bunch of women – I think Italians and foreigners – who were standing on the outside of the crowd, unable to make their way toward the side of the boat.

Because these men had gathered around this collapsible boat? Yes sir. So we helped the officer to pull these men out, by their legs and anything we could get hold of.

You pulled them out of the boat? We pulled out several, each. I should think five or six. But they were really flying before Mr Murdoch from inside of the boat at the time.

They were members of the crew? I could not tell. No, I do not think so. I think they were probably third class passengers. It was awfully difficult to notice very carefully. I got hold of them by their feet and legs. Then they cleared out, practically all the men, out of that boat, and then we lifted in these Italian women, hoisted them up on each side and put them into the boat. They were very limp. They had not much spring in them at all. Then that boat was finally filled up and swung out, and then I said to Steffanson: 'There is nothing more for us to do. Let us go down on to A deck again.' And we went down again, but there was nobody there that time at all. It was perfectly empty the whole length. It was absolutely deserted, and the electric lights along the ceiling of A deck were beginning to turn red, just a glow, a red sort of glow. So I said to Steffanson: 'This is getting rather a tight corner. I do not like being inside these closed windows. Let us go out through the door at the end.' And as we went out through the door the sea came in on to the deck at our feet.

You were then on A deck? Yes, sir.

And did you look on both sides of the deck to see whether there were people? Yes sir.

You say there were none? None, the whole length of it. Not a soul.

How long was that after the collapsible lifeboat that you have just referred to was lowered? Oh, quite a few minutes, a very few minutes.

You remained down there with your friend until the sea came in – water came in – on A deck? On that A deck. Then we hopped up on to the gunwale preparing to jump out into the sea, because if we had waited a minute longer we should have been boxed in against the ceiling. And as we looked out we saw this collapsible, the last boat on the port side, being lowered right in front of our faces.

How far out? It was about nine feet out.

Nine feet out from the side of A deck? Yes.

Was it filled with people? It was full up to the bow, and I said to Steffanson: 'There is nobody in the bows. Let us make a jump for it. You go first.' And he jumped out and tumbled in head over heels into the bow, and I jumped too, and hit the gunwale with my chest, which had on this life preserver, of course and I sort of bounced off the gunwale and caught the gunwale with my fingers, and slipped off backwards.

Into the water? As my legs dropped down I felt that they were in the sea.

You are quite sure you jumped nine feet to get that boat? That is my estimate. By that time, you see, we were jumping slightly downward.

Did you jump out or down? Both.

It could not have been very far down if the water was on A deck, it must have been out. *Witness answers:* Chiefly out, but it was sufficiently down for us to be able to see just over the edge of the gunwale of the boat.

You pulled yourself up out of the water? Yes, and then I hooked my right heel over the gunwale, and by this time Steffanson was standing up, and he caught hold of me and lifted me in. Then we looked over into the sea and saw a man swimming in the sea just beneath us, and pulled him in [Frederick Hoyt].

Who was he? I do not know.

Did you pull anybody else in? No, by that time we were afloat. By that time we were bumping against the side of the ship.

Against the *Titanic's* side? She was going down pretty fast by the bow.

You were still on the port side? Forward, or back, or amidships? We were exactly opposite the end of the glass window on the A deck.

How many men did you find in that collapsible boat? We found one sailor, a steward, and one other man.

And your friend and yourself? And the man we pulled out of the sea.

That made six. *Witness answers:* Yes.

How many women were there in that boat? I did not count them. It seemed quite full of women and children. I should think there were about 30.

How many children? I did not count them, but quite a bunch.

Did you know any of the women, or do you know any of them now? I cannot remember their names. One lady had a broken elbow bone. She was in a white woolen jacket. She sat beside me, eventually.

What officer, if any, did you find in that collapsible boat when you got in? No officer.

Who took charge of that boat? There was a seaman in the stern who steered her with an oar, but when we got out among the other boats, we obeyed the orders of the officer who was in charge of the bunch of boats.

Who was that, if you know? I think it was Mr Lowe, the man who got his sail up. Afterwards, not then, but later. I think his name was Lowe.

How far out from the side of the *Titanic* did you go before you stopped? We got out three oars first, and shoved off from the side of the ship. Then we got her head more or less straightaway, and then we pulled as hard as we could, until, I should think, we were 150 yards [*c.* 137 metres] away, when the *Titanic* went down.

Did you see her go down? Yes.

Were you near enough to recognise people on deck? No.

As she went down did you see or feel any suction? I did not detect any. She seemed to me to stop for about 30 seconds at one place before she took the final plunge, because I watched one particular porthole, and the water did not rise there for at least half a minute and then she suddenly slid under with her propellers under the water.

She went down bow first? Yes.

Did you hear any explosion? No, a sort of rumbling roar, it sounded to me, as she slid under.

Who fired those two shots, do you know? Mr Murdoch, so far as I can tell.

You are quite certain it was not Mr Lowe? I am pretty certain. I think I recognized the voice of Mr Murdoch.

Mr Lowe says he fired three shots as his lifeboat was being lowered. *Witness answers:* I do not remember them.

You got off about 150 yards from where the ship went down, and then you tied up with these other boats. *Witness answers:* We rowed on and on for some time.

Was your boat alone? Yes, for quite a considerable time we simply rowed out into the sea.

For how long a time? I should say a quarter of an hour. We heard other boats around about us, and when the eyes got accustomed the darkness we could see a certain amount.

Did you have any light in your boat? There was a lantern, but there was no oil in it.

After pulling out for 15 minutes or so, what took place? Then some officer came along and said: 'I want all these boats tied up by their painters, head and tail, so as to make a more conspicuous mark' and we did that. There was no call to row much after that because we were simply drifting about.

Did you go back to the scene of the wreck after pulling out this 150 or 200 yards? No.

Was there any attempt made by your boat to go back, so far as you know? Not by our boat, no.

Did the women urge that the boat be taken back? No.

Did you hear any officer say that the boat should be taken back to the scene of the wreck? I did not.

After you got tied together, what did you do? We drifted about for a long time.

Drifted? Yes, just drifted about. There was nothing to do.

And waited until daylight? Yes, and then dawn began to break very slowly, and we could see more.

During the time that you were drifting about did you see any lights in any direction other than those that were on the lifeboats? I could not tell, but there was a green light that appeared, not all the time, but most of the time, down to the south.

How far away? I could not tell, but I should think about half a mile or a mile.

That was probably the green light that was on Officer Boxhall's boat? Very likely. I did not identify it.

Did you see any lights beside that, in any direction that looked like the lights of a ship? No.

Or did you see any rockets? I think I saw a rocket, rather in the direction where the *Carpathia* came up, but it was very distant.

How long before the *Carpathia* came up? Considerably after the sun rose.

After daybreak did you sight the *Carpathia* right away? No sir, we did not sight the ship. Other things happened before then.

Tell what happened. *Witness answers:* An officer came down and said he wanted to empty some of the people out of his boat, because he wanted to go and rescue some people who were on what he called a raft, and they put some people out of the boat, as many as our boat would hold. Probably five or six were put in our boat, which brought us down very close to the water.

That was Mr Lowe's boat? I think it was.

And they took the people out of Mr Lowe's boat? Into other boats.

And did they put some oarsmen into Mr Lowe's boat? Yes. Then he got a crew, mostly of sailors, I think.

He recruited a crew from amongst those lifeboats? Yes, or he may have turned out certain men from his boat and got others.

And you went in the direction of this swamped boat? Yes and took the men on board.

Did you go with him? No, no. We were very heavily laden then.

When it got daylight did you see any icebergs or floating ice? Yes, a number of icebergs.

How near the place where the *Titanic* went down? It is was rather difficult to identify that unless one took the wreckage that was floating away as an indication of where she went down. Taking that, I would say that the nearest was several miles away, but there were a great many of them.

At daylight? Yes, and they were of different colours as the sun struck them. Some looked white and some looked blue, and some sort of mauve, and others were dark gray.

How large were they? It is very difficult to tell.

Did you see any as large as the Capitol Building, here? No. There was one double-toothed one that looked to be of good size.

How high, 100 feet high? I should think it must have been, but it was a considerable distance away.

About 20 or 30 feet higher than the *Titanic*? It may easily have been that.

Did you see any field ice? Yes. I saw a faint line, what looked like a faint line along the horizon, but when we got on the *Carpathia*, we saw it was a huge floe which stretched out, I do not know how far but we were several hours steaming along it.

And did that field ice follow closely these icebergs? No. They looked more like scouts out in front. By out in front I mean to the south.

The *Carpathia* lingered in that vicinity for an hour or so? Yes. She seemed to come up very slowly and then she stopped. Then we looked out and we saw that there was a boat alongside her, and then we realized that she was waiting for us to come up to her instead of her coming to us, as we hoped. Then, just at that time, when we began to row toward the *Carpathia*, Mr Lowe came down with his boat under sail, again, and hailed us and said, 'Are you a collapsible?' We answered, 'Yes.' He said 'How are you?' I said, 'We have about all we want.' He said, 'Would you like a tow?' We answered, 'Yes we would.' So he took our painter and towed us away from the *Carpathia*, and then we looked and saw that there was another little group of people standing up in the sea who had to be rescued.

Where were they? They were standing on an upturned boat.

How many of them were there? I do not know how many at them, but it looked like a dozen or 13.

Were there any women among them? One woman with black hair. A man helped her in the boat first, when it came alongside.

Did you go in that boat? We were only our painter's length away. Mr Lowe took them all on board his boat.

Would you recognize them? One man I saw was a first class passenger whom I had seen in the saloon.

Who had charge of that upturned boat? I do not know, at all.

Did you have any food or water in your lifeboat? We had a water breaker, I think they call it, but there was no water in it.

Did you have any food in the boat? Not that I know of.

Did anybody ask for food? No. A sailor offered some biscuits, which I was using for feeding a small child who had waked up and was crying. It was one of those little children for whose parents everybody was looking [Michel and Edmond Navratil, aged four and two respectively]; the larger of those two.

Its mother was not on this boat? No.

How old was that child? I should think it was about five, as nearly as I can judge.

Do you know of what nationality it was? It looked like a French child, but it kept shouting for its doll, and I could not make out what it said before that. It kept saying it over and over again.

Were there two of these children in the boat? I cannot tell. This is the only one that I had anything to do with. There were several other children in the boat. We handed them into a bag, and they were pulled up the *Carpathia's* side.

Have you seen them since? Yes, I think I saw it once on the *Carpathia*. It had very curly hair, light brownish curly hair.

Was the child identified on the *Carpathia*? Not as far as I know.

From what you say, Mr Woolner, I should judge that you have no complaint to make about the discipline of the crew or the conduct of the officers? Absolutely none.

And you do not know whether these men that crowded up around there, and crowded the women back, were of the crew or were passengers? I could not possibly tell.

That is the only instance where they did crowd? That is the only instance that I saw.

Were you looking at the *Titanic* when she went down? Yes.

As you were looking at her when she went down, do you think she broke in two? I did not think so.

You did not hear any explosions? No sir, only a continuous rumbling noise.

Were you where you could see the funnels? I could not really see a thing when the lights went out. It was all brilliantly lighted at the stem end, and suddenly the lights went out, and your eyes were so unaccustomed to the darkness, you could see nothing, and you could only hear sounds.

You say the speed of the ship greatly increased? Judging by the log.

And you looked at the log? Quite so.

Did you look at it the first day out? I was not very much interested, because it was not a full 24 hours. I do not remember what the figure was.

Did you look at it the second day out? Yes.

What did it record then? As I remember, it was 514. I think it was, either 500 or 400. I think it was 514, and then 546 the next day.

You said 314 before. *Witness answers:* Did I? I meant 514.

What time was that? Do you know? Was it noon, Sunday? Yes, noon Sunday. It was put up at about one o'clock on Sunday in the companionway.

LIFEBOAT B
Port Side, Floated Off *Titanic* 2.15 a.m.

Lifeboats A and B contain some of the most fascinating testimonies of all. These lifeboats were not launched into the sea, but floated off deck when *Titanic* started her final descent. Collapsible lifeboat B was stowed on the roof of the officers' quarters, to the port side. It had been a struggle to cut the boat free and according to Harold Bride a wave eventually swept this lifeboat off the ship, turning it upside down in the process. About 30 people, including *Titanic*'s highest-ranking surviving officer Second Officer Charles Lightoller, managed to climb on to the upturned lifeboat, but with each successive person the boat was sinking lower in the water and those lucky enough to be already on board could accept no more. Archibald Gracie says that there 'were men swimming in the water all around us' and that they 'steered the boat as to avoid contact' with those struggling for life all around them. Bride recalls one of the most well-known stories: 'Somebody said: "don't the rest of you think we ought to pray?" The man who made the suggestion asked what the religion of the others was. Each man called out his religion. One was Catholic, one a Methodist, one a Presbyterian. It was decided that the most appropriate prayer for all of us was the Lord's Prayer. We spoke it over in chorus, with the man who first suggested that we pray as the leader.' This story is corroborated by Gracie and Jack Thayer.

The position of those on lifeboat B was precarious and Lightoller took charge of the boat so everybody worked in unison to ensure collective survival. Many stood in columns two abreast and facing the bow. In this way they could minimise contact with the waves that splashed over the lifeboat and quickly redistribute their weight if necessary. During the night three or four people died and fell into the sea.

The presence of Wireless Operator Bride on this lifeboat offered a glimmer of hope to those struggling to hold on. He was able to report that the *Carpathia* was on its way.

When day broke the occupants of lifeboat B realised that four of *Titanic*'s lifeboats were just half a mile away. Lightoller attracted their attention and surviving passengers were transferred to lifeboats 12 and 4.

57

Archibald Gracie, First Class Passenger

Archibald Gracie was an amateur historian who had just published a book about the American Civil War. Gracie was returning from a visit to Europe where he had been resting and recuperating from a recent illness.

Perhaps the single most important source from amongst the survivors, Archibald Gracie's book *The Truth About the Titanic* is both his vivid account of clambering on to lifeboat B and an analysis of what happened on other lifeboats. Below I reproduce the former only to avoid repetition with the main structure of this book. Gracie never recovered from his extraordinary physical ordeal and died on 4 December 1912 midway through proofing his book. It was published posthumously in America in 1913.

Chapter 1 The Last Day Aboard Ship

As the sole survivor of all the men passengers of the *Titanic* stationed during the loading of six or more lifeboats with women and children on the port side of the ship, forward on the glass-sheltered deck A, and later on the boat deck above, it is my duty to bear testimony to the heroism on the part of all concerned. First, to my men companions who calmly stood by until the lifeboats had departed loaded with women and the available complement of crew, and who, 15 to 20 minutes later, sank with the ship, conscious of giving up their lives to save the weak and the helpless.

Second, to Second Officer Lightoller and his ship's crew, who did their duty as if similar occurrences were matters of daily routine; and thirdly, to the women, who showed no signs of fear or panic whatsoever under conditions more appalling than were ever recorded before in the history of disasters at sea.

I think those of my readers who are accustomed to tales of thrilling adventure will be glad to learn first-hand of the heroism displayed on the *Titanic* by those to whom it is my privilege and sad duty to pay this tribute. I will confine the details of my narrative for the most part to what I personally saw, and did, and heard during that never-to-be-forgotten maiden trip of the *Titanic*, which ended with shipwreck and her foundering about 2.22 a.m., Monday, 15 April 1912, after striking an iceberg 'in or near latitude 41 degrees, 46 minutes N., longitude 50 degrees, 14 minutes W., North Atlantic Ocean,' whereby the loss of 1,490 lives ensued.

On Sunday morning, 14 April, this marvelous ship, the perfection of all vessels hitherto conceived by the brain of man, had, for three and one-half days, proceeded on her way from Southampton to New York over a sea of glass, so level it appeared, without encountering a ripple brought on the surface of the water by a storm.

The Captain had each day improved upon the previous day's speed, and prophesied that, with continued fair weather, we should make an early arrival record for this maiden trip. But his reckoning never took into consideration that Protean monster of the Northern seas which, even before this, had been so fatal to the navigator's calculations and so formidable a weapon of destruction.

Our explorers have pierced to the furthest north and south of the icebergs' retreat, but the knowledge of their habitat, insuring our great ocean liners in their successful efforts to elude them, has not reached the detail of time and place where they become detached and obstruct their path.

In the 24 hours run ending the 14th, according to the posted reckoning, the ship had covered 546 miles, and we were told that the next 24 hours would see even a better record made.

Towards evening the report, which I heard, was spread that wireless messages from passing steamers had been received advising the officers of our ship of the presence of icebergs and ice-floes. The increasing cold and the necessity of being more warmly clad when appearing on deck were outward and visible signs in corroboration of these warnings. But despite them all no diminution of speed was indicated and the engines kept up their steady running.

Not for 50 years, the old sailors tell us, had so great a mass of ice and icebergs at this time of the year been seen so far south.

The pleasure and comfort which all of us enjoyed upon this floating palace, with its extraordinary provisions for such purposes, seemed an ominous feature to many of us, including myself, who felt it almost too good to last without some terrible retribution inflicted by the hand of an angry omnipotence. Our sentiment in this respect was voiced by one of the most able and distinguished of our fellow passengers, Mr Charles M. Hays, President of the Canadian Grand Trunk Railroad. Engaged as he then was in studying and providing the hotel equipment along the line of new extensions to his own great railroad system, the consideration of the subject and of the magnificence of the *Titanic*'s accommodations was thus brought home to him. This was the prophetic utterance with which, alas, he sealed his fate a few hours thereafter: 'The White Star, the Cunard and the Hamburg-American lines,' said he, 'are now devoting their attention to a struggle for supremacy in obtaining the most luxurious appointments for their ships, but the time will soon come when the greatest and most appalling of all disasters at sea will be the result.'

In the various trips which I have made across the Atlantic, it has been my custom aboard ship, whenever the weather permitted, to take as much exercise every day as might be needful to put myself in prime physical condition, but on board the *Titanic*, during the first days of the voyage, from Wednesday to Saturday, I had departed from this, my usual self-imposed regimen, for during this interval I had devoted my time to social enjoyment and to the reading of books taken from the ship's well-supplied library. I enjoyed myself as if I were in a summer palace on the seashore, surrounded with every comfort – there was nothing to indicate or suggest that we were on the stormy Atlantic Ocean. The motion of the ship and the noise of its machinery were scarcely discernible on deck or in the saloons, either day or night. But when Sunday morning came, I consider it high time to begin my customary exercises, and determined for the rest of the voyage to patronize the squash racquet court, the gymnasium, the swimming pool, etc. I was up early before breakfast and met the professional racquet player in a half hour's warming up, preparatory for a swim in the six-foot deep tank of salt water, heated to a refreshing temperature. In no swimming bath had I ever enjoyed such pleasure before. How curtailed that enjoyment would have been had the presentiment come to me telling how near it was to being my last plunge, and that before dawn of another day I would be swimming for my life in mid-ocean, under water and on the surface, in a temperature of 28 degrees Fahrenheit!

Impressed on my memory as if it were but yesterday, my mind pictures the personal appearance and recalls the conversation which I had with each of these employees of the ship. The racquet professional, F. Wright, was a clean-cut, typical young Englishman, similar to hundreds I have seen and with whom I have played, in bygone years, my favorite game of cricket, which has done more than any other sport for my physical development. I have not seen his name mentioned in any account of the disaster, and therefore take this opportunity of speaking of him, for I am perhaps the only survivor able to relate anything about his last days on earth.

Hundreds of letters have been written to us survivors, many containing photographs for identification of some lost loved one, whom perchance we may have seen or talked to before he met his fate. To these numerous inquiries I have been able to reply satisfactorily only in rare instances. The next and last time I saw Wright was on the stairway of deck C within three-quarters of an hour after the collision. I was going to my cabin when I met him on the stairs going up. 'Hadn't we better cancel that appointment for tomorrow morning?' I said rather jocosely to him. 'Yes,' he replied, but did not stop to tell what he then must have known of the conditions in the racquet court on G deck, which, according to other witnesses, had at that time become flooded. His voice was calm, without enthusiasm, and perhaps his face was a little whiter than usual.

To the swimming pool attendant I also made promise to be on hand earlier the next morning, but I never saw him again.

One of the characters of the ship, best known to us all, was the gymnasium instructor, T. W. McCawley. He, also, expected me to make my first appearance for real good exercise on the morrow, but alas, he, too, was swallowed up by the sea. How well we survivors all remember this sturdy little man in white flannels and with his broad English accent! With what tireless enthusiasm he showed us the many mechanical devices under his charge and urged us to take advantage of the opportunity of using them, going through the motions of bicycle racing, rowing, boxing, camel and horseback riding, etc.

Such was my morning's preparation for the unforeseen physical exertions I was compelled to put forth for dear life at midnight, a few hours later. Could any better training for the terrible ordeal have been planned?

The exercise and the swim gave me an appetite for a hearty breakfast. Then followed the church service in the dining saloon, and I remember how much I was impressed with the 'Prayer for those at Sea,' also the words of the hymn, which we sang, No. 418 of the Hymnal. About a fortnight later, when I next heard it sung, I was in the little church at Smithtown, Long Island, attending the memorial service in honour of my old friend and fellow member of the Union Club, James Clinch Smith. To his sister, who sat next to me in the pew, I called attention to the fact that it was the last hymn we sang on this Sunday morning on board the *Titanic*. She was much affected, and gave the reason for its selection for the memorial service to her brother because it was known as Jim's favourite hymn, being the first piece set to music ever played by him as a child and for which he was rewarded with a promised prize, donated by his father.

What a remarkable coincidence that at the first and last ship's service on board the *Titanic*, the hymn we sang began with these impressive lines: 'O God our help in ages past, Our hope for years to come, Our shelter from the stormy blast, And our eternal home.' One day was so like another that it is difficult to differentiate in our description all the details of this last day's incidents aboard ship.

The book that I finished and returned to the ship's library was Mary Johnston's *Old Dominion*. While peacefully reading the tales of adventure and accounts of extraordinary escapes therein, how little I thought that in the next few hours I should be a witness and a party to a scene to which this book could furnish no counterpart, and that my own preservation from a watery grave would afford a remarkable illustration of how oftentimes 'truth is stranger than fiction.'

During this day I saw much of Mr and Mrs Isidor Straus. In fact, from the very beginning to the end of our trip on the *Titanic*, we had been together several times each day. I was with them on the deck the day we left Southampton and witnessed that ominous accident to the American liner, *New York*, lying at her pier, when the displacement of water by the movement of our gigantic ship caused a suction which pulled the smaller ship from her moorings and nearly caused a collision. At the time of this, Mr Straus was telling me that it seemed only a few years back that he had taken passage on this same ship, the *New York*, on her maiden trip and when she was spoken of as the 'last word in shipbuilding.' He then called the attention of his wife and myself to the progress that had since been made, by comparison of the two ships then lying side by side. During our daily talks thereafter, he related much of special interest concerning incidents in his remarkable career, beginning with his early manhood in Georgia when, with the Confederate Government Commissioners, as an agent for the purchase of supplies, he ran the blockade of Europe. His friendship with President Cleveland, and how the latter had honoured him, were among the topics of daily conversation that interested me most.

On this Sunday, our last day aboard ship, he finished the reading of a book I had loaned him, in which he expressed intense interest. This book was *The Truth About Chickamauga*, of which I am the author, and it was to gain a much-needed rest after seven years of work thereon, and in order to get it off my mind, that I had taken this trip across the ocean and back. As a counterirritant, my experience was a dose which was highly efficacious.

I recall how Mr and Mrs Straus were particularly happy about noon time on this same day in anticipation of communicating by wireless telegraphy with their son and his wife on their way to Europe on board the passing ship *Amerika*. Some time before six o'clock, full of contentment, they told me of the message of greeting received in reply. This last goodbye to their loved ones must have been a consoling thought when the end came a few hours thereafter.

That night after dinner, with my table companions, Messrs James Clinch Smith and Edward A. Kent, according to usual custom, we adjourned to the palm room, with many others, for the usual coffee at individual tables where we listened to the always delightful music of the *Titanic*'s band. On these occasions, full dress was always *en règle*; and it was a subject both of observation and admiration, that there were so many beautiful women – then especially in evidence – aboard the ship.

I invariably circulated around during these delightful evenings, chatting with those I knew, and with those whose acquaintance I had made during the voyage. I might specify names and particularize subjects of conversation, but the details, while interesting to those concerned, might not be so to all my readers. The recollections of those with whom I was thus closely associated in this disaster, including those who suffered the death from which I escaped and those who survived with me, will be a treasured memory and bond of union until my dying day. From the palm room, the men of my coterie would always go to the smoking room, and almost every evening join in conversation with some of the well-known men whom we met there, including within my own recollections Major Archie Butt, President Taft's Military Aid, discussing politics; Clarence Moore, of Washington, D. C., relating his venturesome trip some years ago through the West Virginia woods and mountains, helping a newspaper reporter in obtaining an interview with the outlaw, Captain Anse Hatfield; Frank D. Millet, the well-known artist, planning a journey west; Arthur Ryerson and others.

During these evenings I also conversed with Mr John B. Thayer, Second Vice-President of the Pennsylvania Railroad, and with Mr George D. Widener, a son of the Philadelphia street-car magnate, Mr P. A. B. Widener.

My stay in the smoking room on this particular evening for the first time was short, and I retired early with my cabin steward Cullen's promise to awaken me betimes next morning to get ready for the engagements I had made before breakfast for the game of racquets, work in the gymnasium and the swim that was to follow.

I cannot regard it as a mere coincidence that on this particular Sunday night I was thus prompted to retire early for nearly three hours of invigorating sleep, whereas an accident occurring at midnight of any of the four preceding days would have found me mentally and physically tired. That I was thus strengthened for the terrible ordeal, better even than had I been forewarned of it, I regard on the contrary as the first provision for my safety (answering the constant prayers of those at home), made by the guardian angel to whose care I was entrusted during the series of miraculous escapes presently to be recorded.

Chapter 2 Struck By An Iceberg

My stateroom was an outside one on deck C on the starboard quarter, somewhat abaft amidships. It was No. C51. I was enjoying a good night's rest when I was aroused by a sudden shock and noise forward on the starboard side, which I at once concluded was caused by a collision, with some other ship perhaps. I jumped from my bed, turned on the electric light, glanced at my watch nearby on the dresser, which I had changed to agree with ship's time on the day before and which now registered 12 o'clock. Correct ship's time would make it about 11.45 p.m. I opened the door of my cabin, looked out into the corridor, but could not see or hear anyone – there was no commotion whatever; but immediately following the collision came a great noise of escaping steam. I listened intently, but could hear no machinery. There was no mistaking that something wrong had happened, because of the ship stopping and the blowing off of steam.

Removing my night clothing I dressed myself hurriedly in underclothing, shoes and stockings, trousers and a Norfolk coat. I give these details in order that some idea of the lapse of time may be formed by an account of what I did during the interval. From my cabin, through the corridor to the stairway was but a short distance, and I ascended to the third deck above, that is, to the boat deck. I found here only one young lad, seemingly bent on the same quest as myself.

From the first cabin quarter, forward on the port side, we strained our eyes to discover what had struck us. From vantage points where the view was not obstructed by the lifeboats on this deck I sought the object, but in vain, though I swept the horizon near and far and discovered nothing.

It was a beautiful night, cloudless, and the stars shining brightly. The atmosphere was quite cold, but no ice or iceberg was in sight. If another ship had struck us there was no trace of it, and it did not yet occur to me that it was an iceberg with which we had collided. Not satisfied with a partial investigation, I made a complete tour of the deck, searching every point of the compass with my eyes. Going toward the stern, I vaulted over the iron gate and fence that divide the first and second cabin passengers. I disregarded the 'not allowed' notice. I looked about me towards the officers' quarters in expectation of being challenged for non-observance of rules. In view of the collision I had expected to see some of the ship's officers on the boat deck, but there was no sign of an officer anywhere, and no one from whom to obtain any information about what had happened. Making my tour of the boat deck, the only other beings I saw were a middle-aged couple of the second cabin promenading unconcernedly, arm in arm, forward on the starboard quarter, against the wind, the man in a gray overcoat and outing cap.

Having gained no satisfaction whatever, I descended to the glass-enclosed deck A, port side, and looked over the rail to see whether the ship was on an even keel, but I still could see nothing wrong. Entering the companionway, I passed Mr Ismay with a member of the crew hurrying up the stairway. He wore a day suit, and, as usual, was hatless. He seemed too much preoccupied to notice anyone. Therefore I did not speak to him, but regarded his face very closely, perchance to learn from his manner how serious the accident might be. It occurred to me then that he was putting on as brave a face as possible so as to cause no alarm among the passengers.

At the foot of the stairway were a number of men passengers, and I now for the first time discovered that others were aroused as well as myself, among them my friend, Clinch Smith, from whom I first learned that an iceberg had struck us. He opened his hand and showed me some ice, flat like my watch, coolly suggesting that I might take it home for a souvenir. All of us will remember the way he had of cracking a joke without a smile. While we stood there, the story of the collision came to us – how someone in the smoking room, when the ship struck, rushed out to see what it was, and returning, told them that he had a glimpse of an iceberg towering 50 feet above deck A, which, if true, would indicate a height of over 100 feet. Here, too, I learned that the mail room was flooded and that the plucky postal clerks, in two feet of water, were at their posts. They were engaged in transferring to the upper deck, from the ship's post office, the 200 bags of registered mail containing 400,000 letters. The names of these men, who all sank with the ship, deserve to be recorded. They were: John S. Marsh, William L. Gwynn, Oscar S. Woody, Jago Smith and E. D. Williamson. The first three were Americans, the others Englishmen, and the families of the former were provided for by their government.

And now Clinch Smith and myself noticed a list on the floor of the companionway. We kept our own counsel about it, not wishing to frighten anyone or cause any unnecessary alarm, especially among the ladies, who then appeared upon the scene. We did not consider it our duty to express our individual opinion upon the serious character of the accident which now appealed to us with the greatest force. He and I resolved to stick together in the final emergency, united in the silent bond of friendship, and lend a helping hand to each other whenever required. I recall having in my mind's eye at this moment all that I had read and heard in days gone by about shipwrecks, and pictured Smith and myself clinging to an overloaded raft in an open sea with a scarcity of food and water. We agreed to visit our respective staterooms and join each other later. All possessions in my stateroom were hastily packed into three large travelling bags so that the luggage might be ready in the event of a hasty transfer to another ship.

Fortunately I put on my long Newmarket overcoat that reached below my knees, and as I passed from the corridor into the companionway my worst fears were confirmed. Men and women were slipping on life-preservers, the stewards assisting in adjusting them. Steward Cullen insisted upon my returning to my stateroom for mine. I did so and he fastened one on me while I brought out the other for use by someone else.

Out on deck A, port side, towards the stern, many men and women had already collected. I sought and found the unprotected ladies to whom I had proffered my services during the voyage when they boarded the ship at Southampton, Mrs E. D. Appleton, wife of my St Paul's School friend and schoolmate; Mrs R. C. Cornell, wife of the well-known New York Justice, and Mrs J. Murray Brown, wife of the Boston publisher, all old friends of my wife. These three sisters were returning home from a sad mission abroad, where they had laid to rest the remains of a fourth sister, Lady Victor Drummond, of whose death I had read accounts in the London papers, and all the sad details connected therewith were told me by the sisters themselves. That they would have to pass through a still greater ordeal seemed impossible, and how little did I know of the responsibility I took upon myself for their safety! Accompanying them, also unprotected, was their friend, Miss Edith Evans, to whom they introduced me. Mr and Mrs Straus, Colonel and Mrs Astor and others well known to me were among those here congregated on the port side of deck A, including, besides Clinch Smith, two of our coterie of after-dinner companions, Hugh Woolner, son of the English sculptor, whose works are to be seen in Westminster Abbey, and H. Björnström Steffanson, the young lieutenant of the Swedish army, who, during the voyage, had told me of his acquaintance with Mrs Gracie's relatives in Sweden.

It was now that the band began to play, and continued while the boats were being lowered. We considered this a wise provision tending to allay excitement. I did not recognize any of the tunes, but I know they were cheerful and were not hymns. If, as has been reported, *Nearer My God to Thee* was one of the selections, I assuredly should have noticed it and regarded it as a tactless warning of immediate death to us all and one likely to create a panic that our special efforts were directed towards avoiding, and which we accomplished to the fullest extent. I know of only two survivors whose names are cited by the newspapers as authority for the statement that this hymn was one of those played. On the other hand, all whom I have questioned or corresponded with, including the best qualified, testified emphatically to the contrary.

Our hopes were buoyed with the information, imparted through the ship's officers, that there had been an interchange of wireless messages with passing ships, one of which was certainly coming to our rescue. To reassure the ladies of whom I had assumed special charge, I showed them a bright white light of what I took to be a ship about five miles off and which I felt sure was coming to our rescue. Colonel Astor heard me telling this to them and he asked me to show it and I pointed the light out to him. In so doing we both had now to lean over the rail of the ship and look close in towards the bow, avoiding a lifeboat even then made ready with its gunwale lowered to the level of the floor of the boat deck above us and obstructing our view; but instead of growing brighter the light grew dim and less and less distinct and passed away altogether. The light, as I have since learned, with tearful regret for the lost who might have been saved, belonged to the steamer *Californian* of the Leyland Line, Captain Stanley Lord, bound from London to Boston. She belonged to the International Mercantile Marine Company, the owners of the *Titanic*. This was the ship from which two of the six 'ice messages' were sent. The first one received and acknowledged by the *Titanic* was one at 7.30 p.m., an intercepted message to another ship. The next was about 11 p.m., when the Captain of the *Californian* saw a ship approaching from the eastward, which he was advised to be the *Titanic*, and under his orders this message was sent: 'We are stopped and surrounded by ice.' To this the *Titanic*'s wireless operator brusquely replied, 'Shut up, I am busy. I am working Cape Race.' The business here referred to was the sending of wireless messages for passengers on the *Titanic*; and the stronger current of the *Californian* eastward interfered therewith. Though the navigation of the ship and the issues of life and death were at stake, the right of way was given to communication with Cape Race until within a few minutes of the *Titanic*'s collision with the iceberg.

Nearly all this time, until 11.30 p.m., the wireless operator of the *Californian* was listening with 'phones on his head, but at 11.30 p.m., while the *Titanic* was still talking to Cape Race, the former ship's operator 'put the 'phones down, took off his clothes and turned in.' The fate of thousands of lives hung in the balance many times that ill-omened night, but *the circumstances in connection with the S.S. Californian* (Br. Rep. pp. 43-46), furnish the evidence corroborating that of the American Investigation, viz., that it was not chance, but the grossest negligence alone which sealed the fate of all the noble lives, men and women, that were lost.

It appears from the evidence referred to, information in regard to which we learned after our arrival in New York, that the Captain of the *Californian* and his crew were watching our lights from the deck of their ship, which remained approximately stationary until 5.15 a.m. on the following morning. During this interval it is shown that they were never distant more than six or seven miles. In fact, at 12 o'clock, the *Californian* was only four or five miles off at the point and in the general direction where she was seen by myself and at least a dozen others, who bore testimony before the American Committee, from the decks of the *Titanic*. The white rockets which we sent up, referred to presently, were also plainly seen at the time. Captain Lord was completely in possession of the knowledge that he was in proximity to a ship in distress. He could have put himself into immediate communication with us by wireless had he desired confirmation of the name of the ship and the disaster which had befallen it. His indifference is made apparent by his orders to 'go on Morseing,' instead of utilizing the more modern method of the inventive genius and gentleman, Mr Marconi, which eventually saved us all. 'The night was clear and the sea was smooth. The ice by which the *Californian* was surrounded,' says the British Report, 'was loose ice extending for a distance of not more than two or three miles in the direction of the *Titanic*.' When she first saw the rockets, the *Californian* could have pushed through the ice to the open water without any serious risk and so have come to the assistance of the *Titanic*. A discussion of this subject is the most painful of all others for those who lost their loved ones aboard our ship.

When we realized that the ship whose lights we saw was not coming towards us, our hopes of rescue were correspondingly depressed, but the men's counsel to preserve calmness prevailed; and to reassure the ladies they repeated the much advertised fiction of 'the unsinkable ship' on the supposed highest qualified authority. It was at this point that Miss Evans related to me the story that years ago in London she had been told by a fortune-teller to 'beware of water,' and now 'she knew she would be drowned.' My efforts to persuade her to the contrary were futile. Though she gave voice to her story, she presented no evidence whatever of fear, and when I saw and conversed with her an hour later when conditions appeared especially desperate, and the last lifeboat was supposed to have departed, she was perfectly calm and did not revert again to the superstitious tale.

From my own conclusions, and those of others, it appears that about 45 minutes had now elapsed since the collision when Captain Smith's orders were transmitted to the crew to lower the lifeboats, loaded with women and children first. The self-abnegation of Mr and Mrs Isidor Straus here shone forth heroically when she promptly and emphatically exclaimed: 'No! I will not be separated from my husband; as we have lived, so will we die together;' and when he, too, declined the assistance proffered on my earnest solicitation that, because of his age and helplessness, exception should be made and he be allowed to accompany his wife in the boat. 'No!' he said, 'I do not wish any distinction in my favour which is not granted to others.' As near as I can recall them these were the words which they addressed to me. They expressed themselves as fully prepared to die, and calmly sat down in steamer chairs on the glass-enclosed deck A, prepared to meet their fate. Further entreaties to make them change their decision were of no avail. Later they moved to the boat deck above, accompanying Mrs Straus's maid, who entered a lifeboat.

When the order to load the boats was received I had promptly moved forward with the ladies in my charge toward the boats then being lowered from the boat deck above to deck A on the port side of the ship, where we then were. A tall, slim young Englishman, Sixth Officer J. P. Moody, whose name I learned later, with other members of the ship's crew, barred the progress of us men passengers any nearer to the boats. All that was left me was then to consign these ladies in my charge to the protection of the ship's officer, and I thereby was relieved of their responsibility and felt sure that they would be safely loaded in the boats at this point. I remember a steward rolling a small barrel out of the door of the companionway. 'What have you there?' said I. 'Bread for the lifeboats,' was his quick and cheery reply, as I passed inside the ship for the last time, searching for two of my table companions, Mrs

Churchill Candee of Washington and Mr Edward A. Kent. It was then that I met Wright, the racquet player, and exchanged the few words on the stairway already related.

Considering it well to have a supply of blankets for use in the open boats exposed to the cold, I concluded, while passing, to make another, and my last, descent to my stateroom for this purpose, only to find it locked, and on asking the reason why was told by some other steward than Cullen that it was done 'to prevent looting.' Advising him of what was wanted, I went with him to the cabin stewards' quarters nearby, where extra blankets were stored, and where I obtained them. I then went the length of the ship inside on this glass-enclosed deck A from aft, forwards, looking in every room and corner for my missing table companions, but no passengers whatever were to be seen except in the smoking room, and there all alone by themselves, seated around a table, were four men, three of whom were personally well known to me, Major Butt, Clarence Moore and Frank Millet, but the fourth was a stranger, whom I therefore cannot identify. All four seemed perfectly oblivious of what was going on, on the decks outside. It is impossible to suppose that they did not know of the collision with an iceberg and that the room they were in had been deserted by all others, who had hastened away. It occurred to me at the time that these men desired to show their entire indifference to the danger and that if I advised them as to how seriously I regarded it, they would laugh at me. This was the last I ever saw of any of them, and I know of no one who testifies to seeing them later, except a lady who mentions having seen Major Butt on the bridge five minutes before the last boat left the ship. There is no authentic story of what they did when the water reached this deck, and their ultimate fate is only a matter of conjecture. That they went down in the ship on this deck A, when the steerage passengers (as described later) blocked the way to the deck above, is my personal belief, founded on the following facts, to wit: First; that neither I nor anyone else, so far as I know, ever saw any of them on the boat deck, and second, that the bodies of none of them were ever recovered, indicating the possibility that all went down inside the ship or the enclosed deck.

I next find myself forward on the port side, part of the time on the boat deck, and part on the deck below it, called deck A, where I rejoined Clinch Smith, who reported that Mrs Candee had departed on one of the boats. We remained together until the ship went down. I was on the boat deck when I saw and heard the first rocket, and then successive ones sent up at intervals thereafter. These were followed by the Morse red and blue lights, which were signalled near by us on the deck where we were; but we looked in vain for any response. These signals of distress indicated to everyone of us that the ship's fate was sealed, and that she might sink before the lifeboats could be lowered.

And now I am on deck A again, where I helped in the loading of two boats lowered from the deck above. There were 20 boats in all on the ship: 14 wooden lifeboats, each 30 feet long by nine feet one inch broad, constructed to carry 65 persons each; two wooden cutters, emergency boats, 25 feet two inches long by seven feet two inches broad, constructed to carry 40 persons each; and four Engelhardt 'surfboats' with canvas collapsible sides extending above the gunwales, 25 feet five inches long by eight feet broad, constructed to carry 47 persons each. The lifeboats were ranged along the ship's rail, or its prolongation forward and aft on the boat deck, the odd numbered on the starboard and the even numbered on the port side. Two of the Engelhardt boats were on the boat deck forward beneath the emergency boats suspended on davits above. The other Engelhardt boats were on the roof of the officers' house forward of the first funnel. They are designated respectively by the letters, A. B. C. D; A and C on the starboard, B and D on the port sides. They have a rounded bottom like a canoe. The name 'collapsible boat' generally applied has given rise to mistaken impressions in regard to them, because of the adjustable canvas sides above-mentioned.

At this quarter I was no longer held back from approaching near the boats, but my assistance and work as one of the crew in the loading of boats and getting them away as quickly as possible were accepted, for there was now no time to spare. The Second Officer, Lightoller, was in command on the port side forward, where I was. One of his feet was planted in the lifeboat, and the other on the rail of deck A, while we, through the wood frames of the lowered glass windows on this deck, passed women, children, and babies in rapid succession without any confusion whatsoever. Among this number was Mrs Astor, whom I lifted over the four-feet high rail of the ship through the frame. Her husband held her left arm as we carefully passed her to Lightoller, who seated her in the boat. A dialogue now ensued between Colonel Astor and the officer, every word of which I listened to with intense interest. Astor was close to me in the adjoining window-frame, to the left of mine. Leaning out over the rail he asked permission of Lightoller to enter the boat to protect his wife, which, in view of her delicate condition, seems to have been a reasonable request, but the officer, intent upon his duty, and obeying orders, and not knowing the millionaire from the rest of us, replied: 'No, sir, no men are allowed in these boats until women are loaded first.' Colonel Astor did not demur, but bore the refusal bravely and resignedly, simply asking the number of the boat to help find his wife later in case he also was rescued. 'Number 4,' was Lightoller's reply. Nothing more was said. Colonel Astor moved away from this point and I never saw him again. I do not for a moment believe the report that he attempted to enter, or did enter, a boat and it is evident that if any such thought occurred to him at all it must have been at this present time and in this boat with his wife. Second Officer Lightoller recalled the incident perfectly when I reminded him of it. It was only through me that Colonel Astor's identity was established in his mind. 'I assumed,' said he, 'that I was asked to give the number of the lifeboat as the passenger intended, for some unknown cause, to make complaint about me.' From the fact that I never saw Colonel Astor on the boat deck later, and also because his body, when found, was crushed (according to the statement of one who saw it at Halifax, Mr Harry K. White, of Boston, Mr Edward A. Kent's brother-in-law, my schoolmate and friend from boyhood), I am of the opinion that he met his fate on the ship when the boilers tore through it, as described later.

One of the incidents I recall when loading the boats at this point was my seeing a young woman clinging tightly to a baby in her arms as she approached near the ship's high rail, but unwilling even for a moment to allow anyone else to hold the little one while assisting her to board the lifeboat. As she drew back sorrowfully to the outer edge of the crowd on the deck, I followed and persuaded her to accompany me to the rail again, promising if she would entrust the baby to me I would see that the officer passed it to her after she got aboard. I remember her trepidation as she acceded to my suggestion and the happy expression of relief when the mother was safely seated with the baby restored to her. 'Where is my baby?' was her anxious wail. 'I have your baby,' I cried, as it was tenderly handed along. I remember this incident well because of my feeling at the time, when I had the babe in my care; though the interval was short, I wondered how I should manage with it in my arms if the lifeboats got away and I should be plunged into the water with it as the ship sank.

According to Lightoller's testimony before the Senate Committee he put 20 to 25 women, with two seamen to row, in the first boat and 30, with two seamen, in the second.

Our labours in loading the boats were now shifted to the boat deck above, where Clinch Smith and I, with others, followed Lightoller and the crew. On this deck some difficulty was experienced in getting the boats ready to lower. Several causes may have contributed to this, viz., lack of drill and insufficient number of seamen for such emergency, or because of the new tackle not working smoothly. We had the hardest time with the Engelhardt boat, lifting and pushing it towards and over the rail. My shoulders and the whole weight of my body were used in assisting the crew at this work. Lightoller's testimony tells us that as the situation grew more serious he began to take chances and in loading the third boat he filled it up as full as he dared to, with about 35 persons. By this time he was short of seamen, and in the fourth boat he put the first man passenger. 'Are you a sailor?' Lightoller asked, and received the reply from the gentleman addressed that he was 'a yachtsman.' Lightoller told him if he was 'sailor enough to get out over the bulwarks to the lifeboat, to go ahead.' This passenger was Major Arthur Peuchen, of Toronto, who acquitted himself as a brave man should. My energies were so concentrated upon this work of loading the boats at this quarter that lapse of time, sense of sight and sense of hearing recorded no impressions during this interval until the last boat was loaded; but there is one fact of which I am positive, and that is that every man, woman, officer and member of the crew did their full duty without a sign of fear or confusion. Lightoller's strong and steady voice rang out his orders in clear firm tones, inspiring confidence and obedience. There was not one woman who shed tears or gave any sign of fear or distress. There was not a man at this quarter of the ship who indicated a desire to get into the boats and escape with the women. There was not a member of the crew who shirked, or left his post. The coolness, courage, and sense of duty that I here witnessed made me thankful to God and proud of my Anglo-Saxon race that gave this perfect and superb exhibition of self-control at this hour of severest trial. 'The boat's deck was only 10 feet from the water when I lowered the sixth boat,' testified Lightoller, 'and when we lowered the first, the distance to the water was seventy feet.' We had now loaded all the women who were in sight at that quarter of the ship, and I ran along the deck with Clinch Smith on the port side some distance aft shouting, 'Are there any more women?' 'Are there any more women?' On my return there was a very palpable list to port as if the ship was about to topple over. The deck was on a corresponding slant. 'All passengers to the starboard side,' was Lightoller's loud command, heard by all of us. Here I thought the final crisis had come, with the boats all gone, and when we were to be precipitated into the sea.

Prayerful thoughts now began to rise in me that my life might be preserved and I be restored to my loved ones at home. I weighed myself in the balance, doubtful whether I was thus deserving of God's mercy and protection. I questioned myself as to the performance of my religious duties according to the instructions of my earliest Preceptor, the Reverend Henry A. Coit, whose St Paul's School at Concord, N.H., I had attended. My West Point training in the matter of recognition of constituted authority and maintenance of composure stood me in good stead.

My friend, Clinch Smith, urged immediate obedience to Lightoller's orders, and, with other men passengers, we crossed over to the starboard quarter of the ship, forward on the same boat deck where, as I afterwards learned, the officer in command was First Officer Murdoch, who had also done noble work, and was soon thereafter to lose his life. Though the deck here was not so noticeably aslant as on the port side, the conditions appeared fully as desperate. All the lifeboats had been lowered and had departed. There was somewhat of a crowd congregated along the rail. The light was sufficient for me to recognize distinctly many of those with whom I was well acquainted. Here, pale and determined, was Mr John B. Thayer, Second Vice-President of the Pennsylvania Railroad, and Mr George D. Widener. They were looking over the ship's gunwale, talking earnestly as if debating what to do. Next to them it pained me to discover Mrs J. M. Brown and Miss Evans, the two ladies whom more than an hour previous I had, as related, consigned to the care of Sixth Officer Moody on deck A, where he, as previously described, blocked my purpose of accompanying these ladies and personally assisting them into the boat. They showed no signs of perturbation whatever as they conversed quietly with me. Mrs Brown quickly related how they became separated, in the crowd, from her sisters, Mrs Appleton and Mrs Cornell. Alas! that they had not remained on the same port side of the ship, or moved forward on deck A, or the boat deck! Instead, they had wandered in some unexplained way to the very furthest point diagonally from where they were at first. At the time of introduction I had not caught Miss Evans' name, and when we were here together at this critical moment I thought it important to ask, and she gave me her name. Meantime the crew were working on the roof of the officers' quarters to cut loose one of the Engelhardt boats. All this took place more quickly than it takes to write it.

Meantime, I will describe what was going on at the quarter where I left Lightoller loading the last boat on the port side [lifeboat D]. The information was obtained personally from him, in answer to my careful questioning during the next few days on board the *Carpathia*, when I made notes thereof, which were confirmed again the next week in Washington, where we were both summoned before the Senate Investigating Committee. 'Men from the steerage,' he said, 'rushed the boat.' 'Rush' is the word he used, meaning they got in without his permission. He drew his pistol and ordered them out, threatening to shoot if they attempted to enter the boat again. I presume it was in consequence of this incident that the crew established the line which I encountered, presently referred to, which blocked the men passengers from approaching the last boat loaded on the port side forward, where we had been, and the last one that was safely loaded from the ship.

During this very short interval I was on the starboard side, as described, next to the rail, with Mrs Brown and Miss Evans, when I heard a member of the crew, coming from the quarter where the last boat was loaded, say that there was room for more ladies in it. Immediately seized each lady by the arm, and, with Miss Evans on my right and Mrs Brown on my left, hurried, with three other ladies following us, toward the port side; but I had not proceeded half-way, and near amidship, when I was stopped by the aforesaid line of the crew barring my progress, and one of the officers told me that only the women could pass.

The story of what now happened to Mrs Brown and Miss Evans after they left me must be told by Mrs Brown, as related to me by herself when I rejoined her next on board the *Carpathia*. Miss Evans led the way, she said, as they neared the rail where what proved to be the last lifeboat was being loaded, but in a spirit of most heroic self-sacrifice Miss Evans insisted upon Mrs Brown's taking precedence in being assisted aboard the boat. 'You go first,' she said. 'You are married and have children.' But when Miss Evans attempted to follow after, she was unable to do so for some unknown cause. The women in the boat were not able, it would appear, to pull Miss Evans in. It was necessary for her first to clear the four feet high ship's gunwale, and no man or member of the crew was at this particular point to lift her over. I have questioned Mr Lightoller several times about this, but he has not been able to give any satisfactory explanation and cannot understand it, for when he gave orders to lower away, there was no woman in sight. I have further questioned him as to whether there was an interval between the ship's rail and the lifeboat he was loading, but he says, 'No,' for until the very last boat he stood, as has already been described, with one foot planted on the ship's gunwale and the other in the lifeboat. I had thought that the list of the ship might have caused too much of an interval for him to have done this. Perhaps what I have read in a letter of Mrs Brown may furnish some reason why Miss Evans' efforts to board the lifeboat, in which there was plenty of room for her, were unavailing. 'Never mind,' she is said to have called out, 'I will go on a later boat.' She then ran away and was not seen again; but there was no later boat, and it would seem that after a momentary impulse, being disappointed and being unable to get into the boat, she went aft on the port side, and no one saw her again. Neither the Second Officer nor I saw any women on the deck during the interval thereafter of 15 or 20 minutes before the great ship sank. An inspection of the American and British Reports shows that all women and children of the first cabin were saved except five. Out of the 150 these were the five lost: (1) Miss Evans; (2) Mrs Straus; (3) Mrs H. J. Allison, of Montreal; (4) her daughter, Miss Allison, and (5) Miss A. E. Isham, of New York. The first two have already been accounted for. Mrs Allison and Miss Allison could have been saved had they not chosen to remain on the ship. They refused to enter the lifeboat unless Mr Allison was allowed to go with them. This statement was made in my presence by Mrs H. A. Cassobeer, of New York, who related it to Mrs Allison's brother, Mr G. F. Johnston, and myself. Those of us who survived among the first cabin passengers will remember this beautiful Mrs Allison, and will be glad to know of the heroic mould in which she was cast, as exemplified by her fate, which was similar to that of another, Mrs Straus, who has been memorialized the world over. The fifth lady lost was Miss A. E. Isham, and she is the only one of whom no survivor, so far as I can learn, is able to give any information whatever as to where she was or what she did on that fateful Sunday night. Her relatives, learning that her stateroom, No. C49, adjoined mine, wrote me in the hope that I might be able to furnish some information to their sorrowing hearts about her last hours on the shipwrecked *Titanic*. It was with much regret that I replied that I had not seen my neighbour at any time, and, not having the pleasure of her acquaintance, identification was impossible. I was, however, glad to be able to assure her family of one point, viz., that she did not meet with the horrible fate which they feared, in being locked in her stateroom and drowned. I had revisited my stateroom twice after being aroused by the collision, and am sure that she was fully warned of what had happened, and after she left her stateroom it was locked behind her, as was mine.

The simple statement of fact that all of the first cabin women were sent off in the lifeboats and saved, except five – three of whom met heroic death through choice and two by some mischance – is in itself the most sublime tribute that could be paid to the self-sacrifice and the gallantry of the first cabin men, including all the grand heroes who sank with the ship and those of us who survived their fate. All authentic testimony of both first and second cabin passengers is also in evidence that the Captain's order for women and children to be loaded first met with the unanimous approval of us all, and in every instance was carried out both in letter and in spirit. In Second Officer Lightoller's testimony before the Senate Committee, when asked whether the Captain's order was a rule of the sea, he answered that it was 'the rule of human nature.' There is no doubt in my mind that the men at that quarter where we were would have adopted the same rule spontaneously whether ordered by the Captain, or not. Speaking from my own personal observation, which by comparison with that of the Second Officer I find in accord with his, all six boat loads, including the last, departed with women and children only, with not a man passenger except Major Peuchen, whose services were enlisted to replace the lack of crew. I may say further that with the single exception of Colonel Astor's plea for the protection of his wife, in delicate condition, there was not one who made a move or a suggestion to enter a boat.

While the light was dim on the decks it was always sufficient for me to recognize anyone with whom I was acquainted, and I am happy in being able to record the names of those I know beyond any doubt whatever, as with me in these last terrible scenes when Lightoller's boats were being lowered and after the last lifeboat had left the ship. The names of these were: James Clinch Smith, Colonel John Jacob Astor, Mr John B. Thayer and Mr George D. Widener. So far as I know, and my research has been exhaustive, I am the sole surviving passenger who was with or assisted Lightoller in the loading of the last boats. When I first saw and realized that every lifeboat had left the ship, the sensation felt was not an agreeable one. No thought of fear entered my head, but I experienced a feeling which others may recall when holding the breath in the face of some frightful emergency and when 'vox faucibus haesit,' as frequently happened to the old Trojan hero of our school days. This was the nearest approach to fear, if it can be so characterized, that is discernible in an analysis of my actions or feelings while in the midst of the many dangers which beset me during that night of terror. Though still worse and seemingly many hopeless conditions soon prevailed, and unexpected ones, too, when I felt that 'any moment might be my last,' I had no time to contemplate danger when there was continuous need of quick thought, action and composure withal. Had I become rattled for a moment, or in the slightest degree been undecided during the several emergencies presently cited, I am certain that I never should have lived to tell the tale of my miraculous escape. For it is eminently fitting, in gratitude to my Maker, that I should make the acknowledgment that I know of no recorded instance of Providential deliverance more directly attributable to cause and effect, illustrating the efficacy of prayer and how 'God helps those who help themselves.' I should have only courted the fate of many hundreds of others had I supinely made no effort to supplement my prayers with all the strength and power which He has granted to me. While I said to myself, 'Goodbye to all at home,' I hoped and prayed for escape. My mind was nerved to do the duty of the moment, and my muscles seemed to be hardened in preparation for any struggle that might come. When I learned that there was still another boat, the Engelhardt, on the roof of the officers' quarters, I felt encouraged with the thought that here was a chance of getting away before the ship sank; but what was one boat among so many eager to board her?

During my short absence in conducting the ladies to a position of safety, Mr Thayer and Mr Widener had disappeared, but I know not whither. Mr Widener's son, Harry, was probably with them, but Mr Thayer supposed that his young son, Jack, had left the ship in the same boat with his mother. Messrs Thayer and Widener must have gone toward the stern during the short interval of my absence. No one at this point had jumped into the sea. If there had been any, both Clinch Smith and I would have known it. After the water struck the bridge forward there were many who rushed aft, climbed over the rail and jumped, but I never saw one of them.

I was now working with the crew at the davits on the starboard side forward, adjusting them ready for lowering the Engelhardt boat [lifeboat B] from the roof of the officers' house to the boat deck below. Some one of the crew on the roof, where it was, sang out, 'Has any passenger a knife?' I took mine out of my pocket and tossed it to him, saying, 'Here is a small penknife, if that will do any good.' It appeared to me then that there was more trouble than there ought to have been in removing the canvas cover and cutting the boat loose, and that some means should have been available for doing this without any delay. Meantime, four or five long oars were placed aslant against the walls of the officers' house to break the fall of the boat, which was pushed from the roof and slipped with a crash down on the boat deck, smashing several of the oars. Clinch Smith and I scurried out of the way and stood leaning with our backs against the rail, watching this procedure and feeling anxious lest the boat might have been stove in, or otherwise injured so as to cause her to leak in the water. The account of the junior Marconi operator, Harold S. Bride, supplements mine. 'I saw a collapsible boat,' he said, 'near a funnel, and went over to it. Twelve men were trying to boost it down to the boat deck. They were having an awful time. It was the last boat left. I looked at it longingly a few minutes; then I gave a hand and over she went.'

About this time I recall that an officer on the roof of the house called down to the crew at this quarter, 'Are there any seamen down there among you.' 'Aye, aye, Sir,' was the response, and quite a number left the boat deck to assist in what I supposed to have been the cutting loose of the other Engelhardt boat [lifeboat A] up there on the roof. Again I heard an inquiry for another knife. I thought I recognized the voice of the Second Officer working up there with the crew. Lightoller has told me, and has written me as well, that 'boat A on the starboard side did not leave the ship,' [With the evidence on the subject presented later he recognises that lifeboat A floated away and was afterwards utilised] while 'B was thrown down to the boat deck,' and was the one on which he and I eventually climbed. The crew had thrown the Engelhardt boat to the deck, but I did not understand 'why they were so long about launching it, unless they were waiting to cut the other one loose and launch them both at the same time. Two young men of the crew, nice looking, dressed in white, one tall and the other smaller, were coolly debating as to whether the compartments would hold the ship afloat. They were standing with their backs to the rail looking on at the rest of the crew, and I recall asking one of them why he did not assist.

At this time there were other passengers around, but Clinch Smith was the only one associated with me here to the last. It was about this time, 15 minutes after the launching of the last lifeboat on the port side, that I heard a noise that spread consternation among us all. This was no less than the water striking the bridge and gurgling up the hatchway forward. It seemed momentarily as if it would reach the boat deck. It appeared as if it would take the crew a long time to turn the Engelhardt boat right side up and lift it over the rail, and there were so many ready to board her that she would have been swamped. Probably taking these points into consideration Clinch Smith made the proposition that we should leave and go toward the stern, still on the starboard side, so he started and I followed immediately after him. We had taken but a few steps in the direction indicated when there arose before us from the decks below, a mass of humanity several lines deep, covering the boat deck, facing us, and completely blocking our passage toward the stern.

There were women in the crowd, as well as men, and they seemed to be steerage passengers who had just come up from the decks below. Instantly, when they saw us and the water on the deck chasing us from behind, they turned in the opposite direction towards the stern. This brought them at that point plumb against the iron fence and railing which divide the first and second cabin passengers. Even among these people there was no hysterical cry, or evidence of panic, but oh, the agony of it! Clinch Smith and I instantly saw that we could make no progress ahead, and with the water following us behind over the deck, we were in a desperate place. I can never forget the exact point on the ship where he and I were located, viz., at the opening of the angle made by the walls of the officers' house and only a short distance abaft the *Titanic*'s forward 'expansion joint.' Clinch Smith was immediately on my left, nearer the apex of the angle, and our backs were turned toward the ship's rail and the sea. Looking up toward the roof of the officers' house I saw a man to the right of me and above lying on his stomach on the roof, with his legs dangling over. Clinch Smith jumped to reach this roof, and I promptly followed. The efforts of both of us failed. I was loaded down with heavy long-skirted overcoat and Norfolk coat beneath, with clumsy life-preserver over all, which made my jump fall short. As I came down, the water struck my right side. I crouched down into it preparatory to jumping with it, and rose as if on the crest of a wave on the seashore. This expedient brought the attainment of the object I had in view. I was able to reach the roof and the iron railing that is along the edge of it, and pulled myself over on top of the officers' house on my stomach near the base of the second funnel. The feat which I instinctively accomplished was the simple one, familiar to all bathers in the surf at the seashore. I had no time to advise Clinch Smith to adopt it. To my utter dismay, a hasty glance to my left and right showed that he had not followed my example, and that the wave, if I may call it such, which had mounted me to the roof, had completely covered him, as well as all people on both sides of me, including the man I had first seen athwart the roof.

I was thus parted forever from my friend, Clinch Smith, with whom I had agreed to remain to the last struggle. I felt almost a pang of responsibility for our separation; but he was not in sight and there was no chance of rendering assistance. His ultimate fate is a matter of conjecture. Hemmed in by the mass of people toward the stern, and cornered in the locality previously described, it seems certain that as the ship keeled over and sank, his body was caught in the angle or in the coils of rope and other appurtenances on the deck and borne down to the depths below. There could not be a braver man than James Clinch Smith. He was the embodiment of coolness and courage during the whole period of the disaster. While in constant touch and communication with him at the various points on the ship when we were together on this tragic night, he never showed the slightest sign of fear, but manifested the same quiet imperturbable manner so well known to all of his friends, who join with his family in mourning his loss. His conduct should be an inspiration to us all, and an appropriate epitaph to his memory taken from the words of Christ would be: 'Greater love hath no man than this, that a man lay down his life for his friend.'

Chapter 3 The Foundering of the *Titanic*

Before I resume the story of my personal escape it is pertinent that I should, at this juncture, discuss certain points wherein the statements of survivors are strangely at variance.

First: Was there an explosion of the ship's boilers?

I am of opinion that there was none, because I should have been conscious of it. When aboard ship I should have heard it and felt it, but I did not. As my senses were on the lookout for every danger, I cannot conceive it possible that an explosion occurred without my being made aware of it. When I went down holding on to the ship and was under water, I heard no sound indicating anything of the sort, and when I came to the surface there was no ship in sight. Furthermore, there was no perceptible wave which such a disturbance would have created.

The two ranking surviving officers of the *Titanic*, viz., Second Officer Lightoller and Third Officer Pitman, with whom I had a discussion on this and other points in almost daily conversation in my cabin on the *Carpathia* agreed with me that there was no explosion of the boilers. The Second Officer and myself had various similar experiences, and, as will be noticed in the course of this narrative, we were very near together during all the perils of that awful night. The only material difference worth noting was the manner in which each parted company with the ship, and finally reached the bottom-up Engelhardt boat on top of which we made our escape. According to his testimony before the Senate Committee, he stood on the roof of the officers' quarters in front of the first funnel, facing forward, and as the ship dived, he dived also, while I held on to the iron railing on the same roof, near the second funnel, as has been described, and as the ship sank I was pulled down with it. The distance between us on the ship was then about 15 yards.

There are so many newspaper and other published reports citing the statements of certain survivors as authority for this story of an explosion of the boilers that the reading world generally has been made to believe it. Among the names of passengers whose alleged statements (I have received letters repudiating some of these interviews) are thus given credence, I have read those of Miss Cornelia Andrews, of Hudson, N.Y.; Mrs W. E. Carter, of Philadelphia, Pa.; Mr John Pillsbury Snyder, of Minneapolis, Minn.; Miss Minahan, of Fond du Lac, Wis., and Lady Duff Gordon, of England, all of whom, according to the newspaper reports, describe their position in the lifeboats around the ship and how they hear, or saw, with 'ship blow up,' or 'the boilers explode' with one or two explosions just before the ship sank out of their sight. On the other hand, Mr Hugh Woolner told me on the *Carpathia* that from his position in the lifeboat, which he claims was the nearest one to the *Titanic* when she sank some 75 yards away, there was a terrific noise on the ship, as she slanted towards the head before the final plunge, which sounded like the crashing of millions of dishes of crockery. Woolner and I when on board the *Carpathia*, as presently described, had our cabin together, where we were visited by Officers Lightoller and Pitman. This was one of the points we discussed together, and the conclusion was at once reached as to the cause of this tremendous crash. Since then, Lightoller has been subjected to rigid examination before this country's and England's Investigating Committees, and has been a party to discussions with experts, including the designers and builders of the *Titanic*. His conclusion expressed on the *Carpathia* is now strengthened, and he says that there was no explosion of the boilers and that the great noise which was mistaken for it was due to 'the boilers leaving their beds' on E deck when the ship was aslant and, with their great weight, sliding along the deck, crushing and tearing through the doomed vessel forward toward the bow. Third Officer Pitman also gave his testimony on this, as well as the next point considered. Before the Senate Committee he said: 'Then she turned right on end and made a big plunge forward. The *Titanic* did not break asunder. I heard reports like big guns in the distance. I assumed the great bulkheads had gone to pieces.' Cabin steward Samuel Rule said: 'I think the noise we heard was that of the boilers and engines breaking away from their seatings and falling down through the forward bulkhead. At the time it occurred, the ship was standing nearly upright in the water.'

The peculiar way in which the *Titanic* is described as hesitating and assuming a vertical position before her final dive to the depths below can be accounted for only on this hypothesis of the sliding of the boilers from their beds. A second cabin passenger, Mr Lawrence Beesley, a Cambridge University man, has written an excellent book about the *Titanic* disaster, dwelling especially upon the lessons to be learned from it. His account given to the newspapers also contains the most graphic description from the viewpoint of those in the lifeboats, telling how the great ship looked before her final plunge. He 'was a mile or two miles away,' he writes,

'when the oarsmen lay on their oars and all in the lifeboat were motionless as we watched the ship in absolute silence – save some who would not look and buried their heads on each others' shoulders … As we gazed awe-struck, she tilted slightly up, revolving apparently about a centre of gravity just astern of amidships until she attained a vertical upright position, and there she remained – motionless! As she swung up, her lights, which had shown without a flicker all night, went out suddenly, then came on again for a single flash and then went out altogether; and as they did so there came a noise which many people, wrongly, I think, have described as an explosion. It has always seemed to me that it was nothing but the engines and machinery coming loose from their place and bearings and falling through the compartments, smashing everything in their way. It was partly a roar, partly a groan, partly a rattle and partly a smash, and it was not a sudden roar as an explosion would be; it went on successively for some seconds, possibly 15 or 20, as the heavy machinery dropped down to the bottom (now the bows) of the ship; I suppose it fell through the end and sank first before the ship. But it was a noise no one had heard before and no one wishes to hear again. It was stupefying, stupendous, as it came to us along the water. It was as if all the heavy things one could think of had been thrown downstairs from the top of a house, smashing each other, and the stairs and everything in the way.

Several apparently authentic accounts have been given in which definite stories of explosions have been related – in some cases even with wreckage blown up and the ship broken in two; but I think such accounts will not stand close analysis. In the first place, the fires had been withdrawn and the steam allowed to escape some time before she sank, and the possibility from explosion from this cause seems very remote.

Second: Did the ship break in two?

I was on the *Carpathia* when I first heard anyone make reference to this point. The 17-year-old son of Mr John B. Thayer, 'Jack' Thayer, Jr., and his young friend from Philadelphia, R. N. Williams, Jr., the tennis expert, in describing their experiences to me were positive that they saw the ship split in two. This was from their position in the water on the starboard quarter. 'Jack' Thayer gave this same description to an artist, who reproduced it in an illustration in the *New York Herald*, which many of us have seen [see illustrations 52, 53, 86, 90, 91 and 92]. Some of the passengers, whose names I have just mentioned, are also cited by the newspapers as authority for the statements that the ship 'broke in two,' that she 'buckled amidships,' that she 'was literally torn to pieces,' etc. On the other hand, there is much testimony available which is at variance with this much-advertised sensational newspaper account. Summing up its investigation of this point the Senate Committee's Report reads: 'There have been many conflicting statements as to whether the ship broke in two, but the preponderance of evidence is to the effect that she assumed an almost end-on position and sank intact.' This was as Lightoller testified before the Committee, that the *Titanic*'s decks were 'absolutely intact' when she went down. On this point, too, Beesley is in accord, from his viewpoint in the lifeboat some distance away out of danger, whence, more composedly than others, he could see the last of the ill-fated ship as the men lay on their oars watching until she disappeared. 'No phenomenon,' he continues, 'like that pictured in some American and English papers occurred – that of the ship breaking in two, and the two ends being raised above the surface. When the noise was over, the *Titanic* was still upright like a column; we could see her now only as the stern and some 150 feet of her stood outlined against the star-specked sky, looming black in the darkness, and in this position she continued for some minutes – I think as much as five minutes – but it may have been less. Then, as sinking back a little at the stern, I thought she slid slowly forwards through the water and dived slantingly down.'

From my personal viewpoint I also know that the *Titanic's* decks were intact at the time she sank, and when I sank with her, there was over seven-sixteenths of the ship already under water, and there was no indication then of any impending break of the deck or ship. I recently visited the sister ship of the *Titanic*, viz., the *Olympic*, at her dock in New York harbour. This was for the purpose of still further familiarizing myself with the corresponding localities which were the scene of my personal experiences on the *Titanic*, and which are referred to in this narrative. The only difference in the deck plan of the sister ship which I noted, and which the courteous officers of the *Olympic* mentioned, is that the latter ship's deck A is not glass-enclosed like the *Titanic's* but one of the principal points of discovery that I made during my investigation concerns this matter of the alleged breaking in two of this magnificent ship. The White Star Line officers pointed out to me what they called the ship's 'forward expansion joint,' and they claimed the *Titanic* was so constructed that she must have split in two at this point, if she did so at all. I was interested in observing that this 'expansion joint' was less than twelve feet forward from that point on the boat deck whence I jumped, as described (to the iron railing on the roof of the officers' quarters). It is indicated by a black streak of leather-covering running transversely across the deck and then up the vertical white wall of the officers' house. This 'joint' extends, however, only through the boat deck and decks A and B, which are superimposed on deck C. If there was any splitting in two, it seems to me also that this superstructure, weakly joined, would have been the part to split; but it certainly did not. It was only a few seconds before the time of the alleged break that I stepped across this dividing line of the two sections and went down with the after section about twelve feet from this 'expansion joint.'

One explanation which I offer of what must be a delusion on the part of the advocates of the 'break-in-two' theory is that when the forward funnel fell, as hereafter described, it may have looked as if the ship itself was splitting in two, particularly to the young men who are cited as authority.

Third: Did either the Captain or the First Officer shoot himself?

Notwithstanding all the current rumours and newspaper statements answering this question affirmatively, I have been unable to find any passenger or member of the crew cited as authority for the statement that either Captain Smith or First Officer Murdoch did anything of the sort. On the contrary, so far as relates to Captain Smith, there are several witnesses, including Harold S. Bride, the junior Marconi operator, who saw him at the last on the bridge of his ship, and later, when sinking and struggling in the water. Neither can I discover any authentic testimony about First Officer Murdoch's shooting himself. On the contrary, I find fully sufficient evidence that he did not. He was a brave and efficient officer and no sufficient motive for self-destruction can be advanced. He performed his full duty under difficult circumstances, and was entitled to praise and honour. During the last 15 minutes before the ship sank, I was located at that quarter forward on the boat deck, starboard side, where Murdoch was in command and where the crew under him were engaged in the vain attempt of launching the Engelhardt boat. The report of a pistol shot during this interval ringing in my ears within a few feet of me would certainly have attracted my attention, and later, when I moved astern, the distance between us was not so great as to prevent my hearing it. The 'big wave' or 'giant wave,' described by Harold Bride, swept away Murdoch and the crew from the boat deck first before it struck me, and when I rose with it to the roof of the officers' house, Bride's reported testimony fits in with mine so far as relates to time, place, and circumstance, and I quote his words as follows: 'About 10 minutes before the ship sank, Captain Smith gave word for every man to look to his own safety. I sprang to aid the men struggling to launch the life raft (Engelhardt boat), and we had succeeded in getting it to the edge of the ship when a giant wave carried it away.' Lightoller also told me on board the *Carpathia* that he saw Murdoch when he was engulfed by the water and that if before this a pistol had been fired within the short distance that separated them, he also is confident that he would have heard it.

Fourth: On which side did the ship list?

The testimony on this point, which at first blush appears conflicting, proves on investigation not at all so, but just what was to be expected from the mechanical construction of the ship. We find the most authoritative testimony in evidence that the *Titanic* listed on the starboard side, and again, on equally authoritative testimony, that she listed on the port side. Quartermaster Hitchens, who was at the wheel when the iceberg struck the ship, testified on this point before the Senate Committee as follows: 'The Captain came back to the wheel house and looked at the commutator (clinometer) in front of the compass, which is a little instrument like a clock to tell you how the ship is listing. The ship had a list of five degrees to the starboard about five or 10 minutes after the impact. Mr Karl Behr, the well-known tennis player, interviewed by the *New York Tribune* is quoted as saying: 'We had just retired when the collision came. I pulled on my clothes and went down the deck to the Beckwith cabin and, after I had roused them, I noted that the ship listed to the starboard, and that was the first thing that made me think that we were in for serious trouble.' On the other hand, the first time I noticed this list was, as already described in my narrative, when I met Clinch Smith in the companionway and we saw a slight list to port, which gave us the first warning of how serious the accident was. The next and last time, as has also been described, was when Second Officer Lightoller ordered all passengers to the starboard side because of the very palpable list to port, when the great ship suddenly appeared to be about to topple over. Lightoller also corroborates the statement as to this list on the port side. Other witnesses might be quoted, some of whom testify to the starboard list, and others to the one to port. The conclusion, therefore, is reached that the *Titanic* listed at one time to starboard and at another time to port. This is as it should be because of the transverse watertight compartments which made the water, immediately after the compact, rush from the starboard quarter to the port, and then back again, keeping the ship balancing on her keel until she finally sank. If she had been constructed otherwise, with longitudinal compartments only, it is evident that after the impact on the starboard side, the *Titanic* would have listed only to the starboard side, and after a very much shorter interval would have careened over on that quarter, and a much smaller proportion of lives would have been saved.

Chapter 4 Struggling in the Water For Life

I now resume the narrative description of my miraculous escape, and it is with considerable diffidence that I do so, for the personal equation monopolizes more attention than may be pleasing to my readers who are not relatives or intimate friends.

As may be noticed in Chapter 2, it was Clinch Smith's suggestion and on his initiative that we left that point on the starboard side of the boat deck where the crew, under Chief Officer Wilde and First Officer Murdoch, were in vain trying to launch the Engelhardt boat B which had been thrown down from the roof of the officers' quarters forward of the first funnel. I say 'boat B' because I have the information to that effect in a letter from Second Officer Lightoller. Confirmation of this statement I also find in the reported interview of a Saloon Steward, Thomas Whitely, in the *New York Tribune* the day after the *Carpathia's* arrival. An analysis of his statement shows that boat A became entangled and was abandoned, while he saw the other, bottom up and filled with people. It was on this boat that he also eventually climbed and was saved with the rest of us. Clinch Smith and I got away from this point just before the water reached it and drowned Chief Officer Wilde and First Officer Murdoch, and others who were not successful in effecting a lodgment on the boat as it was swept off the deck. This moment was the first fateful crisis of the many that immediately followed. As bearing upon it I quote the reported statement of Harold S. Bride, the junior Marconi operator. His account also helps to determine the fate of Captain Smith. He says: 'Then came the Captain's voice [from the bridge to the Marconi operators], 'Men, you have done your full duty. You can do no more. Abandon your cabin. Now, it is every man for himself.'' 'Phillips continued to work,' he says, 'for about 10 minutes or about 15 minutes after the Captain had released him. The water was then coming into our cabin ... I went to the place where I had seen the collapsible boat on the boat deck and to my surprise I saw the boat: and the men still trying to push it off. They could not do it. I went up to them and was just lending a hand when a large wave came awash of the deck. The big wave carried the boat off. I had hold of an oarlock and I went off with it. The next I knew I was in the boat. But that was not all. I was in the boat and the boat was upside down and I was under it ... How I got out from under the boat I do not know, but I felt a breath at last.'

From this it appears evident that, so far as Clinch Smith is concerned, it would have been better to have stayed by this Engelhardt boat to the last, for here he had a chance of escape like Bride and others of the crew who clung to it, but which I only reached again after an incredibly long swim under water. The next crisis, which was the fatal one to Clinch Smith and to the great mass of people that suddenly arose before us as I followed him astern, has already been described. The simple expedient of jumping with the 'big wave' as demonstrated above carried me to safety, away from a dangerous position to the highest part of the ship; but I was the only one who adopted it successfully. The force of the wave that struck Clinch Smith and the others undoubtedly knocked most of them there unconscious against the walls of the officers' quarters and other appurtenances of the ship on the boat deck. As the ship keeled over forward, I believe that their bodies were caught in the angles of this deck, or entangled in the ropes, and in these other appurtenances thereon, and sank with the ship.

My holding on to the iron railing just when I did prevented my being knocked unconscious. I pulled myself over on the roof on my stomach, but before I could get to my feet I was in a whirlpool of water, swirling round and round, as I still tried to cling to the railing as the ship plunged to the depths below. Down, down, I went: it seemed a great distance. There was a very noticeable pressure upon my ears, though there must have been plenty of air that the ship carried down with it. When under water I retained, as it appears, a sense of general direction, and, as soon as I could do so, swam away from the starboard side of the ship, as I knew my life depended upon it. I swam with all my strength, and I seemed endowed with an extra supply for the occasion. I was incited to desperate effort by the thought of boiling water, or steam, from the expected explosion of the ship's boilers, and that I would be scalded to death, like the sailors of whom I had read in the account of the British battle-ship *Victoria* sunk in collision with the *Camperdown* in the Mediterranean in 1893. Second Officer Lightoller told me he also had the same idea, and that if the fires had not been drawn the boilers would explode and the water become boiling hot. As a consequence, the plunge in the icy water produced no sense of coldness whatever, and I had no thought of cold until later on when I climbed on the bottom of the upturned boat. My being drawn down by suction to a greater depth was undoubtedly checked to some degree by the life-preserver which I wore, but it is to the buoyancy of the water, caused by the volume of air rising from the sinking ship, that I attributed the assistance which enabled me to strike out and swim faster and further under water than I ever did before. I held my breath for what seemed an interminable time until I could scarcely stand it any longer, but I congratulated myself then and there that not one drop of sea-water was allowed to enter my mouth. With renewed determination and set jaws, I swam on. Just at the moment I thought that for lack of breath I would have to give in, I seemed to have been provided with a second wind, and it was just then that the thought that this was my last moment came upon me. I wanted to convey the news of how I died to my loved ones at home. As I swam beneath the surface of the ocean, I prayed that my spirit could go to them and say, 'Goodbye, until we meet again in heaven.' In this connection, the thought was in my mind of a well authenticated experience of mental telepathy that occurred to a member of my wife's family. Here in my case was a similar experience of a shipwrecked loved one, and I thought if I prayed hard enough that this, my last wish to communicate with my wife and daughter, might be granted.

    To what extent my prayer was answered let Mrs Gracie describe in her own written words, as follows: 'I was in my room at my sister's house, where I was visiting, in New York. After retiring, being unable to rest I questioned myself several times over, wondering what it was that prevented the customary long and peaceful slumber, lately enjoyed. "What is the matter?" I uttered. A voice in reply seemed to say, "On your knees and pray." Instantly, I literally obeyed with my prayer book in my hand, which by chance opened at the prayer "For those at Sea." The thought then flashed through my mind, "Archie is praying for me." I continued wide awake until a little before five o'clock a.m., by the watch that lay beside me. About 7 a.m. I dozed a while and then got up to dress for breakfast. At eight o'clock my sister, Mrs Dalliba Dutton, came softly to the door, newspaper in hand, to gently break the tragic news that the *Titanic* had sunk, and showed me the list of only 20 names saved, headed with "Colonel Archibald Butt"; but my husband's name was not included. My head sank in her protecting arms as I murmured helplessly, "He is all I have in the whole world." I could only pray for strength, and later in the day, believing myself a widow, I wrote to my daughter, who was in the care of our housekeeper and servants in our Washington home, "Cannot you see your father in his tenderness for women and children, helping them all, and then going down with the ship? If he has gone, I will not live long, but I would not have him take a boat".'

But let me now resume my personal narrative. With this second wind under water there came to me a new lease of life and strength, until finally I noticed by the increase of light that I was drawing near to the surface. Though it was not daylight, the clear star-lit night made a noticeable difference in the degree of light immediately below the surface of the water. As I was rising, I came in contact with ascending wreckage, but the only thing I struck of material size was a small plank, which I tucked under my right arm. This circumstance brought with it the reflection that it was advisable for me to secure what best I could to keep me afloat on the surface until succor arrived. When my head at last rose above the water, I detected a piece of wreckage like a wooden crate, and I eagerly seized it as a nucleus of the projected raft to be constructed from what flotsam and jetsam I might collect. Looking about me, I could see no *Titanic* in sight. She had entirely disappeared beneath the calm surface of the ocean and without a sign of any wave. That the sea had swallowed her up with all her precious belongings was indicated by the slight sound of a gulp behind me as the water closed over her. The length of time that I was under water can be estimated by the fact that I sank with her, and when I came up there was no ship in sight. The accounts of others as to the length of time it took the *Titanic* to sink afford the best measure of the interval I was below the surface.

What impressed me at the time that my eyes beheld the horrible scene was a thin light-gray smoky vapor that hung like a pall a few feet above the broad expanse of sea that was covered with a mass of tangled wreckage. That it was a tangible vapor, and not a product of imagination, I feel well assured. It may have been caused by smoke or steam rising to the surface around the area where the ship had sunk. At any rate it produced a supernatural effect, and the pictures I had seen by Dante and the description I had read in my Virgil of the infernal regions, of Charon, and the River Lethe, were then uppermost in my thoughts. Add to this, within the area described, which was as far as my eyes could reach, there arose to the sky the most horrible sounds ever heard by mortal man except by those of us who survived this terrible tragedy. The agonizing cries of death from over a thousand throats, the wails and groans of the suffering, the shrieks of the terror-stricken and the awful gaspings for breath of those in the last throes of drowning, none of us will ever forget to our dying day. 'Help! Help! Boat ahoy! Boat ahoy!' and 'My God! My God!' were the heart-rending cries and shrieks of men, which floated to us over the surface of the dark waters continuously for the next hour, but as time went on, growing weaker and weaker until they died out entirely.

As I clung to my wreckage, I noticed just in front of me, a few yards away, a group of three bodies with heads in the water, face downwards, and just behind me to my right another body, all giving unmistakable evidence of being drowned. Possibly these had gone down to the depths as I had done, but did not have the lung power that I had to hold the breath and swim under water, an accomplishment which I had practiced from my school days. There was no one alive or struggling in the water or calling for aid within the immediate vicinity of where I arose to the surface. I threw my right leg over the wooden crate in an attempt to straddle and balance myself on top of it, but I turned over in a somersault with it under water, and up to the surface again. What may be of interest is the thought that then occurred to me of the accounts and pictures of a wreck, indelibly impressed upon my memory when a boy, because of my acquaintance with some of the victims, of a frightful disaster of that day, namely the wreck of the *Ville de Havre* in the English Channel in 1873, and I had in mind Mrs Bulkley's description, and the picture of her clinging to some wreckage as a rescue boat caught sight of her, bringing the comforting words over the water, 'We are English sailors coming to save you.' I looked around, praying for a similar interposition of Fate, but I knew the thought of a rescuing boat was a vain one – for had not all the lifeboats, loaded with women and children, departed from the ship 15 or 20 minutes before I sank with it? And had I not seen the procession of them on the port side fading away from our sight?

But my prayerful thought and hope were answered in an unexpected direction. I espied to my left, a considerable distance away, a better vehicle of escape than the wooden crate on which my attempt to ride had resulted in a second ducking. What I saw was no less than the same Engelhardt, or 'surf-boat,' to whose launching I had lent my efforts, until the water broke upon the ship's boat deck where we were. On top of this upturned boat, half reclining on her bottom, were now more than a dozen men, whom, by their dress, I took to be all members of the crew of the ship. Thank God, I did not hesitate a moment in discarding the friendly crate that had been my first aid; I struck out through the wreckage and after a considerable swim reached the port side amidships of this Engelhardt boat, which with her companions, wherever utilized, did good service in saving the lives of many others. All honour to the Dane, Captain Engelhardt of Copenhagen, who built them. I say 'port side' because this boat as it was propelled through the water had Lightoller in the bow and Bride at the stern, and I believe an analysis of the testimony shows that the actual bow of the boat was turned about by the wave that struck it on the boat deck and the splash of the funnel thereafter, so that its bow pointed in an opposite direction to that of the ship. There was one member of the crew on this craft at the bow and another at the stern who had 'pieces of boarding,' improvised paddles, which were used effectually for propulsion.

When I reached the side of the boat I met with a doubtful reception, and, as no extending hand was held out to me, I grabbed, by the muscle of the left arm, a young member of the crew nearest and facing me. At the same time I threw my right leg over the boat astraddle, pulling myself aboard, with a friendly lift to my foot given by someone astern as I assumed a reclining position with them on the bottom of the capsized boat. Then after me came a dozen other swimmers who clambered around and whom we helped aboard. Among them was one completely exhausted, who came on the same port side as myself. I pulled him in and he lay face downward in front of me for several hours, until just before dawn he was able to stand up with the rest of us. The journey of our craft from the scene of the disaster will be described in the following chapter. The moment of getting aboard this upturned boat was one of supreme mental relief, more so than any other until I reached the deck of the hospitable *Carpathia* on the next morning. I now felt for the first time after the lifeboats left us aboard ship that I had some chance of escape from the horrible fate of drowning in the icy waters of the middle Atlantic. Every moment of time during the many experiences of that night, it seemed as if I had all the God-given physical strength and courage needed for each emergency, and never suffered an instant from any exhaustion, or required the need of a helping hand. The only time of any stress whatever was during the swim, just described, under water, at the moment when I gained my second wind which brought me to the surface gasping somewhat, but full of vigor. I was all the time on the lookout for the next danger that was to be overcome. I kept my presence of mind and courage throughout it all. Had I lost either for one moment, I never could have escaped to tell the tale. This is in answer to many questions as to my personal sensations during these scenes and the successive dangers which I encountered. From a psychological viewpoint also, it may be a study of interest illustrating the power of mind over matter. The sensation of fear has a visible effect upon one. It palsies one's thoughts and actions. One becomes thereby short of breath; the heart actually beats quicker and as one loses one's head one grows desperate and is gone. I have questioned those who have been near drowning and who know this statement to be a fact. It is the same in other emergencies, and the lesson to be learned is that we should 'Let courage rise with danger, And strength to strength oppose.'

To attain this courage in the hour of danger is very much a matter of physical, mental and religious training. But courage and strength would have availed me little had I not providentially escaped from being knocked senseless, or maimed, as so many other strong swimmers undoubtedly were. The narrow escapes that I had from being thus knocked unconscious could be recapitulated, and I still bear the scars on my body of wounds received at the moment, or moments, when I was struck by some undefined object. I received a blow on the top of my head, but I did not notice it or the other wounds until I arrived on board the *Carpathia*, when I found inflamed cuts on both my legs and bruises on my knees, which soon became black and blue, and I was sore to the touch all over my body for several days. It is necessary for me to turn to the accounts of others for a description of what happened during the interval that I was under water. My information about it is derived from many sources and includes various points of general interest, showing how the *Titanic* looked when she foundered, the undisputed facts that there was very little suction and that the forward funnel broke from the ship, falling on the starboard side into the sea. Various points of personal interest are also derived from the same source which the reader can analyze, for estimating the interval that I was below the surface of the ocean and the distance covered in my swim under water; for after I rose to the surface it appears that I had passed under both the falling funnel and then under the upturned boat, and a considerable distance beyond. Had I gone but a short distance under water and arisen straight up, I should have met the horrible fate of being struck by the falling funnel which, according to the evidence submitted, must have killed or drowned a number of unfortunates struggling in the water. I select these accounts of my shipwrecked companions, which supplement my personal experience, particularly the accounts of the same reliable and authoritative witnesses already cited, and from those who were rescued, as I was, on the bottom of the upset Engelhardt boat.

The following is from the account of Mr Beesley: 'The water was by now up to the last row of portholes. We were about two miles from her, and the crew insisted that such a tremendous wave would be formed by suction as she went down, that we ought to get as far as possible away. The 'Captain' (as he calls Stoker Fred Barrett), and all, lay on their oars. Presently, about 2 a.m. (2.15 a.m. per book account), as near as I can remember, we observed her settling very rapidly, with the bow and bridge completely under water, and concluded it was now only a question of minutes before she went; and so it proved. She slowly tilted, straight on end, with the stern vertically upward … To our amazement, she remained in that upright position for a time which I estimate as five minutes.' On a previous page of my narrative, I have already quoted from his book account how 'the stern and some 150 feet of the ship stood outlined against the star-specked sky, looming black in the darkness, and in this position she continued for some minutes – I think as much as five minutes, but it may have been less.' Now, when I disappeared under the sea, sinking with the ship, there is nothing more surely established in my testimony than that about nine-sixteenths of the *Titanic* was still out of the water, and when my head reached the surface she had entirely disappeared.

The New York Times of 19 April 1912, contained the story of Mr and Mrs D. H. Bishop, first cabin passengers from Dowagiac, Michigan. Their short account is one of the best I have read. As they wrote it independently of Beesley's account, and from a different point of view, being in another lifeboat (No. 7, the first to leave the ship), the following corroborative testimony, taken from their story, helps to establish the truth:

> We did not begin to understand the situation till we were perhaps a mile away from the *Titanic*. Then we could see the row of lights along the deck begin to slant gradually upward from the bow. Very slowly the lines of light began to point downward at a greater and greater angle. The sinking was so slow that you could not perceive the lights of the deck changing their position. The slant seemed to be greater about every quarter of an hour. That was the only difference.
>
> In a couple of hours she began to go down more rapidly … Suddenly the ship seemed to shoot up out of the water and stand there perpendicularly. It seemed to us that it stood *upright in the water for four full minutes*. [Gracie's italics] Then it began to slide gently downwards. Its speed increased as it went down head first, so that the stern shot down with a rush.

Harold Bride, who was swept from the boat deck, held on to an oarlock of the Engelhardt boat (which Clinch Smith and I had left a few moments before, as has already been described). I have cited his account of coming up under the boat and then clambering upon it. He testifies to there being no suction and adds the following: 'I suppose I was 150 feet away when the *Titanic*, on her nose with her after-quarter sticking straight up into the air, began to settle – slowly. When at last the waves washed over her rudder, there was not the least bit of suction I could feel. She must have kept going just so slowly as she had been.' Second Officer Lightoller too, in his conversation with me, verified his testimony before the Senate Committee that, 'The last boat, a flat collapsible (the Engelhardt) to put off was the one on top of the officers' quarters. Men jumped upon it on deck and waited for the water to float it off. The forward funnel fell into the water, just missing the raft (as he calls our upset boat). The funnel probably killed persons in the water. This was the boat I eventually got on. About 30 men clambered out of the water on to it.'

17-year-old 'Jack' Thayer was also on the starboard side of the ship, and jumped from the rail before the Engelhardt boat was swept from the boat deck by the 'giant wave.' Young Thayer's reported description of this is as follows:

> I jumped out, feet first, went down, and as I came up I was pushed away from the ship by some force. I was sucked down again, and as I came up I was pushed out again and twisted around by a large wave, coming up in the midst of a great deal of small wreckage. My hand touched the canvas fender of an overturned lifeboat. I looked up and saw some men on the top. One of them helped me up. In a short time the bottom was covered with 25 or 30 men. The assistant wireless operator (Bride) was right next to me holding on to me and kneeling in the water.

In my conversations with Thayer, Lightoller and others, it appears that the funnel fell in the water between the Engelhardt boat and the ship, washing the former further away from the *Titanic*'s starboard side. Since the foregoing was written, the testimony before the United States Senate Committee has been printed in pamphlet form, from which I have been able to obtain other evidence, and particularly that of Second Officer Lightoller in regard to the last quarter of an hour or so on board the ship and up to the time we reached the upset boat. I have also obtained and substantiated other evidence bearing upon the same period. Mr Lightoller testified as follows:

> Half an hour, or three quarters of an hour before I left the ship, when it was taking a heavy list – not a heavy list – a list over to port, the order was called, I think by the Chief Officer, 'Everyone on the starboard side to straighten her up,' which I repeated. When I left the ship I saw no women or children aboard whatever. All the boats on the port side were lowered with the exception of one – the last boat, which was stowed on top of the officers' quarters. We had not time to launch it, nor yet to open it. When all the other boats were away, I called for men to go up there; told them to cut her adrift and throw her down. It floated off the ship, and I understand the men standing on top, who assisted to launch it down jumped on to it as it was on the deck and floated off with it. It was the collapsible type of boat, and the bottom-up boat we eventually got on. When this lifeboat floated off the ship, we were thrown off a couple of times. When I came to it, it was bottom-up and there was no one on it. Immediately after finding that overturned lifeboat, and when I came alongside of it, there were quite a lot of us in the water around it preparatory to getting up on it. Then the forward funnel fell down. It fell alongside of the lifeboat about four inches clear of it on all the people there alongside of the boat. Eventually, about 30 of us got on it: Mr Thayer, Bride, the second Marconi operator, and Colonel Gracie. I think all the rest were firemen taken out of the water.

Compare this with the description given by J. Hagan in correspondence which he began with me last May. J. Hagan is a poor chap, who described himself in this correspondence

as one who 'was working my passage to get to America for the first time,' and I am
convinced that he certainly earned it, and, moreover, was one of us on that upset boat
that night. His name does not appear on the list of the crew and must not be confounded
with 'John Hagan, booked as fireman on the steamer, who sailed for England 20 April on
the *Lapland* whereas our John Hagan was admitted to St Vincent's hospital on 22 April.
In describing this period John Hagan says it was by the Captain's orders, when the ship
was listing to port, that passengers were sent to the starboard side to straighten the ship.
He went half-way and returned to where Lightoller was loading the last boat lowered.
Lightoller told him there was another boat on the roof of the officers' house if he cared
to get it down. This was the Engelhardt Boat B which, with three others, he could not
open until assisted by three more, and then they pushed it, upside down, on the boat deck
below. Hagan cut the string of the oars and was passing the first oar down to the others,
who had left him, when the boat floated into the water, upside down. He jumped to the
boat deck and into the water after the boat and 'clung to the tail end of the keel.' The
ship was shaking very much, part of it being under water. 'On looking up at it, I could
see death in a minute for us as the forward funnel was falling and it looked a certainty
it would strike our boat and smash it to pieces; but the funnel missed us about a yard,
splashing our boat 30 yards outward from the ship, and washing off several who had got
on when the boat first floated.' Hagan managed to cling to it but got a severe soaking.
The cries of distress that he heard near by were an experience he can never forget. It
appeared to him that the flooring of the ship forward had broken away and was floating
all around. Some of the men on the upset boat made use of some pieces of boarding for
paddles with which to help keep clear of the ship.

John Collins, assistant cook on the *Titanic*, also gave his interesting testimony
before the Senate Committee. He appears to have come on deck at the last moment
on the starboard side and witnessed the Engelhardt boat when it floated off into the
sea, he being carried off by the same wave when he was amidships on the bow as
the ship sank, and kept down under water for at least two or three minutes. When
he came up, he saw this boat again – the same boat on which he had seen men
working when the waves washed it off the deck, and the men clinging to it. He was
only about four or five yards off and swam over to it and got on to it. He says he is
sure there were probably 15 thereon at the time he got on. Those who were on the
boat did not help him to get on. They were watching the ship. After he got on the
boat, he did not see any lights on the *Titanic*, though the stern of the ship was still
afloat when he first reached the surface. He accounts for the wave that washed him
off amidships as due to the suction which took place when the bow went down in
the water and the waves washed the decks clear. He saw a mass of people in the
wreckage, hundreds in number, and heard their awful cries.

Chapter 5 All Night on Bottom of Half-Submerged Upturned Boat

All my companions in shipwreck who made their escape with me on top of the bottom
side-up Engelhardt boat, must recall the anxious moment after the limit was reached
when 'about 30 men had clambered out of the water on to the boat.' The weight of
each additional body submerged our life craft more and more beneath the surface.
There were men swimming in the water all about us. One more clambering aboard
would have swamped our already crowded craft. The situation was a desperate one,

and was only saved by the refusal of the crew, especially those at the stern of the boat, to take aboard another passenger. After pulling aboard the man who lay exhausted, face downward in front of me, I turned my head away from the sights in the water lest I should be called upon to refuse the pleading cries of those who were struggling for their lives. What happened at this juncture, therefore, my fellow companions in shipwreck can better describe. Steward Thomas Whiteley; interviewed by the *New York Tribune*, said: 'I drifted near a boat wrong-side-up. About 30 men were clinging to it. They refused to let me get on. Somebody tried to hit me with an oar, but I scrambled on to her.' Harry Senior, a fireman on the *Titanic*, as interviewed in the *Illustrated London News* of 4 May, and in the *New York Times* of 19 April, is reported as follows: 'On the overturned boat in question were, amongst others, Charles Lightoller, Second Officer of the *Titanic*; Colonel Archibald Gracie, and Mr J. B. Thayer, Jr., all of whom had gone down with the liner and had come to the surface again'; and 'I tried to get aboard of her, but some chap hit me over the head with an oar. There were too many on her. I got around to the other side of the boat and climbed on. There were 35 of us, including the Second Officer, and no women. I saw any amount of drowning and dead around us.' Bride's story in the same issue of the *New York Times* says: 'It was a terrible sight all around – men swimming and sinking. Others came near. Nobody gave them a hand. The bottom-up boat already had more men than it would hold and was sinking. At first the large waves splashed over my clothing; then they began to splash over my head and I had to breathe when I could.'

Though I did not see, I could not avoid hearing what took place at this most tragic crisis in all my life. The men with the paddles, forward and aft, so steered the boat as to avoid contact with the unfortunate swimmers pointed out struggling in the water. I heard the constant explanation made as we passed men swimming in the wreckage, 'Hold on to what you have, old boy; one more of you aboard would sink us all.' In no instance, I am happy to say, did I hear any word of rebuke uttered by a swimmer because of refusal to grant assistance. There was no case of cruel violence. But there was one transcendent piece of heroism that will remain fixed in my memory as the most sublime and coolest exhibition of courage and cheerful resignation to fate and fearlessness of death. This was when a reluctant refusal of assistance met with the ringing response in the deep manly voice of a powerful man, who, in his extremity, replied: 'All right, boys; good luck and God bless you.' I have often wished that the identity of this hero might be established and an individual tribute to his memory preserved. He was not an acquaintance of mine, for the tones of his voice would have enabled me to recognize him.

Collins in his testimony and Hagan in his letter to me refer to the same incident, the former before the Senate Committee, saying: 'All those who wanted to get on and tried to get on got on with the exception of only one. This man was not pushed off by anyone, but those on the boat asked him not to try to get on. We were all on the boat running [shifting our weight] from one side to the other to keep her steady. If this man had caught hold of her he would have tumbled the whole lot of us off. He acquiesced and said, "that is all right, boys; keep cool; God bless you," and he bade us goodbye.'

Hagan refers to the same man who 'swam close to us saying, "Hello boys, keep calm, boys," asking to be helped up, and was told he could not get on as it might turn the boat over. He asked for a plank and was told to cling to what he had. It was very hard to see so brave a man swim away saying, "God bless you."'

All this time our nearly submerged boat was amidst the wreckage and fast being paddled out of the danger zone whence arose the heart-rending cries already described of the struggling swimmers. It was at this juncture that expressions were used by some of the uncouth members of the ship's crew, which grated upon my sensibilities. The hearts of these men, as I presently discovered, were all right and they were far from meaning any offence when they adopted their usual slang, sounding harsh to my ears, and referred to our less fortunate shipwrecked companions as 'the blokes swimming in the water.' What I thus heard made me feel like an alien among my fellow boat mates, and I did them the injustice of believing that I, as the only passenger aboard, would, in case of diversity of interest, receive short shrift at their hands and for this reason I thought it best to have as little to say as possible. During all these struggles I had been uttering silent prayers for deliverance, and it occurred to me that this was the occasion of all others when we should join in an appeal to the Almighty as our last and only hope in life, and so it remained for one of these men, whom I had regarded as uncouth, a Roman Catholic seaman, to take precedence in suggesting the thought in the heart of everyone of us. He was astern and in arm's length of me. He first made inquiry as to the religion of each of us and found Episcopalians, Roman Catholics and Presbyterians. The suggestion that we should say the Lord's Prayer together met with instant approval, and our voices with one accord burst forth in repeating that great appeal to the Creator and Preserver of all mankind, and the only prayer that everyone of us knew and could unite in, thereby manifesting that we were all sons of God and brothers to each other whatever our sphere in life or creed might be. Recollections of this incident are embodied in my account as well as those of Bride and Thayer, independently reported in the New York papers on the morning after our arrival. This is what Bride recalls: 'Somebody said "don't the rest of you think we ought to pray?" The man who made the suggestion asked what the religion of the others was. Each man called out his religion. One was a Catholic, one a Methodist, one a Presbyterian. It was decided the most appropriate prayer for all of us was the Lord's Prayer. We spoke it over in chorus, with the man who first suggested that we pray as the leader.'

Referring to this incident in his sermon on 'The Lessons of the Great Disaster,' the Reverend Dr Newell Dwight Hillis, of Plymouth Church, says:

When Colonel Gracie came up, after the sinking of the *Titanic*, he says that he made his way to a sunken raft. The submerged little raft was under water often, but every man, without regard to nationality, broke into instant prayer. There were many voices, but they all had one signification – their sole hope was in God. There were no millionaires, for millions fell away like leaves; there were no poor; men were neither wise nor ignorant; they were simply human souls on the sinking raft; the night was black and the waves yeasty with foam, and the grave where the *Titanic* lay was silent under them, and the stars were silent over them! But as they prayed, each man by that inner light saw an invisible Friend walking across the waves. Henceforth, these need no books on Apologetics to prove there is a God. This man who has written his story tells us that God heard the prayers of some. by giving them death, and heard the prayers of others equally by keeping them in life; but God alone is great!

The lesson thus drawn from the incident described must be well appreciated by all my boat mates who realized the utter helplessness of our position, and that the only hope we then had in life was in our God, and as the Reverend Dr Hillis says: 'In that moment the evanescent, transient, temporary things dissolved like smoke, and the big, permanent things stood out – God, Truth, Purity, Love, and Oh! how happy those who were good friends with God, their conscience and their record.'

We all recognize the fact that our escape from a watery grave was due to the conditions of wind and weather. All night long we prayed that the calm might last. Towards morning the sea became rougher, and it was for the two-fold purpose of avoiding the ice-cold water (temperature of water 28 degrees, of air 27 degrees Fahrenheit, at midnight, 14 April, US Senate Inquiry, page 1142), and also to attract attention, that we all stood up in column, two abreast, facing the bow. The waves at this time broke over the keel, and we maintained a balance to prevent the escape of the small volume of air confined between sea and upset boat by shifting the weight of our bodies first to port and then to starboard. I believe that the life of everyone of us depended upon the preservation of this confined air-bubble, and our anxious thought was lest some of this air might escape and deeper down our overloaded boat would sink. Had the boat been completely turned over, compelling us to cling to the submerged gunwale, it could not have supported our weight, and we should have been frozen to death in the ice-cold water before rescue could reach us. My exertions had been so continuous and so strenuous before I got aboard this capsized boat that I had taken no notice of the icy temperature of the water. We all suffered severely from cold and exposure. The boat was so loaded down with the heavy weight it carried that it became partly submerged, and the water washed up to our waists as we lay in our reclining position. Several of our companions near the stern of the boat, unable to stand the exposure and strain, gave up the struggle and fell off.

After we had left the danger zone in the vicinity of the wreck, conversation between us first developed, and I heard the men aft of me discussing the fate of the Captain. At least two of them, according to their statements made at the time, had seen him on this craft of ours shortly after it was floated from the ship. In the interviews already referred to, Harry Senior the fireman, referring to the same overturned boat, said: 'The Captain had been able to reach this boat. They had pulled him on, but he slipped off again.' Still another witness, the entrée cook of the *Titanic*, J. Maynard, who was on our boat, corroborates what I heard said at the time about the inability of the Captain to keep his hold on the boat. From several sources I have the information about the falling of the funnel, the splash of which swept from the upturned boat several who were first clinging thereto, and among the number possibly was the Captain. From the following account of Bride, it would appear he was swept off himself and regained his hold later. 'I saw a boat of some kind near me and put all my strength into an effort to swim to it. It was hard work. I was all done when a hand reached out from the boat and pulled me aboard. It was our same collapsible. The same crew was on it. There was just room for me to roll on the edge. I lay there, not caring what happened.' Fortunately for us all, the majority of us were not thus exhausted or desperate. On the contrary, these men on this upset boat had plenty of strength and the purpose to battle for their lives. There were no beacon torches on crag and cliff; no shouts in the pauses of the storm to tell them there was hope; nor deep-toned bell with its loudest peal sending cheerily, o'er the deep, comfort to these wretched souls in their extremity. There were, however, lights forward and on the port side to be seen all the time until the *Carpathia* appeared. These lights were only those of the *Titanic's* other lifeboats, and thus it was, as they gazed with eager, anxious eyes that 'Fresh hope did give them strength and strength deliverance.' (Maturin's *Bertram*)

The suffering on the boat from cold was intense. My neighbour in front, whom I had pulled aboard, must also have been suffering from exhaustion, but it was astern of us whence came later the reports about fellow boat mates who gave up the struggle and fell off from exhaustion, or died, unable to stand the exposure and strain. Among the number, we are told by Bride and Whiteley, was the senior Marconi operator, Phillips, but their statement that it was Phillips' lifeless body which we transferred first to a lifeboat and thence to the *Carpathia* is a mistake, for the body referred to both Lightoller and myself know to have been that of a member of the crew, as described later. Bride himself suffered severely. 'Somebody sat on my legs,' he says. 'They were wedged in between slats and were being wrenched.' When he reached the *Carpathia* he was taken to the hospital and on our arrival in New York was carried ashore with his 'feet badly crushed and frostbitten.'

The combination of cold and the awful scenes of suffering and death which he witnessed from our upturned boat deeply affected another first cabin survivor, an Englishman, Mr R. H. Barkworth, whose tender heart is creditable to his character.

Another survivor of our upturned boat, James McGann, a fireman, interviewed by the *New York Tribune* on 20 April, says that he was one of the 30 of us, mostly firemen, clinging to it as she left the ship. As to the suffering endured that night he says: 'All our legs were frostbitten and we were all in the hospital for a day at least.'

Hagan also adds his testimony as to the sufferings endured by our boat mates. He says: 'One man on the upturned boat rolled off, into the water, at the stern, dead with fright and cold. Another died in the lifeboat.' Here he refers to the lifeless body which we transferred, and finally put aboard the *Carpathia*, but which was not Phillips.

Lightoller testified: 'I think there were three or four who died during the night aboard our boat. The Marconi junior operator told me that the senior operator was on this boat and died, presumably from cold.'

But the uncommunicative little member of the crew beside me did not seem to suffer much. He was like a number of others who were possessed of hats or caps – his was an outing cap; while those who sank under water had lost them. The upper part of his body appeared to be comparatively dry; so I believe he and some others escaped being drawn under with the *Titanic* by clinging to the Engelhardt boat from the outset when it parted company with the ship and was washed from the deck by the 'giant wave.' He seemed so dry and comfortable while I felt so damp in my waterlogged clothing, my teeth chattering and my hair wet with the icy water, that I ventured to request the loan of his dry cap to warm my head for a short while. 'And what wad oi do?' was his curt reply. 'Ah, never mind,' said I, as I thought it would make no difference 100 years hence. Poor chap, it would seem that all his possessions were lost when his kit went down with the ship. Not far from me and on the starboard side was a more loquacious member of the crew. I was not near enough, however, to him to indulge in any imaginary warmth from the fumes of the O-be-joyful spirits which he gave unmistakable evidence of having indulged in before leaving the ship. Most of the conversation, as well as excitement, came from behind me, astern.

After we paddled away free from the wreckage and swimmers in the water that surrounded us, our undivided attention until the dawn of the next day was concentrated upon scanning the horizon in every direction for the lights of a ship that might rescue us before the sea grew rougher, for the abnormal conditions of wind and weather that prevailed that night were the causes of the salvation, as well as the destruction, of those aboard this ill-fated vessel. The absolute calm of the sea, while it militated against the detection of the iceberg in our path, at the same time made it possible for all of the lifeboats lowered from the davits to make their long and dangerous descent to the water without being smashed against the sides of the ship, or swamped by the waves breaking against them, for, notwithstanding newspaper reports to the contrary, there appears no authentic testimony of any survivor showing that any loaded boat in the act of being lowered was capsized or suffered injury. On the other hand, we have the positive statements accounting for each individual boatload, showing that everyone of them was thus lowered in safety. But it was this very calm of the sea, as has been said, which encompassed the destruction of the ship. The beatings of the waves against the iceberg's sides usually give audible warning miles away to the approaching vessel, while the white foam at the base, due to the same cause, is also discernible. But in our case the beautiful starlit night and cloudless sky, combined with the glassy sea, further facilitated the iceberg's approach without detection, for no background was afforded against which to silhouette the deadly outline of this black appearing Protean monster which only looks white when the sun is shining upon it.

All experienced navigators of the northern seas, as I am informed on the highest authority, knowing the dangers attending such conditions, invariably take extra precautions to avoid disaster. The *Titanic's* officers were no novices, and were well trained in the knowledge of this and all other dangers of the sea. From the Captain down, they were the pick of the best that the White Star Line had in its employ. Our Captain, Edward J. Smith, was the one always selected to 'tryout' each new ship of the Line, and was regarded, with his 38 years of service in the company, as both safe and competent. Did he take any precautions for safety, in view of the existing dangerous conditions? Alas! no! as appears from the testimony in regard thereto, taken before the Investigating Committee and Board in America and in England which we review in another chapter. And yet, warnings had been received on the *Titanic's* bridge from six different neighbouring ships, one in fact definitely locating the latitude and longitude where the iceberg was encountered, and that too at a point of time calculated by one of the *Titanic's* officers. Who can satisfactorily explain this heedlessness of danger?

It was shortly after we had emerged from the horrible scene of men swimming in the water that I was glad to notice the presence among us on the upturned boat of the same officer with whom all my work that night and all my experience was connected in helping to load and lower the boats on the *Titanic's* boat deck and deck

A. I identified him at once by his voice and his appearance, but his name was not learned until I met him again later in my cabin on board the *Carpathia* – Charles H. Lightoller. For what he did on the ship that night whereby six or more boatloads of women and children were saved and discipline maintained aboard ship, as well as on the Engelhardt upturned boat, he is entitled to honour and the thanks of his own countrymen and of us Americans as well. As soon as he was recognized, the loquacious member of the crew astern, already referred to, volunteered in our behalf and called out to him 'We will all obey what the officer orders.' The result was at once noticeable. The presence of a leader among us was now felt, and lent us purpose and courage. The excitement at the stern was demonstrated by the frequent suggestion of, 'Now boys, all together'; and then in unison we shouted, 'Boat ahoy! Boat ahoy!' This was kept up for some time until it was seen to be a mere waste of strength. So it seemed to me, and I decided to husband mine and make provision for what the future, or the morrow, might require. After a while Lightoller, myself and others managed with success to discourage these continuous shouts regarded as a vain hope of attracting attention.

When the presence of the Marconi boy at the stern was made known, Lightoller called out, from his position in the bow, questions which all of us heard, as to the names of the steamships with which he had been in communication for assistance. We on the boat recall the names mentioned by Bride – the *Baltic*, *Olympic* and *Carpathia*. It was then that the *Carpathia's* name was heard by us for the first time, and it was to catch sight of this sturdy little Cunarder that we strained our eyes in the direction whence she finally appeared.

We had correctly judged that most of the lights seen by us belonged to our own *Titanic's* lifeboats, but Lightoller and all of us were badly fooled by the green-coloured lights and rockets directly ahead of us, which loomed up especially bright at intervals. This, as will be noticed in a future chapter, was Third Officer Boxhall's emergency boat No. 2. We were assured that these were the lights of a ship and were all glad to believe it. There could be no mistake about it and our craft was navigated toward it as fast as its propelling conditions made possible; but it did not take long for us to realize that this light, whatever it was, was receding instead of approaching us.

Some of our boat mates on the *Titanic's* decks had seen the same white light to which I have already made reference in Chapter 2, and the argument was now advanced that it must have been a sailing ship, for a steamer would have soon come to our rescue; but a sailing ship would be prevented by wind, or lack of facilities in coming to our aid. I imagined that it was the lights of such a ship that we again saw on our port side astern in the direction where, when dawn broke, we saw the icebergs far away on the horizon.

Some time before dawn a call came from the stern of the boat, 'There is a steamer coming behind us.' At the same time a warning cry was given that we should not all look back at once lest the equilibrium of our precarious craft might be disturbed. Lightoller took in the situation and called out, 'All you men stand steady and I will be the one to look astern.' He looked, but there was no responsive chord that tickled our ears with hope.

The incident just described happened when we were all standing up, facing forward in column, two abreast. Some time before this, for some undefined reason,

Lightoller had asked the question, 'How many are there of us on this boat?' and someone answered '30, sir.' All testimony on the subject establishes this number. I may cite Lightoller, who testified: 'I should roughly estimate about 30. She was packed standing from stem to stern at daylight. We took all on board that we could. I did not see any effort made by others to get aboard. There were a great number of people in the water but not near us. They were some distance away from us.'

Personally, I could not look around to count, but I know that forward of me there were eight and counting myself and the man abreast would make two more. As every bit of room on the Engelhardt bottom was occupied and as the weight aboard nearly submerged it, I believe that more than half our boatload was behind me. There is a circumstance that I recall which further establishes how closely packed we were. When standing up I held on once or twice to the life-preserver on the back of my boat mate in front in order to balance myself. At the same time and in the same way the man in my rear held on to me. This procedure, being objectionable to those concerned, was promptly discontinued.

It was at quite an early stage that I had seen far in the distance the unmistakable mast lights of a steamer about four or five points away on the port side, as our course was directed toward the green-coloured lights of the imaginary ship which we hoped was coming to our rescue, but which, in fact, was the already-mentioned *Titanic* lifeboat of Officer Boxhall. I recall our anxiety, as we had no lights, that this imaginary ship might not see us and might run over our craft and swamp us. But my eyes were fixed for hours that night on the lights of that steamer, far away in the distance, which afterwards proved to be those of the *Carpathia*. To my great disappointment, they seemed to make no progress towards us to our rescue. This we were told later was due to meeting an iceberg as she was proceeding full speed toward the scene of the *Titanic*'s wreck. She had come to a stop in sight of the lights of our lifeboats (or such as had them). The first boat to come to her sides was Boxhall's with its green lights. Finally dawn appeared and there on the port side of our upset boat where we had been looking with anxious eyes, glory be to God, we saw the steamer *Carpathia* about four or five miles away, with other *Titanic* lifeboats rowing towards her. But on our starboard side, much to our surprise, for we had seen no lights on that quarter; were four of the *Titanic*'s lifeboats strung together in line. These were respectively numbers 14, 10, 12 and 4.

Meantime, the water had grown rougher, and, as previously described, was washing over the keel and we had to make shift to preserve the equilibrium. Right glad were all of us on our upturned boat when in that awful hour the break of day brought this glorious sight to our eyes. Lightoller put his whistle to his cold lips and blew a shrill blast, attracting the attention of the boats about half a mile away. 'Come over and take us off,' he cried. 'Aye, aye, sir,' was the ready response as two of the boats cast off from the others and rowed directly towards us. Just before the bows of the two boats reached us, Lightoller ordered us not to scramble, but each to take his turn, so that the transfer might be made in safety. When my turn came, in order not to endanger the lives of the others, or plunge them into the sea, I went carefully, hands first, into the rescuing lifeboat. Lightoller remained to the last, lifting a lifeless body into the boat beside me, worked over the body for some time, rubbing the temples and the wrists, but when I turned the neck it was perfectly still. Recognizing that rigor mortis had set in, I knew the man was dead. He was dressed like a member of the crew, and I recall that he wore gray woollen socks. His hair was dark. Our lifeboat was so crowded that I had to rest on this dead body until we reached the *Carpathia*, where he was taken aboard and buried. My efforts to obtain his name have been exhaustive, but futile. Lightoller was uncertain as to which one he was of two men he had in mind; but we both know that it was not the body of Phillips, the senior Marconi operator. In the lifeboat to which we were transferred were said to be 65 or 70 of us. The number was beyond the limit of safety. The boat sank low in the water, and the sea now became rougher. Lightoller assumed the command and steered at the stern. I was glad to recognize young Thayer amidships. There was a French woman in the bow near us actively ill but brave and considerate. She was very kind in loaning an extra steamer rug to Barkworth, by my side, who shared it with a member of the crew (a fireman perhaps) and myself. That steamer rug was a great comfort as we drew it over our heads and huddled close together to obtain some warmth. For a short time another *Titanic* lifeboat was towed by ours. My lifebelt was wet and uncomfortable and I threw it overboard. Fortunately there was no further need of it for the use intended. I regret I did not preserve it as a relic. When we were first transferred and only two of the lifeboats came to our rescue, some took it hard that the other two did not also come to our relief, when we saw how few these others had aboard; but the officer in command of them, whom we afterwards knew as Fifth Officer Lowe, had cleverly rigged up a sail on his boat and, towing another astern, made his way to the *Carpathia* a long time ahead of us, but picked up on his way other unfortunates in another Engelhardt boat, boat A, which had shipped considerable water.

My research, particularly the testimony taken before the Senate Committee, establishes the identity of the *Titanic* lifeboats to which, at day dawn, we of the upset boat were transferred. These were boats No. 12 and No. 4. The former was the one that Lightoller, Barkworth, Thayer, Jr., and myself were in. Frederick Clench, Able Seaman, was in charge of this boat, and his testimony, as follows, is interesting:

> I looked along the water's edge and saw some men on a raft. Then I heard two whistles blown. I sang out, 'Aye, aye, I am coming over,' and we pulled over and found it was not a raft exactly, but an overturned boat, and Mr Lightoller was there on that boat and I thought the Wireless Operator, too. We took them on board our boat and shared the amount of room. They were all standing on the bottom, wet through apparently. Mr Lightoller took charge of us. Then we started ahead for the *Carpathia*. We had to row a tidy distance to the *Carpathia* because there were boats ahead of us and we had a boat in tow, with others besides all the people we had aboard. We were pretty well full up before, but the additional ones taken on made about seventy in our boat.

This corresponds with Lightoller's testimony on the same point. He says: 'I counted 65 heads, not including myself, and none that were in the bottom of the boat. I roughly estimated about 75 in the boat, which was dangerously full, and it was all I could do to nurse her up to the sea.'

From Steward Cunningham's testimony I found a corroboration of my estimate of our distance, at day-dawn, from the *Carpathia*. This he says 'was about four or five miles.' Another seaman, Samuel S. Hemming, who was in boat No. 4, commanded by Quartermaster Perkis, also gave his testimony as follows:

> As day broke we heard some hollering going on and we saw some men standing on what we thought was ice about half a mile away, but we found them on the bottom of an upturned boat. Two boats cast off and we pulled to them and took them in our two boats. There were no women or children on this boat, and I heard there was one dead body. Second Officer Lightoller was on the overturned boat. He did not get into our boat. Only about four or five got into ours and the balance of them went into the other boat.

It seemed to me an interminable time before we reached the *Carpathia*. Ranged along her sides were others of the *Titanic's* lifeboats which had been rowed to the Cunarder and had been emptied of their loads of survivors. In one of these boats on the port side, standing up, I noticed my friend, Third Officer H. J. Pitman, with whom I had made my trip eastward on the Atlantic on board the *Oceanic*. All along the sides of the *Carpathia* were strung rope ladders. There were no persons about me needing my assistance, so I mounted the ladder, and, for the purpose of testing my strength, I ran up as fast as I could and experienced no difficulty or feeling of exhaustion. I entered the first hatchway I came to and felt like falling down on my knees and kissing the deck in gratitude for the preservation of my life. I made my way to the second cabin dispensary, where I was handed a hot drink. I then went to the deck above and was met with a warm reception in the dining saloon. Nothing could exceed the kindness of the ladies, who did everything possible for my comfort. All my wet clothing, overcoat and shoes, were sent down to the bake-oven to be dried. Being thus in lack of clothing, I lay down on the lounge in the dining saloon corner to the right of the entrance under rugs and blankets, waiting for a complete outfit of dry clothing.

I am particularly grateful to a number of kind people on the *Carpathia* who helped replenish my wardrobe, but especially to Mr Louis M. Ogden, a family connection and old friend. To Mrs Ogden and to Mr and Mrs Spedden, who were on the *Titanic*, and to their boy's trained nurse, I am also most grateful. They gave me hot cordials and hot coffee which soon warmed me up and dispersed the cold. Among the *Carpathia's* passengers, bound for the Mediterranean, I discovered a number of friends of Mrs Gracie's and mine – Miss K. Steele, sister of Charles Steele, of New York, Mr and Mrs Charles H. Marshall and Miss Marshall, of New York. Leaning over the rail of the port side I saw anxiously gazing down upon us many familiar faces of fellow survivors, and, among them, friends and acquaintances to whom I waved my hand as I stood up in the bow of my boat. This boat No.12 was the last to reach the *Carpathia* and her passengers transferred about 8.30 a.m.

58

Harold Bride, Junior Wireless Officer

Widely celebrated as a hero, Harold Bride's story certainly contains many heroic episodes. He stayed at his post until the very end, defended his fellow wireless operator Jack Phillips against a stoker trying to steal his lifebelt, didn't try to take a lifeboat place but battled for survival in the water, eventually managing to climb on to the upturned collapsible lifeboat B. Once on board the *Carpathia* Bride notably assisted their overwhelmed wireless operator Harold Cottam despite suffering from severe frostbite. Bride had to be helped to disembark from the *Carpathia* and several days later appeared to give evidence to the US inquiry in a wheelchair.

'Chequebook journalism' is nothing new. Bride was still working in the wireless room of the *Carpathia* when he dictated his story to a reporter for the *New York Times*. He received a significant sum (reputed to be at least $1,000) for his story, which would have represented several years' wages. Bride tired of the media attention that his role in the *Titanic* story caused and moved to Scotland in the 1920s, where he remained until his death in 1956.

The second extract comes from Bride's US inquiry testimony and describes Captain Smith jumping from the bridge in the last few minutes before *Titanic* took her final plunge.

New York Times interview 19 April 1912 To begin at the beginning, I joined the *Titanic* at Belfast. I was born at Nunhead, England, 22 years ago, and joined the Marconi forces last July. I first worked on the Hoverford, and then on the *Lusitania*. I joined the *Titanic* at Belfast.

I didn't have much to do aboard the *Titanic* except to relieve Phillips from midnight until some time in the morning, when he should be through sleeping. On the night of the accident, I was due to be up and relieve Phillip earlier than usual. And that reminds me – if it hadn't been for a lucky thing, we never could have sent any call for help.

The lucky thing was that the wireless broke down early enough for us to fix it before the accident. We noticed something wrong on Sunday and Phillips and I worked seven hours to find it. We found a 'secretary' burned out, at last and repaired it just a few hours before the iceberg was struck.

Phillips said to me as he took the night shift. 'You turn in, boy, and get some sleep, and go up as soon as you can and give me a chance. I'm all done for with this work of making repairs.'

There were three rooms in the wireless cabin. One was a sleeping room, one a dynamo room, and one an operating room. I took off my clothes and went to sleep in bed. Then I was conscious of waking up and hearing Phillips sending to Cape Race. I read what he was sending. It was a traffic matter.

I remembered how tired he was and I got out of bed without my clothes on to relieve him. I didn't even feel the shock. I hardly knew it had happened after the Captain had come to us. There was no jolt whatever.

I was standing by Philips telling him to go to bed when the Captain put his head into the cabin.

'We've struck an iceberg.' the Captain said 'and I'm having an inspection made to tell what it has done for us. You better get ready to send out a call for assistance. But don't send it until I tell you.'

The Captain went away and in 10 minutes, I should estimate the time, he came back. We could hear a terrible confusion outside, but there was not the least thing to indicate that there was any trouble. The wireless was working perfectly.

'Send the call for assistance' ordered the Captain, barely putting his head in the door.

'What call should I send?' Phillips asked

'The regulation international call for help. Just that.'

Then the Captain was gone. Phillips began to send 'CQD'. He flashed away at it and we joked while he did so. All of us made light of the disaster.

We joked that way while he flashed signals for about five minutes. Then the Captain came back.

'What are you sending?' he asked.

'CQD' Phillips replied.

The humour of the situation appealed to me. I cut in with a little remark that made us all laugh, including the Captain.

'Send SOS' I said. 'It's the new call, and it may be your last chance to send it.'

Phillips with a laugh changed the signal to 'SOS'. The Captain told us we had been struck amidships, or just back of amidships. It was 10 minutes, Phillips told me, after he had noticed the iceberg, that the slight jolt that was the collision's only signal to us occurred. We thought we were a good distance away.

We said lost of funny things to each other in the next few minutes. We picked up first the steamship *Frankfurt*. We gave her our position and said we had struck an iceberg and needed assistance. The *Frankfurt* operator went away to tell his captain.

He came back and we told him we were sinking by the head. By that time we could observe a distinct list forward.

The *Carpathia* answered our signal. We told her our position and said we were sinking by the head. The operator went to tell the Captain and in five minutes retuned and told us that the Captain of the *Carpathia* was putting about and heading for us.

Our Captain had left us at this time and Phillips told me to run and tell him what the *Carpathia* had answered. I did so, and I went through an awful mass of people to his cabin. The decks were full of scrambling men and women. I saw no fighting, but I heard tell of it.

I came back and heard Phillips giving the *Carpathia* fuller directions. Phillips told me to put on my clothes. Until that moment I forgot that I was not dressed.

I went to my cabin and dressed. I brought an overcoat to Phillips. It was very cold. I slipped the overcoat upon him still he worked.

Every few minutes Phillips would send me to the Captain with little messages. They were merely telling how the *Carpathia* was coming our way and gave her speed.

I noticed as I came back from one trip that they were putting off women and children in lifeboats. I noticed that the list forward was increasing.

Phillips told me that the wireless was growing weaker. The Captain came and told us our engine rooms were taking water and that the dynamos might not last much longer. We sent that word to the *Carpathia*.

I went out on deck and looked around. The water was pretty close up to the boat deck. There was a great scrabble aft, and how poor Phillips worked through it I don't know,

He was a brave man. I learned to love him that night and I suddenly felt for him a great reverence to see him standing there sticking to his work while everybody else was raging about. I will never live to forget the work of Phillips for the last awful 15 minutes.

I though it was about time to look about and see if there was anything detached that would float. I remembered that every member of the crew had a special lifebelt and ought to know where it was. I remembered mine was under my bunk. I went and got it. Then I though how cold the water was.

I remembered I had some boots and I put those on, and an extra jacket and I put that on. I saw Phillips standing out there still sending away, giving the *Carpathia* details of just how we were doing.

We picked up the *Olympic* and told her we were sinking by the head and were about all down. As Phillips was sending the message I strapped his lifebelt to his back. I had already put on his overcoat.

I wondered if I could get him into his boots. He suggested with a sort of laugh that I look out and see if all the people were off in the boats, or if any boats were left, or how things were.

I saw a collapsible boat near a funnel and went over to it. 12 men were trying to boost it down to the boat deck. They were having an awful time. It was the last boat left. I looked at it longingly a few minutes. Then I gave them a hand, and over she went. They all started to scramble in on the boat deck, and I walked back to Phillips. I said that last raft had gone.

Then came the Captain's voice: 'Men, you have done your full duty. You can do no more. Abandon your cabin. Now it is every man for themselves. You look out for yourselves. I release you. That's the way of it at this kind of a time. Everyman for himself.'

I looked out. The boat deck was awash. Phillips clung on sending and sending. He clung on for about 10 minutes or maybe 15 minutes after the Captain had released him. The water was then coming into our cabin.

While he worked something happened I hate to tell about. I was back in my room getting Phillips' money for him and as I looked out the door I saw a stoker, or somebody from below decks, leaning over Phillips from behind. He was too busy to notice what the man was doing. The man was slipping the lifebelt off Phillips' back.

He was a big man too. As you can see, I am very small. I don't know what it was I got hold of. I remembered in a flash the way Phillips had clung on – how I had to fix that lifebelt in place because he was too busy to do it.

I knew that the man from below decks had his own lifebelt and should have known where to get it.

I suddenly felt a passion not to let that man die of a decent sailor's death. I wished he might have stretched rope or walked a plank. I did my duty. I hope I finished him. I don't know. We left him on the cabin floor of the wireless room and he was not moving.

From aft came the tunes of the band. It was a rag-time tune. I don't know what. Then there was *Autumn*. Phillips ran aft and that was the last I ever saw of him alive.

I went to the place I had seen the collapsible boat on the boat deck, and to my surprise I saw the boat and the men still trying to push it off. I guess there wasn't a sailor in the crowd. They couldn't do it. I went up to them and was just lending a hand when a large wave came awash of the deck.

The big wave carried the boat off. I had hold of an oarlock and I went off with it. The next I knew I was in the boat.

But that was not all. I was in the boat and the boat was upside down and I was under it. And I remember realising I was wet through, and that whatever happened I must not breathe for I was under water.

I knew I had to fight for it and I did. How I got out from under the boat I do not know, but I felt a breath of air at last.

There were men all around me – hundreds of them. The sea was dotted with them, all depending on their lifebelts. I felt I simply had to get away from the ship. She was a beautiful sight then.

Smoke and sparks were rushing out of her funnel. There must have been an explosion, but we had heard none. We only saw the big stream of sparks. The ship was gradually turning on her nose – just like a duck does that goes down for a dive. I had only one thing on my mind – to get away from the suction. The band was still playing. I guess all of the band went down.

They were playing *Autumn* then. I swam with all my might. I suppose I was 150 feet away when the *Titanic*, on her nose, with her after-quarter sticking straight up in the air, began to settle – slowly.

When at last the waves washed over her rudder there wasn't the least bit of suction I could feel. She must have kept going just so slowly as she had been.

I forgot to mention that besides, the *Olympic* and *Carpathia* we spoke some German boat, I don't know which, and told them how we were. We also spoke the *Baltic*. I remembered those things as I began to figure what ships would be coming toward us.

I felt, after a little while, like sinking. I was very cold. I saw a boat of some kind near me and put all my strength into an effort to swim to it. It was hard work. I was all done when a hand reached out from the boat and pulled me aboard. It was the same collapsible. The same crowd was on it.

There was just room for me to roll on the edge. I lay there not caring what happened. Somebody sat on my legs. They were wedged in between slats and were being wrenched. I had not the heart left to ask the man to move. It was a terrible sight all around – men swimming and sinking.

I lay where I was, letting the man wrench my feet out of shape. Others came near. Nobody gave them a hand. The bottom-up boat already had more men than it would hold and it was sinking.

At first the larger waves splashed over my clothing. Then they began to splash over my head and I had to breathe when I could.

As we floated around on our capsized boat and I kept straining my eyes for a ship's lights, somebody said, 'Don't the rest of you think we ought to pray?' The man who made the suggestion asked what the religion of the others was. Each man called out his religion. One was a Catholic, one a Methodist, one a Presbyterian.

It was decided the most appropriate prayer for all was the Lord's Prayer. We spoke it over in chorus with the man who first suggested that we pray as the leader.

Some splendid people saved us. They had a right-side-up boat, and it was full to its capacity. Yet they came to us and loaded us all into it. I saw some lights off in the distance and knew a steamship was coming to our aid.

I didn't care what happened. I just lay and gasped when I could and felt the pain in my feet. At last the *Carpathia* was alongside and the people were being taken up a rope ladder. Our boat drew near and one by one the men were taken off it.

One man was dead. I passed him and went to the ladder, although my feet pained terribly. The dead man was Phillips. He had died on the raft from exposure and cold, I guess. He had been all in from work before the wreck came. He stood his ground until the crisis had passed, and then he had collapsed, I guess.

But I hardly thought that then. I didn't think much of anything. I tried the rope ladder. My feet pained terribly, but I got to the top and felt hands reaching out to me. The next I knew a woman was leaning over me in a cabin and I felt her hand waving back my hair and rubbing my face.

I felt somebody at my feet and felt the warmth of a jolt of liquor. Somebody got me under the arms. Then I was hustled down below to the hospital. That was early in the day I guess. I lay in the hospital until near night and they told me the *Carpathia's* wireless man was getting 'queer' and would I help.

After that I never was out of the wireless room, so I don't know what happened among the passengers. I saw nothing of Mrs Astor or any of them I just worked wireless. The splutter never died down. I knew it soothed the hurt and felt like a tie to the world of friends and home.

How could I then take news enquiries? Sometimes I let a newspaper ask a question and get a long string of stuff asking for full particulars about everything. Whenever I started to take such a message I though of the poor people waiting for their messages to go – hoping for answers to them.

I shut off the inquirers, and sent my personal messages. And I feel I did the right thing.

If the *Chester* had had a decent operator I could have worked with him longer but he got terribly on my nerves with his insufferable incompetence. I was still sending my personal messages when Mr Marconi and the *Times* reporter arrived to ask that I prepare this statement.

There were maybe 100 left. I would like to send them all, because I could rest easier if I knew all those messages had gone to the friends waiting for them. But an ambulance man is waiting with a stretcher, and I guess I have got to go with him. I hope my legs get better soon.

The way the band kept playing was a noble thing. I heard it first while still we were working wireless, when there was a ragtime tune for us, and the last I saw of the band, when I was floating out in the sea with my life belt on, it was still on deck playing *Autumn*. How ever they did it I cannot imagine.

That and the way Phillips kept sending after the Captain told him his life was his own, and to look out for himself, are two things that stand out in my mind over all the rest.

US Senate Inquiry (inquiry question is followed immediately by witness's answer) How did you expect to leave the ship? We had to wait until the Captain told us, first.

You had to wait until the captain told you? Yes sir. He came along in a very short period afterwards and told us we had better look out for ourselves.

You waited until the Captain told you that you could leave the ship? Yes sir.

How long was that before the ship disappeared? I should say it was just about a quarter of an hour.

And the Captain said you had better take care of yourselves? Yes sir.

Did he indicate what he was going to do? No sir.

Where was he when he said this? He came around to the cabin to tell us.

Was there anyone else on the deck? Oh, there were other people on the deck.

With you? Yes. They were running around all over the place.

How running around? Several people looking for lifebelts and looking for refreshments.

I want to locate exactly the position of this operating room of yours with reference to the boat deck? The officer's quarters were situated together with the Marconi cabin, the officers' rooms, and other places, [on the boat deck] and the people were running around through these cabins. We had a woman in our cabin who had fainted.

A woman in your cabin who had fainted? And we were giving her a glass of water there and a chair. We set her down on a chair, which she wanted badly, and then her husband took her away again.

Did you see any lifeboats after that? No sir.

Do you know whether there was any on the ship at that time? There were no big lifeboats on the ship at that time. There was a collapsible boat on the top deck at the side of the forward funnel.

When did you last see the Captain? When he told you to take care of yourself? The last I saw of the Captain he went overboard from the bridge, sir.

Did you see the *Titanic* sink? Yes sir.

And the captain was at that time on the bridge? No sir.

What do you mean by overboard? He jumped overboard from the bridge. He jumped overboard from the bridge when we were launching the collapsible lifeboat.

I should judge from what you have said that this was about three or four minutes before the boat sank? Yes. It would be just about five minutes before the boat sank.

Do you know whether the Captain had a lifebelt on? He had not when I last saw him.

Did the bridge go under water at about the same time? Yes sir. The whole of the ship was practically under water to the forward funnel, and when I saw her go down the stern came out of the water and she slid down fore and aft.

The Captain at no time went over until the vessel sank? No sir. He went with the vessel? Practically speaking, yes sir.

59

Jack Thayer, First Class Passenger

The 17-year-old son of Marian and John Thayer. Jack's mother survived, getting away in lifeboat 4. Jack died in 1945, tragically committing suicide after the loss of his son in the Second World War.

Account pieced together by Archibald Gracie, and included in his book, The Truth About the Titanic The experience of my fellow passenger on this boat, John B. Thayer, is embodied in accounts written by him on 20 and 23 April and, just after landing from the *Carpathia*: the first given to the press as the only statement he had made, the second in a very pathetic letter written to Judge Charles L. Long, of Springfield, Massachusetts, whose son, Milton C. Long, was a companion of young Thayer all that evening, 14 April until at the very last both jumped into the sea and Long was lost, as described:

Thinking that father and mother had managed to get off in a boat we, Long and myself, went to the starboard side of the boat deck where the boats were getting away quickly. Some were already off in the distance. We thought of getting into one of them, the last boat on the forward part of the starboard side, but there seemed to be such a crowd around that I thought it unwise to make any attempt to get into it. I thought it would never reach the water right side up, but it did.

Here I noticed nobody that I knew except Mr Lingrey, whom I had met for the first time that evening. I lost sight of him in a few minutes. Long and I then stood by the rail just a little aft of the captain's bridge. There was such a big list to port that it seemed as if the ship would turn on her side.

About this time the people began jumping from the stern. I thought of jumping myself, but was afraid of being stunned on hitting the water. Three times I made up my mind to jump out and slide down the davit ropes and try to swim to the boats that were lying off from the ship, but each time Long got hold of me and told me to wait a while. I got a sight on a rope between the davits and a star and noticed that the ship was gradually sinking. About this time she straightened up on an even keel again, and started to go down fairly fast at an angle of about 30 degrees. As she started to sink we left the davits and went back and stood by the rail aft, even with the second funnel. Long and myself stood by each other and jumped on the rail. We did not give each other any messages for home because neither of us thought we would ever get back. Long put his legs over the rail, while I straddled it. Hanging over the side and holding on to the rail with his hands he looked up at me and said: 'You are coming, boy, aren't you?' I replied: 'Go ahead I'll be with you in a minute.' He let go and slid down the side and I never saw him again. Almost immediately after he jumped I jumped. All this last part took a very short time, and when we jumped we were about 10 yards [*c.* 9 metres] above the water. Long was perfectly calm all the time and kept his nerve to the very end.

How he sank and finally reached the upturned boat is quoted accurately from the newspaper report from this same source given in my personal narrative (see Gracie's account earlier in this section of lifeboat B). He continues as follows:

As often as we saw other boats in the distance we would yell, 'Ship ahoy!' but they could not distinguish our cries from any of the others, so we all gave it up, thinking it useless. It was very cold, and the water washed over the upset boat almost all the time. Towards dawn the wind sprung up, roughening the water and making it difficult to keep the boat balanced. The wireless man raised our hopes a great deal by telling us that the *Carpathia* would be up in about three hours. About 3.30 a.m. or four o'clock some men at the bow of our boat sighted her mast lights. I could not see them as I was sitting down with a man kneeling on my leg. He finally got up, and I stood up. We had the Second Officer, Mr Lightoller, on board. He had an officer's whistle and whistled for the boats in the distance to come up and take us off. Two of them came up. The first took half and the other took the balance, including myself. In the transfer we had difficulty in balancing our boat as the men would lean too far over, but we were all taken aboard the already crowded boats and taken to the *Carpathia* in safety.

One of these lifeboats, lifeboat number 4 contained Marian Thayer, Jack's mother.

60
Charles Lightoller, Second Officer

Charles Lightoller was a key figure in the loading of lifeboats, especially those on the port side. He was a noticeably strict observer of the women and children first rule and only allowed one adult male passenger into a lifeboat. For his adherence to this policy he has received some criticism – when there were no more women available Lightoller would order a boat to be lowered even if there were spaces in it that men could have taken. This criticism needs to be balanced with the observation that Lightoller worked tirelessly that night – only abandoning his duties when the ship took her final plunge, and assuming then again by taking control of the upturned lifeboat B. Lightoller was awarded the Distinguished Service Cross for gallantry during the First World War and would later use his own small boat to assist in the evacuation from Dunkirk.

Charles Lightoller was the highest-ranking officer to survive the sinking of the *Titanic* and was hence a key witness at both the US and the British inquiries. Lightoller's testimonies are generally defensive of the White Star Line, of his own and fellow officers' behaviour. It is notable how he claims that his ultimate boss, Bruce Ismay, was 'bundled' into a lifeboat by Chief Officer Wilde, who would of course be unable to confirm this version of events. Here is what Lightoller said of the British inquiry:

> In London it was very necessary to keep one's hand on the whitewash brush. Sharp questions that needed careful answers if one was to avoid a pitfall, carefully and subtly dug, leading to a pinning down of blame on to someone's luckless shoulders... Personally, I had no desire that blame should be attributed either to the B.O.T. [Board of Trade] or the White Star Line, though in all conscience it was a difficult task, when handled by some of the cleverest legal minds in England, striving tooth and nail to prove the inadequacy here, the lack there, when one had known, full well, and for many years, the ever-present possibility of just such a disaster.

When the inquiries finally finished Lightoller tacitly admits that he had helped the White Star Line, commenting: 'Still, just that word of thanks which was lacking, which when the *Titanic* inquiry was all over would have been very much appreciated.'

Titanic and Other Ships, Lightoller's autobiography, which includes a chapter devoted to his side of the story, was first published in the 1930s but was withdrawn from publication when the Marconi Company threatened a lawsuit.

Lightoller's granddaughter is Lady Louise Patten, who grew up being looked after by her grandmother, Charles Lightoller's widow. Lady Patten worked into the story of her first work of fiction, *Good as Gold* (Quercus 2010), a family secret about what had really happened on the bridge of *Titanic* in the moments after the iceberg was spotted. In the subsequent media interviews Lady Patten fleshed out the details of the family secret. Her grandfather had related to her grandmother that upon hearing the warning of 'ice straight ahead' Quartermaster Hichens had accidentally steered the wrong way, not away from the iceberg, but towards it. Secondly, that Bruce Ismay had insisted on continuing forward for 10 minutes after the collision, a decision that hastened *Titanic*'s demise. These revelations and that White Star Line staff colluded in the cover-up is nothing short of dynamite but it has been questioned by *Titanic* historians.

The exact port-side lifeboat launching sequence discussed in the extract below has since been discredited, with the following sequence now thought to be closer to the truth: 8, 6, 16, 14, 12, 2 (the port-side 'emergency' lifeboat), 10, 4 and lastly, lifeboat D (one of the two port-side collapsibles). Collapsible lifeboat B floated off the port side after lifeboat D and wasn't launched as such. Given this discrepancy, which lifeboats are actually being referred to below is sometimes unclear. We can spot that the 'fourth lifeboat' as described below was lifeboat 6 (the second to be launched) as Major Peuchen is mentioned in relation to its launch. There is no dispute, however, that the last two lifeboats to be launched on the port side were lifeboat 4 followed by lifeboat D.

Adding to the confusion is that in the testimony below only seven lifeboats are discussed, when there were clearly ten lifeboats on the port side. This might be explained by Lightoller's statement that one or two lifeboats on the port side were launched by a fellow crew member and that the tenth and last lifeboat (collapsible lifeboat B) wasn't launched, rather it floated off *Titanic* as the ship sank.

US Senate Inquiry (inquiry question is followed immediately by witness's answer) How long were you in the sea with a lifebelt on? Between half an hour and an hour.

What time did you leave the ship? I didn't leave it.

Did the ship leave you? Yes sir.

Did you stay until the ship had departed entirely? Yes sir.

From what point on the vessel did you leave it? On top of the officers' quarters.

And where were the officers' quarters? Immediately abaft the bridge.

Was that pretty well toward the top of the vessel? Yes sir.

Were the lifeboats gone when you found yourself without any footing? All except one.

Where was that one? In the tackles, trying to get it over.

Did not the tackle work readily? Yes sir.

What delayed it? It was the third boat over by the same tackles.

From what deck? The boat deck.

How close were you to this lifeboat at that time? 15 feet

Was it filled before starting to lower it? It was not high enough to lower.

Why was it not high enough to lower? They were endeavoring to get it over the bulwarks, outboard; swinging it; getting it over the bulwarks. When it was over the bulwarks, then it would hang in the tackles, and until it hung in the tackles it was impossible to put anyone in it.

How far above the boat deck? About four feet six inches.

And it was lowered to the boat deck? It did not get over the bulwarks to be lowered.

The last you saw of it? Yes sir.

Who was managing this tackle? The First Officer, Mr Murdoch.

He lost his life? Yes.

Did you see Mr Ismay at that time? No sir.

Did you, at any time? Yes sir.

Where? On the boat deck.

How long before she sunk? At first, before we started to uncover the boats, when we started to uncover the boat.

How long was that after the collision? About 20 minutes.

What was he doing? Standing still.

Was he talking to anyone? No sir.

He was alone? Yes sir. On the boat deck.

How many lifeboats had been loaded? None had been loaded.

Had the order been given to clear away? Yes sir.

Had you started to clear away? Yes sir. I was walking around the deck then distributing the men all around the deck, taking off boat covers.

What men were you distributing? Seamen.

How many at each boat? I could not say. The watch below was coming up all the time.

Did you get more than three or four? I could not say. About three or four.

You were placing these men at the different stations, removing the covers from the lifeboats, and preparing to load and lower them? No.

Well, the order had been given to clear away, had it not? Yes.

What did that mean? I was in the act of clearing them. There had been no orders to load or lower.

Had there been any orders in reference to the women and children, at that time? No, not to my knowledge.

How soon after that time were the orders given to put the women and children into these lifeboats? I dare say about 10 minutes or a quarter of an hour.

That would be 45 minutes after the impact? Yes.

How soon did you get to loading the lifeboats on your side and under your direction? As soon as the boats were cleared away.

I asked you with reference to time. Did you get ready to lower them within an hour after the boat was struck? I dare say so.

How long was the boat above the water, if you know, after she was struck? I do not know.

About how long? As far as I know, she sank at 2.20 a.m.

And what time was she struck? I am only going by what I have heard. I do not know. About 20 minutes to 12, I believe.

Between the hour she was struck and the time she sank would be 2 hours and 40 minutes, yes. It took an hour to prepare the boats, did it? *Witness answers:* I cannot say, it would only be guesswork.

You are the ranking officer, and I want you to tell us as near as you can. *Witness answers:* Very well. I would have to go absolutely into all the details as to what is required in working the boat. There are a great many details. I think also the circumstances might be taken into consideration. I consider that the seamen did their duty, and were as smart as anyone else, and those boats were put out. But it is very difficult to be pinned down to a question of a few minutes. The boats were gotten out, and they were gotten out with all promptitude, I can say, but further than that I cannot say.

Had the passengers the right to go on the boat deck from below? Every right.

There was no restraint at the staircase? None.

Was that true as to the steerage? The steerage have no right up there, sir.

Did they on that occasion? Oh, yes.

There was no restraint? Oh, absolutely none.

There must have been considerable confusion. *Witness answers:* Not that I noticed.

Was everybody orderly? Perfectly.

How long did you see Mr Ismay there alone? As I passed.

Where were you going at that time? I was attending to the boats, seeing the men distributed, having the boat covers stripped off.

You say you were 15 feet from this last boat when it was lowered? It was not lowered, sir. I was 15 feet from it when they were endeavoring to get it into the tackles.

Did you go nearer to it than that? Did not have the opportunity, sir.

Why not? The ship went down.

Was this boat ever lowered? No sir.

It remained in the tackle? Yes sir.

When did you see Mr Ismay, with reference to the attempted lowering of this boat? I saw Mr Ismay, as I stated to you, sir.

Only once? Yes sir.

And that was about 20 minutes after the collision? Yes sir.

And there were no other passengers on that deck at that time? Not that I noticed. I should notice Mr Ismay naturally more than I should notice passengers.

Why? Because I know him.

Did he speak to you? No sir.

Did he see you? Yes sir. I don't know whether he recognized me.

Do you know where the Captain was at that time? I could not say sir.

Did you see him on the bridge? Previous to that I had seen him on the bridge.

How long before that? About three minutes after the impact.

Did he leave the bridge or did he remain there and leave your point of occupation? I left.

Where did you go? Back to my berth.

What for? There was no call for me to be on deck.

Did you believe the boat was in danger? No sir.

You felt that it was not a serious accident? I did not think it was a serious accident.

What was the force of the impact? A slight jar and a grinding sound.

Where were you when the impact occurred? In my berth.

Asleep? No sir. I was just getting off asleep.

You arose? Yes sir.

Did you dress yourself? No sir.

You went out of your room? Yes sir. Out on deck. A matter of 10 feet, until I could see the bridge distinctly.

You could see the bridge distinctly and the Captain was on the bridge? The Captain and First Officer.

Did you see any other officers at that time? I did not notice them.

Had no alarm been given at that time? None.

How much time elapsed after the impact and your appearance on the deck? I should say about two or three minutes.

Then you returned? How long did you remain on deck? *Witness answers:* About two or three minutes.

At that time who else was on deck at that point? Excluding the bridge, I saw no one except the Third Officer, who left his berth shortly after I did.

Did he join you? Yes.

Did you confer about what had happened? Yes sir.

What did you conclude had happened? Nothing much.

You knew there had been a collision? Not necessarily a collision.

You knew you had struck something? Yes sir.

What did you assume it to be? Ice.

Why? That was the conclusion one naturally jumps to around the Banks there.

Had you seen ice before? No sir.

Did you see Mr Murdoch after that? Yes sir. I saw him when I came out of the quarters after the impact.

Where was he? On the bridge.

With the Captain? One on one side, and one on the other side of the bridge; one on each side.

Did you speak to him after that? No sir.

You were not together when finally parted from the ship? No sir.

You saw him on the bridge at the time? Immediately after the impact, yes sir.

Did he remain there until the end? He was getting the boats out on the starboard side later on.

Did you see him at that work? No sir. I was on the port side.

How do you know that he did it? I saw him at the last boat.

Where did you last see the Captain? On the boat deck, sir.

How long before the vessel sank? I could not say, sir. I saw him about the boat deck two or three times. I had no occasion to go to him.

Was the vessel broken in two in any manner, or intact? Absolutely intact.

Tell us, as nearly as you can, just where you saw the Captain last, with reference to the sinking of this ship. *Witness answers:* I think the bridge was the last place I saw him sir. I am not sure. I think he was crossing the bridge.

From one side to the other? No sir, just coming across. I merely recognized a glimpse. I have a slight recollection of having seen him whilst I was walking. It is my recollection that I saw him crossing the bridge. I think that was the last.

How large was this bridge? How large was it on the *Titanic*? *Witness answers:* It extends the width of the ship and 18 inches over each side.

When you saw him was he giving any orders? I was not near enough to know, sir.

What did he seem to be doing – pacing? No sir, not pacing, ust walking straight across as if he had some object that he was walking toward.

He was walking from one side to the other? Yes sir, from starboard to port.

Did that give him a full sweep of view of the situation? Yes sir.

If he had been giving orders would you have heard them? Yes sir.

And you did not hear any such thing at that time? At that time no, sir.

What were the last orders you heard him give? When I asked him, 'Shall I put the women and children in the boats?' he replied, 'Yes, and lower away.' Those were the last orders he gave.

Where was he at that time? About abreast the No. 6 boat.

How long was that before the ship sunk? Approximately somewhere about a quarter to 1, say. I don't know what time it was, sir. It would be only a guess [lifeboat 6 was actually launched at 1.10 a.m.]

How long was the vessel afloat after this collision? That I do not know either, only from what I was told.

What were you told? I was told she sunk at 2.20 a.m.

Who told you that? We came to the conclusion amongst the officers, by various indications.

Did any officer that you communicated with know the exact moment of this impact or collision? That I could not say, sir.

Of course you had a watch with you? No sir.

You asked the Captain on the boat deck whether the lifeboats should take the women and children first, if I understand you correctly? What did you then do? *Witness answers:* I carried out his orders.

Were all the boats lowered on the port side? They were all lowered with the exception of one, the last boat, which was stowed on top of the officers' quarters.

We had not time to launch it nor yet to open it. And when all the other boats were carried away, I called for the men to go up there, told them to cut her adrift and throw her down.

How did it happen to be stowed up there? Was that an unusual place for it? *Witness answers:* No sir.

Well, what happened to that boat? It floated off the ship, sir. I understand the men standing on top, who assisted to launch it down, jumped on to it as it was on the deck and floated off with it.

What type of boat was it? Collapsible.

Did you see it afterwards? Eventually. It was the boat that I got on.

Did you see the Captain after that final order with reference to the women and children? Yes sir.

Where? Walking across the bridge, sir.

Did you have any further communication with him? No sir, none.

This lifeboat which was taken from the top of the officers' quarters, and that you finally reached, contained how many people? When it floated off the ship?

Yes. *Witness answers:* I could not say how many.

How many after you had gotten into it? We were thrown off a couple of times. It was cleared, it was a flat collapsible boat. When I came to it, it was bottom up, and there was no one on it.

No one on it? And it was on the other side of the ship.

What did you do when you came to it? I hung on to it.

You floated with it merely? Yes sir.

Was that all the service it ever rendered? Was that the only service this lifeboat performed? No sir. Eventually about 30 of us got in it.

Tell us just how it occurred. *Witness answers:* Yes sir. Immediately after finding that overturned lifeboat, and when I came up alongside of it, there were quite a lot of us in the water around it preparatory to getting up on it.

With life preservers? Yes sir. Then the forward funnel fell down

Were there any persons there without life preservers? No sir. Not that I know of. The forward funnel falling down, it fell alongside of the lifeboat, about four inches clear of it.

Did it strike the boat? It missed the boat.

Then what? It fell on all the people there were alongside of the boat, if there were any there.

Injure any of them seriously? I could not say, sir.

Did it kill anybody? I could not say, sir.

Was this vessel sinking pretty rapidly at that time? Pretty quickly, sir.

Do you know any of the men who were in the water as you were and who boarded this lifeboat? Yes, sir.

Give their names. *Witness answers:* Mr Thayer, a first class passenger, the second Marconi operator – I can tell you his name in a minute, Bride. Oh yes and Colonel Gracie.

Was he on the upturned boat before you got it righted around? We never righted it.

Who else was there? I think all the rest were firemen taken out of the water, sir. Those are the only passengers that I know of.

No other passengers? There were two or three that died. I think there were three or four who died during the night.

Aboard this boat with you? Yes sir. I think the senior Marconi operator was on the boat and died. The Marconi junior operator told me that the senior was on this boat and died. She was packed standing from stem to stern at daylight.

Was there any effort made by others to board her? We took all on board that we could.

I understand, but I wanted to know whether there was any effort made by others to get aboard? Not that I saw.

There must have been a great number of people in the water? But not near us. They were some distance away from us.

How far? It seemed about a half a mile.

Was not this the only raft or craft in sight? It was dark, sir.

Yes. But this was the only thing there was to get on at that time? With the exception of the wreckage.

Did you see Colonel Gracie? I don't know whether I saw him, sir. I met him on the *Carpathia* afterwards, of course.

Do you remember seeing him in the water? No sir.

Who took command of that overturned lifeboat? I did, as far as command was necessary.

Did your judgment rule the conduct of those on it? Yes, sir; that is my reason for saying that I believe it was mostly the crew of the ship, because of the implicit obedience.

When you left the ship, did you see any women or children on board? None whatever.

Could you give us any estimate whatever as to the number of first and second class passengers that were on board when the ship went down? No Sir.

Were there any on the so-called boat deck? Yes sir.

Were there quite a number, in your opinion? A number of people - what they were, first, second, or third, crew or firemen, I could not say, sir.

But there were many people still on the ship? Yes sir.

And, so far as you could observe, could you tell whether they were equipped with life preservers? As far as I could see, throughout the whole of the passengers, or the whole of the crew, everyone was equipped with a life preserver, for I looked for it especially.

Were the passengers on those decks instructed at any time to go to one side or the other of the ship? Yes.

What do you know about that? When the ship was taking a heavy list – not a heavy list – but she was taking a list over to port, the order was called, I think, by the Chief Officer. 'Everyone on the starboard side to straighten her up,' which I repeated.

How long before you left the ship? Half an hour or three quarters of an hour.

How were these passengers selected in going to the lifeboats? By their sex.

Whenever you saw a woman? Precisely.

She was invited to go into one of these boats? Excepting the stewardesses. We turned several of those away.

Except the employees? Except the stewardesses, yes.

And did you see any attempt made to get women to enter the lifeboats who refused to go? Yes sir.

How many? Several? *Witness answers:* A few.

What reason was given why they did not? I had not time; I didn't notice. Merely they would not come.

Did they ask that their families be taken? Yes, one or two.

And were families taken, to your knowledge? Not to my knowledge.

How many lifeboats were actually picked up by the *Carpathia*? All accounted for.

One, however, was badly injured, and another lifeboat took the passengers from it, did they not? That was the upturned one that I was on.

And they took you into another lifeboat? Yes sir.

Was the lifeboat full at that time? I counted 65 heads, not including myself or any that were in the bottom of the boat. I roughly estimated about 75 in the boat.

Was the boat safe with that number of people in it? Safe in smooth water only.

How many of those lifeboats did you help load? All except one or two on the port side.

Who determined the number of people who should go into the lifeboats? I did.

How did you reach a conclusion as to the number that should be permitted to go in? My own judgment about the strength of the tackle.

How many did you put in each boat? In the first boat I put about 20 or 25. 20, sir.

How many men? No men.

How many seamen? Two.

Was that sufficient to take care of the boat? We wanted them up on deck.

For what purpose? Lowering away the boats.

Do you mean that there would not have been sufficient on deck and to man the lifeboats at the same time? Not to distribute more than two to a boat, sir. It would not be safe.

That is not the usual requirement, is it – two to a boat? Quite sufficient under the conditions.

As a matter of fact, women were obliged to row those boats for hours? Yes, a great many did, I know.

That indicated that they were not fully equipped? Not necessarily, sir.

How many oars in a boat? I think it is 16, the full, equipment.

How many persons can use an oar at one time? I do not mean how many can, but I mean how many ordinarily would? We would man about five oars a side. In the boat I was in we could put only three oars.

You couldn't pull at all, could you, in your boat? We managed to keep our head to the sea with three oars.

You mean you got hold of three oars after this boat was turned over? No sir. The one that picked us up, afterwards.

You did not have any means of propelling your craft until you were taken from this upturned boat? A couple of bits of wood we picked up, only.

What happened to that lifeboat, the first one loaded? It was loaded and sent away from the ship.

Did it not return to the ship because it was only half loaded? Not to my knowledge, sir.

As a matter of fact it was not much more than half loaded, was it? You mean its floating capacity?

Yes. *Witness answers:* Floating capacity, no.

How did it happen you did not put more people into that boat? Because I did not consider it safe.

In a great emergency like that, where there were limited facilities, could you not have afforded to try to put more people into that boat? I did not know it was urgent then. I had no idea it was urgent.

Supposing you had known it was urgent, what would you have done? I would have acted to the best of my judgment then.

Tell me what you would have thought wise. *Witness answers:* I would have taken more risks. I should not have considered it wise to put more in, but I might have taken risks.

As a matter of fact are not these lifeboats so constructed as to accommodate 40 people? 65 in the water, sir.

65 in the water, and about 40 as they are being put into the water? No sir.

How? No sir, it all depends on your gears, sir. If it were an old ship, you would barely dare to put 25 in.

But this was a new one? And therefore I took chances with her afterwards.

You put 25 in? In the first. And two men.

How were those two men selected, arbitrarily by you? No sir. They were selected by me, yes.

Who were they? I could not say, sir.

How did you happen to choose those particular men? Because they were standing near.

Did they want to go? I did not ask them.

You did not call for volunteers? They went by my orders.

Did you see any lifeboat return to the ship and take on additional passengers? No sir.

How many did the second boat contain? About 30.

How many men? Two.

How many women and children? I should say, roughly 30, and probably grown ups.

You do not know, I suppose, whether they were first or second cabin passengers? No.

Did you see that boat again alongside or any place else? By the *Titanic*, sir? Not to my knowledge.

How many did the third boat contain? By the time I came to the third boat I was aware that it was getting serious, and then I started to take chances.

How long did it take to lower a boat – fill it and lower it? Just filling it and lowering it, and not clearing away?

Filling and lowering and clearing? We clear it away first then heave it out over the side, then lower it down level with the rail, and then commence to fill it with people. Previous to that we have to take the covers all off, haul out all the falls and coil them down clear.

How long do you think it took you to uncover and lower that lifeboat? It is difficult to say sir, 15 or 20 minutes.

Were there any lifeboats being lowered from the other side at the same time? I do not know, sir.

How did it happen that you had charge of that feature? Because I took charge.

And where was Mr Murdoch that time? As far as I know, he had charge of the starboard side.

How many passengers did the third boat contain? I can only guess. I filled her up as full as I could, and lowered her as full as I dared.

How many seamen? Two.

You followed that rule? I followed that rule throughout.

Were the people ready to go? Perfectly quiet and ready.

Any jostling, pushing, or crowding? None whatever.

The men all refrained from asserting their strength and crowding back the women and children? They could not have stood quieter if they had been in church.

If you had filled that third boat full, how many people would you have had in it? *Witness answers:* What do you mean by full?

To its full capacity. *Witness answers:* 65.

Do you think you had that many in it? Certainly not, sir.

How many did you have? 35, I should say, sir.

And two men? *Witness answers:* Yes.

Then the fourth boat. Was there any fourth boat on that side? There were eight boats to a side

As to the fourth boat, you followed the same course? The same order, the same conditions.

You put two men in each? I think I was getting short of men, if I remember rightly. I started to putting one seaman and a steward in. That was the boat I had to put a man passenger in. I could only find one seaman. I had started to lower the boat. I had put two seamen in and then I wanted two for lowering. It is absolutely necessary to have a seaman on each fall. No one else can lower a boat. I was calling for seamen, and one of the seamen jumped out of the boat and started to lowering away. The boat was half way down when the women called out and said that there was only one man in the boat. I had only two seamen and could not part with them, and was in rather a fix to know what to do, when a passenger called out and said, 'If you like, I will go.'

Did you know him? I did not.

Was he an officer of the ship? No sir, a first class passenger.

You don't know who he was? I have found out who he was since, Major Peuchen.

Did he volunteer? He merely said, 'I will go if you like.' I said 'Are you a seaman,' and he said 'I am a yachtsman.' I said 'If you are sailor enough to get out on that fall' – that is a difficult thing to get to, over the ship's side, eight feet away, and means a long swing on a dark night – 'if you are sailor enough to get out there you can go down.' And he proved he was, by going down. And he afterwards proved himself a brave man, too.

Have you seen him since? I saw him on the *Carpathia*. I made it my business to find him.

How many did you say you had in this boat? 35, about the same, as far as I remember.

That is the fourth one. How about the fifth? As far as I know, the conditions were the same.

Did you have to call somebody from among the passengers? No sir. I cannot remember anything in particular about that boat. I was getting along then just as fast as ever I could. I was too quick to bother about things.

How many women were you caring for? How many did you have aboard the ship? *Witness answers:* I could not say.

Do you know whether they were all cared for? I could not say, sir.

All that would go? In the case of the last boat I got out [collapsible lifeboat D], I had the utmost difficulty in finding women. It was the very last boat of all, after all the other boats were put out and we came forward to put out the collapsible boats. In the meantime the forward emergency boat [lifeboat 2] had been put out by one of the other officers. So we rounded up the tackles and got the collapsible boat to put that over. Then I called for women and could not get hold of any. Somebody said, 'There are no women.' With this, several men ...

Who said that? I do not know, sir.

On what deck was that? On the boat deck.

Were all the women supposed to be on the boat deck? Yes sir. They were supposed to be.

Why? Because the boats were there. I might say that previous to putting this Berthon boat [one the collapsible lifeboats] out we had lowered a boat from A deck one deck down below. That was through my fault. It was the first boat I had lowered. I was intending to put the passengers in from A deck. On lowering it down I found the windows were closed. So I sent someone down to open the windows and carried on with the other boats, but decided it was not worth while lowering them down, that I could manage just as well from the boat deck. When I came forward from the other boats I loaded that boat from A deck by getting the women out through the windows. My idea in filling the boats there was because there was a wire hawser running along the side of the ship for coaling purposes, and it was handy to tie the boat in to, to hold it so that nobody could drop between the side of the boat and the ship.

Which one was that? That is No. 4 boat.

That was filled from there? That was filled from there, loaded, and sent away. Then we went to this Berthon boat.

In the fifth boat, how many seamen were there? As far as I remember, two seamen.

How many people did you put into it? I might have put a good deal more. I filled her up as much as I could. When I got down to the fifth boat, that was aft.

You were still using your best judgment? I was not using very much judgment then. I was filling them up.

At that time you felt ... *Witness answers:* I knew it was a question of the utmost speed, to get the boats away.

In that situation you were quite sure that they were filled to their capacity? Yes sir. I don't say to their floating capacity, I don't say 65.

But about the same number of persons were in each boat? I should say 35 or 40.

Was the sixth one loaded in the same manner? I think the sixth one put down was this one from A deck that I spoke of – no, the fifth one would be from A deck. I think the Chief Officer, under his direct supervision, lowered a boat from the after-end. Of course I cannot be absolutely certain. But when I came forward, as I say, I put the one down from A deck which I told you about. Then we went to the Berthon boat, which is the last boat on the port side, the collapsible boat.

The fifth boat was lowered in the same manner? Yes sir. I think it was the fifth from the A deck.

With two seamen? Yes.

And the balance women? Women and children.

Women and children? Up to this time, so far as you recollect, no men had been permitted to get into these boats? *Witness answers:* None had attempted to do so, no sir.

How about the sixth boat? *Witness answers:* That is the collapsible [lifeboat D], the surfboat?

That is the collapsible. Did you take the same course with that? *Witness answers:* That is a much smaller boat.

How many seamen did you put in that? I think there was one seaman and one steward. I could not say.

How many people were put into this sixth boat? Between 15 and 20.

And two seamen? I think one seaman probably, if I had one seaman there. Perhaps it was two stewards. I do not know, sir.

Would the two stewards answer the same purpose? They would have to.

Were any of them officers? No, sir.

Did you have any difficulty in filling it? With women, yes sir. Great difficulty.

But you filled it to its capacity? I filled it with about 15 or 20 eventually mustered up. It took longer to fill that boat than it did any other boat, notwithstanding that the others had more in them. On two occasions the men thought there were no more women and commenced to get in and then found one or two more and then got out again.

How long a time do you think you had been in loading these six boats? I don't know, sir.

If it took 15 to 20 minutes to a boat? About an hour and a half.

The vessel must have been going down? I lowered the last boat 10 feet and it was in the water.

When you began lowering, the boat was about 60 feet up from the water? 70 feet. From the deck, exactly sir.

What did you do with the seventh boat? That was the finish.

What was that? The seventh boat [lifeboat B floated off] was the one on top of the quarters.

That was the last boat that was lowered by your orders? It was the last. It was not lowered.

Did you see Mr Ismay at that time? Mr Ismay, as far as I know, from what I have gathered afterwards, was on the starboard side of the deck wholly, helping out there.

He did not enter the boat from the port side? No sir.

How many people do you think were in the sixth boat? *Witness answers:* The last collapsible boat?

Yes. *Witness answers:* I say about 15.

Wouldn't it hold any more than that? Perhaps 20. They won't hold many. They are canvas. They will not stand many. They are merely stowed in a smaller place. Perhaps you can stow at least three of those where you can stow one lifeboat. You can stow them one on top of the other.

So far as your knowledge goes, the lifeboats on the port side consisted of how many lifeboats and how many of those canvas boats? Seven lifeboats, one emergency boat, which is on the same principle as the lifeboat, practically, only it is a smaller and handier boat, and two collapsible boats.

You must have been painfully aware of the fact that there were not enough boats there to care for that large passenger list, were you not? Yes sir.

Do you know who had charge on the starboard side of the lowering and filling of the boats? No sir. Merely what I am told. As far as I know, and I think it is correct, Mr Murdoch. I was on the port side, and Mr Murdoch was on the starboard side, and the Chief Officer [Henry Wilde] was superintending generally, and lowered one or two boats himself.

From whom did you get information? Of course, I saw Mr Murdoch there when finally I had finished on the port side.

You went to the starboard side? On top, yes sir. I went over to see if I could assist.

From anything you have been told, did he pursue the same course on the starboard side in reference to the filling of the lifeboats, and the complement of seamen as you did? That I could not say.

What was the number of the ship's crew? *Witness answers:* Of seamen?

Yes. *Witness answers:* 71 seamen [of which 43 survived].

What constituted the crew besides seamen? Firemen and stewards [Lightoller would testify later in the inquiry that he counted quartermasters as seamen too].

And their force? Oh yes. They mustered up something like 800, perhaps a little under, perhaps a little over. Somewhere around 800. About 800, roughly speaking, firemen and stewards. A little less than 800. The crew altogether is about 850 or 860; that is, including seamen, firemen, and stewards.

And you had your full complement on this voyage? As far as I know.

How do you account for your inability to get hold of more than nine seamen to man those lifeboats on the port side? Earlier, and before I realised that there was any danger, I told off the boatswain to take some men – I didn't say how many, leaving the man to use his own judgment, to go down below and open the gangway doors in order that some boats could come alongside and be filled to their utmost capacity. He complied with the order, and, so far as I know, went down below, and I did not see him afterwards. That took away a number of men, and we detailed two men for each boat and two men for lowering down.

But you did not have two men for each boat, officer. You had only ... *Witness answers:* So far as they will go.

You only had nine seamen to seven boats? Well, I have only been telling you approximately. As far as ever I could I put two seamen in a boat. If I didn't have a seaman there I had to put a steward there. Sometimes there would be three seamen in a boat. As soon as the boats were lowered to the level of the rail, I would detail one man to jump in and ship the rudder, one man to cast adrift the oars, and one man would see that the plugs were in, and it would take three men.

You said you chose these men and when the lifeboat is swung out from the ship and lowered it is supposed that she has her full complement of officers and seamen, is it not? She is swung out and lowered to the level of the rail, sir.

Level with the rail but not against the rail? No.

When you are lowering the lifeboat you are supposed to have filled it to its safe capacity? Lowering it afterwards from the rail down. You see we have to swing it out first of all and lower it until it is level with the rail, so that the people can have one foot on deck and the other foot to step into the boat. They must be level.

And how many of the crew have been saved altogether? How many survived, altogether? *Witness answers:* 210.

If the same course was followed on the starboard side with the lifeboats that you took on the port side, how were these men saved? I don't know, sir. I know that a great number were taken out of the water. I made it my special business to inquire, and as far as I can gather, for every six people picked out of the water five of them would be firemen or stewards. On our boat, as I have said before, there was Colonel Grace and young Thayer. I think those were the only two passengers. I am speaking of the overturned boat.

There were no women on your boat? No sir. These were all taken out of the water and they were firemen and others of the crew.

How many were there on that boat? Roughly, about 30. I take that from my own estimate and from the estimate of some one who was looking down from the bridge of the *Carpathia*.

Assuming there were 24 of those among the crew? Yes.

That would still leave 190 to get over on these other lifeboats that were filled with women and children? Some of the boats went back and picked people out of the wreckage after the ship had gone down, mostly, firemen and stewards.

Some of the lifeboats went back? That is what I understand, course, I don't know.

From what you have said, you discriminated entirely in the interest of the passengers – first the women and children – in filling those lifeboats? Yes sir.

Why did you do that? Because of the Captain's orders, or because of the rule of the sea? *Witness answers:* The rule of human nature.

The rule of human nature? And there was no studied purpose, as far as you know, to save the crew? *Witness answers:* Absolutely not.

Were there any women left on the deck? On the port side on deck, I can say, as far as my own observations went, from my own endeavor and that of others to obtain women, there were none. I can give you the name of a man who will give testimony, who was working with me, one of our best men, a man I picked out especially to man the falls for lowering away. He went from the port side to the starboard side of the deck, as I did, and after that, when she went under water forward, instead of taking to the water he walked aft the whole length of the boat deck previous to sliding down the aft fall on the port side, and in the whole length of the deck and in crossing the bridge he saw two women. They were standing amidships on the bridge perfectly still. They did not seem to he endeavoring to get to one side or the other to see if there were any boats or not. The whole length of the boat deck, so far as he went, he did not see any women.

Do you know what became of those two women? I do not.

After the ship went down what happened? I was sucked down, and I was blown out with something pretty powerful when the ship went down.

Just describe that a little more fully. You were sucked down? *Witness answers:* I was sucked against the blower first of all. As I say, I was on top of the officers' quarters, and there was nothing more to be done. The ship then took a dive, and I turned face forward and also took a dive.

From which side? From on top, practically amidships. A little to the starboard side, where I had got to and I was driven back against a blower – which is a large thing that shape (indicating) which faces forward to the wind and which then goes down to the stokehole. But there is a grating there, and it was against this grating that I was sucked by the water and held there.

Was your head above water? No sir.

You were under water? Yes sir. And then this explosion, or whatever it was, took place. Certainly, I think it was the boilers exploded. There was a terrific blast of air and water, and I was blown out clear.

I want to ask whether, in your judgment that was from an explosion or from the force of the air through the blower? It was certainly air through the blower, and behind that was a great force, and that force, in my opinion, was from the boilers. I have heard great controversy as to boilers exploding owing to coming in contact with salt water, by men who are capable of giving an opinion; but there seems to be an open question as to whether cold water actually does cause boilers to explode. I was speaking to a gentleman yesterday who said it was very probably the rush of cold water going down below at such a terrific rate, and then, the hot air being forced out. I do not quite follow that, myself. In my judgment, it was a boiler explosion – a rush of steam, anyway.

At least you took your head out of the water? I came up above the water, yes.

And how far from the sinking ship did it throw you? Barely threw me away at all, because I went down again against these fiddley gratings immediately abreast of the funnel over the stokehole.

Was anybody else sucked down at the time? Colonel Gracie, I believe, was sucked down in identically the same manner. He was sucked down on the fiddley gratings.

There must have been considerable suction? That was the water rushing down below as she was going down.

Going down into the ship? Exactly.

How did you get released from that? Oh, I don't know sir. I think it was the boilers again, but I do not distinctly remember. I do not know.

Where did you next find yourself? Alongside of that upturned boat that had been launched on the other side.

Where had you gone at that time? Had you gone around the ship? *Witness answers:* No sir. The boat had come around.

Was there anyone on it? I don't think so. I think they were around it.

Your position had not changed, but the boat's position had? Yes sir.

How much of the ship had gone down when you left it? I went under water on top of the officers' quarters, immediately at the fore part of the forward funnel, so she was under water at the fore part of the forward funnel.

You say that after you came up you attached yourself to this raft the funnel fell upon those who were upon one side of the raft? I say the funnel fell down, and if anybody was on that side of the raft it fell on them.

Then by that time the entire ship was not submerged? Oh dear, no.

What portion of the ship was out of water at that time? The stern of the ship was completely out of the water.

When you said that you twice found yourself against the grating at the blower, when in the water, did you mean that you gravitated back toward the blowpipe, or were you pushed back to it by suction of any kind? It was the water rushing down the stokeholes through this blower, which acts as a ventilator, and therefore gives access to the stokehole, the force of the water rushing down this blower which naturally carried me back with it, and against the blower.

When you last saw the *Titanic* did you see numerous people on the decks? *Witness answers:* Do you mean before I left it?

Before you left the side of the *Titanic*, and while you were in the water? I saw no one while I was in the water.

You could not see the decks very well from that point. You were below the decks, and could not see the upper part of the ship? No sir. I could not see anything when I was in the water, at all. I mean to say, I could not see anyone on her decks.

How far did you swim from the blowpipe to this overturned collapsible lifeboat upon which you finally escaped from the wreck? I hardly had any opportunity to swim. I was blown away from this blower by a rush of air, or it may have been steam. What it was exactly I cannot say, but I was blown a considerable distance away from the blower.

And from that? From there I was sucked in again to what we call the 'fiddley,' which leads down to the stokehole, I may say. I presume I was blown away from there. I really cannot say exactly. Then I came up alongside of this overturned boat.

How long was that before the *Titanic* disappeared? It might be 10 or 15 minutes.

And after getting aboard of this overturned lifeboat, you went out some distance from it? It was the action of the funnel falling that threw us out a considerable distance away from the boat.

You had no oars or other means of propelling that boat? Nothing of any effect. We had little bits of wood but they were practically ineffective.

I have forgotten whether you said that at daybreak you cruised around the place of the wreck? At daybreak we were taken on board by one of our other lifeboats.

No. 14? The number I cannot remember.

Was that Mr Lowe's boat? There was not any officer in the boat until I got in.

And then? Of course, I took charge.

And did you cruise around the scene of the wreck? No sir.

You then bore toward the *Carpathia*? No sir, we held our bow on to the wind. The boat was too full. In fact, she was dangerously full, and it was all I could do to nurse the boat up to the sea.

I understood you to say that. What I particularly desired to know was whether at that time you saw any of the wreckage or floating bodies, dead or alive? *Witness answers:* I saw none.

Witness offers: I may also say, in regard to the testimony in regard to Mr Ismay, although I cannot vouch for the source, yet it was given to me from a source such that I have every reason to believe its truth ... *US Senate inquiry:* Before or since this occurred? *Witness answers:* Since. On the *Carpathia*. Before she arrived in New York.

Give the information. *Witness answers:* It is that Chief Officer Wilde was at the starboard collapsible boat in which Mr Ismay went away, and that he told Mr Ismay, 'There are no more women on board the ship.' Wilde was a pretty big, powerful chap, and he was a man that would not argue very long. Mr Ismay was right there. Naturally he was there close to the boat, because he was working at the boats and he had been working at the collapsible boat, and that is why he was there, and Mr Wilde, who was near him, simply bundled him into the boat.

You did not say that before? *Witness answers:* No, but I believe it is true, I forget the source. I am sorry I have forgotten it.

Did Mr Wilde survive? He did not.

As I now recollect your testimony – and I have it here – you said you were not acquainted with Mr Ismay. *Witness answers:* I have known Mr Ismay for 14 years.

LIFEBOAT A
Starboard Side, Floated Off *Titanic* 2.15 a.m

This is the lifeboat we know least about. Although collapsible lifeboat A floated off the right way up, passengers were not able to fully raise the canvas sides and the lifeboat took on a lot of water during the night. Those who managed to get into this lifeboat spent the next couple of hours with their legs partly in water. There were probably other survivors who clung on the sides but couldn't get in and died later that night.

The stricken lifeboat was spotted late in the morning by Fifth Officer Harold Lowe in lifeboat 14. In both his testimony to the US and British inquiries he stated that he transferred 'about 20' male survivors off the boat and one woman (Rosa Abbott, the only woman to have survived after being thrown into the water) but with a caveat that he hadn't counted how many he had collected. As with many statistics surrounding the *Titanic* there are some contradictions with the numbers saved from this lifeboat. Richard Williams, quoted below, puts the number transferred into lifeboat 14 at only 11.

The lifeboat with three dead bodies still on board was abandoned and found a month later by the *Oceanic*.

61
Olaus Abelseth, Third Class Passenger

The collision woke Olaus Abelseth, whose cabin was deep down in the ship and towards the bow. He jumped from the *Titanic* in the last few minutes and managed to swim to collapsible lifeboat A. Abelseth, a 25-year-old Norwegian who had settled in America a decade previously, was returning from a visit to Norway. This testimony is interesting for its description of the difficulties faced by third class passengers in reaching the lifeboats and for the vivid descriptions of his fight for survival in the water.

US Senate Inquiry (inquiry question is followed immediately by witness's answer) I believe you were a steerage passenger? Yes sir.

In the forward part of the ship? Yes. I was in compartment G on the ship.

Go ahead and tell us just what happened. *Witness answers:* I went to bed about 10 o'clock Sunday night, and I think it was about 15 minutes to 12 when I woke up; and there was another man in the same room – two of us in the same room – and he said to me, 'What is that?' I said, 'I don't know, but we had better get up.' So we did get up and put our clothes on, and we two went up on deck in the forward part of the ship.

Then there was quite a lot of ice on the starboard part of the ship. They wanted us to go down again, and I saw one of the officers, and I said to him: 'Is there any danger?' He said, 'No.' I was not satisfied with that, however, so I went down and told my brother-in-law and my cousin, who were in the same compartment there. They were not in the same room, but they were just a little way from where I was. I told them about what was happening, and I said they had better get up. Both of them got up and dressed, and we took our overcoats and put them on. We did not take any lifebelts with us. There was no water on the deck at that time.

We walked to the hind part of the ship and got two Norwegian girls up. One was in my charge and one was in charge of the man who was in the same room with me. He was from the same town that I came from. The other one was just 16 years old, and her father told me to take care of her until we got to Minneapolis. The two girls were in a room in the hind part of the ship, in the steerage.

We all went up on deck and stayed there. We walked over to the port side of the ship, and there were five of us standing, looking, and we thought we saw a light.

On what deck were you standing? *Witness answers:* Not on the top deck, but on – I do not know what you call it – but it is the hind part, where the sitting room is; and then there is a kind of a little space in between, where they go up on deck. It was up on the boat deck, the place for the steerage passengers on the deck. We were then on the port side there, and we looked out at this light. I said to my brother-in-law: 'I can see it plain, now. It must be a light.'

How far away was it? *Witness answers:* I could not say, but it did not seem to be so very far. I thought I could see this mast light, the front mast light. That is what I thought I could see.

A little while later there was one of the officers who came and said to be quiet, that there was a ship coming. That is all he said. He did not say what time, or anything. That is all he said. So I said to them, we had better go and get the lifebelts, as we had not brought them with us. So my cousin and I went down to get the lifebelts for all of us. When we came up again we carried the lifebelts on our arms for a while.

There were a lot of steerage people there that were getting on one of these cranes that they had on deck, that they used to lift things with. They can lift about two and a half tons, I believe. These steerage passengers were crawling along on this, over the railing, and away up to the boat deck. A lot of them were doing that.

They could not get up there in any other way? *Witness answers:* This gate was shut.

Was it locked? *Witness answers:* I do not know whether it was locked, but it was shut so that they could not go that way.

A while later these girls were standing there, and one of the officers came and hollered for all of the ladies to come up on the boat deck. The gate was opened and these two girls went up.

We stayed a little while longer, and then they said, 'Everybody.' I do not know who that was, but I think it was some of the officers that said it. I could not say that, but it was somebody that said 'everybody.' We went up. We went over to the port side of the ship, and there were just one or two boats on the port side that were left. Anyway, there was one. We were standing there looking at them lowering this boat. We could see them, some of the crew helping take the ladies in their arms and throwing them into the lifeboats. We saw them lower this boat, and there were no more boats on the port side.

So we walked over to the starboard side of the ship, and just as we were standing there, one of the officers came up and he said just as he walked by, 'Are there any sailors here?'

I did not say anything. I have been a fishing man for six years, and, of course, this officer walked right by me and asked: 'Are there any sailors here?' I would have gone, but my brother-in-law and my cousin said, in the Norwegian language, as we were speaking Norwegian: 'Let us stay here together.' I do not know, but I think the officer wanted some help to get some of these collapsible boats out. All he said was: 'Are there any sailors here?' I did not say anything, but I have been used to the ocean for a long time. I commenced to work on the ocean when I was 10 years old with my dad fishing. I kept that up until I came to this country.

Then we stayed there, and we were just standing still there. We did not talk very much. Just a little ways from us I saw there was an old couple standing there on the deck, and I heard this man say to the lady, 'Go into the lifeboat and get saved.' He put his hand on her shoulder and I think he said: 'Please get into the lifeboat and get saved.' She replied: 'No, let me stay with you.' I could not say who it was, but I saw that he was an old man. I did not pay much attention to him, because I did not know him.

I was standing there, and I asked my brother-in-law if he could swim and he said no. I asked my cousin if he could swim and he said no. So we could see the water coming up, the bow of the ship was going down, and there was a kind of an explosion. We could hear the popping and cracking, and the deck raised up and got so steep that the people could not stand on their feet on the deck. So they fell down and slid on the deck into the water right on the ship. Then we hung on to a rope in one of the davits. We were pretty far back at the top deck.

My brother-in-law said to me, 'We had better jump off or the suction will take us down.' I said, 'No. We won't jump yet. We ain't got much show anyhow, so we might as well stay as long as we can.' So he stated again, 'We must jump off.' But I said, 'No, not yet.' So then, it was only about five feet down to the water when we jumped off. It was not much of a jump. Before that we could see the people were jumping over. There was water coming on to the deck, and they were jumping over, then, out in the water.

My brother-in-law took my hand just as we jumped off; and my cousin jumped at the same time. When we came into the water, I think it was from the suction – or anyway we went under, and I swallowed some water. I got a rope tangled around me, and I let loose of my brother-in-law's hand to get away from the rope. I thought then, 'I am a goner.' That is what I thought when I got tangled up in this rope. But I came on top again, and I was trying to swim, and there was a man – lots of them were floating around – and he got me on the neck and pressed me under, trying to get on top of me. I said to him, 'Let go.' Of course, he did not pay any attention to that, but I got away from him. Then there was another man, and he hung on to me for a while, but he let go. Then I swam. I could not say, but it must have been about 15 or 20 minutes. It could not have been over that. Then I saw something dark ahead of me. I did not know what it was, but I swam toward that, and it was one of those collapsible boats.

When we jumped off of the ship, we had life preservers on. There was no suction from the ship at all. I was lying still, and I thought 'I will try to see if I can float on the lifebelt without help from swimming,' and I floated easily on the lifebelt.

When I got on this raft or collapsible boat, they did not try to push me off and they did not do anything for me to get on. All they said when I got on there was, 'Don't capsize the boat.' So I hung on to the raft for a little while before I got on.

Some of them were trying to get up on their feet. They were sitting down or lying down on the raft. Some of them fell into the water again. Some of them were frozen and there were two dead, that they threw overboard.

I got on this raft or collapsible boat and raised up, and then I was continually moving my arms and swinging them around to keep warm. There was one lady aboard this raft, and she got saved. I do not know her name. I saw her on board the *Carpathia*, but I forgot to ask her name. There were also two Swedes, and a first class passenger – I believe that is what he said – and he had just his underwear on. I asked him if he was married, and he said he had a wife and a child. There was also a fireman named Thompson on the same raft. He had burned one of his hands. Also there was a young boy, with a name that sounded like Volunteer. He was at St Vincent's Hospital afterwards. Thompson was there, too.

The next morning we could see some of the lifeboats. One of the boats had a sail up, and he came pretty close, and then we said, 'One, two, three' we said that quite often. We did not talk very much, except that we would say, 'One, two, three,' and scream together for help.

Were you on the top of the overturned collapsible boat? *Witness answers:* No. The boat was not capsized. We were standing [in it]. In this little boat the canvas was not raised up. We tried to raise the canvas up but we could not get it up. We stood all night in about 12 or 14 inches of water on this thing and our feet were in the water all the time. I could not say exactly how long we were there, but I know it was more than four hours on this raft. This same boat I was telling about.

The sailboat? *Witness answers*: Yes. When the *Carpathia* came she was picked up. There were several boats there then. It was broad daylight and you could see the *Carpathia*. Then this boat sailed down to us and took us aboard, and took us in to the *Carpathia*. I helped row in to the *Carpathia*.

Did you see any icebergs on that morning? We saw three big ones. They were quite a ways off.

I want to direct your attention again to the steerage. Do you think the passengers in the steerage and in the bow of the boat had an opportunity to get out and up on the decks, or were they held back? Yes, I think they had an opportunity to get up.

There were no gates or doors locked, or anything that kept them down? No sir, not that I could see.

You said that a number of them climbed up one of these cranes? That was on the top, on the deck; after they got on the deck. That was in order to get up on this boat deck.

On to the top deck? On to the top deck yes. But down where we were, in the rooms, I do not think there was anybody that held anybody back.

You were permitted to go aboard the boats the same as other passengers? Yes sir.

Do you think the steerage passengers in your part of the ship all got out? I could not say that for sure; but I think the most of them got out.

Did that part of the ship fill rapidly with water? Oh yes. I think that filled up, yes. There was a friend of mine told me that he went back for something he wanted, and then there was so much water there that he could not get to his room.

Were the three relatives of yours from Norway lost? Yes, they were lost.

You never saw them after you parted from them at the time you spoke of? No sir.

Do you know how many people there were in that lifeboat that you were in? I could not say for sure; but there must have been 10 or 12. They got saved off this raft. There was one man from New Jersey that I came in company with from London. I do not know what his name was. I tried to keep this man alive; but I could not make it. It was just at the break of day, and he was lying down, and he seemed to be kind of unconscious; he was not really dead, and I took him by the shoulder and raised him up, so that he was sitting up on this deck.

He was sitting on a seat? He was just sitting down right on the deck. I said to him, 'We can see a ship now. Brace up.' And I took one of his hands and raised it up, and I took him by the shoulder and shook him, and he said, 'Who are you?' He said, 'Let me be. Who are you?' I held him up like that for a while, but I got tired and cold, and I took a little piece of a small board, a lot of which were floating around there, and laid it under his head on the edge of the boat to keep his head from the water; but it was not more than about half an hour or so when he died.

62

August Weikman, Barber

Ship's barber August Weikman, aged 51, managed to climb on to a bundle of deckchairs after being washed overboard. He eventually spotted lifeboat A and paddled his 'raft' over to it and clambered in. The following is the affidavit Weikman supplied to the US Senate Inquiry.

I certify that my occupation on the *Titanic* was known as the Saloon Barber. I was sitting in my barber shop on Sunday night, 14 April 1912, at 11.40 p.m., when the collision occurred. I went forward to the steerage on G deck and saw one of the baggage-masters, and he told me that water was coming in, in the baggage room on the deck below. I think the baggage man's name was Bessant. I then went upstairs and met Mr Andrews, the 'builder,' and he was giving instructions to get the steerage passengers 'on deck.' I proceeded along E deck to my room on C deck. I went on the main deck and saw some ice laying there. Orders were given, 'All hands to man the lifeboats, also to put on lifebelts.'

Who gave the orders? *Witness answers:* Mr Dodd, Second Steward. I helped to launch the boats, and there seemed to be a shortage of women. When I was on E deck I met the Captain returning from G deck, who had been there with Mr Andrews, and the Captain was on the bridge at that time. I did not think there was any danger.

What happened after the orders were given? *Witness answers:* Instructions were given to get the passengers into lifebelts and get on deck from all the staterooms.

Did you see Mr Ismay? *Witness answers:* Yes. I saw Mr Ismay helping to load the boats.

Did you see him get in a boat? *Witness answers:* Yes, he got in along with Mr Carter, because there were no women in the vicinity of the boat. This boat was the last to leave, to the best of my knowledge. He was ordered into the boat by the officer in charge. I think that Mr Ismay was justified in getting in that boat at that time.

I was proceeding to launch the next boat when the ship suddenly sank at the bow and there was a rush of water that washed me overboard, and therefore the boat was not launched by human hands. The men were trying to pull up the sides when the rush of water came, and that was the last moment it was possible to launch any more boats, because the ship was at an angle that it was impossible for anybody to remain on deck.

State further what you know about the case. *Witness answers:* After I was washed overboard I started to swim, when there was a pile of ropes fell upon me, and I managed to get clear of these and started to swim for some dark object in the water. It was dark. This was about 1.50 a.m. toward the stern.

How do you know it was 1.50 a.m.? *Witness answers:* Because my watch was stopped at that time by the water.

Did you hear any noise? Yes. I was about 15 feet away from the ship when I heard a second explosion.

What caused the explosion? I think the boilers blew up about in the middle of the ship. The explosion blew me along with a wall of water toward the dark object I was swimming to, which proved to be a bundle of deck chairs, which I managed to climb on. While on the chairs I heard terrible groans and cries coming from people in the water.

Was it possible to help them? No it was not. The lifeboats were too far away.

Do you think if the lifeboats were nearer they could render any assistance? Yes. Had the lifeboats remained close to the *Titanic* they could have take 10 to 15 or maybe 20 more passengers to each boat. There was a great number of people killed by the explosion, and there was a great number that managed to get far enough away that the explosion did not injure them, and these are the people that I think could have been saved had the lifeboats been close.

Did you see the *Titanic* go down? Yes. I was afloat on chairs about 100 feet away, looking toward the ship. I seen her sink.

Did you feel any suction? No, but there was some waves come toward me caused by the ship going own, and not enough to knock me off of the chairs.

63

Richard Williams, First Class Passenger

Williams was a tennis player, who was travelling with his father. He went on to win the US championships in 1914 and 1916, despite having suffered damage to his legs from the icy waters at the bottom of lifeboat A. Martha Stephenson (see chapter 45) reported that Williams knocked down the door of a cabin which had a passenger trapped inside, a steward apparently threatened to report him for damage to White Star Line property.

Letter from Williams to Archibald Gracie and included in his book, The Truth About the Titanic I was not under water very long, and as soon as I came to the top I threw off the big fur coat I had on. I had put my lifebelt on under the coat. I also threw off my shoes. About 20 yards away I saw something floating. I swam to it and found it to be a collapsible boat. I hung on to it and after a while got aboard and stood up in the middle of it. The water was up to my waist. About 30 of us clung to it. When Officer Lowe's boat picked us up 11 of us were alive, all the rest were dead from cold. My fur coat was found attached to this Engelhardt boat A by the *Oceanic*, and also a cane marked 'C. Williams.' This gave rise to the story that my father's body was in this boat, but this, as you see, is not so. How the cane got there I do not know.

The *Carpathia*

The *Carpathia* was travelling from New York to Europe when Wireless Operator Harold Cottam received a distress message from the *Titanic*. The *Carpathia* set sail straight away for the *Titanic*'s last known position approximately 58 miles away. She arrived just after 4 a.m. and took on board just over 700 survivors. Survivors have nothing but praise for the way they were treated on board the *Carpathia*, but it must have been a deeply upsetting scene with survivors hoping to find their loved ones only to realise the awful truth that two thirds of *Titanic*'s passengers had not survived. The *Carpathia* arrived in New York on the evening of Thursday 18 April by which time crowds of people were waiting to meet her; relatives hoping to see their loved ones and reporters sent to interview survivors. The advent of wireless had meant that news now travelled fast and the world had been anticipating the survivors return for several days.

The *Carpathia* was torpedoed by a German U-boat in 1918. In 2000 the wreck site was discovered off the coast of Ireland. The salvage rights to *Carpathia* are owned by the same company (RMS *Titanic* Inc.) who control the rights to the wreck of *Titanic*.

64

Harold Cottam, Wireless Operator on *Carpathia*

That 21-year-old Harold Cottam picked up the *Titanic*'s distress signal was lucky. He was just about to retire for the night and leave the wireless unmanned, as was the practice of the time. Once the *Titanic* survivors were on board Cottam sent lists of surviving passengers out before the *Carpathia*'s arrival in New York. This article was another scoop for the *New York Times* and was headlined '*Titanic*'s CQD. Caught By a Lucky Fluke'.

New York Times, 19 April 1912 I got the *Titanic*'s 'CQD.' call at 11.20 p.m. New York time, on last Sunday night. It was this:

'Come at once. We've struck an berg. It's a "CQD." call, old man.'

Then the *Titanic's* operator followed with his position, which was latitude 41:46 north and longitude 50:14 west.

'Shall I go to the Captain and tell him to turn back at once?' I asked.

'Yes. Yes,' came the instant reply.

I went to the bridge and notified First Officer Dean of the call for help. He roused Captain Rostron, who was taking his turn below, and he issued orders to turn the ship about immediately.

I hurried back to my cabin, and just as I got there I heard the *Titanic* working the *Frankfurt*. The *Titanic* was having trouble getting the *Frankfurt's* signals because escaping steam and air from the expansion joint were making the signals almost indistinguishable.

I tried to get the *Frankfurt*, for he apparently only got the *Titanic's* position, but I couldn't raise him.

I think I received the CQD seven to 10 minutes after the *Titanic* struck.

It was only a streak of luck that I got the message at all, for on the previous night I had been up until 2.30 a.m. in the morning, and the night before that until 3.00 a.m., and I had planned to get to bed early that night.

I thought I'd take some general news, as I didn't know how the coal strike in England was going, and I was interested in it. When I had been taking this some time there was a batch of messages coming through for *Titanic* from the long-distance Marconi wireless station at Cape Cod, which transmits the day's news at 10.30 p.m. New York time every evening.

When Cape Cod had been going some time he started sending a batch of messages for the *Titanic*, and, having heard the *Titanic* man being pushed with work during the afternoon, I thought I'd give him a hand by taking them and retransmitting them the following morning, as I had nothing much to work on.

As I was the nearest station to the *Titanic*, it was more or less my duty to retransmit them. When Cape Cod finished I made up my daily list of communications and reported them to the officer on watch. On returning to the cabin I put the telephones on to verify a time rush which I had exchanged with the *Parisian* early that afternoon. A 'time rush' is the slang wireless word for the exchange of ship's time, which is always made when you encounter another ship to see if your clocks agree.

I put the telephones on and called the *Titanic* and asked him if he was aware that a batch of messages were being transmitted for him via Cape Cod. And his answer was:

'Come at once. We have struck a berg.'

Previous to reporting the communication to the bridge I had been in constant watch, so that I was certain that she must have struck while I was on the bridge, and that was seven to 10 minutes before.

After hearing the *Frankfurt* then, I heard the *Olympic* calling the *Titanic* with a service message, and as the *Titanic* didn't reply, apparently he couldn't hear the *Olympic*. I said to the *Titanic*:

'Don't you hear the *Olympic* calling you? Go ahead and call.'

My wireless wasn't of as late type as that aboard the *Titanic*, so that my calls would have had no effect.

The only other ship I heard at this time was the *Baltic*. She was calling Cape Race. The *Titanic* exchanged sundry signals with the *Carpathia*, but apparently the *Olympic* and the *Carpathia* were the only ships that heard them.

We steamed with every ounce of speed in us in the direction given by the *Titanic*, and we reached the spot just before dawn. One of the engineers told me that the *Carpathia* had been making between 17 and 18 knots. Her usual speed is about 13 to 14 knots.

There was a double watch of men in the engine department, and everything that could be done to hasten our arrival at the location of the *Titanic* was being done.

All this time we were hearing the *Titanic*, sending her wireless out over the sea in a last call for help.

'We are sinking fast,' was one which I picked up being sent to the *Olympic*.

The *Frankfurt* kept calling and asking us what was the matter, but though she must have been nearer to the *Titanic* than we were, she never arrived there until after we had picked up the survivors and left for New York.

Just before we reached the *Titanic* I got this message:

'Come quick. Our engine room is flooded up to the boilers.'

I answered that our boats were ready, and for them to get theirs ready also, and that we were doing out utmost to get there in time. There was no reply. It was 11.55 p.m. New York time when I got this last signal from the *Titanic*.

From 11.55 p.m. until we reached the spot where the *Titanic* foundered I was listening for a spark from his emergency set, and when I didn't hear it I was sure that he had gone down.

The first sign we got, shortly before dawn, was a green light off the port bow of the *Carpathia*. It was a beacon on one of the small boats, and we knew then that the *Titanic* had gone, but that there were survivors for us to pick up.

I was kept busy in the wireless room for the next few minutes, and the first of the rescue that I saw was a boat alongside and the passengers being hauled aboard.

Most of them were women and children. Some were crying, and they seemed overcome by the calamity. As they were raised to the deck several of them collapsed.

I saw wood and debris from the sunken *Titanic* when dawn came, but I did not see a body in the water.

Daylight showed that we were right on the scene of the disaster, for there were 10 or a dozen boats around us when it became light enough to see, and as rapidly as possible their occupants were taken aboard.

We remained near the spot, looking for additional survivors, for about three hours, and then, convinced that there was no human being alive in the sea of ice in which we floated, we started for New York.

65

Arthur Rostron, Captain of the *Carpathia*

One of the real heroes of the night, Captain Arthur Rostron's prompt actions on hearing of *Titanic*'s plight saved lives. Rostron was in the Royal Navy Reserves and went on to active service during the First World War. He was awarded the CBE in 1919. His autobiography *Home from the Sea* was published in 1931 and included the following chapter entitled *The Loss of the Titanic*.

Of the thousand pictures retained in my mind of that tragic night when the *Titanic* was lost, the first that recurs is of a man stooping as he unlaced his boots!

He was the Marconi operator on board the *Carpathia*, and if that officer had not been keen on his job, ignoring the regulation time to knock off, many of the 700-odd lives we were able to save that night might have been added to the appalling list of dead that marks the disaster as the greatest in maritime history.

In those days wireless was but a recent addition to the equipment of ships at sea. We were quite proud of our installation, though it had a normal range of only 130 miles, and just over 200 miles in exceptionally favourable circumstances.

And we carried only one operator.

This man should have finished duty at midnight. Yet here was half-past twelve and he was still listening in. But he was on the very point of retiring. He was, in fact, in the act of bending down to undo his boots when the dread call came, for in his interest he still retained the phones upon his ears.

'SOS *Titanic* calling. We have struck ice and require immediate assistance.'

One can imagine him jerking upright, the alarm growing in his mind, though to be sure, in those first minutes, we none of us permitted our fears to embrace so devastating an accident as it was destined to prove. But it was the *Titanic*, a mammoth ship, proudful in her size and power, carrying over 2,000 souls and making her maiden voyage from England to America! That was sufficient to impress on the operator the magnitude of the danger and, throwing the earphones to the table, he raced to the first officer who was on watch at the time.

It is a dramatic thought, that if the signal had been two or three minutes later we should not have picked it up!

The news was at once brought to me. Curious how trivial things stamp themselves on the mind in moments of crisis. I can remember my door opening – the door near the head of my bunk which communicated with the chart room. I had but recently turned in and was not asleep, and drowsily I said to myself: 'Who the dickens is this cheeky beggar coming into my cabin without knocking?'

Then the first officer was blurting out the facts and you may be sure I was very soon wide awake, with thoughts for nothing but doing all that was in the ship's power to render the aid called for.

So incredible seemed the news that, having at once given orders to turn the ship – we were bound from New York to Gibraltar and other Mediterranean ports, while the *Titanic* was passing us westward bound, sixty miles to our nor'ard – I got hold of the Marconi operator and assured myself there could have been no mistake.

'Are you sure it is the *Titanic* that requires immediate assistance?' I asked him.

'Yes, sir.'

But I had to ask again. 'You are absolutely certain?' for remember, the wireless was not at the pitch of perfection and reliability it is today.

'Quite certain,' he replied.

'All right,' I said then. 'Tell him we are coming along as fast as we can.'

I went into the chart-room, having obtained from the operator the *Titanic's* position. It was Lat. 41° 46' N., Long. 50° 14' W.

I at once worked out the course and issued orders. Within a few minutes of the call we were steaming all we knew to the rescue. The *Carpathia* was a 14 knot ship, but that night for three and a half hours she worked up to 17 knots. One of the first things I did, naturally, was to get up the chief engineer, explain the urgency of matters and, calling out an extra watch in the engine room, every ounce of power was got from the boilers and every particle of steam used for the engines, turning it from all other uses, such as heating.

Fortunately it was night – fortunately, I mean, from one aspect – all our passengers were in their bunks. Many never woke until the drama had been played out, because one of my first instructions was that, as far as possible, absolute silence should be maintained, while every man was told to instruct any passengers seen about to return to their cabins and stay there.

There was much to be done. All hands were called, and then began over three hours of restless activity and never-ending anxiety.

For though, as I say, it was fortunate that our passengers were asleep, the covering of night added to the risks we had to take. Ice! Racing through the dark towards we knew not what danger from bergs, standing on the bridge with everyone keeping a bright look out, I was fully conscious of the danger my own ship and passengers were sharing.

I may say now that the spring of that year was phenomenal in regard to ice. The *Titanic* was on her right course, a course where, it is true, one at times may see ice, but that night was so exceptional as to be unique in anyone's memory. The reason was that two summers before the season had been unusually warm in the far north. Islands of ice had broken adrift from their polar continent and come drifting south. It took two years for these giant remnants to work their way so far south and we were to be amazed when daylight broke to find on every hand berg and floe stretching as far as the eye could reach.

Into that zone of danger we raced the *Carpathia*, every nerve strained watching for the ice. Once I saw one huge fellow towering into the sky quite near – saw it because a star was reflected on its surface – a tiny beam of warning which guided us safely past. If only some such friendly star had glistened into the eyes of the lookout on the *Titanic* … Ah, well, it was not to be.

Before I could take the bridge, however, there were a thousand and one things to be done. They started at once. Even as I stood in the chart room working out the position I saw the bosun's mate pass with the watch off to wash down decks. I called him, told him to knock off routine work and get all our boats ready for lowering, not making any noise. Questioning surprise leapt into his eyes.

'It's all right,' I assured him. 'We are going to another vessel in distress.'

The first officer I called, as I said, was the engineer. Speed was the imperative need. When he had gone to turn out his extra watch – and as soon as the men heard what was wanted and why, many of them went to work without waiting to dress; good fellows! – I had up the English doctor, purser and chief steward and to these I gave the instructions which follow:

The English doctor to remain in the first class dining room; the Italian doctor in the second class dining room and the Hungarian doctor in the third. All to have ready supplies of stimulants, restoratives and other necessities.

Purser, with his assistant purser and chief steward, to receive the rescued at the different gangways, controlling our own stewards in assisting the *Titanic* passengers to the different dining rooms for accommodation and attention. They also to get as far as possible names of survivors, to be sent by wireless.

The inspector, steerage stewards and masters-at-arms to control our own steerage passengers, keep them out of the third class dining hall and to restrain them from going on deck. Chief steward to call all hands and have coffee ready for our men and soup, coffee, tea, etc., for the rescued. Blankets to be placed ready near gangways, in saloons and public rooms and others handy for the boats. All spare berths in steerage to be prepared for *Titanic's* third class passengers while our own steerage occupants were to be grouped together.

To all it was enjoined that the strictest silence and discipline should be maintained, while a steward was to be stationed in each gangway to reassure our own passengers should any hear noise and inquire – such inquirers to be asked politely but firmly to return to, and remain, in their own cabins.

Here I might interpolate the experience of Mr and Mrs Louis Ogden, friends of mine who were on board that night. They occupied a deck cabin and it was only to be expected that they should hear something of the preparations that were going forward. Their experience was duplicated many times, of course, by other passengers, though, while all these things being done, the great majority of those on board slept peacefully, unaware of our exertions. A great credit to the crew.

Mr Ogden told me later that during that night his wife woke and aroused him.

'What's that noise on deck?' she asked,

'Don't worry; go to sleep,' – the average man's reply to the anxious wife at such an hour. But, like other ladies, she was not to be so summarily silenced.

'Open the door and see what's wrong.'

Mr Ogden obeyed the injunction. Outside was a steward. Mr Ogden called him.

'What's the noise all about?' he asked.

'Nothing, sir; doing work with the boats.'

'What for?' Mr Ogden was growing interested.

'I can't tell you, sir.'

Mr Ogden retired and quite naturally only made his wife's suspicions increase. She waited a few minutes listening to the noises which were inevitable as our boats were swung out on their davits.

'Try again,' she requested at length.

This time Mr Ogden, peeping out, encountered the surgeon.

'What's the trouble?'

'There's no trouble. Please return to your cabin. It is the Captain's orders.'

Which didn't allay doubts. Going back and repeating the conversation to his wife, they both began to dress, putting their valuables in their pockets. Then the lady's insistence recommenced.

'Try again.'

Once more Mr Ogden opened the door – and, curiously enough, he again looked into the face of the surgeon. No need for questions, the surgeon ordered him back and told him on no account to leave the cabin until the Captain gave instructions. But the passenger was urgent and at length, as the only method of satisfying him, the surgeon said: 'We are going to the *Titanic*. She's in distress.'

'But isn't this ship in distress?'

'No sir, it's the *Titanic*, she's struck ice.' But then Mr Ogden saw stewards in line carrying pillows and blankets.

'There's something wrong,' he concluded. And somehow he and Mrs Ogden reached the deck. There they found some nook or corner and remained through the hours until, with the coming of the first gleams of dawn, they saw the ice and eventually the first boat.

Meanwhile, we were ploughing on through the night – a brilliant night of stars. I had been able to go to the bridge.

To me there the Marconi operator came reporting he had picked up a message from the *Titanic* to the *Olympic* asking the latter to have all her boats ready. The sense of tragedy was growing. But the *Olympic*, homeward bound, was hundreds of miles away, very much farther than we were. The *Titanic* had also called us. They asked how long we should be getting up.

'Say about four hours,' I told the operator (we did it in three and a half hours), 'and tell her we shall have all our boats in readiness and all other preparations necessary to receive the rescued.'

I then gave the following orders to the first officer:

Prepare and swing out all boats; all gangway doors to be opened.

Electric clusters at each gangway and over the side.

A block – with line rope – hooked in each gangway.

A chair – slung – at each gangway for getting up sick or injured.

Pilot ladders and side ladders at gangways and over the side.

Cargo falls, with both ends clear and bight secured, along ship's side on deck, for boat ropes or to help people up.

Lines and gaskets to be distributed about the decks to be handy for lashings, etc.

Forward derricks to be rigged and topped and steam on winches – to get mails or other goods on board.

Oil to be poured down lavatories both sides to quiet the sea.

Canvas ash-bags to be near gangways for the purpose of hauling up children or helpless.

Company's rockets to be fired from 3 a.m. every quarter of an hour to reassure the *Titanic*.

And, beyond these, detailed instructions as to the various duties of the officers should the situation require the service of our boats.

At about 2.35 a.m. – roughly two hours after the first call – the doctor came to the bridge and reported that all instructions were carried out and everything was in readiness.

While we were talking together I saw a green flare about a point on our port bow.

'There's her light,' I cried, pointing. 'She must be still afloat.'

This looked like good news. An hour before the Marconi operator had brought me a message from the *Titanic* that the engine room was filling. That had looked fatal. It left little doubt that she was going down. So to catch that green flare brought renewed hope.

Almost at once the second officer reported the first iceberg. It lay two points on the port bow and it was the one whose presence was betrayed by the star beam. More and more now were we all keyed up. Icebergs loomed up and fell astern; we never slackened, though sometimes we altered course suddenly to avoid them. It was an anxious time with the *Titanic's* fateful experience very close in our minds. There were 700 souls on the *Carpathia*; these lives, as well as all the survivors of the *Titanic* herself, depended on a sudden turn of the wheel.

As soon as there was a chance that we were in view, we started sending up rockets at intervals of about a quarter of an hour and, when still nearer, fired the company's roman candles (night signals) to let them know it was the *Carpathia* that was approaching. Occasionally we caught sight of a green light; we were getting pretty near the spot.

By this time the hope that their green signals had at first bred in us was gone. There was no sign of the *Titanic* herself. By now – it was about 3.35 a.m. – we were almost up to the position and had the giant liner been afloat we should have seen her. The skies were clear, the stars gleaming with that brightness which only a keen frosty air brings to them, and visibility was as good as it could be on a moonless night. I put the engines on the 'stand by' so that the engineers should be on the alert for instant action. At four o'clock I stopped the engines; we were there.

As if in corroboration of that judgment, I saw a green light just ahead of us, low down. That must be a boat [it was lifeboat 2] I knew and, just as I was planning to come alongside, I saw a big berg immediately in front of us – the second officer reporting it at the same moment. I had meant to take the boat on the port side, which was the lee side if anything, though there was not much wind or sea. But the iceberg altered the plan. It was necessary to move with the utmost expedition. I swung the ship round and so came alongside the first of the *Titanic's* boats on the starboard side.

Devoutly thankful I was that the long race was over; every minute had brought its risk – a risk that only keen eyes and quick decisions could meet – but with that feeling was the veritable ache which the now certain knowledge of the liner's loss brought. No sign of her – and below was the first boat containing survivors.

A hail came up from her. 'We have only one seaman in the boat and cannot work very well.'

They were a little way off our gangway.

'All right,' I told them and brought the vessel right alongside. Then they started climbing aboard. Obviously they had got away in a hurry, for there were only 25 of them whereas the capacity of the boat was fully 40. They were in charge of one officer.

I asked that this officer should come to me as soon as he was on board and to him I put that heart-rending inquiry, knowing with a terrible certainty what his answer was to be.

'The *Titanic* has gone down?'

'Yes,' he said; one word that meant so much so much that the man's voice broke on it. 'She went down at about 2.30 a.m.'

An hour and a half ago! Alas, that we had not been nearer!

But there was no time for vain regrets. Daylight was just setting in and what a sight that new day gradually revealed! Everywhere were icebergs. About a third of a mile on our starboard beam was the one that a few minutes ago had faced us; less than 100 feet off our port quarter was a growler – a broken-off lump of ice 10 to 15 feet high and 25 feet long. But stretching as far as the eye could reach were masses of them. I instructed a junior officer to go to the wheel house deck and count them. 25 there were, over 200 feet in height, and dozens ranging from 150 down to 50 feet.

And amid the tragic splendour of them as they lay in the first shafts of the rising sun, boats of the lost ship floated. From that moment we went on picking them up and as the rescued came aboard their thankfulness for safety was always mingled with the sense of their loss and the chattering cold that possessed them. Many of the women had been hours in those open boats, shielded from the almost Arctic cold only by a coat hastily thrown over night clothes – telling of the urgency with which they had left the ship, suggesting to the imagination awful long-drawn-out anxiety before the slips were loosed and the boat was on the water and away.

Slowly we cruised from boat to boat and as we neared the end of our questing, one gathered the enormity of the disaster. Altogether we picked up 706 persons; but on the *Titanic* crew and passengers numbered over 2,000 – so many hundreds lost who a few short hours before had been members of a gay and distinguished company – halfway through the maiden voyage of one of the world's largest liners!

While we slowly cruised, we held a service in the first class dining room – in memory of those who were lost and giving thanks for those who had been saved.

Except for the boats beside the ship and the icebergs, the sea was strangely empty. Hardly a bit of wreckage floated – just a deckchair or two, a few lifebelts, a good deal of cork; no more flotsam than one can often see on a seashore drifted in by the tide. The ship had plunged at the last, taking everything with her. I saw only one body in the water; the intense cold made it hopeless for anyone to live long in it.

It was not for us to remain, especially as about this time – eight o'clock – we saw another ship coming up. This was the *Californian*. She carried no wireless and all the night had been lying not many miles away, hove to because of the ice. We signalled her now, asking her to continue searching as we were about to make for New York. The sea was rising and I was anxious to get well away from that danger zone in good daylight. So we got as many of the *Titanic's* boats as we could on board, some remaining suspended in our davits, others hauled on the forecastle head, and proceeded.

I may mention here that during the work of getting the boats alongside I happened to look down from the bridge and saw my friend Mr Ogden. The day before he had been trying a new camera he had with him. So I cupped my hands and shouted down: 'What about that new camera?' He glanced my way, threw up his hands as if to say he had never thought of it, sped off and in a few minutes was taking snaps of the boats as they came alongside. They are the only authentic records of the occasion and surely an amateur photographer never had a more thrilling scene to take! The *Carpathia* had stopped in mid-Atlantic. It was a beautiful morning, a clear sun burning on sea and glistening on the icebergs. On every side there were dozens of these monsters, so wonderful to look at, so dreadful to touch. Some boats containing the survivors were alongside; people were climbing up the ship's side, others being pulled up; all wearing lifebelts (and incidentally it was the wearing of these that protected those who had been so long exposed in the boats and prevented many from dangerous chills) ; and then, from every quarter, boats were pulling in, all making for one common objective – the *Carpathia*.

One thing stands out in my mind about it all – the quietness. There was no noise, no hurry. When our passengers at length came on deck they were some time before they seemed to realise the stupendous nature of the tragedy; it was too big to assimilate at once. Their hardly-awakened senses could not respond to the immensity of the scene. But as soon as reality followed on questionings, I must say our people understood that they must not remain spectators; that here was a situation unparalleled in which they must play a part. They set about comforting the rescued, persuading them to take nourishment or stimulant, seeking to soften the grief which wrapped them round about. Our doctors must have been relieved to see our passengers using their persuasion and common sense so successfully.

They saw the survivors required dry and warm clothing, so off they took them to their own cabins to fit them out with everything they could. All our men passengers gave up their cabins and many of the ladies doubled up with others so as to leave their own quarters free for the distressed. Every officer, of course, yielded his accommodation.

In my cabin were three ladies, each of whom were bereaved. Their husbands, all millionaires, had perished and, in addition, one lady had lost a son. On the other hand, one had her son with her whose saving had that touch of the dramatic that was in evidence time and again that night.

This boy [Jack Thayer] had been separated from his mother but later on had found a place in a collapsible boat. These things are like ordinary boats as to the hull except that they are flat-bottomed and their sides are canvas and can be folded down. The sides of the one this boy was in collapsed [not collapsed, this was the *upturned* collapsible B] for some reason and he, with others, was kneeling on the hull. His position was even more precarious than it sounds, for, since they were helpless to propel it in any way, the boat was floating in the near vicinity of the liner and couldn't move away. It was right under her stern and from this boy I heard a graphic account of how the *Titanic* up-ended herself and remained poised like some colossal nightmare of a fish, her tail high in the air her nose deep in the water, until she dived finally from human sight.

That collapsible was fortunate not to have been sucked down with the ship, probably the suction was lessened by reason of the pause and then the sliding movement she took; at all events, the helpless boat merely bobbed a little dangerously and remained afloat.

In a little while a ship's boat came near. It was hailed and the boy was taken into her. And the first person whom he saw in this rescuing boat was his own mother. Imagine the joy of that meeting.

But it was more than matched by another, rather similar, episode of that night.

Some of the first boats may have got away not filled to capacity, but later others certainly were overloaded and there were heart-rending moments when too-well-laden boats pulling about encountered poor fellows swimming in that ice-cold sea.

In this case I am recounting a boat's gunwale was seized for'ard by a swimmer [probably Frederick Hoyt, though the story here differs a little from Hoyt's own account]. It was well before dawn. No one could see who it was, but many voices were raised protesting against him being hauled in.

'We are full; we are full,' they cried. 'Don't let him come in!'

One woman in the stern sheets, however, nursing her sorrow of a husband left behind on the sunken ship, begged for the swimmer to be taken in. The pity in her pleading prevailed and she knew the swimmer had been saved before she sank back into the frozen coma that great tragedy engenders.

Hours passed. At length dawn lit the haggard faces of those who huddled shivering in that boat. Only then did the woman see the features of the drenched man she had been chiefly instrumental in dragging from a death by drowning.

It was her own husband.

It stirred the heart to see the fortitude of the bereaved, just as it sent a glow of pride to listen to some of the tales that were gradually revealed by the survivors of the sights that had been witnessed during those last hours on the sinking ship. Tales of bravery and self-sacrifice that add lustre to the human story, shown by every class. In those hours of trial, facing death, men were equal in heroism, whether they were the humblest or such as had much of this world's possessions. And one wondered, looking into the troubled and sometimes vacant faces of those who were saved, whether they or those left behind had the harder part to play. But it is sure that there were many that night who, loaded with riches and honours, showed they possessed the greater gifts of self-sacrifice and self-command.

We heard then and later of tales of the famous, tales, too, of the unknown. Of them all one remains warm in my memory. It concerns a young girl.

A boat full of women was ready for lowering from the stricken ship. It was found to be too full and the order was given for someone to get out. What a moment! But it had to be done, for the overfull boat endangered the lives of all. A young lady – a girl really – got up to leave the boat. At once some of the others protested, pleading that she should stay.

'No,' she said, 'you are married and have families. I'm not; it doesn't matter about me.'

She stepped out of the boat and returned to the deck. She went down with the ship. She gave her life that others might live. No words of mine can add to the beauty of that action. But that night it was duplicated a hundred times as the boats went off – until there were no more to go and those who remained knew all hope of safety was dissipated.

The night and the morning were crowded with incidents. Here is one that shows how truth can indeed be stranger than fiction. It also throws a light on the amazing quietness and smoothness with which the crew of the *Carpathia* went about their task of preparation and rescue.

We had sailed from New York on 11 April 1912. It had been a pleasant and smooth passage save for the intense cold, upon which we all remarked. On the Sunday – three days out – we were in reach by wireless of the *Titanic*. At dinner that night a message was received from that ship – a private communication. It came from two young ladies who were aboard her and was addressed to their uncle and aunt – Mr and Mrs Marshall – who were on the *Carpathia*. Just a cheery greeting, saying how they were enjoying the crossing on the new ship.

It was that same night she went down.

The Marshalls knew nothing of it. They retired to their state cabin; they went to sleep. The night was calm, the sea smooth, they slept on all through the preparations that were going on aboard. But among the first of the survivors who came up one of the gangways were the two nieces who a few hours before had been wirelessing from the *Titanic* to the Marshalls. While the latter had been sleeping, these young ladies had been through all the agony of the night.

It was about half-past six when the Marshalls awoke. A steward knocking on their door aroused them.

'What is it?' asked Mr Marshall.

'Your nieces wish to see you, sir,' replied the steward.

No wonder he was dumbfounded; hardly believing his eyes when he opened the door and looked upon the girls, not crediting his senses as he listened to their story.

Looking back on that morning I am persuaded to emphasise again as the outstanding feature the silence on board. There was absolutely no excitement. At first no doubt the enormity of the occurrence stunned the sensibilities of our passengers when they knew of it, while the rescued came solemnly, dumbly, out of a shivering shadow. Afterwards everyone was too occupied to think.

The ladies were very soon self-appointed nursing sisters, getting the newcomers to lie abed, others to rest on deck, and doing what they could to ease suffering and console. As many of the second and third class passengers who came aboard were but poorly clothed, blankets and sheets were requisitioned and many of the ladies started to make clothes. Others went to the third class and busied themselves nursing, clothing and feeding the children. The cream of human kindness was surely extended that morning and during the days that followed while we made New York, and through it all that quietness reigned – as though the disaster were so great that it silenced human emotion. It seems incredible that the trying experiences through which so many had passed should not have developed hysterical trouble, in some at least, but it didn't. Indeed, on Tuesday morning Dr McGee came to me and made the satisfactory report that 'all the survivors were physically well!' Marvellous!

I knew that was the reward of endless attention on his part and that of the entire staff. No one relinquished their utmost efforts. Loyally and cheerfully every member of the crew, both officers and men, gave of their best. Doctors, pursers, steward – even the little bell-boys – all entertained no thought of rest from the moment I issued my first orders until we had landed the survivors in New York and had again left to take up our interrupted voyage to the Mediterranean.

In all that large assembly of differing human beings I heard of only one instance of selfishness. A certain foreigner who had come aboard bedded himself down in one of the smoke rooms. With an acquisitive eye, and a disregard of others, he had obtained several blankets for his own comfort. These were draped round his portly figure when other men found they were devoid of any. He was asked to share up, but adopted that old motto of 'What I have I hold.' There was a small council of war among a few men. But the war was soon over – and the blankets distributed.

Which reminds me of another incident in lighter vein – for in the human drama, however near the tragic, there always seems to shoot a ray or two of humour. The man himself told me the experience later and, with the heaviness of the immediate worry off my mind, I couldn't help laughing at the picture his tale called up.

It seems that he, having given up his cabin, was bedless. He wandered about the ship looking for some niche in which to curl up when, mirabile! he espied an empty mattress with some blankets handy. With a sigh of relief he lay down, pulled the blankets over his head and went peacefully to sleep. Can you imagine his disconcerted surprise when in the morning he woke up to find himself entirely surrounded by women? He had camped himself out in a portion of the ship which had been reserved for the rescued ladies and had lain there unnoticed through the night. His retreat was more hurried than strategic.

Well, having left the *Californian* in charge of the search – hopeless as it was that any man could live in that ice-cold sea – we started on our return. We soon found our passage blocked by a tremendous icefield. There surely never was so much ice in that latitude. We had, of course, seen this field before, but had no means of knowing how compact it was or what was its extent. All we could see was that it stretched to the horizon – a remarkable awesome sight with great bergs up to 200 feet in height standing out of the general field, which, itself, was six to 12 feet above the waterline. These little mountains were just catching the early sunshine which made them take on all manner of wonderful aspects. Minarets like cathedral towers turned to gold in the distances and, here and there, some seemed to shape themselves like argosies under full sail.

For nearly four hours we sailed round this pack – quite 56 miles. Then we were clear and could set our course for New York.

I ought to mention that the *Olympic*, which at the time of the disaster was some hundreds of miles to the westward, having left New York on the Saturday, had wirelessed suggesting she should take off the rescued. But I was against any such move. Fortunately, Mr Ismay, the chairman of the White Star Line, was among those saved, and when I informed him, suggesting that it would be unwise to endeavour to tranship these poor people who had just been saved from the boats, he at once agreed and told me to request the *Olympic* to keep out of sight. So on we went, still passing other isolated bergs from time to time. I remember that about noon we passed the Russian steamer *Burmah* who, bound east, made an endeavour to cut through that icepack. But he turned out again and I didn't blame him either!

We were able to communicate to the *Olympic* the bare facts of the disaster, and I also sent the official message to the Cunard Company together with as many names of the survivors as we then had. This offered the first chance we had of dispatching the news to shore. It was – owing to the short range of wireless then in operation

– also the last opportunity we had of establishing communication until Wednesday afternoon, and then we learned how the world had waited in suspense for details and especially a correct and complete list of passengers and crew who had been saved.

After the ice, we ran into that other great enemy of ships at sea fog. For hours it enshrouded us, and again on Wednesday it came down thick, continuing more or less all the way to New York. The dismal nerve-racking noise of the whistle every half-minute must have been particularly distressing to the survivors, and I was sorry for their state of mind, having encountered this after all their other experiences.

We had taken three bodies from the boats and one man died during the forenoon on Monday. All four were buried on Monday afternoon, Protestant and Roman Catholic services being held over them.

During Wednesday afternoon we were in communication with USS *Chester* – dense fog at the time – and through her were able to send a more complete list of survivors and corrections. We picked up Fire Island light-vessel from its foghorn on the afternoon of Thursday 18 April and, about six, stopped off Ambrose Channel lightship and took on our pilot. And now we got some idea of that suspense everyone was in. Press boats literally surrounded us!

I decided that these journalists must not come on board. The comfort of the rescued had to be the first consideration. To have them interviewed by dozens of alert young newspaper men, eager to get the most lurid details, would cause endless distress, making them live it all over again. It was, of course, only in the nature of the reporters' jobs to get news, and when I told them they would not be allowed on board it was amusing to see the tactics some of them adopted to defeat my ruling.

These press boats carried huge placards announcing this was from such and such a paper and that from another. They badgered and pleaded to be allowed to interview me and the passengers, but I could not oblige. Two pressmen adopted the ruse of coming in the pilot's boat. Now he was a friend of mine, and it was not easy to give him a straight refusal.

'Can these fellows come aboard?' he yelled.

I cupped my hands and sang out: 'I can't hear you.'

'They want to come aboard. They have friends on the ship.'

'I can't hear what you say,' I shouted and they knew, I guess, I was prevaricating. When the pilot had the ladder down, however, I expected they would try to get on board after him. So I had a rope bent from the bottom of the ladder and set two boys to haul it in as the pilot came up. You can see what happened. The moment the pilot had lifted his foot from one rung to the next, the boys drew in the rope and the ladder was hoisted right under the man's heels. One of the two in his boat made a jump and tried to follow, but the ladder wasn't there and he fell backwards.

Of them all one pressman only got aboard. That was later, after we were stopped off quarantine. He made a jump that risked his life and landed on the deck. This was reported to me and I had him brought to the bridge. I explained my reasons for not having anyone on board and that I could not allow the passengers to be interviewed. I put him on his honour not to leave the bridge under certain penalties and, I must say, he was a gentleman. After we had docked and the passengers had left I know he made a good story out of his exploit, being the only man to get aboard, and I believe he got complimented – which, after all, he deserved for his temerity.

But before we got to quarantine, the weather made another violent change. It brought the most dramatic ending to the tragic episode. First it began to blow hard, then the rain tumbled down and, as a finale, as though the curtain had to come down under unusual surroundings, it commenced to lightning. Vivid flashes accompanied us all the way up the channel to quarantine and heavy thunder-claps rolled across the skies. This weather held until we were off the Cunard dock.

While on the bridge in the pelting rain a bundle of letters and a number of telegrams were brought to me. I couldn't examine them at the moment and put them in my pocket. During a lull, later on, I ran into my chartroom, dipped a hand into my rather full pocket and drew out one item – only one. It was a cable and came from my wife! Quite satisfied I returned to my bridge.

It was a scene never to be forgotten. Press photographers on the dock let off their flashlights. All round the ship were dozens of tugboats and, before we could tie up, all the *Titanic's* boats had to be lowered because they were in the way of working the mooring ropes. In each of those boats went two of the *Titanic's* rescued crew and to see them pull into the pitchy night brought back to one's mind again the last occasion when they had been lowered from their own great and magnificent mother ship which was destined never to arrive at this harbour.

After nine o'clock at night they left us – those who had come out of the terror of shipwreck – and no one was more glad than I to see them passing on to the land. Not, of course, that they personally were well rid of, but to think that the long guardianship was over and they were safe. We had all been strained to the highest pitch of anxiety and the extent of that concern was now the measure of our relief. The job was done. We at once thought of our own affairs. We had set out to make the Mediterranean; we had a fairly full complement of passengers. I hastily replenished linen, blankets, etc., that the interruption had utilised, from a sister ship, and that same Thursday afternoon – exactly a week from the time of our previous sailing – we left the dock, restored, watered and coaled, and – went on with our job. One of our passengers left us, but we took on two fresh ones so that we had a gain of one!

It had been, indeed, an eventful week – eventful in the history of shipping, it was to prove. One of the results was that the Board of Trade made new regulations that on every ship at sea there were to be carried sufficient boats to accommodate all passengers and crew. Today it seems incredible that it needed this appalling calamity to bring in such a regulation – and it hardly bears thinking about that if there had been sufficient boats that night when the *Titanic* was lost every soul aboard could have been saved, since it was two-and-a-half hours after she struck that she tilted her mammoth stern into the heavens and sank by the head, taking with her all that were unprovided for. Now, yonder from Portsmouth even on the little ferry boats that ply between port and the Isle of Wight there are lifesaving appliances for all the passengers the ferries can hold.

One other good thing resulted from the disaster. Supported by both Britain and America, there is now a constant ice patrol – from March to July or August – always watching along the latitudes where sometimes the ice reaches – and reporting to all shipping whenever there floats out of the icy maw of the far north bergs which might bring to some other ill-fated ship the calamity which met the *Titanic*.

Titanic! Of all the remarkable incidents connected with the short life of that ship of destiny not the least was her name. If you look in your dictionary you will find: Titans - race of people vainly striving to overcome the forces of nature.

Could anything be more unfortunate than such a name, anything more significant?

That would seem to be the natural end to the story. Yet for me the repercussions went on for some time. Having refueled, filled up our water tanks and so on, we took up our interrupted voyage. In July I returned to England overland from Naples to attend the inquiry held in London into the *Titanic's* loss; then followed several weeks of holiday. It was in December that I left the *Carpathia*, leaving on board the testimonials with which we had been presented by the rescued. There followed a round of social functions. I had to be in Washington on 2 March to receive from the hands of President Taft the Congressional Medal of Honour 'with the thanks of Congress.' The British Ambassador, Lord Bryce, took us to the White House to receive this, the highest honour the United States Government can bestow, and afterwards we returned to the British Embassy where I was presented with the American Cross of Honour. My wife and I had a royal time for a few days and then returned in the *Mauretania* – the *Mauretania* which I was to command so long and through such exciting times.

And it was during those exciting times of the war which were soon to be upon us that the gallant *Carpathia* was to end her days. She was torpedoed in May 1918, off the south of Ireland. It was a sorry end to a fine ship, yet it is a fitting end to my tale of her career. She had done her bit both in peace and war, and she lies in her natural element, resting her long rest on a bed of sand.

Further Reading

Books

Unless otherwise stated, place of publication is London

Nick Barratt, *Lost Voices From the Titanic: The Definitive Oral History*, first published Preface Publishing 2009. An excellent compilation, strong on letters written by survivors.

W. B. Bartlett, *Titanic: 9 Hours to Hell the Survivors Story*, first published Amberley Publishing, Stroud 2010. Narrative account of the disaster concentrating on the events of the 14/15 April. Very detailed and weaves into the story survivor testimony.

Lawrence Beesley, *The Loss of the SS Titanic: Its Story & Its Lessons By One of the Survivors*, first published Houghton Mifflin, New York 1912 / William Heinemann Ltd, London 1912. Equally as important as Gracie, this memoir was by an Englishman, travelling second class.

Bruce Beveridge, Daniel Klistorner, Steve Hall and Scott Andrews, *Titanic: The Ship Magnificent: Volume 1: Design and Construction, Volume 2: Interior Design and Fitting Out*, both first published History Press, Stroud 2008,. The definitive two-volume book on the construction of the *Titanic* with hundreds of photographs.

Marshall Everett, *The Wreck & Sinking of the Titanic*, first published L. H. Walter 1912. An instant book, similar in character to Logan Marshall.

Archibald Gracie, *The Truth About the Titanic*, first published Mitchell Kennerley, New York 1913, republished Amberley 2009. One of the two most important memoirs written by *Titanic* survivors, in this case an American first class passenger.

Eva Hart (edited by Ron Denney), *Shadow of the Titanic: A Survivor's Story*, first published Greenwich University Press 1994. Memoir by a survivor who was a girl of seven when the *Titanic* sank. Invaluable child's-eye view of the disaster although was written up long after the event. Currently available in a new expanded edition under the title *A Girl Aboard the Titanic*, Amberley 2011.

Donald Hyslop, Alastair Forsyth, Sheila Jemina, *Titanic Voices: Memories from the Fateful Voyage*, first published Southampton City Council 1994. Book of the *Titanic Voices* exhibition held at Southampton Maritime Museum in 1992. A very useful compilation of survivor accounts, many rare and specific to Southampton. Very well illustrated.

Violet Jessop (edited by John Maxtone-Graham), *Titanic Survivor: The Newly Discovered Memoirs of Violet Jessop Who Survived Both the Titanic and Britannic Disasters*, first published Sheridan House New York 1997. Excellent and interesting but only about 10 per cent of the book is about her *Titanic* experience. Currently available under the title *Titanic Survivor: The Memoirs of Violet Jessop Stewardess*.

Tom Kuntz, *The Titanic Disaster Hearings: The Official Transcripts of the 1912 Senate Inquiry*, first published Pocket Books, New York 1998. Very handy 600-page compendium of edited testimony delivered to the US inquiry.

Jack Lawrence, *When the Ships Came In*, first published Farrar & Rinehart, New York 1940. Autobiography by the ship news reporter of the *New York Times*, contains fascinating insights into the real world of the transatlantic liner industry.

Charles Lightoller, *Titanic & Other Ships*, first published Nicolson & Watson 1939. The Second Officer's autobiography includes five chapters on the *Titanic*. Essential reading. The book was quickly withdrawn after Marconi threatened to sue. Despite this publisher's efforts to arrange a new edition with the literary estate, no agreement has been forthcoming. Several 'bootleg' editions are available on the internet.

Walter Lord, *A Night To Remember: The Minute-by-Minute Story of the Sinking of the Titanic*, first published 1955. The first proper history of the *Titanic* disaster. A bestseller, it was translated into several languages and was made into the film of the same name. Still excellent half a century on.

Geoffrey Marcus, *The Maiden Voyage*, first published 1969. A good solid history of the disaster.

Logan Marshall, *The Sinking of the Titanic*, first published L. T. Myers 1912. One of the 'instant books' published in the USA to cash in on the huge interest in the *Titanic* disaster. Full of survivor testimony, some more reliable than others. Reputedly sold over 400,000 copies.

Louise Patten, *Good as Gold*, first published Quercus 2010. Although a work of fiction, Lady Patten (Charles Lightoller's granddaughter) chose this book to air some of her family's secrets. These sensational claims that the 'hard a-starboard' order was misinterpreted by the Quartermaster Robert Hichens and that he turned the ship right instead of left were splashed all over the British media and deserve further investigation.

Arthur Rostron, *Home from the Sea*, first published Cassell 1931. The captain of the *Carpathia's* autobiography. Now available again as *Titanic Hero: The Autobiography of Captain Rostron of the Titanic* (Amberley Publishing, Stroud 2011).

Jack Thayer, *The Sinking of the SS Titanic, April 14-15, 1912*, privately published 1940, USA. A valuable account now available in an edition published by Academy Chicago Publishers.

Titanic: The Official Inquiry, first published Public Record Office 1999. Transcript of the British Board of Trade inquiry, almost 1,000 pages.

Titanic Disaster: Hearings before a Subcommittee of the Committee on Commerce, United States Senate, Sixty-Second Congress, Second Session, Pursuant to S. Res. 283, Directing the Committee on Commerce to Investigate the Causes Leading to the Wreck of the White Star Liner 'Titanic'. The transcripts of the Senate inquiry, which were published in 1912 and are over 1,100 pages long. Issued as Senate Document 726, 62nd Congress, 2nd session.

Titanic: The True Story, 1999 CD-ROM, PRO Publications. Produced by the UK Public Record Office (renamed National Archives) at Kew. Includes both the British and American Inquiry transcripts.

Jack Winocour (editor), *The Story of the Titanic as Told by its Survivors*, first published Dover Publications 1960. An anthology of key survivor accounts (Gracie, Beesley, Lightoller and Bride's *New York Times* article), still in print today.

Filson Young, *Titanic*, first published Grant Richards 1912. Britain's 'instant book' on the *Titanic* disaster but written by a respected author. Republished in 2011 by Amberley Publishing.

Websites

www.encyclopedia-titanica.org. A fabulous resource of all things *Titanic*.

www.titanicinquiry.org. Contains the transcripts of the British and American inquiries, an invaluable aid to research.

http://dsc.discovery.com/convergence/titanic/explorer/explorer.html. Explore the original blueprints of *Titanic*, deck by deck.

http://www.bbc.co.uk/archive/titanic/. Several audio recordings of *Titanic* survivors recalling their experiences from the BBC's archives.

Societies & Museums

Merseyside Maritime Museum, Liverpool. Holds a small but significant collection of records. Details include photographs of the *Titanic*, survivors' accounts, papers relating to Stanley Lord, captain of the SS *Californian* and the *Titanic* Signals Archive.

National Maritime Museum, Greenwich, London. Major source of records on *Titanic*, including Walter Lord's research papers for his book *A Night To Remember*, which including his correspondence with survivors.

Southampton Maritime Museum. Has a permanent exhibition devoted to the Southampton crew aboard *Titanic* and their families.

RMS *Titanic*, Inc. (a subsidiary of Premier Exhibitions, Inc.). A commercial company created to recover, conserve and display artefacts from the *Titanic* wreck. *Titanic: The Artifact Exhibition* has been seen by more than 25 million visitors worldwide and is currently running in London, Las Vegas and several other major cities. It currently hold over 5,500 artefacts. An example of a commercial firm doing a better job than many museums to enliven the study of history.

Titanic - The World's Largest Museum Attraction, Branson, Missouri, USA. Includes 400 artefacts, a replica of the *Titanic*'s grand staircase a first class stateroom and a third class cabin.

Titanic - The Experience, Orlando, Florida, USA. Includes a replica of the *Titanic*'s grand staircase, first class parlour suite, boilers, and promenade deck. Over 200 artefacts and historic exhibits from private collections. Actors in period costume portray famous *Titanic* notables such as Captain Smith and Molly Brown.

The *Titanic* Museum, Indian Orchard, Massachusetts, USA. Houses the *Titanic* Historical Society collection. Many items were donated by the survivors themselves to THS's founder and president, Edward S. Kamuda, in the 1960s through to the 1980s, the organisation's early years.

Titanic's Dock & Pump-House, Queen's Island, Belfast, Northern Ireland. Is a scheduled monument which includes the dry dock and sliding caisson gate where *Titanic* was fitted out.

Titanic Historical Society, Inc. American-based society established in 1963. Publishes *The Titanic Commutator*. An excellent journal for members filled with original articles and reviews about all things *Titanic*. www.titanic1.org.

Ulster Folk & Transport Museum, Belfast, Northern Ireland. New exhibition includes 500 original artefacts, including *Titanic* objects recovered from the Atlantic.

List of Illustrations

1. Front cover of the first anthology of survivor accounts, *The Sinking of the Titanic*, by journalist Logan Marshall. An 'instant book', it was sold door-to-door across America in the months following the sinking of the *Titanic*. © Jonathan Reeve JR2166b98cvr 1912.
2. *Titanic* was the second of the trio of *Olympic*-class ocean liners built by the Harland & Wolff shipyard for the White Star Line. *Olympic*, pictured, was her virtually identical sister ship. This is an illustration of *Olympic* produced after the *Titanic* sank. Notice the continuous row of lifeboats on the boat deck. Additional lifeboats were added as a result of the *Titanic* disaster © Jonathan Reeve JR2214f140 1912.
3. *Titanic* proceeding down Southampton Water on its maiden voyage, 10 April 1912. Although *Titanic* was the most luxurious ship in the world it she carried 20 lifeboats, enough for 1,178 passengers. On her maiden voyage to New York she was carrying over 2,200 people. © Jonathan Reeve JR2221f147 1912.
4. At 45,000 grt *Titanic* was easily the largest ocean liner in the world. © Jonathan Reeve JR2220f146 1912.
5. Contemporary depiction of the *Titanic* sinking and the survivors on the lifeboats looking back in horror. In reality there was no huge iceberg nearby. Survivor Esther Hart, lifeboat 14: 'The air was full of the awful and despairing cries of drowning men. And we were helpless to help, for we dared not go near them.' © Jonathan Reeve JR2260f168 1912.
6. View from *Carpathia* of the iceberg which sank the *Titanic*. Captain Rostron of the *Carpathia*: 'It was a beautiful morning, a clear sun burning on sea and glistening on the icebergs. On every side there· were dozens of these monsters so wonderful to look at, so dreadful to touch.' © Jonathan Reeve JR2091f81 1912.
7.a. A graphic depiction of the *Titanic* striking the iceberg. From a French journal, April 1912. © Jonathan Reeve JR2355f204 1912.
7.b. 'As I was put into the boat he cried to me "It's alright little girl. You go. I will stay." As our boat shoved off he threw me a kiss, and that was the last I saw of him.' Mary Marvin, lifeboat 10, who was on her honeymoon and pregnant when her husband was lost. © Jonathan Reeve JR2356f205 1912.
7.c. A view of the bridge & crow's nest. © Jonathan Reeve JR2364f213 1912.
8.a. Heartbreaking farewells. Romanticised view of the scene on the boat deck as husbands and wives were parted. Some women chose to remain with their men folk, including Rosalie Ida Straus, who drowned with her husband Isidor Straus. 'Mrs Strauss had hidden from the officers, who were trying to force her into one of the boats.' Lucy Duff-Gordon (lifeboat 1). © Jonathan Reeve JR2175b98fp41 1912.
8.b. Loading of passengers into the lifeboats. It is easy to understand why the accounts of different eyewitnesses often differ so radically when it is remembered that the *Titanic* was over 260 metres in length and that the lifeboats were leaving from widely separated points. Margaret 'Molly' Brown, lifeboat 6: 'It was a strange sight. It all seemed like a play, like a drama that was being enacted for entertainment. It did not seem real. Men would say, 'After you,' as they made some woman comfortable and stepped back. I afterward heard some one say that men went downstairs into the restaurant. Many of them smoked. Many of them walked up and down. For a while after we reached the water we watched the ship. We could hear the band. Every light was shining.' © Jonathan Reeve JR2209b98fp247 1912.
9. Survivor Lucy Duff-Gordon, lifeboat 1: 'The stern of the great ship shot upwards out of the water. For a few seconds she stayed motionless while agonised cries from her decks grew in intensity, and then, with one downward rush, she plunged to her grave and the air was rent with those awful shrieks.' Archibald Gracie, lifeboat B: 'After the water struck the bridge there were many who rushed aft, climbed over the rail and jumped.' © W.B. Bartlett.
10. *41° 16' N; 50° 14' W* by Norman Wilkinson. This painting was commissioned as a frontispiece by the publisher of Filson Young's 1912 account of the sinking, *Titanic*, published in London just 37 days after the disaster. Over the years it has been much criticised for apparent inaccuracies but when *Titanic* survivor Eva Hart (lifeboat 14) was shown the image she said 'That's exactly how it was'. © Amberley Archive.
11. *Titanic* survivors in one of the lifeboats approaching the *Carpathia*. Possibly lifeboat 6, as Quartermaster Hitchens wore a blanket and was at the tiller. The number of occupants appear to match lifeboat 6 too. © Jonathan Reeve JR2014f42 1912.
12. Lifeboat 14 towing collapsible lifeboat D. Lifeboat 14, as it left the *Titanic* (some survivors were transferred to another lifeboat mid-Atlantic), included Charlotte Collyer and her daughter, Daisy Minahan, Esther Hart and her daughter Eva, Joseph

Scarrott and Harold Lowe. Daisy: 'Some of the women implored Officer Lowe, of No. 14, to divide his passengers among the three other boats and go back to rescue. His first answer to those requests was, "You ought to be damn glad you are here and have got your own life."' © Jonathan Reeve JR2015f43 1912.

13. *Titanic* survivors in collapsible lifeboat D, one of the last to be launched at c.2.05 am. Hugh Woolner: 'We hopped up onto the gunwale preparing to jump out into the sea, because if we had waited a minute longer we should have been boxed in against the ceiling. And as we looked out we saw this collapsible, the last boat on the port side, being lowered right in front of our faces.' © Jonathan Reeve JR2016f44 1912.

14. *Titanic* survivors in a lifeboat. Mary Hewlett, lifeboat 13: 'We were alone on the calm sea. It seemed much longer than it really was before we saw the *Carpathia*.' © Jonathan Reeve JR2017f45 1912.

15.a. & 15. b. A view of one of the *Titanic* lifeboats alongside the *Carpathia* showing that some were far from full. Survivor Helen Bishop, lifeboat 7: 'It was then almost impossible to get people to venture into them...The officers implored people to get aboard, but they seemed to fear hanging out over the water at a height of 75 feet, and the officers ordered the boat lowered away with only a small portion of what it could carry.' © Jonathan Reeve JR2002f30 1912 & JR2323f197 1912.

16. *Titanic* passengers coming aboard the *Carpathia*. © Jonathan Reeve JR2108f98 1912.

17. Captain Rostron of the *Carpathia*: 'They started climbing aboard. Obviously they had got away in a hurry, for there were only twenty-five of them whereas the capacity of the boat was fully forty.' © Jonathan Reeve JR2109f99 1912.

18. *Luxuries versus lifeboats*. Cartoon from American periodical, 8 May 1912. A common theme in the reaction to the sinking of *Titanic*. © Jonathan Reeve JR2317f191 1912.

19. George Harder and his wife Dorothy Harder (first class passengers, both rescued on lifeboat 5). The Harders were a honeymoon couple saved from the *Titanic*. The woman weeping, with hand to her face, is Clara Hays (lifeboat 3). Her husband Charles M. Hays perished. When the cry came to get in the lifeboats the Harders, thinking there was no danger, jumped in one of the first boats lowered. © Jonathan Reeve JR2129f119 1912.

20. Group of survivors of the *Titanic* disaster aboard the *Carpathia* after being rescued. Howard Chapin, *Carpathia* passenger: 'Practically everyone was quiet and subdued, apparently stunned by the shock and the cold.' © Jonathan Reeve JR2023f53 1912.

21. Howard Chapin, *Carpathia* passenger: 'Nearly all had on heavy garments, although very few were entirely dressed. Many men had on evening clothes.' © Jonathan Reeve JR2090f80 1912.

22. *Speed! The new terror of the sea*. Front-cover cartoon from an American periodical 1 May 1912. The satire is obvious. © Jonathan Reeve JR2318f192 1912

23. Photo taken before the 'orphans' of the *Titanic* were correctly identified and returned to their mother. The boys are French brothers Michel (age four) and Edmond Navratil (age two). They escaped the sinking ship in lifeboat D; their father perished. To board the ship (in second class), their father assumed the name Louis Hoffman and used their nicknames, Lolo and Mamon. Margaret Hays (lifeboat 7) volunteered once on board *Carpathia* to care for the 'orphans' as she could speak fluent French. © Jonathan Reeve JR2026f56 1912.

24. Left to right: Chief Officer Henry Wilde, Fourth Officer Joseph Boxhall and Captain Edward Smith. Henry Wilde took charge of the even-numbered boats, those on the port side, though he is not referred to very much in the survivor accounts of the sinking. He died in the disaster and was last reported attempting to free the collapsible lifeboats A and B. Boxhall survived on lifeboat 2 and decided against returning to pick up survivors in the water. © Jonathan Reeve JR2137f127 1912.

25. Ida Hippach and her daughter Gertrude, first class passengers, who survived the *Titanic* disaster in lifeboat 4. They explained their escape to the *New York Times*: 'We saw Colonel Astor place Mrs Astor in a boat and heard him assure her that he would follow later. He turned to us with a smile and said, "Ladies, you are next." The officer in charge of the boat protested that the craft was full and the seamen started to lower it. Colonel Astor exclaimed, "Hold that boat," in the voice of a man to be obeyed, and the men did as he ordered. The boat had been ordered past the upper deck, and the Colonel took us to the next deck below and put us in the boat, one after the other, through a porthole.' © Jonathan Reeve JR2263f171 1912.

26. Eva Hart, her mother Esther and father Ben. Esther and her daughter survived in lifeboat 14. Ben drowned. Eva was one of the longest-surviving survivors and died in 1996. © Ron Denney.

27. First class passenger Madeleine Astor (lifeboat 4) the 18-year-old bride of the millionaire John Astor who went down with the *Titanic*. She was pregnant at the time of the sinking and went on to give birth to a son in August 1912. At one stage whilst waiting on the boat deck, the Astors retired to the gym and sat on the mechanical horses. © Jonathan Reeve JR2320f194 1912.

28. Archibald Gracie was one of the few passengers to have survived in the freezing waters before scrambling onto the upturned lifeboat B. He describes vividly how he went down with the ship: 'I was in a whirlpool of water, swirling round and round, as I still tried to cling to the railing as the ship plunged to the depths below. Down, down, I went'. © Jonathan Reeve JR2250f160 1912.

29. Eleanor Widener (first class passenger, lifeboat 4), who left her husband, George, behind on the sinking ship. © Jonathan Reeve JR2192b98fp184T 1912.

30. Marian Thayer (first class passenger, lifeboat 4), mother of Jack Thayer (first class passenger, lifeboat B). They were reunited on board *Carpathia*. Jack, like Gracie, survived in the water and described the moment the *Titanic* went down just metres away from the upturned lifeboat B: '[*Titanic*] pivoting and moving in an almost perpendicular position, was sticking up in the air almost 300 feet. The ship then corkscrewed around so that the propeller, rudder and all seemed to go right over the heads of us on the upturned boat. Of course the lights now were all out. The ship seemed to hang in this position for minutes. Then with a dive and final plunge, the *Titanic* went under the water with very little apparent suction or noise.' © Jonathan Reeve JR2204b98fp209B 1912.

31. Margaret Brown (first class passenger, lifeboat 6), better known as the unsinkable Molly Brown. Molly is remembered for her presence of mind when her fellow lifeboat passengers despaired: 'I rowed because I would have frozen to death. I made them all row. It saved their lives.' Lifeboat 6 was one of the last to be picked up by *Carpathia* at around 7 a.m. © Jonathan Reeve JR2088f78 1912.

32. Eloise Smith (first class passenger, lifeboat 6), one of the first class passengers who was widowed by the *Titanic*. Eloise and her husband Lucien had only been married a few months. © Jonathan Reeve JR2189b98fp152 1912.

33. Charlotte Collyer and her daughter Marjorie (second class passengers, lifeboat 14). Charlotte's account is the fullest we have from a female survivor: 'Something in the very bowels of the *Titanic* exploded... two other explosions followed, dull and heavy,

as if below the surface. The *Titanic* broke in two before my eyes. The fore part was already partly under the water. It wallowed over and disappeared instantly. The stern reared straight on end, and stood poised on the ocean for many seconds – they seemed minutes to me.' © Jonathan Reeve JR1995f23 1912.

34. *Titanic* under construction in Belfast *c*. May 1911. © Jonathan Reeve JR2080f70 1912.

35. Sister ships *Olympic* and *Titanic*. View of bows in shipyard construction scaffolding Belfast *c*. May1911. The *Olympic* was almost identical to *Titanic*, and many more press photographs were taken of *Olympic* than *Titanic* and hence many of the views of the two ships (including those captioned *Titanic* in 1911 and 1912) are actually of the *Olympic*. © Jonathan Reeve JR2092f82 1912.

36. View of one of *Titanic*'s huge propellers, with shipyard workers in the background just prior to *Titanic*'s launch 31 May 1911. © Jonathan Reeve JR2082f72 1912.

37. View of the stern and rudder of the *Titanic* in dry dock. © Jonathan Reeve JR2084f74 1912.

38. The funnel-less *Titanic* in May 1911 just after her launch. © Jonathan Reeve JR2085f75 1912.

39. The *Titanic*. Seven-year-old survivor, Eva Hart (lifeboat 14), described her thoughts when she first saw the ship: 'I had never seen a ship before... it looked very big... everybody was very excited.' © Jonathan Reeve JR2116f106 1912.

40. Filson Young, author of one of the first accounts of the disaster, went to Southampton following the *Titanic* disaster to see her sister ship the *Olympic* leave for America. Having walked around on board he explained later in his book how he could understand the feeling of unsinkability that had given such false confidence to the passengers and crew aboard the *Titanic*. © Jonathan Reeve JR2216f142 1912.

41. *Titanic*'s sister ship, the *Olympic*. © Jonathan Reeve JR2215f141 1912.

42. First class suite bedroom (B59). Lucy Duff-Gordon (lifeboat 1): 'I had been in bed, I suppose, for about an hour, and the lights were all out, when I was awakened by a funny rumbling noise. It was like nothing I had ever heard before. It seemed almost as if some giant hand had been playing bowls, rolling the great balls along. Then the boat stopped and immediately there was the frightful noise of escaping steam, and I heard people running outside my cabin, but they were laughing and gay. "We must have hit an iceberg," I heard one of them say. "There is ice on the deck." © Jonathan Reeve JR2275b101p317TL 1912.

43. Another opulent first class cabin bedrooms. © Jonathan Reeve JR2254f162 1912.

44. Sitting room of a first class suite aboard *Titanic*. This cabin had a view onto the boat deck. © Jonathan Reeve JR2282b101p317TR 1912.

45. Lawrence Beesley (lifeboat 13): 'On the night of the disaster, right up to the time of the *Titanic*'s sinking, while the band grouped outside the gymnasium doors played with such supreme courage in face of the water which rose foot by foot before their eyes, the [gym] instructor was on duty inside, with passengers on the bicycles and the rowing-machines, still assisting and encouraging to the last. Along with the bandsmen it is fitting that his name, which I do not think has yet been put on record – it is [Thomas] McCawley – should have a place in the honourable list of those who did their duty faithfully to the ship and the line they served.' © Jonathan Reeve JR2284b101p317MR 1912.

46. *Titanic* passing through Belfast Lough en route to the Irish Sea for her trials, 2 April 1912. © Jonathan Reeve JR2275b101p313T 1912.

47. *Titanic*'s near miss with the SS *New York* shortly after departing from Southampton on her maiden voyage, noon Wednesday 10 April. © Jonathan Reeve JR2279b101p316L 1912.

48. The *Titanic* ablaze with lights heading out of Cherbourg harbour on Wednesday 10 April 1912. Lawrence Beesley (lifeboat 13): 'In the calmest weather we made Cherbourg just as it grew dusk and left again about 8.30 p.m., after taking on board passengers and mails.' © Jonathan Reeve JR2277b101p314T 1912.

49. One of several candidates photographed in the immediate aftermath of the sinking for 'iceberg that sunk the *Titanic*'. These photographs were reproduced around the world in newspapers and books. This one was photographed near the scene of the sinking. © Jonathan Reeve JR2122f112 1912.

50. A contemporary newspaper depiction of the iceberg alongside the *Titanic* based on a siting of an iceberg in the vicinity by Captain Wood of the *Etonian*. © Jonathan Reeve JR1992f20 1912.

51. Diagram showing the force of the *Titanic* hitting the iceberg. The iceberg punched along the ship's starboard side over *c*. 10 seconds, buckling the hull in several places below the waterline over *c*. 90 metres. This opened the first six compartments (the forward peak tank, the three forward holds and boiler rooms 5 and 6) to the sea. While the ship was designed to remain afloat with the first four compartments flooded, the collision caused flooding of the six forward compartments. © Jonathan Reeve JR2176b98p47 1912.

52. Sunday 14 April 1912, '11.45 p.m. *Titanic* strikes an iceberg with its starboard bow, 12 feet aft.' Jack Thayer (first class passenger, lifeboat B) was one of a number of survivors to describe the ship breaking in two as she sank. This is the first in a series of six illustrations drawn aboard *Carpathia* that show the ship in her dying minutes and clearly show the two halves. It would be over 70 years before Thayer was proved right when the wreck was discovered resting on the seabed in two halves. Series of sketches executed on board *Carpathia* by Lewis Skidmore (a young art teacher), based on conversations with Jack Thayer following the rescue. The timings listed in this series of illustrations have since 1912 been revised. © Jonathan Reeve JR2195b98p201TL 1912.

53. Monday 15 April 1912, '12.05 a.m. *Titanic* settles by head, boats ordered out.' © Jonathan Reeve JR2196b98p201ML 1912.

54. A chart from a 1912 edition of magazine *The Sphere* showing the ships too far away to help the *Titanic*. Note that the *Californian* is said to be 19½ miles away and there is a mystery ship between her and the stricken liner. © W.B. Bartlett.

55. Cutaway drawing of *Titanic* reproduced in newspapers in late April 1912 showing the suspected section (heavy black line) 'torn out' by the collision with the iceberg. Since the discovery of the wreck, scientists have used sonar to examine the area and discovered the iceberg had caused the hull to buckle, allowing water to enter *Titanic* between her steel plates. The illustration also shows much of the layout of the ship. © Jonathan Reeve JR1994f22 1912.

56. Longitudinal section of the *Titanic* from the Harland & Wolff blueprints *c*.1911. Bridge deck B through to lower deck G are marked. © Amberley Archive.

57. Plan of the Tank Top of the *Titanic* showing the 15 transverse bulkheads of the ship's hull which created 16 compartments, each of which could be isolated from the adjoining compartment by a watertight door. Note the forward peak tank, three forward holds and boiler rooms 5 and 6 marked in this plan. © Amberley Archive.

58. Transverse amidship section through the *Titanic* showing the various decks of the ship, the indoor squash court, swimming

pool and third class living quarters. The *Titanic* consisted of ten decks, in order, descending: Boat Deck, Promenade Deck [A], Bridge Deck [B], Shelter Deck [C], Saloon Deck [D], Upper Deck [E], Middle Deck [F], Lower Deck [G], Orlop Deck (the deck the stokers stood on) and Tank Top (the plating forming the inner bottom of a ship hull). © Amberley Archive.

59. A typical wireless room of an ocean liner of the period. Junior Wireless Operator Harold Bride (lifeboat B) relates the last few minutes in the wireless room with his Senior Wireless Operator Jack Phillips: 'Then came the Captain's voice: "Men, You have done your full duty. You can do no more. Abandon your cabin. Now it is every man for themselves. You look out for yourselves. I release you." I looked out. The boat deck was awash. Phillips clung on sending and sending. He clung on for about 10 minutes or maybe fifteen minutes after the Captain had released him. The water was then coming into our cabin.' © Jonathan Reeve JR2136f126 1912.

60. The wireless station at Cape Race was the first to hear *Titanic* transmit CQD, the distress signal, at 10.25 p.m. New York time simultaneously with the ships *La Touraine* and *Mount Temple*. © Jonathan Reeve JR2179b98fp57 1912.

61. The first class gym on board *Titanic*. © Jonathan Reeve JR2283b101p317ML 1912.

62. The first class Café Parisien was a favourite with the ship's younger set. Situated on the starboard side B deck, aft of the fourth funnel and outside the first class À la Carte Restaurant. The café's large picture windows gave diners a view of the sea while dining. Alfred Fernand Omont, a Frenchman, was playing cards in the Café Parisien with Pierre Maréchal, Paul Chevré and Lucien P. Smith when the collision took place. Chevré, Maréchal and Omont were all rescued in lifeboat 7. Omont: 'At about 11.40 p.m. there was a shock. I have crossed the Atlantic 13 times, and the shock was not a great one, and I thought it was caused by a wave... When the shock had happened, we saw something white through the portholes, and we saw water on the ports. When the waiter opened the porthole we saw nothing except a clear night.' © Jonathan Reeve JR2285b101p317BL 1912.

63. Located on A deck aft of the first class smoking room, just off the Café Parisien near the stern, the Veranda Café (also known as the Palm Room or Palm Court). Like the Café Parisien, there was real ivy growing up the walls. Also, there were real palm trees. There were actually two identical verandas on either side of the ship. Archibald Gracie: 'That night after dinner, with my table companions, Messrs James Clinch Smith and Edward A. Kent, according to usual custom, we adjourned to the palm room, with many others, for the usual coffee at individual tables where we listened to the always delightful music of the *Titanic*'s band... From the palm room, the men of my coterie would always go to the smoking room.' © Jonathan Reeve JR2314f188 1912.

64. First class reading room of the *Titanic*. On the promenade deck, as a counterpoint to the men's smoking room, this stylish area was primarily intended for the first class female passengers. After dinner the women could gravitate to this cozy space for coffee and conversation. © Jonathan Reeve JR2310f184 1912.

65. Rear starboard boat deck and the second class promenade area. The lifeboats shown are 15 (nearest), 13, 11 and 9. In the distance can just be seen lifeboats 7, 5 and 3. Lawrence Beesley (lifeboat 13): 'I was now on the starboard side of the top boat deck; the time about 12.20 a.m. We watched the crew at work on the lifeboats, numbers 9, 11, 13, 15, some inside arranging the oars, some coiling ropes on the deck, the ropes which ran through the pulleys to lower to the sea, others with cranks fitted to the rocking arms of the davits. As we watched, the cranks were turned, the davits swung outwards until the boats hung clear of the edge of the deck. Just then an officer came along from the first class deck and shouted above the noise of escaping steam, "All women and children get down to deck below and all men stand back from the boats." The men fell back and the women retired below to get into the boats from the next deck. Two women refused at first to leave their husbands, but partly by persuasion and partly by force they were separated from them and sent down to the next deck.' © Jonathan Reeve JR2188b98fp137 1912.

66. Plan of the boat deck of the *Titanic* showing the position of all 20 lifeboats 1 to 16 and collapsibles A, B, C & D. © Amberley Archive.

67. Forward starboard boat deck. The *Titanic* Good Friday, 5 April 1912, the liner was thrown open to the public for the day in Southampton. This was the only occasion the ship was dressed overall in flags. The lifeboats shown are 3 (nearest), 5 and 7. In the distance can be seen lifeboats 9, 11, 13 and 15. The exit onto the boat deck from the gym and grand staircase is opposite lifeboat 7. Elizabeth Shutes, lifeboat 3 remembered: '... the awful goodbyes, the quiet look of hope in the brave men's eyes as the wives were put into the lifeboats. Nothing escaped one at this fearful moment. We left from the boat deck, 75 feet above the water. Mr Case and Mr Roebling, brave American men, saw us to the lifeboat, made no effort to save themselves, but stepped back on deck.' © Jonathan Reeve JR2139f129 1912.

68. Promenade deck (A) which ran nearly the whole length of the ship. John Astor helped his wife Madeleine to climb through the windows of the enclosed promenade into lifeboat 4 along a steamer chair. Many female passengers were loaded into lifeboats from this deck. © Jonathan Reeve JR2132f122 1912.

69. Port side towards the stern of the ship showing position of lifeboat 16. Stewardess Mary Sloan (lifeboat 16): 'I was still standing when I saw Captain Smith getting excited, passengers would not have noticed, I did. I knew then we were soon going, the distress signals then were going every second, so I thought if anyone asked me again to go I should do so, there was a big crush from behind me, at last they realised their danger, so I was pushed into the boat. I believe it was one of the last boats to leave. We had scarcely got clear when she began sinking rapidly.' © Amberley Archive.

70. This photograph from the *Olympic* reveals how the first class smoking room (A deck behind the fourth funnel) on the *Titanic* would have looked. Hugh Woolner (lifeboat D) describes the collison: 'We felt it under the smoking room. We felt a sort of stopping, a sort of, not exactly shock, but a sort of slowing down; and then we sort of felt a rip that gave a sort of a slight twist to the whole room. Everybody, so far as I could see, stood up and a number of men walked out rapidly through the swinging doors on the port side.' © Jonathan Reeve JR2140f130 1912.

71. First class dining room (or dining saloon). Positioned on D deck between funnels 3 and 4, it could seat over 500 pasengers and was the largest room aboard *Titanic*. Washington Dodge, first class passenger, lifeboat 13: 'So little motion was there to the vessel it was hard to realise, when dining in the spacious dining saloon, that one was not in some large and sumptuous hotel.' Among the passengers that dined there on the last night were Benjamin Guggenheim, Isidor and Ida Straus, and Molly Brown. © Jonathan Reeve JR2218f144 1912.

72 & 73. Forward first class grand stairway immortalised in the *Titanic* film. The top landing led out directly onto the boat deck. Ella White: 'Captain Smith came down the stairway and ordered us all to put on our life preservers, which we did.' Ella escaped shortly after on the fourth lifeboat to leave, lifeboat 8, immediately outside the exit of the grand staircase on the boat deck. Elizabeth Shutes, lifeboat 3: 'How different are these staircases now! No laughing throng, but on either side stand quietly, bravely, the stewards, all equipped with the white, ghostly life preservers.'. © Jonathan Reeve JR2201b98fp208T 1912 & ©

Jonathan Reeve JR2202b98fp208B 1912.

74. A cross section through the *Titanic* showing the forward first class grand staircase, the wireless room, first class gym, first class reception room, turkish bath and boilers. © Jonathan Reeve JR2187b98fp136 1912.

75. Reception room. This was located on D deck between the first class grand staircase and the first class dining room. This is where first class passengers would gather for aperitifs prior to taking their seats in the adjacent dining room. © Jonathan Reeve JR2312f186 1912.

76. Lounge room. Martha Stephenson (lifeboat 4): 'About nine-thirty we went up to the lounge, a most beautiful room with open fire. I, having finished all my books, got the library steward to lend me Sir Ernest Shackleton's book of the South Pole and I spent half an hour looking at pictures of icebergs and ice fields, little realising that I should ever see similar ones.' © Jonathan Reeve JR2309f183 1912.

77. Captain Smith on the starboard side of the bridge. Jack Lawrence, Ship News Reporter, *New York Times*: 'Some of his contemporaries thought that Captain Smith was old fashioned. He certainly looked old fashioned with his rolling gait, his puckered eyes and his white beard.' © Jonathan Reeve JR2004f32 1912.

78. Crow's nest where at 11.40 p.m. lookouts Frederick Fleet (lifeboat 6) and Reginald Lee (lifeboat 13) spotted a large iceberg directly ahead of the ship. Sounding the ship's bell three times, Fleet telephoned Sixth Officer James Moody on the bridge exclaiming, 'Iceberg, right ahead!' The deck at the bow was known as the forecastle. The lower deck to the bottom of the photo is the fore well deck. © Jonathan Reeve JR2311f185 1912.

79. Cartoon from a 1912 newspaper about the *Titanic* disaster showing the despair of wives being physically parted by the crew and put aboard the lifeboats. Olaus Abelseth, third class passenger (lifeboat A): 'I saw there was an old couple standing there on the deck, and I heard this man say to the lady, "Go into the lifeboat and get saved." He put his hand on her shoulder and I think he said: "Please get into the lifeboat and get saved." She replied: "No; let me stay with you." I could not say who it was, but I saw that he was an old man. I did not pay much attention to him, because I did not know him.' Some women were man-handled by crew to force them to enter the lifeboats. Constance Willard (lifeboat 8): 'Women were being placed in the boats, and two men took hold of me and almost pushed me into a boat. I did not appreciate the danger and I struggled until they released me. "Do not waste time; let her go if she will not get in," an officer said.' © Jonathan Reeve JR2268f176 1912.

80. *Titanic* author Logan Marshall's offering for the hymn played as the ship went down, not *Nearer My God to Thee*, but *Autumn* as suggested by Harold Bride (lifeboat B). © Jonathan Reeve JR2185b98p103 1912.

81. A scene depicted in a cartoon from a 1912 newspaper showing children being lowered into the lifeboats. © Jonathan Reeve JR2274f182 1912.

82. Sketch of the lifeboats being lowered based on descriptions from eye-witnesses. Elizabeth Shutes (lifeboat 3): 'Our lifeboat, with 36 in it, began lowering to the sea. This was done amid the greatest confusion. Rough seamen all giving different orders. No officer aboard. As only one side of the ropes worked, the lifeboat at one time was in such a position that it seemed we must capsize in midair. At last the ropes worked together, and we drew nearer and nearer the black, oily water. The first touch of our lifeboat on that black sea came to me as a last goodbye to life, and so we put off – a tiny boat on a great sea rowed away from what had been a safe home for five days.' © Jonathan Reeve JR2181b98p71 1912.

83. The lowering of the lifeboats. Charlotte Collyer, lifeboat 14: 'There came the terrible cry: "Lower the boats. Women and children first! Women and children first!" They struck utter terror into my heart, and now they will ring in my ears until I die. They meant my own safety; but they also meant the greatest loss I have ever suffered – the life of my husband.' © Jonathan Reeve JR1990f18 1912.

84. Survivors look on in horror as the *Titanic* sinks and passengers fling themselves off the stern of the massive ship. Harold Lowe, Fifth Officer, and in command of lifeboat 14, was asked at the British inquiry into the sinking why he didn't immediately return to the wreckage after the *Titanic* had sunk: 'Because it would have been suicide to go back there until the people had thinned out.' © Jonathan Reeve JR2208b98fp246 1912.

85. View from the lifeboats of the *Titanic*. Catherine Crosby (lifeboat 7): 'I heard the terrible cries of the people that were on board when the boat went down, and heard repeated explosions, as though the boilers had exploded.' © Jonathan Reeve JR1999f27 1912.

86. Monday 15 April 1912, '1.40 a.m. *Titanic* settles to forward stack, breaks between stacks'. August Weikman (lifeboat A): 'I was proceeding to launch the next boat when the ship suddenly sank at the bow and there was a rush of water that washed me overboard... that was the last moment it was possible to launch any more boats, because the ship was at an angle that it was impossible for anybody to remain on deck... [I] started to swim for some dark object in the water. This was about 1.50 a.m. toward the stern... my watch was stopped at that time by the water.' © Jonathan Reeve JR2197b98p201BL 1912.

87. Cartoon from a 1912 newspaper about the *Titanic* disaster. © Jonathan Reeve JR2272f180 1912.

88. Cartoon from a 1912 newspaper about the *Titanic* disaster showing the horrific predicament of passengers on the boat deck as *Titanic*'s bow slipped beneath the waves. © Jonathan Reeve JR2265f173 1912.

89. After deck *Olympic* 1911. View towards the decks at the stern of the ship. Helen Bishop (lifeboat 7) describes the last moments of the *Titanic*: 'When the forward part of the ship dropped suddenly at a faster rate so that the upward slope became marked, there was a sudden rush of passengers on all decks toward the stern. It was like a wave. We could see the great black mass of people in the steerage sweeping to the rear part of the boat... Then it began to slide gently downwards. Its speed increased as it went down head first, so that the stern shot down with a rush. The lights continued to burn till it sank. We could see the people packed densely in the stern till it was gone.' © Jonathan Reeve JR2315f189 1912.

90. Monday 15 April 1912, '1.50 a.m. *Titanic*'s forward end floats then sinks'. Archibald Gracie (lifeboat B): 'The force of the wave that struck Clinch Smith and the others undoubtedly knocked most of them there unconscious against the walls of the officers' quarters and other appurtenances of the ship on the boat deck. As the ship keeled over forward, I believe that their bodies were caught in the angles of this deck, or entangled in the ropes, and in these other appurtenances thereon, and sank with the ship.' Charles Lightoller, Second Officer, lifeboat B: 'Striking the water was like a thousand knives being driven into one's body, and, for a few moments, I completely lost grip of myself.' © Jonathan Reeve JR2198b98p201TR 1912.

91. Monday 15 April 1912, '2.00 a.m. Stern section of *Titanic* pivots and swings over spot where forward section sank'. © Jonathan Reeve JR2199b98p201MR 1912.

92. Monday 15 April 1912, c. 2.15 a.m. 'final position in which *Titanic* stayed for several minutes before the final plunge'. Helen

Bishop (lifeboat 7): 'Suddenly the ship seemed to shoot up out of the water and stand there perpendicularly. It seemed to us that it stood upright in the water for four full minutes. Then it began to slide gently downwards. Its speed increased as it went down head first, so that the stern shot down with a rush. We could see the people packed densely in the stern till it was gone. As the ship sank we could hear the screaming a mile away. Gradually it became fainter and fainter and died away.' © Jonathan Reeve JR220ob98p201BR 1912.

93. A *Titanic* lifeboat rowing amongst the icebergs. The 'unsinkable' Molly Brown (lifeboat 6) described what she saw from the lifeboat as the sun rose on the morning of 15 April: 'On every side was ice. Ice 10 feet high was everywhere, and to the right and left and back and front, were icebergs. This sea of ice was 40 miles wide, they told me. Imagine some artist able to picture what we saw from that boat at dawn in that field of ice, with the red sun playing on those giant icebergs.' © Jonathan Reeve JR225ibioop251 1912.

94. The recovered *Titanic* lifeboats on board the *Carpathia*. Catherine Crosby (lifeboat 7): 'We had to row quite a long time and quite a distance before we were taken on board the *Carpathia*; I was suffering from the cold while I was drifting around, and one of the officers put a sail around me and over my head to keep me warm.' © Jonathan Reeve JR2001f29 1912.

95. 1912 illustration of lifeboats among the ice field with the *Carpathia* in the distance. Ella White (lifeboat 8): 'The men in our boat were anything but seamen, with the exception of one man. The women all rowed, every one of them. The men could not row. They did not know the first thing about it. Miss Swift from Brooklyn rowed every mile, from the steamer to the *Carpathia*. Miss Young rowed every minute also, except when she was throwing up, which she did six or seven times. Countess Rothes stood at the tiller. Where would we have been if it had not been for our women, with such men as that put in charge of the boat?' © Jonathan Reeve JR218ob98fp64 1912.

96. A contemporary newspaper depiction of the location of the sinking of the *Titanic* and positions of other ships in the area. © Jonathan Reeve JR1993f21 1912.

97. Captain Arthur Rostron who rushed his ship *Carpathia* to rescue *Titanic*'s survivors and bring them to New York. © Jonathan Reeve JR2120f110 1912.

98. Photograph of the *Carpathia* with the recovered *Titanic* lifeboats. © Jonathan Reeve JR2095f85 1912.

99. Sketch of the iceberg believed to have sunk the *Titanic* by Colin Campbell Cooper. A renowned artist, he and his wife were aboard the *Carpathia* during its rescue mission. He assisted in the rescue, and created several paintings which document the events. The consensus that emerges from the survivor accounts is that the iceberg was 100 feet high (above the water). © Jonathan Reeve JR2327f192 1912.

100. The front page of *The World*, Tuesday 16 April 1912, describing the sinking to a hungry audience. Note the exaggerated claim for the number of women and children saved. © W.B. Bartlett.

101. *New York Tribune*, Tuesday 16 April 1912. © Jonathan Reeve JR2005f33 1912.

102. *Washington Times*, Thursday 18 April 1912. Note the sensationalised headline, no lifeboats was sucked under by the sinking liner. © Jonathan Reeve JR2007f35 1912.

103. Getting *Titanic* news. White Star Office, April 1912. © Jonathan Reeve JR2076f66 1912.

104. A photograph of Mrs Florette Guggenheim leaving the White Star offices in New York after trying to get news of her husband. Mr Guggenheim was accompanied aboard *Titanic* by his mistress, a French singer named Madame Léontine Aubart. On the night of the disaster he put his mistress aboard lifeboat 9. He was last seen, with his valet, seated in deckchairs in the grand staircase sipping brandy and smoking cigars. © Jonathan Reeve JR2214b98fp56det 1912.

105. Crowds wait in New York for news of those who have been saved and who have been lost on the *Titanic*. Firm news took several days to come through. © Jonathan Reeve JR2178b98fp56 1912.

106. Cartoon from a 1912 newspaper about the *Titanic* disaster showing the misery of family discovering that loved ones have perished on board *Titanic*. Hundreds flocked to the White Star Line offices in London, Southampton and New York seeking news. © Jonathan Reeve JR2270f178 1912.

107. Seeking information about lost relatives and friends at the office of the steamship company in New York. © Jonathan Reeve JR2124f114 1912.

108. Interior of the Cunard Line pier all cleared out ready to receive the survivors of the *Titanic* on arrival of the *Carpathia*, where they were met by relatives, doctors and nurses. © Jonathan Reeve JR2131f121 1912.

109. Cartoon from a 1912 newspaper about the *Titanic* disaster showing the family of passengers on board the *Titanic* waiting at New York for the survivors to disembark from *Carpathia*. Jack Lawrence, Ship News Reporter, New York Times: 'The first Titanic survivor to come down the gangplank was a woman, a sailor's oilskin thrown over her shoulders. At the foot of the gangplank a man faced her ith outstretched arms. She collapsed in those arms and he carried her away, a Red Cross nurse trotting after him.' © Jonathan Reeve JR2259f167 1912.

110. Arrival of the *Carpathia* into New York on Thursday 18 April 1912. Carpathia dropped off the empty *Titanic* lifeboats at Pier 59, as property of the White Star Line, before unloading the survivors at Pier 54 where thousands of friends and relatives of the survivors were waiting. © Jonathan Reeve JR2008f36 1912.

111. Harold Bride (lifeboat B), surviving wireless operator of the *Titanic*, with feet bandaged, being carried up ramp of ship. He was washed off the deck of the *Titanic* just as it sank but managed to attach himself to the upturned hull of collapsible lifeboat B: 'There were men all around me – hundreds of them. The sea was dotted with them, all depending on their lifebelts.' © Jonathan Reeve JR2027f57 1912.

112. Stuart Collett (second class passenger, lifeboat 9) survivor of the *Titanic* on board *Carpathia* on arrival in New York. © Jonathan Reeve JR2081f71 1912.

113. Crowd awaiting Titanic survivors April 1912. © Jonathan Reeve JR2073f63 1912.

114. *The Call*, Friday 19 April 1912. Survivor testimony was the stock and trade of most of the new stories relating to the sinking. © Jonathan Reeve JR2011f39 1912.

115. *New York Tribune*, Friday 19 April 1912, the day after the *Carpathia* had arrived in New York with survivors. © Jonathan Reeve JR2009f37 1912.

116. *The Washington Times*, Sunday 21 April 1912. The *Mackey-Bennet*, a ship charted by the White Star line to recover bodies from the scene, had arrived at the scene of the sinking on 20 April. Over 300 bodies were eventually recovered. © Jonathan Reeve JR2010f38 1912.

117. The *Titanic*'s 13 surviving lifeboats in New York. Their nameplates and White Star flags were removed and the lifeboats disappeared. © Jonathan Reeve JR2117f107 1912.

118. Partial list of survivors of the *Titanic* who were taken aboard the *Carpathia*. This page includes the names of John Thayer junior, Emily Ryerson, Martha Stephenson, Eleanor Widener, Elizabeth Shutes and Mary Marvin. © Jonathan Reeve JR2242f152 1912.

119. Noted first class passenger Isidor Straus. His wife Ida reportedly would not leave Isidor, refusing to get in a lifeboat without him. The officer filling up the boat told Isidor that he could get into the boat with his wife, but he refused to do so ahead of younger men but instead sent his wife's maid, Ellen Bird, into the boat (lifeboat 8). Ida reportedly said: 'I will not be separated from my husband. As we have lived, so will we die together.' Isidor and Ida were last seen on deck sitting in deckchairs holding hands when a huge wave washed them into the sea. The couple are portrayed in the 1958 film *A Night to Remember*, in scenes that are faithful to the accounts just cited. In the 1997 film *Titanic*, the Strauses are briefly depicted comforting each other as their stateroom floods with water. © Jonathan Reeve JR2123f113 1912.

120. Noted first class passenger William T. Stead, a well-known author, went down with the ship sitting in the first class smoking room quietly reading a book. © Jonathan Reeve JR2121f111 1912.

121. Charles Hays, a first class passenger, who drowned. An hour before the collision, Hays relaxed with Archibald Gracie in the first class smoking room. Hays never believed the ship would sink quickly and as he put both his wife, Clara Hays, and daughter, Orian Davidson, into lifeboat 3 he assured them *Titanic* would 'Stay afloat for at least ten hours'. His son-in-law, Thornton Davidson, also died in the sinking. © Jonathan Reeve JR2172b98fp31T 1912.

122. The millionaire John Astor who went down with the *Titanic* but not before putting his pregnant wife, Madeleine Astor, in lifeboat 4. © Jonathan Reeve JR2319f193 1912.

123. James Clinch Smith, friend of Archibald Gracie who went down with the *Titanic*. It was Clinch who told Gracie of the collision and collected some of the iceberg fragments. Gracie: 'He opened his hand and showed me some ice, flat like my watch, coolly suggesting that I might take it home for a souvenir.' © Jonathan Reeve JR2255f163 1912.

124. John B. Thayer who went down with *Titanic*. He was Jack Thayer's father, who was one of the few survivors to have survived exposure in the Atlantic before scrambling aboard lifeboat B. © Jonathan Reeve JR2203b98fp209T 1912.

125. George Widener, husband of Eleanor Widener (lifeboat 4), who was lost in the sinking with his son. Archibald Gracie's account states that George had bravely assisted Second Officer Charles Lightoller in the loading of the last lifeboat, D, launched at about 2.05 a.m. and was last seen making his way to the stern of the *Titanic*. © Jonathan Reeve JR2193b98fp184B 1912.

126. Another noted *Titanic* victim, first class passenger Archibald Butt, military aid to two US presidents. He was seen on the bridge five minutes before the last boat left the ship. The reports of him beating back a crowd rushing a lifeboat with an iron bar or a pistol are believed to be media exaggerations. © Jonathan Reeve JR2141f131 1912.

127. Unidentified family who survived the *Titanic* disaster. © Jonathan Reeve JR2083f73 1912.

128. Trevor Allison, 11 months, with his nursemaid Alice Cleaver. Both escaped on lifeboat 11. Trevor was the sole survivor of his wealthy Canadian family. His mother, father and sister all drowned. © Jonathan Reeve JR2328f202 1912.

129. Frederick Dent Ray (lifeboat 13), one of the saloon stewards in the main dining saloon, five decks down. © Jonathan Reeve JR2100f90 1912.

130. Frederick Fleet (lifeboat 6), Lookout on the *Titanic* who spotted the iceberg. He described the moment the *Titanic* struck the iceberg at 11.40 p.m.: 'We struck the iceberg on the starboard bow, just before the foremast. There was scarcely any jar, and I thought and said we had had a narrow escape.' The experience of first impact was very different for fireman Frederick Barratt in boiler room 6 on the lowest deck of the ship: 'There was a crash... I saw a wave of green foam come tearing through between the boilers and I jumped for the escape ladder.' © Jonathan Reeve JR2099f89 1912.

131. John Thompson, Fireman (left) lifeboat A. Thomas Whiteley, Saloon Steward (right), lifeboat B: 'In some way I got overboard myself and found something to hold on to – an oak dresser about the size of this hospital bed. I wasn't more than 60 feet from the *Titanic* when she went down. I was aft and could see her big stern rise up in the air as she went down bow first. I saw all the machinery drop out of her. I was in the water about half an hour and could hear the cries of thousands of people, it seemed. Then I drifted near a boat wrong side up. About 30 men were clinging to it. They refused to let me get on. Someone tried to hit me with an oar, but I scrambled on to her.' © Jonathan Reeve JR2326f200 1912.

132. P. A. S. Franklin, White Star Line Vice President. When the New York office of the White Star Line was informed that *Titanic* was in trouble, he announced, 'We place absolute confidence in the *Titanic*. We believe the boat is unsinkable.' By the time Franklin spoke those words *Titanic* was at the bottom of the ocean. © Jonathan Reeve JR2098f88 1912.

133. Senate Investigating Committee questioning Harold Cottam at the Waldorf Astoria, 29 May 1912. Harold Cottam was the Wireless Operator on the *Carpathia* on the night the *Titanic* struck an iceberg. It was he who alerted Captain Rostron who immediately turned the ship round and put on all possible speed. © Jonathan Reeve JR2071f61 1912.

134. Contemporary newspaper cartoon attacking Bruce Ismay, Managing Director of the White Star Line. His survival on lifeboat C when so many women and children failed to make it into the lifeboats caused a major controversy. © Jonathan Reeve JR1998f26 1912.

135. Bruce Ismay being questioned by the Senate Investigating Committee. When asked by the US Senate Inquiry why he got in the lifeboat he replied simply: 'Because there was room in the boat. She was being lowered away. I felt the ship was going down, and I got into the boat.' © Jonathan Reeve JR2029f59 1912.

Acknowledgements

The publisher and the author would like to thank Nicholas Wade for permission to reproduce the extract from Lawrence Beesley's book, *The Loss of the SS Titanic*. If you have any further information on the survivors of this book or suggestions for additional accounts for any future edition, please contact the author on titanic_voices@hotmail.co.uk.

Also available from Amberley Publishing

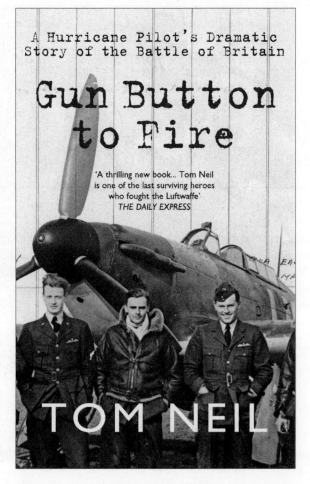

A Hurricane Pilot's Dramatic Story of the Battle of Britain

Gun Button to Fire

'A thrilling new book... Tom Neil is one of the last surviving heroes who fought the Luftwaffe'
THE DAILY EXPRESS

TOM NEIL

The amazing story of one of the 'Few', fighter ace Tom Neil who shot down 13 enemy aircraft during the Battle of Britain

'A thrilling new book... Tom Neil is one of the last surviving heroes who fought the Luftwaffe'
THE DAILY EXPRESS

'The best book on the Battle of Britain' SIR JOHN GRANDY, Marshal of the RAF

This is a fighter pilot's story of eight memorable months from May to December 1940. By the end of the year he had shot down 13 enemy aircraft, seen many of his friends killed, injured or burned, and was himself a wary and accomplished fighter pilot.

£9.99 Paperback
120 Photographs (20 colour)
320 pages
978-1-4456-0510-4

Available from all good bookshops or to order direct
Please call **01453-847-800**
www.amberleybooks.com

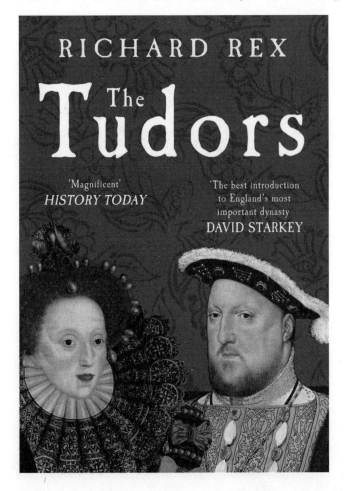

Also available from Amberley Publishing

The story of the sinking of the Titanic based on first-hand accounts collected in the days and weeks following the disaster

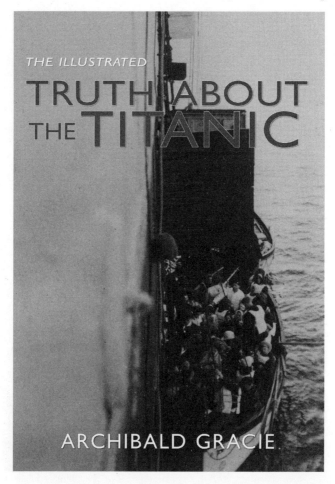

Also available from Amberley Publishing

America's first 'instant book' about the sinking of the Titanic

Published in America within a month of the sinking by the opportunist L.T. Myers and written by journalist Logan Marshall, *The Illustrated Sinking of the Titanic* tells the story of the ship and her final few hours. Often over dramatic and inaccurate, nonetheless the book is now prized among *Titanic* collectors and those interested in the sinking of what was the world's largest and most luxurious ship.

£17.99 Paperback
78 illustrations
192 pages
978-1-84868-053-1

Available from all good bookshops or to order direct
Please call **01453-847-800**
www.amberleybooks.com

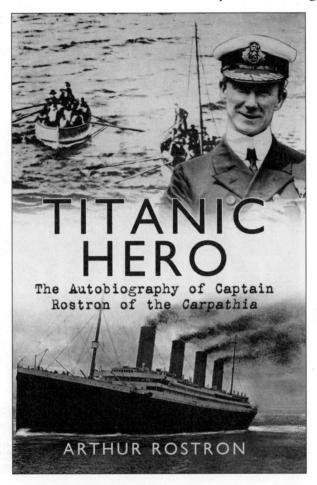

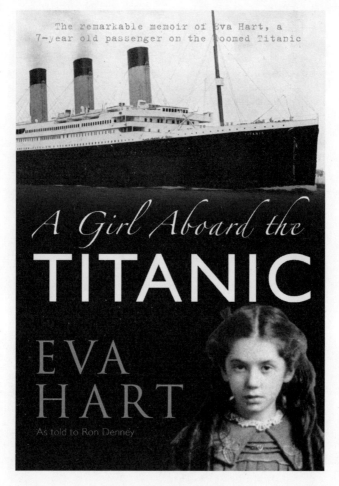

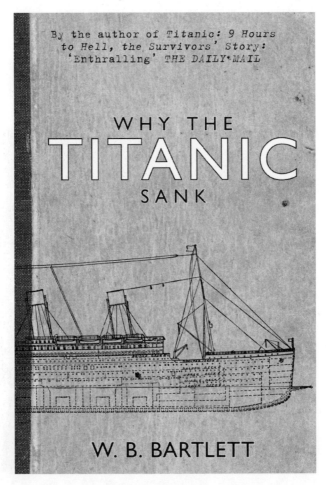

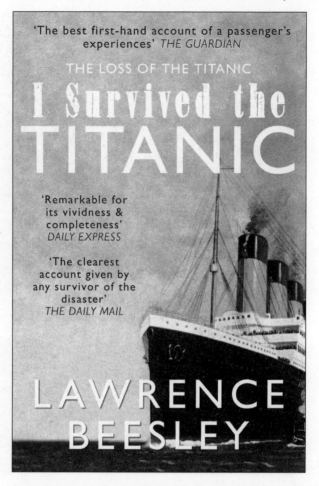

Available from October 2011 from Amberley Publishing

'Quite the best and most level-headed telling of the whole story I have ever read' THE INDEPENDENT ON SUNDAY

W. B. BARTLETT

TITANIC

9 Hours to Hell, the Survivors' Story

'Enthralling'
THE DAILY MAIL

A major new history of the disaster that weaves into the narrative the first-hand accounts of those who survived

'Enthralling' THE DAILY MAIL

'Quite the best and most level-headed telling of the whole story I have ever read'
THE INDEPENDENT ON SUNDAY

It was twenty minutes to midnight on Sunday 14 April, when Jack Thayer felt the Titanic lurch to port, a motion followed by the slightest of shocks. Seven-year old Eva Hart barely noticed anything was wrong. For Stoker Fred Barrett, shovelling coal down below, it was somewhat different; the side of the ship where he was working caved in. For the next nine hours, Jack, Eva and Fred faced death and survived. 1600 people did not. This is the story told through the eyes of Jack, Eva, Fred and over a hundred others of those who survived and recorded their experiences.

£9.99 Paperback
72 illustrations (14 colour)
368 pages
978-1-4456-0482-4

Available from October 2011 all good bookshops or to order direct
Please call **01453-847-800**
www.amberleybooks.com

SHOWING THE LOSS OF LIFE ON THE *TITANIC*

FIRST CLASS

	Carried.	Saved.	Lost.	Per cent. saved.
Men	173	58	115	34
Women . . .	144	139	5	97
Children . . .	5	5	0	100
Total	322	202	120	63

SECOND CLASS

	Carried.	Saved.	Lost.	Per cent. saved.
Men	160	13	147	8
Women . . .	93	78	15	84
Children . . .	24	24	0	100
Total	277	115	162	42

THIRD CLASS

	Carried.	Saved.	Lost.	Per cent. saved.
Men	454	55	399	12
Women . . .	179	98	81	55
Children . . .	76	23	53	30
Total	709	176	533	25

TOTAL PASSENGERS

	Carried.	Saved.	Lost.	Per cent. saved.
Men	787	126	661	16
Women . . .	416	315	101	76
Children . . .	105	52	53	49
Total	1308	493	815	38

CREW

	Carried.	Saved.	Lost.	Per cent. saved.
Men	875	189	686	22
Women . . .	23	21	2	91
Total	898	210	688	23

TOTAL PASSENGERS AND CREW

	Carried.	Saved.	Lost.	Per cent. saved.
Men	1662	315	1347	19
Women . . .	439	336	103	77
Children . . .	105	52	53	49
Total	2206	703	1503	32